LACHLAN MACQUARIE

His Life, Adventures and Times

M.H. Ellis

Angus&Robertson
An imprint of HarperCollinsPublishers

Angus&Robertson
An imprint of HarperCollins*Publishers*

First published in 1947
by Angus & Robertson (Publishers) Pty Ltd
This edition first published in 1973
by Angus & Robertson
Reissued in 2010 with a new introduction
by HarperCollins*Publishers* Australia Pty Limited
ABN 36 009 913 517
harpercollins.com.au

HarperCollins*Publishers*
25 Ryde Road, Pymble, Sydney, NSW 2073, Australia
31 View Road, Glenfield, Auckland 0627, New Zealand
A 53, Sector 57, Noida, UP, India
77–85 Fulham Palace Road, London, W6 8JB, United Kingdom
2 Bloor Street East, 20th floor, Toronto, Ontario M4W 1A8, Canada
10 East 53rd Street, New York NY 10022, USA

National Library of Australia Cataloguing-in-Publication data:

Ellis, M. H. (Malcolm Henry), 1890–1969
    Lachlan Macquarie / M. H. Ellis, Beverley Kingston.
    ISBN: 9780732291488 (pbk.)
    Macquarie, Lachlan, 1761-1824.
    Governors–New South Wales–Biography.
    India–History–British occupation, 1765-1947.
    New South Wales–History–1788-1851.
    Kingston, Beverley.
994.4020924

Cover design by Nada Backovic Designs
Cover image of Lachlan Macquarie, watercolour on ivory miniature, from State Library of NSW
Printed and bound in Australia by Griffin Press
70gsm Bulky Book Ivory used by HarperCollins*Publishers* is a natural, recyclable product made
from wood grown in sustainable forests. The manufacturing processes conform to the environmen-
tal regulations in the country of origin, New Zealand.

5 4 3 2 1   10 11 12 13 14

LACHLAN MACQUARIE

His Life, Adventures and Times

LACHLAN MACQUARIE

His Life, Adventures and Times

LIEUTENANT-COLONEL LACHLAN MACQUARIE, *ætat.* 44
Assistant Adjutant-General of the London District Command

From the portrait by John Opie, R.A., in the possession of the Trustees of the Mitchell Library, Sydney

To
JOHN EDWARD WEBB

AUTHOR'S NOTE TO THIRD EDITION

★

SINCE the first edition of this work was printed the author has revised the text, correcting some small errors in dates, largely due to misprinting, and in quotations; also adding a little material which has come to light within the past ten years, clarifying some passages rather hastily written in the turmoil of the year after the close of the Second World War, and adjusting the account of the rebellion against Governor Bligh and the estimate of the proceedings of John M'Arthur to the facts as made clear in the M'Arthur Family Papers and other research material not available when the earlier editions were issued.

In assembling the matter used in the book the practice was followed as far as possible of working from original documents; but for the convenience of students who cannot have recourse to these references are given in the notes to the versions which are most easily accessible to the public. This in some instances means that the wording of a quotation used in the book may differ very slightly, but not materially, from the text as it occurs in the work to which students have been referred. Where there is any variation between documents which matters in the slightest degree, and which is not patently due to an accident in copying, or to some other fortuitous cause, care has been taken to associate the text with the specific source from which it has been drawn.

AUTHOR'S NOTE TO FIRST EDITION

*

For assistance in preparing this book the writer is indebted to many helpers.

First and foremost he owes acknowledgments to his wife, who has been associated with every detail of the assembly of material and production of the book for many years, and to his sister, Winifred Ellis, for devoted assistance as amanuensis.

To the Mitchell Library Trustees at Sydney his primary thanks are due, because the Mitchell Library owns ninety per cent of the relevant manuscripts and other original documents, and without a very generous helpfulness on the part of the principals and staff it would have been impossible to study the material which it was necessary to sift in the spare intervals of an otherwise busy life.

To the Board of Trustees of the Library, to Mr W. H. Ifould, Mr J. P. Metcalfe, Mr Hugh Wright, Hon. T. D. Mutch, Miss Phyllis Mander Jones, Miss Nita Kibble, the late Miss Willis, Miss Barrington, Miss Joyce Cocks, and to all the senior members of the Mitchell Library Staff during twenty years the author owes his gratitude for continual and courteous assistance which often has gone far beyond the bounds of ordinary duty.

Acknowledgments also are due to the Royal Australian Historical Society, for permission to use material from its journals, to its General Secretary, Mr C. Price Conigrave, F.R.A.H.S.; and to Mr C. H. Bertie, F.R.A.H.S., for his rediscovery of Elizabeth Macquarie's important letter describing her husband's last days and death, and for other important contributions to Macquarie literature.

My colleagues, Cecil Mann and John Brennan, have read and helped to check and correct proofs for me; and I have to thank the late Sir Fitzroy Maclean, Bart, for help in the matter of clan history; Sir William Dixson, for permission to reproduce pictures in the Dixson Wing of the Mitchell Library, Sydney; the Bank of New South Wales, for permission to quote from its Minute Book and for obtaining from South Africa for me the portrait of Judge-Advocate John Wylde, of whom no likeness existed in Australia; Dr Joseph Pearson and Captain Pearse, of the Hobart Museum, for assistance to reproduce Read's fine miniature of Elizabeth Macquarie, of which, together with the miniature of Macquarie himself in the Museum, they had copies painted for my use; Lieutenant-Colonel C. G. C. Jarvis, O.B.E., D.L., for lending the reputed miniature of Jane Jarvis printed in the book, and the Rev. E. Royle, M.A., for his help in establishing the facts about Macquarie's second marriage in Devonshire.

Sydney
2 May 1947

INTRODUCTION

by Beverley Kingston, Professor of Australian and Women's History, 2010

Malcolm Henry Ellis began writing this biography of Lachlan Macquarie in 1926 and he worked on it, mostly in his spare time, for almost twenty years. It was 1947 before it was published, but since then it has been in print more or less continuously.

Ellis spent most of his working life as a journalist, but he became passionate about Australia's early history. At a time when there was little available in print, he researched and wrote a series of major biographies. He had begun with the idea of writing a history of early NSW but decided that biographies of its leading figures would be more accessible than a general narrative. Indeed, his three big biographies — of Lachlan Macquarie, architect Francis Greenway (1949) and entrepreneur John Macarthur (1955) — do provide three different perspectives on life in early NSW.

Ellis was born on 21 August 1890 at Narine Station near Dirranbandi in southwest Queensland. His mother, Constance Jane Ruegg, was an impressive woman and a great influence on her children. Constance was born in 1860 and lived with her grandparents after her own mother died in 1869. When she was about 28, and working as a telephonist in London, she decided to follow one of her brothers and migrate to Australia. Her grandfather Richard Ruegg was a journalist and editor of the *Kentish Independent*. All four of Constance's sons were to become journalists.

On arriving in Brisbane in 1889 Constance quickly found a place as 'lady companion' to Mrs Webber, wife of the owner of Kyabra, a sheep and cattle station in the far southwest of Queensland, near Eromanga. Six months after arriving at Kyabra, she and the station bookkeeper, Thomas James Ellis, travelled to Thargomindah to be married. They had bought a buggy and planned to make their way back to Brisbane (about 700 miles) to start a new life. However, as Constance recorded in her memoir, *I Seek Adventure*, published in 1981, 'Malcolm was well over four years old when we reached there'.[1] He was in fact nearly ten, and there were two younger brothers and a sister by the time the Ellises gave up their wandering life and settled in Mount Morgan in 1899. Thomas Ellis found work in the mines there and the children began formal schooling. They must already have been well taught by their mother, however, because at 14, Malcolm won a scholarship to Brisbane Grammar School.

After editing the school magazine he gained a cadetship on the Brisbane *Daily Mail*. He probably would have liked to go on and study law, but there was as yet no university in Queensland and his family could

1   Constance Jane Ellis, *I Seek Adventure*, Alternative Publishing Co-operative Ltd, Sydney, 1981, p.14

not afford the cost of private legal training. Malcolm quickly gained a reputation as a capable journalist and as a press advisor to the National Party. Disqualified from war service because he was blind in one eye as the result of a childhood accident, by 1920 he had married and moved to Sydney to the *Daily Telegraph* as chief political correspondent. In 1926 he was sent to London to take charge of the *Telegraph*'s office.[2]

He had already begun 'an intensive general reading of the printed historical documents of the period from 1789 when Macquarie went to India with his regiment until he died.'[3] And after he had visited Macquarie country in Scotland, talked to family members and other connections and sought out documentary material, he wrote a first draft of an Introduction to a biography of Macquarie in 1926. An overland car trip to India the next year enabled him to visit sites connected with Macquarie there. Back in Australia in 1928, doing contract and freelance work, he had time to examine the Mitchell Library's relevant holdings and to complete a first draft of the biography. In 1933, however, he joined the staff of the *Bulletin* and had less time for his historical work, and the appearance of substantial books on Bligh[4] and the Rum Rebellion[5] threw doubts on some of his earlier work. By 1939 his draft contained 28 chapters, but when he began revising, checking his sources as he went, he found a lot more material that seemed to warrant inclusion even though it hindered the flow of the narrative. By now he was so proud and possessive of his research that he was unwilling to leave any of it out and the MSS grew ever larger and more unwieldy.[6] Nonetheless, he submitted it for the S.H. Prior Prize in 1939.

The Prior Prize had been established in memory of a former editor whose family still held a controlling interest in the *Bulletin*. The judging panel in 1939, Frank Dalby Davison, H.M. Green (Fisher Librarian at the University of Sydney), and playwright Louis Esson, decided in favour of Ellis's work; but Kenneth Prior at the *Bulletin* who knew Ellis too well, was concerned about its accuracy. So Davison sought an expert opinion from

---

2   There is an entry on Ellis in *The Australian Dictionary of Biography*, Vol. 14 by Brian Fletcher. See also Andrew Moore, 'The "Historical Expert": M.H. Ellis and the Historiography of the Cold War', *Australian Historical Studies*, Vol. 31, No. 114, April 2000, pp. 91–109

3   M.H. Ellis Papers, Mitchell Library, Author's Note in MSS Vol. submitted for the Prior Prize, 1940, Box K21886

4   George Mackaness, *The Life of Vice-Admiral William Bligh*, Angus & Robertson, Sydney, 1931

5   H.V. Evatt, *Rum Rebellion*, Angus & Robertson, Sydney, 1938

6   For the later consequences of Ellis's possessiveness see Andrew Moore, ' "History without Facts": M.H. Ellis, Manning Clark and the origins of *The Australian Dictionary of Biography*', *Journal of the Royal Australian Historical Society*, Vol. 85, Part 2, December 1999, pp. 71–84

Ida Leeson, the Mitchell Librarian.[7] It seems that Davison may also have showed the MSS to Marjorie Barnard, with whom he was then having an affair. Barnard, an honours history graduate from the University of Sydney, was at that time engaged on research in the same period, published in 1941 as *Macquarie's World*.[8] (Charles Currey, another historian with expertise in the area, declined an invitation to read the MSS on the grounds that the fee offered was too small for the amount of work involved.) Miss Leeson was not impressed by Ellis's scholarship and it was decided to award the prize to the next MSS on the list, Miles Franklin and Kate Baker's study of Joseph Furphy, with the understanding that Ellis could clean up his MSS and re-submit in 1940. This he did. In his papers in the Mitchell Library there are three thick volumes of typescript, corrected and annotated in Ellis's hand, with a fourth volume of notes and appendices as submitted for the Prior Prize in 1940.

Although it won the prize — the chair of the judging panel, Davison, described it as 'monumental' — there was some difficulty about getting it published, probably because it was so big. When Ellis submitted it to the Commonwealth Literary Fund for assistance with publication he was advised that it would need cutting by about a third. Meanwhile Ellis was invited to deliver two 1942 John Murtagh Macrossan lectures at the University of Queensland, where he discussed Macquarie's struggle with the brothers Bent over the administration of justice in NSW as well as Macquarie's time in India. Eventually, in 1947, Angus & Robertson published *Lachlan Macquarie* as a large, handsome volume with illustrations in colour. Since then there have been three revised editions, the last in 1965. (Ellis died in 1967.) A fifth edition appeared in 1973 and in 1978 it was re-issued in the Famous Australian Lives series (along with, among others, Ellis's biographies of both Greenway and Macarthur).

From the beginning, Ellis's Macquarie is the son who is destined to rescue the name of his family, once proud chieftains of Ulva, an island in the Inner Hebrides of Scotland, now poor farmers.[9] There are few records of Macquarie's early years, before he became, with the help of his uncle Murdoch Maclaine, 'The Dashing Lieutenant' in the second battalion of the 84th Regiment serving in the Americas. In 1788 he joined a new regiment, the 77th, raised for service in India. Ellis shows him as ambitious, both for promotion and to improve his financial position though winning his share of looted gold and jewels. Ellis was fond of things military. He describes uncritically the British Army in India sacking and plundering wherever they went. Macquarie's involvement in the defeat of Tippoo Sahib at the battle of Seringapatam is a highlight.

7   Sylvia Martin, *Ida Leeson: A life*, Allen & Unwin, Crows Nest NSW, 2006, p. 123
8   By The Australian Limited Editions Society, Sydney, 1941
9   Macquarie's Scottish inheritance is neatly summarised in Malcolm D. Prentis's *The Scots in Australia: A study of New South Wales, Victoria and Queensland, 1788–1900*, Sydney University Press, 1983, p. 36

Besides winning promotion and enough treasure to begin the process of buying back the family estate, in India Macquarie became a 'benedict'. His bride, Jane Jarvis, was heiress to a West Indian fortune and, though her death from consumption in 1797 just before their third wedding anniversary was devastating, her fortune enabled Macquarie to complete the purchase of land in Mull that he named Jarvisfield in her memory.

In 1804, while Macquarie was on a trip home to organise his affairs, 'Lord Ullin's Daughter', Elizabeth Campbell of Airds, agreed to marry him when his next tour of duty in India was over in 1807. Elizabeth was by then 29; Macquarie was 46. It says a great deal about the nature of their relationship that she allowed their first child to be named Jane Jarvis, but the baby survived only a few months. Now a Lieutenant Colonel and second in command of the 73rd regiment, Macquarie was reluctantly 'transported to NSW', to clean up the mess left by the rebellion against Governor Bligh. When his commanding officer could not make the journey, however, Macquarie was elevated, becoming Governor of NSW by default.

After the Macquaries arrived in Sydney on 28 December 1809, a deceptive mood of calm there allowed them 'a wonderful year'. With the departure of both the NSW Corps and many of those involved in the overthrow of Bligh, either to face trial, or to appear as witnesses, or to pursue other interests in relation to the troubles, there was a kind of power vacuum. But the colony was also sadly bereft of men who were capable, experienced, or knew enough to serve in its administration. Macquarie has been given much credit for his broadminded attitude towards former convicts and temperamentally he was probably inclined to encourage those who had reformed and prospered, but in reality he had no choice but to seek out ability among the emancipists. However this also aroused the disgust of those like the Reverend Samuel Marsden and the Bent brothers, who considered that no former convict could ever be trusted.

To this point Ellis's biography of Maquarie has been carefully chronological. The subsequent chapters though become more thematic as Macquarie finds himself at odds with different leading men of the colony on a range of issues, both large and small. Some of the clashes were of personality, others over differing views of the future of the colony. There were now several settlers who had become wealthy beyond their wildest dreams either though the acquisition of land or the construction of trading monopolies: men like Marsden, a poor boy chosen to receive a rudimentary training by a religious charity interested in providing some kind of ministry to the convicts; or John Macarthur, a common soldier with an eye to the main chance. Unlike these contemporaries, Macquarie knew that his service in NSW was costing him money. His power as governor was compromised because it was known that his term in the colony was finite. Furthermore, as a Scot, his command of influence at Westminster was inferior to those who had been cultivating British officials for decades.

Ellis attributes many of the positive aspects of Macquarie's policies in NSW, however, to his Scottish inheritance and experience. After all, his family's estate and the army were the only administrative models he knew. He probably saw NSW as a larger Jarvisfield, a vast estate needing new roads, buildings and villages that he could create with the assistance of his tenants and labourers, the landowners and the convicts. Even the Aborigines became part of his responsibility as the laird: they were the poorest of his people, who needed education for their children if they were to become good tenants. 'In their habits,' Ellis writes, 'the aborigines were uncommonly like the lower order of Highlander of the sixteenth and seventeenth centuries, though in some ways less impish in their mischiefs.'[10] When they became really troublesome Macquarie did not hesitate to send his men against them, just as he sent troops to flush out bushrangers outside Hobart.

The 'mere sassenachs' who knew that the future for them lay in NSW were not sympathetic to the plans of the laird. Nor were they willing to be treated as adjuncts to the military garrison that provided Macquarie's other model for the management of the colony, where commands were to be obeyed and duty done. A serious debate was emerging about the direction the convict colony should take, focussed on the role of law under military rule. And while Macquarie did his best to provide employment for the ever-growing number of convicts by developing public works, there were those both in Sydney and London who believed the convicts would be better employed as cheap labour for capitalists wishing to create local enterprises such as the production of wool.

Though he tried to resign first in 1817, Macquarie served longer as governor than any of his predecessors. Some of the things for which he is remembered were almost accidental, such as his part in the inevitable expansion of the colony after a route was found across the Blue Mountains. But though there can be no doubt that the colony had reached the stage of needing decent public buildings, the conjunction of Macquarie's enthusiasm for building, Elizabeth's sense of style, and their choice of the talented former convict Francis Greenway as architect gave Sydney some beautiful landmarks. Macquarie's vision beyond the daily requirements of administration is evident in his recognition of the potential of Matthew Flinders's use of the name 'Australia' in a report on his circumnavigation of the continent in 1801. Without Macquarie's deft appreciation we may never have advanced beyond New Holland or Botany Bay; with a new name in place it was easier to throw off the associations of those older terms. However, these developments are now usually associated with Bigge's Reports and the beginnings of self-government in 1823 than with Macquarie.

It was 1822, well after his third resignation had been accepted and his replacement had arrived, before Macquarie was able to leave NSW, already

10 Ch XXIV 'The red-spattered Tartans', p. 351 in the 1970 edn (upper case as in the original)

60 and far from well. He died in London in 1824, having struggled to obtain the pension he believed his due, and believing that Bigge had destroyed his name and that he had been a failure even though much of his time in NSW had been personally satisfactory. He had achieved much for the ordinary people, and his happiness with Elizabeth — who had enthusiastically accompanied him on his journeys around his 'estate' and, after many distressing miscarriages, had at last succeeded in giving birth to 'his young posterity' — was unbounded. And as Ellis points out Macquarie's name lived on in NSW.

Ellis concludes with a list of places and things named Macquarie, adding to the 1965 revision Macquarie University, then being built. Since then, the university may have abandoned its symbolic link with Macquarie's lighthouse, and the Macquarie Broadcasting network may have disappeared, but at least two more significant institutions have been added to Ellis's list — Australia's own *Macquarie Dictionary*, now under the aegis of Sydney University, and the Macquarie Bank with its international business.

Macquarie has not been lucky with his biographers, who have been drawn to the romance of his life but struggled to convey an idea of the man. The first doctorate in Australian history, a study of the Macquarie period by Marion Phillips at the recently established London School of Economics under the supervision of Graham Wallas and Sidney Webb and published in 1909 as *A Colonial Autocracy*, described Macquarie as 'a man of very ordinary ability' who for a brief period wielded extraordinary power.[11] Phillips was a daughter of a liberal Melbourne Jewish family, cousin of the artist Emanuel Phillips Fox, aunt of literary critic A.A. Phillips, one of the early women graduates of Melbourne University, and winner of a travelling scholarship to the LSE. There she was able to access the Colonial office records for her study of Macquarie's governorship. She thrived in the Fabian, suffragist and trade union world of Edwardian London, worked as a research assistant for Beatrice Webb, and as a personal assistant to Ramsay and Margaret Macdonald, eventually becoming the organiser of the women's section of the British Labour Party and in 1929 MP for Sunderland. Her judgment of Macquarie was in keeping with her idealistic yet pragmatic embrace of labour politics in Britain. She was more interested in government and administration than in personality. Ellis was more inclined to look for the heroic, and ultimately tragic, individual. He listed Phillips's work in his bibliography, but he was never inclined to bother with secondary sources nor allow that others had also studied the original documents as he had.

In his note on the Prior Prize MSS Ellis wrote, 'The author has relied wholly on contemporary sources and tried to let the subjects speak for

11 Marion Phillips, *A Colonial Autocracy: New South Wales under Governor Macquarie, 1810–1821*, P. S. King & Son, London, 1909, reissued by Frank Cass and Co., Ltd, London, 1971, and Sydney University Press, 1971, p. vii

themselves ... events have been left to describe the natures of those who were involved in them.' He quotes extensively and at length from Macquarie's letters and diaries and other contemporary sources, and it seems as if after immersing himself in the extreme formality of their eighteenth-century prose, he was reluctant to return to plainer prose. Modern readers may find some of his allusions and usages now archaic or puzzling. Latin tags (as a schoolboy Ellis had excelled at Latin), and obscure references, classical, biblical, literary and contemporary are frequent. For example, the chapter on Marsden is headed 'A new Balbus', and while Ellis's contemporaries may have understood his allusions to significant Australians whose mothers were convicts, 60 years later most are quite obscure. (see p. 151 of the 1970 reprint). A later biographer, John Ritchie, also had difficulty escaping the prose of Macquarie's time. [12] Noel McLachlan's 1967 entry in the *Australian Dictionary of Biography* is recommended for a short and simple outline of Macquarie's life.

Ellis hoped that he had written 'a useful source book not only to the historian but to the writer of fiction who delights in picturesque characters ... the whole is full of dramatic situations and characters waiting to be ushered into Australian literature.' It seems likely that Eleanor Dark had read Ellis's biography before writing the third volume of her *Timeless Land* trilogy, *No Barrier* (1953) dealing in part with the Macquarie years. Readers of Alex Buzo's play, *Macquarie* (1971), are referred to Ellis along with C.M.H. Clark's *A History of Australia* Vol. 1 (1962) and the *ADB* as sources. Lysbeth Cohen's semi-fictional *Elizabeth Macquarie: Her life and times* appeared during the feminist rediscovery of Australian history. [13] It lists Ellis among its sources without any specific references. Elizabeth Macquarie is also emphasised in Alan Atkinson's account of the Macquaries as a modernising and humanising influence on her husband. Atkinson suggests trying to understand Macquarie as a 'good king', but unlike Ellis he is not much interested in Macquarie's Scottish background. [14]

We are no longer inclined to bestow on individuals the kind of significance Ellis accorded to Macquarie. Nor do we place so much faith in the ability of the written record to reveal 'the truth'. Modern writer Kate Grenville's impressive use of the sources and the evidence in writing her novel set partly in the Macquarie period, *The Secret River* (2005), would probably have given Ellis apoplexy. [15] Yet his book remains a monument to not only the Macquarie years but also to the views and values of the times in which he himself lived and wrote.

12 *Lachlan Macquarie: A biography*, Melbourne University Press, 1986
13 Wentworth Books Pty Ltd, Sydney, 1979
14 *The Europeans in Australia: A History*, Vol. 1, Oxford University Press, Melbourne, 1997
15 *Searching for the Secret River*, Text Publishing Co, Melbourne, 2006

INTRODUCTION

The Fall of Ulva

I

FOR several hundred years before the eighteenth century a clan, whose members called themselves "The Sons of Guarie"—the Macquaries or MacQuaries[1]—dwelt in the isle of Ulva, which lies in the arms of Mull, in the Inner Hebrides, off the west coast of Scotland.

They were lordlings, also, over some other small lands and isles round about . . . a strip of Mull itself obtained in the early sixteenth century, Little Colonsay and, out to sea, Staffa, with its famous Cave of Fingal.

They were a tough, hardy breed. Much Norwegian sea-going blood, but more of the Celtic ichor, coursed in their veins.

The heraldic achievement of the clan bears the conventional grants of those who took part in the Norse expulsions.[2] It tells plainly their near relationship to the Mackinnons and to the MacDonalds of the main line of Sleat.

The name of their island, Ullfur, "The Island of Wolves", advertised their primeval natures.

Their war cry was a blood-curdling yell of "*An-t-arm breac dearg!*"— "Here come the red-spattered tartans!" Their badge was the *giuthas*, the grim *pinus insignus* of the north, resistant to the strongest gale; their crest, the dagger, which spoke clearly to all islemen with imagination and ribs.

II

Ulva was no nest in which the soft or unthrifty could hope to survive.

It flung itself up, a shaggy, five-mile-long heave of furze and heather and nettle, from the sea to the top of the towering Ben Chreagach, "The Rocky Mountain".

Its weather was dramatically uncertain and inclement.

Savage polar winds howling down from the North Atlantic set its caves rumbling almost every day in winter. Its miserable vegetation was nearly always dripping.

The driving rains which swept it shrieked on across dark Loch-na-Keale to batter the summits of the south Mull bens. But, for all that, it knew days of azure beauty, sombre purple calms when the sea was like a sheet of olive glass, and nights when the summit of Ben More stood in sharp and frostily-white relief against a soft-starred east under the moon.

A race which for centuries dwelt in such a region became involuntarily shaped in form and character to the mould of its environment. Its qualities and tendencies grew fully into tune with surrounding nature. It partook of the gustiness and rudeness which were inherent in the turbulent climate, though its moods were illumined periodically by reflections of the lighter and gayer phases of the seasons.

Men of Ulva were ever ready for a queigh of whisky or for a foray. They sometimes romaticized women and—especially after shedding blood—they indulged lustily in song.

In their prime they were the most acquisitive raiders who ever purloined barley.

They even boasted a collateral ancestor who once had stolen a bishopric![3]

III

At first the lands which these delightful Hebrideans held were regarded as clan properties; but in time the chieftains and their cadet houses secured them as their own under Royal Charter granted by a frugal Crown, whose law officers were not unmindful of the legal, duty to pay taxes attached to established personal titles.

However, after the Old Pretender's Rebellion clans and chieftains in the Scottish West were alike dispossessed and the year of Forty-five put its seal on the disaster.

The sixteenth Chieftain of Ulva, the last and ironically the longest lived, the sire of eight daughters and seven sons, became a mere mortgagor drawing rentals of about three pounds a week from an estate which the Campbell moneylenders sold over his head in 1778 for less than £6000.[4]

"*Aspectum generosum habet*," said Boswell to the Sage of Litchfield, as they tasted of this old man's hospitality some years before his downfall.

"*Et generosum animum*," conceded the Sage, carefully removing his soused foot from a puddle on the clay floor of the chieftain's best bedroom.

But the good old Scottish gentleman's high qualities of heart and mind could not save him from the moneylenders. He was constrained to leave the "mean house"[5]—with its elegant bed and very draughty best bedroom— in which Doctor Johnson discovered him during the journey to the Hebrides.

He abandoned for ever his presumptive claim to exercise the rights of *mercheta mulierum*—a romantic privilege which he was wont to commute for five shillings or a sheep. His offspring were thrown into a pitiless world, which quickly destroyed them all.

There was, in fact, no resource left to him at the age of sixty-three years save to take a lieutenancy in the 74th Regiment and hie him to the American wars, from which he returned to draw half-pay for four decades more.

He died in 1818, at the heroic age of 103, the last Hebridean relic of the age of Sheriffmuir and, to the end, "intelligent, polite and much a man of the world[6]," even while he eked out his pension with the contributions of his relatives.

His clansmen, long before misfortune struck him down, were dispersed, their chieftain's ancient authority forgotten or ignored.

Even when the magic carpet of the middle years of the eighteenth century had begun to unroll, displaying all its richly woven pattern of wars and plunder, the Macquaries were represented in Mull and Ulva only by a few poor farmer landlords and tacksmen, and by a crowd of hungry tradesmen and drovers of the name, the whole clinging like limpets to the patronage of richer connections by marriage or tenancy among the Macleans and Campbells.

Many years before the old chieftain's death, one of the residue of his kin, his cousin-german, who was not so unfortunate as the rest, could write, "Our ancient clan and name are of late years reduced to great poverty, indeed; and I assure you it would afford me the most heartfelt pleasure and gratification to raise a few of the most deserving of them from obscurity."[7]

The author of that mournful passage was born on 31 January 1761.

He himself was not destined to be the plaything of obscurity.

His name, LACHLAN MACQUARIE, is known to every schoolchild in the antipodean continent which he ruled for a dozen years, and for longer than any other single man, but which had held not a single European in the year of his birth.

CONTENTS

★

ILLUSTRATIONS

★

MAP

BOOK ONE

*

1761 - 96

*

The Soldier and His Bride

Mirth! airy child of fond delight!
And Fancy! eldest born of Jove,
Haste to the Syren call of Love,
And now, while health and youth unite
To Beauty in its earliest Prime,
To Worth in radiant armour bright
Inured its Country's Cause to fight,
Swell the loud Symphony sublime!

Let odours from Arabian vales
Breathe gently on the saline gales
And not a sound in aether float,
Save the soft dove's enamoured note,
Till the bright star of evening rise
Auspicious to the Lover's sighs
And Cynthia with her paler fire,
Warns lingering Beauty to retire.

—Michael Massey Robinson, From "Epithalamium".

CHAPTER I

The Dashing Lieutenant

I

THE first month of 1761, on the last day of which Lachlan Macquarie was born on the isle of Ulva,[1] marked the beginning of the long, hard, historical autumn of the eighteenth century as well as the premature arrival of the spring of the year.

Birds nested that January in Coomb Wood near Wimbledon. Primroses and daisies appeared in Sussex well ahead of the snowdrops. Homing swallows were noticed in Wales, and strawberries fruited in Devonshire.[2]

George II, dead of a literally broken heart,[3] had not so long been carried to his grave among six dukes. George III, "the patriot King compleat", was devising excuses to rid himself of that jewel in his crown, the elder Pitt, who was busily engaged in "conquering India on the fields of Germany". The Seven Years' War had spent its greatest heat. France, the arch-offender in it, had become the prime mover in seeking peace. The names of Arcot and Wandewash, Glatz, Minden, and Montreal had risen in the public consciousness to shadow memories of Blenheim and Fontenoy. Men thought for the moment of Wolfe rather than of Marlborough; and nobody had yet discerned that the impending surrender of Canada might start a chain of events ending in the loss of most of Britain's American colonies.

In Pondicherry the forces of the East India Company and of Admiral Stevens were making M. Lally most unhappy. And in Mysore the erstwhile Punjabi peon, Haidar Ali, was about to institute that period of bloodshed and atrocity which closed more than a generation later when Tippoo, his son, lay stripped and slaughtered in the Palace of Seringapatam.

The events with which the period was pregnant promised great advantage to every Highlander who came within the ambit of Pitt's new schemes of Scottish recruitment; but the vital statistics of the hardy and useful northerners were little noticed.

No chronicler recorded the details of the birth and first years of survival of Lachlan Macquarie in the rugged, remote, gale-swept islet off the coast of Mull in which he began his adventurous existence.

II

Young Lachlan seems to have been a member of the poorer of the two main septs of Clan Macquarie, that of Ormaig,[4] whose senior member held a small farm, soon to be lost to the Campbells, on the flattest part of Ulva facing eastward across the water to the lands of Argyll.

There is no positive identification either of his father or of his birth-place. Were there not immutable laws of nature, casual readers of his history might even have deduced that he was the product of a virgin birth. All his parental references till late in life are exclusively to his mother. He makes only three mentions of his father—one to give his name, one his burial place and one to record that his parent, as well as his brother Hector, had died of "a pleurotic fever". The voluminous panegyric[5] on the son's tombstone does not speak of his male parentage.

Lachlan's mother was a daughter of one of the Maclaine chieftains of Lochbuy who owned a castle on a yellow hill in Mull. Her mother in turn was a half-sister of the fifteenth Macquarie chieftain of Ulva, of whose sixteenth and last chieftain her son proclaims himself cousin-german. Such relationships were normal and usual in a community in which scarcely a Macquarie had failed to marry within his own or the Maclean clans for two hundred years,[6] and in which the young man himself was presently to become brother-in-law to his own uncle.

There is no extant physical description of Mrs Macquarie. She was obviously the type of hard-working, self-respecting widow so common in the Isles and Highlands in those days of frequent bloodshed and far-flung adventure. Under the protection of her brother, Murdoch Maclaine, Chieftain of Lochbuy, she eked out a very thrifty existence for herself and her family on a poor farm at Oskamull on Mull, which she rented from 1775 onwards from the Duke of Argyll.

Two of her sons already lay buried with their father at Kilvicheoin. A daughter, Betty, married a Maclaine neighbour. And the remaining three sons—Donald, Lachlan, and Charles—remained on the little farm until Lachlan went abroad with the American War contingents, Charles became an officer of the Black Watch and Donald died in their absence at the age of fifty-one.[7]

After his death the old lady seems to have lived alone during her remaining years, her welfare a matter of constant solicitude to Lachlan, her elder surviving son, whose progress was paved with acts of benevolence towards her whom he described as "my amiable, good, affectionate mother".

He, however, gives us no picture of her, tells us nothing of her nature; and there is no correspondence to clarify their personal relationships. There is, indeed, room for more than a suspicion that, like many a West Highland farm wife entitled to enrolment in the Scottish baronages, she could not read or write a letter; for it was her son's habit to communicate with her, not directly, but through her brother, the reigning chieftain of Lochbuy: ". . . Send for my good mother, on receipt of this, and with my dutiful and affectionate good wishes, tell her of all my good fortunes, and that she must now live for at least twenty years longer."[3]

This injunction the hardy old lady obeyed. She died in her eighty-second year, on 29 November 1810.

III

Young Macquarie's father could at best have been a poor tacksman, dwelling in a rain-seeped cottage, perhaps eking out his resources with a little droving. His own clan, through their misfortune with the moneylenders and the smallness of their patrimony, could have done little for him or for his progeny.

Young Lachlan, therefore, had very good reason to thank Providence for having elected as his guardian his mother's brother, Maclaine of Lochbuy, with whom he shared the streams of the ancient blood of Ulva and of the clans of Gillean.

Thus, from the beginning, he found himself under the immediate and friendly protection of "a great Highland Laird whose grounds for game are the most extensive in Mull . . . the best shooting ground in all the Highlands, for grouse, black game and the red deer"; one who aided him "in getting through the world, from my earliest youth, with credit and honour".[9]

Lochbuy sent him to school—tradition says to sit at the feet of the great Adam, in whose seminary the wonders of the Greek tongue had become manifest to Scottish youth. But the Royal High School of Edinburgh today possesses no record of his attendance, though this is not conclusive evidence, since masters' rolls before 1800 are not available.

It was Lochbuy, too, who by procuring the influence which presently sent him to the wars made it unnecessary for him to remain uneconomically long at whatever school he attended; the same Lochbuy who financed his early expeditions; the same who, though descending later in status to become merely a "pleasant old veteran", remained his ward's friend, left him to be one of the chief mourners at his graveside, and at the end entrusted him with the guardianship of his own numerous progeny.

To tell the truth, young Macquarie had more in common with this helpful relation than with the members of his own clan. Though he had a Highlander's reverence for his chieftain, the family traditions and habits which shaped his life were almost entirely those of his mother's people, through whom he inherited many of the traits of that "facile" old John Maclaine whom Dr Johnson had known, and whose status as a human boundary-mark between the feudal and the modern Isles was illustrated by the facts that he was fined by the Court of Session for exercising his forfeited right to put his clansmen in his private pit, and that he was deprived of his war-saddle by his son Archibald, who rode away upon it behind his drove to Falkirk Fair.

IV

Of young Macquarie's boyhood there is nothing to tell.

It is not even known whether, as a boy of eleven years, he saw and spoke to the restless, scholarly young gentleman, Joseph Banks,[10] fresh home from Botany Bay, who stayed on Mull with Maclean of Drimnin and viewed that strange Macquarie heritage, the wondrous Cave of Fingal on Staffa.

If he did attend the Royal Edinburgh High School, he did not remain long enough to see the old school-house, with its grim turrets from which of yore students had sallied forth to destroy uncongenial burgesses, give place in 1778 to a newer building. But his education progressed till he could write, in a good clear hand, a very average sort of eighteenth-century English and provide the world with absolute evidence that he had read two books at least, though he could plead in extenuation that one of them mentioned his family very favourably. One was Boswell's *Journey to the Hebrides*; the other, *Candide*, which in the last decades of the eighteenth century was to be found in every boudoir.

It is recorded at the War Office that he was familiar with the French language of which, no doubt, he learned something in Canada, but in which he admitted that he was a very "indifferent scholar". He had a mind "not able or inclined to attend much to study"; and a single resolution taken in India in a moment of exaltation to employ, daily, the hours between twelve and two o'clock in improving his knowledge came rapidly to naught.

At any rate, his higher education was cut short by the outbreak of the American War. What young Hebridean would linger in school when there was an influential relative—no less than his cousin Colonel Allan Maclean, son of the Laird of Torloisk—at work recruiting battalions to fall upon the dazzled Americans in full Black Watch dress, diversified with raccoon-skin sporrans, and led by officers armed with claymore and dirk?

The privileged males of the Isles from old MacQuarie of Ulva, who was sixty-three years of age, to his cousin-german, young Lachlan Macquarie, who was something under fifteen, left their farms and colleges in an importunate scramble for lieutenancies and ensigncies.

Old MacQuarie of Ulva marched manfully as one of the oldest lieutenants in the Army; young Lachlan, too young for a commission, preceded him abroad as a volunteer with the 84th Regiment, known as Maclean's Regiment, on the waiting list for the first commissioned vacancy. He landed in Halifax on 31 October 1776, and received his commission as ensign five months after reaching Canada.

He served with the second battalion of his regiment, commanded by Major John Small of Strath Ardle, in Halifax and Nova Scotia generally, till 1780.[11]

In 1781 he was transferred to the 71st Highland Regiment and was stationed in New York and Charleston and finally in Jamaica—where Sir Archibald Campbell held Supreme Command—till the end of the American War.

Three years later he went home, as a half-pay lieutenant, having seen no fighting.

He was twenty-three years of age. He had spent nearly one-third of his life under rough barrack conditions. He had learnt obedience during his most receptive period under stern disciplinarians; and he came back to Scotland to find his family struggling with their farm at Oskamull after the hard famine years of 1781-3.

What he did with himself in the next three years nobody knows. Legend says that he attended lectures at Edinburgh University; but there is no record to support this. From his own reference a few years later to his being, at that time, "so long in Mull" it seems unlikely.

Undoubtedly, he was not idle. It was not in his nature to be so. And he was not unsocial—as witness the number of friends to whom he wrote from India at later dates, the "thousands" of female cousins to whom, for ever after, he must bring small presents whenever he returned from abroad, the platoons of cousins-german and nephews who sought his patronage when he became a dispenser of favours in his after years. His acquaintanceship, in those days while he was immured in Mull, must have been wide.

V

In the early winter of 1787, "the late bustle with France having obliged Government to make an augmentation of the Army, orders were issued to raise four regiments to serve in India".[12]

General Allan Maclean again played the part of patron. He secured that of one of the regiments, the 77th, which was not to be a Highland regiment, Lachlan should be the eldest lieutenant, provided that he could find fifteen recruits for the colonel's company.

It is quite patent, from his elation, that the young man knew that his chance had come. From now onward his career would be worth recording.

He bought a white, vellum-bound book and ruled a line down the left side of each page, another across the top. He carefully numbered and dated every page, and the cover soon bore the inscription in the later well-known handwriting:

Journal—No. 1
Kept by L. Macquarie,
Commencing 15*th Decr* 1787.[13]

From the moment he took his pen to inscribe the first meticulously written page there was no more need to surmise about him for many a year. He chronicled his doings and his reflections. He told his thoughts about his brides as well as those about his battles. He mentioned his generosities and his angers, measured his wealth periodically to a bottle of wine; and did it all with an air of almost comic faith in himself and in his own ethics, which he epitomizes in a letter to a sister-in-law in 1794 during a family quarrel by asserting that he is "conscious of the innocence and rectitude of my own conduct which has yet been unsullied and no one has ever dared to impeach".[14]

Many other young men of his time made a point of cultivating an identical attitude towards their own perfections. The private correspondence of that curious age is rich in the same sentiments expressed in similar formalized phrases.

VI

Macquarie was nearly twenty-seven years old when he received his "beating orders and recruiting instructions"[15] at Oskamull, on 16 November 1787, and went abroad in advance of the depth of the Mull winter, to try to enlist his fifteen recruits.

The rough tracks of the islands already were so wet that a horse might not safely pass over them, and human travellers sank to their ankles in the ooze. Clansmen, shivering over their fires of peat, in such a season preferred whisky to war, and the days were long past when a chieftain might successfully send a fiery cross through the Highlands.

The lieutenant by 15 December had been across the Sound of Lorne and walked the hills of Morven and Ardnamurchan in person, but without success. He had been "equally unfortunate in all parts of Mull". His Uncle Lochbuy, "notwithstanding his powerful interest among his own clan and tenants could not prevail with one of them to enlist". The persuasions of his "good friend Torloisk"—father of Mrs Clephane, later the treasured intimate and adored hostess of Scott and of himself alike— "which was all he could make use of", had no effect.

The human game was equally shy, Macquarie reported, "in the place of my nativity and ancient possessions of my ancestors; among my own clan and namesakes, the Macquaries of Ulva; where every fair and lawful means were used by . . . my relation the Laird of Macquarie, and myself".

"Such," he wrote, "is the aversion of these people to become soldiers or to go abroad, that notwithstanding all the entreaties of their old chief and master, not one of his ungrateful clan, (to whom he had been in the days of his prosperity, a most kind and generous master), would enlist or follow me and his own son Murdoch Macquarie, (a lad about sixteen years of age) who voluntarily offered to follow my fortunes and push his own in India as a volunteer."

He was not, however, much surprised, though at the same time exceedingly displeased. Ulva's tenants had treated their old chief in exactly the same manner when he had obtained his commission to serve in the American War.

VII

The Highlands were evidently hopeless for recruiting; so about twelve o'clock on Saturday 15 December 1787, Lachlan determined to set out for the Low Country without loss of time, to prospect fresh and more fruitful fields.

His equipment for adventure was strictly limited as he took leave of his mother and his friends and, with his brother Charles and the young volunteer, Murdoch MacQuarie, old Ulva's son, strode away from Oskamull through tempestuous rain.

He parted with his brother at Crogan Ferry and tramped in leisurely fashion, farewelling his many friends along the route, through Inveraray and Sonachans, a guide carrying his portmanteau. A hired wherry wafted him over the Clyde on a beautiful moonlight night to Greenock. There, after a fatiguing march, having travelled "all the way on foot from my mother's house hither, being nearly about one hundred miles", he put up at the White Hart Inn, before beginning to beat his next hunting ground in Glasgow upon Christmas Day.

Even now success called for all his energies and for those of his relations who scoured the countryside loyally on his behalf as far away as Oban, on one side, and Edinburgh, on the other. The records of the next three months of his life were made up of struggle and disappointment evolving, in the end, into only a mitigated triumph. It was 21 January 1788, as Phillip was in Botany Bay, before he could line up twenty recruits to be inspected and given refreshment by Lochbuy in the good old Highland style. But at length he marched his troops proudly aboard the *Livingston* packet at Leith, behind a piper. He enjoyed a sober farewell dinner given him at Gibbes's Coffee House by a tableful of Highland chieftains headed by old Ulva. He suffered, in a cabin full of "boys and whores" bound to London to make their fortunes, a voyage to Gravesend which the howling North Sea weather lengthened from the normal four days to a solid month. He met, unflinching, during that period, the frugal and pleading eye of the Scottish skipper who had bargained to give the men "good usage" during the voyage at a guinea a head. He marched triumphantly through the lanes of Kent at the head of his troop, "to set an example"; and he was greeted at the journey's end by his old friend Captain James Dunlop, the redoubtable officer who had given John Moore so much cause for gratitude at Penobscot.

In the week that followed, however, the joy of his reunions gave way to other feelings. Events were certainly not such as to produce any elation in a frugal breast. Lieutenant-Colonel Balfour, a "plain good sort of man", rejected four of his recruits—one too old, one ruptured, and that quaint pair, Waddle and Dick, for being undersized. There was anguish in the deprived officer's heart as he wrote of "the great cruel loss" of recruiting money, expenses and bounties he would suffer; and he showed even more "displeasure and disappointment" when Colonel Marsh "neither received him with that civility and attention" which he had expected from the influence of letters of introduction from Lieutenant-Colonel Alexander Lesslie and Major-General John Campbell, nor with that politeness to which he had always been accustomed from previous commanding officers. The grumpy old colonel, indeed, expressed pained surprise that his eldest lieutenant had not joined the regiment earlier, complaining that "he expected from what he was told, of the great interest and influence, that my friends had in the Highlands, that I would have brought at least a hundred recruits".

Actually, Macquarie's effective contribution to the strength of the regiment had been seventeen men. The financial return from this modest recruitment was such as to allow him to send his Uncle Lochbuy £45 out of the £127 7s. he had borrowed from him to start afresh his military career. And the 5th Company, which he was appointed to command, proved to be "one of the best Battalion Companies in the Regiment".

VIII

At length all was ready for departure to India. Macquarie had enjoyed a fortnight of final leave in London, staying at the Cecil Coffee House in the Strand (kept by a Maclean), wandering here and there among the shops, as his relative and sponsor, Colonel Allan Maclean, "pointed out everything necessary for an Indian voyage". He had met his friend, Allan Park, whose chambers were in Carey Street, and his old comrades of the 84th Regiment. He had indulged one night with acquaintances in a "very droll ramble through *many* very *curious places* in the town", though he regretted that he had lacked time to go to Hammersmith to visit his cousin Betsy Campbell, who was at boarding-school there, and of whom in later years he was to see a very great deal.

All these adventures past, he had set out from the Blue Boar in Holborn at 7 p.m. one evening, and had climbed down from the coach at Dover at 6 a.m. next day.

His kit was complete. Over his well-being presided a Scottish servant, whom a cousin had found for him in Edinburgh, one Donald Campbell who "dressed hair remarkably well, waited table and played very well upon the fiddle".

He ate his last meal in England for many a day at the City of Antwerp Inn at Dover. He marched his company a brisk seven miles to the beach at Deal where he regaled the men with bread and cheese and porter—"a very acceptable treat". Cheering and excited, they stepped into the boats which were to bear them to the East Indiaman *Dublin*.

On 28 March 1788 their ship lay in the Downs, her full complement aboard and ready to sail, but it was ten o'clock on the morning of 4 April before a fine, smart, favourable breeze came up to waft them down the Channel under a cloud of sail in company with several other Indiamen, including the *Northumberland*, which carried the second division of the regiment. At Plymouth they sent their last letters ashore with the pilot.

On 6 April The Lizard faded into the glow of the sunset while three hundred and fifty souls feasted their eyes as long as they could discern it upon the last of old England, which many of them would never see again.

CHAPTER II

A Passage to India

I

THE *Dublin* was a typical Indiaman of the time, a perfect piece of sailing mechanism in which all the experience of centuries of adventuring British seamen was embodied, her interior keyed to match the taste of those who were passengers in her.

She was eight hundred tons burthen. She was coppered and fast-sailing and her gear was the best that the wealth of the world's greatest trading company could provide. She was flush fore and aft with a handsome round-house, a neat cuddy, a balcony over her stern, and a quarterdeck which Lieutenant Macquarie judged sufficiently large for walking or dancing. There were "several neat apartments divided off for the Captain himself and the female passengers". Military officers berthed in the great cabin, which was lofty and well lighted. Here they lived together for nearly five months at sea. During that time only their commanding officer had any personal privacy—a part of the cabin was partitioned for his use.

Out of the great cabin, on either side, led the cabins of the ship's officers, "neatly arranged", while the soldiers were bedded down on what, to Macquarie, not very familiar with the terminology of the sea, was "the hollop deck". To this level in the ship each company had its own hatch for entry and exit; and each man had a "birth" marked out and his own hammock served to him, so that all were "well and comfortably accommodated as to room, air, etc. etc."

Into their tiny ark was packed such a company as would crowd a fairly large modern coastal steamer, even on a short voyage.

Captain William Smith, the absolute autocrat over them all, but a fine-mannered gentleman, had under his command two mates, a surgeon, a captain's clerk, three midshipmen and one hundred seamen to man the ship and the twenty-four nine-pounders which the *Dublin* carried to guard against roving Frenchmen.

To the crew were added three companies of the 77th Regiment, and the passengers—a "genteel looking set of people", whose forum was the captain's table, which was "most plentifully and elegantly served with the very best eatables and drinkables".

With all the officers of the Regiment in their scarlet, with the ship's officers in whatever bright costumes they chose to affect, with the scurrying personal servants, and the red and white wine in the glasses, with the polished silver on the spotless napery, and with the band playing loudly during breakfast and dinner, mealtimes in the *Dublin* must have been brilliant and colourful.

And the presence of (1) Miss Seccome, (2) Miss Blair, (3) Miss Hunter, (4) Miss Lofty, and (5) Miss Charlotte Lofty, all carefully numbered in Lieutenant Macquarie's journal, added a certain elegance to these daily occasions, which were also sanctified by the preliminary devotions of the Misses Lofty's dear and reverend papa.

No wonder that the King's officers felt "every great reason to be pleased with their situation"; and this more especially since the East India Company was paying their passages, "which were costing them nothing at all".

None but Captain Smith could have had reason to be at all dissatisfied. His was the task of making a profit out of the £70 that the Honourable Company allowed him to feed each hungry military captain and subaltern on the voyage, though to meet the more highly developed thirsts and appetites of field officers, he had £30 more.

On that scale, Macquarie thought, "unless we have a very short passage, he can be *no gainer* by the allowances".

But if the captain had any feelings on the matter he did not show them. He was "particularly attentive to everyone".

II

They soon fell into the orderly course of the ship's routine of breakfast at nine and dinner at four—which gave them a long interval over the forenoon for study or for leisure—and supper at ten o'clock, with tea or coffee for the ladies and such males as needed it. To settle down was the easier because the weather across Biscay was fair.

The gentry of the cabins aft lazed and read through the sunny mornings. In the afternoons they walked or danced while the band played on the poop. If the nights were dark, they were able to fall back upon the more confineable diversions of "cards and backgammon for triffles" (*sic*).

It was an Arcadian existence to which only the soldiery lent a stronger flavour. They were divided into watches to help with the working of the ship; but, as common soldiers always have done and always will, they brought their land manners aboard, and the lords of the cuddy were "obliged to hold court martials now and then and inflict corporal punishment according to the nature and degree of their offences".

This was something of a tie upon the freedom of Macquarie himself, for "there being only three of us . . . Tait, Erskine and myself . . . I am obliged to be constant president of every court martial that sits".

The sailors, not to be outdone in iniquity and suffering, also were "some times punished by Captain Smith for any misbehaviour with a dozen lashes".

One wonders what (1) Miss Seccome, (2) Miss Blair, and (5) Miss Charlotte Lofty thought as the whistle of the cat-o'-nine-tails and the groans of the misdemeanants were heard.

To the officers these affairs seem to have been merely a matter of routine—as much so as the "most cleanly and necessary custom of bathing the soldiers every day before sunrise upon the fore-castle under the eye and inspection of the Officer of the Day", which became part of the ship's drill upon reaching the warmer latitudes.

Strange it appears that in the dirtiest century of modern Europe life on an Indiaman was speckless and sterilized. The decks were always holy-stoned to perfect whiteness and, at a steady round of parades—before sunrise, at ten o'clock, for dinner at noon and again at sunset—the soldiers were compelled to appear clean and tidy, or to have their dirt and odours exorcized from their carcasses with a cat.

Daily the bulk of the regimental complement spent most of its hours in the sunlight on deck under compulsion while the wind-sails fed fresh air to the orlop deck below. And, as hammocks and bedding flapped in the breeze throughout the day, the *Dublin* must have presented the regular appearance of a sea-going laundry with all clothes-lines full.

No doubt the soldiery had few complaints. Drawn as they were from "none but the worst description of men . . . the mere scum of the earth . . . all enlisted for drink", as the Duke of Wellington described them on enlistment, they were in process of being turned into "the really fine fellows that they are", as he described them in perfection.

They were being fed for the first time in their miserable lives with plenty of good wholesome provisions, washed down with a dram of spirits every day, or occasionally with punch. The captain gave them "sourcroute to prevent scorbutic infections", and they were, indeed, very healthy from treatment, at the thought of which their officers glowed with pride. Lieutenant Macquarie was moved to write, "I must confess, that during all my travels, I never saw soldiers live near so well, either on shore or on board of transports—indeed, too much praise cannot be given to Captain Smith, for his extremely good and humane attention to the living, etc., of the troops on board the *Dublin*."

III

Nine days out from The Lizard, sailing fast, they were abreast of Madeira, more than 1300 miles from their starting point, and on 6 May their vessel "crossed the *Line* or *Equator* about eleven o'clock this day", the ship's company being "entertained with the ceremony of *Neptune's Visit* . . . practised upon this occasion with great humour by the sailors, to extort money or grog from such passengers as have never crossed the Line before".[1]

They suffered their first death—that of their master tailor. The weather became colder. The sun suddenly appeared to have dropped behind them into the northern heavens. They saw upon the sea "a vast number of very curious sea-fowls—especially the bird called the *Albicross* with immense long wings". They caught several very large sharks with lines trailed over the side. Land appeared high up and very far away, loomed over them, then seemed to reach out its arms to enfold them as they came to anchor in Simon's Bay, the winter-season anchorage of the Cape of Good Hope.

Dutch East Indiamen lay in the roads, with some French ships and "one English Man of War, *viz*—His Majesty's Sloop *The Bounty* commanded by Lieutenant Bligh (who sailed as master with Captain Cook) bound to Ottaheitta in the South Sea in search of discoveries; but particularly sent to carry and transplant the *Bread Fruit* from Ottaheitta to the West India Islands".[2]

At first there was a jovial atmosphere about all their proceedings in Africa. They made the "most delightful and romantic ride round the Bay", winding along the foot of Table Mountain, drinking "the excellent fine flavoured wine" of Constantia on the isthmus between False and Table Bays, jogging on under "a very hot and powerful" sun, like that of midsummer at home, till they thankfully saw Cape Town and its fortifications nestling at the foot of towering hills.

A very agreeable and beautiful prospect they thought it as their guide took them to the lodging house, which replaced the non-existent inns; but on closer inspection Cape Town's attractions proved somewhat variegated. Excellent walks there were at Government House, and a Company's Garden containing wild beasts and birds, even to that strange bird, the cassowary. There were forts of which they saw as much as they wished, though they were unable to approach the long lines of redoubt and battery on the landward side or the "very strong and sufficient" defences towards the sea, which were linked to the Citadel with its good parade ground and its barrack accommodation for two thousand troops.

They noted with pleasure the regularity of the town with its brick houses and with the streets "not paved but straight and crossing each other at right angles". They watched fashionable people walking after church, the ladies "finely and richly dressed up", some "very pretty women". They frequented the beer-gardens full of smoking Dutchmen who played bowls; and they cast astonished eyes upon the Hottentots—once "a very wild, fierce, savage race of men", now become "very tame, quiet and inoffensive"—and Kaffirs dancing and singing.

But the gilt was taken off all their enjoyment by the facts that their accommodation fell very far short, indeed, of the "mighty fine promises and elegant descriptions" their guide had been pleased to give them on the road, and that all Cape Town could offer them was a supper "not very extraordinary" to hungry men, and beds which they shared with the bugs.

They do not appear to have shown further zest for African amusements until they were back on the white decks of the *Dublin* making a very merry day of it "and with a great deal of dancing with the ladies in the evening to fine moonlight on the quarter deck". Lieutenant Bligh and Mr Mason, the famous botanist, who was collecting strange plants for the King in Africa, along with Colonel Gordon, the Commandant of the Dutch troops at Cape Town, dined with them and "staid on board till very late at night".

Macquarie had no words for Bligh; and Bligh had no words for him. For each the Dutch colonel with the Scottish name seems to have been the centre of attraction —"a tall stout soldierlike man . . . a very fine jovial fellow, and a most agreeable companion as can be".[3]

He had lived long in the country. He had travelled a thousand miles into the interior of the dark continent and was full of entertaining travellers' tales. As the wine thawed him, he sang a number of native songs "in their own real manner and language". And finally—"altho not born in the Highlands or even Scotland being born in Holland of Scotch extraction"—he burst into a Gaelic lay.

In the company of this amusing fellow, who remained for ever ignorant that he was to become the involuntary father of the sheep industry of New South Wales, to which his estate after his death sent the first merinos, Bligh experienced no premonitions at the sight of Macquarie; Macquarie none at the sight of Bligh.

Each sailed his separate way leaving the world to wait another quarter of a century for mutual comment.

IV

The *Dublin* hurried from Africa on the wings of a turbulent breeze which, in some degree, atoned for the eventlessness of the continuing voyage.

For a while, as she passed through the channel of Mozambique, she kept company with another Indiaman, the *Raymond*, which carried the 75th Regiment.

Sometimes the officers went off in boats to dine with those on board the other ship, their hosts returning their calls. They put in at one or two islands. On 24 July they crossed the Line for the second time, still "wonderfully well content".

"We continue to be very merry and happy one with another," writes Macquarie. ". . . We want for nothing, being well supplied with everything —and the whole of our society are cheerful, pleased and happy in their situation."

So, with no more events to break the monotony than some rough weather, an occasional sermon and prayers by the Reverend Mr Lofty on the quarterdeck on Sunday mornings, and another poor soldier drowned when the ship was "going very fast through the water under full sail", the pilot at last brought them, on 3 August 1788, safely into Bombay Harbour, which seemed to the traveller to be "a very fine one—commodious and capacious as well as secure".

Nine months after Lachlan Macquarie had walked out of his mother's humble dwelling at Oskamull, he and his fellow officers sat down to dinner in sight of the Indian shore. They "ate and drank heartily and congratulated one another upon our safe arrival in India, after a very pleasant and most agreeable voyage" of exactly four months from England. It was easy indeed to understand why the traveller gazed "with full heart" on the "exceeding fine view" of the "many surrounding islands and continent at sunset, the whole forming a most beautiful prospect from on board ship".

The harbour was full of the bustle of trooping Indiamen. The *Northumberland* and the *Asia* had come in on 26 July with Dunlop's com-

B

panies and with a section of the 75th Regiment under Captain Craufurd. There were great goings and comings.

Brigade-Major Auchmuty, with Lieutenant Erskine, came aboard to say that the 71st Regiment was on the Island with Lieutenant-Colonel Elphinstone. Lieutenant-Colonel Balfour was rowed ashore to call on the Governor, while the reverberation of the *Dublin's* saluting guns rolled back from the mainland.

The officers busied themselves fitting out their men with arms and accoutrements, pausing only to bury another poor fellow who had died in harbour.

On 4 August the tall *Raymond*, which they had left in the Indian Ocean, glided into the roads.

And next morning—5 August 1788—between five and six o'clock, the three companies of the 77th Regiment from the *Dublin* landed at the Dock Pier, and thence marched, with drums beating and colours flying, through the Fort to Culaba.

Bombay saluted them with a tremendous shower, and they arrived at their first Indian cantonments drenched to the skin.

It is sad to know that (1) Miss Seccome, (2) Miss Blair, and (3) Miss Hunter, (4) Miss Lofty, and (5) Miss Charlotte Lofty all continued their travels to Bengal, "notwithstanding, some of them, had very tempting offers, in the way of matrimony to remain in Bombay".[4]

CHAPTER III

On the Threshold of Glory

I

IN 1788 Bombay boasted a population of 100,000 souls,[1] variegated in hue and almost unanimous in their abstention from the use of soap and water.

Thousands of them seethed inside the brown walls of the Fort, which was about three miles in circumference, very strong and sufficient, dominated by a citadel, and with wet ditch and raveline complete. Subalterns' guards in scarlet stood at the three drawbridge gates which provided communications with the outside world.

Seen from a distance through vistas of green palm-fronds, the settlement had a romantic air. Brown, irregular buildings rose above the topmost level of the frowning walls. Loyal flags fluttered, fully extended in the brisk Indian breeze. A single church steeple marked the position of Bombay Green, which served the island as a Piccadilly and Hyde Park combined.

Upon a near view the town was "exceedingly irregular and crouded with old, nasty, dirty looking houses"; excepting, of course, "Government House and a few others belonging to the Company and gentlemen of fortune, which are pretty neat and handsomely built".[2]

Its dominant feature was that it was "amazing populous, especially in natives". And with natives the European exile soon became sated.

Outside the Fort much that was one hundred and fifty years later garden suburb and teeming slum was then rural.[3] Malabar Hill was fashionable only with the snakes, and with the vultures hovering above its single burning ghat. Girgaum was a plantation, the Esplanade a rural walk and racecourse, Parel the Arcady of Governors.

Culaba, formerly the home of the Company's antelopes, was still an island.[4] In Macquarie's day it displayed on its green levels the cantonments of the sweating King's regiments—the Highlanders driven by the mosquitoes out of kilts into trousers—some supple palm-trees, a mosque, a slimy tank of Indian dimensions, and that primary necessity of all tropical garrisons, a surgeon-general's department, completely ignorant of bacteriology, but well equipped with mercury (for fevers) and nitrous compounds (for the itch).

Official prudence had set down this facility conveniently near to a capacious cemetery.

II

Viewed by watchers who did not have to partake of its monotony and suffer its itches, Bombay, with its harbour full of outlandish ships, with its *polygars* and its palanquins, its palm-trees and its *kooee-hai*,[5] its strutting officers and its pig-tailed soldiery, all done up neatly in scarlet coats and stocks like bright-hued parcels, must have seemed a sort of Joseph's coat, full of rainbow colours and fancy stitches.

But to those who suffered its amenities at close quarters, life was staled by custom and suffering. It was tolerable only because it formed a purgatory from which an enterprising subaltern or writer might emerge enriched and refined in a few years into fitness to enter the ranks of the British county families.

A more articulate Scot[6] than young Macquarie from Mull found the society poor in comparison with that in the back room of a London book-shop. And even for Macquarie himself, certainly no Mackintosh, scenes which Zoffany deemed worthy of his brush must have lost their charm as he wrestled with the problem of the "enormous expense" of the Punch House—"the only tavern a gentleman might be accomodated in"—or debated whether he could add to the weekly half-guinea for general mess the cost of a guest's dinner at a rupee, with the necessary bottles added at a profit of threepence over cost to their messman, Sergeant MacDowell.

The beauties of the view were apt to shrivel when seen by an officers' guard, undefended by mosquito net or punkah, which had been on duty for seventy-two hours while the enterprising rank and file of the 77th and 75th Regiments settled their differences. The life could not appear otherwise than dull when appraised by a company commander engaged on the tedious monsoon-season task of seeing that two hundred potentially scorbutic private soldiers had green vegetables for the sake of their skins and daily tots of arrack for the promotion of their morale.

III

However, to one who had never known the discursive brilliance of the back room of a bookshop, the regimental company was congenial enough. Fellow-veterans of the American War were there in abundance, stout lads, touchy and adventurous, handy with a bottle at night as with a pistol at dawn . . . Montresor, after whose father an island in the Hudson River had been named, James Dunlop and Robin Craufurd of the Peninsula, Archie Campbell of Burma.

And there were ladies who, during the "season" when the ships were in with news of the "recovery of our good and amiable sovereign from his madness" or of the "*Civil War* prevailing in France between the Court and the Country Party", rendered a ballroom floor almost as variegated as the jungle.

One never knew, upon any of those evenings when the "tutelary days" of Britain's saints were remembered, whether one would be called upon to foot it through "a couple of country dances with Mrs. Capon . . . a country born lady of the type sometimes called Blueskins"; or whether it would be more appropriate to appear in full Highland costume borrowed from Lieutenant Roderick Mackenzie, the historian of Tippoo's wars, to "dance with Miss Rose".

There was Christmas to be celebrated, not as a holy festival but as the anniversary of the day upon which the Regiment first went upon full pay; dinners at the Sans Souci Club at the Grove; symposia with senior officers at one of which it was recorded: "Smoaked for the first time out of an Indian *Hooka*".

Also, naturally, there were mornings when one walked on the Glacis or the Esplanade to clear the head, especially after the celebrations that followed when the British Army of Bombay, at a sedate trot, pursued to complete subjection a routed native corps, whose defeat had been achieved according to the cast-iron tradition that it should begin running in panic at the sound of the first British round of blank cartridge.

All these things were part of existence in the Bombay in which young Lachlan Macquarie began to spend the better part of twenty years in exile, depressed by its climate and its diseases, but sustained by the inspiration provided by men like the Governor, General Medows, a veteran of the West Indian Wars to whom European Bombay of the last ten years of the eighteenth century might well have been grateful for summarizing its ambitions and its spirit.

It was he who exclaimed, when he learned that his aide-de-camp, the admirable George Harris, had saved for him in three years, out of a stipend of £1146 a month, the modest nest-egg of £40,000, "Harris knows how he scraped it together . . . I don't."

IV

For the moment such states as that of General Medows were only faint aspirations to young lieutenants. Pitt and his followers had sadly cramped the style of would-be nabobs. Warren Hastings had been noisily impeached. Parliamentary critics at home inveighed persistently and thunderously against the presumed greed, opulence and extravagance of the John Company and its fatted commanders, collectors, and writers. Old gentlemen at Fort William to a man could agree over their madeira that the world was hurtling precipitately to the devil.

And even the presence of so shining a pattern in official acquisition as General Medows himself was not an advantage to King's officers. For, unmindful of his own good example, the General felt constrained urgently to "make very great changes . . . for the better in both Civil and Military Departments; especially in the latter".[7] And his increases and improvements could be achieved only through "vast deductions and reforms", paid for in part by members of the King's Army whose allowances, "ever *far inferior*" to those of Bengal and Madras, were "now reduced very low indeed". Arrears, "paid at home once only in three years", were struck off allowances in India. The sustenance allowances of subalterns dwindled in September 1788 to a beggarly twenty rupees for lodging and twenty-eight rupees for living monthly.

There were to be no luscious pickings of "language money" and "share of off-reckonings" which came the way of Company Army officers but not of those in the King's Service. The position, in fact, called for the direst pessimism— ". . . our golden dreams, and the flattering prospects we had formed to ourselves in Britain, of soon making our fortunes in the East, must now all vanish into smoke; and we must content ourselves, with merely being able to exist without running into debt."[8]

Fortunately promotion, if it could be obtained, offered a means through which one might improve one's position; and the lieutenant, forlorn as he might feel, was not backward in seeking it.

He importuned Madras; he worried Fort William. He led his commanding officer, Lieutenant-Colonel Balfour, to Government House to sponsor him as he presented a memorial to the hearty Medows, who gave him a promise that he would, "as far as it depended upon him, do everything in his power to forward my promotion". After another rocket shower of supplication had fallen in high places, the suppliant found himself, on 30 March 1789, conning a chit which told him that, a year less by a day since he had set out from Oskamull, he was a captain-lieutenant.

This was lucky. There were at least thirty lieutenants in the King's Army in India who were older in the rank than he, but they lacked his persistence. Thus, a fortnight later, on 14 April 1789, he did duty "as captain in the garrison for the first time, being captain of the day, and in consequence, having the command and charge of all guards in garrison; the detail of which is upwards of five hundred men, that march off the Grand Parade daily".

Despite the weather and under the influence of such advancement, the first faint aspirations of his incipient period in the Orient began to give way to more shining ambitions, which stirred from their dormant condition the mind "not able or inclined to attend much to study" and the body which found the climate "trying to one so long in Mull".

In this development he had a special incentive in that his social progress if anything outstripped his promotion. He advanced all too rapidly for his pocket from the neophyte's seat, at "Mr Vice's" end of the dinner-table, to places on the committees of the balls, suppers, assemblies and concerts which formed the staple amusements of the Bombay season. Two years after he had stepped ashore in India it must have seemed a far cry to the day when his friend Captain Campbell had been "so obliging as to introduce me to the most genteel and fashionable circle of acquaintance in Bombay . . . from all of whom I receive particular attention". For here he was on jesting and familiar terms with near-admirals:

> Sept. 3, 1790—Friday . . . I had laid a bett of a Chevouz and Ball for forty ladies and gentlemen with Commodore Nesbitt, that the *Princess Royal* would arrive on or before the 15th September; it gave me no small degree of satisfaction that I won this bett.

What was now needed of Fortune was a sound war, preferably against some rajah with cellars full of rubies, so that an increased share of prize-money appertaining to a captain's rank might be exploited to the full. While he had waited for one, however, and watched a suitable quarrel wend its slow way to a fruition in arms, he had not done so badly.

By November 1790, two years and two months after he had reached India, he had paid off in full his debt of £127 to his Uncle Lochbuy. He had sent a substantial surplus home for the relief of his mother and sister and his ailing brother Donald. He had transmitted to his younger brother Charles, "for his sole use and behoof", a still further £30. And even after these dispersals of funds his bankers held a thousand rupees to his credit, a fact all the more extraordinary since the martial circumstances of the country had put him to added expense in preparation for the hostilities which had stood imminent but unrealized for several months.

V

Pitt's India Act[9] of 1784, which had proclaimed schemes of conquest and the extension of the Company's Dominion in India to be "repugnant to the wish honour and policy of the nation", had very obviously not ended wars in India. Neither had the death of Haidar Ali, who never more would be able to hang a minister in a cage and feed him on bird-seed in performance of a promise to "cherish him as kindly as a parrot". Neither, again, had the Treaty of Mangalore under which his son Tippoo, ostensibly a reformed character though the author of many a past horror, including the poisoning of British prisoners, agreed to keep his claws off the Carnatic.[10]

That Medows, who earlier had fought over Tippoo's country with the gallant 73rd Regiment, was sent to mould the Bombay forces did not look like a mere accident, especially since Lord Cornwallis himself had openly inveighed already "against the unavoidable inconvenience of the system of neutrality". And surely enough, with no warning, right in the middle of the Bombay season, Tippoo struck at the lines of Travancore, a rich little kingdom under the protection of the Company.

Quite by accident, of course, a battalion of Madras establishment sepoys was at Travancore when the blow fell. A Company's officer and some Madrassis were killed, but the defenders gave Tippoo more than he bargained for.

The Travancoreans and the Madrassis chased him out of their lines so quickly that he ran his forehead against a bamboo fence, which did not improve his looks or his temper.[11] It seemed to Macquarie that "the King of Travancore, our best ally", had fought a "pretty smart action".[12]

Made fluent by indignation, the King wrote his views on the invasion to General Medows in a letter in which he referred to Tippoo as "the accursed tyrant" and rejoiced at having slain heaps of fleeing Mysoreans.

Thus, when the news of Mysorean events filtered through to Bombay on 13 January 1790, one Ulvan felt he had reason to hope that "our Government in India will support her Allies; and not suffer the enterprising spirit of Tippoo to repeat his attacks of this nature with impunity".[13]

It was, however, some months before Medows informed the smiling tyrant that "the English equally incapable of offering an insult, as of submitting to one, have always looked upon war as declared from the moment you attacked their ally, the King of Travancore".[14]

Still more months passed while the doughty general performed those remarkable strategic evolutions in which he slid with his army across the plains to the passes of the Deccan—from Aracouch to Deniacottah; from Gopalchittypalam to Sheelamootapalam; from Singalore to Satiamungalan; from *lootie* gang to *lootie* gang.

But in time Dindigul fell to Stuart's column. The dashing leader, Floyd, was through the pass at Oocarro, while the wicked Tippoo, apparently abashed before General Medows and the Almighty—whom the General had invoked as his main ally in his declaration of war—retreated precipitately with a large army, after throwing some of his guns into the Paniani River.[15]

So far did good fortune seem to favour the British arms that the war appeared to be almost over.

A cry of disappointment was heard from Captain Macquarie in the mess of the disgruntled 77th Regiment—"the only *King's Regiment in India*, either not on active service or *Full Batta*"—when General Abercromby on 20 September told Colonel Balfour that his troops were "not to go at this time on service, nor any of the troops from Bombay for the present".[16]

It was, Macquarie vowed, "a most cruel mortification and disappointment to us all"—especially as the officers of the 77th had "incurred immense expence in equipping and compleating themselves and their companies, with clothing, necessaries and camp equipment fit for taking the field".

"Hard cruel fate!" exclaimed the indignant Scot.

The Regiment, two days later, marched out of the Fort, where it had been kept ready to sail, to the cantonments on Culaba, where it seemed that it was due for an interminable sojourn in idleness.

The redoubtable Dunlop, Dr Anderson, and Macquarie resignedly began to form a new mess for themselves.

Fortune, however, was already at work on their side.

On the very day on which General Abercromby spoke to Balfour, the "abashed" Tippoo had appeared out of the silence of Mysore on the flank of Floyd's advance column with a mere matter of 40,000 horse and foot and a modicum of elephants and guns, and a few hours later Floyd was in full flight with dragoons covering the well-tucked-in and slightly singed tail of his retreating column.[17]

How Medows, a splendid man in a charge, proved himself to be no scout; how he crossed the line of Floyd's march as he hurried to rescue him and was put right only in the nick of time by Captain Dallas; how Tippoo almost spoilt the General's vital junction with Colonel Maxwell and the Carnatic guard force; how the General chased the Mysorean army all over the interior valley of the Cauvery and round in several rings without catching it, and finished the campaign breathing heavily at Vellore, while Tippoo's motley host laughed at him from a spot twelve miles off the east coast and Pondicherry, is all forgotten now except by military historians; but it is an entertaining story.

It was clear that Tippoo's case demanded stronger medicine than the mere power of righteousness and a flying column.

Cornwallis up at Fort William soon made up his mind.[18]

The task called for his own intervention, for the use of every soldier and sepoy available and for converging armies marching from Malabar and Coromandel. He came in person to supersede Medows, who, a little relieved, assumed the position of second-in-command.

VI

On 10 November 1790, nearly eleven months after the first smell of battle had become evident in Bombay, Captain Macquarie was recovering from the effects of a "very pleasant and agreeable evening in the country at the house of Lawyer White's where the nuptials of Miss James and John Fell Esq. (of the Bombay Civil Establishment) were celebrated with great festivity, mirth and good humour".

That day he wrote in his journal:

> *Nov.* 10, *Wednesday.* In this days General Orders, the very agreeable and pleasing intelligence, was announced to us, of our Regiments being ordered to hold themselves in readiness on the shortest notice to embark for *immediate* and *actual field service.* What made this Order the more agreeable, was, that we had almost despaired of being employed during the present war at all;—having at the commencement of it, put ourselves to very great expence in providing camp equipage and necessaries for the field, and being buoy'd up with a full and certain hope of going on service we were all extremely mortified and much hurt, after all our preparations, to be informed some months ago, that we were not going.—but this days Order, fortunately reversed that cruel decree, and very agreeably dispelled all our doubts and fears.[19]

There is no need to ask what sort of emotions the news produced in the captain's heart, or what he and his companions had been doing to celebrate the change in their fortunes. The state of his handwriting itself makes the exploration explicit.

Early on the morning of 24 November the 77th Regiment, as part of the Malabar Army, marched out of its cantonments on Culaba to the dock pier-head. At nine o'clock, under command of Major Stirling, it embarked in the *Hercules*, Captain Galloway, a "very civil, obliging, gentlemanlike man".[20]

The Commander-in-Chief of the Army, Major-General Robert Abercromby, with all his suite and staff, boarded the *Drake*, cruiser, Commodore Robertson. Lieutenant-Colonel Balfour joined the *Scorpion*, cruiser.

The *Hercules*, very fine and large, was "prodigiously crouded", for she was certainly "not sufficiently large to accomodate six hundred and fifty Soldiers and twenty four officers", especially since Mrs Stirling "made

one of our society, but had a part of the round house allotted to her".
At four o'clock the fleet set sail with a fair wind, steering southward.

The Captain's table proved to be good and well served. The officers,
in order to make the expense easier for juniors, agreed to pay for their
living according to rank, so that Captain Macquarie's proportion for
eleven days' diet amounted to the modest sum of fifty-eight rupees.

On the morning of 4 December 1790 they were in Tellicherry Roads
on the southern part of the western coast. One of the oldest of the western
factories dreamed along the green-fronded shore in the missionary India
of the story books. Above the enchanting scene hung the slippery Ghauts,
rain-washed and steep, which presently they must climb.

And somewhere between the sea and the foothills the Bibbee (or Queen)
of Cananore was busily preparing for battle.

CHAPTER IV

Moving Day in Canaan

I

On the wet Malabar coast the enemy forts frowned across the approaches to Cananore, in the defences of which, with their master's son the Prince Ali Rajah and his consort, the resourceful Bibbee, were five thousand not very ardent followers of the Mysorean tyrant.

Many grinning victims of Tippoo, the legions of the Nairs, the cohorts of Coorg and Cherica, of Cottiote and Cartanad, had augmented the force with which General Abercromby proposed to root out this nest of Indian villainy in short order.[1]

And the eagerness of all these, as well as that of the Highlanders, had been stimulated by a rumour that emeralds lay in heaps amid bags of gold and pearls on the floor of the Bibbee's treasury; this, despite the fact that the prudent lady had long since sent her valuables to the Laccadive Islands, far out of the reach of ambitious British officers on the hunt for prize-money.

British officers, luckily for their peace of mind, knew nothing of this unsportsmanlike proceeding; and thus they faced the imminent future with a hope far brighter than the listless sun which they beheld one morning nine days after their arrival, crawling over the Ghauts in weary fashion in the perspiring Malabar dawn.

Daylight saw the whole army astir. The General and his suite took their places in front of the right brigade. The columns of half-companies in scarlet coat, stiff black stock and tight-drawn pigtail, marched forward machine-like towards the foe's position.

On the outskirts of the main masses rode the Indian cavalry of the rajahs, spearmen and firelock men, their spurs jingling, and their muslins rustling with the breeze of their progress, as they more than kept pace with the rolling mass of elephants which, behind the advance guard, were dragging the siege guns under the urging of Major Jones, the army's artillerist.

On their left, as they advanced, the British saw the slow wash of the ocean; on their right, the mountains; and in front an unpleasing assortment of ravine and jungle, the monotony of which was relieved by rows of unfriendly Oriental noses poked discreetly out of masonry redoubts and formidable stockades.

The running commentary of the enemy was loud and continuous but, muted by distance, it had little chance of competing with the clamour from the attackers' rear, which represented the concerted observations of some thousands of camp-followers upon the chances of loot.

It needed a sweat-drenched march of two miles to bring them on to a hill about fifteen hundred yards from Fort Avery, one of the enemy's crucial positions, which was defended by a numerous garrison supported by some small cannon.

A creek or valley, parallel to the advancing columns, cut across the landscape, separating the attackers from Carley Hill, on which there was another strong fort.

Here was their battle-ground, upon which, as the clank of ramrods died away along the loading line, the gruff voices of Major Jones's eighteen-pounders spoke the prologue to Captain Macquarie's first taste of actual war.

Throughout the smoke-clad morning the cannon roared, filling the landscape with fumes and noise and the foe with a competitive spirit which induced him to turn on some guns of his own.

It was not out of keeping with the nature of Indian warfare that both were firing in vain. Major Jones's artillery found fifteen hundred yards "too great a distance for battering in the breach", and so his "shot did little execution"; and the Indians in Fort Avery did no more hurt than those in Fort Carley who were dropping their ball three hundred yards in front of the British centre.

This in no way discouraged either set of combatants, nor robbed the Indians of their desire and resolution to wipe Captain Macquarie and his companions off the scene of battle, an ambition they sought to gratify in a very persistent manner by every means then known to Asiatic warfare.

They sent into the jungle in the valley ahead of the British array snipers, who fired at so short a range that their bullets fell at the very feet of the astonished British soldiery, one of whom actually "had a Biscuit that was in his Pocket, broke to Pieces by a spent Musquet Ball". They tried rockets. They sent from Fort Avery against Major Jones some enterprising shock troops. These ran headlong into the screen of free-riding Nair cavalry who drove them home screaming, though suffering casualties themselves which they could well afford, seeing that they were great populators.

However, all hostile efforts proved in vain. The scarlet lines stood firm, as if they were a fact of nature. Major Jones and his opponents banged away, and the *hathis* swayed in the shade, switching their ears. The staff posed gorgeous in the van of the brigades, its members peeping occasionally through their spy-glasses, and watching anxiously while the sun, in its own good time, made its way past zenith to three o'clock, an hour which no eighteenth-century officer could allow to pass without due celebration, since it was the period of tiffin.

As it approached General Abercromby became at last convinced that "the battery was errected [sic] at too great a distance to demolish Avery Fort". He "ordered the guns to cease firing altogether, and the line to ly upon their arms during the rest of the day and ensuing night".

II

From the respite which ensued Captain Macquarie, two subalterns, and sixty stealthy men were perforce excepted. They were ordered out to build a new battery for Major Jones, four hundred yards nearer to the enemy than his old one.[2]

It was far from pleasant work. From the moment they moved forward the enemy fired a good deal in their direction; and they could not reply since they had piled their arms when they were served out with working tools.

As the evening grew clearer, and the moon rose to full brightness at midnight, the workers' situation became even more precarious. The men hastily carried forward their sandbags to the new position. Their foes, more and more emboldened, crept so close that they could be heard speaking to each other in the undergrowth.

Tippoo's sepoys saw very plainly what the Chief Engineer and Captain Macquarie were up to. They "kept up a very heavy fire of musquetry" upon the working parties during the whole night. But the pioneers, Europeans and sepoys alike, under the captain's command, "behaved remarkably well, working hard and very steadily notwithstanding the very galling fire from the enemy:—One poor sepoy was mortally wounded just as he was laying down his sand bag on the ground; except this man, who died next morning of his wounds, I had no more of my party hurt, which was surprising considering the unremitting heavy fire kept up by the enemy."[3]

About three o'clock in the morning, when the new emplacements were almost finished, a party came out to relieve Macquarie and his "much fatigued" labourers, who marched off to enjoy repose until, about 7 a.m., the curtain rose upon the second act of the drama of Cananore.

Thanks to Captain Macquarie's nocturnal efforts, Major Jones with his eighteen-pounders and elephants had become far more dangerous than yesterday. He opened a "very heavy bombardment". The occupants of Fort Avery had dust and flying masonry for breakfast, and, within an hour, their responsive salvoes had ceased. A great part of the walls of the Fort had been in that time demolished; and when a party advanced with cannon to storm it, the inmates abandoned it "with precipitation".

At the same time the Bombay Left Brigade flowed into the valley which stretched, jungle filled, along their front. Without halting, they possessed themselves of the heights of Carley, on which a large body of the enemy "made but a very short stand behind their stockadoes and dykes". The Right Brigade, which included the 77th Regiment and Captain Macquarie, advanced rapidly up the hill in front of them, driving Tippoo's men under the shelter of Fort Carley's guns.

That night another breaching battery was set up, and at daybreak the defenders of Fort Carley joined those of Fort Avery in retreat or surrender.

III

That, for all practical purposes, was the end of the siege of Cananore and of actual fighting. Tippoo's forces retired hurriedly, then capitulated on 16 December, sixty hours after the first shots had been fired. They were completely trapped between the Bombay Army and the Belliapatam River. Unless they surrendered, they must inevitably be slaughtered in hundreds.

Inside Cananore the troops were no more anxious to be killed than those beyond the Belliapatam. They knew that, in submission, they would be called upon to sacrifice only Tippoo's property, and not their own personal effects.

Only one obstacle to peace existed after the destruction of the two guardian forts—the Prince Ali Rajah, the Mysorean tyrant's son, who felt "so strongly attached to the interest of Tippoo Saib that he never would hear of or allow the Bibbee to surrender the Fort of Cananore to British troops while he was alive".

Luckily, the Bibbee was no less vigorous in averting disaster than she was prudent in anticipating it.

During the night she and her cabinet decided that "it was necessary in order to save many lives and the Fort being taken by storm, to dispatch the poor old Rajah". He was, so 'twas said, "carried off by poison by the private directions of his now afflicted consort".[4]

Next day Belliapatam Fort and the Cananore Heights were surrendered to Abercromby and his allied troops. As soon as the British line formed in front of them Tippoo's battalions "marched out opposite and laid down their arms". Hostages had been sent to Tellicherry to plead for terms and, after the "humiliating ceremony" of surrender was over, the vanquished were placed under guard and supplied with provisions "until they were sent away to their own country".

Mir Mahomed, Tippoo's commander-in-chief at Cananore, his second-in-command, Said Mahmood, between four and five thousand fighting men and "a prodigious number of followers", thirty-four stands of colours, two field pieces and four thousand muskets were at General Abercromby's disposal. The Bibbee surrendered her town and main fort immediately afterwards.

At last Macquarie and his friends were able to lick their wounds and survey the results of their triumph.

It had been cheaply gained. Not a single officer had been killed and none wounded save a Mr Cochrane, a surgeon of the 2nd Native Infantry, who had been struck by a spent cannon shot, which "bruised and stunned him a great deal". The casualties among the rank and file had numbered only ninety, and they were mostly Nairs.

The only fly in the ointment was the paucity of divisible spoils.

These were "not likely to be much"; but despite this Captain Macquarie was happy and active enough after his martial adventures.

Unexhausted by his midnight efforts of a week agone, sharing a tent with his friend, Dr Colin Anderson, he attended a sale of captured *circar* horses, and bought "a very pretty chestnut coloured mare, between five and six year old and between fourteen and fifteen hands high, for ninety rupees". He secured the loan of a "very elegant" saddle and bridle from his "old chum Honble Lt. Cochrane", so that he was now "handsomely mounted". He was "lucky enough to have hired a very good horsekeeper, whom I procured among the prisoners of war lately taken, and also a pair of very good bullocks for eighteen rupees to carry our tent".

Lastly, he had settled to act as Regimental Paymaster during the absence of Captain Montresor, who was attached to native infantry.

Lord Cornwallis, so Macquarie heard presently, was arrived from Fort William at Madras. By January 1791 his brigades lay at Vellout—22,000 fighting men and 130,000 camp followers, poised ready to assault Tippoo's stronghold of Seringapatam.

General Robert Abercromby, on their own side of India, was preparing to face the tremendous task of moving his force of 9000 men, with a host of camp-followers and an all-too-small supply of guns, up the slippery passes into Mysore. It was work to daunt the bravest heart.

IV

An Indian army of the eighteenth century on the march, isolated from its main bases by long stretches of wild land and sometimes wilder sea, necessarily must be self-sufficient or perish. Its leaders brought within their ambit every kind of available supply and transport facility, which assured the officer the comforts of home, the private soldier his domesticity, and the enemy the maximum degree of hostile attention.

Not merely was it necessary for Bombay's Commander and his officers to move three brigades of fighting men, equipped with artillery and siege trains, baggage trains and escorts. The private soldier went forth to war with all of his prized possessions which he could carry or persuade someone else to carry. His officers braved the rigours of the Indian climate in capacious tents, six-ply and rainproof, furnished with elaborateness, equipped with stocks of wine and sometimes with a lady, and transported and managed by *ménages* which might well have been a source of envy to the owner of a travelling circus.

Thus, even Macquarie, who had left his mother's cottage on Mull three years before with no luggage save his cloak and his portmanteau, set out for Seringapatam with a riding horse, a *doolie* to sleep in or be borne in if wounded, a very good tent, four good bullocks to carry his baggage and a retinue which consisted of a cook, a *massaljee*, a horse-keeper and four coolies.[5] But this was modest. It was not abnormal to see forty servants in the retinue of an Indian Captain on campaign.[6]

The native soldiery travelled equipped as comprehensively as the British. Every sepoy joined the ranks with his wife, his children, his bedstead, his cooking pots, his sacred cow or his goat, his pi-dogs and his poultry, and perchance even his grandfather and grandmother. Camp-followers swarmed and seethed in tens of thousands in the army's official bazaars, in which named and ordered streets were moved forward as the army advanced and daily set down at each new camp in their original patterns.[7]

All trades followed the bazaars, the fortune-teller and the silversmith, the horse-coper and the moneylender, the baker and the man with the dancing bear, the conjurer with his cobras, Phryne with her charms,

Lazarus with his sores. All had their own peculiar type of transport from Shanks's pony upwards, strange and makeshift by comparison with the immense official tide of pack-bullocks, at least three to a man, provided by the East India Company; puny beside the ponderous elephants, hired from large-minded stock owners in Malabar, which hauled battering trains, siege equipment, and the eighteen-pounders, which could be dragged along with their tumbrils, when the *hathis* were not available, only by sixty bullocks to a gun.

In and out among the surging throng threaded *polygars* on highly sensitive camels and, precious beyond rubies, the horses of the dragoons.

Round the edges of all this moving mass of men and beasts hovered the *looties*, gentlemen of the highways who robbed whom they might, be he friend or foe.

No Indian army escaped the depredations of the *looties*. They had drawn first blood against General Medows's men the year before. They were a plague and a burden now to Captain Macquarie and his friends. They knew no fear; they were not fastidious in their plundering.

V

At intervals all this array, human and animal, flowed forward as the weather and the nature of the countryside allowed, carrying Captain Macquarie with it towards the Indian hills.

The aim was to rouse the men before daybreak, to have them on the road at six o'clock, to bring them into camp at noon before the full impact of the Indian midday heat had had time to beat them down. But nature and the rains, hunger and mud, exhaustion of man and beast were alike elements in the game.

Sometimes they laboured from daylight till dusk to cover a few miles of hillside. Sometimes weary stragglers were still splashing into the disordered and tentless lines well on into the darkness of the rain-drenched nights.

However, when circumstances allowed, the soldiers in their absurd three-cornered hats, their strangling neck-stocks, their long scarlet coats and their tight cross-belts, marched grimly along of a morning while the grease melted out of their pigtails and the sweat poured out of their tired, overloaded, fever-stricken bodies, to the intense satisfaction of illimitable hordes of Indian flies.[8]

It is easy enough to believe with Captain Macquarie that, marching in close-packed columns of half-company, twelve miles was a long enough stage. As often as not, it was much shorter—eight, seven, sometimes even only five miles in the day.

Soldiers and sepoys grew weaker as they advanced. The transport animals shared their weariness. Only the well-chosen oaths and whip-cracks of the baggage masters could urge along the little, white, lumbering Mysorean bullocks of the supply train placed for safety in the centre. And there were necessarily frequent calls for help from the siege train, bugbear of all campaigning generals, rumbling and bogging itself at intervals in the rear.

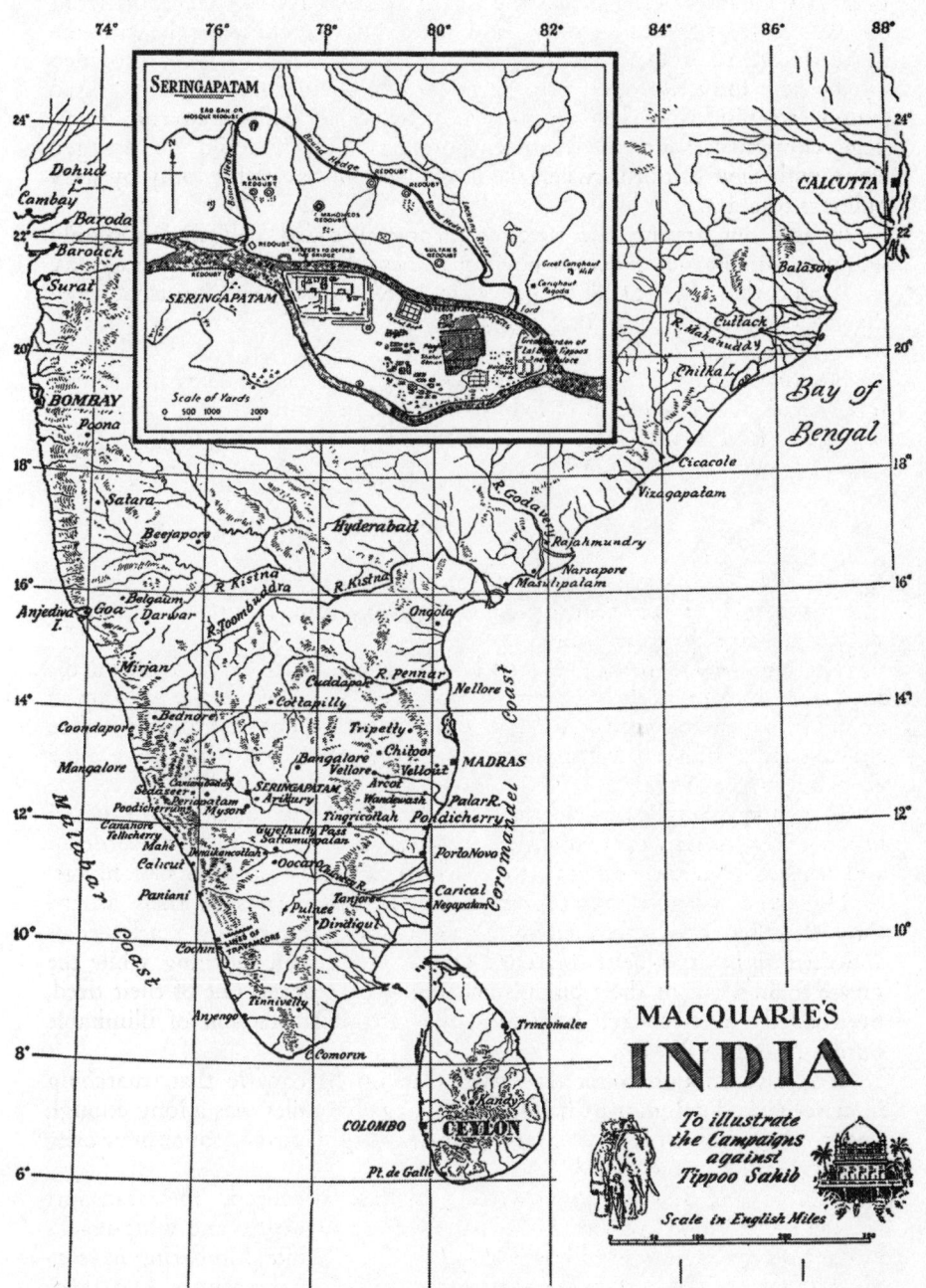

SERINGAPATAM

EAO BAN, OR
MOSQUE REDOUT

N

Mill Redout

Hedge

REDOUBT

LALLY'S
REDOUT

REDOUBT

MANOUEGS
REDOUBT

SULTAN'S
REDOUT

REDOUBT

SERINGAPATAM

BATTERIES TO DEFEND
THE BRIDGE

REDOUBT

Great Carnghaut
To Hill

ford

Carnghaut
Pagoda

Ford

Scale of Yards

0   500   1000   2000

Dohud
Cambay L.

Baroda

Barouch

Surat

CALCUTTA

Balasore

BOMBAY

Poona

Cuttack

R. Mahanuddy

Chilka L.

Bay of
Bengal

Cicacole

Satara

Vizagapatam

Beejapore

Hyderabad

R. Godavery

Rajahmundry

R. Kistna

Anjediva
I.

Belgaum
Darwar

Goa

R. Kistna

Narsapore
Masulipatam

Mirjan

R. Toombudra

Ongola

Coondapore

Bednore

Cuddapah

R. Pennar

Nellore

Cottapilly

Nellore

Mangalore

Tripetty

Coromandel Coast

Bangalore
Vellore

Chitoor

Yellout

MADRAS

Cananore

Sedaseer

SERINGAPATAM

Mysore

Arcot

Poodicherrum

Aritury

Wandywash

PalarR.

Cananore
Tellicherry

Gugelkutty Pass

Tingricottah

Pondicherry

Mahé

Satamungalam

Calicut

Doraikencottah

Oocatra

PortoNovo

Paniani

Tanjore

Carical

Pulnee

Negapatam

Cochin

Dindigul

Tinnivelly

Anjengo

Trincomalee

C. Comorin

Kandy

COLOMBO

CEYLON

Pt. de Galle

MACQUARIE'S

INDIA

To illustrate
the Campaigns
against
Tippoo Sahib

Scale in English Miles

On the flanks of the more compact portions of the force, the happy, mounted Nairs scouted for *looties* like a swarm of gaily coloured flies; while the servants and the merchants, the fortune-tellers and the harlots travelled by a process of infiltration through the forests, though keeping as closely under the shadow and protection of infantry and guns as possible.

Thus, in the early months of 1791, *doolie* and palanquin bearer, loaded humans and more heavily-burdened pack bullocks, barefooted families and sore-footed half-companies of cursing Highlanders struggled towards the passes from Malabar Coast into Mysore, each fresh mass floundering the more heavily and cursing the more loudly as they found themselves wading in the slough created out of the wet countryside by the countless feet rising and falling in front of them.

The Bombay Army on the march was a living picture of moving day in Canaan, with all the traditional amenities.

But, though progress was exhausting to all, there is no memorial to show that the privations were greater than those of some later and better-furnished imperial hosts.

Even when Arthur Wellesley had set new standards in Indian logistics, Lord Lake, twelve years after Tippoo's war, once found himself fighting the perfidious Mahrattas, "without claret for twenty-four hours".

VI

It was on the day in January 1791 on which Cornwallis marched out of Vellore on the opposite side of India that Abercromby, four hundred miles away on the Malabar Coast, prepared to move.

He and his army left the very pleasant ground six miles from Cananore facing the Ghauts, and on 23 February they were on the march.

Slowly the columns wound on, now across fords in the rivers, now through pleasant woods in romantic situations, up steep hills, down steeper ones, rough into the bargain, where the corpses of wretched bullocks worn to death with toil lay stiff and bloated, feet to sky as they had been cut loose from the tumbrils or the wagons.

The heavy battering train was left behind them to come on, Captain Macquarie knew not how.

His musical servant, Donald Campbell, whom Maclean of Scallastle had found for him in Edinburgh—"so excellent a servant, and so faithful and attached a follower of my fortunes"—perished of fever, as did many another soldier.

Starvation struck them down as well as fever. Rations were often left behind in the slough, and they were forced from time to time to send men into the jungle to shoot bullocks for food. When these hunters came back to camp empty-handed, the poor drenched privates had nought for supper but a little biscuit.

Sometimes the country blazed into flame around them, bringing a stern reminder that not all the local inhabitants loved them.

At last they came to a quiet resting ground, where, in a "*pleasant* rural retreat", they gathered their strength for the final effort which was to take them over the worst of the passes.

Then the Command began to send Macquarie out at break of day to toil with two subalterns and a hundred men building, mile by mile, the roads which were to carry the artillery park and the battering train and the heavy stores up on to the plateau.

Every morning while the infantry plodded and floundered by, they built a mile of road in five hours. And thanks to this labour, and by the mercy of Heaven, they were on top of Poodicherrum Ghaut on 21 March, but not without tremendous effort.

Though the distance was only ten miles, the ascent for half of it was "exceedingly steep, almost up a precipice", and "very fatiguing to the soldiers", who were loaded, at that stage, "besides their arms, accoutrements and necessaries, with *thirty six rounds* of ball cartridges, and *five days allowance* of *biscuit* and *rice*".

They, however, performed their march "with great chearfulness and arrived in high health and spirits".

VII

In a few days, the first rain of a heart-breakingly early monsoon season fell. The regular work of road building was now varied by expeditions to forage for straw to thatch huts, and by pauses to watch the artillery dare the Pass. . . .

"Two brass field eighteen pounders brought up the Ghaut this evening with immense labour"—a task which "could hardly have been effected without the powerful assistance and exertions of these noble and sagacious animals the *Elephants* hired by the Company from Mooser the Black Merchant of Tellicherry".

It was 4 April before they heard of Cornwallis's capture of Bangalore one hundred and fifty miles away, after a bloody rout of Tippoo's garrison. Royal salutes were fired, while Abercromby's men were still hauling some of his guns up the Pass with "inexpressible labour".

General orders announced on 12 May Abercromby's intention to march forward on the following day with the whole army. They were leaving the head of Poodicherrum Ghaut at last, men, baggage and gun-park complete.

The King of Travancore scouted in advance with his cavalry; but Abercromby moved more slowly. There were endless halts, while fatigue parties were formed to relieve the knocked-up bullocks of the task of dragging the big cannon, a couple of which they found left behind by the Advance Guard. At five that day they were at Ahmutna; next evening twelve miles on at Seedasur, still plagued with bad tracks and obstinate eighteen-pounders.

They rested a while. They saw behind them from the steep hill, whence eight years later Montresor's staff spied Tippoo's green tent rising at their feet, the sea and the towns of Tellicherry and Cananore and the shipping fifty miles away; but their eyes turned more interestedly to the scenes for which they were bound, "clothed with the most beautiful verdure; with the fine large tanks, or large ponds of water and elegant gardens interspersed through these extensive plains as far as the eye could reach".

"I have had many fine views and prospects," Macquarie wrote, "but the *one* I was gratified with today from the top of this hill surpasses in beauty and variety everything of the kind I ever yet beheld. . . . The Fort and Town of Periapatam; and the rich luxurious fertile plains of *Mysore*."[9]

He feasted his eyes for a full hour and "would have staid much longer, were I not afraid of being benighted".

The mutter of distant firing was heard on that quiet Sunday as Floyd and Maxwell slew Mysoreans at Arakury. The Bombay Army wound through the Seedasur Pass to occupy, without a shot, the abandoned Fort of Periapatam, which the enemy had undermined by way of welcome. Abercromby had advanced too quickly for his foes, who had time to blow up only two bastions. Cornwallis and Tippoo were burying their dead nine miles from Seringapatam.[10]

The Bombay Army was in Tippoo's country at last; but no sooner had they reached the plain than it began to rain with such violence that in two hours they were drenched to the skin.

Macquarie confessed that he never yet had felt greater cold from rain in all his life; and what made the situation doubly disagreeable was that they had had to stand to arms all the time, while the Advanced Brigade felt its way forward and took the Fort.

That night he mounted the outlying picket of the Right Brigade, with one hundred and fifty men, a mile in advance of the line, but they were not disturbed by the enemy, though the rain continued to fall increasingly, while the officers sat in their *doolies* and "the poor soldiers had no cover".

At sunrise on 20 May they fired more salutes for the victory at Arakury; but there was not really much to feel triumph about, though they heard "all was well" before Seringapatam.

As they loitered in the rain of Periapatam they presented a miserable spectacle. Dysentry and malaria were prostrating the soldiers in droves. They were surprised and puzzled by the sudden appearance on their front of bands of horsemen whom they, at first, took to be *looties* and whose impudence knew no bounds. The raiders invaded the square at Periapatam and stole an elephant. They wounded foragers. Presently they revealed themselves as part of a large body of reconnoitring horsemen who could belong only to Tippoo.

Abercromby's artillery was in such a miserable state that a gun could not be quickly found to disperse these enemies; and want of proper cavalry prevented the General from dealing with them by "going out immediately to feel their force and punish them for their temerity".[11]

All this bred fretfulness and discontent among the regiments of Bombay. But, as they were soon to learn, their weaknesses were their salvation.

Between them and disaster in those early days of May 1791 was interposed only the incalculable will of Fate.

CHAPTER V

The Spoils of Mysore

I

By 23 May every nerve in the Bombay Army was on edge. There was no news of the proposed junction with the Grand Army of Cornwallis except through rumour.[1]

It rained incessantly as the Malabar troops watched their foes scouting along their front. The nights continued bitterly cold; the floors of their tents remained covered with water, despite the trenches dug round them.

A vague air of apprehension began to pervade the camp. The pickets, shivering in the bitter wind, were doubled. They were ordered to be ready to turn out with their arms at a moment's notice.

Fortunately their troubles were not made worse by a knowledge of the Grand Army's real position before Seringapatam; for it was an unhappy one. Cornwallis, as he had advanced across the Deccan, had seen again and again the highly-coloured sterns of Tippoo's baboon-like squadrons; but all attempts to catch them had been in vain, till Floyd's dragoons had broken leash, killed one thousand Mysoreans and lost two hundred valuable horses for their pains.

The British later had swept forward, after leaving the gateways of Bangalore choked with Tippoo's dead. They had been ambushed at Arakury, nine miles from the tyrant's lair, and had confounded their ambushers with devastating effect. They had reached the walls of Seringapatam to be met with the kind of luck which had dogged Cornwallis throughout his military life.

He knew that in the north his allies, the Mahrattas and the legions of Hyderabad, were on their way to his aid, 120,000 strong, not to mention 360,000 camp-followers, but he knew not where. He knew that the Bombay Army only a few miles away was in bad fettle. He saw the Cauvery and other rivers already swelling with monsoon rains, which had begun to fall earlier in the season than any man could remember.

His bullocks could no longer haul their heavy loads through such mud as that which was growing underfoot. His cavalry horses could not carry their riders.

The prudent General did not hesitate.[2] He burst his siege guns, destroyed his surplus stores, and while the officers of the Bombay Army waited eagerly for the glorious day when they would help the Grand Army to storm Tippoo's fort, he began to lead his sick and straggling formations back to Bangalore to recuperate and refit.

This, of course, the Bombay Army did not know. When one evening its troops received orders "to *strike tents immediately* and send all the *sick and baggage* to the rear" to be taken charge of by the Baggage Master, the vast rain-soaked camp woke with an enthusiastic splashing. No one doubted but that they "were going out under cover of night to surprise the enemy, or at all events to fight them". And the thoughts of "giving them a handsome drubbing before, or by daybreak", put them, Captain Macquarie wrote, in the highest spirits.

Many officers were so certain of the issue that they disobeyed the order to send away their baggage. They expected to return at dawn; so they left it where it lay and walked about among their men waiting excitedly for orders.

Macquarie was not among the optimists. He did the sensible thing, taking "about an hour's nap" in his *doolie*.

At midnight the brigades fell in under arms. The pickets were called in. The army, in columns of companies, at one o'clock in the morning began to steer happily towards Periapatam; but when they came to the fort, instead of wheeling to the right against the enemy as they had expected, they wheeled left. They began to retreat as fast as the bad roads would permit towards the Ghauts, over which they had climbed with so much sweat and loss.

This was a "most sensible mortification to the whole army". It "most completely damped all their fond and sanguine hopes of acquiring *laurels, fame, honour, riches* and *promotion*" at Seringapatam where, they had felt certain, they would arrive in time to share with the Grand Army "in the glorious Siege of Tippoo's great Capital".

All their dreams, Macquarie decided, must now give way to gloom and desponding thoughts on their being "obliged to retreat or *fall back* (as it is called)" from an enemy whom they had been in hopes of "fighting and conquering by the dawn of day".

It had been Abercromby's real intention to attack, after he had reconnoitred Tippoo's positions on his front. He had formed the plan of assailing them silently with the bayonet before daybreak, but an order received from Cornwallis while he was on the march had quickly changed the General's mind; the Commander-in-Chief was "peremptory".

Tippoo's cohorts in the vicinity, it became plain to Macquarie, were "no trifling body of skirmishers, but one capable of giving us a pretty warm reception"; no less, indeed, than 10,000 picked cavalry and 10,000 specially chosen infantry sent out under Cummer-ud-Deen Chawn, Tippoo's best general, to annihilate Abercromby's much smaller force.

The troops seen by the British pickets were the outposts of this hostile array, against which the Bombay Army's tired brigades and miserably-conditioned artillery would have stood little chance.

All thoughts of a siege were now to be forgotten till next season.

The knowledge of these facts did not reconcile Captain Macquarie's martial soul to the ignominy of "being obliged to *retreat* in the face of an enemy we so much despise"; nor did it increase his admiration for his commander as an organizer:

I am sorry to say, I cannot here, pay any great compliment to our General for the judgment and coolness he ought to have shewed in conducting our retreat; altho' to do him justice, I do believe that if his orders had been strictly complied with, no private property would have been lost or left behind; but, from not attending to the orders, and every one supposing that we were only going out to fight the enemy, a vast deal of baggage was lost; and what was worse, the most part of the sick belonging to the different corps were left on the ground for want of doolies to carry them and fell into the hands of the enemy. . . . the whole about one hundred men.[3]

These unfortunate prisoners included an ensign, a sergeant and eleven privates of the 77th Regiment, of whom three belonged to Macquarie's own company.

The flight of the army had been precipitate. There had not been even time to destroy the guns and large quantities of stores, as could have been done had Abercromby held for a few hours longer his position on the strong encampment ground which he had occupied.

The bleak dawn saw the great, straggling Bombay columns wading in deep mud two miles from the fort which they had left behind, and still in sight of the enemy, who luckily made no attempt to attack or molest them.

II

Of the progress to Malabar, the less said the better. Bullocks bogged down as they approached the passes and soldiers dragged the guns. When they entered the jungle, *looties* and Tippoo's horsemen pursued them, stealing much of Captain Macquarie's equipment and frightening his cook almost to death, though leaving behind the regimental paybooks.[4]

The march to the delightful green hill at Seedasur was the "most fatiguing and most unpleasant" the captain had ever endured. Beyond that point he could not even march. Suffering from fever and bowel complaint he rode, ill and dizzy, through the rain to the Ghaut, along a road on which the water was often knee-deep and which sometimes was almost impassable.

As he hobbled down the precipitous decline of the Pass as best he could, with the help of a strong pole, a "truly most horrid and melancholy sight" met his eyes.

Guns were axle-deep in mire. Writhing and struggling bullocks and horses lay in heaps, among or under the heavy loads which had fallen with, and sometimes upon, them.

Great numbers of animals, both public and private, were dead along the steep track from the summit to the foot of the declivity. Immense quantities of stores protruded from the mud. "In short," declared the narrator of the tragedy, "it was a distressing scene to look at, and I made the best of my way through it."

It was some days before he reached the coast ahead of the main body of troops. He had ridden wearily to the banks of the Belliapatam River. He had sailed down the river, watching the corpses of soldiery drowned out of capsized boats float past in a dreary swirl. He had limped on fifteen miles to the base cantonment at Durmapatam, wading through many a creek and nullah on the way—rather a long tramp, he meditated, for a convalescent.

He had no servants, no dry clothes, no horse, no *doolie*, nor anything to eat or drink. And he felt too tired and dirty to brave the civilization of Tellicherry, three miles away.

Still in pain, therefore, he was obliged to "take up my abode this night, in an old ruinous bungaloe, wet, dirty and hungry as I was, my only attendant my *massaljee* who carried my camp cloak which was my only bed".

On a "hard wooden cott that happened to be in this ruinous habitation" he suffered through one more wretched night, before his baggage arrived, soaked and spoiled, with a bedraggled swarm of refugees, behind whom the no-longer gilded staff of the Bombay Army was presently tossed up very weary and bad-tempered.

"*Thus*," writes Ulva's young hero, testily, "ended our campaign! Our next, it is hoped, and expected will be a more prosperous as well as, a more brilliant and successful one."

III

With the resilience of youth he struggled towards recovery. The bloodshot eye cleared, the yellow parchment skin assumed something of its natural hue. His interest quickened as he read his letters from Scotland, full of tidings of auspicious weddings and fortunate inheritances.

Almost with relish he helped to court-martial and cashier Lieutenant John Brown of the 77th Regiment for "conduct at different times unbecoming to the character of an officer and a gentleman", and chiefly "for not having in a proper manner resented a public insult he received in company from a brother officer, Lieut. M'Crea".

He sent to old Lachlan MacQuarie, Chieftain of Ulva, the prize-money of his dead son, John, earned in the Rohilla Campaign, £261 10s. 3¾d., which to his chieftain, in his present necessitous situation, was "quite a little fortune".

He drifted gradually into the social life of Tellicherry, where there were "no less than nine of the gentler sex who danced, which, for so small a place, was thought an extraordinary thing".

He was seen with some of them at a turtle feast, watching from afar the celebrations at the first full moon in August, which the natives called "Coconut Day". He was in correspondence with his friend, Mrs Coggan, in Madras. She wished him to sell for her among his military friends copies of an English version of that famous Scots pastoral, *The Gentle Shepherd*, which her sister had lately published in London.

His complete renaissance at last was marked by the entry in his Journal: "I danced *a reel* with pretty Agnew, Mrs. Taylor and General Abercromby."[5]

Family affairs more often exercised his mind than of yore. He had given a great deal of thought to the future of his brother Charles. He felt "a repugnancy in my own breast, in being the cause of bringing him from home", since their "worthy affectionate good mother" was "so anxious to detain him to be the comfort of her old age".

At the same time, he thought it very much against young Charles's interest to let him remain a farmer in Mull. With his Uncle Lochbuy's concurrence, he decided to "get him out to India, in the military line, as soon as possible, it being the only line, I can possibly be of assistance and service to him in". A draft for £200 on London or Edinburgh was ordered from Bruce, Fawcett and Company in Bombay for Charles's benefit.

And, even after that had been provided for, the fortune of Lachlan Macquarie stood at 4000 rupees.

IV

Four months after the sick and sorry Bombay Army reached the coast, India slid into a new autumn.

They heard that 10,000 bullocks were on their way from the Carnatic, and in a few weeks regiments serving in India found their strengths ominously increased to one thousand rank and file.

By the end of October 1791 Abercromby and his suite had returned from a visit to Bombay. The more domestic type of preparation went ahead steadily in Macquarie's quarters: "I received a letter from my Agent at Bombay with *five coolies* for the *field*. I discharged my head servant Francis . . . I purchased a very fine looking bullock for carriage of my baggage in the field . . . I only paid twenty rupees for this bullock, which is remarkably cheep."[6]

On 11 November the whole Bombay field force, augmented, refreshed, well supplied with stores and livestock, was ready to march again for Mysore, "on the shortest notice".

December 5 saw the Regiment on its way "towards, (as is supposed), the Ghauts", stepping it out for the customary first day's march of twelve miles.

There was some hitch about Macquarie's getting his tents down, but his new Europe-servant, Malcolm M'Innis—"whom I this very day took into my service"—arrived to marshal his employer's belongings, which had grown most noticeably since the earlier campaign:

> I reckon myself very well equipped for taking the field this campaign: being provided as follows *vizt*, a horse to ride occasionally.— Six bullocks for carriage of my baggage.— a dooly to sleep in or to be carried in case of sickness.— Four dozen of Madeira, four doz. brandy, some gin, two maunds of fine biscuit, a cheese, spices, two thirds of a tub of sugar, eight pounds of fine tea, some fowls and a small quantity of salt beef, composed my eatables and drinkables.— Two small light trunks contained my clothes, linens and boots and shoes. I have a new tent, a table, a chair, lamps or lanthorns, and ten pounds of wax candles; these and several other little equipments unnecessary to mention cost me upwards of ———. I have at present ten servants and coolies. . . .[7]

This *ménage* was little comfort to him. The bullocks were restive and troublesome from the start, the servants incompetent. The rear of the army became thoroughly familiar with the spectacle of Captain Macquarie rescuing his derelict belongings with the aid of soldiers borrowed from the regiment. Sometimes he was without a tent, occasionally without even a cloak. The rest of the army was in much the same fix. It was raining again. It was colder even than during their earlier campaign, if that were possible. The road had not been improved by their previous exertions.

They arrived at the top of Poodicherrum Ghaut without food, without anything to place between themselves and the wet ground, or any cover to protect themselves against the rain. A general order had forbidden servants and baggage to be taken to the summit "for fear of crouding the Ghaut too much untill the guns were brought up".

They froze and starved but they were there, after Macquarie with a pair of subalterns and two hundred and fifty soldiers had dragged the guns and tumbrils up the now familiar slope.

In a drizzling February, after two months on the road, they were passing out of the lines at Ahmutna and Sidapore above the Ghauts to form the much-wished-for junction with the "Grand Army and our own allies before Seringapatam". In six days they toiled through eighty-five miles of fords and slush while the *looties* made "terrible havocks" of the baggage train, killed a few soldiers who were leading bullocks and cut down several followers, before flanking parties dispersed them. Then, with Floyd and his 19th Dragoons and the Nizam's Horse, who had joined them as a rearguard when they crossed the Cauvery, they reached their final camping ground at noon on 15 February 1792.

V

The sight which met their eyes made them "exceedingly happy indeed".

Cornwallis, his soldiers preening themselves after carrying the *pettah* and outworks in the most peculiar nocturnal affray, at a cost of eleven officers killed and twenty-one wounded, and about five hundred men killed and four hundred wounded, lay outside the frowning fortress of Seringa-patam.[8]

Macquarie conceded that Cornwallis's attack on the *pettah* had been "very brilliant and successful"; but he has no descriptive touch.

Only love and indignation could lift his words above platitude. He mentions the "great and dreadful slaughter of the enemy" and their "bold and desperate" resistance which could not prevent the British from establishing themselves on the banks of the Cauvery "within gunshot of the Tyrant's capital". "Since the 6th inst. the Grand Army have only been busily employed preparing materials for the siege . . . which is not yet commenced, the Army not having even *broke ground*; so that the Bombay Army have made the much wished for junction at the most critical and most interesting period of the whole war."[9]

There is no detailed picture of that victorious host or of its exciting surroundings and neighbours. That, camped two miles away on Cornwallis's right, were "my old American friends, Major Skelly and Captain Madan, *aides-de-camp* to Lt.-Genl. Earl Cornwallis", seemed to be more worthy of notice than the pageantry; but he had a great joy in being where he was: "I cannot help observing here, that this is one of the happiest days I ever experienced in all my life, as there is nothing I ever so much wished for, as being present at the Siege of Seringapatam and joining the Grand Army."[10]

He catalogued the sights with a careless disregard for the spelling of words. He rode to the captured *pettah* on the island, admired the old palace and Haidar Ali's tomb and "the Garden (called the Loll-Bang)", and was "very highly gratified with the superb magnificence and grandeur of these places; particularly so with the elegance of Tippoo's New Palace in the Loll-Bang" (*lal bagh*, red garden), as yet only half finished, but which "being airy and healthy" had been turned into a hospital.

It housed, among others, his "very worthy friend and old 84th acquaintance, Lieut. James Robertson, who was wounded in the head, but recovering very fast".

Presently, the army broke ground within six or seven hundred yards of the walls. Upwards of five hundred men were sent from Macquarie's brigade to dig trenches. Abercromby, with the Reserve and 3rd Brigade, crossed to the south side of the river, while the 1st Brigade covered their crossing of the ford.

Little action followed. There was time for Macquarie to visit *aides-de-camp* at the Grand Army Headquarters, and Colonel Harris and Major Hunt. These last two shared the role of *fidus Achates* to Medows, whose despondency was now not so great, after a mishap in the recent battle for the *pettah*, that he could not receive young Captain Macquarie "very politely" at dinner.

On 22 February the "enemy attacked the picquets of Genl Abercromby's Corps, which were posted in a *tope* [wood] on the west side of Seringapatam Fort; but were repulsed and driven back on a part of the line being sent to support the Picquets". Next day the 77th went into the trenches for the ensuing twenty-four hours. "I was sent with my company to a detached post."[11]

At daybreak on the twenty-fourth there was a "pretty smart fire of long shots". Those in trenches did not suffer, but a few among the working parties were killed and wounded. It was thrilling to feel that "many of their shot struck very close to where our men were stationed"; but that firing was the last that Seringapatam heard for many a year.

At noon that day they learnt with a shudder of disappointment that "cessation of hostilities was to take place immediately, and that preliminaries of peace were signed by the *Confederate* powers and Tippoo Sultan".[12] The news "damped the spirits of every one who wished the downfall of the Tyrant and who hoped to have the satisfaction in a few days more, of storming his capital". However, the Peace was "an honourable as well as an advantageous one for the British Nation" and it seemed that Tippoo would relinquish for ever half of his present Dominions, and pay in ready money three *crores* and thirty *lakhs* of rupees towards the expenses of the war.

Earl Cornwallis was "pleased to announce in General Orders, that he would pay the Army, out of the first part of this money, a handsome gratuity in lieu of prize money". That, at any rate, was ground for general satisfaction.

For some days it seemed as if hostilities might break out again. The Sultan obviously felt a certain difficulty—due to the widespread choice of offspring and relations offering—in selecting a pair of hostages to guarantee his good behaviour.

General Medows, in particular, appears to have supported a hope that he would in the end need to lead the assault on the citadel and thus atone for having become lost during the attack on the *pettah*, to his great discredit in his own eyes.

When the two young princes who were to act as sureties for their father actually arrived in the British Camp, he gave way to despair, placed the muzzle of a pistol against his heart, and fired.

The faithful Harris had guessed his intentions and forestalled them, making sure that the weapon held no ball. Instead of producing a death, the shot merely bred another anecdote; for it is told that the intended victim himself summed the incident up to Colonel Knox, by saying that "Mr Medows had had a fight with General Medows, but honour was now satisfied".

Macquarie inaccurately recorded that the General was "severely wounded, but the balls were immediately extracted, and he is again in a fair way of recovering". The incident "made a great noise and astonished every one".

VI

Not a single man in the 77th Regiment was killed in Tippoo's War of '92, but one Hebridean captain nearly left his £308 10s. in prize money to his relatives without handling it. A few days before the definitive treaty with Tippoo was signed, General Abercromby's army marched out to Caniambaddy to the west of Seringapatam; but Macquarie was taken very ill, so that he could not travel with it, and followed it next day.

The 77th Regiment started for home at daybreak on 26 March 1792 . . . "ten miles . . . a very tedious march, having frequent long halts. I rode during the cool of the morning, but was under the necessity of being carried in my *dooly* during the rest of the day, being still much indisposed and extremely weak. . . . Doctor Ker, the Surgeon General, having kindly obliged me with the loan of eight men . . ."

They hurried him coastward in front of the army, and "my friend Doctor Anderson always rode with me in the mornings, to bear me company untill I betook to my *dooly*".

At the end of the month he improved. At Sidapore Captain Gray of the 77th Regiment supplied him with good milk, and some egg curry, which refreshed him very much and "for the first time, these *five weeks* past", he found "a desire, tho' not a great one, *to eat*; having been for that time, deprived of all appetite whatever".

He reached Cananore on 6 April 1792, "much fatigued and tired", but he had now "the consolation to think, that my disorder is removing fast, and that I shall improve and recover daily, in my health. I feel quite overjoyed, to breathe the sea air again."

On 10 April he wrote, "I gave up using mercury this day, finding my mouth sore, and consequently, the habit affected;— I have been constantly using this medicine for these five weeks past."

There was nothing left for him to do in connection with the campaign save to pay out the "gratuity of *six months batta*" to each man in the Regiment, along with pay and allowances.

Unfit in his "present weak condition to transact business", he was due for a shock, since he was handed the money—"near one lakh of rupees"—in "*Hydrie* and *Sultanie pagodas*, at the rate of 4⅛ rupees each pagoda; upon which we are likely to lose much money, as these coins do not pass at Bombay, for near what they are issued to the Army at".

However, he hoped that "upon a proper representation being made, the deficiency or difference will be made up by Government".

He presented his tent, *doolie*, and all his bullocks, "excepting one favourite one, which I gave Capt. Cameron", to Lieutenants Cameron and M'Coll, of the 75th Regiment. He sold his mare and saddle for what they had cost him. His servants received a fortnight's extra pay.

The war was over. They rowed him to the *Hercules* which was to carry five hundred men of the Regiment, in Captain Galloway's own boat, and he occupied the captain's own cabin, because the great cabin was so crowded and half of it was divided off for Major Stirling and his wife.

Early one morning, six days later, on 20 April 1792, he was once more gazing upon the calm roadstead at Bombay and the green sweep of Culaba.

CHAPTER VI

The Soldier's Wedding

I

LITTLE had changed in Bombay in the sixteen months since Macquarie had sailed for Tellicherry.

The young palm-trees had grown taller. A few faces were missing. There were a few new ones, some of them looking out from under cropped and ungarnished thatches; for under the influence of the new democracy the paint and powder of the eighteenth century were wearing thin. But Bombay, when it hailed the returning Army of Seringapatam on 21 April 1792, was, in the main, its old familiar self.

From its amenities, though "mending fast" after the fevers of his campaigning, the Hope of Oskamull held aloof for some time, moving restlessly from the Fort to Culaba and back again, or visiting the country, and almost always shadowed by the faithful Dr Colin Anderson.

The military life around him since his return was something apart from his own. He does not even seem to have shown apprehension at the news which the Indiamen of the Season[1] brought that His Majesty the King was delighted with the affectionate attachment of his subjects to his person—despite the need of dragoons in the Midlands to assure it—and was disposed to view the chances of peace with such optimism as to meditate "some immediate reductions . . . in our Naval and Military establishments".[2]

When he did recover completely he had a preoccupied air, as he prepared himself for the rigours of the Christmas season festivities in "the very neat small house or bungaloe, the property of Mr Robertson, at the rent of forty rupees per month", in which a new head servant ministered to his needs.

The returned captain was, in truth, in a state bordering on enchantment at the close of 1792. A fragrant and delicious object was claiming his whole concentrated attention; a "Dulcinea", as he himself described her . . . . "in plain words, Miss Jane Jarvis".[3] He had become "sincerely and deeply in love" with her, although his native Scottish caution led him for long to refrain from confessing it.

He first had met the lady among "Mr. Morley's family", to whose members his commanding officer, Lieutenant-Colonel Balfour, introduced him in the house of John Forbes, the banker, on 7 November.

The Morley family, it appeared, was "seemingly a very pleasant one to be acquainted in". Mr Morley himself was truly "a gentleman of very high rank and opulent fortune here, being the Senior Civil Servant in the Honble Company's Service on the Bombay Establishment"; one who had "gone home several years ago with a large fortune to England, but having married a most elegant and amiable woman there . . . returned again to Bombay in the year 1790 to increase his fortune". This nabob dined jovially *en famille* with the Governor on days when His Excellency "entertained privately". His wife was "a well bred elegant woman"; and so, too, was her sister, Miss Jane Jarvis, who had accompanied her "merely from attachment as a companion, and not to look for a husband in this country, (as young ladies in general do who come out to India), her fortune putting her far above such views".[4]

Miss Jarvis was described a year later as "young and handsome (being just twenty one years of age)—an excellent figure, rather above the middle size, with a most comely pleasing face and countenance (what I call pretty) . . . but, above all, a most amiable disposition and temper; with a good understanding, and a mind well cultivated and instructed by the best and finished education."[5]

In a word, he believed, she was a "most pleasing companion", and what his Uncle Lochbuy would call "*an agreeable Sonsie*"; in fact, "a most amiable good girl as ever lived".

Though "West Indian by birth", he recorded, "she was of a "very genteel, respectable and opulent family in that country", born in the Island of Antigua, where her father had been Chief Justice and First in Council.

The old gentleman, who had been dead for some years, had "left behind a large family of sons and daughters, all very handsomely provided for". His eldest son, Mr Thomas Jarvis, had an estate worth £2000 sterling per annum in Antigua. The delectable Jane's mother was possessed of "a very handsome jointure" which "enabled her to support her widowhood in London in a very genteel stile". And her male parent had not forgotten to provide for Jane's future. She had inherited from him, beside those of his qualities which he had contributed to mould her charming disposition and agreeable manners, a "private fortune of six thousand pounds sterling".

Captain Macquarie "became deeply enamoured from the first moment I was introduced to Jane; and, indeed, was very partial to her even before then". A little closer contact with the damsel's amiable qualities of mind and disposition, while he danced a reel with her a fortnight after he met her, served to "rivett his chains and entirely win his affection".

II

It was one thing, however, to be in love with her; quite another thing was the problem of "how he was to get possession of this jewel". He conceived her to be "so very far beyond anything he had a right to expect that he could not muster up sufficient courage to pay his addresses to her, or even to hint to her his partiality in her favour"—this, though he "could plainly discover that she had sufficient penetration to see what was going on in his bosom".

What was a poor Hebridean captain to do in such a dilemma? Jane, he pointed out, had "a tolerable *good fortune*; he had NONE", and the situation was worse because even delay was dangerous. Already there were "*young men* and *old* men, some of them of high rank and large fortunes, who had made proposals of marriage to her, but were all rejected".

For all its colour and its professions of sentiment, the eighteenth century was an age of realism. The young man had to confess, "Poverty made me a coward lover", though he was far from a despairing one. There was every hope that promotion and preferment would solve his problems. His heart was none the less stout because it must have been obvious to him that he was engaged in a breathless race to produce, out of the cap of Fortune, conditions in which he could propose marriage to his lady-love before the censorious eyes of Bombay compelled her guardians to inquire formally about the nature of his intentions, or hand her over to some richer suitor. But he thought he could solve the problem.

His eyes fixed upon the eligible and pleasant appointment of Major of Brigade to the King's troops, Captain Macquarie set out upon one of the most strenuous campaigns of his life.

It is easy to see that the normal social occasions of that Bombay season were to him shadowy episodes and not part of his real life.

He was inducted into the local Lodge of Freemasons as one in a dream. Dinner with the Governor—"sitting on his right hand, which is reckoned a particular mark of distinction and favour"—was merely a skirmish in the battle for preferment. A review, at which His Excellency praised the military virtues and appearance of good order of the 77th Regiment, was the signal to order up the guns to bombard authority with requests. Captain John Abercromby, the Governor's nephew, was sent to conduct an outflanking movement to capture his uncle's goodwill; General Allan Maclean, the lover's patron at home, was invoked as an ally.

III

The first ships of the 1793 season brought him news far more ominous than that of the previous year, but far more pleasing to aspiring King's officers.

The King's Speech gave an "affecting description of the times and savoured of war with France". There were a great number of disaffected persons in Britain who were endeavouring to foment tumult and disorder among the lower classes, thus generating riot and insurrection. The Army and Navy were being augmented, a hundred independent companies of foot raised, and the Militia embodied. All this was due to the actions of the "*National Convention* or Executive Government [of France], alias the violent infamous Republican leaders", who were well on the way towards making their country what Mr Ben Cooper, the Secretary of the English Revolutionary Society, was pleased to call "the instructress of the world".

Captain Macquarie noticed these events, but he was inattentive to them, for upon the day on which the intelligence of them arrived, he was deep in his own campaign; was, in fact, entertaining "several respectable

friends" who might further his interests, all of them commanding officers
or commodores save only Mr Morley, and all persons from whom he
had "received very great civility and attention".

It was a pleasant party, and no doubt it served a useful purpose in
influencing events towards the end which was becoming urgent to the
host, as he was being seen more and more in the company of the lady of
his choice; the end which was of more import to him than all the caperings
of the Dantons and their like.

He had come to the stage at which, on a day of pageantry which
signalized the investment of Sir Robert Abercromby with the insignia
of knighthood, he not only had had the felicity of dancing two dances
with Jane in a single evening but had "handed her to supper", before he
returned to the new home which he had acquired a few days before—"a
neat little upstair house adjoining the Ramparts in the rear of the Garden
Ravelin, for fifty rupees per month".

Three weeks later, having dined at Government House on "one of
the Governor's private entertaining days when he invites only ladies and
particular friends", he was asked by His Excellency to be one of the managers
of his farewell ball and supper. He felt it was an omen.

The ball was not a great success. A civil servant, choosing that evening
of all evenings to become "intoxicated and mad", quarrelled with "another
queer customer" (known as the Russian Bear) and had to be thrown out
by a guard of sepoys.

Macquarie did not dance because Miss Jarvis had a "bad head-ach
and could not be prevailed on", and because he had "no desire to dance
with any other".

It is possible that Mr Morley knew something of the reasons for Miss
Jarvis's headache. Conduct such as that of her swain was enough to set
every wagging tongue in Bombay to work. It was too much for Mr Morley,
who gave battle with swift vigour. At ten o'clock on the morning after
the ball he was upon Captain Macquarie's doorstep to tell the gallant that
if his income did not admit of his making proposals, he "should desist
from paying his sister such assiduous pointed attentions, as such conduct
might engage her affections and be the means of preventing her from
accepting any other offers that might be made to her".

True love was little understood in the circles in which Bombay *kooee-hais*
moved, and Mr Morley sternly intimated that the captain must be not
merely seriously attached to the lady, but also sufficiently endowed with
worldly goods to prove it, if he wished her favours. Then, and then only,
the captain narrated, would Mr and Mrs Morley be "very happy to forward
my views and think themselves much honoured in being connected with
me".

As the young man was unprepared for the ambush, he was, he wrote,
so much embarrassed that he answered his visitor in very awkward and
incoherent manner; but he "confessed his partiality and love for Miss J."
and said that he "should have made his sentiments known long ago had
his situation in life with regard to fortune authorised him to do so".

"THE GOOD, AMIABLE GIRL"

A reputed portrait of Jane Jarvis, from a miniature in the possession of
Lt.-Col. C. G. C. Jarvis, D.L., O.B.E., Doddington Hall, Lincoln

But, said he, his circumscribed income precluded such a declaration at present, seeing that he had but £1000 saved and his income was a mere £500 a year.

At this stage an armistice seems to have been signed. Jane's guardian was content to exact an undertaking from the Scot "not to be so particular in his attentions" until he should be able to propose marriage; and Mr Morley himself promised not to disclose their conversation to anyone save Mrs Morley.

He left Captain Macquarie—having drawn a secret from him which he had not meant to make known to anyone for some time to come—"in the most perplexed, painful and awkward situation that can be conceived", greatly at a loss how to act, and with his mind "tortured between hope and fear".

It was clear to him that he could not support the amiable good girl in the style and manner she was entitled to. So he determined to renew his flank attack on the Governor to win the spoils of promotion. Those secured, he could with propriety, he felt, "propose marriage to my dearest and loveliest of women, Miss J."

In ten days the prize was his. The Governor, about to leave for Bengal to take up the post of Commander-in-Chief, invited him to dinner. ("This augurs well.")

In less than a week, he was able to write:

> In this day's General Orders, I have the happiness to find myself appointed to act as Major of Brigade to His Majesty's Troops on the Coast of Malabar in room of Major Auchmuty untill the Commander-in-Chief's pleasure is known:— I cannot express the joy and satisfaction I felt on being informed by Major Auchmuty of my succeeding to this appointment. . . it affords me now the privilege of disclosing my attachment to my dearest and loveliest Miss J. . . . I supped this evening at Mr. Morley's but had not an opportunity of saying anything to Miss J. respecting my attachment for her; therefore, I have come to a resolution to write to her on the subject tomorrow.[6]

IV

He rose very early next morning and wrote a letter "to the object of my sincere love and affection, of which letter, I kept a copy. . . . . God grant that it may prove successful!"[7]

He waited on General Abercromby to give thanks for his new appointment, was received very kindly and informed that the General had a great desire to serve and befriend him. The General conversed in a very friendly manner with him and told him that "notwithstanding many applications made to him for the post . . . he preferred me to them all".

The new official learned, moreover, from the General's staff, that had His Excellency remained in Bombay he had proposed to make him an aide-de-camp; and he felt that for all his blessings he "owed gratitude and obligation to his worthy and much esteemed friend Captain John Abercromby".

C

As soon as he had returned to headquarters, at about eleven o'clock, off went the Moor-man, Bappoo, with his note to his lady-love, with orders to deliver it into Miss Jarvis's own hands; "which he did, but got no answer only to make compliments".

Soon came a message from Mr Morley making an appointment for nine o'clock next morning.

Before then there was dinner to be got through with Mr O'Donnell, the Deputy Auditor-General, with the Governor and his suite present . . . "a very genteel agreeable party . . . . we sat till seven o'clock". And there was supper at Mr William Simpson's where the anxious lover spent "as pleasant an evening as the state of my mind at present would admit of; for my anxiety between fear and hope is greater than I can well describe".

At the appointed time—it was the Sabbath—Mr Morley attended him at his house and told him that he had seen his letter to Miss Jarvis and that she wished to take a little time to consider the proposals, before she could give a decisive answer.[8]

The good old man advised the suitor to consider seriously the step he seemed so desirous of entering upon. He repeated his former arguments, and explained how expensive it was to maintain a wife and family in a genteel way in Bombay. He said Miss Jarvis's fortune must, of course, be settled on herself, in case of their being united.

The swain replied that he had never even thought of the lady's fortune and that he had "not been guided or influenced by sordid or mercenary motives". His attachment to her, he said, proceeded "from real love and admiration for herself and the pleasing manners and qualifications she was endowed with". Her fortune, he declared, should "run on accumulating without his even touching the interest unless she herself desired it".

He even offered himself to settle his thousand pounds on her—"which was *all* I had to bestow", and that whenever fortune threw more in his way, he would add to it to convince her and her friends how dear she was to him and how warmly and sincerely he was attached to her.

Punctiliously he presented Mr Morley with a card on which he had noted down his different allowances per month as Captain-Lieutenant, Paymaster, and Major of Brigade, adding as he gave it into his visitor's hand, that it would show his real monthly income, which was only 603 rupees (£67 9s. sterling) and that it was not his intention to impose or deceive, but on the contrary to give as candid and explicit an account of his present circumstances and future prospects as possible.

Mr Morley thanked the lover ceremoniously. He promised to consult Mrs Morley and then state the position to his sister-in-law. He paid "a number of compliments", saying that he should be exceedingly happy to see the pair united, but that it was his duty "to prevent his sister from connecting herself but with one who could support her in a genteel comfortable style". He departed, declaring that he would now place everything before Miss Jarvis and leave it entirely to herself to decide how to act. He promised an answer in two or three days.

Miss Jarvis, however, did not temporize. In about an hour and a half

Mr Morley was on the doorstep of the Macquarie home to announce "the most delightful, acceptable and pleasing intelligence that I ever yet was made happy with—*vizt.*—that he had talked to Miss Jarvis and that she was resolved to accept of my offers, to which he added, that she had declared that she preferred me to all other men in the world. What heavenly news this! Oh delightful glorious and generous girl!"[9]

The bemused suitor "had some friendly and interesting conversation on this subject with Mr. Morley", and the old gentleman beat a hasty retreat from his transports of joy and begged him to come that evening to deal with the lady herself.

The accepted lover could not contain himself. He rushed to tell the news to Dr Anderson, "who I know to be my real and sincere friend, and who heartily participated in my good fortune and happiness". He took a short walk on the Esplanade. After an age he was at the Morley's door and most kindly received by the master of the house himself.

Soon afterwards the ladies made their appearance, but there were no scenes of passion. He held a "pleasing and interesting conversation with the delight of my heart and soul—but some strangers coming in obliged us to break off our discourse abruptly".[10]

This he believed fortunate, for he "was so agitated and overcome with joy, that he did not well know what he said to Miss Jarvis". He must have spoken very incoherently indeed, he thought, for he never felt himself so much discomposed.

Major and Mrs Oakes called and were asked to stay to supper, which he was very glad of, because he was engaged to them for that meal. At any rate, they stayed and they all spent what to him was "the happiest evening of my life in company with my beloved and dearest of women".

He did not "sit next to her or offer to hand her to table, for fear of being taken notice of"; but he took the opportunity of asking her permission to wait on her next morning, which she "declined, saying she would rather see [him] in the evening", in which wish he "most readily acquiesced".

Oblivious of what some other August the fourth of the future held for the world, Lachlan Macquarie, benedict-to-be, went to bed at midnight.

V

It was Monday, the day after his acceptance by his betrothed. It was still the eighteenth century, and it was, also, five years to the day since he had disembarked in India from the *Dublin*.

He awoke, feeling that "thanks to God . . . he had no reason to complain of his success and prosperity".

He looked up, he declared, "with humble and pious gratitude to a good Providence, who has so wonderfully conducted me through the difficulties of my youth to a station of credit and respect, such as I am now in".

He was on the threshold of a new epoch in his life and felt that, with military precision and exactitude, he must set down rules for his future conduct in solemn form:

August 5, Monday: It is five years this day since I disembarked along with Colonel Balfour etc. etc. on board the *Dublin* at Bombay; on reflection, and looking back how I have spent my time since then, I am convinced I have spent the greater part of it very unprofitably and idly—and after serious consideration and minutely weighing my present situation and pursuits, I am thoroughly convinced I ought to alter my line of conduct, and live henceforth more regularly temperately and rationally than I have hitherto done; being fully persuaded that it is absolutely necessary as well for the preservation of my life and health, as for my future happiness through life; and I am also sensible, that I have not attended to my own improvement, by reading and study, near so much as I ought to have done:— THEREFORE, I have this day very seriously resolved and determined, to divide my time and live in the following manner. *vizt.*

First.—Whether I am late out over night or not, I am always to rise and get up at sun-rise; or at farthest at six o'clock; and if not for any duty or obliged to attend parades, I am to employ the morning from six till seven o'clock, in exercise of walking or riding; to read from seven till eight o'clock; and breakfast precisely at eight o'clock.

Secondly.—If I have any duty or business to transact, either as Major of Brigade or Paymaster of the Regiment, or Capt of the Company I command, the hours between nine and twelve O'clock, always to be devoted entirely to such duties or occupations as my offices may require . . .

Thirdly.—The time from twelve to two o'clock, to be always employed in improving my mind by serious reading and study;—a part of this time is always to be devoted to reading such military books, as may tend to teach me my profession and instruct me in a further knowledge of it.

Fourthly.—I am always to dress at two o'clock or at half past two o'clock at farthest.

Fifthly.—When I dine abroad, I am never to drink more than equal to ONE BOTTLE of WINE—that is to say, twelve glasses, three of those only to be Madeira, and the rest Hock or Claret;—to avoid drinking Malt Liquor as much as possible, but on no account to drink any at night, nor never to exceed one Lumba of strong beer even at dinner.

Sixthly.—While in Bombay to make it a rule, in order to keep up my acquaintance to visit the families I am acquainted with in Bombay, each once in the fortnight;—for this purpose, the evenings of Mondays and Fridays, are to be set apart for visiting those families that I am only slightly acquainted in; and to visit those I am more intimate in, on the other nights of the week or as it may suit my conveniency; but, to eat suppers as seldom as possible, and then, never exceed two glasses of wine.

Seventhly.—When I spend the evenings at home, to amuse myself with music, or light reading until bed-time; and if possible always to go to bed before eleven o'clock.—There may be exceptions now and then to the foregoing rules or distribution of time, but care must be taken to make as few deviations as possible from them:—this I am resolved and determined to adhere strictly to, in testimony whereof I subscribe my name on this the fifth day of August, 1793.

L. Macquarie

N.B. Punctuality with regard to time and appointments, to be particularly attended to, as well as the foregoing rules from this day henceforth. L.M.Q.[11]

VI

This was a fit prelude to taking over the Brigade Office and its books from Major Auchmuty next day.

On 7 August Sir Robert Abercromby left for Fort William with his suite by the *Swallow* Packet and appeared "much affected" as he was going into the boat. He was pleased to shake the new Brigade-Major cordially by the hand when he was descending the stairs.

In the afternoon that hero again had the happiness of "dining with my charmer *en famille*". But this was a little thing compared to the felicity which had awaited him when Mrs Morley "had had the goodness to invite him to ride out with them in the carriage".

When the carriage was ordered he was most agreeably surprised to find that Mrs Morley was to ride with Mr Morley in a buggy and that he was to accompany his Jane and little Charles Morley in the chariot. "Oh! what felicity,—I actually thought for some minutes I was in a dream!—blessed adorable girl.— We had a delightful interesting conversation untill we reached the Buffaloe Tank . . ."

As they walked there they were "joined by Mr. Stevenson, an elderly gentleman, one of the visitors at Mr. Morely's House, and a great admirer of Miss Jarvis", who appeared "much discomforted and displeased, to judge by his Gorgon looks, to see me so happy".

At dinner they were obliged to be reserved because visitors appeared; though the happy lover believed it was "now in vain to conceal our intended union any longer—for, in Bombay a gentleman and a lady in a carriage together marries them immediately".

"What a fortunate fellow I am," exclaimed Miss Jarvis's swain, as Mr Morley secured for them a house which should have been the perquisite of "one of Miss Jarvis's lovers and great admirers".

The prospective bridegroom wished to God that the occupier was already removed from this dwelling; for it was painful to a man when he "had so much bliss in view, but could not attain it for a certain time". Haste in such matters, however, was unknown to Bombay where Society loved to enjoy the full lingering flavour of a courtship. So the bridegroom must wait, bound by convention and resigned to the many irksome duties which must be gone through before this "most blessed of marriages" could take place.

There was Private John Stevens to be shot for desertion, for instance, as the first assignment of the new Brigade-Major; but he performed this "awful and solemn" duty with the same detachment as he showed on most serious official occasions. "As soon as I came home from the execution I wrote a note to my lovely dear, to enquire how her headach was—I also sent her Mr. Boswell's *Journey to the Hebrides* to read;—in return, I was made happy by a tender note,—but this happiness was greatly damped by the information it contained of her having had a bad nights rest and her headach still continuing."[12]

By midday thoughts of Private Stevens lying under the wet Indian soil were completely banished by the vision of Jane's "headach", which cleared up during the evening. She presently appeared among a large company, still sick, though "her face beamed benignity and love" and her conversation was as usual, "pleasing, charming and interesting".

From now onward, it was his habit to call regularly every morning at Mr Morley's—in blank defiance of Clause Two of his anniversary resolution—to converse with his "dearest of women", who made him a present of "her own dress watch, seals etc." which she had received from her mother, and which she insisted he should wear for her sake—"a very elegant watch and goes on a diamond". He was even "allowed by my Angel to cut off a lock of her hair to wear about my neck as a *chain*—What a happy fellow I am!"

The Morleys came to dine at his bungalow and he showed his beloved "his little stock of plate, furniture, etc.", of which he sent her a list. As a prospective family man, he subscribed to Mr Hall's newspaper, the *Bombay Courier*. He attended the launching of Mr Tasker's ship, *Upton Castle*. He borrowed a riding horse for Jane and pranced with her *coram populo*.

The last day of August saw him in possession of the keys of his "new, excellent house" near the Ramparts "in a clean, airy undisturbed part of the town" (but three times the rent of his previous nest), with which his betrothed and her sister were "much pleased". The marriage settlement had been drawn up by Mr Constable, appointing Messrs Morley and Tasker as trustees. He moved into the new abode. On 7 September 1793 George Dick, the acting Governor, gave him his marriage licence.

On 8 September he was married.

VII

To the incidents of his wedding night, what better witness than the bridegroom?

Septr. 8 *SUNDAY.* My beloved and dearest Miss Jarvis, having consented to crown my felicity, by being united forever this day, in the holy banns of matrimony, a numerous and very respectable company of our mutual friends and acquaintances were invited by Mr. and Mrs. Morley to an evening entertainment in their house; where it was agreed our nuptials should be solemnized by the Reverend Mr. Arnold Burrowes, the Minister of Bombay and who was accordingly warned to attend at Mr. Morley's House, precisely at seven o'clock this evening.—

I spent a great part of the forenoon with my beloved at Mr. Morley's house, seeing her baggage removed from thence to her intended place of residence, which I got put into the best order that circumstances would permit; and having arranged everything preparatory to the happy event, I took my leave of her untill the evening, and went to the Barraeks where I took a sober farewel and last bachelor's dinner with my good and much esteemed friend Surgeon Colin Anderson of the 77th Regiment, with whom I had some agreeable conversation on my approaching happiness.—

I left my friend Anderson a little before six o'clock, and went home to my own house to dress.— I dressed as quick as possible, having very little time to spare, as I promised Mr. Morley to be at his house before seven o'clock, so as to have the ceremony over before the whole of the company should assemble, it being intended to have only a few particular friends present on this happy occasion; but notwithstanding all my haste in dressing, it struck seven o'clock before I arrived at Mr. Morley's house, where, I found all the friends, intended to be there, assembled, except Mr. Tasker who soon afterwards appeared.—

Having first seen, and paid my respects to my beloved Jane, who had just done dressing herself as I entered the house; a few minutes past seven o'clock, she was led out, elegantly attired, (her lovely countenance beaming full of beneficence, beauty and unaffected modesty) by her brother-in-law, James Morley, Esq, followed by Mrs. Morley and the rest of the ladies, to the outer hall or veranda, where the Revd. Mr. Burrowes and the gentlemen waited to receive us.— The rites of matrimony were solemnized with all due form; Mr. Morley having given away his sister, as her nearest male relation in Bombay;— I had provided a wedding ring some days before for this happy occasion; and the ceremony [was performed] with great regularity and decency, my beloved having conducted herself during the whole of it with the most correct propriety and fortitude.—

The following ladies and gentlemen were present at the celebration of our nuptials—*vizt.*—Mr. & Mrs. Morley, Mr. John Morley, Mr. Jas. Morley, Major and Mrs. Stirling, Major and Mrs. Oakes, Major and Mrs. Woodington, Mr. & Mrs. Halliday, Colonel James Balfour, Lt. Colonel Nicholson, Surgeon Colin Anderson, Mr. John Forbes, Mr. John Tasker; besides the Revd. Mr. Burrowes; all these gentlemen had the pleasure of kissing the bride and the rest of the ladies, as is usual on these occasions, I having myself set them the example as soon as the ceremony was over.— The usual compliments and congratulations being received by the bride and myself from the company present, the ceremony of baptism was performed on Mr. Morley's youngest daughter who was christened by the name of Hariot, and, General Carnac, who was to have stood as Godfather being absent, I stood as proxy for him and my beloved stood as Godmother.— There was also a little country-born girl, a distant relation of Mr. Morleys, christened at the same time, and named Sarah or Sally—(the daughter of a Mr. Richardson) I was requested by Mrs. Morley to stand Godfather to this girl which I accordingly did;— after which the company sat down to cards; and in addition to our former society which I have already named, the following gentlemen who had been invited to spend the Evening joined us—*vizt.*— Mr. Thistleton, Mr. Stevenson, Mr. Harding, Mr. Reeves, Doctor Scott, Mr. Boag, Mr. Charles Forbes, Captain Romney;— Mr. Seton, Mr. Paddock, and the Revd. Mr. Wade were invited but sent excuses on account of their having been engaged.—

Mrs. Morley had prepared a most elegant supper, to which the company sat down twenty eight in number, a little after ten o'clock. Mr. and Mrs. Morley paid Mrs. Macquarie and myself a most handsome compliment in placing us at the head and foot of the table, to preside at and do the honours of it in their stead; waving [sic] their own right, to do the honours of their table for this night in our favour, as a testimony of their regard love and respect for us:— this mark of kind and polite attention, was very pleasing and flattering to us both; and will not fail of making a strong and lasting impression on our minds, of grateful and just remembrance, for the favour and honour conferred on us.—

The company were well chosen on this joyous occasion, and appeared, one and all, to participate in our joy and felicity—all was mirth and good humour, tempered by strict decorum, politeness and temperance— Several songs were sung, and we sat till past twelve o'clock at table; when the company broke up, and the whole retired to their several homes, in good spirits, and highly pleased with each other, and the entertainment of the evening.—

Mrs. Morley was kindly pleased to accompany her sister home to her new lodging, where she staid to see her bedded, and then took leave of her sister;— I handed Mrs. Morley to her chair and saw her off; then undressed as quick as possible and flew on the wings of love to my dearest of women, to finally crown my measure of happiness and bliss!— My felicity and delight, on this joyous and fortunate night, can only be conceived—but impossible, to be described! Suffice it to say—no Benedict was ever happier, or better pleased with his lot and good fortune, in the choice of a WIFE!—[13]

VIII

He was thirty-two. He was married. The year had added £260 to his annual income.

"In short, my dear Madame," as he wrote to his old friend, Mrs Clephane of Torloisk, "I have become all at once a Benedict and a man of fortune."

Which was something to be proud of, seeing that all the machinery which he brought to the accomplishment of these good things had been his own personality and limited influence.

What the sonsie Jane thought about it all nobody knows. With a complete lack of consideration for a curious future the amiable, good girl failed to keep a diary.

CHAPTER VII

Escape from Fortune

I

THE wedding was over. The bride and bridegroom, not wishing to have "their own little interesting society" interrupted, retired into what they seemed to regard as profound seclusion. Nobody visited them during the first five days of this retirement save Mr and Mrs Morley, who called every day and spent two or three evenings with them, and "a very few select friends"—thirty-eight of them to be exact. But these were *sub rosa* proceedings, pending the time when they "should sit up in form to receive visits agreeable to the custom of Bombay".[1]

Eight days after the wedding they appeared at Mr Herring's ball, riding thither in Mr Tasker's carriage, and the next day they began their period of three "sitting up evenings".

The Morley family and a galaxy of thirsty military officers and their wives supported them in this ordeal, while "all the Ladies and Gentlemen of the Settlement" came to pay their compliments or to offer congratulations.

Bombay society took them to its bosom with a warmth and thoroughness which was even more expensive than it was flattering. The bridegroom at first bore up bravely. Every mail to Britain carried accounts of his "happiness and prosperity". He proclaimed himself "a truly happy Benedict", and 1793 as "a lucky year for me".[2]

He made haste to clasp his bride's family to his bosom as closely as the interposition between him and them of twelve thousand miles of water would permit, opening relations with a letter to his mother-in-law which must have entranced the good lady had she lived long enough to receive it.

He addressed her as "My dear Mother".[3] He told her that she would not be a little surprised when she cast her eye on the subscription of this letter, to find that the writer had addressed her by such a tender name; but to satisfy her with respect to the propriety of the address, he asked her to give him leave to inform her that he had the happiness and felicity of being married to her amiable and charming daughter Jane.

> It is unnecessary for me, my dear Madam, to attempt giving you the panegyrick of your charming daughter;—you already know her worth and excellencies, which are far beyond my praise; and therefore, I shall only observe, that I reckon myself not only supremely happy, but also, the most fortunate and happiest of men, to be in possession of so great and valuable a blessing. . . . My fortune is very small, but I believe, I may say without vanity, that my character and connexions are unexceptionable and will bear the strictest enquiry.

He asked her to "believe me with great truth and regard, my dear Mother, your affectionate Son"; he begged her to sit for her miniature and "allow the cost of drawing and setting it neatly in gold to be at my sole expense". Lastly, he entreated her "to allow some of your hair to be set in the back of the picture, and, also, in a breast locket", which he had commissioned, and in which he proposed to insert some of the locks of Jane herself and of her "lovely sister".

To his overtures the Jarvis family responded in a friendly manner, save Mr Thomas Jarvis of Antigua, who showed a regrettable lack of gentlemanly spirit. He exhibited a definite reluctance to hand over to the trustees Jane's modest fortune which was in his charge. And his new brother-in-law eventually wrote to Mr Tasker that "any further delay in payment of it, and investing of it in the funds, will be attended with very serious inconvenience to us; and I trust you will have the goodness, to send directions to Messrs. Goslings, to compel him, by law, should it be found necessary, to make immediate payment".[4]

II

Engulfed in the social whirl of Bombay, Macquarie soon suffered convincing proof that his was "the best and consequently the most expensive society in the place".

Morleys circulated through it very close to governors. Commandants and rear-admirals moved hospitably among Rivetts and Carnacs—the dear old General who had driven across the Jumna and signed the Treaty of Allahabad in company with Clive was still alive. And there was not one of the great of Bombay who baulked at eating the bread and drinking the wine of Captain Lachlan Macquarie and his bride, Jane. As for colonels and majors, these and their consorts came in swarms. It was quite clear that Mr Morley had not exaggerated when he had issued his warnings about the costliness of Indian matrimony.

The newly wedded pair at first were quite overwhelmed by all the festivity. The Benedict wrote to his friend Captain Zachariah Hall in December 1793: "Really until these few days past, I have hardly had a moment of time to myself since our marriage, being constantly engaged in a round of great *chevoes* and entertainments given to us by our numerous friends in Bombay."[5]

They danced at Government House at Parel; they footed it at Mr Tasker's Admiralty House and at the mayoral mansion of Mr Bruce, the banker. They watched, with interest, amid a flutter of femininity in palanquins, gigs and chariots, and among an imposing array of uniforms, while "a race was run over Back-Bay sands, from the General Hospital to the Arbour, between Mr. Morley's Arab horse *Sheik* and Mr. O'Donnell's Arab horse *Sultan*; the latter horse won the race; the sport was highly pleasing, and a very numerous company of ladies and gentlemen attended. My dearest Mrs. M. rode on horse-back, and I went thither in my *palanquin*."[6]

Now, that waggish aide-de-camp and undistinguished Persian interpreter,

Mr Samuel Wilson, whose name appears on so many historical Indian documents of the day, organized a *nautch* or a ball for Miss Bellasis. Merry, mellow, all-day-long parties of colonels and collectors assembled on birthdays and festival days and sometimes on the Sabbath; or there might be a great drinking of sillabub on the Ramparts in Lieutenant-Colonel Balfour's tent, while the Bombay scene acquired variety from an ever-changing flow of new faces.

Once Rear-Admiral "Blue Billy" Cornwallis asked Captain Macquarie to break bread with him and savour his wines. He proved to be "a plain honest blunt man, and quite the gallant brave sailor in his appearance".[7]

Once a penitential-sounding entry creeps into the Journal, written in faint ink in the margin, after dinner with a medico who, later, nearly pickled Arthur Wellesley in nitric acid: "No beer for three months."[8]

When there were no wilder excitements, there was lunch at the Sans Souci Club at the Grove, or officers and civil servants, "very elegant and respectable" but painfully hard on the bottle and their host's pocket, gathered round the Macquarie dining-table assembling the "Bombay Gup", which was in time retailed in "lucubrations in the way of epistolary correspondence"[9] to "recluse" friends in isolated military stations round the Indian coast, or at Fort William or Madras:

> Captain Alexander Macdonald of the 11th Battalion of Native Infantry died suddenly of a few hours illness on the 1st instant . . . Captain Bell of the Artillery died last night of a liver complaint. . . . Colonel Kerr has renewed his addresses again to Miss Dick and it is currently reported is soon to be married to her; Mr. Page is arrived from the coast, and I suppose he will soon be buckled to Mrs. W. Freeman . . . I believe our friend Wilson is once more shot with one of Cupid's darts . . . he wants to get married to Miss Bellasis (daughter of the Major of Artillery lately come out) a pretty smart girl enough, but an *imprudent* match for Wilson. . . . Mrs. Oakes is delivered of a very fine boy . . . Mrs. Oakes's small boy is dead of the small pox.[10]

Wide-eyed friends in the army and relatives in Mull and adjacent parts of Scotland heard often of the young couple's progress:

> All the good things in the world flow in upon me at once:—a good and amiable wife with a tolerable fortune—a Major of Brigade-ship—and a company coming all in the course of a few months, is more than comes to everyone's share, from that slippery *Goddess, Fortune*;—but she has been threefold kind to me, and I must be very ungrateful indeed, not to be thankful for all her good gifts.[11]

All his stories of the "most suitable, eligible and happy match that was ever made in Bombay"[12] were salted with the recital of the grandeur and opulence of Jane's family, with his triumphant emphasis on the fact that so genteel a piece of femininity should have "preferred the poor captain lieutenant to *all* the great and mighty offers" she had received.

Presents which the ships of the season carried homeward were lavishly distributed—"an Indian shawl (the finest that could be got in the Guzerat country)", for Mrs Maclaine Lochbuy[13]; "two shawls of an inferior quality" for his mother and sister Betty; a sandalwood box for Mrs Clephane of Torloisk, whose thanks were a shrewd lecture on the wanton, un-Scottish habit of bestowing gifts.[14] His token to Mrs Maclaine, his aunt, was accompanied by congratulations on the birth of a new sprig of the Lochbuy blood and with the "devout" wish that she "might annually add one more of the same sex to the *Clan Maclaine* for many years to come".[15]

Poor Lochbuy, weighed down with his debts and thus compelled to take a half-pay majority in the Western Fencibles, was so impressed with his ward's "nabobery" that he promptly offered to sell him some of his mortgaged lands;[16] but that even before the letter with this proposal reached India, this "great Chieftain in Mull" had fallen in his nephew's eyes from the status of one who "has ever shown me a paternal kindness and attention and aided me in getting through the world, from my earliest youth, with credit and honour", to that of "a pleasant old veteran".[17]

The captain's own immediate family benefitted by his superficial prosperity. He remembered that his mother's lease of the Oskamull farm was due to be renewed. He urged Lochbuy that:

> I have no objections to make any annual allowance that you may judge necessary and sufficient . . . to enable her and my brother Donald to live comfortably and pay the rent of her farm punctually. Say what it is I should allow her yearly and it shall be done—I could also wish to give my sister Betty and her young family a little assistance. Pay one or even two year's schooling, for my nephew Murdoch, in any part of the low country, you may think proper to send him to. . . . [18]

His brother Charles, needing money, drew on Lachlan for £300, as if it were the most natural thing in the world for so rich a fellow to meet bankers' demands for such trifling amounts.

It was all flattering but remarkably hard on the pocket.

III

The Benedict, for a time, undoubtedly was rather above himself in his new surroundings, till it became evident that all was not well with his financial concerns.

Jane was a "great economist and manager" in her family and domestic affairs. His "income now in *this country*" was very handsome, "about £700 sterling per annum", which, he told his Uncle in Mull, "would enable him to . . . live well . . . comfortably and genteely . . . with *economy*".[19]

But the truth was that, "if they were to live as others lived", it was "not in their power to save a sixpence".

The bare walls of their house cost them £200 a year; their servants another £150, and the balance of their income (£350) was "little enough to defray other expences—especially when we keep a carriage which we mean to do;—for there is no doing without one in this country, when there is a lady in the question".

Only six weeks after his wedding Macquarie was 4200 Bombay rupees in debt, even though the bulk of the debit had gone "in purchasing and paying for plate, household furniture and stores and liquors for housekeeping".[20] He discovered, in short, as he related afterwards, that "my expences far exceeded what we at first imagined they would amount to, owing to the large and expensive circle of society we move in in Bombay, where every family of any consequence must live as their neighbours do". This was "a bad way of becoming richer".[21]

For a time the generosity of their friend, John Forbes, the banker, relieved the situation when he presented Jane "in the most delicate and handsome manner imaginable" with 4000 rupees, which he had obtained as commission in settling the estate of a dead colonel who had "sincere regard for her"; but it stopped pursuit by the spectre of debt only for a little while, as they moved from the expensive sheriff's house, which was their bridal home, to a smaller nest near the Dockyard, for which Daddy Napper Wanjee charged them £65 a year less rent than their former landlord. Before long bankruptcy was again almost at their heels.

They gave up the thought of the carriage, which they had ordered from London, in favour of a "new Bengal built gig from Mr. Joseph Harding, for which I am to pay him 500 Bombay rupees". Instead of sitting behind a prancing team they would have to do with merely "a good strong, well tempered, white coloured horse from Nasserwangee Monackerjee".

They cut their household expenses to the bone.

All in vain. The captain's load already had become almost unbearable when he had discovered that Sir Robert Abercromby had expressed the wish that he should let a company in the 77th Regiment, with which he believed he had been presented free of cost, "go as a purchase", a suggestion with which he felt bound to comply, though it added another £550 to his encumbrances.[22]

At last no expedient could take them out of the toils of debt save flight, since, as Macquarie wrote, in retrospect, from first to last, "The whole of my income did not exceed five hundred rupees a month, and upon an average every month since I became a Benedict, I spent at least eight hundred rupees a month."[23]

Plans which they had made to double their present fortune in eight years and return to England were abandoned and the Benedict was forced to reflect gloomily that "when we shall return to Europe God only knows".

They yearned to "quit Eastern luxury for Scotch or English frugality".

He made attempts to secure promotion to the vacant office of Deputy Paymaster-General, but arrived at the conclusion that "the Army is a perfect lottery, in which there are very few prizes, and those are very seldom, indeed, bestowed on those justly entitled to expect them".[24] His old friend Dunlop, a determined careerist, snatched the office from under his hand. The hard-pressed Macquarie bore no grudge. He was "exceedingly well pleased, that [the office] is so well bestowed".

IV

Three months after they were married the immediate days of their perfect happiness were over. It was then that Mrs Morley sailed for England in the *London*.

To her Scottish brother-in-law, who with his friends farewelled her "with heavy aching heart", as if they were consigning her body to the deep instead of to a comfortable East Indiaman, "it was a most beautiful sight to see her in the stern gallery surrounded by her sweet babes, more lovely than ever in her tears, waving her hands to us, after we had quitted the ship's side and taken leave of her".[25]

Poor Jane suffered exceedingly. "My lovely girl was overcome with grief . . . we were obliged to tear them from each other's embraces," and Mrs Stirling, the new regimental commandant's wife, was compelled to lead her weeping away and to watch over her for days while she mourned for her lost companion and for her mother's house at 49 Welbeck Street, where there were no blackamoors, prickly heat or Indian livers.

They had, indeed, at that stage, good cause to know the condition of one Indian liver. Its owner was Mr James Morley, and because of it Mrs Morley, before she sailed, had exacted from her brother-in-law a promise to keep on good terms with her husband, who already had begun to show violently his disapproval of Jane's marriage.[26]

Lachlan and Jane did their best to conciliate the irascible fellow. They even went on a voyage to Goa with him on the trial cruise of his new ship, the *Maria*. But the shared memorable experiences of that excursion did not bring them closer together.[27]

They were rowed ashore at Goa in the Captain-General's barge by twelve oarsmen in rich uniforms, the stern sheets of their boat covered by "a very rich and superb awning", the inside of which was lined with "yellow sattin", with which material the cushions were also covered. They dined with the Captain-General in almost medieval state in his Hall of Assembly. A lady abbess showed them her nuns through a grate—"several very good-looking young women . . . what a sacrifice to so abominable and absurd a custom of secluding for ever from the world and their friends these poor unfortunate girls ! ! !" They met a "pretty little woman" from Madras who had been confined in the convent by her husband for infidelity.

They viewed the tomb of Saint Francis Xavier, with its "most superb black marble monument, the top of which is silver and gold". And, finally, they were chased home by the Mulwan pirates, in time to hear of the execution of Marie Antoinette.

Instead of improving their relations with "Old Morley", as his irreverent brother-in-law now designated him, constant association seemed to have widened the rift. So far as Old Morley was concerned, they might have been pirates themselves, and the spectacle of a certain Scottish captain hanging on a yard-arm might well have delighted him, judging by his conduct.

Before Old Morley's wife had been away four months, the breach was an open one.

Macquarie had commissioned Mrs Morley to arrange in London the purchase of his chariot and silver and to have them adorned with the "arms of Ulva, the supporters not to be upon the carriage or plate".[28]

He had given her an order upon Messrs Francis and Gosling, the bankers who held his and Jane's fortune for their trustees, to provide the money out of the accrued interest on Jane's six thousand pounds. He had told the bankers that, having "the strictest reliance upon their integrity", he had no doubt that they would attend to the matter and also to a letter from Jane "relative to your corresponding in future with me; as well as transmitting to me, by the ships of the next season, a stated account of her affairs, made up to the 31st December, 1794". He hoped, he said, to "hear regularly and receive accounts as to how his interest stood".

Nobody seems to have thought of telling their trustees, Messrs Morley and Tasker, of these proceedings, though Macquarie agreed that, when the marriage settlement had been drawn, he had "allowed Old Morley to settle all money matters as he thought proper".[29]

He was under the impression that the result of the arrangement was that Jane's £6000 and his £1000 were to be now "invested by our Trustees in the English funds; from whence we draw the interest annually, for our mutual support; but cannot remove the principal *without the consent* of our Trustees, so as to secure it for our offspring in case we have any".[30]

Old Morley thought differently. When he heard what had been done he flew into a violent passion such as was only possible to a well pickled *kooee-hai* on the edge of the monsoon season. He expressed fear lest Mrs Morley would spend *his* money in buying carriages and plate for the captain. He said that Goslings could not comply with Macquarie's instructions to them. He shouted that the poor Benedict had acted illegally, and "very soon convinced him that his conduct had been improper and irregular".

"Ingenuous" confession failed to mollify him; he was unattracted by the theory that it was all an "innocent mistake"; nor would he be placated by pleadings "not to mind it or to be concerned about it in the least", or by promises that security would be found immediately for any money which Mrs Morley might spend on behalf of the Macquarie household.

Old Morley, in fact, almost gibbered with rage whenever he saw his victim, who bore with him patiently, reflecting sadly in his disillusionment that "I am now nominally a *man of fortune* without having the power of making the least use of it".[31]

His apologies meant nothing to the trustees. They hastened to their notary public and had him serve upon the Benedict a formal protest "in very harsh language, desiring to be discharged from their trust", a procedure, their wretched victim remarked, which "always implies some fraudulent intention in the person to whom it is addressed".[32]

"Conscious of the innocence and rectitude of my own conduct, which has yet been unsullied and no one has ever dared to impeach", the captain decided that he would cut with his brother-in-law for ever and never more speak to him, as a measure of resentment against what he conceived to be "imperious caprice and marked illnature".[33]

And when Old Morley went roaring home to England in his ship *Sarah*, Jane's husband wrote to the nabob's spouse that he must refer her to her husband "for *his account of it* all", which, he trusted, "for the sake of his veracity, will in substance, be the same as I have given you of it".

However, he believed it "not improbable" that the old gentleman would "fret himself to death before he reaches England", and, when his own contemporary troubles are known, it seems to show great power of restraint in him that he told Messrs Francis and Gosling that "the whole blame is mine . . . all originated in our not being fully acquainted with the nature of our marriage settlement".

Apart from the harassment caused by his debts and his quarrel, he had to deal with the situation caused by the death of his mother-in-law. That "hale, healthy, cheerful woman", fifty-six or fifty-seven years old, "blessed with numerous children by her only husband", had in February, they were informed by letters on the ships of the season, contracted St Anthony's Fire of the brain, of which she seems to have been the only victim in England that·year, and departed from 49 Welbeck Street, Cavendish Square, to another Elysium, leaving behind a far-flung and respectable offspring "to mourn and bewail her loss".[34]

It was twenty-four hours before even a bold officer could muster up "sufficient resolution, or command of himself, to disclose the afflicting tale to his dearest Jane".

When she did receive the "heartbreaking communication", with "religious and pious fortitude", her tears flowed in a solid stream for days while the ladies of the Regiment coped with her grief and her spouse devoted himself to the battle with Old Morley and his creditors, who were looming ever larger in his life.[35]

V

Disaster had seemed imminent when, on 15 July 1794, the 77th Regiment had been ordered out of Bombay to Madras, though fortunately the order was countermanded nine days later.[36]

This brought home to him the peril he was in. If he left Bombay permanently with his regiment, he must forfeit his office of Major of Brigade. And if he abandoned his regiment to keep his Headquarters office, he must lose his paymastership.

It was a terrible dilemma. Of course, if his brother Charles, for whom he had secured an ensigncy, had come out to India, all would have been well, for he could have been nominated acting paymaster as his brother's deputy.

But the ungrateful Charles, who would have been promoted lieutenant had he arrived—in a corps in which he had drawn pay for a year without having been within the width of the globe of it—preferred to remain at home in another regiment, despite the fact that his passage on the *True Briton* was paid.

Such behaviour caused his patron and sponsor in Bombay to be "excessively angry, displeased and disappointed":

> Oh! Charles! Charles!— You have indeed hurt my feelings very much. . . . My word, which, as yet, has been held sacred, is forfeited:— I pledged myself in the most solemn manner to Sir Robert Abercromby, that you *certainly would*

come out this season. I once stood high in his esteem:— I shall now be affronted and degraded in his opinion:— and never—never—shall I have the face, to ask him for another favour, as long as I live.—[37]

Since it was certain that his regiment presently must leave Bombay, as it proved for Calicut down the coast, his last resource was Colonel Balfour, who had succedeed as acting Commander-in-Chief in Bombay that "rather singular character . . . a mild inoffensive man",[38] Colonel Howson, who had died leaving behind a *lakh* of rupees.

It fell to the Benedict, who had already received many favours from his colonel, to recall Colonel Balfour from a voyage which he had begun and "acquaint him with the dissolution of Colonel Howson"; so that it seemed reasonable that Colonel Balfour might "prove agreeable to make a choice of me as one of his staff".

Colonel Balfour accepted the invitation of his aspiring junior, upon his arrival in the *Queen* Cruiser, to "live with us until his own quarters in the Tank Barracks should be fitted up for him", and went ashore with his delighted host in a bunderboat. But his suppliant wrote that the colonel's attitude was "rather a disappointment to me as I really imagined . . . [he] had a sincere friendship for me and a wish to serve me, but I am now fully persuaded he has neither".

Told that Macquarie was truly sorry for having made a request to him, Balfour muttered "some very lame and awkward excuse".

Indeed, the colonel's conduct was such that the captain remarked that he proposed in future to consider him as he really was—a "most selfish, sordid, avaricious, unfeeling character".

"As such," he wrote, "I withdraw my friendship entirely from him from this day henceforth." He exclaimed, "Thank God I am independent of him!" But all this did not prevent him from resolving to treat his senior "with every attention while he stays in my house".

Perhaps the colonel was not so selfish as he seemed. He may have smiled to himself about his good deed, for Macquarie was, after all, "happy to quit [Bombay] in an . . . easy manner, without it appearing that I was forced to do it". As the Colonel watched, Captain Macquarie, who mysteriously had "paid off all his debts", set out in the ship *Endeavour* on his retreat from bankruptcy to the lines of Calicut. It was a journey to which there was "no alternative after being disappointed in my expectations from Colonel Balfour".[39]

The exile was able to bring himself later to write to the colonel that perhaps his vanity had led him too far in expecting that an offer would be made him, but that on cooler reflection he was wrong, and that he had no claim whatever on his commander's good offices beyond "the kind notice you have ever been so good as to take of me, and the intimacy you have been pleased to permit me, to be upon with you for upwards of six years past".[40]

Upon that note he appears to have put aside his animosity. When Colonel Balfour visited Calicut he was again Macquarie's guest. They remained lifelong friends.

VI

After a merry voyage, during which Colonel Bowles, the Brigadier, "sung every night for the ladies and contributed very much to our amusement",[41] they were five hundred miles from Bombay and a little south of Tellicherry in the lines of Calicut, four or five miles from the town. Jane, who had been ill for several days before sailing from Bombay, was recovered.

They found themselves dwelling in a "sweet spot", ideally situated and equipped for wiping off liabilities which now totalled 5200 rupees—in spite of the payment of "all his debts" before leaving Bombay—"a place where we can live more retired for a while", and from which they rarely visited the town.[42]

Their bungalow, which he had bought from Dr Ker, surgeon to the 75th Regiment, who had given it up out of consideration for Jane, was some distance back from the road.

Its lord and master christened the place "Staffa Lodge" after part of his ancestral possessions—"a title I should be proud to have in another country".[43]

There were "high airy beautiful hills commanding a charming view and prospect of the country round and of the sea at the distance".[44] The bedrooms of the bungalow were large. It had an excellent garden.

Dr Ker left behind for them a large stock of bullocks, goats, and pigeons. If the roof leaked and the hall was lined with plain bamboo, 700 rupees and native labour could soon put that right with mud and *chunam*; and 15,000 *cajans* made the place watertight before the advent of the monsoon rains.

The gardens provided vegetables and fruit. Beef and mutton were reasonably priced. And they did not need a chariot here, being "so well provided in cavalry".

His friends would know that the captain was "not the best horseman in the world and, therefore, that he could not possibly be better mounted than on the Old Grey".[45] And for Jane there was a "new Turkai, very quiet and gentle, but sufficiently lively for a lady", and well worth the 300 rupees which it cost.

Indeed, they found their other expenses so moderate that they could even indulge themselves in the luxury of "two very fine well-looking healthy black boys from Cochin between six and seven years of age". Well washed, their hair cut and combed and well clothed, the stouter named Hector after Macquarie's nephew, the other named after Jane's brother George, the dusky pair were dirt cheap at 170 rupees.

Poor Hector, kidnapped years afterwards in Calcutta, disappeared ultimately into the black void of India. George remained Macquarie's faithful servitor all his life, crossing the world with him again and again, the last living soul able to remember with him the sound of the guns of '99 before Seringapatam and the happy life with Jane at Calicut.

All in all, Captain Macquarie and his wife, relieved to be "out of the expence of Bombay", thought society while "most undoubtedly desirable", to be "too dearly purchased when people are under the necessity in order to enjoy it of exceeding their income".

The captain was "willing, as matters have turned out to think with *Candidus*—that—everything that is—is best",[46] even though he and his wife were restricted in the matter of their surroundings and associates.

After Mrs Shaw had been sent post-haste to Bombay for a happy event, Jane became the only lady on the station, and they were bound to show a guarded hospitality. Their table became the stock resort to which all officers were welcomed for a "sober repast" of a Sunday, but there was no extravagance.[47]

There was reborn, in place of the dancing staff officer, the Scottish farmer and improver of Mull, exercising the talents which he was later to apply on a grander scale to a corner of a then savage continent. He was seen making a "most complete fence or enclosure round the whole of *my Estate*"; taking in "a good deal of the *Lawn* in front which I mean to plant with trees"; adorning with more timber "the *Park* in the rear of the house, having made cross walks in both the front and rear parks, which gives them a very neat appearance".[48]

Jane, in her turn, was "charmed with the beauty of the countryside and the novelty of carrying the knapsack and roughing it as a soldier's wife".[49] She was much improved in health and her husband went about, "stout and hearty as he ever had been in his life", though preoccupied at intervals about the fact that "there is no appearance of my being made a *Papa*". He meditated to his friends that he had "not yet had the honour of increasing and multiplying the Ancient *Sheol Alpin* . . . but all in good time; if never I am determined to be content", seeing that they were "as happy without any, tho' I believe, most married people naturally wish to have children".[50]

And though their watchword was "frugality", the fare of the exiles was not rude, as witness their grocery orders:

Macquarie to Nash Grantham & Co.

Be pleased to send me per the first boat that comes down the coast, after the arrival of the ships of this Season from England, the following articles, *vizt.*—

  12 Dozen of Madeira in Bottles of the same kind I had from you in December last at Eleven Rupees per Dozen.
  2 Casks of good Pale Ale,
  4 English Hams of the smallest Size,
  6 Good Pineapple Cheeses,
  1 Case of Pickles,
  2 Bottles of Pickled Mushrooms,
  6 Bottles of Ketchup,
  1 Box of Fine Raisins,
  1 Maund of Fresh Almonds in the Shell,
  1 Keg or Firkin of Salt Tongues,
  1 Kit of salt Salmon,
  10 Pounds of Coffee,
  10 Pounds of Barley,
  1 Maund of Wax Candles.

I beg that the above articles may be of the best quality and carefully packed up; directing them for me at Calicut, accompanied with an account of their amount.

VII

O simple life in Arcady! In no time there would be no debts if living continued on the initial scale, more particularly as Dr Colin Anderson, his friend and fellow Scot, who had preceded him to the south had laid the foundation for him of a regimental financial system, which enabled him to turn many an honest penny, and which seemed to produce "additional proof that his friendship for me evinces a warmth and sincerity of heart, that is rarely to be met with in this selfish world".

The scheme was instituted with the friendly connivance of his friend Dunlop, the Deputy Paymaster-General in Bombay.

No sooner had Macquarie settled down in Staffa Lodge than Dunlop received a letter from him which disclosed the weakness of this ingenious budgetary artifice:

> I find my deputy, Colin Anderson, has drawn on you for *ten thousand rupees* on account of King's Subsistence commencing 25th December;— tho' it is not in your estimates, I request the favour of you to honour his bills; and by some means, procure cash for them when they become due. I will cheerfully pay any interest that the *shroffs* may demand from the time the bills become due until you can receive the money, as I should be exceedingly sorry if they were returned unpaid. In future nothing of this kind will happen, as, I shall take care to send you our estimate in full time to be included in your general one.[51]

There were, it transpired, other bills for 1300 rupees on the same account drawn against the Deputy Paymaster-General. "A rather awkward piece of business", the Laird of Staffa Lodge admitted; but he should be "excessively hurt", nay, "affronted", if the bills were not met, and it would "also hurt our credit here in future with all the native merchants".

He was anxious about the situation, particularly since he found that it would be attended with "considerable advantage" to himself and also of "some little advantage" to his correspondent, "to draw . . . for . . . the whole of the subsistence of the regiment on the day it becomes due, at thirty days sight, in favour of such people as may have occasion to use the bills". He was assured, he wrote. that "I shall always be able to get vent for my bills and receive three *per cent* premium for them . . . Anderson got *me* six per cent on the ten thousand rupees he drew on you."

The enterprising paymaster issued, as it were, a public loan for his own benefit using the security of the regiment's next month's charges. Local *shroffs* were willing and eager enough to discount his issue of bonds, to the profit of the issuer. So, "You see, my good friend, what an advantageous thing it is to be even a *regimental paymaster on the Coast*, and I trust, you will smooth the way for my availing myself of all the fair advantages annexed to it."[52]

Dunlop was so long in replying to his friend's stream of naive letters from Calicut on the subject, that it seemed as though he intended to emulate the historic silence of his mother, whose desertion of Robert Burns, after he had tickled her eye with many an original manuscript, stands in the front rank of literary apostasies.

At length, after drawing bills with frequency and diligence, Macquarie was constrained to ask Dunlop, "What can you be about?—Are you in love or so occupied with business that you cannot drop a few lines to a poor man at this solitary place?"

Actually, Dunlop's slow Ayrshire mind was merely devising a safe *modus operandi* and, when his advice did arrive, it convinced Macquarie that "the reasons you assign in your letter of the 14th Instant, for discontinuing the mode I at first adopted of drawing bills on you at thirty days after sight" were valid.

Dunlop could be assured, wrote his friend, that "it never was my wish or intention to allow you to run the least risk on my account; and, I am very sorry that I should have drawn on you in the way I did lately in favour of the Arab".

Not that Dunlop was unaccommodating or smitten with any moral scruples. He was merely concerned with their safety; and he suggested three other expedients for carrying on the business with less danger.

One, which Macquarie adopted, was "that the bills for the first muster should not become payable until the day of receiving and drawing the following one". This method, which provided him with a longer margin in case of accident, the Calicut financier thought was one in which "neither ran any risk".

If Dunlop grew cold about it all, it was probably because all the profit seemed to go to Calicut and little to him. In the end, a prospective army reorganization made it wise to drop the scheme altogether, but not before it had borne sufficient fruit to make the inmates of Staffa Lodge solvent. In some months the yield was more than that of Macquarie's normal salaries.

Six months after he had reached Calicut, he was able to inform John Forbes, his new banker, that:

> from our economical mode of living since we came down the coast, I have nearly cleared off all my little debts; and, by going on in the same course, only for a few months longer, I shall not owe one single rea to any one. I must even be frank enough with you to acknowledge, that, when I talk of being in debt, I always consider Mrs. Macquarie as my *principal creditor*, as the sum of Rs 4000, you were kindly pleased to make her a present of, and which she gave me, I merely considered as a *loan from her* and as no part of my own money . . . a few months more will relieve me of even this *encumberence*.[53]

He had cleared off 5200 rupees of his debts. But in an army of which the Paymaster-General in England in some years recently had had a balance of £900,000 of public funds in his hands, on which the interest was his perquisite; on a station on which commander argued with commander as to who owned the bazaar profits, who could condemn the captain's proceedings as abnormal, or as out of accord with the regimental ethics of the day?

He was a virtuous fellow—especially where the East India Company's employees were concerned. His indignation with public servants who sent false tales of civil strife and native rebellion to Bombay to cover their peculations set a standard in righteousness which even Arthur Wellesley would have approved.

No, he wrote, there was no truth in certain rumours heard in Bombay. Mr Stevens, Jr, the Collector of the Southern District, had called on him lately and "did not say one word of his being obliged to collect the revenue at the *point of the bayonet*". He was even collecting it without a guard.[54]

The natives, both Moplahs and Nairs, especially the former, were "very inimical to our Government", and, he believed, were very much disposed to be refractory and troublesome, but:

> I am also sure they are often said to be so, when they are not, in order I suppose, to give the Civil Dogs a plausible excuse to say, that the Province is not so productive as *it was supposed to be*, and consequently to enable themselves to keep a few of the pice that ought to be placed to the credit of the Company. I believe it was about two months ago, that it was reported that the Cartinaud Rajah was in a state of rebellion—that he had taken possession of one of his old forts which he had filled with armed men stores and provisions. When a company of sepoys was sent from Mahé to take this Grand Fort, they found one old lame sepoy and two rusty muskets in it taking care of the Rajah's house.[55]

It was one thing to do this sort of cheating and quite another to use one's normal opportunities to make something out of the army, so long as there was no peculation and individuals were not injured.

A few days after writing of the "Civil Dogs", he had been filled with scorn of "the gallant Captain Ringrose" who "has been endeavouring to make money at the expence of the soldiers of his company by charging them most exorbitant prices for necessaries". He added, "It is supposed he will be smashed."[56]

That virtue, frugality, and industry pay was shown by the results of his policy. By strict adherence to the principles of judicious economy, and an enterprising use of his financial opportunities, Captain Macquarie was free of debt—even had paid off the £550 owed on the purchase of his company—which had been reduced by not a single stiver up to April 1795[57] when the New Year of 1796 dawned.

During the whole of the rest of his life he was never in such straits again as he had been in Bombay in the months after his marriage.

CHAPTER VIII

The Governor of Galle

I

IN Europe history was moving to a disastrous climax.

Rumours earlier had reached Bombay that the Allied Powers were "victorious and triumphant in every quarter over the French"; that "there had been an insurrection by Royalists in Paris"; that "the whole of the infamous convention had been extirpated and put to death as its members merited"; that "the Monster and Chief of Crimes, Robespierre, was broke on the wheel, after seeing the ashes of the murdered King marched in solemn and mournful procession round the street"; that the Dauphin was crowned "on condition that he should swear to govern by the British Constitution".[1]

These tales had proved to be as unreliable as most war rumours, whether relayed by the sensational newspapers or the Busrah *Dawk*.

France still had revolutionaries who were as much devoted as of yore to the tenets of the newfangled "democracy".[2] With the zeal of amateurs they had challenged the old order in Europe to mortal combat and had issued a rousing invitation to the people of adjacent lands to "drive out your tyrants, show yourselves freemen and let France protect you". Then they positively had leapt into Belgium—making war with Britain inevitable —while from all quarters came the loud complaints of Ancient Pistols of the age of Dettingen about their flagrant disregard of the most elementary niceties of military punctilio.

They went up in balloons to spy upon Austria's paladin, poor General Latour, about whom they floated down pink notes to their artillery. They conquered time and space by communicating, within an hour, by means of a newfangled instrument called the telegraph, between the region of Menin and the Hill of Sacre Coeur in Montmartre. They outraged all the canons of good breeding by refusing to grant leave passes through their hostile territory to British officers who desired to spend the Christmas holidays with their families in England.

When it became certain that these savages even were bent on fighting in winter, an uncomfortable proceeding to which no ageing general could look forward with equanimity, there was but one course left open to respectable British commanders.

In October 1794 the Dutch of the United Provinces, "giving loose to an intemperate rage against the Stadholder", had made peace with the villains and had begun to speak of themselves as "delivered from the English", their pledged protectors and the guarantors of their security. Thus "to the shattered remnants of the British armies surrounded in this manner, by open and hostile enemies, the only resource remaining was, to effect a total retreat from what might be justly considered as a hostile country."[3]

The Duke of York forsook Nijmegen and went home. General Abercromby went home; so did Colonel Arthur Wellesley. In their wake on New Year's Day 1795 came the Stadtholder, compelled "to flee with all diligence from the fury of his people", and pursued by the raucous exhortations of Citizens Van Lang and Van der Zoo, of the Amsterdam Revolutionary Committee: "Brave citizens . . . By the mighty aid of the French Republic . . . you have cast off the Tyranny that oppressed you . . . *You are free, you are equal!*"[4]

England, that "home of tyranny", received the prudent prince with hospitality, not to say with alacrity. Mr Pitt was soon inspired through his arrival to a generous impulse. He proposed to seize the Dutch possessions overseas and hold them in trust for the panting visitor until bloody revolution should be defeated.

The fact that realistic governors like Mynheer Van Angelbeck of Ceylon and Van Spall of Cochin might not be very confident that Dutch territory or property taken under trust by the British East India Company would ever be returned to the rightful owners, made promising food for thought in Indian military quarters.

II

In due course the situation had its impact on the life of Calicut. Macquarie from afar watched events unfold as the ships of the season brought news of the "rapid strides of Democratic progress in Dutch Brabant, the conduct of our Prussian Ally, the critical situation of the Spanish Crown tottering under subjects ripening for revolt, and the exhortations of the Prince de Saxe-Coburg without effect, to the Germanic body".

He had noted with alarm the portents of these developments. He perceived that "the war is not likely to terminate with honour to the Confederacy, or to Great Britain, with the *éclat* that an honest man could wish"; also, that "the infernal and destructive principles of Democracy"[5] seemed to be daily gaining ground in all countries in Europe. He prayed that his "own land might be preserved from following the horrid and detestable example of the worse than canibals [sic] and savages of France", whose atrocious crimes he found "shocking beyond description".

But in a sense he welcomed these things amid the quarrels and irritations of a scene in which the inhabitants were "doomed to a slugish [sic] inactive life" while expeditions, moving in princely fashion from the Madras coast upon native states which fairly dripped with spoils, inspired his envy.

Here in Calicut were no excitements to enliven the dull routine of existence, save the "sad stew" of the Brigadier, Colonel Bowles, apprehensive lest he should be recalled to England before he became rich enough for so permanent a transition; or the disputes between the Brigadier and the Commandant of the 77th Regiment as to which should take the profits of the soldiers' bazaar[6]; or the indiscipline of the regiment, which, from "being one of the finest in India was going to the devil", the men, disorderly and licentious, burning down their barracks and indulging in scenes of drunkenness so disgraceful as to move their paymaster to display the unusual weakness of asking somebody for sympathy. "I am sure," he wrote to Colonel Stirling, a former commandant, "that *you* will feel for, and deplore our situation."[7]

And there was, of course, the annoyance of the "unjust Marquis's unjust proposals" to be put up with. For Cornwallis, in blending the King's Army and the Company's Army in India, failed to give the King's men an expected "few of the crums". He was cruel enough even to "attempt to injure those by whose gallantry and intrepid exertions he had acquired his fame and character as a general and statesman!"; and it appeared that he proposed to award the "Company's lads", who hitherto had "run away with all the loaves and fishes", an "unjust accession of rank" before the amalgamation. "This," exclaimed his indignant Calicut victim, "is the sense I extract from and put on what he calls his *fundamental principle*."[8]

There was obviously need for a new war, especially to one who had it in mind to accumulate enough pelf to betake himself permanently to retirement in England. "I am not quite so much of a patriot as to wish for a long peace in this country. War is always the soldier's harvest. The Company can now pretty well afford the expence of one, and I sincerely wish to be once more, in a serious manner, in the tented field before I quit India."[9]

He found it hopeful that Tippoo was "still a restless dog". But his contemplation of the prospect of a war to protect the Dutch was at first lack-lustre. "There is to be sure a chance that *we* may be sent to Cochin, but I am afraid there is neither honour, glory or profit to be reaped there."

III

Meanwhile, all intelligence from Britain without doubt indicated that the King's regiments in India might soon be involved in some sort of hostilities, if not in that kind of recompensing onslaught on bejewelled native states which meant so much to the future prosperity of combatant officers.

There were vast promotions of officers of all senior ranks. Press-gangs, rum money, pretty decoys were all doing their part at home in the expansion of Pitt's extraordinary new British Army, in which colonelcies were sold to seventeen-year-old schoolboys, and infants in arms, for a price, became cornets.

The protests of the trepanned and of their bereft relatives rent the air unheeded. English boroughs, when they could, rescued their citizens from crimps' hide-outs. British troops, whose officers hitherto had been content to follow in the wake of Vegetius and Caesar, and who for long had won their wars by moving forward a solid column of half-companies shielded by flank forces of bolder spirits, were now expected to incorporate in their instruction the lessons learned from the skirmishing tactics of the North American Indians. The shadow of Old Pivot with his "Damned Eighteen Manoeuvres"[10] darkened the lives of colonels and subalterns as well in India as in England, as they struggled with the intricacies of Britain's first drill book, under the supervision of Major Whitelocke, their commandant.

In Calicut, as Captain Macquarie recorded, the 77th Regiment was busy indeed "practising the new exercises and movements lately ordered . . . the regiment twice every day; the officers every morning and some times in the evening also".

Discipline went on "in great stile", so that the

> Austrians and the Prussians will be nothing to us!—everything is Dundas—and Germanicus all over! Our commandant is torturing his poor unfortunate brains in studying the new system, and in endeavouring to make us perfect in it—but, all to very little purpose; for, he makes a most miserable hand of it, notwithstanding the fine subject he has to exercise his bright talents upon.—[11]

Colonel Bowles, in the guise of a "magnanimous commander", was "highly pleased or at least expressed himself so with their *soldierlike appearance* as well as with the *great progress* they had made in the new exercise and movements"; though, "*entre nous*", Macquarie wrote, "there was nothing but their cleanliness that deserved praise; for their movements were slovenly executed and their firing was neither close nor regular".

Their manoeuvres —"echelon of grand divisions, with the left in front; retiring in two lines by alternate companies" and many more complications and gyrations—concluded with "a very confused, impetuous charge, or rather race, each striving who could run fastest after poor Colonel Bowles, who with all his military ardour, narrowly escaped being run down in the charge".

Nevertheless, the captain wrote that "Our Commandant was highly flattered with ye compliments paid him by the *Reviewing General*, and boasts of having made a *most capital Review*—in this opinion, however, he is unfortunately in the singular number, as none of us are blind or stupid enough, to subscribe to it . . ."[12]

Matters were improved by the arrival of Major Petrie to replace the contentious Whitelocke, who was so coarse, brutal, and antipathetic to the smell of powder. He proved to be "a very sensible clever man and in whom is blended the soldier and the gentleman".[13]

After his arrival there was a sort of lusty cheerfulness about the life in Staffa Lodge. It found an outlet in unaccustomed bursts of Gaelic wit in which friends in Bombay were twitted with being "lazy dogs", and in which Jane became "the Lady of the Isles" or "Lady Mull" in the ceaseless correspondence which her lord carried on throughout the rainy season, when, during a month, it was "impossible to venture out at all".[14]

He wrote for pleasure, to be sure, but always with one eye on advantage and promotion. He wrote often to Calcutta, where a new supporter had been added to the circle of influence, in Sir John M'Gregor Murray, head of the Clan M'Gregor, who was applying his inherited acquisitiveness as Military Auditor-General on a staff which had just returned after a highly fatiguing but, as usual, glorious and profitable victory over the Rohillas.

He wrote to Dunlop and Balfour in Bombay; to Lieutenant-Colonel Stirling, who was dealing with that "most accomplished and dexterous villain", that "dangerous and artful character", Monsieur Fumeron, and other "restless and intriguing Democrats" at Pondicherry where, his correspondent in Calicut believed, the colonel was "fortunate to escape from the Frenchman's machinations and deep laid schemes".[15]

He wrote of politics, of war, even of love. He wrote of the Calicut and Bombay gossip:

Macquarie to Robert Gordon

I must remind you, I believe that I am still *alive*. . . . What can you be about you lazy dog? Are you as much occupied in attendance on the Fair Sex . . . that you cannot devote a few minutes to enquire about your old friends at this recluse corner of the world? . . . I never go into Calicut unless on real business, consequently know very little of what passes there or in any other part of the coast. We have a few friends to dine with us every Sunday. *Lord George* is one of our party on these occasions. . . . I suppose our good and amiable friend Mrs. Oakes will very soon be in the straw—I am told she can hardly walk.—tell her, with my kindest Salam, that I shall postpone receiving my uniform coat, until I have occasion to wear a *staff one* again at Bombay. I must then have *my coat*, as well as a kiss from herself, and the young Adjutant General.[16]

They were gay and social. They had visitors in the shape of Jane's brother George from the healthy 36th Regiment at Trichinopoly, with a "stout recruit", Alex Campbell, to add to the jollity of the recluse life.[17]

IV

All this happiness and domesticity gave way completely to more serious preoccupations when the definite duty was thrown upon the regiment's shoulders of taking possession of Cochin "in the name of the Prince of Orange", providing the Dutch were disposed to receive them in a friendly and pacific manner.

On 21 July 1795 Major Petrie set out to reason with Governor Van Spall to this end, leaving behind him only the "skeleton of the 77th Regiment", whose companies had been "completely gutted", to bring up the flank companies, the mainstay of the expedition, supported by a native grenadier battalion, to one hundred rank and file. As an evidence that they were merely "embassadors of peace", the force marched out "unattended by a single field piece".[18]

They had "no orders to act offensively nor even to enter the Dutch Territories, but merely to negotiate and act upon the defensive in case of their being attacked by the Mynheers, which is not at all likely". However, it was taken for granted that if "the amicable terms" offered were not accepted, a stronger detachment would be sent "to force the Dutch to a compliance in a hostile way".[19]

It was an anxious time waiting for the result of the expedition. The portents were favourable and at first the Benedict remarked buoyantly that "we, who call ourselves on this occasion *the precious remains*, flatter ourselves we shall not be long behind the guardians of our right and left wings"; but doubt crept in as to whether Governor Van Spall and his mynheers "might open the gates and receive our detachment as friends—in which case, all our preparations for field service, and all our hopes of laurels and *plunders* will soon fall to the ground".[20]

The Dutch are a reasonable people. By the middle of August "the gallant remains of the invincible 77th heroes" learned with delight that they were about to follow, "with the animating sound of war", the amicably intentioned flankers under Major Petrie's command.

Yet not, at the last moment, with so much delight after all.

One Scot discovered when the hour of parting from his Jane approached that he would prefer to "continue where I am than go to *live* in Cochin", and wrote with lingering regret to his friend Captain George Mackenzie, "This is an exceeding pleasant place in my opinion, and I have been at very considerable expence to render my house and situation here at large, neat and comfortable—I shall therefore quit it and all my improvements at Staffa-Lodge, with very great regret indeed—but I am a soldier and must obey."[21]

Four days later they marched out.

Jane was left behind in a house in Calicut, "very well situated, and in a good neighbourhood, being close to Colonel Bowles' house and Mr. Wensley's the Paymaster Generals". She was suffering from "inexpressible pain" at her first parting from him. While he lay before Cochin she besought his permission to come up to "see me here and live with me for some few days in the camp". But such entreaties were repelled with an exhortation to "drop every idea of the kind". The poor, desolate girl was compelled to be satisfied with the letter which he wrote to her every day and with the knowledge that he spent the anniversary of their wedding day before Mynheer Van Spall's unyielding fortress, "jovially and pleasantly, drinking the health of my dearest Jane in many overflowing bumpers", in the company of Dr Anderson, Captain Grant, and that tall ancestor of Indian heroes, Lieutenant Lawrence.

Once the Governor made up his slow mind that he was "positively determined not to admit a British garrison to Cochin—but on the contrary to defend it to the last extremity"—the captain could hope to return to Calicut in "about a fortnight".[22]

The obliging satrap had considerably postponed this decision, vacillating while Captain Macquarie with two companies of the regiment and two of Grenadier sepoys held "pleasant [reconnoitring] expeditions" within half a mile of his walls, until the siege train had time to arrive from Bombay and to be placed in position to bombard him!

Even after that he showed great delicacy and refrained from molesting the British working parties which set up the batteries, or Captain Macquarie and his junior officers who were living on the fat of the land in the Jewish quarter of Muttoncherry, within easy reach of the enemy's guns, and under the roof of "Mr. Wredé, a man of considerable Property in Cochin, but attached to the Stadholder and the English Government".[23]

It was not till the British had been digging and emplacing for five weeks that Governor Van Spall let loose his attack. He launched a tornado of fire, which had "fortunately no effect", except that "the noise of the cannonading and the light of the shells in the air, was grand and awful to a degree to us who were spectators of it all night".

The captain's part in the response to this aggression was oblique. His was the duty to open fire on the fort "with my little six pounder from behind the empaulement thrown up for its security, pointing the gun every time myself, in order to distract, and in some degree, to divert the attention of the enemy from our grand breaching battery", of which the emplacements were not quite complete.[24]

He "had the satisfaction to see that every shot I fired reached and fell into the town of Cochin, not being quite five hundred yards distant from it".

This was not surprising, perhaps, seeing that the town was some thousands of yards in circumference.

At any rate, the enemy was "very much provoked at this minor attack of ours"; so much enraged that he opened and kept up a most "tremendous fire" upon the post for two hours from every gun he could bring to bear. His shots, "very well directed", lodged every time close to the little entrenchment, throwing "heaps of earth and dust" about the British ears, though not a single man was killed or wounded.

When the brave master of the six-pounder, however, discovered, through a cloud of dust, that the Lost Tribes of Muttoncherry were suffering a wholesale loss of their dwellings, which were being hit instead of himself, he considerately ceased fire, just in time to be relieved by Captain Grant, who immediately became the only casualty of the engagement through being struck on the shoulder by a splinter from one of the wooden houses of the Jews.

Before long Macquarie had a chance to ride to where the eighteen-pounders were throwing out a fire "very dreadful indeed", which had knocked out all the defences and silenced the Dutch guns.

The Governor suddenly became quicker in making up his mind than in any previous proceedings. He sounded the *chamade* and hung out a white flag on a bastion. Capitulations were signed that night. The Dutch surrendered and a thousand of them—Europeans, native regulars and irregulars—marched out "with the Honours of War in a most shameful noisy disorderly unsoldierly manner, behaving most brutally and insolently to their officers" and being "most abusive to their poor fallen Governor for surrendering". They told their commander "that he ought to be hanged; and they needed to be restrained from cutting him down with their swords".[25]

Colonel Whitelocke and Captain Macquarie marched in through the Muttoncherry Gate and the latter gave a dinner in the evening to celebrate "a very easy conquest", in which the attackers had "lost during the whole siege by the enemy's shot one European artilleryman and one native follower", in exchange for "considerable ordnance and military and naval Stores", out of which, the convivial artillerist remarked, "we, the captors hope to *share handsomely in prize money*."[26]

V

Indisposed and fatigued from his exertions "for the last five days successively" he soon was speeding in a *pattamar*, one hundred and forty miles down the coast, to a "truly happy meeting" with Jane, in which their "mutual joy and felicity was easier conceived than described after such a separation".[27]

But he had cause for worry. For it was forced upon him as they returned to Staffa Lodge in the bright tropic moonlight, Jane in her palanquin and he and her brother on horseback, that she "had a severe bad cold through getting her feet wet".

Her illness overshadowed in importance the social occasions and rejoicings of Calicut lines as they christened their plate, newly arrived from London and emblazoned with the Macquarie arms copied from old Ulva's signet ring, to welcome General Balfour to the station.

The poor girl's high spirits, which, according to her husband, "fortunately never forsook her at any time", and which "made her society not only much liked—but also greatly admired", could not disguise her increasing sickness.

She left a great blank in the otherwise womanless lines of Calicut as they sailed for Bombay, whither Macquarie was ordered to appear as a witness before a court martial.

Her cough grew worse. She did not sleep. Her appetite failed. Her husband had, at length, perforce to write that she had been "extremely ill for some time past".

The medical profession of Bombay was original, as ever. Her doctor constrained her husband to take her out along the Esplanade in ominous red dawns to drink warm buffalo milk. He treated her with mercury. But she was low in her spirits, which fell still lower when she knew that Mynheer Van Angelbeck, the Dutch Governor of Ceylon, was as obstinate as Governor Van Spall of Cochin, and that ere long her soldier would have to join the persuasive forces which were to change his mind for him. The nearer the time came for his departure, the more often she wept.

She begged her spouse to be allowed "to share the toils and hardships of a soldier's life during the campaign". She became "most earnest in her entreaties and solicitations" that he should avail himself of his situation as Major of Brigade as an excuse to remain in Bombay, but though it went deep into his heart to see her so unhappy, he was not to be tempted:

> . . . She says she cannot survive my absence a second time; and she poor dear soul, conceives my character can not suffer from remaining at the Presidency, where I have a public duty as Major of Brigade to the King's Troops to perform.— These, poor dear girl, are fair arguments enough for her to use but alas!—they

will not satisfy the malicious world; and however wretched it makes me to part and thus so soon leave her a second time—yet Honour—Honour calls—and I must obey.[28]

So, a few days afterwards, farewelling her whom he called "all I hold dearest in life", first placing her in the care of "good dear Mrs. Oakes", he sailed, after a "very elegant Tiffing", upon the conquest of Ceylon. She was in good hands. Friends were all round her. He had bought her a very good milch cow from Surat; but he was sad that "she could not be comforted" in their parting hours "by any mirth".

On his birthday, 31 January 1796, the Regiment was in the *Epaminondas*, "a very large ship", in Tuticorin Bay. Four days afterwards, they were at their final rendezvous, Negombo, on the Gulf of Manar, where they were joined by General Stuart and the Madras Army.

Thence they marched steadily towards Colombo, twenty-four miles away.

Only rarely was the even tenor of their progress disturbed by the ugly flash of a kris or a flying ball. There was but one "little brilliant occasion", in which Jane's brother distinguished himself, "being warmly engaged during the whole time of the attack".

They lay, soon, two thousand yards outside Colombo's walls, getting ready for a siege. Under a flag of truce, Major Agnew, the Adjutant-General, called on Ceylon's Governor and summoned him to surrender—"or take the consequence". Followed a twenty-four hour armistice. After two days, the white flag fluttered on a rampart.

The rich island of Ceylon, with great stores of treasure, had been bought for Britain at the small cost of the lives of one ensign and eighteen men. Within a few hours a force under Colonel Whitelocke was on the glacis. The Dutch laid down their arms, their rank and file, as at Cochin, full of good liquor, disorderly, tumultuous and abusive and insolent to their officers, who were "very much ashamed of their noisy and unruly conduct".

At length they were lined up in some order, piled arms, and were marched to barracks under strong guard—1200 Europeans and 1800 Asiatics, mostly as drunk as lords.

The Stadtholder's property was now safe from socialism, republicanism and all other diabolic and predatory creeds . . . so safe, indeed, that he would never see any of it again, for, as Captain Macquarie saw its rescue:

> This is a most important and valuable capture and acquisition to not only the East India Company in a commercial point of view—but also to the British Nation at large in a political one, in as far as it contains the only good harbour for our Navy on this side of India—and the French being prevented from possessing themselves of this valuable island. There are immense quantities of cinnamon, pepper, arrack, and various other goods and merchandize, belonging to the Dutch Company, found in Colombo, the guns, ordnance and naval stores, are also of very great value; so that there is good reason to hope the CAPTORS will share very handsomely indeed in the prize money on this occasion.—[29]

VI

None, indeed, had more reason to be happy at the outcome of the affair than Captain Macquarie.

General Stuart sent for him to tell him of the "very high character he had heard of him from Colonel Petrie and others". He was at once entrusted with the command of a detachment which was to march south next day "to take possession of the town and fortress of Point de Galle—and the dependencies thereunto belonging in that district, between 80 and 90 miles to the southward of Colombo".

The General said "that as there were public property of great value in the stores and arsenals at Point de Galle he wished to send an officer of capacity and experience there to take possession of that important place—and that he therefore *had selected me* for this service if it was perfectly acceptable and agreeable to me to go."[30]

The delighted Scotsman replied that "he was ready at a moment's notice to receive his orders or commands for this or any other service".

On 19 February 1796 at three in the afternoon, he found his detachment with three subalterns, thirty artillerymen and seven companies of Madras sepoys—seven hundred odd men in all—ready paraded for him on the Esplanade near the south gate of the Fort.

They marched each day in two easy stages, remaining on the road till late at night. On 22 February they were at Genderé, four miles from Point de Galle, after a march that day of twenty-one miles.[31]

He sent to the Dutch Governor, in charge of his Dutch interpreter, Sergeant M'Kenzie, a letter announcing his arrival, along with a missive from Mynheer Van Angelbeck.

Here were no boorish hesitations and drunken soldiery, but an elegant consideration for the feelings of a conquering expeditionary.

Mynheer Fretz, the Governor, answered thanking the invader for his polite attention and saying that he would be ready to deliver over the fortress and town at twelve noon next day—"or earlier if I wished it, as every preparation was already made for that purpose".

When they marched towards the gates in the morning, they were met half-way, wrote Macquarie, by "two gentlemen in a carriage belonging to Governor Fretz—who announced that they were two of the Members of Council of the Government of Galle", and that they were sent by the Governor "to conduct me in his carriage into the Fort, where he and the rest of the Members of Council were ready to receive me at Government House".

Lieutenant Harris was left behind to halt the invading force two hundred yards from the gates. Its commander in the Dutch carriage went ahead in state.

> I arrived at the Government House in the Fort at ½ past 11 a.m. and was there received by Governor Fretz, all the Members of Council and the Heads of Offices Military and Civil of the Dutch Administration, and principal officers and other gentlemen belonging to this settlement.— These gentlemen were

all individually introduced by the Governor to me commencing with the Members of Council and the Commanding Officer of the Troops.

The Governor then came up to me and presented me, in a most solemn and formal manner, on a large silver salver, with the keys of the different gates of the Garrison, making a short but very appropriate speech on the occasion—in doing which, however, he was very much affected and shed tears—as did also several of the gentlemen around him.

I was very much moved at this scene, and wished it over as soon as possible since its being further prolonged would only add to their distress.—I therefore made a short reply to the Governor, assuring him that I was most sincerely disposed, as well from motives of duty as inclination, to make his own particular situation and that of all the Members of Council and other gentlemen of the settlement of Point de Galle as easy and comfortable as possible, and that they might rely on their wishes being attended to in every respect as far as was consistent with my duty while I continued in command of Galle.

The Governor thanked me in his own and the name of the whole.— Wine and cake was then carried round—and healths were drank. The Governor invited me and the officers of my detachment to dine with him at 4 o'clock, inviting all the gentlemen now present at the same time to meet us.[32]

The Dutchman also offered to leave Government House with his family in the morning; but his Scottish successor begged that he would not think of doing so. He must insist, he said, that his predecessor remain with his whole family, so long as he himself continued in command of Fort de Galle. A couple of rooms were "quite enough for him, and full as much as he had occasion for, the house being very large and quite sufficient for both their accomodation".

The British detachment marched in through the South-east Gate to the Grand Parade in the middle of the fort, drums beating, colours flying. The six hundred and fifty Dutch troops, already assembled with their colonel at their head, saluted. The Dutch guards were relieved, the Dutch flag struck. The British, formed up opposite, returned compliments. Formal possession was taken in the name of His Britannic Majesty. A Royal Salute was fired; and the ceremony went off with perfect decorum and with no ill feeling.

The British marched to barracks and were given a double ration of arrack to drink His Majesty's health. The new Governor appointed his second-in-command, Lieutenant Harris, to take charge of the Fort and District of Matura, a few miles to the south. And then off he went to dinner with the old Governor and his company in "the great hall or dining room". About sixty gentlemen were present.

We sat down at ½ past 4 o'clock to a most excellent and plentiful dinner; we sat at table exactly an hour having got up and retired to drink coffee in another room at ½ past 5.— There was however plenty of wine drank during the hour we remained at the dinner table, the Dutch gentlemen wobbernobbing very frequently. . . .[33]

He wrote a long dispatch—his first as a "Governor"—to Colonel Stuart.[34]

Afterwards he took a ride in the country in an open carriage, a walk along the ramparts to visit guards and prisoners. He supped with the Fretz family—a son and four daughters, two of whom were married.

"Mr Fretz," he reported, "is a widower, the three eldest daughters very pleasant agreeable women." They very politely asked him if he would do them the honour to be their guest during his stay.

And so, at half past ten, his predecessor lighting the way for him, to rest in his chamber, in which "a very elegant bed had been made up and prepared for him".

It was next day—24 February—before "I wrote letters of this date to my beloved Jane, giving her an account of my proceedings here—and of my being now dubbed *Governor of Galle*!"[35]

VII

He was not to hold his new post for long. He spent a busy month cataloguing stores, writing, dining and talking with Fretz, adjusting the local monetary exchange. There are scarcely any signs in his journal of his having thought of Jane during those days, but suddenly she intruded herself into his immediate life again with painful urgency.

Colonel Kerr, Surgeon General of Bombay, wrote to him to say that she had been "in a very delicate state of health for some time back".[36]

He applied for leave immediately. The Dutch were sorry to see him go when he rushed off in a palanquin. Such was his haste that inside forty-eight hours his twelve bearers had covered the eighty miles to Colombo.

His last act connected with Fort de Galle was to write a letter in which he told poor Fretz that he considered himself "peculiarly fortunate in having gained and secured the friendship of so very respectable a character as yourself, and you may rest assured, Sir, I shall ever have particular pleasure and satisfaction in cultivating and maintaining a friendly correspondence with you". [37]

He was happy to report to his new friend that General Stuart was able to allow "your own civil court of justice to take cognizance of your daughter's present very unpleasant situation with her husband Mr Van Spall;—and I trust that an eternal separation will shortly be the consequence".

In the whole business he had given a foretaste of the amiability and conciliatory spirit which were his outstanding characteristics as a ruler in later days. His conduct obviously fully justified the thanks which General Stuart rendered him for his "very able and officer-like proceedings". He was promoted to a brevet majority.

His commander promised to report "what he was pleased to call my very able and officer-like conduct and judicious arrangements . . . in the manner it deserved" to the Commander-in-Chief and Government.[38]

Gently refusing the Town Majorship, he joined the ship *Jane* on 30 March 1796, a fortnight after he left Point de Galle, bound for Bombay with the left wing of his regiment.[39]

He was looking forward to the not-far-distant day when he and the amiable, good girl would be home once more in Staffa Lodge, which was to be "re-*cajanned* and put in complete repair", under Colin Anderson's supervision, against their coming.

They would come free of worry, their debts paid, the new accessions of prize money lodged safely with Forbes or Bruce, Fawcett in Bombay to draw a steady nine per cent interest.

When they had accumulated sufficient capital they would retire to the green and placid land of England, far from *kooee-hais*, mynheers, and mercury.

So soon as he reached Calicut, where the ship put in, Macquarie rode out to his Lodge to arrange to have the garden put in order and to survey the loved scene of their future tranquil life.

As he trotted back to the coast, he met a man with letters from Jane, and sat down on the road to read them "with a joy and real delight that cannot possibly be expressed".

The triumphs of his campaign faded into the background and everything else in his life momentarily was dwarfed beside the news which Jane's letters brought him; that her health was much improved by her living in the country and that—to his "inexpressible joy"—she had every reason to believe that she was pregnant and would soon make him "a happy, happy father".

> I believe I read these Letters over and over at least twenty times—almost devouring them with kisses! At length I was roused from this state of felicity and profound reverie these tidings had thrown me into, by my horse-keeper reminding me it was getting late, since he knew I had some business to do at Calicut before I embarked. I therefore got up, and mounting my horse, pursued my way to Calicut with a lighter heart than I had ever done before; being now more anxious than ever to get to Bombay to fold my darling Jane to my heart.[40]

The ocean, however, delayed him with baffling and contrary gales and kept him "five long—long days" at Mahé; but at length the current chapter of his adventures closed, as so many other ones closed during his life, by his coming to Bombay:

> May 6. *Friday*!— At 3 o'clock this afternoon the *Jane* anchored in Bombay Harbour, after a most tedious tiresome passage of 21 days from Calicut! ! ! !—[41]

The reader turns confidently the succeeding page of the returning husband's diary, to share in the flush of gladness at his homecoming, victorious over his enemies and over his personal troubles, and out of the toils of those fears about his beloved wife which had so thickly beset him.

But after those four excited exclamation marks many an ivory-coloured sheet has remained virgin to this present day.

BOOK TWO

*

1796 - 1808

*

Canvas Still Unriven

Man, like a ship with many a sail
Spread to a favouring breeze,
Embarks before Hope's flattering gale,
Upon the world's wide seas,
Right sure he will not, cannot fail
To gain his port with ease.

But, like a vessel far at sea
Struck by a sudden squall,
If Fortune (fickle dame!) should flee,
Or Passion should enthrall,
Right soon the hapless youth may be
Engulphed and lose his all.

Then let thy spirit, Lord! be given,
Like a fair breeze to blow
And keep my canvas still unriven,
While here I sail below,
Till safely in the port of Heaven,
I let my anchor go!

        —JOHN DUNMORE LANG, "The Voyage of Life".

CHAPTER IX

"All For Ever Fled . . ."

I

In 1797 European India was emerging from the age of cow-dung floors and oyster-shell windows. The punkah had been invented. There was a growing battalion of sybarites who took their rest beneath the newfangled mosquito nets.

Lord Mornington, who had been so much moved by the opulence of the East India Company during the trial of Warren Hastings, would soon arrive at Fort William, bringing to it for the first time an air of imperial splendour.[1] Before long, the new Governor-General's palace, a second Kedleston, was to rise in Calcutta with the lush crop of sentries and minions which so much amazed and bewildered the frugal Cornwallis during his second reign.

But on the incipience of these grandeurs Captain Macquarie, to whom earlier they might have been a joy and an excitement, could only gaze with a tear-dimmed eye.

From the growing throng of the "best and consequently the most expensive society" of Bombay a "tall girl above middle size . . . and what I call pretty" was missing, and her inconsolable husband for the time being had ceased to be a member of the Indian beau-monde.

Jane was dead, and he walked apart, self-pitying and beside himself with grief.

He had landed in Bombay that fateful day in 1796 to find that the poor girl's account of herself was all delusion.

She was not with child, as she had believed and as he had hoped. She was not improving in health through living in the country air. She was, in fact, "just in life and that is all".[2]

On the day he came home to her he was almost demented.

Macquarie to Dr. Colin Anderson

Indeed, my dear Anderson, tho' I do not think I am deficient in courage, I confess to you I have not fortitude enough to sustain this dreadful shock with manly resignation.— I sink under it, and I am actually at this moment as miserable a wretch as any that lives on the face of the earth.— O my dear Anderson, if you saw her, how you would pity me! She cannot live! Alas! I must say so!—and of course I shall ever [be] most miserable and wretched. In short she is in the last and worst stage of deep consumption, and probably will not be many days in this cruel world. . . . My Angel is in good spirits, and fancies herself *pregnant*, which gives her great pleasure and contributes to render her insensible to the unhappy and cruel malady with which she is at present afflicted.—But alas!—it is only a temporary and pleasing delusion. Great God! what have I done to deserve so much misery? Success, prosperity and happiness have hitherto attended me from my infancy!—All is now forever fled from me, and this cruel world will very soon have little in it to make life at all supportable and desirable to me!³

The doctors recommended sea air for the patient, a voyage to a suitable and healthful destination. They chose Macao which, like Bombay, was in the Tropics, a degree or two further north. It looked across the teeming Canton River mouth. The island of Lantao was at its front door, the wild deserted peak of Hong Kong beyond. Macao was older, dirtier, lonelier, more insanitary than Bombay.

A nightmare time began. East Indiaman captains adopted an attitude which "certainly does no credit to the feelings of those gentlemen". With "a degree of inhumanity and want of feeling" which the distracted husband hoped was only peculiar to themselves, they had "the barbarity to refuse us a passage".⁴

At last Captain Lestock Wilson, a "very genteel, sensible, pleasant man", obliged without the slightest demur. *He* made one condition only—that "we should not think of offering him the smallest compensation or payment of any kind; as he gave us a passage to China from very different motives to that of *gain*".⁵

Affairs at Calicut were placed in the hands of the faithful Colin Anderson, who was told to do as he pleased with the house, the garden, the horses and the servants, though the cook Andrew, "being an idle useless fellow, and also a drunkard", must be paid off and discharged.

The dream of Staffa Lodge was over.

II

In a few days they were on the *Exeter* bound for China. Jane laughed and chattered and made pathetic little lists of toys which she wished to buy for the children of her friends in Bombay.⁶

By the time they reached Macao on 2 July her husband almost believed she would recover. He wrote "pleasing and flattering accounts of my Angel's improving health"; but he "was indeed fatally deceived".

On the day they landed Jane rose at daybreak and packed all her trunks. She was cheerful while going ashore, though wind and water were against them and they were four hours in the boat. British exiles from the English factory came to meet them—William Drummond who became Lord Strathallan and Macquarie's executor, as well as Mr Cumine, Dr and Mrs Beale, Dr Duncan and others. Jane was "so stout and hearty as to be able to sit up to dinner with the company".

She tore at his heart with her merriment; for she never at any time apprehended she was in danger—"or at least if she did, she never once mentioned it".

She went through a regular household routine. She left her bed for breakfast, made tea herself, sat all day in an easy chair or on a couch while her husband read to her; walked arm in arm with him on the terrace and spoke of the child she expected and of the good things the future held for them.

She took, with patience, the doctor's neguses of red wine and spices and the three daily doses of tincture of yellow bark which they prescribed, but within a week Dr Duncan told Macquarie that "there are no hopes" and that "it is impossible she can recover". The poor man endeavoured to reconcile himself as well as he could "to what a few days more must decide —an eternal separation".

Twelve days after they landed, she discovered with apparent surprise that "her feet were no use to her". She could not stand without help.

At five o'clock one morning the end came, leaving him alone with but one consolation; that he had to the best of his abilities and judgment discharged his duty in every respect to an excellent, tender and affectionate wife.[7]

> Yes! my heavenly darling Jane is gone!—she is gone and lost to me and you forever!—and with her all my earthly happiness is forever fled! This fatal and most mournful event took place here on the morning of Friday the 15th July. She died as she has always lived—like an angel and a saint—with perfect ease and tranquillity, resigning her soul to Heaven without pain or struggle or even a sigh, and retaining the entire and perfect use of all her senses and faculties to the very last moment of her existence. Thus then died in the prime of her youth and beauty the best of women and the best of wives. . . . Oh! dearest and loveliest of women! Who shall ever efface from my remembrance the fearful and distracting horrors of these seven eventful sorrowful days.[8]

Her wretched husband was "stupified with horror and affliction". He had not sufficient fortitude or strength of mind to bear it as he ought, either as a man or as a Christian. For some moments he was "lost to all recollection of what passed after she breathed her last in my arms".

In ten days he did not stir out of the house. At intervals he embraced her coffin, bathing it with his tears. The only relief he could find was in solitude.

Sometimes Jane's Indian maid, Marianne—"poor little creature"—heard him yield to his sorrow "by crying and sobbing in bed". She would "come to the side of it", he reported, "and take hold of my hand, and endeavour by her innocent prattle, to console and divert my attention". All in vain. Attempts at comfort in all forms had "the opposite effect".

During terrible months he wrestled with the red tape of Chinese officialdom and wrote long, grief-stricken epistles to his friends. In these he set out, over and over again, the details of his sufferings, bursting into paroxysms of hysterical words. One letter of that period to Mrs Morley covers forty-eight pages of foolscap.

He wrote that he was fallen from a perfect state of bliss and the summit of all human felicity into the most profound abyss of misery and everlasting despair. He reproached himself that he had not sent his poor bride to England. He cried out in a strain of passionate desolation, "Oh Memory forever dear!—forever to be mourned honoured and adored."

III

Before he left Macao he wrote to her brother George, "As a small testimony of my love, affection and respect for the memory of my dear and excellent wife, I have got a coffin constructed—after the Chinese manner of preserving their dead—which preserves the body sweet and incorruptible for many years; and also admits of its being removed from one place to another without injury to anyone."[9]

Towards the end of the year he took all that was left of his wife home to Bombay. They went in Captain M'Intosh's ship, the *Sarah*, "touching at many places for information respecting the enemy's cruizers, into whose hands we were in hourly fear of falling, but whom we very fortunately never saw". They reached Bombay on 13 January 1797, more than six months after they had set out for Macao.

John Forbes came on board and took the wanderer at once to his house, where he had first met his bride only a little more than four years earlier.

In the cool of the evening at half past five on 16 January 1797, as the sun was sinking out to sea, they went through "the last awful and mournful ceremony" of depositing all that remained of "the amiable good girl" in the dank Burying Ground of Bombay, out by the Esplanade.[10]

John Forbes, her old friend, walked as chief mourner, by her husband's special request. Two major-generals, a commodore and three colonels—"six of her most particular and intimate friends"—were her pall-bearers, followed by a "very numerous and respectable company of friends and acquaintances of the first rank and consequence in this settlement". Indeed, the "whole of the respectable part" of the population was in her train; by which sign, her husband "had the consolation to find, she was universally and sincerely regretted".[11]

A dozen years afterwards there could have been almost none in Bombay to think of Jane, though an anguished soul far off remembered sometimes to cry, "O dearest and best of women . . . never never shall other fill her place."

Sincere as that cry undoubtedly was, it was not to be taken too literally; for though he made a solemn vow on 31 July 1796, a fortnight after she died, which he carried out to the letter, it was merely that he would never marry again *in India*, nor bring another spouse to that land of death.

IV

The period after the funeral found him living in a sort of vacuum.

He wrote that this "mournful and fatal event has not only unhinged and affected my mind most deeply and severely—but has, also, deranged all my present plans and pursuits in life—and rendered me indifferent to all future ones.—I feel myself perfectly undetermined and irresolute as to what plan to adopt and pursue in the present exigency of my affairs."

The society of his friends was something he was "unable to support", and for over a fortnight he did not venture out of Mr Forbes's house, in which he remained until he sailed to join his regiment at Cochin.

He seemed to have difficulty even in communicating his thoughts orally to his host; for he wrote to him on the Sabbath after the funeral, "It will doubtless appear extremely odd to you my addressing you by letter when living under the same roof with you;—but I really find it easier, in my present unhappy and agitated state of mind, to express my sentiments in writing than by word of mouth."[12]

He begged Forbes to decide his future for him. "I will gladly conform myself to whatever plan of life you may judge most conducive to my interest and *welfare*:—for, I fear, *happiness* is forever beyond my reach."

But, however devastating the outward effect might seem to the spectator, the rock of his personality—his shrewd Scottish practicality—remained as solid as the core of Ulva itself. The substance of his ambitions was merely submerged and not destroyed. If need arose, his hard-headed self came quickly to the surface, sometimes lending an air of paradox to the parallel emanations of his despair and of the perfectly controlled manifestations of his purpose.

His grief might run the whole gamut of Gaelic emotions, but business-like indeed was the manner in which he paid his last duties to his dead.

He sent to Cox and Greenwood, the army agents in London, an extract from the *Bombay Courier* describing Jane's obsequies which, he said, "mentioned in a pleasing manner the regard in which her excellent memory is held by this settlement". He begged them to have it "published in the principal papers in London" for the comfort of her relatives.[13] He composed an epitaph to be placed over Jane's tomb and entreated of John Forbes the favour that he should "send home the inscription, with directions to have it put on one of the *best and most elegant black marble slabs that can be procured in England*; and order it to be sent out to Bombay by the ships of next season".[14]

A very large slab was needed for his purpose; Jane's memory was not to be slighted by parsimony in verbiage.

In four hundred and fifty-seven words, linked by strange punctuation, he told of his wife's life, of her long sufferings, of her voyage to China, of the ships in which she had sailed, living and dead, together with the names of their captains. The record exists today in his careful, faded handwriting.

Her virtues he extolled in detail:

". . . She was laid to rest on the 16th day of January 1797 Her funeral being attended by her numerous friends, and the highest and most respectable characters in this settlement. To those who knew her modest worth no Panegyric can be necessary: and to those unacquainted with her, suffice it to say that she possessed in a most eminent degree all the virtues that adorn the female character and render it worthy of universal admiration. As a wife, a Daughter and a Sister, she was pre-eminently conspicuous, and an excellent pattern for others. In her manners, she was mild, affable and polite;— In her disposition sweet and even; In her opinions, liberal; and in her appearance elegant without extravagance—True Christianity gave a superior lustre to all her virtues:— She was an excellent model of every female virtue:— and those of her sex who

make her their Pattern may with confidence anticipate a glorious immortality
—and look forward with pleasure to virtue's best reward—the applauding
smile of HEAVEN."[15]

He ended with an assurance that he wrote not only in honour of his
lady's memory and in testimony of his sincere grief for her loss, but also
as "a lasting monument to their mutual disinterested love". He could
"safely and without vanity affirm that never yet lived a happier or more
contented couple in WEDLOCK!"[16]

He wrote to his brother-in-law, George Jarvis, "You will perhaps think
it too long and no doubt you will also observe that it is not elegantly or
well written;—but it is the no less true and sincere—and at least expresses—
tho' not elegantly—the sincere effusions of a deeply wounded and distracted
heart."[17]

He did not rest until—the first slab of marble consigned to him having
been destroyed on the voyage to India—the remains of his beloved rested
beneath his sombre encomium.

V

Jane's will, drawn by Mr Phineas Hall, had been signed at Calicut on
5 May 1795.

Being "in sound health and body", the amiable girl had bequeathed
to her just and lawful husband and his heirs for ever £6000 in English
funds. To a sister, Mrs Wilkins, not prosperously married, she bequeathed
£1000. To one brother in Antigua she gave her slave, Cassius, "forever",
along with a looking-glass and a cedar press; to her brother, George, some
pieces of plate which he refused to accept because they bore the Macquarie
Arms. Five Antiguan slaves received their freedom.[18]

That was all; but, in a codicil drawn on their leaving Calicut, Jane
had proposed to divide Macquarie's share between his family and that of
Mrs Wilkins in the event of her husband's death before her own.

Neither will nor codicil was witnessed, and when the documents
reached England they were recognized to be void. Jane being intestate,
the whole estate was her husband's. But he refused to take advantage,
save that it enabled him to deal with the ne'er-do-well husband of
Jane's sister, Mrs Wilkins, to whom it was made plain that *he* had no chances
of laying hands on his spouse's legacy.

The widower seemed even to think that his wife's "singularly strong"
affection had led her to be "over-liberal" to him, and he set out to redress
the balance.

He was perfectly convinced, he wrote, that she would have left some
small remembrances to Mrs Morley's "three little dears" in particular if
she had felt at liberty to do so in the unhappy footing on which they stood
at that time with Mr Morley; for she was "doatingly fond of her god-
children, sweet Maria, Charles and Harriet"; and hardly a day had passed
in her married lifetime "without her naming them with marks of the
strongest affection".

Macquarie to Mrs Morley

May I therefore, in the name of my heavenly adorable Jane, take the liberty of earnestly entreating the favour of you and Mr. Morley to permit me to fulfill what I know were her wishes in regard to leaving some trifling memorandums to these little dears as tokens of her affection and love for them. . . . One hundred pounds sterling to each of them.[19]

He brushed aside Mrs Morley's objection that "the sums are too large and instead of them a remembrance of muslins or shawls would be more acceptable"; and, with the "greatest deference to her excellent judgment," he "beseeched her to do him the favour of receiving the money" since he believed that such trifles as *she* suggested were "not sufficient to the occasion—as these things are now so common and so easily procured in England".

He gave £300 more to George Jarvis; £40 to Miss Morley; £30 each to the Misses Louisa and Anne Morley, "to be laid out in any manner they may think proper in the purchase of some jewel or trinket to be worn in remembrance of their dear deceased aunt". There was £200 for another Jarvis brother in Antigua, a victim of Gallic "democracy"; and there was a shroud and £10 for Jane's old Mammy, Dinah, also in Antigua, whose freedom he was prepared to buy at any price Mr Jarvis might choose to put upon it. This, he wrote, he "would gladly pay with much pleasure"; for he "did not suppose the sum he could demand would be very great" and it was his own wish that "the poor old woman should spend her declining years, in ease, freedom and peace".

Other slaves received guineas; and to Jane's little maid, Marianne, who had sought to comfort him in Macao and who must be schooled and cared for, "not only for her own intrinsic worth, but also on account of her fidelity and strong attachment to my late beloved wife", he gave a "certificate of her being perfectly free and no slave which she has locked up in her little box with her clothes".

From time to time, he held correspondence about her with her school mistress, her employers, and with Mrs Morley.

VI

From the moment of his arrival in Bombay he seemed to be involved in a perfect orgy of giving.

Within two days after the curtain had come down upon the final act of his tragedy in Bombay Burying Ground, his friends had begun receiving the presents which poor Jane had bought for them in Macao and some more which his own feelings dictated that he should send them.

Matrons in the more fashionable quarters of Bombay—the Grove, the Mount—answered the *kooee-hais* of his Moor-boy to find themselves the recipients of "toys for your little boy and a fan for yourself"; or "a fan for yourself and some toys for your sweet little Marianne". Jane's doctors received, each, a "breakfast set of china and some Buglepore coat pieces". He sent more toys for her little godson, Mrs Oakes's boy.[20]

Captain M'Intosh, of the *Sarah*, who had refused to take a fare for bringing the bereaved captain and his "dear corpse" home from Macao, returned a thousand rupees sent him to buy a piece of plate, but was rewarded with a lifelong friendship. All the friends in Macao received gifts. Orders poured in on Mrs Morley in Wimpole Street for more and more mourning rings. Jewellers in London worked busily on lockets backed with pieces of his darling's hair. George Jarvis, Jane's favourite brother, was offered copious loans, of which "payment will be time enough twenty years hence", with the privilege "of not standing on any difficulty should he need funds for any purpose".

George's brother-in-law was for ever thinking of new ways to provide pleasures and promotions for him. It might, for instance, occur to him that a grand tour among scenes more jovial than those of southern India would delight the young man. If so, how easy now to write: "If you really wish to go to see Bengal . . . avail yourself of it by all means . . . do not let the expence . . . be any consideration whatever; as it is only drawing on me for a few hundred rupees more which I shall consider as extremely well laid out . . ."[21] Largesse even pursued George to England in the form of an exotic gift which Jane had bought for him:

> A hooka bottom, three ditto snakes complete, one silver surpoose, one silver mouth-piece, one composition ditto, and two *china chillums*.— These articles are all handsome of their kind and of the newest fashion—One of the snakes is truly elegant, and the surpoose and chillums are equally so.— They will all be much admired, and I am sure they will be doubly beautiful in your estimation when you recollect that they are the choice and gift of your heavenly angelic sister Jane!—[22]

George's mourning patron apparently felt that such equipment might be an urgent need in the bizarre world of London.

Upon Jarvis relations a perfect stream of inlaid boxes, rattan canes, lockets, rings, jewels from the sack of Seringapatam poured in during the succeeding years Nor were his own relatives forgotten, for he reflected, "Since I cannot be happy myself in this cruel world, I shall at least endeavour to make others so; by doing all the good I can to my poor relations, in raising as many of them as I possibly can from obscurity and want, and placing them in respectable and eligible situations in life."[23]

So there were fresh annuities for his mother and sister and his brother Donald; aid for needy female cousins and nieces; schooling for the boys of poor kinsmen in Mull and Ulva; help for the son of his cousin John, of Ormaig, who was named Lachlan, after his own father, and there was a continuous bombardment of military headquarters with requests for commissions for friends and relations so young that some of them had only just grown beyond the need of a cradle on parade.

All this generosity was not, however, undiscerning or wasteful. Colonel Gore took home with him on the *Sulivan* Indiaman early in 1798 "a large red trunk containing the cloathes and wearing apparel of my heavenly Jane that are worth sending home, a great many things having been spoiled and damaged by the *white ants* and wet weather". If they were not acceptable to Mrs Morley, he thought her sisters, Mrs Scott and Mrs Wilkins, might relish them; or they might be serviceable to the Morley girls; or, "if not of use in fashionable England", they possibly would gladden the hearts of old Black Dinah and her daughter in Antigua.[24]

All he asked from his own clan in return for his favours was that they should hold their heads up. And he demanded nothing of the Jarvis family, which had indirectly given him so much, save that they should have copied for him "by the very best and most eminent artist in London" an only portrait of Jane, of which he had known nothing during her lifetime. News of its existence at this juncture "afforded him a more real and heartfelt joy than if he had succeeded to an estate of ten thousand a year".

For the rest, he received his recompense in kindly advice and friendship. He made up his quarrels with Old Morley. Mrs Morley's letters in particular at length became to him "perfect cordials to my spirits . . . and make me feel contented with myself and the world around me".

VII

The prime objective of the poor "unhinged" widower—for so he described himself—was now to avoid being yet awhile sent home from India.

This was a change not easy to circumvent. Hostilities in the Orient had ceased. The East India Company was suffering once more from a fit of parsimony and had become reluctant to maintain regiments which were not earning their cost in profitable campaigns. The rising clamour in Europe heralded the shifting of the vortex of war.

Among the corps selected to be drafted for home was the 77th Regiment, now stationed at Cochin.

Macquarie heard this bad news on his arrival from China. He begged Sir Robert Abercromby to allow him to stay in India on the ground that "the present state of his private fortune rendered it of double importance that he should remain in Bombay as Major of Brigade". This excuse was sheer dissimulation. He admitted that Jane's legacy had left him "a very independent man", though he professed his "great surprise and mortification" at Abercromby's refusal of his plea for "at least a couple of years more" in the Presidency, which was firmly denied. He had actually resigned himself to his fate, and to sharing with his brother officers "this very severe stroke upon us all", when rescue came.

Two months after he had arrived in Bombay from China the Government changed its unstable mind on the grounds that Spain had declared war on Great Britain and that "an expedition is soon to take place from India against the Spanish settlement of Manila". The order for the withdrawal of the regiment was cancelled before Macquarie reached Cochin on 4 March, five weeks after Jane's burial.

The expedition remained a dream, but the mourner now could delay his return to England. With Bombay given over to as fine a coterie of Scots as had ever managed a colony—Jonathan Duncan, the new Governor,

Major-General Stuart, the Forbes and Bruce families, financial magnates and his near friends—he soon had good reason, indeed, to meditate that India was become "beyond any doubt the best country for a *soldier of fortune*",[25] though he became indignant when it was suggested that this was the factor which was keeping him where he was.

Macquarie to Lochbuy

Excuse me—my dear and much revered uncle—when I very sincerely assure you that you have *quite mistaken my character* in entertaining any such poor opinion of me for a moment.— *There was a time*, I proudly confess, that I very much wished to become a *rich man*!— that it might enable me to secure and promote the happiness of *one* whose temporal ease and comfort were ten thousand times dearer to me than my own!— The motive and cause that excited that wish—being now alas! no more!—my desire and ambition for riches are both annihilated!— I have already much more money that I shall ever, I hope, live sufficiently long to spend.— Why therefore plague myself in collecting—to me at least—such *useless trash?*—For, it cannot in the smallest degree add to my happiness.—farther than enabling me to help and provide for some of my poor relations. It is not therefore to *collect money*, my dear uncle, that I now remain in India;—but *solely because I am unfit* in my present temper and disposition of mind to enjoy happiness or comfort *anywhere*—and it is entirely with a view of being able, in the course of time, to dissipate and dispel melancholy and mournful impressions that I am *now* induced to prolong my stay in India—and *not by any means* from motives of lucre.[26]

Adjustments to secure his end—on a properly economic basis of course— were a little complicated. But it was possible to achieve the seemingly impossible when, in the right quarters, pity and sympathy were mingled with friendship and respect for his talents and honesty.

His main anxieties lay in the fact that his interests were in two widely separated spheres. At Cochin he was Paymaster to the Regiment, and Whitelocke, returned to the command, now presented him with its profitable grenadier company—an act which was "very kind and civil", since the pair had not been upon very good terms in the old days at Calicut.

At Bombay, six hundred miles and more away to the north, he was still Major of Brigade.[27] There, too, he had become the incumbent of the "very respectable and honourable situation of Deputy Paymaster-General to the Army", which he had bought from his friend Dunlop, in the course of some strange bargaining which did both parties great credit. Macquarie was to act in the office and perform its duties. But for two years he was to pay the emoluments of about £700 a year to Dunlop as capital purchase price.

A skilled conjurer might have envied the easy dexterity with which he made barriers to his wishes disappear and coaxed his interests in Bombay and Cochin within the limits of the same dimension.

Whitelocke was quickly cajoled to "allow me (tho absent) to retain my Grenadier Company, the payment and charge of which I gave to Archy Campbell".

The paymastership was offered to Captain Weston, "at half the annual salary, as well as every emolument to June 24, 1799". The terms, he believed, might appear hard to Mr Weston, but he "asked him to consider the circumstances".[28]

When obstacles arose to prevent him from returning to Bombay he arranged that his friend John Forbes, who was a civilian, should keep the books and carry out the duties for him in the Deputy Paymaster-General's Office, of which, in the end, he was robbed of all the gains by the economizing Wellesleys, who abolished it before he benefited financially from it.

Though he had gained no profit by it, it certainly had given him advantages on such occasions as that on which he needed to transmit funds to George Jarvis upon his travels in regions where he had "no acquaintance I can draw upon":

Letter of Credit[29]

My dear Brother,   COCHIN, 18th March 1897 [sic]

    I do hereby authorize and empower you to draw upon me at sight (—if necessary—) for the sum of fifteen hundred Bombay rupees; which I do hereby promise to pay on demand to whomever you may find it convenient or necessary to draw in favour of for the aforesaid sum.—I remain

My dear Brother
Yours very affectionately
L. MACQUARIE
DY Paymr. Genl. King's Troops.

To
   LIEUT. G. R. P. JARVIS,
   36th Regt
   Negapatam.

George obtained the money; if the copy of the date is accurate, a century was nothing to an Indian banker, when the signatory was "Yours very affectionately", and Deputy Paymaster-General to a King's Army.

VIII

Having settled all his affairs with the Regiment at Cochin to his own satisfaction the widower set out for Bombay, where he now thought that "more than probably he should pass the remainder of his days", instead of two years. He felt, nevertheless, an "unconquerable repugnance" to returning thither.

He paused at Calicut to rid himself of Staffa Lodge.

His poignant memories of the place kept him company; and when he tried, in the house in which he had "passed so many days of delight and felicity", to sort out Jane's clothes and linens to be sent to England, he became "perfectly unmanned" and could not complete the task.

All his belongings were packed together somehow; his silver in "two plate chests covered with gunny", his "books and papers" in a "small deal box". He took with him everything else portable "excepting the two poor old horses", the old grey and Jane's Turkai, on which they had ridden together. These he gave to friends.[30]

The wreckage from the only personal home which in all his life he had a chance to love and improve, with his Cochin slave boys, George and Hector, his head servant Bowmanjee and his staff, was crowded into the brig *Active*.

But they did not reach Bombay.

On 25 April 1797, lying in Mahé Roads, they heard that Governor Duncan and Lieutenant-General Stuart were at Tellicherry, come to deal with the Pyché Rajah, an obscure but active chieftain of the Malabar coastal fringes.

This miscreant and his followers in the previous year had ambushed and murdered three British officers in a pass in the Wynaarde district a few miles from Tellicherry. They now had added to their outrages, their victims being Macquarie's friend Captain Donald Cameron and most of his battalion.

To subdue and bring back of obedience the guilty potentate, it was proposed to send out an expeditionary force of 3000 regular European and Native troops, with 4000 irregulars—"too small a command for General Stuart himself to take the field at the head of; more especially on such a blackguard triffling [sic] kind of service."[31]

Colonel Dow was to be in charge, and Captain Macquarie brushed aside all the objections and hastily volunteered for service with him. It mattered little to him that he was "very far from being in good health at the time, having hardly sufficient strength to undergo the fatigues of the campaign". He was so anxious, he declared, to be actively employed, in order to banish—if possible—melancholy reflections, that he had made "a point of going into the field contrary to the advice of friends who wished to see his health restored".[32]

What better specific for a badly wounded heart than that which a swift sortie could provide?

It was proposed to plunge into jungle, "seize the rebellious rajah's person if possible", and, if not, "to drive him up to the Ghauts and burn and destroy all his houses, towns and villages" in the Cottiote country, which had "never been explored much by Europeans".

This certainly was "a blackguard trifling kind of service", though not without its perils.

To exact reprisals Colonel Dow's detachments were taking with them large bands of those enthusiastic irregulars, "the friendly Nairs and Moplahs", who were "famous for the cruel work of destruction and devastation and ... accordingly employed on it to great good purpose ... but in a fighting way no use to us at all".

While these adventurous followers trailed in the rear, burning and looting, Macquarie marched in the van. He showed the first gleam of enthusiasm for anything in his immediate surroundings since Jane's death in his expressions of satisfaction that General Stuart had "made a particular arrangement" to appoint him to the command of a "very pretty little detachment of which I am very proud", the Advance Guard of seven hundred men, made up of four companies of the 77th Regiment and a battalion of the 3rd Native Infantry Regiment.

Theirs was the honour of bearing the brunt of the hardships along the rougher tracks, and if necessary of the imminent rainy season. Dunlop was on the right wing in command of the infantry forces in general, while the staff and the guns upon the left travelled by an easier route.

It was the kind of war which so astonished American correspondents in Malaya in 1942, and which led them, in their confident innocence, to instruct the Indian Army in systems of infiltration with which British officers had been painfully familiar for nearly two hundred years. It was, indeed, the sort of campaign in which the British always appear to blunder to inconclusiveness but in which they always are decisively successful at the second or third attempt.

They endured all the normal experiences of such expeditions. They faced a harrying fire from the jungle. They were peppered from trees and nullahs. They fought their way through the ravine in Wynaarde in a battle in which Sergeant Wilson, "a fine active fellow", was shot close to Macquarie, and Captain Browne, a volunteer, was killed.

They assaulted Mananderry, "a considerable Nair village, situated in a large, beautiful valley, surrounded by pretty high hills". Against it they deployed into line, with a galling fire breaking upon them from all sides, charged various bodies of the enemy, put them all to rout and assailed the village fort, by Dunlop's permission,

> which being granted and some scaling ladders having been sent me at same time, I moved on rapidly with the Advanced Guard to storm this little fort accordingly; but the enemy posted within it perceiving our design, abandoned it in a great hurry and confusion . . . setting a few houses within it on fire. . . . We had five men killed and wounded in this attack, but luckily no officer materially . . . I received a slight contusion on the upper part of my left foot, where I was struck with a spent ball, and which I picked up; but which only left a blue mark on the skin, and did not even penetrate through the leather of my boot.[33]

It was the only bullet-touch he received during all his years of service. His companies lost the bulk of the day's casualties in the force apart from "about 15 of the Irregulars who accompanied us—but *who fought very shy*".

They pushed on, harassed everywhere among the "fine rich well cultivated villages", suffering great losses among the irregulars who insisted in action on being "huddled together in great confused crowds". They seized the Rajah's capital of Todicollum, but the bird had flown.

The tracks became narrower, the jungle thicker and wetter, and more infested with the enemy.

Unencumbered with equipment, other than their loin-cloths and lethal weapons, the Rajah's villains showed themselves as mobile as they were invisible. Not a man of them was

> to be seen with the naked eye; but on watching and looking with our spy glasses at the particular spots from whence the smoke of their fire issued, this dastardly enemy were seen sitting *like monkies* in the tops of the thickest and highest trees in the jungle, from which they fired in perfect security to them-

selves—and unperceived by us.— In this way they continued to annoy our camp the greater part of the day, killing and wounding a few soldiers and several public and private followers.[34]

The British did not succeed in catching these "intrepid warriors", as the indignant commander of Dow's vanguard force in sarcasm called them. A few rounds fired at random would send the miscreants scurrying to their lofty nests, to be seen no more.

Thus the expeditionaries could but leave them to the jungle and carry on with fire and sword. They took Canote, after a fight in which Brigade-Major Bachelor was shot through the head while handing orders and speaking to Macquarie. They wiped out the town and ravaged the country to the south of it.

Houses were sent up in flame; grain, goods and cattle were seized by the Nairs and Moplahs with a thoroughness which would have done credit to experienced Maclean or MacDonald partisans of the Elizabethan age.

In a few days the "short but successful little campaign" was at an end, with the result that the Rajah's troops

> must now be fully sensible that they never can stand us in the field, even in their own extraordinary mode of warfare and *monkeylike-way of fighting from the tops of trees!*—It is true we cannot say to a certainty that we have killed many of them on this last service. . . . [Their dead] are instantly carried off the moment they fall.— But if we may judge from the dreadful *yells and screams of the enemy* every time our troops fired at them into the jungle, tho' generally at random, there must have been a considerable number of them killed and wounded on this last service.[35]

The elusive Rajah they had been unable to find. He was saved to be numbered among the earlier prey of Colonel Arthur Wellesley three years later.

"The principal object of the expedition having been accomplished— as far as the present advanced stage of the season would admit", Macquarie squelched back at the head of his companies to Cottiamgurry and, less than a month after leaving Mahé, he was meditating in his new quarters with General Stuart's staff at Tellicherry that "notwithstanding my being exposed on every occasion to the fire of the enemy, during our short late campaign in the jungle, I am returned unhurt and in whole skin".

IX

He still was in low spirits and two days later he was in the grip of a new bout of fever which kept the pages of his journal once again blank for many a day.

His convalescence was a miserable business. His view of his illness in retrospect had an air of cheerless disappointment.

"Had I fallen in the jungle," he wrote, "it were perhaps the most fortunate circumstance that could have happened me:—but you see I am still reserved for enduring more misery in this life . . . if you knew what anguish tears and distracts my unhappy heart both night and day, you would hardly—out of pity to my sufferings—wish me to live much longer. But alas!—live I must as long as God Almighty has ordained that I should do so."[36]

In August 1797 he appeared, at first glance, more than ever to be a man headed for an early grave. In that month he wrote to his sister-in-law, Mrs Morley:

> I am exceedingly reduced in my appearance with these last fourteen months. I never was very stout since you *first* saw me at Bombay; but alas! there is a terrible change in my appearance since then.— and that change is far from being occasioned by bad health alone!— I am persuaded, my dearest sister, if you were to see me at this moment, you would hardly know me to be the same person you took leave of at Bombay, on the 16th of January, 1794!— Some months ago I was so very ill, and so altered in my looks, that I had a melancholy pleasure in contemplating the rapid strides that Nature was making on me towards a dissolution!—which—I am forced to own—however sinful such a sentiment may be considered—I did not wish to avert.[37]

All through the rains Governor Duncan and General Stuart lingered dealing not only with the Rajah who had come to "submit himself to the will and discretion of the Company", but with "the most extraordinary scene of peculation and mismanagement" in the Province of Malabar. And throughout that season the patient's correspondence is flavoured with malarial melancholia, though his interest was stimulated a little when he heard the confession of his brother, Charles, that he had fallen in love in London with "the lovely and amicable Sarah Morley". His lucubrations on the subject showed that his body might be in process of dissolution, but his sense of caution was very much alive.

He told his brother that "most sincerely do I wish you were married to that delightful girl", possessed of "every good quality and every accomplishment necessary to make a man happy *in the married state*". But he wrote that he feared the smallness of Charles's fortune would prove an insurmountable barrier, since he knew Mr Morley so very well that he was convinced he would "never allow his daughter to marry anybody that has not *a very large fortune*—and who cannot make a *very handsome* settlement upon her".[38]

Presently, his spirits turned towards recovery and his benefactions became more varied. Particularly did he become absorbed in altruistic schemings due to the fact that he had become "*deeply engaged in the commission way*",[39] bent, apparently, upon inducting every young Macquarie and Maclean on Mull or Ulva into the British Army, sometimes by the most curious devices.

Murdoch, the heir of Lochbuy, aged six years, John his brother, aged five; the infant sons of Ormaig, Ballighartan, Laggan, and Scallastle, twigs off old Ulva's tree, his sister Betty's sons—all these were upon his list and found an advocate, who was sometimes as ingenious as he was zealous.

Lachlan Macquarie to Charles Macquarie

In respect to what you propose of giving the commission in the 73rd Regt (that was intended for our nephew Murdoch) to our cousin Lochbuy's eldest son

Murdoch, I cannot possibly have the least objection, and most willingly and readily give my assent to it if it can possibly be done; providing the boy Hugh (our sister's second son—) has not already assumed the name of *Murdoch*, and claimed the commission in the manner I directed and advised it to be done in my former letters to yourself and Lochbuy on this subject; and which could very easily have been done—without injury to anyone—in case you have not informed the *Agents*, or *the War Office*, that the commission in question *was actually intended for the lad in* the 37th Regiment— The commission was given at my solicitation, by Sir Robert Abercromby *to my relation* Mr. *Murdoch Maclaine*;—but neither he—nor the War-Office care one pin about *who that Murdoch Maclaine is*—if he is a gentleman and otherwise properly qualified for holding the commission.— It was under this idea, and on the supposition that the Agents did not know *what Murdoch Maclaine* the commission was intended for, that I desired my nephew Hugh to assume the name of *Murdoch* so as to entitle him to take up the commission in question.—[40]

There were pages more of the letter tendering sage and guileful advice to cover procedures in all contingencies and to leave no loophole in his plans. He suggested arrangements for financial adjustments and supplied proper certificates to prevent the War Office from catching him napping. Enough, in fact, did he do to assure that Murdoch Maclaine in due course should be inducted into uniform, and that Murdoch (Hugh) Maclaine should become an ensign on half-pay and should rise to the command of the 77th Regiment.

On 4 January 1798 the ailing captain had returned to his own house on the Ramparts in Bombay, and was engaged in dealing with Jane's will as her executor, and in giving friendly answer to the overtures of Old Morley, who had written a "very kind and affectionate letter".

He lived almost as a hermit, as he felt that he "could not have done with propriety and decency in the midst of his relations in Scotland". His was, he declared, "a most retired and sequestered kind of life", in which he indulged his fancy, "entirely excluding himself *from all public society* and very rarely going into any private company". His intimacies were limited almost entirely to those associated in his memory with his wife's last days.

Colin Anderson still was first among all of them—"my dearest friend", for whom, he said, "this miserable poor life of mine would be willingly and cheerfully sacrificed in your defence"[41]; John Forbes and his nephew, Charles Forbes, the pioneer of women's suffrage; Governor Duncan, with whom he was drifting into personal friendship; John Abercromby, the conqueror-to-be of Mauritius.

Also, such newer ones as Captain Lestock Wilson, who had conveyed them in the *Exeter* to Macao, and William Drummond, later Lord Strathallan, who was to join Charles Forbes in defending him in Parliament many a year later, and who lived to become his executor and the guardian of his son:

Macquarie to Drummond

I have now travelled over many parts of the world, and have formed acquaintance with a variety of characters;—but the generous, disinterested, and truly benevolent attention I experienced from you, during my unfortunate and unhappy residence in China, surpasses anything I have ever yet met with in my travels—and does honour to human nature.[42]

His experiences in that fateful year of 1797 coloured the whole of the rest of his existence. It was then that there opened into full flower his weakness for standing by the underdog, which eventually grew to be an obsession with him and destroyed much of the happiness of his last years.

He became all too lenient in his first judgments of men, and slow to generate suspicion of them in his mind.

CHAPTER X

Corn in Egypt

I

THE few months after he returned from the Cottiote campaign cover the period in which history knows less of Lachlan Macquarie than during any other time in the thirty-six years which elapsed between his arrival in India and his death.

He had begun to have serious thoughts of home, especially after letters of sympathy began to arrive from Mull in reply to the lengthy and heart-stricken epistles which he had written from Macao. He told his uncle that he looked forward very soon to making his appearance as a guest at Lochbuy, whenever he could reconcile himself to a different mode of living.

There seems to be in his writings evidence that he was very lonely and not a little homesick. He wrote almost with abandon of his suffering to his brother Charles, to Mrs Morley, and more particularly to Mrs Maclaine Lochbuy, whom he described as "near and dear to my heart". To her he declared that though he had had many correspondents in his time, he could say—without paying her a compliment—that she was "the best, most attentive and most intelligent one he had ever yet had, either at home or abroad". He found her "arguments just and sensible, her consolation and comfort real". But even her ministrations could not produce an absolute effect upon his spirits, and he told her that, though both religion and philosophy instruct us to conform and resign ourselves to the decrees of the Supreme Ruler of Universal Nature, it was nevertheless "a most difficult task for even the firmest and most philosophic mind to reduce these sage and wise rules to the practice of sober life and frail human nature". For, he wrote,

> however exalted and sublime our notions may be of a Supreme Being, we *must* both feel and lament the crosses and calamities he pleas[es] to inflict upon us in this life; more especially when they deprive us of our *greatest happiness* and *dearest interests in it*! No one can entertain a more sublime or a more devout reverence for an Almighty Power than I do;— but I am no philosopher, and must ever feel and lament the decree of Providence that has deprived me of all my worldly happiness, and the dreadful and awful eternal separation from a most deservedly dear and beloved wife.[1]

Among all his benefactions he had a special list of favours for his "dear aunt's" growing brood—her family in the end swelled by annual increments to the healthy number of nine, of whom seven were girls. He enjoined their mother not to allow her husband "to spare expence on giving a most complete education to all his children; for since he could not leave them *fortunes*, he could not do them too much justice in the other way".[2]

He demanded minute particulars about "all names, ages, size, general appearances, dispositions, talents and progress in education", which he knew she would not deny him since he "only required it *annually*".[3] He assured her that he felt a "fraternal love and affection for all of them"; and that he "was inviolably bound to protect and promote their interests, and advancement in life to the utmost of his power and poor abilities". He gave solemn assurances that the sons of Lochbuy *would never want a friend and protector as long as I exist*". He was even prepared, across half the globe, to take a personal part in the education of the young female Maclaines himself.

> My Cousin *Jane* (—a name that will ever sound sweet and dear to my Ear—!) is now, I believe, between eleven and twelve years of age—and I suppose must be by this time far advanced in her education. If she has learnt *French*, I should be glad to commence a correspondence with her *in that language*;—for tho' *I am* a very indifferent French scholar, it may be useful to her to begin early to correspond in that language with a relation who will not hesitate to point out her errors and inaccuracies in style, orthography, &c.— Should she however not feel yet inclined to correspond *in French*, I have no objection to challenge her to correspond in *English*, which perhaps will be easier for us both;—so that she may take her choice. She may safely and without scruple write to me with the same freedom and familiarity that she would do *to a brother*, had she one so old; and she may rely upon [it] that her confidence in this respect will never be abused.[4]

Even with this advance, his solicitude for the Maclaine children had yet to soar to its supreme manifestation; for he presently announced his readiness to go far beyond saving these young relatives from "that great prejudice to both men and women" of "not beginning an epistolary correspondence with their confidential friends earlier in life".

> It would perhaps sound ungracious and repulsive in your ears, were I to propose to you that two of my fair young cousins should be educated and destined for Indian brides!—that is—that they should be extremely well educated and accomplished in all the present fashionable branches of female education; and after being thus educated, and when of proper age, if they should feel inclined one day or other to undertake a voyage to India under my protection, I do very sincerely assure you that I would with great pleasure and readiness go home on purpose to bring two of them out to this country, and take a brotherly care of them until they are well and handsomely settled in the world.[5]

He declared that he would pay for a year's schooling for each at some London seminary, in view of his firm opinion that, though the Edinburgh system of education might be good, London was superior for finishing a young lady's training and "giving her that confidence and certain air of fashion which the Scotch schools never do".[6]

His "dear aunt" did not share his enthusiasm. She soon had him agreeing that "there are many serious objections to the *high fashionable boarding schools* of London", and that her observations on the subject were "extremely just and well founded".[7] He did not press his offer.

After all, his interest in females was secondary, as he proved in a letter to the lady's husband:

> I find the last addition to your family was a *daughter* but I hope the next will be of a different sex—and bring to life again my *grand-father*—the so much wished for young Lachlan!—When *he* makes his appearance, most happy and proud shall I be to have the honour of being considered his *god-father*—as well as his *future protector*.[8]

There is no record to suggest that any one of Lochbuy's seven daughters married a nabob.

II

By the end of 1798 his mind was "considerably easier"; he was "more reconciled to life".

He noted, absent-mindedly, the destruction of Napoleon's fleet at the Battle of the Nile and rejoiced at the tyrant's forces being cut up by the Arabs.

Always the optimist in public affairs, he hoped that he would "now very soon be gratified with the pleasing tidings of all our domestic disturbers and foreign enemies being entirely crushed and subdued".

French principles, "abhorred as they must now be all over the world, by every feeling mind", were, he trusted, "nearly extinguished". And never might they be renewed for the sake of humanity; for they "disgraced human nature!"[9]

His wish was vain. The "Corsican monster" had no intention of abandoning his design of attacking India, "if he could procure sufficient craft for this purpose in the Red Sea". The English in the Presidency were well assured that "his *first object* is Bombay; where we are prepared and ready to give him a warm reception".

To this prospect local happenings added dessert, for Macquarie reported, "It is also highly probably that *we shall very soon be at war in this country* with our old enemy *Tippoo Sultan*."[10]

This, he said, he was very glad of—this active kind of life would do him a great deal of good. His health and spirits were "much better than they had been for a great while past". At the end of January 1799, as he reached the beginning of his thirty-ninth year, he was looking forward eagerly to a "campaign under canvas" and to the task of "stripping him [Tippoo] at once of all or the greater part of his rich valuable dominions".[11]

In this he was at one with all other ambitious Europeans of Bombay, who were "lately become military mad—from the Governor downwards to the youngest civilian—in forming Military Associations and Fencible Corps for the defence of Bombay, in case of the French coming to attack us from Egypt".[12]

Tippoo, of course, had no inclination to disappoint their longing to try a fall with him. Had he not heard from Napoleon himself that the latter was arrived on the borders of the Red Sea "with an innumerable and invincible army, full of the desires of delivering you from the iron yoke of England"?[13] Had not the fat despot of Mysore actually informed M. Malartic in Mauritius that he awaited the arrival of the bearers of the Eagles, whom he was prepared to furnish with every article necessary for carrying on the war, wine and brandy excepted, before he himself proceeded with the work of "purging India of these villains"?[14] Was not a tree of Liberty—a strange exotic growth—rooted already in the soil of Mysore?

Tippoo seemed utterly captivated with the portents and with his new allies, more especially since he knew the East India Company's war chest to be half empty.

He found the English dull dogs in any case. They had nothing much to offer him save a list of cold and querulous inquiries about his activities and intentions, and unsupported assurances that "no people on earth are so baneful and insidious in the arts of intrigue as the French".

And they evidently opened his mail, for they politely enclosed in their own correspondence with him one of his treacherous letters to the "Grand Seignor of Constantinople", a monarch whom he himself described as "the Prince in a Station like Jamshyd, with angels as his guards, with troops numerous as stars; the Sun, illumining the World of the Heaven of his Empire and Dominion, the Luminary giving splendour to the Universe of the Firmament of Glory and Power, the Sultan of the Sea and Land and the King of Rome".[15]

He had no raptures like this for Lord Mornington. The latter, in turn, was not mesmerized by Tippoo's "hope that you will continue to gratify me with friendly letters notifying your welfare". Neither was he entranced with Tippoo's suggestion that he should send into Mysore an ambassador without, or almost without, escort. But he was deeply interested in a jeering sentence in the Sultan's letter which read, "Being frequently disposed to make excursions and hunt, I am accordingly proceeding on a hunting expedition."

The trump card of the British is always action rather than words. Mornington, with reckless disregard for the emptiness of the Treasury, hastily formed a large Company Army. Soon his enterprising brother, Colonel Arthur Wellesley, was spurring on a host of agents to the collection of bullocks, while at the same time he stimulated the predatory hopes of a body of seasoned looters who were prudently brigaded with his own 33rd Regiment.

The campaign was the old game over again. The Bombay Army tramped through the mud up to the Western Ghauts. The Madras Army, infinitely larger and more diverse, moved up the eastern slopes of the Mysore Plateau, a vast hollow square three miles wide and seven miles deep, with a surging city of 150,000 camp-followers in its centre.

On 9 February 1799, without having made his will, since he was "not in a disposition or temper of mind to undertake a task of so serious a nature", Macquarie followed General Stuart's staff to Tellicherry in a cruiser, in charge on the Bombay Army's treasure chest, and marched with the Bombay force up the familiar Ghauts.[16]

This time his view from the Green Hill of Seedasur was even more engaging than upon the occasion of his first survey of Mysore's landscape from it eight years previously. From where he and Colin Anderson in 1791 had looked down upon the rich plains of the Cauvery country, the most intriguing feature of the scene now was a vast, green tent.[17]

It rose to catch the vigilant eye of the pickets of Lieutenant-Colonel Montresor's native advance guard; and it advised all too clearly that, in the ill-omened region of Periapatam, Tippoo himself was assembling an army of nearly 18,000 sepoys and cavalrymen to crush the Bombay Army, as he had attempted to crush Robert Abercromby's force in 1791. It fell to Macquarie's lot to tell the official story.

Tippoo proposed to throw six thousand men against the British front. To infiltrate through the jungle on either wing to catch the British flanks in a death grip and assail them in their rear, he arranged two more forces each of the same strength. But "no part of his scheme succeeded".

Montresor's natives, after a battle lasting from nine in the morning till two in the afternoon, flung back the frontal onslaught.

Dunlop dealt effectively with the outflanking moves in his usual thorough manner. The foe was utterly routed. For miles in an expansive arc his dead and wounded were to be seen "scattered through the jungle in great numbers", apart from those who fell in front. A Mysorean deserter told them that twelve principal officers and two thousand rank and file of Tippoo's army were casualties in the enemy camp the day after the battle.

The Bombay Army's loss was only two officers killed and three wounded. The total of the killed, wounded, and missing was 143. They had captured two *buckshees* of *cutcheries* or brigades and were sure that they held prisoner, badly wounded, Said Goffar, a commander of one of the enemy frontal forces, but this was not true, as later events proved; for Said Goffar died on the day of the final assault on Seringapatam, killed by a roundshot as he turned from the sight of advancing scarlet columns, vowing to drag Tippoo to the walls to see his danger.[18]

All Tippoo's schemes at Seedasur were "completely frustrated". He had had a smart drubbing which must have made "a very sensible impression upon himself and his whole army". He retired incontinently to his lair, followed by the Army of Bombay with Captain Macquarie, sick as ever, obstinately bringing up the rear in a *doolie*, and determined to be in at the death.

III

The Battle of Seringapatam was one of the romantic engagements of British Indian history. As the purchase-price of control of a rich kingdom and mountains of jewels and spoil, and of the destruction of an ever-present menace to the safety of the Company, the British losses were a cheap investment. Over a period of days in those sweltering weeks of April and May 1799 only 203 Europeans and 119 natives were killed, and 622 Europeans and 420 natives wounded on the British side.[19]

Viewed from the lines of the Bombay Army, however, the operations were "brilliant" and vivid with event.

There was the excitement of their junction with Floyd's cavalry on 10 April at the fort of Periapatam, where they had once known so much disaster and chagrin; there was the crossing of the seven-hundred-yard-wide stony bed of the Cauvery on 15 April, which brought them into a position north of the Tyrant's grim-looking fortress, of which the opposite side was invested by the army of Lord Harris—he who had proved so great an economist in the interests of General Medows a decade earlier in Bombay.[20]

They watched the two claws of the nutcracker inching forward to crush the shell of the defences and pulverize the kernel of Tippoo's kingdom. Each night they saw new siege platforms rise. The breaching and enfilading guns pushed closer to the walls under cover of darkness. The hordes of squealing Mysorean rocket men were driven off, and the preparatory operations culminated on 2 May in the opening of a "most tremendous peal of fire" from all the batteries on both sides of the river, with "no less than fifty two pieces of ordnance, including eight howitzers" breaking a way into Tippoo's fortress.[21]

What defence work—in the eighteenth century—could withstand so violent a blast? By sunset, they noticed, across the grey Indian landscape, afire from the bombardment and sultry with the imminent promise of the rains, a large breach in the south-west curtain wall.

This each day grew wider, until the blazing noon of 4 May, on which the sleek, mutton-chop-whiskered Tippoo sat at tiffin in the cool hall of his palace. He was arrayed in a jacket of fine white linen and loose drawers of flowered chintz, set off with a crimson cummerbund, his purse supported by a red and green silk belt.

He was in a boastful mood. When he was told that outside in the heat four thousand British troops in scarlet coat and high stock were forming up for an assault, he refused to leave his meal. He knew the English were mad but he did not believe that they could be so mad as to give battle in the high noon of a sweltering day in Indian May.

So the convalescent Macquarie, like Arthur Wellesley—the latter still subdued after his curious nocturnal adventures in the Sultanpettah Tope—had a fine view when David Baird waved his sword and emerged from the British trenches, grinning dourly at the thought of the old scores that he was about to pay off.[22]

He was a terrible fellow, whose old mother had exclaimed in deeply sympathetic tones when she heard years before that he was manacled to another of Haidar Ali's prisoners, "God help the chiel wha's chained tae oor Davie!" And he was followed by a noble band consisting of the 73rd Regiment, and of the flank companies of the 77th Regiment and other eager troops, drawn forward by the shoutings of Lieutenant-Colonel James Dunlop.

The onlooker saw them cross the river, above two hundred yards broad, and the outer ditch waist deep; saw them thin out and mount the breach in the space of a few minutes, and then, like distant ants, swarm through the gap in the wall with bayonets glinting.

He watched the vast hordes of Tippoo's followers burst from the gates of the fortress like escaping bees out of a smashed hive.

He heard, afterwards, many a tale of gallantry. Dunlop, for example, had nearly had his hand cut off by a *sirdar* but had slashed his foe to ribbons. Then he had pushed on, cheering his men till loss of blood stopped him in his tracks, so that he missed the sight of Tippoo's mangled corpse, still gaudy in its flowered chintz, lying in a pool of blood amongst a heap of slain—it was never known who killed him.

Macquarie voted the battle "a grand and memorable occasion".

> The final result of this glorious and memorable day was that our troops were in complete possession of Tippoo Sultan's Fortress and Capital in less than an hour from the commencement of the assault; the Sultan himself, and a great many of his principal officers, killed in the storm; his sons and all his family our prisoners—and all his immense riches and treasure in our possession:—for he had neither sent his family—or treasure—out of the Fort;—being, as it is said, fully confident that he would be able to defend it against all our efforts.[23]

Also, he was constrained to record the almost inevitable aftermaths of his campaigning. His health was "indifferent", and his share in the prize money, which he expected to be between £2000 and £3000 sterling, was a disappointment to him, since his moiety of captured jewels, which included seventeen ruby rings, was grossly overvalued, and his ultimate reward was a mere £1300.[24]

IV

Macquarie's return from the campaign against Tippoo seems to have marked the turning-point of his mental sickness and the presence of Jonathan Duncan in Bombay worked a revolution in his life.

Duncan had become Governor of the Presidency in the days when Jane lay ill in the Settlement on the eve of the Ceylon campaign in 1796. Macquarie had found him, when he courteously called upon Jane, "rather a good looking man". He had noted that he "does not appear to be above forty or forty two years of age, which is a young period of life to be appointed to so high and very distinguished [an] important situation. His salary as Governor is a *Lack of Rupees*—or £12,500 Str. pr. annum."[25]

On Cornwallis's special recommendation, Duncan had been brought from Benares, where he had put down infanticide and discouraged peculation to such effect that "his character for superior talents, honour and integrity stood very high indeed".[26] His fellow-countryman from Mull wrote heartily that "every good and honest man on this side of India is happy that so honourable and upright a character, as Mr. Duncan is universally allowed to be, has succeeded to this long vacant Government". Macquarie's attention was riveted a little more firmly upon the new administrator, because he learned that "My friend Sir John M'Gregor Murray (the chief of Clan M'Gregor)" had recommended him to his new senior. That he hoped to gain something by the reference was proved by the strain in which he wrote to Sir John Murray from Ceylon and "took the liberty to entreat of you, my dear Sir, to mention my name again to him".[27]

Four years after he had first met the Governor, their association flowered into friendship. Macquarie was recovered and refreshed in spirit, stimulated by his adventures on a leave tour in the fashionable and exciting regions of Fort William and the Ganges. Even before he had left Bombay he had mustered up sufficient high spirits to dine several friends at the Bombay Tavern, to attend the play, and even—on 13 June 1799, at the onset of the monsoon rains—a ball. On 12 March 1800 he wrote to his brother Charles:

> I had once a serious intention of quitting the army after the war, and of sequest-ering myself from the world and public society in some remote part of Great Britain where I might indulge my grief and ruminate on my unhappy loss of the dearest and best of wives. I have, however, relinquished this mournful and melancholy scheme, and have determined to remain as I am, being resolved to try to bear up against my misfortune with as much resignation and fortitude as I can. This of course being more rational will be more acceptable to my friends.

On his journeyings he had braved the rich curries and the wines of many a dinner table. He had dined with the Commander-in-Chief, Sir Alured Clarke, and had gone "riding in my *palanquin*" to Barrackpore, "where the General and his staff generally go every Friday and remain there till Monday following"—a custom as yet not much practised in Scotland. He had dined with Lord Mornington in Calcutta and attended one of his levees, at which "His Lordship spoke to me for some time and was very gracious indeed". He had visited a lady relative in romantic Kippengunge, four hundred miles up the Ganges, and breakfasted on an "elegant *budgerow*" with General Rawstone, while the General's band played music and a teeming staff ensured that the guest should be "elegantly accommodated with suitable apartments to dress and sleep in and most magnificently entertained at dinner, etc."

Lord Mornington gave him a confidential message to General Stuart. Sir Alured Clarke gave him two ensigncies for his sister's son, Hector, and old Ulva's son, Lachlan. And after that, dinner with Lord Clive and Generals Harris and Floyd in Madras and a visit to Trincomalee were mere passing incidents of travel in a journey which had been marred only by kidnapping of one of his two Cochin slave-boys, Hector, in Calcutta.

He came back to a militarily busy Bombay in which there were no less than five King's regiments, resumed his offices of Major of Brigade and Deputy Paymaster-General of the Forces, but his circumstances soon changed:

Macquarie to Charles Macquarie

In my last letter of the 1st of July I forgot to inform you that I had lately obtained a most honourable and highly respectable situation in *Governor Duncan's family*, on being appointed *his confidential Military Secretary*—which I had the honour of being on the 18th of April last, perfectly unsolicited and unasked on my part which of course rendered it the more grateful and flattering to my feelings: and it was offered in so handsome and friendly a manner by Mr. Duncan that I could not with any propriety decline accepting it and I am now living entirely in Mr. Duncan's family on the most friendly and confidential footing with him. —I must however, inform you that this appointment, honourable and flattering as it certainly is, *does not add one farthing to my income*—farther than saving me the immediate expence of house-keeping which—bye the bye—is of itself a very great consideration in this country.—The gentleman (Major Wilson) who was my predecessor, from his holding various other offices, was unable to discharge the duties of *Military Secretary* to Mr. Duncan's satisfaction, and was therefore obliged to resign it.—But being a married man and not rich—and also being a very old and particular friend of my own; I could not reconcile it to my feelings to be the cause of any diminution in his income . . . I made a positive stipulation with the Governor that my predecessor should continue to draw the pay and every allowance attached to it.[28]

He had taken the oath of secrecy in his new office in Surat, where the Company's oldest factory in India sweltered beside the river Tapti, in a nawaubate which had seemed to Lord Mornington to be ripe to have "a new model government and constitution" imposed upon it.[29]

To invest Surat with its freshly acquired blessings the Governor's suite had arrived in state. They were welcomed by the Nawaub's sons, his old Buxshy (a former Prime Minister) and "an immense *swary* of guards and attendants". They had trained themselves for the stern task ahead at many elegant entertainments among the factory's officials, while the Nawaub treated them to such samples of his opulent rule and goodwill that it seemed almost discourteous to contemplate measures against him.

He was seen, "a very fine, handsome-looking man about 44 years of age", very richly apparelled and with his great officers of state mounted on "large beautiful elephants most elegantly dressed and decorated", celebrating the feast of Bakr-Id, while an immense and enthusiastic retinue shouted in his rear, drawn along by a generous practice which could not but appeal to a true Scot: "He every now and then threw handfuls of small pieces of silver among the crowd."

It was a spectacle, however, which led to the melancholy reflection: "Alas! poor man, he yet little thinks of the fate that is hanging over him, or that he is about to very soon be stripped of all his power and consequence."

There was, indeed, some doubt whether the Nawaub would submit to the Company's will without unpleasant incidents. Against the chances of his resisting, it was thought necessary to provide by having the new Military Secretary ride out at daybreak to take "as near and accurate a view as possible of the Nawaub's Palace and also of all his other public buildings where he has guards", and to select a site for a sepoy cantonment outside the city and survey the ground for siege works. British diplomacy, however, triumphed. Though the Nawaub showed "infinite regret and reluctance" at the change, he was "prevailed on to relinquish his sovereignty and principal authority and control in and over the city of Surat; on condition of his receiving a pension from the Company, in lieu of all the taxes, tolls, and customs, heretofore collected by his people within the said city".

The Treaty was signed. The Governor was in high spirits at having achieved his purpose amicably, after the Nawaub had sworn that he would only yield his authority with his life. The monarch was placed on his puppet throne with pomp and splendour. A British judge was sworn in in the new Court of Adawlat, ere the Bombay *tappal* summoned Duncan home to Parel, a journey for Macquarie of one hundred and eighty-three miles and twelve days of intimacy with the Governor in a palanquin closed against the incessant rain.

The news of active hostilities with France, evidence of which was in the fact that Colonel Murray had been forced to evacuate Suez precipitately, was their spur to haste. By the time they reached the capital the Governor had become "my friend" in Macquarie's thoughts and correspondence, having offered him sanctuary in Government House with all that the move entailed in comfort and relief from expense.

V

On 18 September 1800 he sat for the first time as president of the convivial Sans Souci Club at the Grove and wore the uniform of his office.

On the same day, with some rejoicing, he occupied his new quarters and ceased to wear the black crape band which had been round his arm, in memory of Jane, for four years and two months—"the least respect I was bound to pay to her beloved memory".[30]

The poor girl's great black marble tombstone had stood, at first, sheltered from the inclement monsoon weather by a *cajan* building. But this had been removed, revealing a sepulchre "very elegant . . . by far the most so in the Burying Ground". He had unveiled it with much ceremony on Jane's birthday, 16 October: "It is in honour of it that I have had her tomb uncovered and displayed to public view.—Had Heaven spared her precious dear life—she would only be this day twenty-eight years of age! But alas! I was not doomed to be so happy."

He seems to have been almost happy now, despite this earlier gloom.

He showed his good humour by giving his *purvoe* a thousand rupees "as a reward for his great attention, zeal and fidelity, in the honest and faithful discharge of his trust and duty", and attended the wedding of the daughter of the faithful old man. And he did not forget those in Mull. He told his uncle that he had resolved to settle £30 a year on his mother and brother Donald for life:

> Lay your strictest injunctions and commands on my worthy dear good mother to abstain from all laborious work; and in future to attend *MORE* to her own ease, health and comfort than she has hitherto done. She ought to keep *at least ONE female servant* about her, and a man servant to attend to the business of the farm. . . . I also entreat you to recommend strongly to her to allow my brother Donald every comfort his forlorn and helpless situation requires, in regard to good diet and good clothing. This is a subject I naturally feel most warmly interested in, and I cannot therefore too strongly solicit your most earnest attention to it; lest as my mother herself gets old, my poor dear helpless brother may be neglected.[31]

E

VI

The year 1800 ended. The nineteenth century had entered in turmoil, giving no indication that it was quick with the embryo of a new sort of world, Macquarie was forty years old. He still held the brevet rank of major, and he told Mrs Morley that he would return to Britain when his rank became effective. There was eager talk in India of expeditions to Java and Mauritius. Admiral Blankett's squadron had sailed for the Red Sea with a detachment of the 86th Regiment. On 21 March 1801 Bombay and Trincomalee were full of red-coats. Ralph Abercromby and the Royal Highlanders were fighting the second battle of Aboukir Bay. The *Suffolk*, 74, lay in Bombay Harbour with a large fleet of transports for the "Secret Expedition". Colonel Arthur Wellesley, with his suite, was at Government House, "indefatigable in his exertions" to prepare the expedition which Macquarie declared that he himself "had known from the beginning" was destined for the Red Sea and Egypt, instead of the East Indies.[32]

But the arrival of the terrible David Baird to take command surprised them all—though the reason is a mystery, since the prospect had been known in Calcutta three months earlier.

Colonel Wellesley was "still to continue *Second in Command*" but he found the news "very unexpected", and of a nature to "affect [him] very sensibly indeed, he being much hurt at this supersession". Seconds-in-command always were anathema to The Peer.

Baird—in his moods of peace courteous and politic, like all really terrible and dangerous men—was, however, no less a thorn in the side of the future Duke of Wellington than Captain George Molle, whom he brought with him, was in that of Major Macquarie in a later and farther-flung phase of British colonial history.

At the moment roses were far more prominent in the life of Macquarie than thorns. For on the afternoon of Baird's arrival, as they all walked upon the veranda, the stormer of Tippoo's stronghold called him aside. To his "agreeable surprise" he asked him if he would go to Egypt as "head of his Staff as Depy. Adjt. General of his Army".[33]

Such an offer, "made in so very handsome and friendly a manner", was too tempting and too flattering to be rejected. And all his friends were soon rejoiced at the honour conferred upon him by so distinguished an officer as General Baird. Colonel Wellesley was not nearly so pleased at the turn of events. He ostensibly intended to "follow . . . himself with the last Division of transports not yet arrived from Ceylon". Macquarie, "from the Colonel's present bad and delicate state of health", was "rather doubtful of seeing our *Second in Command* at all in the Red Sea"; and this, the narrator added, they should all much regret, as he was "a most valuable and most excellent officer on actual service, and General Baird is particularly anxious that he should follow him".

Macquarie was, for once, a true prophet. Colonel Wellesley remained in Bombay while his harassed medical advisers restrained his military ardour and burned his towels with the nitric acid in which they bathed him. His politic brother, Henry, applied balm to his affronted soul. Yet, though "his anxiety to embark was with difficulty repressed by [Dr] Scott", he was not so preoccupied that he could not leave for history a crumb of comment on a new Deputy Adjutant-General who had spoiled the chances of a candidate of his own—Major Colman, of the Guards, whose company in the 77th Regiment Macquarie had bought with profits of his ingeniously designed usury in the happy days of Calicut:

Col. Arthur Wellesley to Lieutenant-Colonel Campbell

You must have heard that Colman was dismissed from his situation, and the General offered to make him Deputy Quartermaster-General. No man can decide upon the propriety of the feelings of another; Colman thought that the appointment of Macquarie was a preference against him, and that the situation of Deputy Quartermaster-General has in that manner become inferior to that which he was to lose; he therefore determined not to accept that which was offered to him. The General was very candid, and told him that Macquarie had been recommended as a man of business, and he wanted a person having that qualification. However, I doubt whether Macquarie will answer: he is an excellent man, but has bad health, and, I think, wants that decision in difficult cases which is the life of everything, although he has habits of business. Colman was improving fast; latterly I had made him do almost all the business, and he had got into a better habit than he had been in before; and if he had agreed with the General, which I almost doubt, he might have been more useful to him even than Macquarie.[34]

Later, he was not so definite in his own mind about the appointment:

Wellesley to Lieutenant-Colonel Robertson

Macquarie, who is gone with him, is a good man, but I think a little undecided. I may be mistaken, however, in my notion of his character, as I saw him during but a few days in office, and it was natural for him to be diffident and undecided at first.[35]

Baird had no fears. He appointed Macquarie "from a conviction that he was eminently qualified for the duties of that important department".[36] A lifelong friendship blossomed from the seed then sown, though it was nearly interrupted when the army reached the Red Sea. There it was discovered that the Horse Guards had appointed Lieutenant-Colonel Auchmuty by special commission to be Adjutant-General and Chief of Staff to the Indian Army without first advising its commander. It took all the latter's power of persuasion to deter Macquarie from at once returning to India, but eventually he gave way to the General's insistence that he should retain his position.[37]

VII

This was the first Indian Army to serve outside Asia.[38] It was landed on the burning shores of the Gulf of Suez at Cosseir, after they had called at Mocha and Jedda, where the Shereef of Mecca presented Major Macquarie with a shawl.

But Cosseir, he wrote, "was the poorest and most wretched miserable looking place I have ever seen in any part of the world". They were glad to leave it even for the "wild, dreary, arid desert" through which they marched one hundred and twenty miles to the green oasis of Kenné on the Nile—opposite the celebrated temple of Isis—where the grapes were refreshing but the dancing girls disgustingly lascivious.

It was a pleasant change from the desert and even from India, for food and fruit were abundant and cheap, and just as cheap along the banks of the Nile, down which they made a swift voyage of six hundred miles in nine days, pausing occasionally to admire classic wonders or to buy "good fat geese" at fourpence apiece, and eggs, 1200 for a Spanish dollar.

They reached their headquarters on the island of Rhoda in the Nile to find General Baird already there, at dinner with Lord Blaney of the 89th Regiment and a large company. They explored the "celebrated and ancient city of Grand Cairo" which appeared to be "altogether such an assemblage of grand and beautiful objects of Nature and Art", the visitor wrote, as I had never seen combined before", and in which delight followed delight, according to the sober Scottish taste.

Not for a Deputy Adjutant-General the dissipations of Egyptian bagnios. He preferred to descend into that "most extraordinary piece of human labour and art . . . Joseph's well", rather than into the wells of vice. The halls of dancing girls enthralled him less than the "Great Hall in the ancient Citadel", where Joseph (as he learned) saw his brethren when he came down to Egypt for corn; and he was much attracted by the Nilometer and even more by Pompey's Pillar, which he adjudged "truly the most magnificent and most beautiful object I have ever seen". "After staying for near an hour feasting our eyes with this elegant and most beautiful object, Colonel Abercromby and myself bent our steps homewards."

Even those "wonderful and stupendous monuments", the Sphinx and the Pyramids, could not oust Pompey's Pillar from his affections, though one of the pyramids ran in the race for favour with a clear start, since his brother, Charles, had climbed it.

VIII

The presence of Charles was the fact which crowned his satisfaction in being in Egypt. He had not seen Charles since the raw week in which he had left him, a youth, in Leith early in 1788. Now, here he was in Egypt, a stout captain, and if not in the completely prime condition in which Scots desire to see their relatives after long absences, nearly intact and almost as much a wonder as the Sphinx itself. For, on the fateful eighth of March at Aboukir, as he had urged on his Royal Highland Grenadier company, "a musquet ball had entered a little below his left eye and came out at the back of his neck". Thus, "poor dear, he had had—thank God—a most miraculous escape indeed ! ! !"

Already he was sufficiently recovered to have returned to the command of his company in John Moore's reserve, and to welcome the Indian visitor when the latter reached General Hutchinson's camp to learn—as in each of his other campaigns—that the war was almost over at his coming.

His brother found Charles sitting at sundown alone in his tent, still tangibly marked with the evidence that a French Trojan had fired at the wrong end of a Scottish Achilles.

The Indian brother opined that, after his having come "above 3,000 miles, and after a long separation of fourteen years", their meeting must be "allowed to have something of the appearance of romance and to have consequently produced in both of us a variety of interesting and uncommon emotions".

Indeed,

> To attempt to describe the scene that took place at this most happy and most unexpected meeting is impossible, and would convey but a very imperfect idea of the delightful transports of real joy and unfeigned felicity we mutually received and conveyed on this most happy occasion. Tho' words cannot describe it, hearts of sensibility and true affection can very readily conceive, what the feelings of two most affectionate most loving brothers must have been at such a meeting, in such a country, under circumstances of such recent danger *to him* and his *miraculous escape from death*; *my* having come hither so unexpectedly, over seas and deserts from so remote a quarter of the globe. . . .[39]

For days the untutored Egyptians were treated to the unusual spectacle of a lean Indian staff officer—his weight was eleven stone three pounds—and a slug-marked captain of the Black Watch, embracing each other in various stages of exaltation and sometimes of inebriety, or breakfasting with "my old American friend" John Moore or Hildebrandt Oakes, Moore's second-in-command, to talk over mutual adventures of American days and discuss the small matter of ensigncies for Mull infants.

Charles seemed to absorb the whole mind of his brother for a time—Charles leading his grenadiers to occupy Cleopatra's Redoubt in evacuated Alexandria; Charles approving of the regularity and neatness of the Indian Army's cantonments and of its officers' tents and especially of Lachlan's, which was "at least twice the size of those of the *General Officers* of the *Grand Army*".[40] There was only a bare mention of their elder brother, Donald, of whose death at fifty-one years they heard, and who was speeded into eternity with the encomium that "he had always enjoyed good health and had been a regular temperate man", and with the consolatory reflection that he was "now in a happier world" than that of Mull.

IX

The main body of the British Army sailed for home and Mediterranean stations, leaving the Indian Army brigaded with some of its detachments, under the Earl of Cavan and Macquarie as Deputy Adjutant-General to the whole force. Charles was off to Minorca with a present of £2000 to buy an estate, and a rattan cane. Lachlan was left behind consoled by a gift of a pair of pistols from his brother and "a fine large camel" from Colonel Dickson, of the Black Watch—a beast which he humorously named "the Laird of Kilbuckie", and which, within a year, was "no more".

In January 1802 his misfortunes smote him with their normal regularity.[41] The first blow was one from which he seemed to recover quickly—a horse kicked him in the thigh, but by his forty-first birthday he was once again in high spirits, chaffing Mrs Morley because the lovely Sarah Morley "could not wait any longer for him", but had married an Ogilvy of Angus; chiding the lady for having "*naughtily given me the slip*", and doing a little match-making between Mrs Morley herself and his friend, John Forbes.[42]

Promotion came to him again—on 11 February 1802 he found that he had been appointed as from 15 January 1801 to an effective majority in the 86th Regiment—then a Shropshire corps, but later handed to the Irish as the County Down Regiment.[43]

About him, while he vainly begged the Duke of York to make him a lieutenant-colonel, history slipped by. They celebrated a first anniversary of the Battle of Aboukir Bay, which inspired him to write an emotional letter of thanksgiving for Charles's survival, with a dinner held in a mosque, during which he presided at a table.[44] Turks killed mamelukes. The armies continued to drift away. It was a signal that the war was really over when Dr M'Grigor of the 88th Regiment was seen preparing mercury in large quantities for a military patient "—4 pills at night and 3 in the mornings—and to *rub in* besides twice in the day!" As mild measures had no influence on the sufferer's condition during seventeen days, more heroic expedients obviously were called for—a daily dose of nitric acid and a "chirurgical operation".

These specifics seem to have had effects which were almost mortal. The newly fledged major was one morning discovered unconscious with his bed full of blood—he had burst some blood vessel. If his servant, Stewart, had not found him in time he assuredly would have died.

He was nursed back to feeble health by three doctors, aided by a daily course of consolation administered by General Baird, a stimulus which had so good an effect that in May he was well enough to be borne by twenty *hamals* in a *doolie* to the ship *William*, on which he made an uneventful voyage to Bombay.[45]

July found him living once more at Government House, in command of the 86th Regiment, concerned with its routine, sicknesses and missing uniforms. The Acting Governor tried to send him to Madras to report on an affray in which an unlucky Persian ambassador was killed by two companies of sepoys. We find him securing the appointment of his relation, Lachlan, as aide-de-camp to the Governor by dint of representing him as a "steady, sober and good young man without friends or money". He was, also, playing chaperon to Louisa Wilkins, Jane's niece, who had come out to Bombay on his advice to seek her fortune as an Indian bride. He was noticed ordering for her from his old friend, Francis Wredé, of Mutton-cherry, "a couple of smart little slave girls, each about twelve years of age . . . the cheaper the better, as it was not my wish to go to a high price for them", to be dispatched "by the first good sea conveyance that offered".[46]

But his heart was no longer in Bombay.

X

On 6 August 1802, almost fourteen years to the day since his first landing in India, he told Duncan of his long-formed intention to return to Europe the following January. He was tired of India—"this vile country".[47] In Mull his poor Uncle Lochbuy, with his growing habit of devoting too much time to the hunting of the black cock and the hare, was fast losing his "vast estates", of which ten thousand acres already had been transferred to Macquarie himself while he was still in Egypt. The purchase price was £10,060, guaranteed by John Forbes and officers at home who had snatched it for him from the impending clutches of the Campbells and other avaricious mortgagees.[48]

Verily, there had been corn in Egypt, for his fortune which at the end of 1796 had consisted only of the £7000 in London with Francis and Gosling was now more than £20,000. Of this he had acquired £10,000 in little more than two years.

Thought of his lands around Callachilly, Gruline, and Bentella seemed to fill him with yearning; and particularly those of Callachilly, "on account of the large river passing through it, and being immediately on the beautiful Sound of Mull".

The queer fellow made it clear that he was chafing with eagerness to take over his new patrimony for the benefit of his heirs. For heirs it seemed, there were still to be, and, surprisingly, their intended production was his "principal motive in wishing to become a landed proprietor in my own native country".

He was granted leave on the ground that urgent family business called for his attention in England.

He wrote in his journal:

> Dec. 30 (1802). *Thursday!* I visited for the last time the sacred and venerated tomb of my late angelic and beloved wife, and paid her adored memory the tribute of my tears:—Peace be to her angelic soul in Heaven!—This mournful farewell brought all my former happiness fresh to my remembrance.[49]

Lastly, he made his will; then sailed at length for London in the *Sir Edward Hughes* on 6 January 1803, not comforted even by the fact that Governor Duncan gave a farewell dinner in his honour and promised that he would not fail to bring his services to the notice of the Court of Directors in his Public Letter, in the most favourable terms.

The wretched man "felt extremely low and melancholy" as he looked back on Bombay where he had spent "by far the happiest period of my whole life" but where "all that constituted that happiness lies mouldering dust".[50]

CHAPTER XI

The Laird of Jarvisfield

I

THE *Sir Edward Hughes* sailed southward with her twenty-eight passengers
—Carnac ladies, the new-made widow of an officer with her little children,
invalided soldiers, yellowed East India Company clerks, and Major Lachlan
Macquarie, commanding officer of the 86th Regiment of the Line.[1]

It was fifteen years since he had journeyed from England. Then, his
fare had cost the Company £70. Now, he was going home, forty-two
years old, in luxurious quarters for which he had paid the captain £400.

The atmosphere of his travel was sober and responsible. The very ports
at which they touched seemed to float in a different dimension from that
in which he had encountered them on his outward voyage in 1788.

At Cape Town, they saw Sir Roger Curtis's British Squadron weigh
anchor as a signal that Cape Colony was once more Dutch territory.
There all was hospitality on the highest social plane, with nothing to mar
the stranger's intercourse with the inhabitants save the extortion of the
laundryman who charged him £4 8s. to do his washing—"sixpence for
every piece from handkerchiefs". At Constantia, where, fifteen years before,
he had merely sipped the local vintage, he bought his wine with lavish
gestures—a red Pontac from a Mauritius grape, "of a most luscious rich
quality", a white wine of "remarkable fine flavour and quality"—60
gallons for £52 sterling.

At St Helena he differed from a later visitor about "The Briars". "A
most beautiful and romantic place", he pronounced it, with "a very elegant
house, a beautiful prospect, an excellent garden and fine shrubery [*sic*],
laid out with great taste". Sir Arthur Wellesley might write of Governor
Patton, who inhabited this demesne, that he was "a good man, but a quiz,
of a description that must have been extinct for nearly two centuries.
I never saw anything like his wig and coat."[2] To Major Macquarie he was
the head of "an amiable agreeable family", and his daughter Sally, recently
married to Major Torrens, and soon to be the mother of one of the first of
Wellingtonian godsons, "a very well educated, accomplished and agreeable
young woman; and whom I think will prove a great acquisition to the
society of Bombay".

But she and St Helena were forgotten at the sight of wild spume beating
on The Lizard on a May day, and of the pilot-boat, *Stag of Dover*, tossed
about in the Channel on the way to bring them the news that there was
"a great probability of Britain being at war again immediately with France."

It had been "a prosperous and pleasant short voyage of 4 *kalender months*", during which only five of their passengers had died. He had won a bet on the length of it from Major Heath; and his landing was not less satisfactory than his journey.

The Customs man at Brighton "behaved most civilly and obligingly in passing *all our baggage* without any noise or trouble", for the reward of a ten-guinea tip.

It was 7 May 1803, and, as the visitor's postchaise bowled up the road to London through Cuckfield, Crawley, Sutton, Reigate and the County of Surrey, Nature was in her springtime green, and the flowers and the bees were in the hedgerows. London was at its gayest when he arrived, considerately bringing with him the widow Gray and her little brood; but the whole town was crowded "on account of the Parliament being still sitting", and it was only after he had driven about for three hours that he found lodgings in Jacquiere's Hotel in Leicester Square, not far from where his brother, Charles, sojourned at Old Slaughter's Coffee House in St Martin's Lane.

The life of London seemed all so heady and fashionable that he felt somewhat out of his element and was constrained to send a distress signal to Mrs Morley:

> You know what an *awkward, rusticated Jungle-Wallah* I must appear at first amongst your friends;— You must therefore prepare them for beholding a very uncouth and unpolished Indian.— After our first interview, I must place myself *entirely under your direction* to be a little *humanized* and *modernized* . . . I shall prove at least a willing and obedient pupil—tho' I fear a very dull and stupid one.[3]

Outwardly, however, he maintained the opulent pose of the Indian "nabob":

Macquarie to Lochbuy

> I hope you will be able to make room in your *wine-vault* in Moy-Castle for a pipe of *excellent fine, old, Madeira* that I have brought home for you and my aunt all the way from India.— You will be able to form some judgment of the quality of it, when I tell you that this pipe of Madeira will have cost me one hundred and thirty pounds sterling by the time I have it cleared out from the Custom House in London—I beg you will communicate the news of my safe arrival in England as soon as possible to my dear good mother with my most affectionate and most dutiful remembrance:— I hope in God she is alive and well![4]

II

He had intended to make his way at once to Mull, but Europe was in an uproar, and trained field officers as scarce as fine gold. The Horse Guards at once put its clutches upon him. It could not trust him as far away from Whitehall as Scotland. The most it would allow him to do when he had been in London a month or so was to palliate the exhaustion caused by his first unaccustomed plunge into the life of the capital by making an excursion to Cheltenham and Gloucester. There he found the cathedral to be a "most noble elegant structure", distinguished by the presence within its walls of "a very handsome monument to the former wife of the late Mr. Morley".

And his excitement at the sight of the "New Gaol, the Berkley Canal, etc., etc." vied with that which rose up within him as he contemplated the tomb of Catherine Parr, last wife of Henry VIII, who, he recollected, had "lived and died at Sudley Castle after her divorce from that Prince".[5]

Meanwhile, his Commander-in-Chief had been pondering his future. The result was the conclusion that the obvious task for a yellowed Indian officer, detached from Europe for nearly sixteen years, would be to "enquire into and report upon the present state of the troops" of Britain's ancient and original allies, the Portuguese. But the Duke's proposal that he should be brigaded with Lieutenant-Colonel Stuart and Major Lowe to form a mission composed of *"experienced officers"* for this purpose, was defeated with a single salvo of protest.[6]

He could not, the returned jungle wallah wrote, reconcile it at all to his own feelings to accept "a situation of so much national and political importance, to which I am conscious I am totally inadequate on account of my being entirely unacquainted with the Portuguese and all the other foreign Continental European Languages".

To this there could be no valid answer, and after an attempt to exile him to Guernsey in command of a battalion of recuperating Indian veterans[7] —a fate from which the arrival of his friend Dunlop rescued him—his royal superior decided that the proper post for him was that of Assistant Adjutant-General on the staff of the London District, which was under the command of Lord Harrington, a descendant of Charles II and Barbara Villiers, "blessed with a lovely charming family of seven sons and three daughters".[8]

"A very honourable but very troublesome and laborious situation", its incumbent pronounced his new office; and so urgently in need of an occupant that he again was refused a month's leave to go to Scotland before entering upon his warlike duties. These largely consisted in break-o'-day trottings round Blackheath and Hyde Park, as reviewing Royalty romped down unflinching lines of crimped patriots, and somewhat swifter subsequent canterings towards the points at which lavish collations had been prepared to refresh the staff after these loyal and arduous exercises.

He fitted easily into the new atmosphere. He had no family ties to hamper his comings and goings. He had sufficient money to enjoy the fashionably frugal life of the twilight years of Farmer George's London. And he had enough acquaintances — the Jarvis family, the Earl of Breadalbane, and all his returned Indian friends—to assure him a place in the gay round of the season.

His journal for the years 1803 and 1804 reads like a record of the social calendar. To dance at the Lord Mayor's Ball with a pretty girl; to have his name mentioned by the Government of Bombay "in a very handsome and flattering manner"; to dine with the Company's Court of Directors, with the Earl of Breadalbane and with that budding paladin of Cintra, General Harry Burrard, or with Lord Harrington and the Prince of Wales; to be carried to Court by his old, irascible commander, Colonel Marsh, and to take part in the birth throes of a "regular monthly Staff Club at the

Thatched House"—such occasions became commonplaces in the life of Lachlan Macquarie, now a lieutenant-colonel on the staff, but not in his regiment, with his promotion dated back to 7 November 1801.

He was painted—very debonair—by Opie. He rode on a black charger —fortunately, in view of his equestrian limits, "warranted sound and perfectly free of vice"—which had cost him eighty guineas. He was lost at dawn in the fog at a parade in Hyde Park. He attended a Queen's levee— "a grand and most pleasing spectacle of the finest women in the world". He viewed the ballet, *Achilles et Deidamia*, and saw Mrs Siddons and Kemble act in *The Tragedy of Pizarro*. Grassini warbled to him in her role in *La vergine del sole*—in exquisite derision of the future.

He gazed with attention on the "grand exhibition of paintings and pictures at Somerset House" and on the Panorama of Paris, and, with something like rapture, upon the skeleton of the mammoth.

Lord Castlereagh called him to Cleveland Row to discuss the affairs of India—about which His Lordship seemed "already very well informed". The Chairman of the East India Company, Mr Bosanquet, had had a long conference with him. Lord Teignmouth, Marquis Cornwallis, Sir Alured Clarke, Sir Walter Farquhar all received him with attention. The Duke of York sent for him and discussed with him at length his regiment and his service.

What wonder that there was a growing air of assurance about him and that he sloughed off very quickly the rough hide of the jungle wallah, revealing underneath the smooth and polished carapace of the habituated military courtier whose regular orbit and diversions were those of the world of Society? He could circulate as a matter of right with the rest of the great ones to hear the King—"sitting on his Throne in the Great State Presence Room"—receive the Address in Reply on the war with France. He could loiter at will in the House of Commons galleries, so instructed and amused by the oratory of the "great Mr. Pitt and Mr. Fox" on the Volunteer Bill that he stayed till two o'clock in the morning and heard the debate closed by a startlingly familiar apparition from his Bombay days—no less than "Colonel Craufurd".

In his benefactions[9] he assumed the air to be expected of one who has paid £215 in duty on his imported possessions, and who has been presented to the Queen by the Earl of Morton, the Lord in Waiting. To him it was quite natural to distribute to people whose names, while he was in India, were known to him only as faint echoes from a greater world, lavish little gifts scented with the odours of the East, which he insisted that he had brought home "on purpose" for each recipient—a cornelian necklace and earrings, "being of rare quality from Cambay in the East Indies", for Mrs Harry Calvert, the Adjutant-General's wife; a "set of white Cambay cornelians" for the Countess of Breadalbane; rattan canes for the Duke of York and Lord Harrington; an ivory and sandalwood inlaid box for the Duchess of York, "as a humble testimony of my very high respect and great veneration for her high and amiable character"; and even a gift for Majesty. He hoped that her Majesty the Queen will be graciously pleased to forgive his presumption in offering for Her Majesty's Royal and benignant acceptance the accompanying ivory and sandal-wood inlaid work-box, being the manufacture of Bombay, in the East Indies, from whence he lately brought it for the express purpose of being thus presented to Her Majesty as a humble testimony of his high veneration and most respectful attachment for Her Royal Sacred Person, and for her innumerable, great, and exalted virtues.[10]

Such was his confidence in himself and his station that he even could show a courtly blandness towards the newer blights of civilization, such as that which reared its ugly head in Half Moon Street at the residence of "Charles Reeve, Esq., Collector of the Income Tax":

Macquarie to Charles Reeve

Being at a loss how to fill up the enclosed printed paper received by me on the 30th ultimo, I take the liberty of returning it to you, and of requesting that you will be so obliging as to take the trouble of filling it up yourself in the proper manner from the following statement of my property—*vizt.*—[11]

There followed a slightly mendacious catalogue of his wealth in which he assigned £3000 of his stock as belonging to his brother, Charles, and £1000 as the property of his servant, Stewart.

III

All the time his thoughts were upon Mull, but it seemed to grow more distant. It was a full year before he could obtain leave to go thither, though his own health was not good and three days before Christmas 1803, Doctor Everard Home, of Sackville Street, and his assistant, Doctor Nicholson, had been compelled to perform upon him an operation "of a very delicate nature" at a cost of twelve guineas.[12]

England's fears were passing into the phase in which, he reported, "the Government are now *in daily expectation* of Bonaparte's paying his long threatened visit".

Even though the era of *Rejected Addresses* had not yet dawned, the brooding figure on the Boulogne cliffs seemed to pervade every corner of British life in which something went wrong. It would have been as easy to find an answer then, as nine years later, to such queries as:

> Who, while the British Squadron lay off Cork
> (God bless the Regent and the Duke of York!)
> With a foul earthquake ravaged the Caraccas,
> And raised the price of dry goods and tobaccos?
> Who makes the quartern loaf and Luddites rise?
> Who fills the butchers' shops with large blue flies?
> Who thought in flames St James's Court to pinch?
> Who burnt the wardrobe of poor Lady Finch?

Naturally, in all the circumstances, the Government was prepared to burn up the last fevered relic of the Indian wars to assure that "Gallia's stern despot shall in vain advance from Paris the Metropolis of France".

But hearts at the Horse Guards softened as June came. There was no attack across the Channel, but a battalion of Maclean medicos, doctoring Lochbuy in his castle at Moy, raised the alarm of his absent nephew by asking him to secure from a London specialist the advice which he sent by express at once to Dr Alan Maclean, along with a flexible gum catheter.[13]

Even a royal duke could not gainsay pleadings for leave made upon such portents. His Royal Highness was pleased to observe that it "was but reasonable after absence of near 17 years".

In June 1804, a year and a month after his return from India, Macquarie was bound upon a four-day journey to Edinburgh in a roomy, clean postchaise hired by the month, carrying with him his sister-in-law, Mrs Scott, and Miss Carnegie, sister of Sir David Carnegie of Southesk. And in Edinburgh, he learned from his relative John Campbell of Airds, as he baited at Dumbreck's Hotel in the New Town, that he had come only just in time. Poor Lochbuy was beyond recovery and his two boys had left their school in Musselburgh under the care of Miss Elizabeth Campbell, on their way to see their father for the last time.[14]

The two kinsmen followed without haste. Airds had business in Edinburgh which delayed him for two days. Then they were off to Mull in Macquarie's postchaise by a route known to every modern tourist to the Western Highlands.

They slept one night at the Luib House in Glen Dochart; the next they passed over the Black Mount, and were through Glencoe at Ballachuilish. On the third, they were at Airds House in Appin, inspecting its new improvements. After five days of travel they sailed from Lochspelve Head, and in the evening were holding a rational conversation with the poor old Chieftain of Lochbuy. Supported by his two sons and seven daughters, he was sinking fast, but hanging to life with true Scottish tenacity.[15]

Each day the ancient Ulva, Maclean of Coll, Airds, and Macquarie sat by his bedside in turn, holding the old man's hands. After Charles Macquarie, long awaited, had arrived from Ireland, he passed into the shadows at a quarter before three o'clock on the misty midsummer morning of 5 July 1804.

At once Macquarie rode away with old Ulva to break the news to his mother, the dead chieftain's sister. In his first sight of her since December 1787 he came upon her unexpectedly, and in a reunion which it was "more easy to conceive than express", he seems to have spent a resourceful evening allaying her tempestuous Gaelic sorrow, with the help of his sister Betty, "a most amiable affectionate creature as ever lived", and giving "a brief sketch" of his own adventures.[16]

Five days later all Lochbuy's friends from Mull, from Lorne, from Morven, and all the common tenantry of the estates of Lochbuy, gathered at the ancient family seat of Moy. They laid the last Maclaine of the old tradition "by his own particular desire . . . in the family burying place of *Capelle-Fubier* at Laggan, under the great Center Layer or Tomb-stone, within the chapel".[17]

The chieftain's eldest son, Murdoch, still a schoolboy, and Macquarie walked as chief mourners at the head of the coffin; his younger son, John, and Charles Macquarie at the foot of it. The pall-bearers were ancient lairds. Three hundred tenantry followed their master to his grave.

For the commoners an abundance of meat and drink was laid out in a field near the Castle, in the true old Highland style. Within the great dining-room of Moy Castle itself, the relatives and gentry sat down to loaded tables presided over by old Ulva and other near relations of the dead chieftain.

The influence of Lochbuy had permeated the weave of Macquarie's life since his boyhood; but if he felt severe grief at the old man's passing, there was no outward sign of it. He remained a few days at Lochbuy, until he felt that he could leave his aunt with "safety and propriety". Then he went off upon his own special business.

IV

He first of all hastened, at an appropriate period, to carry out some duties which eight years ago he had pledged himself that he would one day perform.

The anniversary of Jane's death fell almost immediately after that of Lochbuy. And though, for once, he did not record the shedding of a single tear, she was far from forgotten. Upon that day he and his brother set out on a "pleasant and romantic ride" over their recently acquired estates— Charles's at Pennygown; his own surrounding Callachilly, where they put up their horses at the inn and bespoke dinner for a large number of friends.

He and Charles and their new factor, one M'Tavish, walked over the principal parts of the farms at Callachilly and Kilbeg, which included the Great Moss and Crofts of Salen, thus taking possession of his estate, which, he said, he intended at this day's meeting to "name and christen JARVISFIELD, out of grateful respect and sincere affection for the beloved and revered memory of my late angelic excellent wife and in due conformity *with my solemn vow of date* 31 st July, 1796".[18]

At six o'clock on that evening nineteen people sat down to dinner at the Callachilly Inn, all Maclaines, Macquaries, Campbells, and Mackinnons. Some were lairds, some were ancient family pensioners, some were drovers and small farmers; but all did justice to the repast and good liquor, and old Ulva, in spite of his years, was not behind the rest.[19]

The host solemnly explained to them that he now took the opportunity in their presence of consecrating his property to the memory of his Jane—"it being with the fortune she was so generous as to bequeath me on her ever-to-be-lamented death—that I was enabled to purchase the estate in question".

Then he proposed "that a *bumper* toast should be drank standing to the memory of my late beloved wife—and success to the estate of Jarvisfield! —which was accordingly done". They drank another bumper to his brother's new estate of Glenforsa and success to his "title of Glenforsa"—given standing with *"three times three"* by all present. The host recorded that the company "sat till a late hour at table and spent a very jovial, sociable, and pleasant evening, not having broke up till after 12 o'clock at night".

All that remained for him to do to become a laird was to have himself registered as a freeholder in Edinburgh, whence his agent, John Campbell, writer to the signet, presently assured him that he should be recognized under the title of "Jarvisfield".[20] And accordingly, he arranged for publication of a paragraph in three Edinburgh papers, "as an article of intelligence in order that our friends may know the names we have given to our respective estates".

His only regret was that the Callachilly farm, on which he wished to "build his mansion and make his family seat" was under lease for nineteen years to an adhesive clansman, Dr Donald Maclaine, who was unmoved by his landlord's earnest pleas for the surrender of the property.

To that particular Maclaine, as to most others, a lease was a lease. The pair bargained through agents. They met at Colin Campbell's house at Auchnacruish "with some friends to consult upon the terms under which the lease might be surrendered".[21]

But "after many *warm professions*, and a variety of proposals, nothing could be agreed upon". Macquarie offered five hundred pounds but without avail. In the end he had no more satisfaction than that gained through his ultimate tart postscript which closed a rapidly heating exchange of correspondence: "As postage of *double letters* come very high, I'll thank you to write your letter *on one sheet only without an additional cover.*"[22]

He was compelled to fall back on his second choice of a home-site, Gruline, which lay towards the south of the little valley which cuts clear across the narrow centre of Mull, north from Loch-na-Keale. There, past Salen Moss and Torosay, the Jarvisfield lands stretched to the Sound.

It was not so bad a selection. Hard by Gruline a fine fishing stream found its way into the lovely freshwater Loch Ba. Inchkenneth was scarcely more than a stone's throw away. Behind the site which he had chosen were thriving enclosed woods. Ben More towered above the scene to the south.

The surrounding countryside was studded with the farms, the houses, the villages and burial grounds of a score of the cadet families of Macleans, Campbells, Mackinnons, and Macquaries. No part of the British Isles left its mark more clearly on the maps of the British Dominions than the land and sea within thirty miles of Ben More. From inside this magic circle came the original names of two capitals, Calgary in Canada and Duntroon (the site of Canberra) in Australia, along with those of Airds, Appin, Ardmore, Aros, Glengorm, Glenmore, Glenforsa, Inchcolm, Inchkenneth, Dunolly, Knock, Laggan, Lorne, Ormaig, Ulva, Morven, Barcaldine, Kilmore, Lochnell, Lismore, and a hundred others which have sprung up anew in the farthest corners of the earth.

Many of those names Macquarie himself placed upon his foundations in the southern wilds and his connection with them is well remembered by Antipodeans.

In Mull, the population of which has dwindled until in the twentieth century it is less than that of the Lochbuy Estates alone in the eighteenth century, there is still a memorial to his "intention to drain and improve the Great Moss of Salen, and to build a neat village there for crofters and a certain number of useful tradesmen, together with a new good inn, a smithy and a shop for merchandise".

Salen is the only hamlet in Mull which has grown since Macquarie's time. The first settlement which he founded in his fruitful life of foundations, it still survives in its modest way with its inn and its smithy and its other small amenities which he planned.

V

Summer drew towards its close as his leave began to run out. There were a few idle days at Lochbuy, visits to Ulva where a usurping MacDonald had replaced the ancient owners of the isle, and finally a breathless tour of the clans far afield, four hundred and fourteen miles on horseback, not halting for a whole day anywhere save at Lindertis House, near Glamis in Angus, the seat of Captain William Ogilvy, R.N., who was there married to the lovely Sarah Morley.[23]

Then to Oskamull to say farewell to his mother, who seems to have played a singularly small part in his adventures in the Isles, though now, as he left her, he was all zeal to see that the old lady's situation at Oskamull became "more comfortable as well as more respectable", since he judged that she must be nearly eighty years of age. He had improvements and additions to her farmhouse carried out and he instructed the widowed Mrs Maclaine Lochbuy to advance her whatever money she should need and to supply her with wines and groceries necessary for her use—"which last Mrs. Maclaine has very kindly undertaken to commission along with her own family stores from the low country annually".

Before he left Oskamull he promised that when the war with France was over he would certainly come to live permanently in Mull and build a good house there.

At length, with scarcely a backward glance, he was off to London in a series of stages, each marked by some fresh hospitality. First, he was dining with the Duke of Argyll—a "good old Duke" who "eat and drank heartily" at half past six in the evening and who was "very sociable and attentive to everyone" as he sat, with a daughter on either hand, and listened to Mr Sheridan, junior, singing "two or three most excellent songs". Next, he renewed acquaintance with Sir Robert Abercromby at Airthrie, four miles from Stirling, and almost at once was discovered dining with Lord Moira and his amiable young wife in Edinburgh after a well-fed journey, in which his companion had been his aunt's sister, Miss Elizabeth Campbell of Airds, who was taking his two wards, Murdoch Maclaine, Laird of Lochbuy and the latter's younger brother, John, to Mr Taylor's school at Musselburgh.

Late in September he was once more in the centre of the gay whirl of London, dining at Lord Harrington's house where, he recorded, the Prince of Wales sat at table till a very late hour and "was pleased to address a good deal of his discourse to me, and did me the honour to ask me several questions respecting Mull and those parts of the Highlands through which I had lately travelled".

But he was not quite the same man as had gone to Scotland. He was more thoughtful. He felt the weight of his lairdship and his guardianships. Before long he was giving evidence, especially, that he did not intend to take his duties to Lochbuy's brood lightly:

Macquarie to Murdoch Maclaine, 19th Laird of Lochbuy

. . . It gives me very sincere concern, my dear Murdoch, to hear from very good authority, that, *you* in particular have been very negligent, careless and inattentive to your studies, since you returned to Musselborough. What this can be owing to I cannot conceive—as—surely you are old enough to know that it is very wrong to be thus idle and careless; and that nothing is more disgraceful and shameful *to a gentleman*, than to be a bad scholar when a boy—and consequently ignorant and illiterate when grown up as a man.— . . . I must therefore call upon you peremptorily to pay in future the strictest attention to your education and to the instruction you receive from your Master Mr. Taylor and his ushers or assistants;—assuring you, that, if I ever hear any more complaints of this kind, I shall think it my duty—as *your near relation and guardian* to desire Mr. Taylor to *punish you most severely whenever you are careless,* or refuse to apply properly and closely to your several studies.[24]

Moreover, he proceeded with greater vigour and tenacity than ever with his constant efforts to use the army to better the condition of his relatives, even extending his blessing and assistance to his chieftain, old Ulva, whom he represented to the Horse Guards as "wonderfully stout and active" at eighty-two—he was actually eighty-nine—but "too old for any active employment".[25] His tender solicitude for the ancient lieutenant, who had served a year or two in quiet American towns twenty-five years before and had been drawing half-pay ever since, should surely have won the sympathy of some royal heart. But the measures which he suggested to rescue the veteran from the poverty to which he had been brought by his "merciless creditors" evoked no response. The Royal Duke who was the dispenser of such favours was not attracted by the ingenious suggestion that he should place the old man "*upon full pay* in one of the Royal Veteran Battalions, and obtain for him the King's leave to remain always absent". And His Royal Highness was even less impressed with the outcome of some other applications by the new Mull laird which had been long since granted.

VI

At the end of 1798, on the verge of the campaign of Seringapatam, the jungle wallah (so he had informed Mrs Maclaine Lochbuy) had written to his friend Captain John Abercromby, then commanding the 53rd Regiment, entreating him if possible—before the end of the war—to "procure an ensigncy for my Cousin John", without saying anything about his age. He meditated that if the young candidate, who was Lochbuy's second son, were commissioned, he must "immediately *exchange upon half pay*". This was indeed a highly necessary precaution; for although he thought the matter "could be settled and arranged very easily", John was a mere five years old.[26]

Now, in 1803, when John was ten years old,[27] he was no longer an ensign. He had been promoted to be a lieutenant, along with his coeval, "Charles's *young hero* Hector".[28] And both of them were drawing the half-pay of their ranks while imbibing such education as was possible at the seminary of Mr Taylor in Musselburgh.

It was at this stage that the royal Commander-in-Chief called the pair up for service on the Reserve. It placed their sponsor in something of a dilemma. So far from being fit to lead a company, Lieutenant John Maclaine could not even be trusted to lead himself home to Mull when his father lay dying and went thither shepherded by Miss Elizabeth Campbell in the role of nursemaid. Hector Macquarie was delicate into the bargain. Both would undoubtedly have been *de trop* even upon an Indian battlefield and infinitely more so on one upon which there were Frenchmen. Even their sponsor admitted that it would be impossible for them to appear in the flesh at barracks as they were "still much too young to join any corps".[29]

At first, however, he seemed equal to dealing with the awkward predicament. He merely informed the Horse Guards that, about six months ago, the youthful pair had left for the West Indies, "with a view to settle in that country as planters".[30] He pleaded that "it would be attended with great loss and inconvenience to their private affairs to be obliged to return to Europe and join any regiment at this particular juncture". He hoped earnestly that "His Royal Highness the Commander-in-Chief will be graciously pleased to dispense with their services for the present".

His Royal Highness was graciously pleased to do nothing of the kind. The royal nose seemed to have smelled a rat, and the royal will was not weakened even by the representation that both the gallant fellows were "the sons of old officers in the Service". The Duke followed the scent he had struck like a dachshund after a badger. The *"true facts"* came to light. The unhappy warrior who had been responsible for the tarradiddles which had secured the pair their commissions was compelled to acknowledge that they were in reality at school in Scotland.

He had the effrontery even after this revelation to write that it would materially injure and retard the education of Lieutenants Macquarie and Maclaine to be obliged to join at present such corps as His Royal Highness might be pleased to appoint them to on full pay, as it was the earnest desire of their friends to have them properly educated for some time longer at school.[31] The Duke showed himself deaf to such arguments. His correspondent then pleaded, on behalf of the parents, that since the boys could not be allowed to remain on half-pay he would be graciously pleased to allow them to realize the money they paid for their lieutenancies. He wrote that it was "all the patrimony they had", and it "must consequently prove ruinous to their future prospects in life in the event of their being superseded".[32]

It was of no avail. The pleas were being addressed to a duke from whom sympathy might have been expected, since he himself had been appointed a bishop—at a modest stipend of £50,000 a year—at the age of six months. But he now lived his life in the midstream of a roaring current of appeals from deceitful officers. They pursued him through the day. And when he realized the ambition of his evenings ("O my angel . . . two whole nights before I shall clasp my darling in my arms!")[33] Mrs Clark pinned more of them upon his bed curtains.

Besides being adamant, he became annoyed. He gave Macquarie cause to be "exceedingly sorry that he had made a request which should have caused any surprise or displeasure in the mind of His Royal Highness or caused him to think that I have done anything improper or inconsistent with the rules of the Service":

> *Macquarie to Colonel W. H. Clinton, the Duke of York's Secretary*
>
> I should not have taken the liberty of thus trespassing on your time, with any reply to your last letter were it not for the concluding paragraph of it which has given me a great deal of pain; as, you therein state *"that, in the event of Lieutenants Macquarie and Maclaine not joining the Regiments they may be appointed to, His Royal Highness cannot but consider the whole of the statement concerning them as a misrepresentation."*
>
> I am beyond measure grieved to find that His Royal Highness should entertain so very unfavourable an opinion of me as to suppose me capable of such conduct; and I must therefore entreat, sir, that you will do me the favour to assure His Royal Highness that, I *have made no misrepresentation* . . . that I am incapable of such conduct, and that I indulge a fond hope His Royal Highness will not entertain sentiments so prejudicial to my character.[34]

His Royal Highness did entertain such sentiments. He cast the two young Mull heroes forth from the British Army. He turned a deaf ear to their supporter's plea that he himself was but an agent for parents so remote that they had no access to the royal ear—perhaps he knew that the father of one of them, Charles Macquarie, was in London while the flurry was going on. And though Macquarie himself in the end bested his Commander-in-Chief and brought both his nephews back into the forces to be his aides-de-camp in Australia, it availed him little in the meantime.

The Duke in time recovered from his resentment, though for long he treated the jungle wallah with a distant air. He received his application for a transfer to the Guards in a manner which made the applicant greatly fear that he had "injured himself in his opinion by my illtimed precipitancy—a circumstance which I shall ever deeply deplore".[35]

All the pleadings of his friends, including those of Lord Harrington, could not deter the Duke from a conviction that as Major Torrens, the acting-commandant, was ill, the luckless Scot must return to India and rejoin the 86th Regiment with which there were no effective field officers.[36]

The only concession which Macquarie could gain was an assurance from the Duke that he might "make his mind easy" about the anomaly that though he was "a lieutenant-colonel in the army, he was only an *effective major* in the 86th Regiment after 28 years in the King's Service", and that "he would avail himself of the first opportunity of promoting me".[37]

However, the Duke proved to be not so hard of heart as his conduct at first seemed to indicate. One might almost suspect him of having dealt with the culprit under the influence of a grim sense of humour. Until a last interview, as the sorrowful officer was about to leave for India, "he never gave *anything like a positive* promise" of advancement; but his final reply to his victim's supplication regarding his rank sounded "as it if might be considered as such".[38]

Promotion would inevitably have meant immediate exchange from the 86th Regiment in India into another regiment at home, and the Duke was determined that the sinner should suffer at least temporary exile.

He waited until Macquarie was in Bombay, and then gave him effective advancement to command the 73rd Regiment, which had already returned to England, and which its new commander could not join for some time, firstly because he could not leave the 86th Regiment, since it was on active service against the Holkar, and secondly because he was compelled to wait till the official notification of the change reached India.

It would be wrong to imagine, however, that his royal senior's displeasure caused more than a passing cloud in the sky of Lieutenant-Colonel Macquarie, or that he was in any way abashed, or that his will to ask favours was inhibited by what had happened.

He even threw out, at a venture, an intriguing suggestion that his brother Charles might succeed him as Assistant Adjutant-General to the London district. But the Horse Guards greeted the proposal with a haughty silence.

VII

The time for him to return to India was fast approaching. The demands of society in the last months were unceasing. The Earl of Breadalbane invited him to an elegant entertainment at which the Duke of Sussex, the Earl of Strathmore, Lord Montgomery, Sir Sidney Smith, Macleod of Macleod and others were present.[39] He attended a Highland Society dinner in full staff uniform, acting as one of the managers and presiding at the table which the Duke of Sussex graced in full Highland costume—a "most respectable meeting"; but, sitting up till midnight, next day he found he "must stay at home to eat chicken broth, owing to my yesterday's debauch".[40]

At last he tore himself from Britain after he had paid Captain Landon £264 for a passage in the *City of London* for himself and his faithful Cochin slave-boy, George, who had seen many wonders and heard many strange accents and had even acquired a sound Scotch education since the quiet days when he had been well washed by Jane's orders in the lines of Calicut.

His servant, Stewart, remaining in Britain, wept, poor fellow, at saying good-bye.

The postchaise stopped at the door to take him and a young Rivett-Carnac away. The roads to Portsmouth, where they found his old Bombay friend, Oakes, installed as Lieutenant-Governor, were so crowded that they travelled part of the way in a fishcart. The Admiral and the men-o'-war escorting the India ships nearly led them off without him.

But once he was aboard the *City of London* Captain Landon gave him the whole larboard half of the round-house for his cabin, because he was entitled to it "not only on account of my superior rank, but also on account of my having paid him a higher sum for my passage than anyone else on board of his ship".[41]

On 25 April 1805 Admiral Tonbridge hoisted his flag over the convoy. A vast expanse of sail, the *Blenheim* seventy-four leading twenty-two Indiamen with the 53rd, 56th, and 67th Regiments on board, set out from Yarmouth to brave the ocean and the French. Villeneuve was out, the Malta convoy on its way, and Nelson was preparing for the first phase of the long chase which would end at Trafalgar. There was promise of an eventful voyage; but no aggression marred its smoothness.

They called at no ports. They touched no land. Once or twice ships hailed them with news of the seaways. Occasionally the passengers on one ship dined with passengers on another. Thus Macquarie met Lieutenant-Colonel Ralph Darling on the *Dorsetshire*, just as he had met Bligh on his earlier outward voyage, neither of them being conscious that they would one day make history as governors in the self-same continent.[42]

In three months and sixteen days—two years and five months since he had left India—he was in Bombay Roads again, "in very indifferent health", he remarked, and also "in exceeding low spirits on my arrival once more at a place where I had passed by far the happiest days of my whole life". The retrospect of long-past years occasioned in his mind "the most painful and mournful emotions and reflections on a most calamitous and irreparable event that can never be erased from my heart". He was back in India not only in the flesh, but in mood.[43]

This was strange. For on the very night before he left London, he had spent the evening exchanging locks of hair, "as tokens of our mutual affection", with a young lady who had promised to become his wife.

As in every other crisis of his life, the situation was "better to be conceived than described".

CHAPTER XII

Lord Ullin's Daughter

I

To Lachlan Macquarie, lieutenant in the 77th Regiment, Elizabeth Henrietta Campbell, of Airds, was only a ten-year-old schoolgirl relative, acquiring English refinement at Hampstead, when he was entrusted with a parcel to carry to her on his way to India in 1788.[1] He did not then go to see her; and during the next sixteen years he made no mention of her in his journals or his letters.

When, however, he reached London in 1803 he met her aunt, Mrs Campbell of Corwhin, whose son—through the ill fate which so often deprives titled Campbells of direct heirs — had become Earl of Breadalbane.

To all Mrs Campbell's friends Breadalbane's house opened its doors. Macquarie had not been in London long before she took him thither in her carriage. The Earl approved of Macquarie. He invited him to dine with royal dukes. Macquarie reciprocated the liking. To be an earl in any case was something to earn his approbation; and anybody who introduced him into the presence of a royal duke, even if only the Duke of Sussex or the Duke of Cumberland, was accounted worthy of his highest personal regard. Not that he was a snob, but he shared the veneration of all Scottish lairds of that age for a title.

Elizabeth was the youngest daughter of his second cousin, Campbell of Airds. Her brother had inherited her father's small estate in Appin where she had spent most of her life. When she burst anew upon Macquarie's sight in 1804, she had just turned back from Edinburgh towards the west, having abandoned a journey to London to see her aunt so that she might bring Lochbuy's sons from school to the bedside of their dying father.[2]

Macquarie, we know, went westward with Airds. The latter, a Campbell of the old school, called himself the Baronet of Ardnamurchan, but the Crown refused to restore the title, which had been lost by attainder in the Stuart wars, till more than a hundred years after his time.

The family was vigorous and long-living. Two of its later scions were Vice-Admiral Campbell, V.C., of the Q-ships, and Brigadier Lorn Campbell, V.C., of the Wadi Akarit.[3] The baronet of the 1914-18 period married an Australian and fought in the Great War with distinction.

These heroes were still to be born and one gathers that the Campbells' greatest glory, in Macquarie's age, was Elizabeth.

When Macquarie first noticed her she was in her late twenties. No portraits of her in that day exist. But there is, in Hobart Museum, a miniature[4] of her, by Read—no flatterer, as his likenesses of her husband show. It was painted in 1819. Then she was a pleasant-looking woman about forty-one years of age with whom time appeared to have dealt very kindly.

Her hair was bronze and curled slightly. Her dress was a little primmer than the mode. Her brow was broad and serene, with honest eyebrows arching over widely-set blue eyes. Her nose looked as if it had been meant for the purposes for which God made noses.

Below, there was a wide, sensitive, rather humorous mouth, and a round, somewhat wilful mound of a chin.

Hers in middle age was a capable, friendly face, full of dignity and sensibility, holding some beauty, but still marked with the traces of the earlier youthful sprightliness and humour which must have given it sparkle in the period when it first attracted Macquarie's eye.

Not that her mere vivacity by itself captured the visiting Indian. Elizabeth's charm for him seems to have lain neither in her looks nor in any lighter qualities. She might have been merry and sportive. She might even have been beautiful. If she was, he never dwells on the fact. All his earlier notices of her tend to show that Elizabeth's chief merit in his eyes was that she was made for business rather than for pleasure.

He had had his Dora Spenlow, and had loved her even to the point of letting his imagination endow her with practical virtues which she never had possessed in her feverish young life. But in Elizabeth it was soon obvious that he recognized his Agnes Wickfield. She, he seems to have felt, could bring calm and peace to his later days and be the mother of the posterity which would ensure that the name of Jarvis should be perpetuated in the Macquarie family, as he had vowed in 1796 that it should be.

In fact, before he set eyes on her, when he was waiting for her brother at Airds on his way to Lochbuy in June 1804, his instinct was at work on the virtues of Elizabeth. He walked about the grounds with her relatives. He went to look at "a very pretty new gravel walk" planned by and executed under her direction—a pleasant walk round a point of land jutting out into the sea called the Black Rock.

He thought that it "showed the good taste of this young lady for ornamental improvements of this kind".[5]

II

At Lochbuy, he met her:

> I also found Miss Elizabeth Campbell of Airds here, who had lately arrived from Edinburgh with Lochbuy's two sons; and who had come here on purpose (tho just then on the eve of going up to London . . . to her aunt, Mrs. Campbell of Corwhin), from the benevolent generous motive of affording all the consolation and assistance in her power to her sister Mrs. Maclaine and her young family in their present great distress. I had the pleasure of being introduced to this very amiable young lady by her sister Mrs. Maclaine previous to sitting down to dinner.[6]

Elizabeth was the prop and mainstay of that household during the succeeding days of sorrow. She managed everything.

When the time came to distract the grief-stricken they organized water parties. They sometimes went out in the boat to fish "with the long line", and Elizabeth was particularly expert and successful.[7] She was good company; she could be amusing. But she was coy when he suggested that she should share his postchaise on the way to Edinburgh, and it was only after much importunity that he persuaded her to join him with the young Maclaines on the journey.

Then they lost her for a time.

> We were this morning deprived of the agreeable society of this most amiable agreeable and very sensible girl, whose departure occasions sincere regret to all of us. She set out early this morning before anyone was stirring, in a small open boat for *Crinnan*, without any other company or society than the boat's crew! ! !
> This girl is quite a heroine! What a most excellent soldier's wife she would make—and happy—in my mind—will that man be whose good fortune it may happen to be to get her.[8]

By the time Elizabeth joined him in his postchaise at Inveraray she had become "our amiable relation and friend".[9] He saw her virtues growing. They viewed Loch Lomond together and she proved "a most excellent traveller, ready to put up with any fare and fatigue, as well as a most pleasant, cheerful and agreeable companion".

He left her in Edinburgh on 1 September 1804. Presently, she reached London. He met her at dinner at Mrs Campbell's house on 2 December 1804, and again on the evening of 8 January 1805. That night he returned to find awaiting him orders to be ready to return to India. He was not heading for a burning romance. Elizabeth does not seem to have entered into his existence very largely. She, poor girl, had had no defunct Antiguan papa to leave her slaves and a fortune of £6000. She was merely the poor daughter of a West Highland laird, who in London unobtrusively stayed with her aunt in Wigmore Street or with her friends, the Misses Stewart, of 49 Albemarle Street.

Macquarie appears to have thought her case over very carefully, until one day he wrote in his journal for the year 1805:

"*March 26, Tuesday* ! ! !"

The occasion for this special display of exclamation marks was that "after very mature and deliberate consideration and reflection on all the consequences of so important a step", he had "taken the opportunity this forenoon of waiting on Miss Elizabeth Henrietta Campbell, the youngest daughter of my late second cousin John Campbell Esquire of Airds in Argyleshire, at the house of her aunt, Mrs Campbell of Corwhin in Wigmore Street".[10]

There, finding her alone, he wrote, he "made a full avowal to her of my sentiments, and of my sincere love and ardent affection for her, explaining fully to her at the same time previous to her giving me any answer to this declaration of my sentiments in her favour, the utter impossibility of *our immediate union, nor until after my return from India, which I* promised should not, if possible, be delayed beyond four years at farthest".

He could not carry her *to India*, even if they were now to be married. This, he told her, was "in consequence of a most solemn vow and unalterable resolution I had been induced to make very soon after the irreparable loss of my late angelic and beloved wife in the year 1796; alluding to the vow I made on the 31st July of that year!"

That was, of course, that he would never marry again in India or take a wife to India.

Elizabeth heard all *he* had to say "with the kindest and most good natured attention" and then, her suitor reported, "to my infinite joy and delight, with a degree of noble candour, and delicate liberal frankness, peculiar to herself, declared a most flattering return to the sentiments I had avowed in her favour, and most kindly consented *to be mine* under all the untoward circumstances that opposed our mutual wishes for immediate union."[11]

Her readiness in yielding to the unavoidable delay of the happy event, he added, had endeared her to him more than ever, "notwithstanding the high and exalted opinion I had already formed of her rigid virtue, refined delicacy, and most excellent judgment and sound understanding".

They discoursed for a long time on "this very interesting and delicate subject", and perfectly explained their wishes and sentiments to each other. Then, her lover ventured to kiss Elizabeth, who surely must have felt that she had earned the caress. They "embraced affectionately—and took leave for the present, agreeing to meet as often as possible".

They spent occasional hours together; but there is less of Elizabeth in his journal than of the £264 cabin which he had bespoken on the Indiaman, *City of London*, and of the elegant entertainment he attended at the invitation of Breadalbane, at which the Duke of Sussex toasted the Earl of Strathmore.

Before sailing for Bombay he spent his last day in town with her. He dined with her and her favourite friend, Miss Meredith, and he and his new love "exchanged reciprocally locks of our hair" as tokens of mutual affection. Then, he took "a tender, affectionate and most affecting leave" of her. And when he retired to bed his mind "was too full of future prospects to admit of my sleeping much *this night*!"[12]

However, though it was "reckoned by everyone who has seen it very like me", he did not leave with her the half-length portrait for which he had lately sat to Mr Opie, "one of the most eminent artists now in London", and for which he had paid twenty-eight guineas.[13]

He intended it for his poor old mother should anything befall him; but he entrusted it to Mrs Morley, since she expressed a particular desire to keep it. This was not treachery to his beloved, for only she and he were in the secret of their betrothal, though he feared that other people had guessed the truth.

He had his reasons for his silence, and he had been some time in India before he broke the news to his friends, the Morleys, and to Airds and Breadalbane.

His vow *"never to marry again in India nor to bring a wife to India"*, he told Breadalbane,[14] might seem a very odd, capricious, and romantic resolution, but to himself *"it was a most sacred one*, and *one* from which no earthly considerations should ever induce me to depart".

Those who had "never felt the acute and afflicting pang of separating from a beloved object—on going on active and dangerous services" would, he was aware, ridicule it.

It might, indeed, be said that his vow formed no bar to his marrying Miss Campbell and leaving her at home; but the interval between his proposal and departure was so short that it was scarcely possible.

Besides, a war was imminent in India when he left England and the chances of the campaign or the bad climate might cut him off, "leaving her, in such event, in a much more wretched and unhappy situation, than she could possibly be in by remaining in her present condition" until his return.

Also, though his income was sufficient to support a family "with great and rigid economy", he was so placed that he "could not make such a liberal settlement and genteel provision for Miss Campbell's maintenance as my wife—as her birth and rank in life" dictated; nor such as his own inclination prompted. Whereas by remaining single for three or four years longer his little fortune would be considerably increased. His reasons seemed to him, he wrote, sufficiently conclusive; and if anybody thought he had acted unfairly or clandestinely, his belief in his own righteousness was his armour against his traducers:

> I am equally incapable of duplicity as I am conscious of never having swerved from those principles of rectitude and integrity, which ought ever to guide and influence the conduct of a gentleman and a man of honour, in every action and concern of his life—and in all his dealings with mankind—Those who know me, will, I trust, bear testimony to my character being yet unsullied by any unworthy action incompatible with true honour and honesty—which have ever been my governing principles through the whole course of my progress hitherto through life.—[15]

He was firmly persuaded, he assured his lordship, that if he was ever again to enjoy any portion of real happiness, he would find it united to Miss Campbell. In her "he saw everything excellent, good and amiable". His mind was perfectly made up on the subject, and "of all women living, I love her the most—and, in fact I consider myself . . . as much her husband as if I were ten thousand times married to her".

III

India, however, presented itself as a disturbing and newly intricate field of existence. Between the French and the Holkar life was hard and uncertain, and conflicting loyalties made it more complicated.

He had proposed that he should remain in India four years. Yet he wished once more to exchange into the Foot Guards, so that he might return to England post-haste. The Duke's attitude to this proposal when he had mooted it earlier had not been encouraging. But Greenwood, the banker, the Duke's particular friend, was asked to reopen the matter of exchange.

His present regiment, however, naturally looked for the presence of its commanding officer in the field in which it was preparing to shed the blood of more Indians in the region of Guzerat. Duncan, who had installed him in one of the most elegant rooms in Government House when he arrived, desired that he should again become his military secretary and settle down until January 1808, then travelling with him to Europe overland. Macquarie agreed to this. In consequence "he felt *bound* in honour to accompany the Governor to England at the time fixed".

The Duke of York, now exercising the privilege which every commander-in-chief possesses of changing his mind, suddenly decided to appoint him to the effective lieutenant-colonelcy of the 73rd Regiment, which had sailed for England after twenty-seven years of contests with the Company's enemies and the Indian mosquitoes. The new commander was "agreeably surprised" at "this gratifying and highly flattering mark of my most gracious Sovereign's approbation and reward of my services", as well he might be in all the circumstances.

But the appointment produced a tantalizing situation. The news of his promotion was published in the Madras press, but no coincident official notification reached India.[16] The promoted officer felt that he must for a time at least, for the sake of honour and propriety, join the 86th Regiment, a project which involved precarious financing and an "enormous" outlay of £650.[17]

Moreover, return to Bombay had reminded him once more of Jane; and though he might burn to be with Elizabeth, he was soon to be seen in Bombay Burying Ground venting his sorrows and the overflowings of his heart, in which his first bride's memory "was still and evermore would be deeply engraved".[18]

IV

The Holkar's activities quickly dragged him from the peace of Bombay to Guzerat. So far, the contest with the northern ruler had been full of disaster for the British forces.

Marquis Cornwallis, who had returned to India to be bewildered by its new pomp and circumstance, had taken command of the Grand Army and within a month had died at Ghazipore on the banks of the Ganges.[19]

Seven days later Macquarie with his servants, horses, and baggage was in Baroach. He left behind with Forbes and Company one ticket in the Calcutta Town Hall Lottery 1805—No. 4221—and one in the Bombay Lottery of 1805—No. 45—with instructions that "if they should come up prizes, the amount to be received by your firm and placed to my credit". From Baroach, he travelled to Dohud, ninety-two miles from Baroda, and assumed there temporary command of 1300 men, on the way to making a visit of ceremony to the Gaikwar.[20]

To his new command he proceeded to administer a thorough spring-cleaning, and though there was nobody available for them to fight, the occupations of the Dohud forces for a little while were far more arduous than those of most eighteenth-century wars. For nearly two months during December and January 1805-6 an insistent Scottish voice was heard establishing arduous rules for extra parades, talking firmly to companies which were all behind in their discipline, and calling for them to be marched and exercised in small squads till further orders for two hours every morning and evening. In the intervals of more serious work, he admonished *killadars*, regulated bazaars and dined his officers with amazing energy.[21]

No hostilities followed. The only war affecting the Dohud front was fought between the commandant and the East India Company Army Headquarters; but that was later, after he had returned to the coast with a proper escort of *silladar* horse.

The issue was whether the warrior should be paid table money on a full colonel's scale for his entertainments at Dohud. His table expenses were heavy—1558 rupees 2 annas for "wines, liquors, etc.": "I might urge as an additional claim to the favourable notice of Government that, even for the short period of my Command at Dohud, I saved the Honble. Company *between three and four thousand rupees* in the article of gram alone to the public draft bullocks . . . the allowance of gram . . . I reduced *four* to *three* seers each bullock per day."[22]

The Government split the difference with him and paid the cost of his entertainments.

V

The Dohud campaign was Macquarie's last taste of active service in the field, and when it was over early in 1806 half a year was devoted to consideration of the problem whether he should try to persuade the Duke to allow him to remain in India with Duncan for the time being, or go to join his new regiment in Scotland.

There was a confused and sometimes specious correspondence about the matter. He had told Greenwood that before returning to England previously he had "had no less than *three severe attacks of the liver*", which had very much undermined his constitution and rendered him incapable of "bearing the heat of a vertical sun" in the manner he was able formerly. He had asked to have the question of exchange into an English regiment reopened.

Then his transfer to the 73rd Regiment made an early homecoming possible for him, though it did not fill a new gap in his banking account which saddled him with a strong temptation to remain in India, and to return to Europe with Duncan not earlier than the beginning of 1808, with a further £3000 which he could save in the interval.

His need of money and his friendship for Duncan seemed to lead him to reverse his earlier views and he began to plead, through various agencies, with the Horse Guards to let him exchange the command of the 73rd Regiment for that of a King's Regiment in Hindustan, where the vertical sun had somehow lost its terrors for him.

Yet, following this course, he was faced with the problem of Elizabeth.

Reaching Bombay from England, he had written a thirty-page letter giving her "the whole history of himself".[23] Thereafter, no ship sailed homeward without a few salutary injunctions bearing on the conduct of her life, and on her training and deportment.

He dealt firmly but clandestinely with her limited finances. He wrote secretly to their mutual friend, Miss Jane Stewart, "soliciting her kindest good offices and friendly attention to my dearest Miss Campbell . . . to supply all her pecuniary wants *as a loan from herself privately*". He remarked that he "should punctually repay her for all her advances—but for the world not to mention to Miss C. *my name at all*—nor that she made such advances by my desire".[24]

Elizabeth, he hoped, would chiefly reside in London till his return in 1808. He asked her to write to him "*once every two months*" and to keep all the letters she received from him carefully till they met again never to part. Later, he demanded that she should write each month. And he told her that he was "promised a good command in Gujerat at the end of the present war—and *to have at least three thousand pounds in 3 years! in case I stay so long in India!*"[25]

On the whole, that part of the correspondence which the ungallant French failed to capture—they filched twenty-eight of his letters from the *Hercules*—seems to have had a disturbing effect on Elizabeth, especially when he wrote to her that, though he left it to her to decide whether he should remain on in India, he had made a solemn promise to Governor Duncan to do so before he knew of his appointment to the 73rd Regiment, and that he must honour it. Later he entreated her forgiveness for remaining so long away from her in order to go home with Duncan.

It was at this point that Elizabeth showed some of that strength of character which later become obvious in all her actions. Her lover was to be discovered writing to her—the good man had a methodical habit of entering a précis of his notes to his sweet in his letterbook—that he regretted that his letters were giving her uneasiness and making her sad, since "hers had quite the contrary effect on him".

He unbent from his customary uxorious air of authority to rally her about some "old hoary lover" whom he meant "to call to account for making a conquest of her heart". He advised that his "ancient rival must keep out of his way for safety's sake unless his beautiful daughter undertook to intercede for him".[26] At the same time, would she please remember that he did not like her retiring to Devonshire, where she had been living for a time? While he instructed her to keep up her spirits and take great care of her health, he noted that he would "wish her rather to live in London in order to have the advantage of the best masters to improve her in *Music, Drawing and French* in all three of which elegant accomplishments, I am anxious she should excell".[27]

It was to forward these studies, which he knew to be expensive, but which he expected to pay a profit since he hoped to travel on the Continent after he retired from the Army, that he had proposed that Miss Stewart should lend money to Elizabeth.

The next time he heard from that lady, however, she had been admiring the beauties of Epsom and Box Hill. He at once told her to look out for "a snug pretty little cottage within fifteen or twenty miles of London for us to purchase and live in occasionally when tired of Mull". For that he was prepared to pay as much as two or three thousand pounds.

This was after Elizabeth, following a long silence, had written a few tart remarks about the proposed length of their engagement, accompanied by a "dear pretty little present of a toothpick case".[28] Her communication seemed to serve the dual purpose of issuing a solemn warning and of softening his heart. A further silence on the part of his lady seems to have raised his fears. He wrote of a new intention to abandon some of his previous plans and hasten home before March 1807 by the overland route, a decision which was due partly to his being "sadly teased" by slow fever. He asked her again to look about for a small, neat cottage near London for their winter residence. And he wrote that every hour made him more uneasy at "not hearing from her for so very long a time".

Long before that point he had already importuned a fellow-countryman in Canton to purchase an imposing array of home-coming presents for "a thousand female cousins, at home, a great many of whom will expect me to bring them some little eastern bawble or other". But among these gifts were "a laquered-ware lady's work box, middling size, inside sandal wood and neatly finished, to be marked on top with the following name, viz. 'Mrs. Macquarie of Jarvisfield' "; and "a fan of a very handsome new pattern with the initials 'E.H.M.' ". Also, he required a middle-sized Chinese gong with which to call his workmen together when he settled on his "lately-acquired property in the Isle of Mull which I have named Jarvisfield".[29]

The cousins had little of the booty. The Harringtons, Morleys, Bread-albanes, and Stewarts scored most heavily in fans and muslins. . . .

VI

He resolved to leave Bombay for ever early in January 1807 and to reach England in the summer, and he hoped that Elizabeth would be in London to greet him, but if in Scotland, he said, she was not to leave there on his account. October 1806 found him appealing to the Company's Resident at Busrah to arrange his passage overland with a single servant and to buy him Shirazwe wine for his friends in England.[30] He was in haste to be gone. He hoped his wedding would take place at the latter end of July.[31]

His life in India was something he wished to put behind him as quickly as possible.

There was no zest in his services as master of ceremonies at the Governor's Christmas Ball.

On Christmas Eve 1806 he attended, without much sadness, the last review there of his favourite old corps, the 77th Regiment, for which he had recruited his first men on Boxing Day 1788. They, too, were going home after eighteen years of exile.

He could hope at the turn of the year that "this is *the last New Year's Day* I shall ever spend in Bombay!"[32]

Of the close friends he had known when he first married, poor Colin Anderson was dead and nearly all the rest were scattered. Only Charles Forbes lingered and him he made the object of his final India generosity, asking him to accept

> a trifling New Year's gift, as a small token of my sincere friendship, affection and regard: namely— a Gibson's saddle, bridle, martingal, etc., together with a military saddle cloth; which were purposely made for myself and which, I believe, are the best of their kind.—
>
> It is hardly a compliment to offer them to you, being no longer of use to me, since I shall now very shortly quit this country—I hope, forever!—two pair of *true blue royal* rosettes accompany the bridle which, if you will allow your favourite horse *Mughill* to wear a pair of when he runs for the *Cup*, will be highly honouring them, and prove also gratifying to me.—[33]

Almost his last duty was a moral one. That irritating chit, Louisa Wilkins, Jane's niece, whom he had left behind in Bombay still searching for a nabob and a marriage portion when he had journeyed to London in 1803, had unwisely fallen in love with his ne'er-do-well relative, Captain Lachlan MacQuarie, the Governor's aide-de-camp.

With him she contracted what her late protector was pleased to call an "impudent union",[34] to which he could not give approval. While she was busy adding to the Macquarie clan as fast as nature would allow, her spouse had involved himself in other occupations, which led to a sad conference just before the Laird of Jarvisfield finally left India:

> This day had a most serious conversation with my relation and namesake, Captain McQuarie of the 86th Regt. on the subject of his late very improper conduct and intemperance, having for several weeks past neglected his duty at the Government House as aide de camp, and entirely abandoned himself to tippling and low drinking all-day-long. I have lectured and admonished him most severely and seriously on this shameful and disgraceful low-lived practice; pointing out the inevitable ruin, misery and ignominious fatal effects of it! The result of this severe lecture was Captain Macquarie's solemnly pledging *his word and Honour to me*, in presence of his wife, that he would discontinue this vile practice; *promising never to be intoxicated again before dinner*!—[35]

Bombay's dinner, of course, was an afternoon meal.

The tenth anniversary of Jane's burial saw him for the last time at her graveside. He ordered the iron railing round her tomb to be painted, the tomb itself to be whitewashed and repaired in the neatest manner when necessary. He wished that he might have the melancholy pleasure, on his speedily approaching final departure from the country, "of having it in the same state it was in originally".[36]

Poor Jane! If her astral self could look down upon her man at that moment she must have smiled gently. For the Macquarie of 1807 was little changed essentially from the Macquarie of 1793.

He was a man of steadfast mind; and mingled with his ten-year-old grief was the hopeful reflection that within seven months he would "crown his felicity" by being united to Elizabeth in marriage.³⁷

It was the same phrase in which he had referred many a year before to the transports of his wedding night with Jane.

VII

He sailed from Bombay for the last time on the *Benares* cruiser on 19 March 1807 and was nearly drowned off Bushire when a wave filled the boat in which he travelled. His party landed at Busrah in country then prosperous looking, studded with date-palms and grazing immense flocks of cattle and sheep and great numbers of Arabian horses.³⁸

He learned that Turkey had attacked those faithful allies of King George, the Russians, that all British intercourse with the Porte had ceased, and that there were rumours of a fierce naval battle fought in the Dardanelles. So the Aleppo road was closed to him. This left no route to England open save that across the Caspian Sea and the plains of Russia.

Spurred on by an advance of 5000 rupees from the East India Company's agent, to enable him to "use every despatch and celerity" to deliver letters to the Court of Directors in London, he did not linger. Neither the Hanging Gardens of Babylon nor the beautiful Mrs Manesty, of Busrah, who had presented her husband with thirteen children, could detain him. The "sacred grounds" of the "real site" of the Garden of Eden could hold him back for no more than a passing half hour to pluck a grain of wheat as a relic. His gaze even upon sundry encountered lions was casual.

He was wafted up the Tigris at two and a half miles an hour by "three *nockadars* and twenty trackers" in a boat clean out of the Arabian Nights.

He slid through the Eastern Gate of Baghdad with his own caravan, cast a not very attentive eye upon the Alvand Range and its "immense wild scenery . . . terrific . . . truly magnificent . . . sublime". And he was content to pass ancient Ecbatana at midnight, with a mere comment on its size. The dust cloud raised by his progress did not decrease even when his companion, Captain O'Neill of the 65th, was taken by "vile inhuman wretches", beaten, threatened with death and slavery and abstracted from his trousers.

For a few days the Shah's officials prevailed upon the traveller and his party to tarry before Kazvin, "a very filthy town", while he romped with viziers who tossed him onward with an offer of a bribe and loaded down with gifts of keen weapons, but with no sight of the Shah, and with an injunction to return to them as King George's ambassador.

There followed an almost royal progress over the ranges to Baku, a long interlude while the Russians kept him in that region, which smelled strongly of naphtha and blue flame, a voyage across the Caspian with glimpses of the mighty *baluga* fish, an arrival in Astrakhan, a wild drive behind relays of three careering horses across the Kalmuk Plains to the Don Cossack country (where a Mackenzie ministered to a Cossack General's flocks), a week in the hands of the Russian police in Kolomna. After twelve

ELIZABETH HENRIETTA MACQUARIE

*From a portrait attributed to Richard Read the Elder in the possession of the
Hobart Museum and Art Gallery*

days' actual racing across the Continent he had reached St Petersburg, 1500 miles from Astrakhan, and was there playing *milord* in the Dhaimond Hotel, with a *valet de place* (at two roubles a day), and a carriage and four (at four roubles a day).[39]

Finally, after he had been prised loose from the retentive soil of Holy Russia by the joint exertions of the British Ambassador and the Foreign Minister, there were fleeting glimpses of him in the Baltic—at Kronstad viewing the forts mounting seven hundred cannon and the great dockyard in which eight ships of the line could be docked or built at once; on the fleet *Calypso*, carrying one hundred and twenty prime seamen and twenty guns; and finally gazing across the narrowing seas at the church spires of Copenhagen, a capital which looked slightly unusual by reason of the British cantonments in its environs and of the "noble and animating" sight of twenty-four British sail-o'-the-line and three hundred transports dragging at their cables in the anchorage in company with the captured Danish Fleet.[40]

There, on board the *Prince of Wales*, ninety-eight guns, Admiral Gambier, smiling and affable, greeted the wanderer. And well might he be affable. He had risen in rank from lieutenant to admiral in a long career during which he had spent only five and a half years at sea, most of it apparently in prayer. He had just reached the culmination of his fame by the capture of the Danish capital, with a loss of only two hundred men out of thirty thousand and without ship casualities. And he was about to divide £300,000 in prize-money with Lord Cathcart, the military commander, one of Macquarie's acquaintances of London days.

The Admiral sent the voyager ashore with great *éclat* to be welcomed affectionately by his old Scottish friend and commander, Sir David Baird, who had followed his custom of being in the thick of the battle, in which he had been wounded by musket balls in the left breast and in a forefinger.

Old-time London staff comrades appeared with news that Charles now commanded the 2nd Battalion of the Black Watch; that the 73rd was at Dundee awaiting its new commander. Lord Blantyre was in Copenhagen to introduce the Indian visitor to the Earl of Rosslyn; and Lord Cathcart, feeling as good-natured as his naval partner, had him on his right hand at dinner and gave him another bundle of dispatches before the *Calypso* sailed on to Elsinore.

Thence, while a calm held their ship, the traveller crossed to Helsingborg, and the King and Queen of Sweden bowed to him as they walked among vast crowds of the Swedish nobility who had developed the curious habit of coming to the seaside for health's sake.

At Elsinore he strolled in Hamlet's Garden, which, as the wraith of Shakespeare belike would have been glad to know, was within half a mile of the town, a most delightful walk and "very extensive and most beautifully laid out in the finest taste". Interest, indeed, urged him on even farther, for he saw the "*Cave-and-Tower* named after the same illustrious Danish Prince so famed in story".

On 30 September a fair wind blew, but not till twelve days later could he make out the coast of England off Sunderland. After four days more he was in a coach on his way from Yarmouth to London. It had taken him seven months to reach England.

At two o'clock on 17 October 1807 he delivered into the hands of Mr Parry and Mr Grant, Chairman and Deputy-Chairman of the East India Company, in Leadenhall Street, the dispatches he had brought from Busrah.[41] At half past three he knocked at a dingy door in Downing Street and was admitted to the presence of George Canning, Lord Liverpool's Foreign Minister, who invited him to dine.[42]

As he left to take up his abode at the St Albans Hotel, "in a very convenient quarter of the town", his active Oriental career was almost ended. But not quite.

He still had the task before him of arranging for the education of his friend Governor Duncan's son—whose birth seems not to have been quite in accordance with the requirements of the Church—thus starting upon his course in life a very queer character who produced many queer volumes; who once described Robert Peel as a "silly optimist"; and who was a pioneer of the anti-gold movements with which the world was later to become infested.

Macquarie owed, too, a last duty to himself in connection with his Oriental adventures. Had not the Government had some advantage from him through his carrying dispatches from Persia—even though the East India Company had paid him for doing it? Had not the whole journey cost him full £600? Could he not with truth assert that the expedition with which he had travelled had injured and affected his health most severely?

The strange fact about it is that it was eighteen months after his arrival in England before he thought to write a request to Canning, who sent for him at once, apologized, and "speaking in a very handsome and flattering manner on the occasion and of his services", directed that he should receive £750 in compensation.[43]

VIII

Elizabeth was not in London. He was forced to pursue her to Holsworthy in Devonshire, where he married her in the ancient Church of Peter and Paul on 3 November 1807. A month later he was discovered lodged at Miss Stewart's House, 49 Albemarle Street.[44] He had taken command of the 73rd Regiment and his wine bill with Messrs Maclaine and Gilchrist, of Leith, had mounted up to £271 7s. 11d.

March 1808 had found him at Perth addressing the Duke of York "respecting a young relation of mine who is desirous of going into the Army",[45] and "very anxious and ambitious" to obtain a commission in His Majesty's Foot Guards—no less a young relation than Murdoch Maclaine, Lochbuy, now sixteen years old and, as he had told Colonel Wallace a year before, "born of European parents".[46]

The youth had now become "the head and representative of one of the most respectable families in the County of Argyle—being Chieftain of the *Clan Maclaine*".

A few months later the wanderer was seeking the admission as "a cadet into the Junior Department of the Royal Military College" of that "young hero, Hector", Charles's son, who had been a lieutenant on half-pay at ten years old, expelled by the Duke from the Army, and who was now "14 years of age, well grounded in the knowledge of Grammar, in the first four rules of Arithmetic, and writes a good hand".[47]

Hector, he wrote, was "intended for the Military Profession"!

In August Macquarie was reorganizing his estate through the offices of Mr Dugald M'Tavish, his factor and Charles's, who was paid a joint salary of £20 a year, of which Lachlan was to find £13.

These great rich tenants of his, he told Mr M'Tavish, had no excuse for being in arrear, and therefore he would request him to insist that they paid punctually when the rents became due, so that there could be passed over, out of the proceeds every year, £10 each to his mother and his sister Betty and 10s. 6d. to a certain Mrs Flora Macquarie, of Salen, to defray the expense of bringing manure to her croft.[48]

At the same time he was at work, founding his first township.

Salen had been divided into sixteen crofts. Mrs Flora Macquarie was there, and the blacksmith, MacDonald, and the carpenter, Ferguson, and the shoemaker, Campbell. Murdoch Macquarie, the tailor, was preparing to come over from Ulva and settle down with his goose, and two Donald Macquaries, one from Tobermory and one, a wood keeper, at Gruline, were ready to immigrate. The community was even to be completed by the provision of an "oldest inhabitant"; for room was to be found for Hugh Macquarie, who was "a poor old man".

And if all the new tenants of the village would build themselves comfortable, good houses, nearly all of the same size, pointed with lime, each having high stone gables and two glass windows, their new lord of the manor was prepared to contribute towards the cost.

In October 1808 Elizabeth had made him a father when he was nearly forty-eight years old. But the child was a daughter and it died immediately.

He would have to wait a little longer for Elizabeth's posterity which was to make his beloved Jane's name immortal; perhaps even till the French wars were over; but perhaps not, since the war, in the year of Cintra, showed no sign of becoming so all-demanding as to force the recuperating 73rd Regiment to leave its comfortable barracks at Perth and bare its serried ranks of manly bosoms to the fire of Napoleon's infantry in Portugal or Spain.

One thing, however, must have seemed certain to the Laird of Jarvisfield and to all around him in the summer of that year of 1808: there would be no more crossing of "the dark and stormy water" of the world's wider oceans for one scion of Ulva's Isle.

Nearly fifty years old, in poor health, yellowed with fever, blotched with curative acids, racked with long courses of mercury, permanently saddened under the strain of grief, and marked in every way with the evidences of twenty years spent in tropic climes, he must have judged that his public career was near to its end.

He could hope that in a very few years, at most, he would be able to retire in peace to the new mansion-house which he proposed to build at Gruline and live out the end of his life among his farms.

But no man can tell what she whom he called "that slippery goddess, Fortune" has in store for him till she waves her wand.

INTERLUDE

★

The Barren Wood

... *this fifth part of the Earth,*
Which would seem an after-birth,
Not conceived in the Beginning,
(For God blessed his work at first,
And saw that it was good),
But emerg'd at the first sinning,
When the ground was therefore curst;—
And hence this barren wood!

—BARRON FIELD, "Kangaroo".

The Barren Wood

I

IN 1787, while Macquarie tramped the hills of Lorne and Ardnamurchan searching for recruits, a sylvan stream poured itself into a sheltered cove on the southern side of Port Jackson, on the east coast of New Holland.

The cove bit sharply into the hilly margin of the port. Its waters were so deep that ships of the largest burden could have found anchorage next its shores. It was sheltered from every prevailing wind save the north-easterly, which in summer chased foam-laced wavelets up the small yellow beaches beneath the sandstone cliffs on its western side.

Dark-skinned natives fished from canoes on the still waters of the cove. Seagulls quarrelled on its sandbars. The rivulet, a few hundred yards inland, was almost completely hidden by a tangle of boronia and erica, above which the spears of the grass-trees and the flower-stems of the red waratahs rose in the shadows of giant turpentines and silvery eucalypts.

Along its banks ferny grottoes drank from tinkling waterfalls. The bush, usually dappled with sunlight, was gay with the song of native birds. Imprints of the paws of soft, furry things marked its sandy trails.

Through the ages, as with the Europe-sized continent behind, the only humanity the port had known had been the small body of dusky nomads who lighted their corroboree fires beside an adjacent bay,[1] and who would have been adjudged primitive in any other land in the days of Romulus.

In twenty-two years, however, the coming of Europeans had vastly changed this Eden. As Macquarie finished enlisting his recruits in Glasgow in January 1788, Phillip with his fleet had reached Sydney Cove. In the two succeeding decades convicts under the impetus of the lash had cleared the "barren wood" from the hillsides on either bank of the little stream, and much of the turpentine and the boronia and the erica had made way for the stone-and-brick-walled enclosures of the convict settlement of Sydney.

This was not without its charms, even though it might be still another few years before it would regard itself as "a second rising Rome"[2] or "excite the wonder of the spectator when he contemplates the prodigies of advancement and improvement, which the art and industry of man are capable of performing"[3] in such a spot. The voyager after his tedious months at sea on the way from Europe was even then likely to be enchanted by the surroundings of the settlement to the point of failing to notice its dilapidation. As he neared the land he found himself yielding to a sense of joyous elasticity. The air was clear and bright, the sky blue. At every breath "hope was inhaled" with the aromatic perfumes of strange trees and shrubs. The sense of life quickened. And, "rude and irregular" though Sydney township itself might be, "an irregular village of houses, cottages and bark huts", with perfectly naked savages peeping through unguarded windows at the very gates of Government House itself, it had a certain vivid liveliness when one viewed it from the peninsula to the east of the cove, where endless generations of aborigines had left great mounds of half-buried sea-shells from their feasts.

Every house had its trees and its garden; and to the diversity of white-washed stone, reddish brick, and wattle-and-daub was added the brilliance of high-running ensigns above the Fort and public buildings and sound and movement from the swinging sails of windmills etched against the skylines above the ridges.

At the left of the onlooker Government House rose, clothed in white plaster, the Union Jack floating from a staff in its four acres of shrubbery and garden, which sloped down to a paling, a wharf, and a half-moon of sandy beach.

Below this modest palace, on the east of the central stream, the high white mansion and warehouse of the "emancipated" merchant, Mr Simeon Lord, triumphed over the habitations of law and order—the Judge-Advocate's ruinous dwelling, with its neglected orchard and garden and untidy back yard, the guard-house, the dwellings of various military and civil officials, and the lesser cottages of fellow-Britons who had found an enforced exile pleasant and remunerative.

Beyond Mr Lord's imposing pile, a rickety bridge across the stream connected the eastern part of the town with the western near the modest asylum of the little orphan girls. This was surrounded by its wall, which had acquired in parts a certain polish not intended by its reverend trustees, since the little orphans occasionally slid over it of an evening to drink rum with their betters and to learn those social arts which would fit them to do battle presently in an exacting world.

Next to them dwelt Mr James Underwood, the Colony's first substantial shipbuilder, his pretentious mansion half hiding from the north-east the low white bungalow of Mr Garnham Blaxcell, an adventurous naval purser who was Mr John M'Arthur's partner.

His dwelling across the road on rising ground southward from the Jail, formerly had sheltered the Lieutenant-Governor. On this retreat fell the shadow of unfinished St Philip's—the ugliest church in Christendom —which Bligh had "got done with eight bells in the tower, a thing never known before"[4] in Australasia.

The ground about it climbed ruggedly towards the western heights between the Cove and Cockle Bay, upon which Fort Phillip and its outpost buildings kept guard over the scene.

An unwalled military centre lay immediately to the south lined with rotting barracks inhabited by the New South Wales Corps. Here the spring of rebellion had gushed two years earlier.

II

Mostly clustered near the harbour, particularly in what later became known as George Street North, there were shops which the inhabitants considered "particularly respectable, and decorated with much taste".[5] They were crammed with pieces of jewellery which might have seemed strangely familiar to some Londoners of the Upper Ten, and with brightly coloured silks from China and muslins from India.

There was a dejected-looking official gazette office, a rotting hospital whose walls had been put together in England and carried twelve thousand miles across the ocean, and an unfenced burial ground, upon which citizens of a later age built a town hall scarcely less gloomy than the precedent institution. A gallows tree, always fitted for business, waited on a southern sandhill at convenient walking distance from the burial ground.

The other outstanding architectural features were some stern-looking commissary stores, and the huts and shanties of the Rocks stretching towards Dawes Point, from the northernmost end of which, beyond the Battery, the steel-clad rainbow of the Sydney Harbour Bridge was to rise more than a century later.

There were no streets in the true sense of the word, and the general effect, though pleasantly informal, was not orderly. Across frequent green spaces, in which the stumps of the forest and sometimes axe-defying turpentine-trees still stood, straggling red paths meandered along courses dictated by the contours of the landscape. Some of these tracks were impassable after rain. Where the inhabitants had put up dwellings beside them they had scorned to follow regular alignments. Fences made detours to avoid trees or gullies. Houses shrank out of line with their neighbours to avoid being perched upon hummocks of rock.

Along the banks of the stream in the valley, which a few years ago had been so sylvan and unfrequented, members of the population drew their water or washed their pantaloons.

Drays and carts abounded. Pigs were everywhere. Armed sentries paraded the highways at night, and were well needed, since the keepers of abundant boozing kens and dives were lavish in their efforts to mitigate the sufferings of their patrons. Even the tender-hearted jailer of the County Prison, Mr Cubitt, maintained his taproom opposite the dungeon gate, in an erection surmounted by the scales of Justice. Thither the confined felon might send for a pint to wet his penitence. There was nearly one licensed house to every hundred inhabitants of all ages. The result lent a convivial air to Sydney and in the night dark deeds were often done.

Outside the man-made town rolled endlessly-timbered, monotonously-coloured ridges that reminded one who viewed them of a tempestuous sea transfixed into leaden stillness.[6] They "inspired melancholy sensations", but there was no escape from them, no matter where one dwelt or laboured.

The roystering denizens of the Rocks gazed across Cockle Bay to the illimitable wilderness beyond what would one day be Balmain. The millers on the eastern ridge, above Government House, saw nought between them and the Pacific Ocean save Woolloomooloo House and tangled woods rising to the heights of Bellevue Hill.

The signalman on Dawes Point looked northward across the harbour at tumbling cliff-face and wildly-wooded declivity. Towards the ocean his view was of a league-long, wood-bound sweep of water, broken by Pinchgut island, which could have been the prototype of an illustration for *The Swiss Family Robinson*, had not a departed gentleman on a gibbet sometimes formed its admonitory frontispiece.

Such was the hub of civilization on the continent of New Holland and in the Colony of New South Wales. It held in 1810 6156 souls, convicts and otherwise.[7]

Sixteen miles out, at Parramatta, a few officers' houses edged away from two or three rows of hovels which converged on the church of St John, one hundred feet long and forty-four feet wide, the largest holy fane in all the Australasian antipodes.

This tiny intrusion in the wilderness held 1807 inhabitants. And there were 2389 more in the clearings roughly carved out of the scrub around Green Hills on the Hawkesbury River, and on the Nepean River which ran along the base of the Blue Mountains as the limit of settlement in the west.

At the Coal River, a day's sail to the northward, a hundred villains of a wickeder vintage than their fellows burned lime or crawled into an adit in the cliffs above the sea and dragged out as much coal as their empty bellies, their double irons and their flayed backs would permit them to haul.

This was all upon the mainland. But Van Diemen's Land, far across the rolling leagues of the Tasman Sea to the south, boasted settlements at Hobart Town (population 1062) and Port Dalrymple (population 259).

Governor Bligh swore on oath that, in August 1807 there appeared in New South Wales to be only one hundred and sixty-six men outside the New South Wales Corps, which formed the military guard, who had not been convicts.

III

Mrs John M'Arthur[8] who had known Sydney almost from its birth called it "an expensive place, the population vicious". The dashing belles who would have caught her eye as they wended their ways to the further slopes of the western ridge, where the bulk of the convictry hid its nocturnal sinning from official scrutiny, must have helped by their demeanor to confirm her view. They "spared no expense ornamenting their persons"; but although "the costliness of their exteriors there, as well as in most other parts of the world, was meant as a mark of superiority", it "conferred very little grace, and much less virtue, on its wearer".[9]

The worst of the convict women, of course, were vile—"so very depraved that they are frequently concerned in the most dreadful acts of atrocity".[10] But this was far from true of all. One had become the mother of a father of the Constitution. A Governor cherished the offspring of another. Yet another, whose husband, also, was of the "transported" brotherhood, gave birth to the first Australian-born-and-bred Privy Councillor, the first New South Wales minister sprung from his native soil, the first to send troops overseas to help in British wars, and the first Australian who was vouchsafed a memorial tablet in St Paul's, where a British Prime Minister, one of the proudest of Scottish peers, unveiled it.

On the whole, the population of New South Wales was not so wicked as it might have been, though the yeast of villainy which activated sections of it could compete with the blackest that Alsatia had to show, and undiscriminating persons like Mr John M'Arthur were apt to pretend to judge the whole by its vilest parts.

There were Irish rebels by the score.[11] There was, at one time, a discharged sergeant fresh from the wars, transported for seven years, for stealing a broom. There was an Oxonian blackmailer, turned government clerk and poet. There was an Irish baronet who had abducted a Quakeress. The postmaster whose son became one of the earliest of Australian cabinet ministers had narrowly escaped being sent for fourteen years to Norfolk Island for having received stolen goods, though there was some suspicion that well-wishers—and highly exclusive ones at that—had manufactured the evidence against him. The Assistant Surgeon had suffered sentence of death at nineteen years of age as a naval mutineer. A felon had lived in the Colony so hardened that, at his trial at Edinburgh, when kindly old Lord Justice Clerk Braxfield asked him, "Hae ye ony coonsel, mon? Dae ye want ony appointit?" he had replied, "No, I only want an interpreter to make me understand what your lordship says."[12]

And there had been a man—no "sunshine patriot" he—serving a fourteen-year sentence, for irredeemable enormities of behaviour which mainly consisted in "distributing or circulating or causing to be distributed and circulated in the towns of Glasgow, Kirkintilloch, Milltown and Lennoxtown and elsewhere, a number of seditious and inflammatory writings or pamphlets, particularly a book or pamphlet entitled *The Works of Thomas Paine, Esq., etc.*"[13]

Clustered round this nucleus of infamy were the devotees of every form of offence which an English judge could find to catalogue to the extent of thirty-eight octavo pages in the relevant work upon criminal laws—prigging handkerchiefs and stockings, filching a pie, burning haystacks, assisting in cutting down trees at night, stealing carp out of somebody else's pond, assaulting the keepers of deer, destroying rabbits after sundown, marrying clandestinely, snatching fish out of private rivers, and forging postage franks.[14] And though the British Government spoke of reform and had its own code, most of the stern naval governors after Phillip could see clearly that evil was inherent in the natures of most transported convicts, so early did some of them turn to turpitude.

What could be done with a "pretty accomplished girl . . . of respectable family"[15] sentenced to transportation in 1802 for stealing lace from a Bond street haberdasher, or with a schoolgirl who "stole" a pony from a neighbour in a frolic? What influence could remove the canker from the blackened souls of the five infants of eleven years, the seven of twelve years, the seventeen of thirteen years, the thirty-two of fourteen years, and the sixty-five of fifteen years of age who during a five-year period were sent out under sentences of transportation for from seven years to life, as befitted such dangerous characters?[16] What but life-long villainy could be expected of a "very little boy of thirteen", whom a visitor somewhat later discovered on a British hulk awaiting export, double ironed with twelve-pound irons?[17]

It was no wonder that, in an earlier and juster age, a merciful Providence sometimes took a fifty per cent toll of such sinners before they reached the Colony, mowing them down with fever and foulness during an eight-months-long voyage in holds awash with stinking bilgewater.

Those who survived, however, earlier had formed an awful democracy of redemption. Tender youth and hardened burglar leg-ironed together; "pretty accomplished girl" and prostitute rotten with disease, the mutual prey of drunken soldiery and sailors—all had the consolation to know that their indignant but forgiving country designed to afford them an equal chance of reform in new surroundings which surprised and delighted most of them.

When they arrived they became part of a community which looked much like other communities. No broad arrows marred their dress. Save for those who added new crimes to their records and membership of the chain-gangs to their experiences, they seemed as other men and women at first casual glance, and often they were freer in supposed captivity than they had been in their London slums and cellars.

The men received blue kersey jackets, raven pantaloons, woollen caps; or duck frocks for summer wear with trousers or breeches; or gaudy military uniforms which a frugal government had retrieved from defeats inflicted on continental foes in Europe. The women wore brown serge jackets and petticoats. The clothes of the bond were so often so much better than those of the free, that the original owners sold their issues for rum and reverted to their second thin tatters to cover themselves.

The convicts dwelt in lodgings in the town and were to be seen wandering of a morning after bell-ring to the lumberyard or the public buildings or gravel pits and quarries where their work lay. This work was of infinite variety. They were the staple labourers. They were assigned as servants to the owners of estates. They groomed the Governor's horses, they tended the sick. They built every early church and public building. They even provided a chaplain from among their number. Freed on tickets of leave, they were constables and overseers of road gangs. They kept the grog-shops. They argued in the courts. They were the heart and fibre of every exploring expedition.

But upon their bowed shoulders there ever fell the shadows of the lash and of the gallows.

IV

Above the scandalized chorus of some of their betters who debauched the convicts with concubinage and rum, growing rich in the process, a few sober voices raised themselves in favour of the general run of the Botany Bay population.

John Palmer, the Commissary, Squire of Woolloomooloo, told a House of Commons Select Committee in 1812 that free settlers received convicts tolerably well and that some few were admitted to the society of the free but not in general.[18]

D. D. Mann, an emancipist himself, who in 1810 wrote a most common-sense account of New South Wales, declared that "the morals of the colony are by no means so debauched as the tongue of prejudice has too frequently asserted".[19] On the contrary, he said, virtuous characters were not rare, and honourable principles were not less prevalent in the Colony than in other communities of equal extent and limited growth. Instances of drunkenness, dishonesty, and concomitant offences were not more common than in the mother country; and those amongst the convicts who were disposed to return to their old habits, were deterred by the threat of severe punishment. Mann wrote:

> There are many also amongst the prisoners themselves who are now striking examples of probity, industry, temperance and virtue; and some have obtained a remission of the punishment which occasioned their residence in the Settlement, in consequence of the signal and radical change which had taken place in their inclinations and behaviour. Where there is society their [sic] must exist offences; but, on the whole, considering the nature of the colony of New South Wales, the morals of the people are as free from glaring defects, as those of any other tract of equal population in the habitable world; and the characters which are celebrated for their virtues are as numerous, in proportion, as those which are to be found in other countries, where civilisation and prosperity have made greater progress, and where individuals have greater inducement to labour, and the prospect of a brighter reward for their industrious exertions.[20]

Their children stood as references for their innate virtues. Mann thought them "very robust, comely, and well made . . . remarkably quick of apprehension; learn any thing with uncommon rapidity; and greatly improve in good manners, promising to become a fine race of people".[21] Even John M'Arthur a little later said of young Australians bred from this convict stock that they were "active, intelligent, and I think will be enterprising whenever a proper field is opened to their industry".[22]

The bulk he found capable of greater exertions in the Australian climate than Englishmen; and he noted in them a disposition towards sobriety and marriage. He had never known, he said, an instance in which any of them were not sober and honest, and he believed there were but few who were not. Also—the greatest compliment he could pay them—"when educated in the right way they were exceedingly modest and disposed to be properly obedient".

New South Wales held many abandoned criminals "vicious, hardened, and callous in disposition", as did all other communities in that age,—men and women who had escaped the noose by the strength of their own cunning; but they formed a small original infusion. Asked to arrest most of the Australian prisoners of 1810 for the kind of "crimes" which caused their transportation, a modern constable would have turned away smiling.

But this, when convicts had been freed and claimed the right to be regarded as respectable, did not prevent the growth of bitter class animosities between the free "exclusives" and the freed "emancipists".

These enmities were fanned to fever heat by one evil influence—the Demon Rum.

V

Influential colonists had established a wide trade in rum within ten years of the foundation of the Colony.[23] This business was in the hands of a few persons who, though almost exclusively officers, both civil and military, were not always "gentlemen". By virtue of their official positions, these held a watertight control over the ship-loads of goods which the Government imported, or permitted to be imported, to feed and clothe the population and provide it with tools and implements. They also controlled the only money negotiable outside New Holland, which came to them for distribution from the Treasury in the shape of army paybills and Treasury Bills for civil purposes. And they were not slow to exploit their opportunities. Former convicts soon joined the traders.

Not a pound of tobacco, not an ounce of flour nor a gill of spirits, not a pick or shovel or an axe, not a shilling in sterling currency found its way to the public until ships' captains, officials or traders had squeezed out of it the last farthing of profit for themselves.

Their positions enabled them to buy all consignments of arriving merchandise, often with bills secured upon assets which, in fact, were the property of persons to whom they intended to sell their purchases at an exorbitant advance on the landed cost.

To the common soldiers and the general populace they traded the purchased goods for the paybills or produce, at prices often almost forcibly obtained. And they enhanced their gains by using spirits as a tempting intermediate currency. Of rum, again, they, of course, fixed the rate of exchange.

Bligh, who became Governor in 1806, had written with righteous indignation, "It [rum] has been a great evil in this country; but its being used by way of barter has added to its pernicious effects more than by the quantity imported beyond all conception."

He professed to have discovered many cases in which "a few individuals who secured large quantities [of liquor] had afterwards disposed of it as high as 800 per cent profit". He declared that two or three bushels of corn sometimes was bought for a bottle of spirits which cost half a crown; that farmers were "ruined by the high price of spirits or the high price of labour".[24] He thundered that it was inconceivable what money had been made through the means of bartering spirituous liquors and the sufferings of the multitude on that account. Yet he himself made at least one purposeful distribution.

Beef and mutton, he wrote, were selling at 1s. 6d. a pound. A person with liquor procured at 8s. a gallon could, therefore, disposing of it for barter at the retail rate of £2 a gallon, obtain 26⅔ pounds of meat to the gallon of liquor. A person who had no liquor, with his 8s. could buy only 5⅓ pounds of meat. Two gallons of rum could buy an acre of wheat.[25]

This summary was written long after rum had established its clutch on the Colony. Ten years before the air had become strident with the wails of honest settlers as they paid 5s. a pound for tobacco which they knew had been landed at 7d. The widow Bray had keened loudly at being forced to disgorge 25s. a bottle for a fiery brew to burn away her thirst. And the claws of monopoly had closed even upon the cherished pig of Mr Kellyson which "weighed thirteen score and was his all; but only [was] afflicted with the flea".[26]

In short, the soldier or settler, if buyers or employers paid him at all, received his meagre due in spirits or groceries. These a grinning retailer transferred to him on a scale of prices under which he often was "obliged by forestalling . . . to pay 400 per cent for every article of consumption". If he were a soldier or an employed convict he dared not resist. If a settler, his alternative to submission was to let his land go uncultivated until it fell into the clutches of ambitious officers or members of the greedy commissary staff or emancipist merchants.

Did he show himself reluctant to deal with these, his credit dried up; his grain and pork were no longer received into store; the prices of his necessities soared above Everest; but this did not matter since he had nothing with which to pay. Ragged and gaunt, and afflicted with a parching thirst, he either died of starvation or embraced High Toby and presently perished in suspension from the tail of a cart, a horrible example to deter stout hearts. Such, at any rate, was the tale.

Usually, however, sellers and customers alike had thirsts sufficiently urgent to spur them to accept with alacrity an offer of liquor, be the rate of exchange what it might. This was the tale of Hunter and Bligh.

VI

Each Governor from Hunter onwards had used the legend of the "rum monopoly" as a stick to beat his enemies, though the viceregal official families harboured ardent spirit traders who distracted attention from their own evil operations by accusing less privileged persons outside Government House.

Hunter had at first pleaded for a supply of spirits to be used as incentives for government labourers; but later he had wrung his hands over the alleged ruin caused by rum, in order that he might try to pin the odium for its distribution on John M'Arthur, who had criticized official toleration of a general moral laxity.

Hunter was recalled, discredited by his own inconsistencies of statement, to be superseded by the gout-ridden King.

The latter had told the Home Government that "a Governor has very little chance of justice where he is so situated, having only one corps and but a sufficiency of officers to sit a Courtmartial and being unable to manage the prosecution in person".[27]

King did, in vain, all that his nature and habits and his own acquisitiveness would allow to curb his officers. Hunter's former aide-de-camp, Major Johnston, was sent to England for trial, for "paying spirits to a sergeant as part of his pay at an improper price, contempt and disobedience of orders".[28] The major had come back, untried and unscathed, in a ship loaded with his livestock and merchandise, after nearly two years in arrest. He had a powerful patron—the Duke of Northumberland.

Captain John M'Arthur, denounced as ringleader of all the Colony's discord, "the Botany Bay Perturbator", King had sent also to England for trial, after he had nearly killed his colonel, Paterson, in a duel, to which Paterson had challenged him, forcing him to fight.[29]

He had returned with a grant of five thousand acres of land and with concessions and indulgences gained through Lord Camden. The letters he carried virtually made the Governor the servant of his wishes; and it was obvious that, despite his previous denunciations, King was soon M'Arthur's humble servant.

Almost every other officer[30] of the Corps had suffered court martial or had been marked down for court martial, without effect.

So King eventually fled, with a sigh of relief, after having neatly feathered his nest with land grants, the derisive rhymes of regimental satirists still ringing in his ears. He might well have been grateful for the chance to leave his task; for matters in the Colony were fast approaching a crisis.

With the arrival of privileged settlers like the Blaxlands and Dr Townson the free community had grown in power to resist authority. Tempers were rising.

To follow King, the Government thought fit to send out Governor Bligh, a broad, red-faced, pompous, irascible little naval captain who had been thanked by Nelson before Copenhagen, who had suffered the *Bounty* mutiny, and who had commended himself because he had shown himself capable of sternness at the Nore.

Sir Joseph Banks, acknowledged arbiter in all things antipodean, esteemed him as "one who has integrity unimpeached, a mind capable of providing its own resources in difficulties without leaning on others for advice, firm in discipline, civil in deportment and not subject to whimper and whine when severity of discipline is wanted to meet emergencies".[31]

All these things Bligh certainly was not. He was not a strong man. He was not equable in temper. He shared with those whom he was sent to discipline a capacity for feathering his nest. He had spent much of his life in ships in which his word was law. The solitariness of a naval captain's state had inhibited his capacity for taking counsel. He had an old salt's natural contempt for landlubbers. He was, in fact, a typical seadog of the time, though a little more irritable and arrogant than the common run. Seadogs were peculiar persons. The sea "cut up a man's youth and temper

SIMEON LORD

From a miniature in colour in the possession of the Trustees of the Mitchell Library, Sydney

most terribly and the naval officer grew old sooner than any other man", so that Jane Austen's Admiral Baldwin, at forty, was "the most deplorable looking person . . . his face the colour of mahogany, rough and rugged to the last degree, all lines and wrinkles, nine grey hairs of a side, and nothing but a dab of powder on top". Many of the population of New South Wales would have agreed with Sir Walter Elliot of Kellynch Hall that all admirals should be knocked on the head before they reached forty.

Bligh was over fifty. He was not capable, out of his experience, of bringing about change without force. And though, in the opinion of an observer who professed to be unbiassed by prejudice and untainted by corruption, his "meaning was for the general interest of the Colony", he was "not thoroughly acquainted with the disposition of the people, was deficient in policy, and erred in judgment".[32] He was soon generally hated.

So Bligh's reign soon saw exclusive officer and emancipist trader and the rank and file of the population in temporary alliance to smite a common enemy.

Bligh did not realize the dangers of the situation. Within a few months after his arrival he felt that the evils under which the Colony had laboured by reason of the spirit traffic "were now done away with to the great satisfaction of the people . . . except the persons alluded to at the head of whom is M'Arthur and the officers". His own chief advisers were spirits traders.

Fourteen months of experience of New South Wales and of the effects of his blustering regime, in fact, satisfied Bligh, that "everything seemed to be propitious", that his rebellious subjects were "quiet at present", and that he had succeeded in dividing them, "so that they cannot unite without our knowing it in time".[33]

He seems to have been little conscious that already the stream of venomous letters which rocketed homewards, telling of his threats against the life of poor Mr John Blaxland and of his visions of feathers inserted into the most unusual parts of sergeants' anatomies, had given birth to London rumours of his projected withdrawal.[34]

Londoners felt more than a little sympathy with the settlers. They knew their Bligh; and tales of his reported peculations and corruption seemed to have some confirmation in the stories that the Governor preferred the company of emancipated Hawkesbury River settlers to that of military gentlemen.

VII

John M'Arthur produced the inevitable explosion. That resourceful "arch fiend"[35] was the central figure in a series of dramatic incidents which culminated in his arrest.

Bligh ordered him to be arrested and sent to trial on a number of charges, which ranged from illegal possession of stills to sedition and resisting arrest.

On most of these indictments history since has unjustly found M'Arthur guilty. But he had on his side every "monopolist," whether of the old ex-clusive school or of the new breed of emancipist merchants and dealers. Every officer, every householder seemed to be with him. All he needed to do to provoke actual insurrection was to set fire to the fast-forming resolutions of the mob.

For weeks before his trial he bustled about the settlement on bail, lustily quarrelling with his accusers, complaining of his "ignorance of the nature of the accusations"[36] against him, crying out that Judge-Advocate Atkins, who was to preside over the court which would try him, "was deeply interested to obtain a verdict" and like to "be called upon to defend himself at the very bar to which he is about to drag me, for the false imprison-ment I have suffered under the authority of his illegal warrant". He had good ground for genuine complaint and fear that Atkins was plotting his ruin.[37]

His masterly preparations, conducted apparently with the knowledge and connivance of his future judges and of the commandant of the New South Wales Corps, Major George Johnston, culminated immediately before the sittings of the court.

On the eve of the trial, having secured by the grace of Bligh himself a pipe of wine to inaugurate a regimental mess, the six officers nominated to sit in judgment on their old friend and others joined M'Arthur's son Edward and his nephew Hannibal, his bondsman Nicholas Bayly, and his partner Garnham Blaxcell in a convivial party, while their captive, stalking the parade ground outside their banquet hall, gave ear to the strains of the band and to their tipsy choruses.

It would not have been out of their ordinary judicial habit if the celebrants had entertained the prisoner as their guest; but he himself was a poor diner-out, a teetotaller and a dyspeptic. Thus the court's members had to be content to become themselves mellow without him, a fact which next day tended to accentuate the sharp divergencies of viewpoint already existing between themselves and their President, Judge-Advocate Atkins.

Mr Atkins took the presidential seat amidst "a most violent altercation and uproar",[38] caused by the prisoner's objection to his sitting. He himself was, as was normal, in a sodden condition; for he was a man "accustomed to inebriety . . . the ridicule of the community . . . his determination weak, his opinion floating and infirm". Even the need to pronounce a death sentence could not keep him sober, though now he probably was in no worse state than the soldiers with side-arms who filled the tiny, fetid court-room, or the six officer judges, who, no doubt, came fresh from their precautionary consumption of a "hair of the dog".

The prisoner found them all an easy prey. While the Judge-Advocate threatened him with the consequences of contempt of court and one of the other judges, Captain Anthony Fenn Kemp, from Aldgate, who in his private moments kept a store by the Barrack Gate, broached a popular suggestion that the Judge-Advocate should himself be committed to the jail, Mr M'Arthur became master of the situation in short order.[39]

Untroubled by the aftermaths of wine and dinner, he declaimed in tones and language suitable to the outlook and condition of the Bench, of which part appeared to be vaguely under the impression that it was involved in the proceedings of a revolutionary tribunal.

Cheers shook the building as the Perturbator told his audience of the viceregal plot to destroy him—a plot which in their sober and less excited moments some of those now cheering most gladly would have aided and abetted.

In Bligh's version the ensuing events smell strongly of stale carouse: The Governor sent for Johnston, the New South Wales Corps Commandant, who had dined with his officers before the trial with such success that he had fallen out of his chaise on the way home, and now proclaimed himself to be *hors de combat* in his suburban manor house at Annandale.[40]

To Bligh's summonses he failed to respond. It needed a stirring message from the Corps to induce "temporary forgetfulness of my bruises", after which he had a horse harnessed and drove to the Barracks, marking upon the way that everything in the streets denoted "terror and consternation". And at the Barracks he ordered the drums to beat to quarters, while respectable inhabitants begged him, he wrote later, "with importunate clamour", to arrest Bligh and avert certain "insurrection and massacre", and the immolation of the tyrant himself at the hands of a mob incited by "popular fury".[41]

Johnston released M'Arthur from jail on a warrant which he signed illegally as "Lieutenant-Governor". There was "great movement in the Barrack Square", with all the military under arms. Botany Bay, tradition declares, saw Bligh's erstwhile prisoner high upon a gun-carriage, the *deus ex machina* of the scene, as he accepted signatures to a requisition to Johnston to capture Bligh. And as the day was hot and naturally had not been passed without the adequate refreshment of the actors in the quaint drama, the assemblage was all for action.

One still seems to scent the odour of Bengal Spirits upon the air as the crowd yells lustily, "Down with Bligh!", the band strikes up "The British Grenadiers", and the Corps, over four hundred strong, muskets loaded with ball, bayonets glinting in the last rays of the summer evening's sun and waving uncertainly as in a strong breeze, marches off up Bridge Street to Government House, followed by a populace bent upon missing no tittle of the fun.

According to Bligh, the brave fellows—"creatures . . . more like jailbirds than anything else"—set a cordon of steel round Government House and sent skirmishing parties to hunt down its shrinking occupant.

History has disputed ever since whether Bligh was found beside a bed in an attic, or under it. Bligh said beside it. The soldiery said under it, and professed to be deeply shocked that an officer and a gentleman should thus hide from a mere four hundred bayonets. Bligh characterized the soldiery as a "daring set of ruffians under arms, intoxicated by spirituous liquors, which was given to them for the purpose, and threatening to plunge their bayonets into me if I resisted".[42]

Mr M'Arthur certainly was not intoxicated; neither was Mr John

Blaxland. The evidence of their sobriety stamps itself upon their work. Under their direction mutineers allegedly burgled the colonial repositories with meticulous thoroughness. When all was finished almost no written evidence of the alleged earlier peccadilloes of the mutineers remained in the official archives. How many documents Bligh, who admitted having spent two hours tearing up papers, likely to anger his foes, had destroyed no one ever knew.

The rebels had on their hands a "prisoner of State"—for Bligh had been "arrested" with ceremony "for crimes that render you unfit to exercise the Supreme Authority for another moment"[43]—who resembled more than anything a stray mule whom a convivial householder has led home and tethered in a kitchen area. He was red-eyed with anger; and, with reversion to a state of sobriety, his captors tried in vain to induce him to leave his prison house and retire to England.

Bligh refused, then hedged. He made it clear that he intended not to leave New South Wales before succour arrived, except upon his own condition. He hoped, it was evident, to be present at the last moments of a few of his adversaries. And, every time he looked at the necks of some of the leading rebels cold shivers must have run down their spines. His conquerors were vastly relieved when in March 1809 he set off for Hobart Town, there to plague Lieutenant-Governor Collins in place of themselves.

VIII

The Botany Bay populace, of course, had enjoyed itself hugely during the "revolution". It welcomed any diversion, especially when accompanied by free rum and riot. It laughed tipsily as its lords and masters burned piles of embarrassing records. It danced as "the phrensy of Party bigotry blazed forth in illuminations, bonfires, burning effigies, roasting sheep, and in all manner of riotous dissipation".[44]

With fuddled glee Sydney settlers signed the *post facto* requisition to Major Johnston to implement a mutiny already in full flood. They swaggered in and out of the grog-shops, which displayed crudely executed posters celebrating the "ever memorable 26th January, 1808", and embellished with happily conceived paintings of Johnston being crowned by a beautiful female, Liberty, while his heel ground, or his sword pierced, the hateful snake of Tyranny.

The country settlers did not take to the change even from the first; and when the excitement was all over, and it was found that the rebel administration proposed to keep a tighter rein on the rum trade even than Bligh, many saddened promoters of insurrection joined in cursing the tyrant M'Arthur, who masqueraded as Colonial Secretary, as heartily as ever any of them had cursed the tyrant Bligh.

Very soon all the clamour and excitement faded. Lieutenant-Colonel Foveaux and old Colonel Paterson in turn took charge. As Johnston and M'Arthur fled the Colony,[45] disorganization began to make its mark. The colonists felt the pinch of hunger gripping them ever harder. Every day, before long, they watched the almost empty harbour more longingly for relief from England.

The provisional Government hanged or flogged some of them. It was accused of granting pardons to the convict section. It freely immured those who resisted it "in the dungeons of Sydney Jail", or transported them to the Coal River.

This was the story as the Home Government heard it from Bligh and his supporters. That there was another version of it all they did not yet know for certain.

The actual facts were that the rebellion had a general backing, that it had been conducted in good order and without a single shot fired, much less any record of death or injury or ravage. Indeed, the insurgents—if they justified such a title—in the end produced sufficient justification for their action to induce the Crown to limit the punishment of their official ringleader almost to nothing.

Nevertheless, the results to the Colony were dire.

The stores became empty. Bandits, black and white, infested the highways. Clothes were in rags. Another flood brought the spectre of complete starvation nearer.

Within eighteen months a stranger would have smiled at the idea that this dejected, hungry, tatterdemalion community could have been guilty of anything so violent as "insurrection".

In the meantime, the "slippery goddess, Fortune" had waved her wand.

Lieutenant-Colonel Lachlan Macquarie, of the 73rd Regiment of the Line, who had been coping with the circumlocutory Persians when the seeds of the rebellion were being sown in 1807, had been drawn from one of the most northerly of British outposts in Scotland, to shoulder, in Bligh's place, the heavy burden of authority in the most southerly ones in the antipodes.

BOOK THREE

*

1808-15

*

Numa Pompilius

When infant Rome—earth's future Queen
To grow above her hills was seen,
A Numa rose—brave, sage, serene,
To rule her iron race;
A motley, heterogeneous brood,
For crimes from different lands pursued,
Of courage fierce, of manners rude,
First laid her Empire base.

And lo!—within this Austral zone,
In regions unexplored, unknown,
Till time has into dotage grown,
An infant state appear;
Like Rome, whose motley exiles stand,
A lawless, daring, desperate band,
Expelled from Britain's parent land,
Their crimes to expiate here!

What force, what wisdom can restrain
Such fierce, unruly souls or gain
To Law's, and order's social reign,
And savage natures tame?
Brave chief! tis thy illustrious doom,
To rear for these a dearer home
And in a second rising Rome,
To rival Numa's fame!

—MICHAEL MASSEY ROBINSON, "Laureate Ode on New Year's Day, 1820".

CHAPTER XIII

Southward Ho!

I

THE year 1808 passed from thunder cloud to thunder cloud.

Napoleon seemed to be in every part of Europe at once. Wellesley, home from helping to plan the taking of Copenhagen, had provided the one hopeful interlude by winning, at Vimiero, a battle which his seniors promptly lost again at the convention table. Intelligence of the disastrous Treaty of Cintra reached England almost at the same time as a belated report from the other end of the world of the queer rebellion in the colony of New South Wales.

The news that self-styled revolutionaries had arrested Governor Bligh, had usurped the government and were carrying it on to their own great profit, with loud protestations of loyalty to His Majesty the King, caused little stir in Britain. The *Annual Register* for 1808 does not mention the affair.

Young Edward M'Arthur, reaching London as advance guard for the rebels in September 1808, found all eyes concentrated on Portugal; even he himself soon "burned to be there".[1] Only the Duke of Northumberland proved to have time to listen to him.

England was ready to expect anything of Botany Bay, and it had been for long evident—as Mr Caley, the botanist, had remarked—that Bligh was a man whom nature intended to be the subject of abuse.[2]

Still, something had to be done about it. It was resolved to vary a long course of control by naval captains by appointing a military governor. Arthur Wellesley was consulted. A young, war-worn soldier, Miles Nightingall,[3] who was generally believed to be a natural son of Marquis Cornwallis, was chosen to be Bligh's successor. He had returned to England after commanding a brigade in Portugal. In an earlier career, he had seen much fighting in India. He was forty years of age.

The Government decided to send with him the 73rd Regiment. The New South Wales Corps (the 102nd Regiment) was to return to England, "because of the share it has had in the late revolution".

The commandant of the 73rd Regiment, Lieutenant-Colonel Lachlan Macquarie, brought his wife and his corps to England late in December, in the depth of the winter of 1808. He did not relish the adventure for which he had been selected any more than did his men. He was "shortly to be transported", he wrote to Charles Forbes in February 1809. The Government of New South Wales was "to be entirely new modelled and made a military one".[4]

The War Office "had most kindly selected the 73rd" to accompany the new Governor "to restore order and tranquility [*sic*] in that Colony":

Macquarie to Charles Forbes, Bombay

This is not fair, it not being our tour by roster to be sent thither, after having already served 25 years in India—and only two years yet at home. We are however, now in a great degree reconciled to our banishment and I determined from the first to accompany my Regiment thither.—Mrs. Macquarie of course goes out with me, and we must endeavour to make ourselves as happy as we can in our exile for 3 or 4 years, at the end of which I suppose they will allow me to return home again to my native country. Do not be greatly surprised if Mrs. McQuarie and myself should pay you a visit at Bombay; . . . once we become tired of our exile at Botany Bay. We expect to sail in about 15 or 20 days, and I am only here now for a few days fitting ourselves out for our long voyage.[5]

Nightingall, with the help of Lord Castlereagh, had selected a Judge-Advocate, Mr Ellis Bent. He accepted the selection by Macquarie of Lieutenant Henry Colden Antill, who had carried the colours of the 73rd Regiment into the breach at Seringapatam ten years before, as his aide-de-camp.

The aide-de-camp, a young man of such sensibility that his pangs at parting from his friends in Glasgow were "sufficiently acute to draw a *tear* even from the eye of a soldier", bought a staff uniform and went for long walks from Suffolk Street, Charing Cross, to Blackheath.[6]

The Government had become unhurried in its proceedings. A mysterious dispatch was expected from New South Wales, said the Colonial Office confidentially, though in reality, from the news it had received, it was actually hoping that Bligh himself would arrive. Joseph Banks was fighting hard to have his deposed protégé retained in office.[7]

Having temporized since September 1808, the Government in March 1809 became suddenly infected with a zeal for swift action. It, however, failed to infect the Governor-elect with its enthusiasm.

Perhaps the changed prospects for young generals on the Spanish Peninsula, incidental to Arthur Wellesley's appointment to command, had something to do with Nightingall's alteration of mind.[8] He could not go to Botany Bay at once, said the gallant soldier. He was afflicted with rheumatism of the right arm and wrist, so violent as to prevent him from using a pen. He asked for time—after all the salary was only £2000 a year, little enough for the son-in-law of the Chairman of the Court of Directors of the East India Company.

The more he felt the need for delay, the more the Colonial Office—after the traditional manner of its inhabitants—saw the need for haste. Nightingall at last declined the appointment and, with a perfectly healthy right arm, was presently to be seen in Spain spurring on to victory, firstly a Highland brigade, and then a Division at Fuentes D'Oñoro. A few years later, in the British East Indies and Java, he made history by his strong support of Stamford Raffles.

His aide-de-camp bewailed, with a heavy heart, the wasted expense of his staff uniform and was not unduly cheered by a mysterious attitude of hopefulness which was visible in the outlook of his regimental commander, who advised him "not to despair".[9]

The latter was hard at work. He had been told that there would be no appointment for the moment of a successor to Nightingall; that he was to sail for Sydney as Lieutenant-Governor and await the coming of a superior.

Conceiving, however, that the situation of Governor was still vacant, he "took the liberty to offer himself as a candidate for it", and earnestly solicited Castlereagh's "patronage and protection on the occasion". He would remind his lordship, he wrote, that his recommendation for his appointment as Lieutenant-Governor came from the Duke of York himself; and he believed "my friend Sir Arthur Wellesley likewise recommended me to your Lordship's favour and protection".[10]

The Colonial Office was bland and non-committal. On 22 April its suppliant was able to tell Charles Forbes only unpromising news:

Macquarie to Charles Forbes

When I last wrote you I thought I should by this time have been half way on my passage to Botany Bay; but here we have been ever since detained in anxious suspence, expecting every day to receive orders to embark for that Land of Exiles . . . I believe we shall certainly sail in 8 or 10 days hence at farthest . . . our numers [sic] are now increased to 800 men by draughts and volunteers from the Militia Regiments lately; so we shall go out a very respectable Battalion, and complete in a very good and genteel Corps of Officers; several of whom are married, which will add much to our comfort and society in our exile to the Land of Convicts! I am happy to inform you that I am appointed Lieut. Governor of New South Wales, (alias Botany Bay!) with the rank of Colonel in that Colony, and shall have the chief charge of it until such time as a Governor is sent out from this country—no one going out in that capacity at present;— I was at first in some hopes that they would appoint myself Governor, but I find there is no chance of their doing me that honour; so that I shall probably have all the trouble, plague, responsibility and odium of new modelling the Government of New South Wales, and restoring order and tranquillity there; and most likely be immediately afterwards superseded by a Governor sent out from England— which, I must confess, I shall think rather hard; but I must however be contented—and do my duty.— We go out in two very fine ships—large and commodious—named the *Hindostan* and the *Dromedary*—both being troop ships. The latter was formerly our old Bombay friend—The *Shah Rai Ruperoo* and afterwards called the *Howe*. Mrs. Macquarie and I myself embark on the *Dromedary*, as being by far the finest ship of the two.[11]

Four days later he was presented to the King on his being officially appointed Lieutenant-Governor. The presentation was made during the holding of a private Chapter of the Order of the Bath at which his friends Sir David Baird and Lord Cochrane were made knights. Next day Lord Castlereagh, whom he met by accident in Berkeley Square, told him that he was a full-fledged Governor.[12] His Minister obviously hoped that he would remain Governor for a long time. He promised him a pension if he stayed in New South Wales eight years.

Observing the good news presently in the *London Gazette*, Macquarie felt he could "not forbear intruding on your Lordship's [Castlereagh's] time to express how gratified I feel at being thus noticed by my Sovereign with this highly flattering appointment". It did not, however, inspire him with any goodwill towards the rebels, Messrs Johnston and M'Arthur, to whom he owed his preferment. He trusted there would be "sufficient evidence in England to convict them both at home as soon as Governor Bligh arrives in England".[13]

Otherwise, his difficulties appeared mainly to consist in the solution of the problems concerned with the comfortable berthing of his troops on shipboard.

Between four and five o'clock on the afternoon of 15 May 1809, having received his dispatches from Lord Castlereagh, Macquarie set out from London with Elizabeth for New South Wales.[14]

At Portsmouth, H.M.S. *Hindostan*, under the command of Captain Pasco, R.N., Nelson's flag lieutenant, who had hoisted the signal at Trafalgar, waited for him with the storeship, *Dromedary*, commanded by a master, one Pritchard.

On the latter ship, among 592 souls, the Governor-elect embarked with his entourage to begin the seven months' voyage which was to take them to Rio de Janeiro and Cape Town on their way to New Holland. After one false start they sailed at noon on 22 May.

He would not see England again for thirteen years.

II

The voyage began as a happy Odyssey, despite the strain caused by the fact that war was everywhere and that Captain Pasco found in the taking of an early prize—after a little unanswered firing of his nine-pounders—an incentive to chase hither and thither hopefully each time he sighted a sail.

Their journey was marred, too, in the early period by the illness of Elizabeth. But her indisposition fortunately did not affect her spirits or her zest as a diarist. Thus she preserved for posterity her pictures of the squalors of Funchal and of her pilgrimage up the hill there in a hammock to the Church of Our Lady of the Mount,[15] during which her appearance shocked her husband, though that did not altogether displease her.

Her spouse remarked that she looked exactly like a corpse; and she flattered herself that, as he apparently "did not like my resemblance, he could have no wish to see me in that state"; though, to tell the truth, she wrote, she never dreaded for a moment that he did, for he was "not of a nature to wish ill to anyone, much less his own wife, who indeed during this voyage has been a troublesome charge", because of her indisposition.[16]

On the whole they had reason to think "being at sea a very agreeable life". The ship sailed steadily. The crew and passengers were very healthy. The Governor worked most of the time at his papers. Elizabeth plied her needle. At intervals they catered for Captain Pritchard's fondness for whist, though he proved to be "one of those men given to severely reprimanding a partner who made a mistake".

On Sundays the young and as yet amiable Mr Ellis Bent performed divine service in a most agreeable manner.

There was just enough incident to prevent tedium. They called at Madeira for wine. They fell in with a great, menacing-looking vessel which displayed her colours so awkwardly that it was only when they hove alongside that they found her to be a friendly American, Canton bound.

They met a horrible Portuguese ship bound from Bengola to Rio, crowded with female slaves and smitten from stem to stern with the Yellow Jack. The captain and some of the slaves had died. To put an end to the epidemic, the commanders had "resorted to a precaution at which humanity shuddered, namely, that of throwing the unfortunate slaves overboard as soon as they were taken ill". ("When we heard of this we all thought on Mr. Wilberforce.")[17]

Soon after leaving St Jago, a wretched port in Cape Verde Islands, the sea seemed to be deserted by every living creature. The immense stretch of silent ocean showed not even a bird to keep them company. They met no ships. It seemed "as if they had the whole world to themselves". When they boarded a small American sloop they felt quite rejoiced at the sight again of human beings. It gave rise in Elizabeth to "a kind of feeling new to me till that moment, connected with the idea of being totally separated from our country and the people belonging to it, seeing that here we were in another quarter of the globe, with a new race of beings which I could not help regretting were not our own people . . ."[18]

One day she saw something fall past her cabin window, and had no idea that it was a man till she heard him cry out, which he did in a most distressing manner. Macquarie, on the poop, ran forward and encouraged him by every means in his power to keep hold of a line which he had grasped. Presently he was rescued from the desert of water. . . .

III

On 6 August the heights which guard Rio de Janeiro towered over them. They put in there because dysentery had broken out in *Hindostan*.

To Macquarie the entrance seemed "most grand and magnificent" and the whole scenery near the town and round the harbour "beautifully picturesque".[19] To Elizabeth it appeared that no description could convey the impression produced by this harbour and its wonderful beauty on those who had not seen it, and she felt that she saw the entrance—the finest in the world, she believed—to the best advantage, since they arrived on a fine clear evening. A steady landing breeze carried them in, as they watched the sun setting in a riot of colours behind the Sugarloaf.

Macquarie went ashore with Rear-Admiral de Courcy, whose *Foudroyant* lay proudly in the heart of Rio Bay, to call on Lord Strangford, the British Ambassador. The Prince Regent of Portugal took them to the opera, where it was remarked that the Princess bestowed some very cold looks on Strangford, who told Macquarie philosophically not to be surprised at that, as he had incurred the lady's displeasure by preventing her from becoming Queen of Mexico, which Sir Sidney Smith had proposed.[20]

The opera proved a respectable performance, well attended, but it was very evidently not appreciated by Royalty. The Prince, a heavy fat man, slept most of the time, engagingly leaning on his princess.

The entertainment of the visitors by Sir James Gambier, the British Consul, was better. He lived in a mansion furnished in the most magnificent style, feeling it his duty to keep open house for all the English who cared to sit at his table. He insisted on giving a ball for the 73rd Regiment, and out of that arose an incident which showed how little sea captains change through the centuries. For Captain Pritchard, having refused to attend, on the ground that he would not leave his ship on any pretext after nine o'clock at night, met an old shipmate and, in the small hours of the morning, retired with a headache which he had acquired out of a bottle.

A character out of Smollett, this Captain Pritchard. He made an excursion with them—having been at great pains to assure them that he was a first-rate horseman—a ponderous load on a weak, half-famished nag, travelling at full speed. A mile out from town, by his account, the poor prad "got sick"; and all the remedy he could contrive was to "give it wine and everything he could think of", which was so little effective that he had to reverse the natural order of things and support or almost carry the poor beast back to town.[21]

In the meantime, Macquarie, Elizabeth, and Major Cleaveland had packed themselves into a small sort of carriage "exactly like Gil Blas when he went to take possession of his country home".

It was drawn by two mules; and the driver, a "monkey looking black, man", who could not speak a word of English, held them up in the middle of the street, while the rabble gaped. He was apparently annoyed at having to carry three passengers, instead of the customary two.

IV

Their thoughts often turned to New South Wales and to the state in which they should find the Colony. They had not the smallest hope of learning much before they reached the Cape of Good Hope, but to their surprise they found that Lieutenant-Colonel Johnston, "the usurper", who had headed the rebellion, had been in Rio de Janeiro with John M'Arthur, who had apparently planned it, and had sailed away only four days before their arrival. This, Macquarie averred, relieved him of a "very unpleasant job", since the Government had ordered him to "send home Johnston *in close* arrest and to try the other for High Treason before the Criminal Court in New South Wales". He was most happy to be quit of such gentry.

Bligh, they learnt from Thomas Jamison, the elderly Surgeon-General of the Colony and Dr John Harris, who still tarried in Rio, had left his prison in Sydney for H.M.S. *Porpoise* and had proclaimed a long list of specially guilty rebels headed by John M'Arthur, Nicholas Bayly, Garnham

Blaxcell, Richard Atkins, Gregory Blaxland, Alexander Riley and others.[22]
Elizabeth reported:

> We had a good deal of conversation with Dr. Jamison regarding the extraordinary
> events which had taken place in New South Wales, and it appeared to us that
> *even by their own account* the conduct of those persons who had acted against the
> Government was not to be justified or even excused; we felt sorry that a man
> such as Col. Johnson [*sic*] was described to us, should have committed himself
> as he has done, by an act of the most open and daring rebellion, by which in as
> far as it appears to us, he will probably forfeit a life, which has till this unfortunate
> period, been spent in the service of his King and Country.
>
> Colonel Macquarie felt it quite a relief to him, his having quitted the Colony
> before his arrival, and by that means having spared him the pain of taking
> measures which the service required, but which no officer could feel easy at being
> obliged to have recourse to, particularly on this occasion; Col. Johnson [*sic*]
> being a man of amiable character, and in their early years an intimate companion
> of his own.[23]

The two voyagers gave them a favourable account of Botany Bay and
they saw a drawing of Dr Harris's fine house about a mile from Sydney,
standing in a park stocked with deer and "altogether in much higher style
than anything we expected to find in the new world". Elizabeth observed
the words "*Ultimo Place*, the seat etc." at the bottom of the drawing and,
being struck with the oddity of it, asked what it could mean. On which
the doctor, with an air of the utmost importance, strutted up to her and
said:

> I can explain that to you, Madam. I was once summoned to attend a Court
> Martial. The Gentleman in reading the charge happened to say this court being
> convened on the 12th ultimo, instead of instant; they were not clasical [*sic*],
> but I, Madam, being clasical, immediately perceived the mistake; I ridiculed
> them, and wrote verses on the subject then; and afterwards called my house
> Ultimo Place.[24]

Surgeon Harris was a type quite outside the Macquaries' experience.
Mr Bent named him "Major Sturgeon", from his resemblance to that
character. He came to call on the Governor of New South Wales dressed
in a new uniform coat and seemed to think himself a very great man and
to wish that other persons should think the same.

But one morning, after he had been in the ship arrayed in his usual
grand style, some of the passengers were surprised to see him in Rio,
"dressed like a Jew, in a shabby little shop making merchandise of some
precious stones he had brought for sale from New Holland".[25]

The wonder that this transformation engendered was not greater
than that with which it was discovered that Dr Jamison, the Surgeon-
General of New South Wales, "had brought a venture of *shoes* and *stockings*
and various other articles of traffic" which he disposed of at Rio. It seemed
strange to the Governor and his lady that a surgeon-general of a colony
should be concerned in such matters, though they conceded that such
dealing was "highly respectable to those to whose province it belongs".[26]

They little knew that one august person in their own entourage would find himself unable to avoid the same sort of temptation within a few months to come. Even judge advocates traded in Botany Bay.

V

With these fleeting glimpses of those whom they were to govern, the voyagers passed on to the Cape, where their landing at Table Bay on 23 September was not without event. A great swell was running. When they came to the pier Lieutenant-Colonel O'Connell was amused to see Elizabeth climb the steps on all fours and remarked that he saw that the lady had not been brought up in the Highlands for nothing. She was not well pleased at being laughed at, but this speech "made up for the insult, if such it could be called".[27]

Moreover, the stillness and quiet of the large comfortable room in which they breakfasted with Macquarie's old friend Mr Pringle, whom he had met at Jedda on his journey to Egypt in 1801, was in marked contrast to the continual motion and confinement of the ship.

Cape Colony, too, was looking its best. Wild heath flowered round Table Mountain and everybody was in the highest spirits. And when Elizabeth remarked that she did not wonder that the soldiers of the 93rd Regiment were well behaved since they came from Scotland and were all gentlemen, everybody chaffed her for the rest of the visit and the Sutherlands' rank and file were "gentlemen" to Cape Town society for ever after.

Lord Caledon, the Governor of the Cape of Good Hope, was an extremely good-looking young man with pleasing manners, but very diffident. At his ball to welcome the visitors and the 73rd Regiment he did not dance, though Admiral Bertie, who commanded the naval squadron, "figured away with great industry in every number". Lieutenant-Colonel Sorell, of whom they were to see a great deal more as Lieutenant-Governor of Van Diemen's Land, acted as steward at the ball, and Elizabeth "liked him by far the best" and thought him the most gentlemanly looking man she saw at the Cape; "which was saying a great deal for there were several very pleasant persons there", and particularly Captain Hawkes of the Dragoons, who had come aboard at sea to dine with them.[28]

The captain's assets were extreme good looks combined with the most engaging manners and a young wife who had exchanged the opulence of the London home of her wealthy father, Mr Borradale, for a voyage on which she "often cried for want of something to eat".

This was a hardship which the Macquaries had not suffered. Their table on the *Dromedary* had never been neat and elegant, Elizabeth reflected, nor their cooking of the delicate kind; but they had "always been furnished with what any person inclined to eat could make a good dinner of" and they had a luxury which was rare on so long a voyage—"very fine water".[29]

Captain Pasco of the *Hindostan* and his wife were ashore and they in themselves proved a diversion, for they loved a lord with a great love.

Once, when they were abroad on the slopes of the Mountain, it seemed that they "must have exchanged the canter of their horses into a gallop" to enable them to reach town in time to dine with Lord Caledon. Then "Mrs. P. being desirous of enjoying as much of his Lordship's company as she could, declined playing cards, but sat down most boldly to attack him at chess". To his great consternation, the young governor soon found that his willing antagonist hardly knew the moves. He did all he could to lose the game but failed. So presently, having refused another game, he sent the ladies home in his carriage, and by this time Mrs Pasco felt herself so much gratified, by her morning drive, by dining at a lord's house, playing chess with the Great Man, and being sent home in his grand coach with a coronet on the door of it, that she "fairly burst out in exclamations of joy, clapping her hands and dancing with her feet" as she exclaimed, "I vow! I vow! this has been the happiest and the best day of my life."

All very vulgar, no doubt, thought Elizabeth, but who, she added, could "avoid being pleased at this natural conduct, called forth by sensations of gratitude and satisfaction"?[30]

Macquarie himself was in high spirits. He could even be humorous at the expense of poor Pringle, when he observed him cringing under the onslaught of the post-prandial bagpipe at a mess dinner given by the 75th Regiment. For he wickedly begged his host, Major Campbell, to have the playing continued, since "Pringle liked nothing better on earth".[31]

They sailed on 13 October. They had seen the dawn rise all too often and it was a relief to be at sea again.

VI

The weather in the Indian Ocean was bitterly cold; and at breakfast one morning Captain Pritchard, who had risen hastily to look at a phantom landfall, fell ill.

He had always expressed an abhorrence of doctors, stoutly affirming that when ill he wished to be left entirely to himself. Acute rheumatism quickly altered his attitude. Elizabeth said that he was more impatient and restless than any one she ever saw sick.[32] His attendants had no rest. Two or three hovered continually about him. When Macquarie suggested that he should move out of his little cabin into one of theirs, he accepted the offer with alacrity.

Two of Macquarie's servants, Joseph Big, the prospective coachman, and Mrs Ovens were drawn in as the "most able bodied men" to effect the transfer of the poor, inert mariner, which was performed amid roars of "Avast—Avast—Avast—Vast heaving! . . . Now lower me handsomely! . . . Haul me forward, I say and take care of my larboard side! . . . Now, hoist me, slew me round to starboard! Steady!"—all this with a few expressions which Elizabeth thought it "as well to forget".

But next morning he was back in his own cabin, sending for the doctor every hour and "insisting that he is *never to be left alone*".

To make matters worse Mr Ellis Bent, too, was ill with rheumatic fever, his weeping wife ever in attendance beside his cot. .

G

Their voyage then was drawing to a close, "having been in every respect prosperous except in expedition", their detention having been caused by the bad sailing of the *Hindostan*. Sick soldiers on the *Dromedary* rarely exceeded five or six; the deaths from accidents were few. There were no contagious disorders; but then, Elizabeth reported, "nothing could exceed the minute care and attention paid by Coll. Macquarie to his men at all times; twice each day he visits every part of the ship. The men are regularly paraded morning and evening, the women are also obliged to appear clean and well dressed at regular parades appointed for them."

When the weather was damp and cold, stoves were kept burning between decks all day, while in warm weather wind-sails were always over the hatchways. Care was always taken that hammocks were kept dry. The provisions served to the men were of the best quality and well cooked. And in every object for the health and comfort of the soldiers they always found the old sea-dog, Pritchard, ready to oblige and help.

Far different were conditions on the *Hindostan*, and it shrewdly appeared to Elizabeth that the service such as these ships engaged in was more likely to be successfully executed under command of a master in the Navy than by a captain.[33] Captain Pritchard, a master, was his own purser. His credit and character depended on the manner in which persons on board were accommodated. He knew what was required and that if anything needed was wanting the blame would attach solely to him. Any great neglect on his part would probably be the means of depriving him of his ship; beside which his situation in life did not put him above attending minutely to the wants of persons in his charge.

In the *Hindostan*, commanded by a captain in the Royal Navy, the stores and provisions were supplied by a purser, who happened to be a rogue. The company of that ship, before the end of the voyage, were in want of everything, and particularly were they short of firewood. Ere they reached the Australian coast "casks, spars, hencoops, pig styes, cow-pens, trunks, etc., were obliged to go to wreck to cook their dinners", in spite of the fact that the *Dromedary* was for ever supplying them with fuel.

On 10 December land birds, the first inhabitants of the new world which they had seen, came to pay their compliments, and Macquarie hailed the appearance of a seal as a sure sign that they were at no great distance from shore.[34]

Pasco proposed to make his first call at Port Phillip, but Macquarie wished to hasten on in the hope of meeting Bligh. Judging that he might be at Van Diemen's Land settlement, they passed as closely as possible to Hobart Town; but wind hampered their movement and a thick fog kept the ships from sight of each other for a whole day.

Presently the sea cleared. Whales and big bonito appeared. On 15 December it was recorded that "at half past 10 o'clock this morning we have with the mercy of God made the land".

Macquarie immediately ordered the band to play "God Save the King". When it struck up, he felt himself "particularly affected".[35]

They had "made the land in most favourable manner possible" and true to reckoning. Fifteen miles away they could see the New Stone, a striking object named after a rock on the coast of Cornwall. They thought it in shape like the Bass in the Firth of Forth, and Cape Pillar "exactly like part of Gruline in the Isle of Mull opposite to Oskamull". Elizabeth "did not know of any place the resemblance to which would be so gratifying to me"; for some of the happiest days of her life had been spent at Mrs Macquarie's house at Oskamull.[36]

The day was marked by tragedy. A sailor, whose birthday it was, drank too much grog and fell to death off the yardarm . . .

VII

Towards the end, Macquarie was inclined to be unwell. The new movement of the ship gave Elizabeth a confused motion in her head which, with anxiety for him, made her feel out of sorts. They sailed along the New South Wales coast, on which they could plainly perceive the smoke of the natives' fires.

On Christmas Day 1809 they still had some way to go, but Elizabeth was cheered by the "kindest congratulation I ever received" from her beloved husband who, she thanked God, felt himself better.[37]

They dined with the officers and it was pleasant to meet them all once more before they landed and she felt attached to them and happy in their company.

The officers themselves, though greatly daring, were not nearly so comfortable about the repast. For their fresh provisions were exhausted, and they had nothing to give the viceregal guests for dinner but salt beef and pork and part of an old goat which was killed for the occasion.

There was but one unpleasant incident to mar the Christmas festivities. The second master of the *Dromedary* and two midshipmen got drunk and riotous. The second master hit a Highland officer in the eye. And all three miscreants found themselves presently in irons before the mast in *Hindostan*.

The soldiers were now paraded in full marching order in their new caps and uniform. "No body of men could possibly appear cleaner or in better health." Only six were on the sick list for trifling causes after seven months at sea.

Captain Pritchard handed out an extra helping of grog and they became "very jovial but were quiet and orderly, looking forward to going ashore", a consummation which was too long delayed, since baffling winds held them back so strenuously that in four days they covered only one hundred and thirty-eight miles.

On their last night at sea they endured the terrors of a hurricane seamed through with fearsome lightnings, their cabins awash, their cots swinging from bulkhead to bulkhead. And then, upon a lovely Sydney morning, they saw the long roll of a wide ocean dashing against majestic cliffs. The

sky was enchantingly blue, the *Hindostan*, swaying to the gentle roll, was
seen leading them in through the Heads, her full canvas set. Their colours
rode to the masthead. A puff of smoke spread over the sea, a reverberation
echoed back from the precipices of the shore. *Hindostan*, her number up,
had fired a gun for a pilot. The band once more played the national anthem.

At ten o'clock on the morning of 28 December 1809 they found themselves anchored safely inside the mouth of Port Jackson. Bush, empty and
lonely, lay all about them, and the wind was right ahead from the west,
"an extraordinary thing at that time of the year", so that they could not
continue to Sydney Cove.[38]

Presently a pilot boat came down bearing Isaac Nichols, the assistant
to the naval officer.

Lieutenant-Colonel Foveaux, the acting commandant at Sydney,
fat, debonair, Irish, and brisk as a bee, followed with Paymaster Mell
of the 102nd Regiment. The Lieutenant-Governor's secretary brought
the news that poor Colonel Paterson was ill.

A constant dribble of visitors came aboard till a change of wind made
it possible for them to sail up the harbour on 30 December and anchor
ten fathoms off the Governor's Wharf in Sydney Cove. That night they
stretched their legs on land.

On the last day of 1809 they went ashore officially with Foveaux and
the officers and their ladies in the *Dromedary's* barge.[39]

So soon as the Governor left the gangway the harbour echoed to salutes
of fifteen guns fired from the ships, on which all the yards were manned.
The men gave three cheers. Colonel Paterson and Lieutenant-Colonel
Foveaux were at the Pier Head with the 102nd Regiment, attended by the
chaplain and "the gentlemen of the settlement". The 73rd Regiment
and the ruddy ancients of the New South Wales Corps under arms, formed
a guard all the way to the adjacent newly painted Government House.
Inhabitants bowed as the party passed.

Presently they drove with Foveaux in his carriage through the park-like
lands within the tiny township. Night fell. Bonfires blazed. Rockets rose
from the ships. There was a general air of rejoicing.

In New Holland the Macquarie Era, which was to leave so strong a mark
upon the history of the continent, had begun, and the new Governor had a
chance to look round him and consider his domain.

CHAPTER XIV

"Arise, Anoint Him ..."

I

WITH relief the ragged, half-starved colonists saw the *Hindostan* and the *Dromedary* gently rocking at anchor in the swell inside Sydney Heads.

No doubt they gazed on Macquarie as he came ashore from the latter ship with curiosity, though most certainly not with more earnestness than that eager administrator devoted to a scrutiny of themselves, who, he hoped, were to be his charges for not more than three or four years.

His first glimpses of his surroundings failed to please. Laxity was everywhere evident amid advancing ruin.

The new arrival beheld a community "barely emerging from infantile imbecility, and suffering from various privations and disabilities"; the country impenetrable beyond forty miles from Sydney; agriculture languishing; commerce in its early dawn; revenue unknown. The population, he found, was threatened with famine; the public buildings in a state of dilapidation and mouldering to decay. The few roads and bridges formerly built had become almost impassable. People in general appeared to be depressed by poverty. There was no public credit, nor private confidence.[1]

And, to cap it all, the morals of the great mass of the inhabitants seemed to him to be "in the lowest state of debasement, and religious worship almost totally neglected". But the atmosphere was subdued and submissive. All wished the Governor well. Even Mr M'Arthur, now pining in London, wrote of him, "If he prove on trial at all equal to the universal character he has here, his government cannot but prove a blessing to the Colony."

The incoming 73rd Regiment, clothed in the new uniforms which had replaced its kilts, could spread the news of his kindness and consideration for its welfare during a long and trying voyage.

The new man's mien and his glittering entourage were such as to command respect. His tone and manner warned all to be wary as he proclaimed His Majesty's "utmost regret and displeasure on account of the late tumultuous proceedings" and "mutinous conduct" towards his predecessor. It was clear to even the most insolent that the days had gone when one might indulge in altercation with Botany Bay's ruler or pluck him by the sleeve and importune him in the street, as had been done of yore to the horror of Governor Bligh.[2]

Around him was a hedge of ceremony, and he was closely guarded by a gilded but completely unauthorized staff, with which, pending the agreement of his London superiors, he had provided himself. He had an aide-de-camp and a private secretary appointed on the recommendation of Lord

Caledon—Mr J. T. Campbell, trim, dour, combative, efficient, faithful, an Ulsterman between thirty and forty years old, who had managed the Bank of the Cape of Good Hope. Macquarie proposed in vain to have him appointed Colonial Secretary by the Home Government.[3] He also boasted an impressive coachman who had learnt his art in the employment of the partly-royal Lord Harrington.

The inhabitants on New Year's Day 1810 found themselves watching, open-mouthed, the proceedings of this imposing group, seen against the serried ranks of two regiments on the Grand Parade sweating in the mid-summer glare, while the racket of the troops' incessant volleyings set rocks running in the gullies of the North Shore and the military bands lustily played "God Save the King".[4]

Agreed procedure had been departed from, for the Home Government had intended that Bligh should have his part in initiating the new era. The orders to him which exist in Macquarie's own handwriting were emphasized in their salient parts by the latter's vigorous underlinings:

E. Cooke, Under Secretary to the
Colonial Office, to Governor Bligh

Lord Castlereagh, however, desires it to be understood by you that when liberated from arrest, you are not to proceed to the general exercise of the functions of Governor, *but the day after you shall have been so liberated, you are to receive Colonel Macquarie as your successor at the Government House, when he will open his Patent, and you will swear him into office.*—[5]

Bligh, by being at the Derwent, however, missed his chances.

The state of the Colony and of its government brooked not a moment's delay in the establishment of some firm authority with proper legal right of initiative. The Governor-designate, upon the Judge-Advocate's advice, hastened to assume his powers upon the Grand Parade, no doubt the more readily since it was plain that Bligh's restoration was to be a mere empty formality.

With due dignity he broke the wax upon the Patent, and handed the royal missive to the youthful Judge-Advocate, Ellis Bent, who displayed the Great Seal of the Territory to the admiring onlookers.[6]

The bands once more played the National Anthem while the Governor and his suite stood immobile and the January sun beat down on the loyal polls of all—save the bald one of Mr Bent, who read on interminably beneath an umbrella. The solemn music of the drums rolled across the Parade Ground. Guns thundered once more in royal salutes.

"George the Third: To our Trusty and Well-beloved Lachlan Macquarie."

The Colony had heard most of the words recited to other potentates; but, within a few minutes after the Governor's Commission had been read, they had cause to recognize in his own less ceremonial injunctions a note novel to the atmosphere in which for so long every proceeding had been tainted with factious irritation.

"Fellow citizens and fellow soldiers . . ."[7] began the rich, Scottish, soldierly

voice which Indians of a decade earlier would have recognized with amazement as issuing from the throat of one of the world's most consistent haters
of the "infernal and destructive principles of Democracy".[8]

It was his firm intention, the voice's owner said, to exercise the authority
vested in him with strict justice and impartiality, and he asked for the
cordial support of heads of departments.

He was sanguine that "all the dissensions and jealousies which had
unfortunately existed in the Colony for some time past would now terminate
for ever, and give way to a more becoming spirit of conciliation, harmony
and unanimity among all classes and descriptions of inhabitants".

He strongly recommended *all classes* to a strict observance of all religious
duties and a constant and regular attendance at divine worship on Sundays
and other holidays set apart for the purpose. He trusted that the magistrates
and all other persons in authority would exert themselves to the utmost
in checking and preventing all species of vice and immorality.

He need not, he hoped, express his wish that the natives of the country,
when they came in the way in a peaceable manner, might not be molested
in their persons and property by anyone, but that they should always be
treated with kindness and attention, so as to conciliate them as much as
possible to the British Government and manners.

From the troops, he said, he should at all times expect a most vigilant
discharge of every part of their duties, and he fondly hoped that their
steadiness, sobriety, and strict discipline would preclude the painful necessity
of resorting but very rarely to any punishment.

Lastly, he assured them all that it would be the fault of the inhabitants
if they failed to be as comfortable and happy as any others of His Majesty's
subjects.

To make them so, so far as depended on him, he said, was not only
his duty but would at all times constitute his chief happiness. The honest,
sober, and industrious inhabitant, whether free settler or convict, would
ever find him a friend and protector.

II

Thus he entered upon his new satrapy and a few glances at his Commission
and instructions from the Colonial Office would have assured any doubter
of the amplitude of his power as a locally unchallengeable despot, to carry
out his promises throughout a land mass half the size of Europe and a
delightfully large and vague expanse of oceanic island groups.

His territory stretched, on the eastern side, from Cape York (10° 37′ S.)
the northmost cape of the Australian continent, to South Cape (43° 39′ S.),
the southernmost extremity of Van Diemen's Land, a distance of about
2700 miles.[9]

It reached inland from the east coast to a line drawn along the 135th
parallel of east longitude. This, in the twentieth century, runs through
Stewart's Bay in Arnhem Land on the north, only a few hundred miles
from the Equator, and between Coffin Bay and the Investigator Group

where it leaves the Commonwealth in the south, only a few hundred miles from the Antarctic Circle.

With royal lavishness His Majesty had thrown in "islands adjacent in the Pacific Ocean", between the Colony's latitudinal limits, leaving it to his viceroy's modesty to define—subject, as in all things, to correction—the meaning of the word, "adjacent".

The new satrap presently did this as occasion arose. Among other trifles which he took under his wing were Tahiti, a mere 3800 miles away, the Solomon Islands and Fiji, as well as New Zealand, 1200 miles from Sydney Cove.

He was the first man to endow the Cannibal Islands with the services of a justice of the peace, but this was a modest exercise of authority in one empowered to build forts, platforms and fortified castles, cities and towns, and provide them with ordnance and ammunition; to raise troops and armed forces to vanquish the King's enemies and to apprehend, take, put to death or preserve alive at his discretion such foemen as might fall in his way; to pardon all offenders against the law save those convicted of murder and treason, whom he might reprieve, subject to the King's pleasure; to grant lands; to explore coasts at will, and to proceed with a patriarchal benignity to "grand objects" which in New South Wales might have daunted Saint Paul himself—the improving of morals, the encouragement of marriage, the provision of education, the assurance of a food supply, the weaning of the population from the use of spirituous liquors.

Although he "did not exactly possess the unlimited authority of an eastern despot", a discerning native could justly ask, "Should he invade the personal liberty of the subject, where are the oppressed to seek retribution?"

It was no wonder that he himself jokingly wrote of "my reign". Subject to the long-distance interference of his masters in London, he could "do what he liked and no one could say him nay".

Generally speaking he, in common with other New South Wales Governors of the early period, assumed in emergency the powers of an absolute monarch within his own region, subject, not to constitutional and statutory limitations, but only to what were believed to be the necessities of the situation in hand and the elasticity of the Colonial Minister's tolerance.

Bligh had summed up the viceregal ideal fairly accurately: "What I wish them—i.e. the British Government—to understand is that the Governor in this remote settlement must act according to circumstances . . . If they send orders, they may be assured I act up to them. If anything is left to my own will, I trust it will not be misapplied."[10]

Bligh said that the arduousness of the Governor's situation was more than could be well described. Magisterial, civil and criminal courts "all ultimately rested with him in decision, all the concerns of Government in public works and issues of stores and distribution of convict servants; nothing could be trusted to be done but under the Governor's orders".

There was "an absolute omission of Parliamentary sanction for the greater part of the Colonial Government". As the constitutionalists of the

New South Wales Corps and their poet had sung of Governor King, who had been flabbergasted by the novel proposition that "no order or regulation is binding or legal unless sanctioned by Parliament":

> To every law he, boasting, did defiance,
> Made local laws to suit his own occasion.[11]

III

As the echoes of the Governor's first speech on New South Wales soil died away the scarlet ranks of the regiments stood ramrod-straight and still in general salute. The Battery burst into another roar, which was answered from the ships. The harassed seagulls wheeled aloft again. The day ended in a blaze of light under a heaven sprayed by skyrockets. The "general sentiment promised universal conciliation and peace".

The congregation of St Philip's on the hill celebrated with unusual fervour when young, thin, mathematical Mr Cowper diffidently preached from the text 1 Samuel XVI. 12: "Arise, anoint him: for this is he"—[12] while the blushing David sat below in the Governor's pew with Elizabeth. The preacher omitted that portion of the verse which reads, "Now he was ruddy, and withal of a beautiful countenance, and goodly to look to."

Seamen and marines lent colour to the scene as they paid "their duties of respect and adoration to their beneficent Creator".

And Heaven itself sent a token of notice in a violent storm studded with fireballs, one of which toppled the publisher of the Sydney Gazette off his stool as he read a proof in his printery that Sabbath afternoon.[13]

The colonists hastened off to pen their address to their new ruler in which they declared that they cherished an anxious hope that the union and harmony so forcibly recommended by His Excellency (to whom they knew the bare mention of the late differences in the Colony to be painful) would unanimously prevail and that all party spirit might be buried in oblivion. He in his turn had expressed his belief that, if they rigidly adhered to the line of conduct which he had laid down for them, "the country must inevitably increase in consequence, opulence, and respectability and importance".[14]

Elizabeth Macquarie, faint as always at the smell of fresh paint, settled down to wrestle with the problem of fitting all their viceregal state into a Government House which consisted of two small rooms, a business-room and a dining-room, on either side of a passage, with the bedroom opening into the dining-room, and attics above, in which of an evening the trampling of servants could be heard. That her kitchens were detached did not make it the easier for her to keep house in a country in which diners at the Governor's table expected quantity as well as quality in their victuals; where, in fact, the repast was looked on as a little meagre when she gave her guests only soup, roast beef, a turkey, a fricassee, chickens, kidneys and a tongue and vegetables, with a second course of oysters, wild ducks, tartlets, jellies and more vegetables.[15]

For a full fortnight Sydney was full of strange and beautiful sounds and sights, and the arrival on 14 January of the ship *Marian*, loaded down with grain and putting starvation far astern, lent a sort of second wind to the rejoicing at the Governor's arrival and unexpected lavishness to its culmination.[16]

The celebrations did not close until the night of 16 January and the succeeding morning, when the town ran with good liquor and was full of the stench of burning tallow and whale oil. The ships in the harbour twinkled to their topmasts. Ashore every pane had its loyal sentiments stencilled in light. A bonfire blazed on every height.

Mr Underwood, who had left his country for his country's good—and for his own, as his opulent condition testified—vied with Mr Garnham Blaxcell in inventing fiery mottoes to adorn his parlour and bedroom windows.

A band on his veranda noisily played "Rule, Britannia!" His tables groaned under his offerings of provender. His floors creaked under the load imposed upon them by the crowd of youth and beauty who, according to the ever-poetical *Gazette*, "kept the merry dance alive until Aurora joined the festive scene".[17]

At some shadowy hour after midnight, Commodore Bligh may have gazed from the poop of the wallowing *Porpoise*, which was bringing him from the Derwent, and noticed the smoke rising from the dying embers of the fires which celebrated his final eclipse as Governor of New South Wales.

As an anticlimax he arrived that day to say his vengeful farewells.

IV

Macquarie had sent the *Estramina* to the Derwent in Van Diemen's Land to bring Bligh to Sydney, but Bligh arrived instead in the water-logged old *Porpoise* in a very bad mood. He was feeling "embarrassed to know how to act in bringing rebel offenders to justice", and surprised and pained that his successor "took command *without waiting for my return*".

He was little mollified by Macquarie's assurance that he would be "most happy to bestow on you every respect and attention in my power while you find it necessary to remain in the settlement",[18] or by the salute of thirteen guns and the invitation to dine which greeted him.

He rudely declined dining with Macquarie in favour of the table of the Lieutenant-Governor.

He insisted at once on taking over as Naval Commodore the two ships *Hindostan* and *Dromedary*. He demanded that he should receive viceregal honours. He hired a cottage at ten pounds a month hard by the Tank Stream and there dwelt in high dudgeon.

The chagrined soldiers of the rebel New South Wales Corps were always turning out guards and presenting arms for him, when they did not happen to be doing the same courtesies to the Governor or old Colonel Paterson and Lieutenant-Colonel Foveaux, Bligh's usurping successors, who were being treated as brigadier-generals, or to the Lieutenant-Governor, Lieutenant-Colonel O'Connell, who had been dowered with local rank as a full colonel.[19]

Bligh pestered Macquarie and the new Judge-Advocate with demands for the prosecution of available rebels.

Mr Ellis Bent, the Judge-Advocate, diplomatically expressed doubt whether the law of treason ran in the Colony and whether it would be politic to prosecute for misdemeanours without instructions from home, and presently became mortally offended when the Commodore failed to invite him to his parties.

Macquarie showed a profound disinclination to act as referee in any faction fight surviving from the past, and a complete lack of interest in anything which had transpired before his coming, unless it were likely to influence future events.

His whole attitude and policy were based on conciliation.

In consonance with his orders from the Colonial Office he annulled the trials which had taken place during the Usurpation, revoked land grants, pardons, and emancipations made by the "revolutionary" administration;[20] but he made one of his first social calls on Mrs M'Arthur, wife of the "arch-rebel", John M'Arthur, whom he had been instructed to arrest should he be in the Colony.[21]

He inveighed strongly against the action of M'Arthur and Johnston, but he showed no animosity towards the New South Wales Corps or its officers, even though he accused them of mutiny. For those who wished to remain in New Holland he organized a veteran company which he attached to his own regiment. For convenience of members of the Corps who were to sail for England he made every provision and became thoroughly annoyed when he discovered that, through Bligh's intervention, he could not complete his plans for their comfort on the voyage. When a number of martyrs who had been cast into durance by the usurpers showed a disposition to go to the courts for damages, he assured them graphically that those who sought revenge in that way would be faced with his grave displeasure.

He was more concerned about the emptiness of the public stores, from which practically the whole of the ragged population needed to be fed, than about the eagerness of opposing factions for each other's destruction. His first important executive act was not, as many loyal citizens had piously hoped that it might be, to set a few rebels dangling. Instead he sent the agricultural superintendent post-haste to Castle Hill to plant more potatoes and wheat.[22]

The population noted that he was moderate in all things except in zeal and energy, of which he possessed too large a share to make him a comfortable neighbour.

Bligh became more and more appalled by his successor's attitude, staggered that "so obnoxious a character" as Foveaux—who had taken over the government on his arrival from England in July 1808, he being then the senior officer present—should become the Governor's temporary right hand man. Most angry was he to find that officer "in power", "loyal persons least attended to", the "New South Wales Corps doing duty in great glee" and "visiting between the parties as if nothing had happened". Indeed, although he professed himself on good terms with Macquarie, he "could not account for such phenomena".[23]

He trotted round with a sergeant's guard, being hooted occasionally by the populace, importuning unwilling colonists—who wanted nothing better than to forget the past and settle down to earn a living—with requests that they should follow him to England and assist in bringing about the executions of Messrs Johnston and "the archfiend M'Arthur".

He cried out for his lost papers. M'Arthur had taken some of them to England and the Commodore's repositories at Government House were empty, and the contents among the cold ashes of almost forgotten bonfires, or in the corners of the attic where Bligh had torn them up.

He wrote eloquent dispatches to Lord Castlereagh. He encouraged his friends in the ill-conceived project of calling a public meeting to testify to his virtues—a meeting which was captured by his foes, who impelled it to consider and, after some trouble and reference for direction by the presiding Provost Marshal to Macquarie, to approve the new Governor's policy of forgetting the past and establishing harmony and tranquillity.[24]

The only course, indeed, which seemed open to the Commodore was to "act with mildness and avoid any altercation or appearance of displeasure."[25]

However, in a role of mildness he was a dismal failure; to "see all the poor loyalists in the background" placed too great "a strain upon his temper". Soon all anybody wanted of Bligh was that he should leave New South Wales, but this he seemed reluctant to do, despite his declaration that he hoped that God would grant that he should soon be clear of "this wicked place".[26]

Even the respite which Sydney enjoyed after he had left on St Patrick's Day to tour the Hawkesbury, to see his farms and rouse his followers there, proved an evil in disguise and a stimulant to his arrogance and bad temper.[27]

While he was away, "it being fine weather, he chose to get out of his coach and ride on horseback for twenty miles". He was "a corpulent man and for some time unused to exercise"; so on the following day his leg swelled, fever came on. He took to his bed; and so uncertain became his manners, so violent his conduct and so eloquent his diction, that he "overpowered and affrighted every person that might have dealings with him, expecting from all a deference and submission that the proudest despot would covet".[28]

He returned to Sydney more angry than ever, and, no doubt finding the atmosphere on shore thoroughly uncongenial, he betook himself aboard his ship. There, under his Broad Pennant, he could make it plain to members of the New South Wales Corps that, if they suffered no other punishment for their treatment of him, they would at least learn how much discomfort could be packed into a voyage round the Horn under the thumb of "so boisterous and ostentatious a little old man as Commodore Bligh".

The *Hindostan* became as ceremonious "as if commanded by an Admiral". In a single week he was saluted no less than six times by the guns of the forts and ships, and he made it a practice never to leave or come aboard—as he did several times a day—without guards presenting arms and all the officers standing with their hats off. "And all this humbug," a passenger wrote, "must continue until we arrive in England."[29]

Bligh's disinclination to sail, however, was not entirely due to a desire to flaunt his arrogance in the face of a hostile population. He had received a sudden blow.

Mrs Putland, his daughter Mary, "not more than 22, small and every [sic] accomplished", a pretty, imperious little lady, whose dresses were so diaphanous that shocked observers noted that she wore trousers under them in the interests of decency, had deserted him.[30] Fresh from her grief at the death of her handsome young naval officer husband, she had stood staunchly by her parent throughout the last two years of trial and ignominy. She had been his constant and loyal companion, the one person who showed love for him, his never-failing resource. Now, while he had been absent at Green Hills, she had made a match with Maurice O'Connell, the debonair Irish Lieutenant-Governor after she had been drawn closely into the Government House circle by the fact that upon the staff she had found her cousin, in the person of the aide-de-camp, Captain Antill, the grandson of "Old Governor Colden" of New York. All unknown to her father, the dashing O'Connell had won her affection. Bligh knew only after her cabin had been prepared.[31]

In vain her choleric parent gave the suppliant for his daughter's hand "a flat denial". Though his consent "could only be extorted", it must be given; and, to add wormwood to the gall, the ceremony at Government House at which Bligh gave her away, his last social act in New South Wales, was dressed with "the most public tokens of respect and veneration" by the new Governor and Elizabeth, "who did the honours of the ceremony with an extraordinary degree of pleasure and even exultation".[32]

There were decorations. There were illuminations. There were fulsome speeches. The Government's gift to the penurious, extravagant bridegroom was 2500 acres of land.

Mr Michael Robinson, poet laureate *in cathedra* and a noted blackmailer, carolled in his Oxford accent at the nuptials of the happy pair, devoutly hoping that "children's children would crown their virtuous love", and declaiming:

> *In Australasia's genial clime proclaim,*
> *That LOVE and VALOUR blend their spotless flame,*
> *And wreaths of sweetest flow'rs prepare*
> *For lovely P . . t . . d's flowing hair.*[33]

But he could not comfort Bligh. That squat, hard-bitten, determined officer was "completely overwhelmed" by the disaster involved in "the loss which he could not retrieve" of her whom he called "his inestimable treasure". He was shattered to his very soul, and he looks out of the letter in which he gives his wife the news of his Mary's marriage as a pathetic, stricken old man, rather than as the brutal despot of tradition.

V

In the Colony many who were impatient with Bligh were by this time equally impatient with Macquarie.

Doctor Arnold, for one, despite his experience with the Commodore at Green Hills and his dread of the voyage to England under his command, regarded with alarm the attitude of the new viceroy. "It appears to me," he wrote, "that Governor Macquarie is of too peacible [sic] a nature for his situation, he endeavours to conciliate all persons, and instead of showing a marked disapprobation of the principal men in the late revolt, he invited them to his table at Government House, put some of them in responsible situations and made others his confidants . . ."[34]

Macquarie, nevertheless, did not feel that he was at all mild in his proceedings. He wrote to Charles Forbes that he "had been under the necessity of adopting *some very strong measures*".[35]

He told Castlereagh that he had taken particular pains to discover the causes surrounding Bligh's arrest but found it "extremely difficult to form a just judgment on this delicate and mysterious subject, Party rancour having run so high as to preclude the possibility of arriving at the truth without a very minute and legal investigation".[36]

In justice to Bligh, he wrote, he could not discover any act of his which could in any degree form an excuse for, or in any way warrant, the violent and mutinous proceedings pursued against him, "very few complaints having been made to me against him, and even those few are rather of a trifling nature".

On the other hand, he personally found the Commodore "certainly a most disagreeable person to have any dealings, or public business to transact with; having no regard whatever to his promises or engagements, however sacred, and his natural temper . . . uncommonly harsh and tyrannical in the extreme"; undoubtedly, in fact, "a very improper person to be employed in any situation of trust or command . . . very generally detested by high, low, rich and poor and especially by the higher class of the people". For himself, he could aver, the Commodore had been "a great plague to me" and, when he departed, he was "heartily glad to be quit of him".[37]

He set out his further views on his predecessor in a private letter to Castlereagh and trusted that he might be excused from entering more fully into the merits of the transactions and disturbances connected with the Commodore's arrest.

He repeated to Charles Forbes that Bligh was certainly very unpopular in his mode of administering the government and was very obnoxious to the inhabitants of the Colony; but he was not guilty of any criminal or sanguinary act that could possibly justify or sanction the violent and mutinous measures which were pursued against him by Colonel Johnston at the head of the 102nd Regiment and the party inimical to his Government. M'Arthur, Macquarie branded as being "at the head of the malcontents and real author of the Revolution and disturbances". Both Johnston and M'Arthur, he thought, would be tried "at home for mutiny and treason".[38]

He believed, he wrote, that the trial of the rebels would make some noise in England, and they would all afford fine food for the lawyers. But he was insistent to Castlereagh about the merits and usefulness of Lieutenant-Colonel Foveaux. He even informed his Minister that Foveaux "could not with safety have adopted a different line of conduct from that he pursued" during the rebellion period; that he was a man of very superior talents, of strict honour and integrity, the fittest person he had ever met with in any country in thirty years for improving and conducting an infant colony to maturity. He proposed fruitlessly that Foveaux should forthwith be made Lieutenant-Governor at Hobart Town.[39]

He offered that "obnoxious character" his most cordial thanks for "the very useful and able advice and assistance I have already derived from you", and asked for a continuance of it.[40]

VI

On the afternoon of 12 May 1810, ranged along the cliffs of the South Head of Port Jackson, the colonists of New South Wales watched Bligh and his ships, loaded down with New South Wales Corps soldiers and witnesses for the trial of Johnston and M'Arthur, setting out to face the rigours of the voyage round Cape Horn to London.

Soon all that momentarily mattered of the Old Regime in Botany Bay had departed. The Old Corps had embarked, wholly engaged on the way to the ship "in exchanging the melancholy term *Adieu*!"[41] Old Paterson, the former Lieutenant-Governor, had crept feebly aboard his ship, supported by his shrewd Scottish wife, to die on the voyage; Foveaux had sailed on 17 March in the *Experiment*. The erstwhile Judge-Advocate, Atkins, staggered aboard. He was old and mellow with much secret drinking, though all but a few admitted him to be a polished, courteous, much-travelled man of the world, whose manners spoke of his having seen better days and whose three illegitimate daughters answered for his morals. He was in such shape that opinion prophesied that he might arrive in England like the wife of one of Bligh's victims, poor Mrs Short, carved up and in a cask of pickle; but this expectation he disappointed.

David Collins, the Lieutenant-Governor in Hobart Town, so long established as to be almost the Colony's oldest official inhabitant, died suddenly on 24 March of a stroke. He had perished, sitting in his chair, after offering his doctor refreshment, and had been escorted to his grave like a royal prince by Lieutenant Edward Lord, at a cost of something over £400 to the State.

Bligh would never realize his longing to see *him* grinning through a halter. Society would never again view him "walking with his kept woman, (a poor, low creature), arm-in-arm about the town", and in full view of Bligh's scandalized daughter.[42]

No more would the *élite* of Hobart Town gather in the candlelight which shone so dimly in Government House, that "miserable shell" of a viceregal palace builder's art, while he told them tales of Bunker Hill and exercised his ready wit to embellish his copious and good-tempered reminiscences.

M'Arthur sat in London. His venom was not directed against Macquarie. It was still too much concentrated on Bligh. On a diet of water and vegetables, constantly bemoaning the condition of his unstable interior, he was planning the complete destruction of the latter and many other foes, to the irritation of a British Civil Service pre-occupied with events in Spain.[43]

He gave emus to Lady Castlereagh, swans and geese to Lady Camden. Now and then, he paused to indite a few words about "that unprincipled man, Mr Foveaux", to throw off a few heated sentences of objurgation against his fellow Australians, and particularly against some of his warmest supporters during the rebellion. Stung to the quick by an article seemingly of clerical authorship in that "most virulent paper", the *Morning Chronicle*, he prayed that His Excellency might "speedily detect that arch-hypocrite Marsden", who certainly had done more mischief in the settlement, he believed, than any one of the worthless characters who had had influence in the direction of public affairs.

The field seemed clear for the start of the New Order.

Bligh's ships cleared Port Jackson Heads to the salute of guns; and ere long the guns roared again, even as they had been wont to do in India, to celebrate the royal birthday of Farmer George, which was marked with favours for all those worthy who could be reached, and with opulent entertainments in the best Highland style at a Government House singularly bare of ladies and in which Mr Robinson, now well established as poet laureate, sang like a pompous old lark of his new master's rule, seeing "pity move with melting eye led by her sister charity", and industry "stride with study and perseverance by her side":

> Then comes RELIGION, heav'n-born child,
> With look divine and accent mild.[44]

The omens were auspicious. The god-in-the-machine of Botany Bay could write that everything was "going on quietly and peaceably here",[45] despite the fact that the continued presence of Bligh's daughter kept the limited society of the capital in a state of uneasy faction.

Those of the population who had been most troublesome to his predecessors were either fled to England or momentarily cowed or won over to the support of authority.

But already large sections of the more privileged classes of the remaining New South Wales inhabitants were discovering that his zeal made this Governor an uncomfortable neighbour and that his rectitude was a thorn in the flesh.

CHAPTER XV

The Wonderful Year

I

THE cleaning up of New South Wales was thorough and orderly and conducted at a pace which was apt to stun the beholder accustomed to the quarrelsome lethargy of the rebellious interregnum.

By the end of 1810 it would have been a disgruntled naval captain indeed who could have repeated the strictures which one of the breed had passed upon Sydney seven years agone as he floundered—"over the shoes"— through the miry tracks, muttering that the place was like a miserable Portuguese settlement and wondering whether the piece of timber over the Fort was a flagstaff or a leaning derrick.[1]

The starched grip of civil service methods had suddenly descended on the shoulder of Botany Bay and government ran according to strict timetable, which must have seemed strange in a community in which association with the bottle had often been the governing factor in deciding whether or when the day's work should be done.

Each day from 10 a.m. to 11 a.m., the Governor was to be found in the sunny north saloon of the somewhat battered Government House facing the harbour, communing with his civil servants. The next hour he devoted to military matters.

Land grants, for which applications must be received strictly before noon, he dealt with punctually upon Mondays. He received gentlemen of the settlement at his weekly levee between the hours of noon and two on Tuesdays.

Apart from this, he announced that he would "be ready at all hours, and on all days" to accept pressing applications and "give immediate answers". Urgent requests might even be made to him orally and at any time, though he warned his suppliants that, if their demands should prove frivolous and unimportant, "no notice whatever will be taken of them".[2]

He had been fortunate in that his greatest problem, feeding the starving community, had been partly solved a fortnight after his arrival by the coming of the ship *Marian* with grain.

A mild autumn and winter and a bounteous spring unmarred by floods had helped his plans; but to himself had been due in the greatest degree the salutary changes which had been wrought. It had been hard work. He had been forced to scold, to cajole, to threaten; and he had needed to have order as well as method in his progress.

He had attacked firstly the moral weaknesses of the community. He endeavoured to build up personal self-respect before he applied his subjects to the liquidation of their untidiness.

In the early months of 1810 his pen was busy with orders in which he impugned the "shameful and indecent custom", which prevailed both in Sydney and in the country, "of settlers carrying on their avocations and labours on Sundays", a practice which made it almost impossible to recognize the Australian Sabbath without reference to a calendar. He directed constables to arrest offenders against Sabbath-breaking laws.[3]

Startled inhabitants heard of his determination to "reprobate and check, as far as lies in his power, the scandalous and pernicious custom so generally and shamelessly adopted throughout the territory of persons of different sexes cohabiting and living together unsanctioned by the legal ties of matrimony".[4] Such proceedings, though they were so much the normal colonial fashion that all were brazen about them, he characterized as a scandal to religion, to decency, and to all good government.

Although this seemed a somewhat revolutionary commination the populace soon learned that his threats to withdraw patronage and favour from the guilty and his proposed encouragement of sober and industrious citizens joined in wedlock were not idle. He evidently meant it when he announced that he was resolved to wipe out "this immoral and illicit intercourse", as being not only highly injurious to the interests of society at large, "but oftentimes attended also with grievous calamity to the parties themselves, and the innocent offspring of their misconduct".[5] Obedience quickly was proved to be the easiest and most profitable course. Many a young couple, happy in a bird-like condition of unsanctioned dalliance, reluctantly spent the three guineas needed to achieve matrimony. Many more felt they had gone far enough when they had secured the necessary permission to marry, and had left it at that—especially after the marriage fee had been increased to five guineas.

The products of marriage, and all too often of other kinds of association, —the "rising generation of this infant Colony . . . wholly neglected in their education and morals"—were catered for immediately by the establishment of charity schools. In these the little inmates were to receive instruction in those principles which alone could "render them dutiful and obedient to their parents and superiors; honest faithful and useful members of society and good Christians".[6]

Parents showed no enthusiasm; but Mr Matthew Hughes agreed at once to open a school free to pupils at Kissing Point, at a subsidy of eight-pence per week per scholar for spelling and reading and one shilling for accounts. A relic of the system survives in the twentieth century in Australia's oldest school—that of St Philip's Church in Sydney, which bears the date "1812" over its portals.

Next the Governor turned his attention to those who "in defiance of all law and decency scandalously kept open during the night, the most licentious and disorderly houses, for the reception of the abandoned of both sexes, and to the great encouragement of dissolute and disorderly habits". He "made known his indignation" at the proceedings in such places; and, hoping that his measures would produce morality and decorum, "the want of which was so disgraceful and detrimental to society", he promised offenders "punishment to the utmost extent allowed by law".[7]

With his approach to this subject he found himself face to face with the root of nearly all the Colony's evils, the Demon Rum.

II

The Colonial Office had enjoined him to prevent the use of spirits as an article of barter; to ensure that no rum was landed save by his express permission.[8]

His first measure, taken in February 1810, a month after he arrived, with a view to prevent the destructive and too free use of spirituous liquors as much as possible, was to reduce the number of licensed houses in Sydney from seventy-five to twenty. He made a similar reduction in proportion to population in the other towns. He came down with a heavy hand on illicit stills. He also later decreed the closer control over the conduct of licensees when it was made possible by the institution of a police force.[9]

All the same he saw at once that it was "impossible to suppress the use of spirits, a certain quantity being essentially necessary for the accommodation of the inhabitants".[10]

As under previous regimes, there was no other satisfactory portable medium in universal and perpetual demand which could serve as currency.

By the time he had been four months in the Colony, the Governor had evolved a simple scheme. It would, he wrote to Castlereagh, be good and sound policy to sanction the free importation of good spirits under a high duty of not less than three or four shillings a gallon. He was persuaded that the adoption of the measure would put an end to all further attempts at monopoly and bartering spirits for corn and necessaries, as likewise to private stills, which, in defiance of every precaution, were still numerous in the Colony.

As the free importation of spirits would greatly reduce the general price, the private distillers would be undersold by the fair licensed traders. He believed that, instead of promoting drunkenness and idleness, this would tend rather to lessen both; for it had generally been observed that "the avidity of the lower orders of the people was in the inverse ratio to the quantity of spirits imported". However, he proposed to defer action until he should receive his Lordship's further directions.

He increased the duty on rum from 1s. 6d. to 3s. a gallon as from 3 March 1810; and he joined Foveaux and others in advocating the establishment of a distillery to deal with grain surpluses.[11]

Then the old system continued. He bought houses with spirits, "at the most earnest request of the parties themselves".[12] He continued to pay his workmen in spirits up to 3000 gallons a year, while the new Judge-Advocate, Mr Ellis Bent, provided him with judicial support by selling in the open market for £142 10s. fifty-seven gallons of brandy which he had bought for £17. He early entered into contracts of which liquor was a highly necessary ingredient with Messrs Lord and Williams and others.

Mr Lord and his partner engaged, under an indenture, "to import into this Territory from Bengal for the use of Government, two hundred tons of wheat fit to be issued as a ration to troops and others, at the rate of sixteen pounds sterling per ton weight". They were, also, to bring in twenty-five tuns of good Bengal rum for Government use at 7s. 6d. a gallon and no more, free of all Customs House fees. They were to sell at the prices mentioned. By way of consideration, they were to have liberty to indent ten thousand gallons of rum on their own private account and not subject to any stipulated price.[13]

This was a type of transaction well understood by the Colony at large; but it was not long before even the most hardened rum trader gasped, as he was introduced to a new application of contractual technique on which was based what appeared to the the father of all spirit deals known to Botany Bay history.

This extraordinary piece of business was concerned with the building of a new Colonial Hospital, which became known to future generations as "the Rum Hospital".

III

The original Colonial Hospital in Governor Phillip's day had been tenderly shipped from England in sections. It had been set up in 1790. It was now in "a wretched state of decay . . . tumbling down". In fact the need for its replacement would "not admit of any possible delay which can be avoided in the erection of a new one".[14]

At first Macquarie decided to call tenders to rebuild it, but the resources of the Government were scarcely equal to an adequate building, what with the urgent need for stores, barracks, roads, and other essentials.[15]

However, Messrs Alexander Riley and Garnham Blaxcell offered a proposal. Mr Riley was a very prosperous merchant and indenter; Mr Blaxcell, a retired naval purser's assistant who was Mr John M'Arthur's partner and agent. Both sponsors of the scheme were ignorant of hospitals and architecture, but they were both venturesome and sanguine of temperament.

They were prepared to build a hospital 287½ feet long and 28 feet deep, 38 feet high and double-storied "with a viranda round each story of the building 10 feet wide; the pillars of the lower story to be of stone, and the upper story of wood". In fact it was to be "one of the finest public buildings in any of His Majesty's colonies"—with a stone wall round it enclosing seven acres of land, and two surgeons' barracks, which the enemies of the administration for ever afterwards insisted on describing as "palaces".[16]

The three amazing structures, fitted with mahogany doors and "every sort of judicious ornament", were to rise in the new Macquarie Street, upon the heights of the eastern hill.

All the would-be builders required in return for their work was a qualified monopoly of the spirit trade—the right to import 45,000 gallons of rum and dispose of it within the three years, during which the hospital was to be completed. They were even prepared to pay duty. The material consideration the Government was to find consisted merely of eighty oxen for slaughter, the use of twenty draught bullocks and of twenty convicts for the period of the contract.

Such a plan naturally brought uppermost all that was frugally Scottish in the Governor. The arrangement would put much of the liquor traffic largely into the hands of a couple of the most trustworthy and respectable of New South Wales citizens, thus increasing his power to regulate it. The contract would be nearing completion by the time he could expect to hear from England the view of the Colonial Office on his recommen-. dation to permit free trade in spirits.

And Government rights were preserved. An absolute monopoly was avoided. The indenture stated that, save for the average of 15,000 gallons of spirits a year which the contractors were to be allowed to introduce, imports should be limited to "only what Government may deem it necessary to import for their own use and occasions, and without prejudice or reference to the importation of any quantity of spirits which may be brought into this country by promiscuous ships touching at or using this Port". Also excepted from the monopoly clause were shipments for which permission already had been given, and the regular issues of liquor by the Government at its special landed price, to officers, free settlers and inhabitants as scheduled, 9500 gallons a year.

Everybody involved was pleased with the tentative arrangement till the prospective contractors took a general census of incoming liquor, admission of which was already authorized. Then, a fortnight after they had lodged their offer, they gave tongue urgently. Now that they had been made aware of the full circumstances, they considered them "of such serious importance that they confidently trusted His Excellency would excuse the liberty they took in submitting them to him".[17]

The contractors complained that against their own three year permissive importation of 45,000 gallons—of which they had received 4000 gallons before the contract was signed—Messrs Lord, Wilson, Underwood, and Robert Campbell, and the officers of the 73rd Regiment between them had rum on the water totalling 67,000 gallons, which was due in Port Jackson within five months. This was exclusive of any that might be imported as "ships' stores and in vessels arriving from England and India"—say 8500 gallons.

The contractors calculated the cost of this liquor to the importers at £49,400 landed minimum, including duty. They submitted that, in framing their own previous calculation, they "by no means had considered that so large a quantity of spirits as 76,000 gallons could possibly be brought into the market in the space of time"; and especially the 27,000 gallons which Mr Lord was immediately landing.

It was agreed that Mr Lord might sell 20,000 gallons of his imports to the contractors. And a third contractor was added to the list—Mr D'Arcy Wentworth, principal surgeon, soon to be police magistrate.[18]

His Excellency was "much pleased" to find him concerned. His presence would give the scheme greater security, more especially as, besides being "an opulent man", he was one whose "rectitude of conduct and zealous attention to the faithful execution of the contract I could safely rely on".[19]

The contract was signed on 6 November 1810. It was one of the agreements which Macquarie in later years had most cause to regret having made. The actual facts have never quite overtaken the slander started by his enemies that he had given an absolute monopoly in liquor to the enterprising three, far as this was from being the case.[20]

IV

The Governor's measures quickly produced a healthy impact on Botany Bay opinion—a community spirit which led Mr Hassall, the missionary, to write that "deferances [sic] of our Colony are nearly at an end and we begin to live more in peace and unity"; and that he did not "know whether the Colony could have had a better man for Governor".[21]

Macquarie, indeed, had within the first few months of his reign reached the point from which he might turn to practical reform and, by the end of the year, the colonists, as they gazed backward, must have been astonished at the physical transformation which had taken place.

Only the harbour and the hills were much the same, the former still uncluttered with teeming commerce.

The town of Sydney had ceased to be a merely military camp, but in many ways life was not so free as it had been. It had been made more onerous by the rescript which had enjoined the printing of promissory notes, thus hampering the happy profession of forgery which once had been profitably rife.

No more might the criminal, on the eve of his tryst at the gallows, pass his last hours at a joyous levee, with light conversation and the flowing bowl brought from the jailer's house, "The Cat and Fiddle", at Brown Bear Lane corner.[22]

A regular post office was established.[23] The postmaster had been placed upon bond of £500. Bakers of Parramatta were shocked by a pounce upon their weights, which proved to be tokens rather than standards. Military officers were forbidden to resort to low and unmilitary occupations either mercantile or agricultural.

But the settler gazed with pride round his newly ordered town with its rising buildings and its increasing flow of Government currency, still chiefly contained in kegs and bottles.

The old "rows" had given place to named streets, all at least fifty feet wide—George Street and Prince Street, York, Gloucester, Kent, Clarence, Cumberland, Sussex Streets for the King and the royal dukes; Harrington Street after the Governor's former military commander in London, Argyle Street for his native county, Castlereagh Street for the War Minister, Phillip, Hunter, King and Bligh Streets for former Governors, Bent Street for the

Judge-Advocate, Macquarie and Elizabeth Streets for himself and his wife, and Bridge, Park, Market, and Spring Streets to mark the sites of civic utilities;[24] O'Connell Street for the Lieutenant-Governor.

The open space on the south along the ridge of the hill, on whose slopes lay much of the embryo town, which had been known as "the Common", the "Exercising Ground" or the "Cricket Ground", had been reborn and grandiloquently renamed Hyde Park.

Where Mr John Blaxland's cowyard had been there was now an embryo market square with a bell, governed by the most fearsome regulations against forestallers.[25]

And the numbers of acts which it had become either necessary or illegal to do were enough to make an honest citizen dizzy.

Houses must not be built unless approved by the Governor. Those which encroached on the streets must be moved back into line at public expense. Each must be numbered at a cost of sixpence to the owner.[26] Neat frontal palings four feet high must guard all dwellings.[27] Bricks must not be made in the public park. Wood must not be cut in the Church Glebe.[28] Shirts no longer might be washed in the Tank Stream. Ashes and rubbish must not be cast into the roadways. Pigs and the filthier forms of industry must be removed to the suburbs.[29] And sportsmen must not fill the air of the Domain with buckshot.

The absent-minded and heated citizen might no longer remove his clothes on the main Government wharf or in the dockyard in the heart of commercial Sydney and bathe, *au naturel*, in the broad light of day.

New roads were being built by soldier labour to South Head and the Colony's first turnpike to Green Hills on the Hawkesbury had reached Parramatta. The two bridges in Sydney had been widened at the cost of much good liquor currency.[30]

Everywhere, from Government House to the beginnings of the new stone wharf on Sydney Cove; from the wastes beyond Brickfield Hill to the new court dealing with small debts hard by Macquarie Place, were to be seen the marks of the Governor's determination to "do everything in his power that can in the least degree contribute to the ornament and regularity of the town of Sydney, as well as to the convenience and safety of the inhabitants thereof".[31]

Even the sore-tried carters and bullock wagoners, those hardy fellows who had shaped the streets and ways in the pristine decades of the Colony, did not escape his attention. For soon they must be registered and numbered; they were denied the use of footpaths for their oxen on pain of severe punishment, and they were sternly ordered to pass along the streets and the roads within one mile of Sydney vigilant on foot beside their cattle.[32]

V

All in all he had reason to be pleased that he had so easily surmounted the "very ungracious task I had to perform at the beginning of *my reign* in the Colony".[33] He could write even in March, while Bligh still haunted Port

Jackson, that his own situation "tho' at present a very troublesome one, will, I trust, when I get things into a more regular train, prove a very pleasant and comfortable one".[34] In July he already had "made considerable advances in improving the religion and morals of the lower classes of the people", who had been shamefully neglected by his predecessors in office; but a wide field, he felt, was "still left open to him if he had sufficient talent and abilities to profit by it", though he was sensible that his talents and judgment were "inadequate to the task" of improving the Colony "so effectually or to that degree that the present backward state of everything here would admit of".[35]

His new subjects submitted to his whims the more gracefully because he showed himself humane and because it was evident from the first that he would take no lead from Governor King, who had begged to offer to Lord Hobart his annual list of punishments "as a proof that the morals of the inhabitants and the punishment of vice is not neglected".[36] Did he not celebrate the first King's Birthday by throwing open Government House gates so that the public might see the decorations?[37] Did he not order that corporal punishment should be inflicted as seldom as possible, and never save on clear and distinct evidence?[38] Did he not personally and scrupulously inspect and hold out hope to every fresh batch of prisoners arriving from England?[39] Some there were, in fact, who felt that his kindliness and that of Elizabeth went too far.

Those with memories of the Irish rebellion, for instance, were inclined to shake their heads when they heard, on the day that Bligh had gone to Green Hills and Foveaux to England, that "this being St. Patrick's Day Mrs. M. gave a dinner to all the convicts employed about Government House, Gardens and boats and making the new road—in all about 58 including overseers".[40]

But even the critics noted that, though something of a zealot, their lord and master was no puritan but delighted in earthy amusements, and that his bark was often far worse than his bite. The official *Gazette*, which his secretary censored, rejoiced on a bright May Day when Parramatta held its fair that "ladies raced in sacks for a cheese" and that the population in general then indulged in "feats of humour and fun so congenial to the temper and to the spirit of Englishmen".[41]

His popularity rose when it was announced that, "in order to encourage the rearing of good horses in the Colony", he had given his sanction to setting races on foot, and that he had begun "preparing an elegant race course close to the Town of Sydney"—indeed in Hyde Park, with starting and finishing posts not far from the gallows.[42]

With good reason he could in October sum up his preliminary work to Lord Liverpool, the new Colonial Secretary, in a highly cheerful spirit. There was every prospect of a good and plentiful harvest. Horned cattle and sheep were fast increasing and the general state of the Colony was prosperous and improving. He wished to establish a loan bank on the lines of that at the Cape of Good Hope, under the fullest conviction that "such an establishment would be attended with advantages of the utmost impor-

tance to its [the Colony's] increasing trade and prosperity".[43] In the meantime he asked for copper coin to stop the shameful traffic in valueless notes.

The out-stations of Port Dalrymple and Norfolk Island, he heard, were
well supplied with provisions, and the inhabitants peaceable and happy,
but he thought the latter settlement should be evacuated.

Though his expenses were heavy he had been compelled to replenish
stores which had been in an exhausted and almost empty state, but which
now carried at least five months' supply of grain. He had been forced to
buy clothing for convicts whom he found in a wretched state of rags and
nakedness. Also, he had had to buy materials indispensably necessary to
complete barracks, stores, and public buildings in course of construction.

There were other needs, of course, outside those which he had mentioned before—schoolmasters, a government architect. And some more
printing equipment.

Always in a precarious condition, the printing office furniture of
the *Sydney Gazette* was breaking down under the weight of his flood of
general orders and proclamations, not to mention the reports of a devastating tide of local happenings.

The Governor requested therefore that there be sent from London at
public expense, *inter alia*, "one printing press, three composing sticks, two
of common length, 14 lines Long Primer, and 400 weight of Long Primer
with a double complement of capitals, etc."—to which he was much
addicted—with appropriate quantities of italic, double primer, hackle-
tooth bodkin blades with six handles, flowers, stars, quotations and celestial
signs, and the "Royal Arms of the United Kingdom in brass, supporters
couchant, about the size and form of the arms that head his Majesty's
speeches to Parliament".[44]

Was the last order due to a high-stomached lordliness on the part of
the Governor or to the homesickness of the printer for a familiar symbol
upon his sheet? The latter, of yore, had been a humble servitor of *The Times*,
which bore the Royal Arms on its title page, and had done his little share
to prove the versatility of the staff of that great journal by getting himself
transported![45]

VI

The results of all the bustle were most certainly gratifying, but the processes
by which they were achieved were exhausting both to the Governor and
his lieges.

Colonists were a little breathless with well-doing when, in the late
spring, they were bidden for the first time "to function in a conjoint
manner", as established communities should do for their own pleasure
and profit.

Officially recognized community effort had never before aspired beyond
the delivery of periodical addresses to viceroyalty, and those addresses
were always sectional affairs. Now convict and free, townsman and settler,
emancipist and exclusive, soldier and civilian found themselves rubbing
shoulders in Hyde Park, where all the gentry and all the lower orders of

Botany Bay's very mixed society gathered at the continent's first Spring Race Meeting.[46]

"Entertainments were given all over the town, to welcome our friends to our first *jubilee*." The excitement continued for days. Captain Ritchie's Chase, grey gelding, six years, speeding round the circular course, just one mile and forty yards in circumference, won Australia's first public race at a meeting, a Subscriber's Plate of fifty guineas, with eight stone twelve up. Every day, during the meeting, Mr Wentworth's b.g. Gig (Mr William Charles Wentworth up) strove for honours and a fresh stake with Mr Broughton's bl.g. Jerry, after a preliminary match for sixty guineas which "Gig won easy".

Elizabeth made a pretty speech presenting the first of all antipodean Ladies' Plates to Captain Ritchie: "In the name of the ladies of New South Wales, I have the pleasure to present you with this Cup. Give me leave to congratulate you on being the successful candidate for it; and to hope that it is a prelude to future success, and lasting prosperity."[47]

The doughty Dicky Dowling gave the horses a point or two by carrying fourteen stone to victory on his back for fifty yards, while an unloaded adversary ran once backwards and once forwards over the ground. Two private mains of cock fighting were held in a discreetly sheltered spot.

But all other wonders of the festival gave way before "Mr. Benn's bl.h. Scratch", from the Hawkesbury, a noble equine, rousingly victorious on the last day of the meeting in the event free for all horses and forced to "submit to fraternal embraces" from his many admirers, among whom he became the subject of "copious libations".

There was a subscribers' ball at which the band of the 73rd Regiment played "excellent music", and the evening was full of diversions, which, as the ever-graphic *Gazette* recorded, "could not fail of diffusing a universal glow of satisfaction—the celebration of the first liberal amusement instituted in the Colony, and in the presence of its Patron and Founder".

The dancers were at it till two o'clock in the morning, when they sat down to supper. They were still abroad when

> the rosy Deity asserted his pre-eminence, and with the zealous aid of Momus and Apollo, chased pale Cynthia down into the western world.— The blazing orb of day announced his near approach; and the God of the Chariot reluctantly forsook his company. Bacchus drooped his head and Momus could no longer animate. The *bon vivants* no longer relishing the tired Heathens, broke up, and left them to themselves.[48]

The company trailed homeward in the late spring heat of dawn, cheerful, no doubt, though probably not so happy as the male guests at two dinners held by the bloods at Mr Wills's in George Street, at which Mr Francis Williams sang one of Mr Robinson's most musical lyrics to the tune of 'To Anacreon in Heaven" ("The Star-Spangled Banner"):

> *When these plaudits are lost in the arch of high Heav'n,*
> *A strain more exalted shrill echo shall send—*
> *"Tis the suffrage of Gratitude, cordially giv'n,*
> *To our Patron—our Chief—our Protector and Friend!*

To Him whose calm voice Makes his people rejoice—
That the Friend to Mankind is their Sovereign's choice.
And long may his mild and beneficent sway,
Enhance—whilst its sanctions the sports of today![49]

But the chorus was even louder when the new hero of the Botany Bay populace attended the Bachelors' Race Ball at Mr Simeon Lord's mansion, the first Governor to appear under the roof of that former convict even on a public occasion.

VII

Spring brought an ominous fresh in the Hawkesbury River and promised a repetition of the floods which had set the Colony starving the year before; but while the Governor, happy and in perfect good health, stood godfather to the first Australian child to be named after him—William Macquarie Cowper[50]—and meditated on the abounding virtues of a generous and grateful emancipist who, dying, had been impelled to endow his ruler with a quarter share in his substantial worldly goods, the threat of the rains evaporated.

The turnpike road to Parramatta was complete.[51] It was two rods wide, with a ditch on either side, and built of stone with a gravel surface. He hastened to use it. There had been no swift, smooth road travel hitherto and the astonished dwellers among the scrubs along the wayside long remembered 6 November 1810 for the spectacle of the opulent equipage which they beheld that day chasing the sun towards the west.

Joseph Big pulled it up about half past seven in the evening, with a flourish only possible to one who had been coachman to a lord, before the front doorway of the little Government House which stood on the western hill at Parramatta. Presently lanterns came, casting shadows of the local magistracy and other potentates. But these dignitaries scarcely glimpsed the Governor and his lady save by night light. When morning dawned, the pair set out with a retinue on horseback for George's River, which they crossed in a boat to breakfast with Mr Moore, a pious local resident and their familiar for the rest of their stay in the Colony. They were rowed up the stream, landed near the house of Mr Laycock, a superannuated relic of the New South Wales Corps.

The Governor climbed to high ground above the stream. He looked round. He saw that the site was "thick forest". "*I determined to erect a Township on it, and named it LIVERPOOL for the Earl of that Title.*" As surely as if the Deity had spoken, a new town was in being.

Later they trotted through the countryside, down to St Andrew's near Minto, then through park-like, timbered hills, losing themselves for a time in the wilds of Bankstown, and wandering as far abroad as the Field of Mars, Mr Marsden's farm at One Tree Hill, Liberty Plains, Dundas, and Baulkham Hills.

On 16 November, the viceregal equipage again rolled majestically southward towards the Cowpastures, winding among the trees, Joseph Big on the box; Macquarie and Elizabeth inside; outside, the viceregal train—

Captain Antill, Captain Cleaveland, young Ensign John Maclaine of Lochbuy, Gregory Blaxland, Dr Redfern, and Meehan, the Deputy Surveyor-General.

A squadron of servants travelled ahead with carts bearing five hundred and fifty pounds' worth of Bengal tents and all the paraphernalia of an Indian nabob on tour. Behind and on the flanks clattered the dragoons of Sergeant Whalan's viceregal guard, which just then, like the Bengal tents, had become an object of astonishment to the frugal Colonial Secretary in London.

Beside the track emus and kangaroos and other strange fauna scattered out of the way of the carriage and its escort, while those curious indigenes, Bootbarrie and Young Bundle, stood goggle-eyed and mute with astonishment at the sight of the procession.

Soon the cavalcade was passing through "fine rich country and open forest" on the outer marches of the Governor's realm. Not so far away the fires of savages who had seen no white man rose in coded columns to the south and there was something Olympian about the high heaven and ever-rolling hills with their park-like covering of timber. Herds of wild cattle unused to and unafraid of men came curiously up to them. They saw wild bulls fighting. The nights were full of eerie bellowings, so that they must keep fires burning round the camps for which Elizabeth, "though so young a campaigner", had "provided every requisite to make their tour pleasant and happy".

In spite of all the strangeness they were at ease, "much pleased with one another and with our manner of life", in which they found time for laughter as they watched an agile aboriginal climb a tree to catch a goanna, and stimulated satisfactorily with spirits the tempo of a corroboree—"an extraordinary sort of dance after their own (native) manner".

Presently the men of the party were at Stonequarry Creek beyond which all was unknown, but lying in "beautiful rich country" in which a new Jarvisfield would later rise. After they had turned back a few miles they found Mrs M'Arthur, as ever cheerful, friendly, and courageous, at Benkennie, in the process of selling beef and mutton said to be worth £15,000 a year to the Government, without affecting the breeding stock of her fugitive husband's herds.

When they all sat round the fire together that evening they had no whisper of the letter which her husband, twelve thousand miles away in London, had only a week before written to this devoted woman sojourning there in a "small miserable hut" on the fringes of a savage wilderness and within reach of raiding tribes: "Depend upon it, the Colony will soon undergo a radical reform. I think I shall be obliged to procure a seat in Parliament. . . . We must, therefore, be very economical in every other expenditure and you must exert yourself to remit me all you can."[52]

They did not know that he had asked her to preserve a guarded silence on the measures of the new Governor, since he had found a powerful body of friends in England, not only able but willing to give support to his endeavours to obtain satisfaction for the past and security for the future.

The Governor, therefore, parted from the recipient of this advice with no shadow of constraint to move to a new camp on the Nepean at Kirboonwallie near the ford. He and some of the party rode twelve miles to Nowenwong, opposite Menangle, where Robert Campbell's sheep were grazing. They had been and still were plagued by frequent bursts of rain.

On 20 November they broke camp to visit St Andrew's on Bunburry-Curran Creek, near the country called Minto in a later age—the farm of that recently dead citizen, Andrew Thompson, of whom their thoughts were tender, since his gratitude had lately impelled him to bestow upon them so generous a legacy.[53]

Here were waving fields of wheat and corn and many flocks. Elizabeth in particular was delighted with the situation of the farm, with the picturesque scenes around it and with the "great order and regularity in which the worthy deceased owner had left it".

In contrast to the "miserable hut" of M'Arthur's outland colonizing the place was plentifully supplied with mutton, fowls, butter, milk, eggs and vegetables. They drank to Mr Thompson's memory over an excellent dinner.

On the second day after their arrival the Governor and his men took another ride at 5.50 a.m. In four miles south-east by east, through fine rich land, they reached a "very deep extensive stony creek or gully, close to the bank of which the rocks appeared". They rode three miles north-east by east till they found George's River half a mile off their track, a "very pretty little stream of clear well tasted running water".

Leaving their horses, they scrambled down the steep banks and crossed the rivulet. Their investigations satisfied them that George's River came from a "more westerly point than has hitherto been supposed, and approaches towards its source within a few miles of the Nepean River".

They trotted to St Andrew's, gratified at having travelled between fourteen and fifteen miles before breakfast "through some of the best and finest country I have yet seen in the Colony, and by far the most eligible, centrical and fittest in every point of view, for small settlers to have allotments of land assigned them in".

He intended forming this tract of country, Macquarie wrote, into a new and separate district for the accommodation of small settlers and to name it "Airds" in honour of his dear, good Elizabeth's family estate.

VIII

Back in Parramatta they rested for a day or two "both a little indisposed after our late fatigues", before starting for the Evan District on the right bank of the Nepean, "to explore the new or Western River lately discovered by Mr. Evans, the Deputy Surveyor in that part of the Country". They set out in company with Gregory Blaxland, a "pleasant, facetious companion".

Beyond Prospect Hill they halted to admire the neatness of Mr Nicholas Bayly's barn and stockyards at Bayly Park on South Creek, and a small farm of Gregory Blaxland, where there was a hut, soon to be the starting point of the first expedition to cross the Blue Mountains.

They saw Mr Badgery's farm, at South Creek, too—"a fine good farm house built, a good garden and a considerable quantity of ground cleared"; also the farms of Doctor Wentworth, of Mrs O'Connell at Frogmore, and of Mrs King, widow of the former Governor, on whose land they paused to inspect "her fine numerous herds of horned cattle, in high condition, of which she has upwards of 700 head of all descriptions"—the trophies of old King's upright and self-sacrificing reign.

Then, with George W. Evans, Deputy Assistant Surveyor-General and first of the real land explorers, they went on, and before evening Elizabeth had added to her experiences that of being the first governor's wife, and possibly the first freely arrived white woman, to bivouac west of the Nepean River, under the foothills of the Blue Mountains; for Ensign John Maclaine had brought his boat, which they "launched into the wide river, naming her the *Discovery*", and rowed across.

They noted that the river at this point was "near a mile broad" and had great depth of water, and that opposite Dr Jamison's farm, which lay on the eastern bank, was a rich tract of country called Emu Island. They rowed next day up the Nepean at 6 a.m., so as to have the more time to "enjoy the beautiful scenery of this large river, the banks of which were very lofty and clothed with wood to the very top". After four hours they came to a circular basin where a new stream poured its waters into the dwindling main Nepean, a tributary, swift and broad, the channel being perfectly clear of rocks, and of considerable depth for a few miles farther up.

They halted about half a mile from its confluence with the Nepean, at "a beautiful romantic spot on the right bank of it, forming a sort of natural terrace at the foot of a prodigious cliff, in order to take our breakfast, and view the grand surrounding scenery". Here the banks of the river were almost perpendicular, not being less than four hundred feet in height, and wooded to their very summits, "beautifully grand and picturesque to look at, but extremely difficult to pass or travel through on foot from their great steepness and ruggedness".

Macquarie wrote in his journal:

> One of the natives born near this part of the country, and who made one of our party on this day's excursion, tells us that the real and proper native name of this newly discovered river that we are now exploring is the *Warragombie*, by which name I have directed it to be called in future.— The immense high hill directly opposite to the terrace we breakfasted on, is called *Cheenbar*, and is well known to the natives.[54]

After another three miles of rowing the first fall arrested the party's progress about two o'clock that afternoon, but they were "highly pleased and gratified with our day's excursion to the 'Warragombie', which we had explored two miles higher up than Mr Evans or any other person had ever before attempted to do. This day's journey by water was at least thirty miles backwards and forwards."

IX

They went northward, for the Governor intended leaving little of his domain out of his tour. Appledore and Westmore, Cheshire and Landrine, Stockfish and Oldwright and many more had glimpses of his figure on horseback silhouetted on rising ground to the east of their farms.

He planted the township of Castlereagh upon the map. His camp-fires blazed beside the Yellow-Mundie Lagoon, "a noble lake of fine fresh water". Now he was at Lieutenant Bell's fortified farm on Belmont Hill, now crawling ant-like up the hills of Kurrajong on his lame horse Cato, feasting his eyes upon "a grand and noble prospect", while the leeches dined heartily off Elizabeth's ankles.

Finally they reached beautiful and extensive fields of wheat and maize and prepared to cross the Hawkesbury in the dead Andrew Thompson's barge to Green Hills, where they were to rest in the Government Cottage, "a sweet delightful spot" on the summit of a terrace rising above the broad river.

On the morrow the Reverend Mr Cartwright, a shepherd who devoted most of his days to the soil, gave a most excellent discourse and read prayers "extremely well".

Richmond was marked out—"on the extremity of the Common near Pugh's Lagoon". The ground for the township was filched, with some bargaining, from Mr Nicholas Bayly, the grantee. The site of Richmond Church and burying ground was fixed "on a beautiful elevated bank immediately above this fine basin of fresh water, and within about 200 yards of it".[55]

All the small settlements along the Hawkesbury were visited in turn. The Governor's energy was unbounded. It was not uncommon for him to ride thirty-five miles in a single day in the course of his duties.

By 6 December the viceregal exploration was finished for the time being. Twenty-one friends with their own official family dined with them, including the pioneer magistrate Dr Arndell, Simeon Lord, and Moore from Liverpool. It was a historic meal:

> After dinner I christened the new townships, drinking a bumper to the success of each.— I gave the name of *Windsor* to the town intended to be erected in the District of the Green Hills, in continuation of the present village, from the similarity of this situation to that of the same name in England;— the township in the Richmond District, I have named *Richmond* from its beautiful situation, and as corresponding with that of its District; the township for the Evan or Nepean District, I have named *Castlereagh*, in honour of Lord Viscount Castlereagh; the township of the Nelson district I have named *Pitt-Town*, in honour of the immortal memory of the late great William Pitt, the Minister who originally planned this Colony; and the township for the Phillip District on the north or left bank of the Hawkesbury, I have named *Wilberforce*—in honour of and out of respect to the good and virtuous Wm. Wilberforce, Esq., M.P.— a true patriot and the real friend of mankind![56]

Five townships were thus added to a continent which previously had possessed only three, and five cooling bumpers to the interiors of all the company.

Before long Macquarie was posting back to Sydney[57]—from which he had travelled to the nethermost boundaries of civilization without ever being more than fifty miles from home, next extending his inquisitions to Toongabbie and Seven Hills, to Concord and to Cook's River; but the echoes of the addresses the men of Hawkesbury had read to him had scarcely died away before he was riding through that district again, twenty-five, thirty, forty miles a day, galvanizing the population to energy, putting up signboards on high posts, planning avenues and streets and burial grounds and glebes, and giving an allotment to Mr Fitzgerald in the Great Square at Windsor, on the express condition of his building immediately thereon "a handsome commodious inn of brick or stone to be at least two stories high", which according to an almost natural law became the "Macquarie Arms".[58]

Parramatta was turned inside out, mapped, remoulded and reformed. Each new centre acquired a Macquarie Street, but Parramatta was graced as well with a principal thoroughfare to be called George Street and with Marsden, Pitt, and Phillip Streets.

X

Before the end of 1810 the settlers had become familiar with a new paternal type of government and general order in which the Governor took the whole colony into his confidence about his movements and his views.[59]

He told them how he was much gratified by the beauty of the country and its natural fertility; how he found much to commend in the general industry of the settlers—"in this widely extended colony"—and in the progress they had made in clearing their lands and preparing them.

He was happy in observing the increased amount of land under grain, giving "promise of a most luxuriant harvest". But he could not forbear to express his regret that settlers paid so little attention to domestic comfort. They had not erected commodious residences for themselves, nor suitable housing for their grain and livestock. He could not refrain from observing the miserable clothing of many of the people, whose means of providing decent apparel, at least, were sufficiently obvious to leave them no excuse.

He hoped they would pay more attention to these important objects and that, by strict regard to economy and temperance, they would give him the chance on his next annual tour to show a more unqualified approbation of their exertions.

To some degree he was even prepared to fill their deficiencies.

He noticed that landholders of the lower classes were inadequately supplied with livestock—so they should have a cow each from the Government upon their thirty acres, to be paid for in grain or money as they chose, inside eighteen months, though none need apply who could not bring unquestionable vouchers of honesty and industry. They must keep the cow for three years. They could, also, have sheep from the Government flocks on the same terms.[60]

He believed that with such assistance from the Government, and the exertion of their own steady industry, they "might very shortly become as happy, thriving, and prosperous a people as any other throughout His Majesty's extensive foreign Dominions".

To meet the inundations of the Hawkesbury and the Nepean, he adjured settlers to seek sanctuary in his high-level townships, in which every one of them would be given a site for a dwelling house, offices, garden, corn-yard and stock-yard, proportioned according to farm sizes. Dwellings in these havens were to be veritable mansions beside some of the bark shacks erected by the farmers on their thirty-acre emancipation grants. They were to be "either made of brick or weather-boarded, to have brick chimneys and shingled roofs, and no dwelling house less than nine feet high". But they were refuges and were not to be sold.[61]

Liverpool was to have a church, a jail, a school-house, and a guard-house. Leases were to be granted to free mechanics who settled there, and Mr Thomas Moore, that most devout and steady citizen whose infinite piety later had expression in the foundation of the Moore Theological College, was to be that town's chief magistrate. All the towns were to have commons.

One of his last acts in 1810 had been to have St Philip's completed, and to make it Sydney's first consecrated church.

The year of 1811 was ushered in with a chorus of watchmen's rattles, for the Governor was dividing Sydney into seven police districts, getting ready to build watch-houses, to man them with constables—under Dr D'Arcy Wentworth as chief magistrate—creating new police powers, reading the proofs of many folios of regulations which were in a few days to be spread like a wet blanket over the whole landscape of Sydney wrong-doing. . . .[62]

As he celebrated the day with an excursion in his new barge, the *Elizabeth*, there seemed to be nothing to suggest that his governorship would last much longer than the next two or three years, or that those years would differ much from the first, in point of view of his viceregal experiences.

CHAPTER XVI

A Molehill Rises

I

THE seasons continued bountiful, the rainfall steadily copious till in March 1812 the Hawkesbury River rose twelve feet, threatening once more to flood out the farms.

The comments of the settlers at the beginning of 1811, were "very handsome and flattering" to the Governor's "*mild* and auspicious administration".[1] The country was "in a progressive state of improvement". This he saw for himself as his carriage rolled ever more frequently over the bush roads. Farmers were "making considerable progress in the cultivation of their lands, taking much greater pleasure in honest industry than heretofore, and becoming daily more temperate and religious".[2] He had all the encouragement he needed for expansion of the settlement to the outlands of the Bunburry-Curran country towards the south-west where, on his first tour the previous year, he had been at much pains to select a suitable tract of good land for the accommodation of small settlers.[3]

No less than two hundred and forty-nine couples had entered into holy matrimony in the second year of the new era, to the great profit of the clergy,[4] though proof that the course of true love did not always run smooth lay in the fact that the Governor was compelled to deter, with a helping of lashes, a miscreant who sold his spouse in the open market with a halter round her neck for £16 currency and some cloth.[5]

By midwinter the "dining room or Great Saloon" at Government House had been completed, and was ready for the entertainment at dinner on King's Birthday of no less than seventy-two persons, including five ladies—Elizabeth, Mrs O'Connell (Bligh's daughter), Mrs Palmer, the Commissary's wife, Mrs Cowper and Mrs Ellis Bent.[6]

In October he laid the foundation stone of the new hospital at an imposing ceremony at which the higher orders feasted in a large marquee and the contractors presented their benefactor with a box commemorative of the Jubilee of George III.

Brick walls were rising abundantly. He established a town common. He was arranging to build vast red barracks for the troops. He and Ellis Bent had planned and were sending to England their ambitious schemes to reorganize justice and the courts, and to establish a large measure of civil government.

They had longed-for mails late in 1811, carrying intelligence nearly a year out of date. There were letters from Drummond, Macquarie's intimate of the days when Jane had been dying in Macao, who hoped that the heats and heart-burnings within the Colony would have subsided into rational and proper sentiments.[7] Drummond was quite confident that his distant friend's "steady and equitable rule will prove of the greatest utility, tho' it may not immediately produce a conversion or a Government of Saints". He spoke of operations against the red deer and believed that "the present government would survive if it did not founder on the Walcheren shoal".

William Wilberforce could not doubt "that attention to ye religious and moral state of ye Colony would in a few years produce improvement which men would scarcely anticipate", and that the Governor's encouragement of marriage and of the domestic virtues would be of unspeakable benefit to everyone in the rising settlements.[8]

His old friends Sir Robert Abercromby and General Balfour were keeping him in touch with the affairs of Britain; Charles Forbes with those of India.[9]

All news was not so good. In August his friend and mentor, Jonathan Duncan, had perished in Bombay. The September mail brought the "mos: afflicting and distressing intelligence of the death of my most beloved and deservedly revered dear good and amiable mother", who had breathed he, last on the evening of 29 November 1810, at the advanced age of 82, "esteemed and beloved and respected by all who knew her".[10]

The old lady had been "interred at Kilvickewan (in the Isle of Mull) and buried in the same grave with her husband and three sons on December 5 1810, with every mark of honour and respect, her funeral being attended by all the gentlemen and 125 of the commoners of Ulva and the neighbouring country, and her own dear, good son Charles".

Thank Heaven, he comforted himself, his good and revered aged parent was now in the blessed regions of the good and virtuous, though he felt that they must ever deplore the loss of her.[11]

On the whole, even apart from his personal troubles, it had been an uneasy year. There had been none of the good fellowship which had flavoured the events of the previous spring. There was anxiety at Government House when the Governor's Secretary, Mr Campbell, and the Commissary each proved his civilian prowess by shooting a military officer, almost mortally, in a duel. These encounters followed dissensions at the August races, during which some miscreant robbed Mr Justice Bent's Matchem of the Cup by bloating him with green feed—the first doping case in Australian racing history. There was scandal in Van Diemen's Land, where an adventurous lieutenant had made too free with his commanding officer's all-too-willing spouse. There were constant wagers upon when Bligh's turbulent daughter, who had worn a fevered and anxious expression throughout the year, would add to the Clan O'Connell. And, generally speaking, personal relationships within the higher ranks of society were unsettled.

II

In November the Governor was, one feels, quite happy to be off to inspect Van Diemen's Land. It was a hazardous and, some thought, a very foolish, enterprise. The only available vessel was the eighty-ton *Lady Nelson*, but the accommodation arranged by Elizabeth in person called for "great praise for the taste and judgment she has displayed on this occasion", for it was "neat, clean and comfortable".[12]

Her arrangements unfortunately did not extend to the perverse Tasman Sea, which made them glad of a serene interlude on shore, during which they walked the mainland beach of Jervis Bay under the friendly eyes of "stout well-made, goodlooking natives" who seemed quite at ease and devoid of fear.

Afterwards they had good reason to thank their stars that the vessel was light, sound, well-found and well-manned and the "best sea-boat I ever sailed in". For the sea became so wild that cooking was impossible for two days and two nights and the viceregal travellers were "obliged to eat on the cabin floor on very common fare", while the gale changed to a tremendous storm through which "our tight little bark . . . swam on top of those terrific billows like a feather and surmounted all the dangers that threatened her".

Elizabeth, of course, made "a *most excellent brave* sailor", never expressing the least fear or apprehension, though Mr Overend, the master of the vessel, confessed it to be one of the worst and most violent gales he had ever encountered.

After four days they were all once more "assembled socially to a very comfortable breakfast in our own little snug cabin", but they were nineteen days out from Sydney before they were carried ashore in the Derwent to be greeted by a "great concourse" of cheering people. They lodged in a little cottage with the thunder of the saluting guns still ringing in their ears, while the inhabitants prepared to illuminate the township and set light to bonfires, round whose blaze rejoicing convicts danced till dawn.

The Governor himself wasted no time in dancing. He journeyed to Newtown and named Macquarie Point; he decreed that a township to be called Elizabethtown be established for New Norfolk. He rode up a mountain by the harbour with Captain Antill, named it Mount Nelson and ordered a flagstaff and a guard-house to be established on the summit.

Within a week he had issued a general order that Hobart, for which no regular plan had yet been laid down, should be subdivided into a principal square and seven streets, and had enjoined his scheme of buildings. He pointed here, and lo, a barracks and a hospital were to arise on Barrack Hill. There, he said, would be a new general hospital, there a new jail.

The speed with which he created a metropolis had something delirious about it, but his touch was sure and commanding:

> I had the names of the great square and principal streets painted on boards and this morning erected on posts at the angles of the square and streets to define and mark out their respective limits and direction; naming them as follows: viz. "George's Square—Macquarie (Main) Street—Liverpool Street,—Argyle Street—Elizabeth Street,—Murray Street,—Harrington Street,—and Collins Street; being 3 long and 4 cross streets as per Plan of the Town.[13]

The inhabitants were plainly awed and enchanted. They dwelt, in their addresses to him, on his many privations and on the dangers of his voyage. They referred to the natural stimulation to merit which must be excited in their breasts by "invincible attachment to the laws and adherence to the regulations, the patronage, favour and protection of an unequalled governor". And they promised in a body that their gratitude at being allowed to draw rations from the King's stores would move them to "instruct their children as soon as their articulation should commence, to lisp the name of Governor Macquarie", who—surely smelling strongly of bonfire smoke—passed out of their sight but not of their ken through scarlet ranks as he, Elizabeth, and Antill ceremoniously rode away, followed by the plodding feet of J. T. Campbell, his secretary, Meehan, the Deputy Surveyor-General, and that young sprig of Lochbuy, Lieutenant John Maclaine, bound upon the first viceregal expedition across Tasmania.

If any evidence later was needed that they had succeeded in their journeying it was there in black and white upon the map.

From Glenforsa, named after his brother's estate, they wandered to Elizabeth Valley;[14] from the valley to "Governor Macquarie's Resting Place"; thence to Mount Dromedary, called after the ship which had borne them from England; to Table Mountain and Western Table Mountain, to remember their sojourns in Cape Town; to Ben Lomond, to Jericho, to the River Jordan; to Macquarie Springs, Governor's Second Resting Place, to Meehan Valley and York Plains; thence to Antill's Ponds and Mount Henrietta—that was Elizabeth's second name.

They made their way to the Argyle Plains, the Macquarie River, Mount Campbell, Maclaine Plains, Antill Plains, Elizabeth River, Macquarie Plains and Gordon Plains, Honeysuckle Beach and the torrent of Corri-Linn—"so named now by me in honour of the Patriot Chief of Scotland, Wm. Wallace".

At last, beyond a wild romantic view they came upon the village of Launceston, its colours fluttering on the new flagstaff on the hill, above the troops drawn up to form a lane to Government House.

The moment the weary travellers appeared round the hill in sight of the town, a salute of nineteen guns began to shake the cliffs and echo through the gorges: "The major's highly officer-like conduct in this ceremonial is highly creditable to him."

Launceston was as much addicted to bonfires as Hobart, and its landscape proved impressive, even to one who had seen the Pyramids, Ben More and the Alvand Ranges. No scenery ever could avoid Macquarie's encomiums:

> The grand view, and noble picturesque landscape that presented themselves on our first coming in sight of Launceston and the three rivers and fertile plains and lofty Mountains by which they are bounded, were highly gratifying and truly sublime; and equal in point of beauty to anything I have ever seen in any country.[15]

The settlement was healthy, with no sick, civil or military. Its situation, however, seemed to the Governor to be too far inland.

He proposed to move it nearer to the sea, and a little more journeying—

on which there had been more renaming of localities and Brumbey's Plains became Breadalbane Plains—found them in his newly envisaged northern capital on York Cove, dining comfortably in their tent and drinking prosperity to "George-town".[16]

They slept where he marked out the proposed principal square, but Georgetown did not progress much beyond the signboards with which he decorated it for many a day.

He left Van Diemen's Land feeling that "the country far exceeds any description I can attempt to give you of it". And before long he was busy providing the sailors with drink "with which to celebrate the holy and sacred day" of the birth of Christ, while their little barque wallowed up the funnel of Bass Strait bound past Sydney for Port Stephens, beyond the Coal River on the New South Wales coast. There they named Inchkenneth (after the Maclean island near the Isle of Mull on which Boswell had tarried with Dr Johnson), and Meredith Island, after the lady who had been Elizabeth's girlhood friend in London.[17]

Port Stephens seemed a very good harbour, but the Governor felt that it could never be of any importance, as the country round it looked to him barren and unfit to be settled. Newcastle was more promising. He journeyed twenty miles up the Hunter River to view the Lime Kilns, seven miles from the town, and to see cedar and rosewood growing.[18]

Then, after two months and two days away, he returned to Sydney Government House, between lines of welcoming soldiery, to discover that Lieutenant-Governor O'Connell had carried out the details of administration with great zeal and regularity during his absence.[19]

It was remarkably gratifying that even exclusives were prepared to rejoice at the chieftain's return, meeting him with a pious expression of the hope that his absence had not caused him to feel "diminished regard for those inhabiting this part of the territory forming your seat of Government".[20]

Immediately after his return the Governor sent G. W. Evans, of the Survey Department, away in the *Lady Nelson* upon the first real exploring expedition of the Macquarie age, an expedition during which the huge ex-purser of the Royal Navy made a survey of Jervis Bay and he and his party became the first Europeans in history to travel overland from the Shoalhaven to Appin through the rich and fertile Illawarra. Theirs was a starved, arduous and perilous journey.

III

The grass still grew long and green in that summer of 1811-12. The markets were stocked with all sorts of vegetables. Potatoes were being sold at seven shillings a hundredweight, the finest peaches for eightpence a dozen. The stalking spectre of hunger limped ever farther behind a community whose new abundance had not yet felt the full strain of feeding the hundreds of unexpected mouths which were soon due to arrive.

Elizabeth "set agoing" Mr West's watermill for grinding wheat[21];

her husband stood godfather to O'Connell's small son, the first president-to-be of an Australian Legislative Council born in the Colony.[22]

January brought them news that Macquarie's old Bombay friend, Sir Samuel Auchmuty, had taken the Isle of Java,[23] intelligence which called the ebullient Michael Robinson, who was now ensconced safely in the Government Secretary's Office and whom the *Gazette* described respectfully as a "lauriat bard", to "give birth to imaginations which pronounce themselves the work of Nature and refinement":

> *Hail Britannia's Warriors glorious,*
> *Still unrivall'd, still victorious!*[24]

Mr Robinson had, indeed, ceased to be merely a horrible example to his fellows or interesting as a character only to the students of *Leach's Cases*. His stature since the Governor had appointed him the antipodean "poet laureate" had increased. The *Gazette* even feared that should he, at such a season, "neglect the twining of a Parnassian wreath", he might "give umbrage to the Muses".[25]

But there was little chance of that. Mr Robinson seemed to fairly burst with song. It scarcely needed "the request of the Governor made with affable kindness to be the reciter of his own performances" to set him off at full blast in the ballroom of Government House in praise of his involuntarily adopted country; a country, it seemed, of "cheerful hills, golden vales, verdant fields" where:

> *. . . . . . sheltered from the martial storm,*
> *Where no rude Hands our Vales deform,*
> *Where worth, with Dignity presides*
> *Where Truth directs, and Wisdom guides;*
> *Where Mercy bends with graceful Mien,*
> *And hope looks on with Smile serene . . .*[26]

Unfortunately, the colonists who lined up to present the (1812) New Year addresses, under the leadership of Mr William Charles Wentworth, the young Acting Provost-Marshal, could not go all the way with Mr Robinson in his raptures. A later generation might have recognized in the colonists' addresses the beginnings of W. Wentworth's life work—his first wary approach to the advocacy of self-government for the Territory.

They professed to feel exultation "at the happy period that was dawning on their prospects" and declared that they were spurred to hope for the antipodean future by the transformation which had expanded the American colonies within two centuries into "now vast States".[27]

They viewed their pioneer land "elevating with hasty steps from the weakness of infancy, and vying with dignity in the great family of the world displaying an importance that shall not disgrace the nation from whence we sprung and setting at rest the long agitated question whether it acted with policy in settling New South Wales". They described the place modestly as "becoming already a creditable epitome of the United Empire which gave us birth".

As their spokesman intoned, having "witnessed His Excellency, regardless of difficulties, personally setting the example of exertion, and proffering patronage of every effort to surmount those obstacles, so long considered sufficient to retard further discovery", they wished to venture the idea that the Governor's thoughts about development were "in unison with the ardour of their own". They remarked that they could not fail to advert to the reflections that "however early you may be called to more splendid or comparatively important duties, you fortunately assumed our government at the early period when its pliant form was capable of receiving every bias your extended experience enabled you to affix". And they showed appreciation of their ruler's "approaches already made to model the laws that rule us after that revered original", the British Constitution.

The Governor assured them of his faith that perseverance in the system of British Government would most effectually render the Colony an effective and beneficial member of the great Empire to which it owed its existence. He concurred in the thanks of Hawkesbury settlers to Divine Providence for an abundant harvest and modestly accepted the compliments of the Parramattans who hailed him as their "sincere protector and friend":

> It being my most ardent wish, at once to call forth the energies of the Colony for the benefit of its inhabitants, and to obtain for them the unshackled advantages of the British Laws; I have great pleasure in informing you, that in pursuance of these sentiments, I have recommended to His Majesty's Ministers such alterations in the present system of our Courts of Justice, both Civil and Criminal, as the increasing wealth and respectability of the Inhabitants at large so justly demand.[28]

IV

Whatever the ultimate ambitions of the various classes in the Colony and of the Governor, however, there existed already the kind of differences of opinion that have wrecked many rainbow schemes in the history of colonization.

Firstly, the Governor believed in development by means of small land settlement on a policy initiated by the Home Government and linked with the redemption of the wicked; but there was a very large proportion of his flock, even among the redeemed wicked themselves, who were at variance with him on that point.

Secondly, he believed that, as a prelude to orderly rural settlement, he must build firm bases from which to colonize, in the shape of well-organized towns. But on this the Home Government, though he was merely developing its own theory, looked with a stinting and parsimonious eye.

The Government was involved in a war which menaced the existence of the Empire. The idea of loading the British taxpayers with the burden of building roads, bridges, and town halls for a distant convict settlement filled its Ministers for the time being with bitter amazement.

These subjects were soon a matter of contention. The exclusives agreed that the convict, bond or freed, had a place in the future of the Colony, but their conception of his role was that of a humble penitent labouring for a meritorious aristocracy, which, they proposed, should consist of their worthy selves.

They had not in general earlier complained very bitterly about the small-settlement policy which had given the emancipated convict thirty acres of land, a cow, and some other help in starting life afresh. For while rum had ruled the colony and commerce had been in the hands of the Military and the Civil Service, there had been ways and means of unfastening the grasp of the reformed villain upon his small holding and possessions.

But those days were nearly over. The Governor himself by early training was a small farmer who had been brought up upon "tacked" land. And his long experience in the broad sub-continent of India, of which this new realm must have reminded him, was the feature in which he differed most from his forerunners in office, all of whom were of the rolling main. He thought that he knew what could be done in the pristine soil which he had found below Liverpool beyond Bunburry-Curran Creek and near George's River, and whatever similar tracts might come to light. And he had no intention of allowing his settler-farmers to fall into the grip of "exclusives" while he could hold out a helping hand by granting them cattle, implements on credit, and government rations, if need be, and by buying their produce.

He was prepared to foster the immigration of free farmers of the lower class, whose industry, he believed, would turn them into a yeomanry, they "being real improvers and cultivators of the soil".

He was not altogether averse to the grant of larger estates, on conditions. He regularly made land grants to officers according to established custom and Home Government policy. The Judge-Advocate received grants; his children had grants. The Lieutenant-Governor he dowered with 2500 acres when he married. The Chaplain was rewarded with substantial grants for magisterial services. So, too, explorers. Jaded travellers, after their contests with three oceans on their return from England to their native or adopted home in Botany Bay—old Johnston, the rebel, young William Charles Wentworth—were generously endowed with broad acres. If the wife of a temporarily deranged paymaster or of a delinquent major succeeded in touching the viceregal heart, the suppliant need be no longer landless.

Against the grasping landlord and the lazy and privileged free settler with influence the Governor set his face; for certain types of gentlemen settlers, he discovered, after securing all the favours and indulgences to which their orders from home entitled them, often set up as merchants without cultivating a single acre of their lands, which they sold immediately in defiance of the conditions of their grants.[29]

And it was now "becoming almost a constant practice for persons who wish to get rid of some troublesome connections, to obtain permission at the Secretary of State's Office for their being allowed to come out here". By this means fell upon the Colony "the weight of a most troublesome and useless set of persons".[30]

Therefore, the Governor told his Minister in his last dispatch of 1812, emancipated convicts seemed to him the best description of settlers. Indulgences to persons of this kind had the best effects, for six emancipist families could live off one normal "gentleman's grant".[31]

V

Certainly, if emancipists were the best for the purposes of development, there was to be plenty of raw material.

The British Government had resumed transportation in full spate in 1810, though the villains male and female whom they were now transporting were of a very different vintage from the 5958 who had been sent out in the first ten years of Botany Bay history and from the 3247 males and 1231 females who had followed them between 1797 and 1810.[32]

In 1810-11 about 500 had arrived, and in the years 1812-17 their grateful country consigned 3978 males and 681 females to the antipodes, apart from the Irish. The total for thirty years was 15,794.[33]

The first 3500 had included a large proportion of agricultural labourers, adventurous young stack-burners, poachers, and political Irish and Scottish. Such men, given a handful of seed potatoes and maize, a pig, a kangaroo dog, a tin to make a still, and a few snares, had discovered in New Holland a golden land of leisure in which man could live with scarce a care. But these types had become precious gun-fodder for the Peninsula and in their place the Home Government exported to Botany Bay London thieves and the halt and the disabled from the battlefields. Among them were few of the mechanics needed for the growing building programme or to supply the wants of the seasonally opulent farms of the great landowners.[34]

The new types made poor farmers and artisans. Only a small percentage of them could recoup to the Colony the £30 a year which it cost to maintain each of them; and the improving communications and increased flow of traffic, which the existence of new turnpikes through the dark bush had brought into being, added to their opportunities for highway robbery and every kind of villainy.[35]

Largely through their influence the 73rd Regiment threatened to become as depraved as its predecessor corps. This could only be expected in a scene in which the men were subjected to so much inactivity and the influence of so many bad examples, especially since O'Connell, the commanding officer, though a good soldier, was a lax administrator.

In 1811 the soldiery had committed more than one act of violence which had attracted public attention, though it had remained for the New Year to mark the drift from grace with an awful example.

In the heat of February Private John Gould murdered a woman named Margaret Finnie, whose body was found "in a state too horrible to be either described or conceived".[36]

Mr Gould had very short shrift. His victim's body was found on 25 February 1812. The Coroner committed him on 26 February. He was sentenced to death on the evening of 6 March. On 9 March he was hanged in a hollow regimental square.[37]

The Governor's subsequent lecture to the Regiment should have armoured its members against further evil-doing. He pointed out how the immoderate use of liquor had led to the crime. He assured them that "the strong arm of justice fails not to avenge the wrongs thus done to society, but it is much better to guard against the commission of crimes than to punish them".

Troops, he ordered, must above all things refrain from over-indulgence in the use of spirituous liquors, which not only incapacitated them from their duties but vitiated and depraved their minds.

Came his peroration:

> Soldiers! You once by valour obtained the honourable badge of Mangalore. You have been selected on account of your long and justly established character for gallantry in the field and regularity of conduct in quarters, for the purpose of protecting the peaceable and well behaved inhabitants of this country. The still higher honour of being called the Defenders of Peace and Good Order in New South Wales awaits you. It only rests with you to obtain it by steady and soldier-like good conduct.[38]

VI

It was while the Governor pondered the problems connected with the new rush of convicts that news came that Lord Liverpool had succeeded Castlereagh as Colonial Secretary. The new minister had little time to waste on convict colonies, while "war's infuriate roar" was audible across the English Channel. He had French experience behind him which apprised him that one could expect nothing from the lower classes save ingratitude.[39]

He had found that he and his officials could not bully his new commander in Spain, who poured scorn upon the "futile drivelling" of official correspondence. Thus he looked for somebody more easily bullied to attack.

And his attack seemed to put a damper on the Governor's vision of a rapidly expanding colonization of New South Wales.

The Governor, despite his enthusiasms, had shown himself nervous at "being under the necessity of drawing so largely on the Treasury since my taking charge of this Government"[40]; but he had explained that "the exhausted and almost empty state of the public stores at the time of my arrival left me no practicable alternative". He claimed that he had not ordered nor "authorised a single purchase, either here nor at the out settlements, which was not imperiously necessary for the subsistence and support of the Colony, or for the carrying on the public works now on hands, and other unavoidable expences of the Public Service". He could "not avoid expressing some anxiety to know whether the line of conduct which I pursued" had been such as to meet the approbation of his Sovereign and his Ministers; but he was optimist enough to hope that the Colonial Office would give his administration and government credit at least for rectitude and integrity of principle.

Long before his missive had reached London, Lord Liverpool fired on him with two barrels loaded with astonished wrath. The first shot was aimed, so to speak, past his ear; but the second was directed straight to the midriff. Lord Liverpool, it seemed, was "very angry" with him. His lordship was commanded by the Prince Regent to acquaint Governor Macquarie that the burden of the Colony to the Mother Country had been so much increased, since the latter's assumption of office, that it became necessary to have a more satisfactory explanation than had yet been received.[41]

Why, said the irate Minister, only £13,873 had been drawn against the Government by New South Wales in Governor King's last year (1806) and £31,110 in Bligh's last year! The rebel administration of Johnston, Paterson and Foveaux had called for only £23,163 in 1808 and £49,514 in 1809.

Yet in 1810 expenses had come to £72,600 6s. 10¼d.—the Treasury had a weakness for farthings—and from 1 January to 12 March 1811 there were Bills dated for £21,214 11s. 8¾d.

His Lordship wished it known that he would have expressed his surprise in much stronger terms if he had not concluded that a great proportion of the expenses would not occur again.

In giving his opinion to the Treasury that the Bills should be accepted, he had been "governed solely by a consideration of the hardships which individuals would sustain, and the additional expence to which the Government might be eventually liable had they been protested".[42] The only conclusions to be drawn from a comparison between past Governors' expenditures and the present one's, he thought, were not in the latter's favour:

> I am to repeat to you the positive commands of His Royal Highness that while you remain in charge of the Colony of New South Wales you use the most unremitting exertions to reduce the expence at least within its former limits, that you undertake no public buildings or works of any description without having the previous sanction of His Majesty's Government for their construction, or without being enabled to prove most clearly and satisfactorily that the delay of reference would be productive of serious injury to the Public Service.[43]

He demanded endless information and data of the kind which irate Ministers are wont to demand. Why had there been no returns of convicts and inhabitants since King's time in 1806? Let them be counted and their oxen and their asses, their wives, concubines, and grain be assessed as before. A detailed revenue statement must be drawn up every quarter. The appropriation of revenue from the Police and Orphan Funds for the purposes for which they had been created was to be looked on as only temporary.[44]

What was this unauthorized charge of £551 10s. 7d. for "camping equipage, tents, etc., purchased in India for your accommodation during your tour of the interior of the country"? The Governor's bodyguard must not be increased at a cost of £25 per quarter. Let it be disbanded forthwith.

Buy two brigs? Yes, but he hoped that he would have no reason to regret having relied implicitly on the Governor's authority in the matter. And what about this rent of a house for the Judge-Advocate?

He repeated that "before you incur any expence of an unusual nature, it is desirable that you should receive a previous authority for it".

Finally came a warning never to lose sight of the necessity of "relieving the Mother Country of a proportion at least of that expence which is incurred in supporting the Colony"[45] and an expression of the Minister's pious hope that "the period is not far distant when a very considerable part of the expenditure of the Colony can be defrayed out of the Colonial Revenue":

If the expence of erecting quays, wharfs and bridges, and of making streets and roads cannot be borne by the free settlers and by those who are to receive the immediate benefits from these improvements, it may be presumed that the Colony is not yet in a state sufficiently advanced to render the constitution of such works necessary. I am to desire therefore that your first object should be to make the Colonial Revenue applicable to that part of the expenditure of the Colony which now falls so heavily upon the Treasury of this country.[46]

Most of all the plan for the new "rum hospital" seemed to incense him. He brushed aside Macquarie's plea that the scheme was

very advantageous, and the necessity for a new building of this kind so imperious that I flatter myself the measure I have adopted will meet Your Lordship's fullest concurrence and approbation; on perusal of the contract itself, Your Lordship will perceive that a spacious, elegant, and indispensibly necessary public building will be erected, without any tax proportional to its magnitude being laid on the Government. The oxen given for slaughter to the contractors forming almost the entire of the expence that Government will be at for its erection.[47]

His Lordship thought "many objections might be urged to an engagement of this nature under any circumstances". He was "surprized that you did not foresee the embarrassment which would inevitably be occasioned in the execution of this contract by the adoption of the suggestions contained in your despatch of 30 April 1810 . . . you distinctly express your opinion that it would be 'good and sound policy to sanction the free importation of good spirits under a high Duty of not less than 3s. or 4s. per gallon'".[48]

The position was awkward mainly because the Privy Council for Trade had rushed to adopt the Governor's view and had granted licenses in Britain for the export of liquor to the Colony. Already several eager sea captains, with official patrons, were on their way to Sydney with vessels loaded down to the line with overproof beverages.

"It would have been adviseable," wrote Lord Liverpool, "that an engagement of this kind had not been entered into, until you had an opportunity of learning the sentiments of His Majesty's Government upon the propriety of adopting the measures which you had proposed and had so strongly recommended."[49]

His lordship, however, washed his hands of the whole matter. It must be left to the Governor's own discretion to take such measures as might appear to him calculated to do justice to all concerned.

VII

Politics, of course, were behind this meticulous display of heat, for a Parliamentary Committee on Transportation was about to sit on the affairs of New South Wales. The unlucky recipient of Lord Liverpool's dispatches knew naught of politics. He was staggered, unable to express "the sincere sorrow and mortification which I feel on account of the severe censure and strong animadversions on my conduct".[50]

He declared that he could "safely affirm, without the least apprehension or fear of contradiction, that no Governor has ever yet been here, or in any other of His Majesty's Colonies, who has been more rigidly vigilant and watchful in the public expenditure of money, provisions, and stores belonging to the Crown; nor a greater economist in every branch of public expenditure" than himself.

> Conscious therefore of my own integrity and rectitude and of the honourable purity of my motives, I shall now proceed to give your Lordship such full and clear explanations of the grounds upon which this unusual expenditure has been sanctioned by me, that I indulge a confident hope your Lordship will be pleased to admit that the apparent great increase of expense has been unavoidable, and that the sanctioning of it by me was imposed by an imperious necessity.[51]

He painted a picture of stores emptied by the usurping government, of an increased number of mouths due to the ingress of the 73rd Regiment with its eight hundred men and its five hundred dependants; of the need to reclothe the almost naked population, of the need to make advances to new settlers to increase cultivation; of all his multitudes of problems of dilapidation and decay.

In his humble opinion the expense would be repaid or compensated for by the important result of securing the Colony for ever from risk of want and famine. The fertility of the new lands he had opened up had already fully answered the expectations he had formed of them.

In two and a half years, when he completed all outbuildings, he thought he could reduce the present expenditure. In fact, he was ready to give assurances that the expenses of the Colony would gradually and annually decrease, and promised to make every practicable retrenchment in all branches of public expenditure.

Macquarie to Lord Liverpool

> In the comparative statement transmitted me by your Lordship, of the amount of Bills drawn by my predecessors, from the year 1806 to 1809 inclusive, when contrasted with the great amount of those drawn by me from the first of January, 1810, to the present time, the *conclusion*, as Your Lordship observes . . . "*is not in my favour*"; I willingly admit that appearances, on a slight or superficial view of the subject, and without due allowance for the change of circumstances and for the various items of expenditure the necessity for which I have already dwelt on, are indeed very much *against me*, and greatly *in favour of my predecessors*. But I fully trust and hope that the full and explicit explanation I have herein submitted . . . will prove satisfactory. . . . I believe I may also without vanity and with great truth assert that I have already done more for the general

amelioration of this colony, the improvement of the manners, morals, industry, and religion of its inhabitants, than my three last predecessors, during the several years they governed it . . . there could be no good reason for their drawing Bills for a greater amount than they did as no works or public buildings of the least consequence, except the church at Sydney (which was not entirely completed at the time of my arrival and of course was finished by me) were ever undertaken or erected since the departure of Governor Phillip, who to do him justice did a great deal with small means.[52]

As for the new hospital, he wrote, he must confess that when he proposed a plan for such an elegant building, "not only free of expence to the Crown, but in itself producing a revenue of six thousand seven hundred and fifty pounds" (in duties on liquor) in three years, he had "expected nothing short of your Lordship's highest commendations on the subject".[53]

VIII

Save for his one brush with the Duke of York over the commissions of his young relatives, a decade earlier, this was the first occasion in Macquarie's life on which he had been officially criticized with severity.

He wrote to Thomas Coutts, the banker, friend of the Duke of York and his own correspondent for many years:

> . . . Here I am happy to say, we are in full enjoyment of peace and plenty. The Colony has improved equal to my most sanguine expectations; my situation is one of considerable fatigue and exertion, but this, I do not consider any hardship.
>
> The only circumstance I have felt hurt by, is the unpleasant nature of the communications I received from Lord Liverpool; although his Lordship must certainly be aware, (if he reads the despatches which I send him) that I found the Colony in a state of rapid decay, in such want of provisions that if ships had not seasonably arrived we should have had a famine, that I immediately set about building all necessary stores and barracks, and have been under the necessity of purchasing food and clothing for the prisoners and soldiers at a great advance on the usual price. I have had also many more to feed than were formerly victualled by the Crown.— Notwithstanding all this, and many other circumstances too tedious to trouble you with, His Lordship expresses himself surprised that my draughts should exceed those of any of my predecessors. By this ship I have sent an explanation, which I considered the wants of this country too obvious to be required, and if His Lordship's sense of justice to me bears any proportion to his desire for saving money to the Crown, I hope I shall certainly receive a very different letter in reply.[54]

It was clear that he was yet unaccustomed to the routine of discipline which prevailed between the Colonial office and its senior servants and to the naked frankness of ministerial communications. He was apt at times to mistake admonition for reprimand and disapproval of specific courses for censure on his conduct. His exchanges with Liverpool left him both depressed and discouraged. He even seemed to feel little elevation of spirit when, for the first time wearing his new brigadier-general's uniform, he reviewed the troops in Hyde Park on 31 October 1812, the thirty-sixth anniversary of his landing in Canada as a very youthful volunteer.[55]

He need not have worried his head in the matter.

Within a month after writing his second critical dispatch Liverpool had been translated to a higher sphere as Prime Minister of England, and the politic Bathurst had begun his long reign at the Colonial Office.[56] His was a more equable and reasonable method of approach, though this did not mean a more lavish outlook on the Colony's finance. Financial policy was dictated by the ever-niggardly Treasury and occasionally the new Minister was to be heard voicing his pleasure that the Governor was directing his efforts towards promoting economy, "although the statement of the Annual Accounts . . . gives me no reason as yet to congratulate you upon the success of your exertions".[57]

For the time being he had more reason to fear the growth of local opposition to his policies than the attitude of his superiors in London.

As he made his summer progress through the outlands of the County of Cumberland, he heard everywhere mutterings of a storm which would soon rage round his devoted head.

Towards the end of the year, when Macquarie had been nearly three years in the Colony, Elizabeth was to be seen, quill in hand, writing, in the guise of "your true and sincere friend" to that curious lady-killer, Captain John Piper, whom somebody described as one "who set an example to everyone which they do not follow":

> I suppose all your friends are writing to you, but I am determined at all events that *I shall*. We are all well here, and the Colony continues prosperous. A small attempt has been made by some of the old faction with a view *as I think* to make it appear that the Colony is not quiet, notwithstanding the absence of the old head. All I have to say to you on this subject is that those who act with impropriety must suffer for it, let them be who they may, which if they continue to be troublesome they certainly will. But the probability (now they see it won't do) is that the people will be quiet and all will go on as heretofore, well . . . this particular to you and because I think some of *your* friends will probably magnify this mole-hill into a mountain, when in fact it is only a molehill, and a very small one too. This letter is *beautifully* written, the despatches are just about to be closed which is the cause . . . I wish you would come back to us and keep your ladies in order. They have all gone to sixes and sevens. Since your departure we cannot now get above two of the B's. to speak to each other. Farewell, may every good attend you. [58]

If one could accuse Mrs Macquarie of anything so vulgar as a pun one might imagine that her use of the word "molehill" was not haphazard. For one of the "Bs" in the colony was Mr Ellis Bent, who was just then falling into a queer, rebellious mood. He glared at Bligh's daughter whenever he met her. He showed himself sour at the tedium of life in general. He was irritated by the over-abundance of viands at Government House dinners and racked by the effort needed to carry his fourteen-stone bulk on a pair of creaking, rheumatic knees. Mr Bent was for ever regretting the happy days when he had lived beside the river Mole on the northern confines of the county of Surrey.

London exclusives soon became conscious of the growing unrest in Sydney and began to turn it to their own accounts. Mr John M'Arthur heard it whispered at the end of the year that "his [the Governor's] withdrawal is determined upon. If it be so, he will probably get certain information on the subject by the *Fortune*."[59]

Though it was not true, Macquarie would not sleep so easily in "our new bedroom", of which they took possession a week before Christmas Day 1812.[60] An issue had arisen which could not be baulked and which loomed larger every day as more convicts arrived, more were freed and more rose to prosperity or a competence and earned their own self-respect.

CHAPTER XVII

The Most Meritorious Men

I

THE issue of convict policy, which had added substance to the disputes between Macquarie and the exclusive elements in the Colony and in London, had begun to develop only a few days after he had reached Port Jackson. Within three years the molehill of opposition which it threw up was growing like one of the great pyramids.

When he had been first chosen to take his regiment to New South Wales, Macquarie had known little of the settlement, save through the conventional gossip which treated it a little humorously, jails, for some reason, having comic implications for the English. He himself joked about being "transported". He regarded Botany Bay as a place which one reached only by one of two means. It was possible to travel there as a warder on appointment or on a passport issued by a Judge of Assize.

It did not enter his head that in such a place there could be a small community with ideals of freedom, or a body of former convicts who had regained their self-respect. He could not be aware that most "prisoners" were little if any more under control in the antipodes than they were when free in their native country; that the jail walls there were the oceans and the endless leagues of bush which surrounded the settlements.[1]

Had he been asked, before he came to New South Wales, to sum up the inhabitants of the Colony, he might well have replied in the words of one of his most distinguished public officers, Mr Ellis Bent, that they were mainly "thieves, rascals, vagabonds and missionaries".

He was unaware, till he observed the phenomenon in person, that hundreds of convicts were political prisoners and that of this they were actually proud.

He was not seized of the fact that the convicts, and persons of convict origin, forming about nine-tenths of the population, were taken for granted and treated with toleration accordingly by all but a few of their neighbours[2]; that, indeed, if it had not been so, life would have been unbearable in a small, cramped, and sometimes starving community, isolated from Europe and civilization by twelve thousand miles of water and waste.

But, after his arrival, the Governor's views very soon took decisive shape. He wrote to Commissioner Bigge a decade after his own coming:

> At my first entrance into this Colony, I felt as you do, and I believe I may add, everyone does; at that moment I certainly did not anticipate any intercourse but that of control with men who were, or had been convicts; a short experience shewed me, however, that some of the most meritorious men of the few to be found, and who were most capable and most willing to exert them-

selves in the public service, were men who had been convicts! I saw the necessity and justice of adopting a plan on a general basis which had always been partially acted upon towards these people, namely, that of extending to them generally the same consideration and qualifications, which they would have enjoyed from their merits and situations in life, had they never been under the sentence of the Law, and which had been partially or rather individually adopted towards them by my predecessors.[3]

The "consideration" shown by his predecessors to the convict classes, save for their own selfish ends, had been painfully restricted. King had dwelt in his reports to Whitehall on the Colony's "vice", and punishments inflicted in his time had been limited only by the power of the human frame to endure.[4] Bligh had believed that "transports" could not be expected to earn the advantage of mixing in superior society "until after generations when they deserve it".[5]

Upon the convict in durance Macquarie, by contrast, tried to exercise a reasonably firm discipline, according to strict rules, which his humanity and natural urbanity more and more often diluted so that they were frequently applied very loosely.

He ever more severely curbed and supervised magisterial inflictions of corporal punishment, and showed an outraged horror of the old-time type of flogging, which had laid bladebones bare in the process of instructing young wrongdoers in the principles of virtue.

Before he pardoned a felon or mitigated his sentence, he made it known, he would require "the most unquestionable proofs of rectitude of conduct for a long series of years",[6] even if the person concerned had shown himself "industrious, sober, honest and truly meritorious"; but he was not always very diligent or searching in his examination of the virtues of some to whom he was disposed to extend pardon or leniency, being, with convicts as with others, inclined to be too friendly and trusting in his initial judgments of men.

His most exacting official critic could agree that "if he erred in carrying a humane principle too far, he has done so under the belief that he was acting under the sanction of very high and respectable authority".[7] His disposition led him to view his charges' crimes in the light of misfortunes, which they were to repair in New South Wales by success, rather than as violations of the law, for which they were to atone to their country by the bitterness of exile or by the severities of toil and privation.

Once a man had been set free by pardon or completion of his sentence Macquarie claimed that his own practice towards him became that the sinner's "former state should be no longer remembered, or allowed to act against him".[8] Let the erstwhile convict then, said he, "feel himself eligible for any situation which he has, by a long term of upright conduct, proved himself worthy of filling".

As that "veteran bard", Mr Robinson, sang not very lucidly—apparently after reading *Marmion*—the new man

> *. . . was the friendless culprit's friend,*
> *And where he saw the wish to mend*

Deigned to the outcast felon bend,
Who former faults deplored;
Foster'd the wish, but newly formed;
Matured the blessed design, and warm'd,
With generous zeal, the wretch reformed,
To long-lost peace restored![9]

Mr Robinson believed, at least on suitable occasions, that "whate'er a noble mind exalts" was his master's; that "from every wrong his soul revolts; his faults are human nature's faults; his virtues all his own".

II

Many emancipists before 1810 had in process of reform become substantial citizens. Their stores and mansions towered over most others in the main settlement. Mr Mann averred that there were many, who, "by their good conduct are now considered as respectable characters, and are in possession of horses, carriages, and servants, with a sufficiency to secure their independence during the remainder of their lives".[10]

Unfortunately, with the exodus of officers of the 102nd Regiment, of gentlemen settlers rushing to London to save their skins at the trials of rebels, and of witnesses taken to England to support Bligh or Johnston, Macquarie found the Colony largely denuded of residents to whom he could look for normal civic services.[11]

The only freely-come civilians of executive and administrative ability on whom he could call were his own officers, who were new to the Colony and ignorant of its personalities and atmosphere, and a few freely-come respectable citizens whom the rebellion had left in a state of intense partisan rancour.

Thus the censorious world was shocked to find that the Governor quite readily turned for help to the richer and better educated emancipists. Without hesitation or a qualm, they noticed, he adopted a policy of choosing for offices within his power of appointment the men whom he considered best fitted to fill them, irrespective of their origin, though actually it was only to a very few former convicts that he opened higher offices.

He applied his method of choice throughout the period of his governorship. Colonists found themselves occasionally compelled to go to emancipist magistrates for justice, to see their land grants surveyed by emancipists. Their best public buildings and churches, which in the twentieth century enchant the modern architect, were designed by one of the class, partly while he was still a prisoner. Their constables had gained some of their experience of crime "on the inside".

As a practical move, the elevation of these "reformed" characters to positions of trust was not so ill conceived. Only a fraction of the populace objected.

The erstwhile prisoners certainly could be no worse in the view of the Governor himself or of respectable settlers than those persons who constituted themselves their ruler's chief critics.[12]

Over the former bondmen the Governor held the stronger control. Members of the military caste, the Blaxlands, Marsden, and the rest of the privileged upper crust might cheat or resist, secure in their intimacy or kinship with sly, friendly clerks in the Colonial Office, with deluded British politicians whose aims they furthered, or with powerful patrons in the peerage or prelacy. Influence in official quarters was the breath of life to most of them and they were difficult for an administrator to manage.

On the other hand, emancipists of position had, in the main, climbed to their eminences by dint of industry, diligence, ability, and willingness to submit to discipline. Sometimes they were more cunning than virtuous; but whatever their private morals and failings might be, the great number of them were "not worse in this respect than their unconvicted fellow colonists".[13]

When they merited it, they were easier to reward than men who had come as free settlers or officials to the Colony. When they transgressed the Governor's standards of honesty and competence, they could be brought at once to heel. If they wished to maintain their status, their behaviour must ever be impeccable. The same hand which raised them from the dust could thrust them back into it by reviving their pasts.

Truth to tell the emancipists as a whole proved loyal and faithful and, above others, grateful. Even if some of them profited privately by their positions and succumbed to human weaknesses, there was no instance in which the Governor had real cause to regret the elevation of any of those who held higher offices. He quarrelled with one or two, and minor officials like his clerk, the ingenious Mr Robinson, occasionally betrayed him and the government.

But then Mr Robinson was "a veteran bard". In mundane affairs such, it is well known, are allergic to ordinary moral laws.

III

The reactions to the Governor's methods did not develop comfort for himself, for those whom he sought to redeem and use, or for some of those exclusive opponents, whom young Mr W. C. Wentworth described as "more cruel than vultures . . . eagerly watching the progress of surrounding misery and . . . preying upon the living victims sinking around them".[14]

As Macquarie pointed out, the most rigid exclusionists were prepared to waive their prejudices when self-interest was strongly enough involved. Even John M'Arthur did not hesitate to procure for a privileged employee, who once had worn leg-irons, "an admission to the society of his own most respectable family upon the same footing on which a family agent would be admitted in England".[15]

But the indignation of those "oppressors" who had "built their greatness on the thraldom and miseries of their fellowmen"[16] was not long in rising. It quickly reached boiling-point when they discovered that they would not be free from contact with the convict element within the precincts of Government House.[17]

Even those who had not hesitated to risk the displeasure of their fellows by associating with the miscreants in the open air were stricken with nausea when they came upon any of them in a vice-regal salon. Lieutenant Bell, who had been court-martialled during the insurrectionary period for riding abroad with the emancipated Andrew Thompson, Chief Constable of the Hawkesbury, drew a breath of pained astonishment as he noted that the Governor and his lady treated persons, whom *he* considered "tainted, unfit for associating with", with peculiar attention and "an evident desire of introducing them with marked esteem to other visitors".[18]

The pair showed these convicted persons, he thought, a "decided preference and notice" beyond that shown to other inhabitants, with the exception of the Lieutenant-Governor and the judges. Mrs Macquarie had actually passed Lieutenant Bell, though he was in the uniform of his regiment, without recognition, but had held out her hand to persons who had been prisoners.

Lieutenant M'Naughton, another young purist of the 73rd Regiment, had risen from the Governor's dining-table rather than eat in such company.[19]

The Governor "utterly disclaimed", of course, that he attempted to force officers and free and unconvicted colonists to associate with convicts or former convicts in their private and unofficial lives. The most he ever had done was to warn military and other officials in the pay of the Crown against "making insolent comments on his administration, and on the society he kept".

To the charge that he and Elizabeth showed a "general preference to persons who had been convicts", he responded with a counter-question, "To what object does the word *preference* allude?"[20]

If it referred to appointments to places of trust, honour, or emolument, the present occupancy of those places would sufficiently refute the charge; if to the character of his private friends and associates, the charge was "equally unfounded". All he had done, he averred, had been to give a few emancipated persons of conspicuous merit the full advantage of their virtues. And so far as the accusation affected his wife, he hoped that it would not be needful to dwell upon it.

Whatever her views and sentiments he could not be responsible for them more than for those of any other lady; and he therefore objected to her case being put forward, in spite of the fact that he felt no difficulty on her behalf in disavowing any partiality or undue favour towards the emancipated classes. "It has ever been her wish to bestow the greatest share of her regard where she finds the greatest share of merit. . . . She considers it her duty during her residence in this Colony to show as much kindness towards those persons as their good conduct can justify."[21]

No disclaimer could silence criticism of his methods. To the end of his reign the officers of the garrison continued to complain loudly of those they were forced to meet under his roof.

Peculiarly enough, his military staff, that haughty and exclusive body, set the worst examples by following his practices, and the regimental messes themselves were not always scrupulous in observing the principles which they professed to accept as rigidly necessary.

Lieutenant Wright had been cashiered—temporarily—for sitting down with an emancipist postmaster; yet the mess of the 73rd Regiment itself showed no qualms about entertaining Sir Henry Browne Hayes, even while he was still a convict, but that was a cat of another colour.[22] Whatever you could say about Sir Henry he was at least a gentleman and no odious rebel. He was a baronet, and the petty act which had exiled him to the shores of Botany Bay was scarcely fit to be entered in the calendars of Irish crime. It was well known that he had merely abducted a young Quaker girl; and abductions of maidens, Quaker or otherwise, subject to the observance of due punctilio, were no felonies in the eyes of full-blooded officers and gentlemen, but rather deft exhibitions of a gallant accomplishment. Stack-burners, assaulters of the keepers of deer, and circulators of the pernicious works of Mr Thomas Paine were, of course, of a different standing.

Soon the rage of the exclusives had sacerdotal backing—a rare distinction since there always had been in the Colony a rivalry between Church and Military.

In February 1810 the Reverend Samuel Marsden, the Senior Chaplain, had reached home from London, where he had consorted with the King and the Archbishop of Canterbury. He came near to apoplexy when he discovered that the board which was to control the new turnpike road to Parramatta was to consist of himself and two emancipist justices of the peace—Messrs Simeon Lord and Andrew Thompson.[23]

Mr Marsden forcibly expressed his view of the matter. He believed that the Governor's linkage of his priestly name and duties with these two persons was evidence of a viceregal resolve "to unite the free and convict population"; to adopt measures tending to "raise one class and lower the other, and to bring bond and free to a common level".[24]

This, he considered, was "a peculiar system", one which required him to accept an appointment "totally incompatible with his sacred functions" and to submit to "a degradation to his office as Senior Chaplain of the Colony".[25] He himself at the moment was not a magistrate.

Very angry words were used. The Governor told him, Marsden said, that he "would not forget him"; that his refusal to sit was an act of hostility to the Government, of disrespect to the viceregal person; that it was well for him he held a civil commission, as otherwise he would have tried him by court martial for disobedience to an order.[26]

Marsden wrote a heated protest to the Colonial Office. He wrote to the Archbishop of Canterbury. He declared that, "whatever the opinion of His Majesty's Ministers", he would relinquish the public service altogether rather than be obliged to act in any public capacity with "men whose characters were notorious for improprieties"; for it was a thing he "could never bring his mind to do".[27] He represented to William Wilberforce that it was "not consistent with morality, religion or sound policy to nominate men magistrates who have been convicts and who are still living in open profligacy".[28]

And whatever the Governor's motive was, he said, he could not conceive.

IV

Two emancipists, before Macquarie's coming, had received full countenance. The friend of all, the Reverend Henry Fulton, was "zealous, useful and respectable". Of Richard Fitzgerald the Governor could write, "No individual in this or any country has performed more useful and faithful services than this excellent man."

Within his first half-year of office, on Foveaux's advice, Macquarie had elevated to the magistracy, the one in Sydney, the other virtually in the role of administrator of the Hawkesbury outlands, Messrs Simeon Lord and Andrew Thompson.[29]

Neither would have very much shocked a modern Assize Judge. Mr Lord had been sent out for seven years when he was nineteen years of age for a crime so "insignificant" that nobody seemed to remember what it was.[30] Mr Thompson's one engagement with indignant justice had been at the age of sixteen years, when the constables had netted him for burning some straw.[31] His offence probably had a political origin.

If Mr Lord had any relatives, none heard of them; but Mr Thompson's meticulous Scottish border kinsmen, "extensive merchants in a muslin way, who principally exported to France", had had no hesitation in declaring him to be "an outcast goat" and in washing their hands of him.[32]

Mr Lord, even upon the voyage to New South Wales in 1791, had drawn from the ship's commander "the most humane and indulgent treatment, and almost paternal kindness".[33] And within a score of years he had become a merchant whose stores and factories were the largest in the antipodes, one whose vessels were as well known to the whales of the Antarctic and the cunning savages of New Zealand as to the *shroffs* and *purvoes* of Bombay.[34] Governor King had praised him. Seventeen years after his country had shipped him abroad in ignominy he had signed his name beside John M'Arthur's on the requisition to Johnston to depose a British Governor.[35] Mr Bigge later admitted that no magistrate save Mr Marsden had objected to associating with him on the Bench.

And now, a year or so after being steeped in rebellion, he was in favour with the Government. Macquarie declared him industrious and enterprising. He later admitted that he was reputed litigiously inclined; but he vouched that he had never known him to oppress a poor man, and credited him with having applied his money to the support of distressed settlers, from whom he received payment, "as it suited their convenience at distant periods and without interest".[36]

It did not worry the Governor apparently that his new magistrate was an auctioneer,[37] prone to jest with his crowds in the veritable Doric and on the most familiar terms. And if it was whispered that Mr Lord was somewhat addicted to orphan girls,[38] one could at any rate have wagered that, with his opportunity, so also would have been the Prince Regent and the Duke of York.

Mr Andrew Thompson (in whose district there were no aggregations of orphans) was also a man of "loose morals", though "his conduct in his several official capacities was considered correct".[39] He dwelt, though discreetly, with a lady to whom he was not bound in holy wedlock. But the Reverend Mr. Cartwright would "not have considered him worthy of a funeral sermon had he been so loose and immoral". He was esteemed a "very industrious and bustling character . . . extremely avaricious and astute", though "the common friend and patron" of all.[40]

His career had, if anything, been even more meteoric than that of Mr Lord. Every Governor had leant upon him from Phillip onwards. Four years after he had arrived, at the age of twenty-one, he had changed his prison garb to fill a niche as "a constable of sober habits and good character in other respects" upon the Hawkesbury.[41] Governor King had made him Chief Constable of the Hawkesbury at the age of twenty-six.[42] At thirty-three he was receiving the praise even of the Reverend Samuel Marsden for having, in the floods of 1806, "in one of his own boats saved the lives of 101 persons, whom he took off the tops of houses and rafts of straw".[43]

In Bligh's time—Dr Arndell, the Hawkesbury magistrate, being infirm—he had become virtually the deputy-ruler of the district. He had charge of Bligh's farms and private affairs.[44] It was at his house that the settlers had met to organize against the prospect of Irish insurrection in 1807[45]; and there, greatly daring, he had called the assembly which, on the eve of the Rebellion, had declared the fealty of the outlands to Bligh.[46]

What with his farms with their hundred to two hundred acres of grain, their fine cattle, their heavy-fleeced sheep—St Andrew's, St Ives Bank—his ships, his tannery, his salt-works, and the rest, Mr Thompson was, at thirty-seven, a man whom his neighbours believed to be worth £50,000. He was hated and maligned by the exclusives, but adjudged by his ruler "ever ready and willing to promote the public service", even if his foes did accuse him of making moonshine liquor upon Scotland Island.[47]

Ellis Bent's opinion was that "he was one of the first, if not the first, man in the Colony". His town house, in Macquarie Place, hard by the gates of Government House itself, was considered the best in the town outside those of the Governor, the Lieutenant-Governor, and Mr Simeon Lord. There, in easy comfort, the Judge-Advocate lodged while his own mansion was being built.

Macquarie "made Mr Thompson a justice of the Peace and Chief Magistrate on the Hawkesbury in consequence of his merits" and of "being the only person at that time in his neighbourhood to fill the office"; and in this post, he asserted, "though not invested with the title of Magistrate", Thompson had acted "for eight years previously".[48]

This pair were, of course, only the foundation of the Governor's emancipist policy. Settlers must have their boundaries traced by Meehan, the Irish rebel, Acting Surveyor-General, his works little hallowed by the Governor's glowing description of him—"eminently well qualified . . . a most excellent land surveyor" of strict honour and integrity.[49] He had "done the whole actual duty of surveyor since 1803"[50]—though of course others had taken the profit—and, recommended by British friends of influence, he had dined at Macquarie's table several times before the end of 1810,[51] plotting the schemes under which he would become the parent of most of the pioneer roads out of Sydney, and of the main streets within it.

If he was somewhat incongruous with his Irish brogue and wit among the rest of the "Government House gang", he at least could claim to be own brother to some of them in past rebelliousness. Was not Redfern, the tawny, strange-looking Assistant Surgeon, sponsor of convict ease and of the sacrilegious cow-pock, a very monster of insurrection, one who, as a nineteen-year-old surgeon's mate at the Nore, had earned a sentence of death by urging his mutinous comrades to be "more united" among themselves?[52] Even the fact that his Gracious Majesty had pardoned him and declared him "right trusty" in a surgical commission[53] had not redeemed him in the eyes of loyal King's officers, who hated to see such plums as Mr Redfern's in the clutches of a felon.

The only member of the Governor's much execrated "convict" *ménage* who seemed to receive public countenance from the *élite* was Mr Michael Robinson, the chief clerk and poet laureate, Oxonian, blackmailer, meat for *Leach's Cases*,[54] and a poet almost as good as Farmer George's shining Pye. But he was to be forgiven, for "the mode of despatch of business in the Secretary's Office was not always of the most respectable kind",[55] so that one might sometimes gain a furtive advantage by acquaintance with Mr Robinson. His habit of concluding his odes on state occasions "with a pointed compliment to the clemency and virtuous example of Governor Macquarie"[56] could well be passed over. Mr J. T. Bigge could report, a few years later, that in the ethereal and exclusive circles in which he moved in the Colony, he had "heard many testimonies given of the general attention and respectful demeanour" with which Mr Robinson acquitted himself "in situations strongly calculated to encourage in him an insolent and unbecoming deportment".[57]

V

At one appointment to the Bench, outside the emancipists, all the pure and holy of Botany Bay professed particular surprise and pain—that of Dr D'Arcy Wentworth, principal surgeon, now in quick succession also chief police magistrate in Sydney, superintendent of police, hospital contractor, and treasurer of the Police Fund.[58]

These were perquisites to make the mouth of the most opulent exclusive water. That they should fall into the lap of such a one as Mr Wentworth was scandal which brooked no palliation.

Vain for Mr Wentworth to hold the King's Commission, vain for Macquarie to dine him and wine him and to authorize him to inform his noble relative, Lord Fitzwilliam, that "the Governor has strongly recommended him to Lord Castlereagh".[59] The dictum of Governor Hunter that his conduct had been "correct and honourable"[60] was a mere empty echo of the past. Mr Wentworth's dramatic cry, "Did I not arrive here as free and uncontrouled as Major Grose or any of his officers or Lieutenant-Colonel Molle himself and have I ever been otherwise?" fell on inattentive ears.[61]

Of no effect was the potted biography adduced some years later by young Mr William Wentworth, who told how his parent, "descended from an unsullied race of illustrious progenitors and, feeling that the glory of his ancestors was in some degree tarnished by the mere imputation that had been cast upon his character . . . sought a voluntary exile to a distant shore to efface for ever the recollection of an unjust accusation."[62] Dr Wentworth's reputation could not be retrieved by such rhetoric. "Vain hope! Twenty-six years of unimpeachable rectitude . . . risen by his single merit to the highest point of distinction and respectability abroad have not sufficed to silence the venomed tongue of slander at home."[63]

Did not Sydney know, despite all his palaver, that Dr Wentworth was a "notorious highwayman"? Had not Dr Harris, that impeccable witness, been present at the Old Bailey and seen him, a tall, dark-eyed, humorous young man, *acquitted* of the charge of dallying with High Toby?[64] What better proof was needed of his guilt? And did not fell circumstances give testimony that he had not reformed? Call, once more, Dr Harris, late of the Old Corps, that queer fellow who had astonished the Macquaries in Rio de Janeiro by putting on old clothes and peddling his wares like a Jew. Dr Harris could testify that even when Dr Wentworth had achieved the distinction of sitting on the Supreme Court Bench of New South Wales, he had never met him "in general society here or anywhere but at Government House".[65] But he *had* seen him "standing at the door of his large store and receiving money for the spirits that he sold there".[66] Dr Harris had used all his ancient authority as an old-time magistrate to remonstrate with Dr Wentworth, who had replied, with a Milesian grin, that his habits were "good for trade and good for the Police Fund".

One fears that his Irish sense of humour was almost as much an offence as his record, and the worst of it was that his sons scarcely provided evidence that the Wentworth breed was likely to improve.

Two of the boys were fresh home from school at Bexhill, in Kent, the younger, Iberian of countenance like the elder Wentworth himself.[67] This one, presently, was to become through Macquarie's favour the first Australian-born to receive a commission in the British Army.[68]

The elder son, William Charles, was something of an enigma and there was a good deal of muttering when, on his presumed twenty-first birthday, the Governor appointed him acting Provost-Marshal during the absence of Mr Gore, then in London enthusiastically promoting the destruction of Johnston, who had thrown him into a dungeon during the rebellion.[69]

A rugged, untidy youngster with a cast in his eye,—which made it inadvisable that he should follow his father in the medical profession[70]— thatched in curious auburn hues, heavy shouldered, carelessly attired, young William Wentworth, fresh from school in England, soon rolled round the town and back and forth to his farm on the banks of the Nepean River,[71] inditing resounding rhymes of love and patriotism and uttering sarcasms which plain men found it difficult to comprehend or appreciate.

As he appeared to possess ideals and took a pleasure in abstract things he was a natural object of suspicion to most of the healthy-minded military.

VI

In October 1810, with Marsden already in open revolt against his policy, Macquarie added more fuel to the fire by his especial social attention to Dr D'Arcy Wentworth and to Mr Meehan;[72] and very soon he was providing, through an extraordinary accident, even more dangerous ammunition for the enemies of his policy.

Andrew Thompson perished suddenly. His illness was due to the two days and two nights of exposure during which he had rescued men, beasts, and chattels from the floods of the Hawkesbury.[73]

Four days after his death Mr Francis Williams reached Sydney with news to prove that Mr Thompson had included in his composition other virtues than industry and faithfulness. He had, giving "a most extraordinary instance of friendship and gratitude", performed what the beneficiary believed to be the "kind and generous action of a worthy good man".[74] In fact he had bequeathed to Macquarie a quarter of his estate, which was adjudged to be worth between £20,000 and £25,000. Antill, the descendant of royal American governors, was numbered among his executors. Gregory Blaxland, descendant of Saxon thanes, Lieutenant William Cox, erstwhile paymaster of the 102nd Regiment and his successor as Hawkesbury magistrate, Thomas Arndell, surgeon of the First Fleet and his predecessor as a magistrate, and Francis Williams walked as his pall-bearers when he was laid to rest at Green Hills.[75]

The private mourning of the Governor for his benefactor was so thorough and heartfelt that it was just as well for him that it was locked away in his journals for several decades.

When he visited Mr Thompson's farm of St Andrew's, after its owner's death, he wrote of how Thompson had in a few months of possession "built an excellent farm house with suitable offices, garden, stockyards, etc., felled a great quantity of timber and cleared and enclosed a field of ten acres for corn". He wrote of the farm's "ninety head of cattle and fourteen hundred head of sheep . . . all in very high order and most excellent condition as I ever saw cattle in any country I have ever visited".[76]

He mourned to think how much more happy he and Elizabeth should have felt themselves, "had the kind valuable deceased owner of this estate been alive on it now, to receive and entertain us under his hospitable roof":

> This reflection affected Mrs. M. and myself deeply—for we both had a most sincere and affectionate esteem for our good and most lamented departed friend Andrew Thompson!—But alas! How vain are our regrets!—He is lost to the world and to us forever—and we must console ourselves with the well grounded hope that he is happier now than if he had remained among us.[77]

Next the Governor had gone in person to the spot where the remains of his "late worthy and high esteemed good friend" had been deposited, in a situation "the most beautiful and convenient that can be imagined".[78] He had decided to improve his sepulchre and "render it more elegant and conspicuous as a tribute of regard and friendship for his memory". He had written an epitaph second only in ornateness to that which he had composed to place over poor Jane in Bombay, telling how he had raised the departed to the magistracy in consequence of his good conduct; how this promotion had restored him to that rank in life which he had early lost; and how it had made so deep an impression on the emancipist's grateful heart, as to "induce him to leave the Governor one fourth of his fortune" after his death had been caused by his tendency to "indulge the generosity of his nature in assisting his fellow creatures".[79] Even when, by the base defaults of the poor exile's creditors, who knew that the Governor and his associate legatees would scarcely dare to sue them, his estate dwindled till Macquarie's share promised to be less than £500, the latter exclaimed philosophically, "Poor man, he intended well, and we must take the will for the deed."

Others were far from viewing Mr Thompson's demise and his acts in the same light as Macquarie. Many an interested exile in London had felt secretly, until the moment news of these doings reached him, that events in New South Wales had taken a turn in favour of the military class—a turn that presently might be capitalized.

Birds of a feather, the roving officers had reasoned, would flock together. The difficulties which military men in New South Wales hitherto had encountered through the antagonism of naval governors would now evaporate with a judicious officer of their own service at the head of affairs.

There were thus plenty of members of the New South Wales Corps and the faction whose bitter disappointment at the actual course of events made them only too ready to interpret, for Whitehall, with feelings of rage, the new Governor's surprising apostasies and desertion of the military caste.

They had been prepared to shelter quietly, biding their time until the trial of Johnston, leader of the rebellion of 1808, should have been concluded and there was assurance that a too loudly-opened mouth might not bring dire consequences to their erstwhile leader which would presently react against themselves. They kept their thoughts within their families and events showed how prudent they had been.

Johnston, of course, had been cashiered as the result of his court martial, and a belated letter from Macquarie's old friend and commander, David Baird,[80] the terrible captive of Tippoo, showed by how slender a thread his continued existence in the world hung:

Sir David Baird to Macquarie

I was a member of the Courtmartial that tried the late Commander of New South Wales (Col. Johnston). I was able to attend untill the day that *sentence* was to be passed and on that day I was so ill (from my wound) as to be obliged to have an operation performed—This I believe was very fortunate for Johnston for I never heard as connected an evidence proving him guilty of mutiny—without the least palliation that was in my mind worthy of consideration.[81]

Johnston not only escaped with his life, but had been able to return to New South Wales in a ship loaded with his merchandise and with the stock which he had acquired by dint of extensive borrowing from sympathetic friends, who afterwards were to be heard gnashing their teeth.[82] The Governor greeted him as an old American comrade and granted him more land to implement the expansion of his already considerable estates. Upon these he prudently withdrew himself for ever from the public gaze.

Not so his old fellow-conspirators. Those in the Colony already were busy with their pens, and others no less busy in Britain. Most of them there were—each with a patron or two supporting his demands—poised for a return flight to the antipodes.

Captain Anthony Fenn Kemp—he who had made so much to-do from the Bench at M'Arthur's trial—had crept under the wing of Sir James Shaw, M.P., and of "Mr. Robert Peele" and Colonel Gordon, the Commissary General, "an old school fellow of mine". He1 had sold his commission and proposed to set up as a mercantile and shipping agent.[83]

His idea was that the new Governor "is supposed to be a humane man but has been wonderfully *misled*". He thought Macquarie would have an arduous task to fulfil respecting his plan of conduct towards Bligh's "villainous and perjured" party whose supporters were going out with a determined, rancorous, and hostile disposition towards any person connected with Johnston.[84] He understood that the Government expected a good deal from Macquarie's prudence in conciliating all parties, and that he might succeed was his earnest prayer.

Bligh, of course, under the wing of Sir Joseph Banks, was railing against Macquarie's partiality for Johnstonian rebels.

Lieutenant Edward Lord, who had bought mourning for the whole of Hobart Town when Collins had died, and whose bills suggested that he had subsisted during his own brief reign as acting Lieutenant-Governor principally on rum, port wine, and yellow soap,[85] was instructing Britain on the urgency for colonial reform and especially on the need to establish himself in New South Wales as a large-scale landed proprietor. He had the willing aid of a brother in the House of Commons.

The queer Dr Harris, who had amused Elizabeth at Rio de Janeiro, had brought himself to the friendly attention of two Royal Dukes. Mr William Wilson, agent for the house of Campbell, was fulminating against the restrictions which prevented free export trade between Botany Bay and the outside world.[86]

But the most active of all naturally was John M'Arthur.

Mr M'Arthur earlier had had almost a gloating air as he waited in London basking in the smiles of Lord Camden,[87] the father of his fortunes, and wondering what changes a Governor of the highest character would work among some of his fellow-colonists—"wretches who have long insulted every honourable and virtuous feeling by the unblushing display of infamy and vice".[88]

The news which reached him, therefore, in the last mails to leave Sydney in 1810 came as a shattering blow. The full significance of what was happening in the Colony was almost too dire to be grasped; and Mr M'Arthur, spurred on by his dyspepsia and his natural choler, very fairly voiced the thoughts which were running through many exiled brains.

John M'Arthur to Elizabeth M'Arthur

Every paragraph increases my amazement, and every circumstance you relate adds to the perplexity of my mind. God alone knows how such a state of things as you describe may terminate, or how operate upon our affairs. Would to God I could withdraw you from the Colony . . . Is it possible (it is said) that Governor Macquarie can . . . bring to his table men who have been convicts—who have amassed fortunes by the most infamous frauds and have and continue to set the most shameful examples of dissoluteness and vice?[89]

Thompson had been M'Arthur's mortal enemy, having, in a difference with him which was the germ of the rebellion, been supported by the courts. So M'Arthur felt that there never had been "a more artful or a greater knave" than the lately dead Hawkesbury magistrate; that his last stroke of leaving the Governor part of his estate, whether viewed in the light of an act done in the expectation of death, or in the hope of raising himself to high favour should he live, was the deepest the fellow ever had attempted. In short, he was convinced that the departure of his emancipist adversary to another sphere was "an earnest of the interposition of Providence to save the Colony from utter ruin".

"How could Governor and Mrs Macquarie have been imposed upon as they have been?" the Perturbator asked[90] in a dazed way; but, however that might be, the events which had developed and the results of the trial of Johnston had persuaded him that "many and great changes must take place and numberless prejudices be overcome" before he would be "allowed to reside in New South Wales exempt from danger and persecution".

He believed that a pass had been reached at which a man of his own known principles must be hated and decried in self-defence in such a colony, and if to those feelings were added envy at his prosperous circumstances, what could he expect of a society so constituted? Whether he thought of returning or withdrawing from the Colony, a "hundred frightful objects" presented themselves to his harassed mind.

Only the knowledge that he and his family, if in England, would find difficulty in realizing the pittance of between £1300 and £1400 per year which they would need to live, deterred Mr M'Arthur, it seemed, from casting off the dust of the ungrateful place. But he was holding the fearful prospect of his departure over the heads of the English. He adjured his wife, "Whatever may be your sentiments . . . I earnestly recommend that you speak of leaving the Colony as a decided thing and entrust *no one* with your real opinion should you think it impracticable. I have for some time spoken in that way here and I am convinced it has been beneficial."[91]

It was encouraging indeed for Macquarie that Foveaux could write later from "that infernal dirty place", Waterford, that "Mack makes very little figure in this part of the world. I have heard that his family are on the point of returning to this country."

VII

It was not long before Macquarie's strange humanity and liberal outlook had become a matter of earnest political discussion in England, especially because of some facets of it exhibited in his recommendations about judicial and land settlement reforms.

Whether the export of felons should be continued had been under debate ever since the outset of the American War of Independence. Transportation had not been originally a punishment in the ordinary sense. The germ of the practice had evolved from the ancient right accorded persons who were accused of felony, and who fled to sanctuary, to plead guilty before a coroner and abjure the Realm; but by a muddled series of laws "guided by no principle whatever" and "utterly destitute of any sort of uniformity", the ambit of its operation was gradually widened to become a sort of alternative penalty to the death sentence.[92] The onset of the American war had robbed the Government of the only receptacle it had possessed into which "transports" could be deposited.

It had, for a time, consigned them to the hulks, until it had begun to send them to Botany Bay. Whether transportation as a system might not be altogether superseded by penitentiaries, which had been tried experimentally, was now a very lively issue. The penitentiary idea was ardently supported by many humanitarians—zealots who, in the course of their advocacy, naturally adduced every possible fact and argument which they believed would discredit the transportation system and convict colonies.

Conveniently to those who wished to discuss Macquarie's leniencies, a Select Committee of the House of Commons had been appointed in 1811 to inquire into the whole matter of transportation. It had begun to hold its sittings in February 1812.[93]

An assortment of witnesses was examined about New South Wales. They ranged from Matthew Flinders to Governor Hunter, who had abandoned his governorship to become captain of a seventy-four of the Line; from Maurice Margarot, very fiery and critical, to a highly contented officer's servant. The evidence had been seasoned with a little pepper from Rear-Admiral Bligh.

The Committee had finished its hearing in a tangle of inaccurate chronology, but the hearts of its members remained in their right places. They were gloomy about New Holland's economic geography. They believed that beyond sixty miles from the coast New South Wales "appeared nowhere practicable for agricultural purposes, and in many places the diameter of the habitable country is less".[94] In length, it extended "from Port Stephens to Port Jervis, comprising from North to South about four degrees"; beyond the confines of these latitudes, it was stated, "the Colony will not be capable of extension". Their report arrived just in time to appear ridiculous in the light of that of the Blaxland party and of other explorers.

They "cordially" concurred with Macquarie's views on convict redemption. They saw "with satisfaction" that the Governor had adopted it as a principle "that long-tried good conduct should lead a man back to the rank in society which he had forfeited, and do away, in as far as the case will admit, with all retrospect of former bad conduct".[95]

It had an important bearing on the Governor's future actions that they professed themselves "the more anxious to express their opinion, as under a former Governor, transports, whatever their conduct might be, were in no instance permitted to hold places of trust or confidence, or even to come to Government House".

They noted one of his requests that as many male convicts as possible should be sent out, since the prosperity of the Colony depended on the numbers available for public works and agriculture; but they did not see eye-to-eye with him in the idea that "on the contrary female convicts are as great a drawback as others are beneficial".

To this "they could not accede". They were aware that the women sent out were "of the most abandoned description", and that in many instances they were likely to whet and to encourage the vices of the men, whilst but a small proportion would make any step towards reformation.

They, however, believed that convict females should be treated in accordance with the knowledge that they were the only stock from whom a rapid increase in the New South Wales population might reasonably be expected.

The Committee called for facilities to permit women whose sentences had expired to return to England at the end of their terms, if they wished to do so, without the need of paying their fares by prostitution.

Generally, however, they were convinced that "when the several beneficial orders lately sent out from this Country, and the liberal views of the present Governor" should have time to operate, "the best effects were to be expected".[96]

They favoured the appointment of a Governor's council. They believed "it could not be expected that the sight of so much authority and responsibility thrown into the hands of one man, would not at times create opposition and discontent among men, unused in their own country to see so great a monopoly of power".[97]

Of course, they said, the wisdom might be doubted of limiting the authority of the Governor over such a colony. In it, more than in any other, the Government ought to be free and unfettered; but the acquiescence of the council would give popularity to the Governor's measures, and its expressed disapprobation might have the effect of checking such as were inexpedient.

Lastly, they believed that permission for distillation of spirits in the Colony and the reform of the courts of justice along civilian lines—matters on which Macquarie had made strong recommendations to the Colonial Office—would stimulate agriculture and give the inhabitants that confidence and legal security which would render them contented.[98]

This was a pleasant surprise to both the Governor and the colonists.

I

VIII

Receiving the report, Macquarie was moved by a desire to "communicate my sentiments on this highly important and most interesting subject with candour, truth and sincerity, and to the best of my judgment, according to my local knowledge and experience".[99]

The findings provoked in him mixed feelings. He felt flattered and pleased at the general endorsement of his ideas; but he did not favour special provision to send women convicts back to England when emancipated.[100]

If the Committee were at all aware of the characters of the ladies, he thought, they would not be so desirous of providing them with facilities to return home, when their sentences had expired. He considered the Honourable Gentlemen, having the good of their country at heart, would rather be inclined to adopt every legal means to keep them out of England.

The honest and industrious ones, he said, could earn enough during their terms of exile to pay their passages. Most of the average of the unhappy creatures, if repatriated, would merely put the Government to the unnecessary expense of trying them again. If they remained in the new land, and were inclined to work, they were sure of employment. If they were sick, they would be looked after; and if they could be kept in order *anywhere*, it must be in New South Wales, where each individual was known and treated on her merits.

No people in the world lived better or had less to complain of than the convicts, both male and female, in New South Wales, he declared, so long as they conducted themselves with common propriety.[101]

He stressed the reasons why the Governor must retain power to grant pardons, which the Committee had wished to take from him. On this Lord Bathurst agreed with him, though at first they were at variance about the matter.

The very suggestion of a council seemed to affect the poor Governor with incipient apoplexy. He was not averse to consultation. He called the magistrates together often to hear their views on local questions; and he had early acknowledged himself fortunate in having two such "able and respectable officers as the Judge-Advocate and the Lieutenant-Governor to support my Government and to consult and advise with in all difficult and important cases".[102]

He had his regular levees for departmental heads and military officers. But the vision of himself presiding over a body consisting of a couple of irate rum-runners, a land-grabber, an emancipist merchant or two, perhaps some military officers, the Judge-Advocate and Mr Marsden, as head of the Church, was too much for him to swallow.

Bathurst, luckily, felt "no disposition to accede" to the Committee's suggestion. The difficulty of selecting proper persons as councillors; the dissensions and disputes to which their opposition to the Governor must give rise, the parties which might then spring up, the length of time during which public tranquillity would be interfered with before the Home Government could deal with a deadlock when differences were serious, "the danger of weakening the higher authorities in a society composed of such discordant materials"—all these factors contributed to make the Colonial Secretary decide, amid applause from his satrap in New Holland, to "leave the Governor unfettered".[103]

His Excellency felt great satisfaction at his lordship's attitude. "So far from being an assistance, if unhappily tried, it would in my opinion, most assuredly, be productive of all the evils and inconveniences Your Lordship so justly observes as likely to result from it. I therefore indulge a fond hope that this measure will never be resorted to in this Colony."[104]

Lastly, Macquarie was rejoiced to learn of the Committee's proposal to new model the courts of justice, "a measure of primary importance".[105] Bathurst had acted speedily on the Governor's initiative and was able to dispatch at once a scheme approved at home.

With it both the Governor and Ellis Bent, the Judge-Advocate, were dissatisfied. They were at one with the Committee in a desire for a civilian system of courts.

The Committee and Macquarie were strongly for trial by jury, in both civil and criminal cases; so were Bent and many free colonists, John Blaxland and Mann among them. These saw no obstacle in the need to mingle free settler and emancipist in the panels. As Mann had pointed out, it seemed no more unreasonable to accept a freed man's judgment as a juror than the oath of a convict under sentence. On convicts' oaths men were hanged every year. And the legal machinery already had provision for coroner's juries.[106]

Bathurst refused assent. Before a change was made he thought they would have to consider whether there were sufficiently numerous settlers who were capable and willing to undertake the duties of jurors.[107]

Neither would he sanction local distillation, even at the repeated requests of the Governor and the inhabitants. In that matter the hidden hand of vested interests was at work.

IX

The discussion of the jury problem had served as a basis upon which the new Colonial Secretary and the Governor could exchange views on the emancipist question.

The latter had previously referred to the attempt to counteract "this extension of just and humane indulgence to those persons (who had formerly been convicts), whom I have brought forward and patronized by admitting them to my society, but whom these factious persons herein alluded to found it advantageous to their interests and illiberal prejudices to consider as outcasts beneath their notice and for ever doomed to oblivion and neglect".

He had postulated that the "improvement, welfare, and happiness [of the convicts] should form the first and chief object of attention in the important duties entrusted to the Governor".[108]

Now he wrote:

Macquarie to Bathurst

No doubt, many of the free settlers (if not all) would prefer (if it were left to *their* choice) never to admit persons who had been convicts to any situation of equality with themselves. But in my humble opinion in coming to New South Wales they should consider that they are coming to a convict country and if they are too proud or too delicate in their feelings to associate with the population of the country, they should consider it in time and bend their course to some other country, in which their prejudices in this respect would meet with no opposition. No country in the world perhaps has been so advantageous to adventurers as New South Wales. The *free settlers*, who have come out as adventurers, have never felt their dignity injured *by trading* in every way *with convicts*, even while they are such, but, further than it suits their interest to have intercourse with them, they would rather be excused.

I must, however, in justice to the original free Settlers, observe that I believe they are not all of one mind in this respect. Amongst them, some few liberal minded persons are to be found who do not wish to keep those unfortunate persons for ever in a state of degradation.

It therefore remains for His Majesty's Government to consider whether they wish the internal policy of this Colony to be so conducted, as to please the minds of the generality of *free persons* coming to settle in it *as such*, or whether they wish so to construct it as to hold out the greatest possible rewards to the convicts for reformation of manners, by considering them, when this is the case, in every way entitled to the rights and privileges of a citizen, who has never come under the sentence of transportation.[109]

He told the Colonial Office that his policy had been crowned with considerable success; that every care was taken of convict health; that marriage was given every encouragement.

He told it that he himself mustered the Sydney contingents of felons every Sunday at St Philip's; and it was perhaps as well for him that some of his critics could not view, in person, this accustomed Sabbath scene, which was described so graphically by the Reverend Pasco Crook.

X

On any Sunday morning before Matins, as Farmer George's eight bells rang out lustily above the church on the hillside in Charlotte Place over which the cross of St George fluttered, the convicts were to be seen dressing into line, grumbling, anecdotal, restless, but stiffening at the clatter of hooves approaching from the east.[110]

"Look out, cullies, here comes the Old Gent! Here comes Sandy!"

Plugs were stowed in cheeks for future reference. The chattering ceased.

Up rode the gilded staff with Macquarie at its head, awkward and uneasy, as always, on his Arab. He passed down the lines, hearing complaints, asking a question here, uttering a reproof, saying a kind word to the sick or diligent in a rich Scottish accent. Then he rode away to Government House, while the bells pealed on and the convicts fidgeted in the sunshine.

Presently, on an order, they doffed their woollen caps and shuffled into church. In the aisles the stands of colours guarded by captains in scarlet made a gaudy splash. In the choir the perspiring band stood ready. A bonnet or two seen above the top of a pew marked the positions of the ladies and the gentry for the felons as they filed into the gallery. Below them a few highly pious soldiers knelt. You could hear a pin drop. There came the crisp sound of wheels on the gravel outside, followed by much activity, as the Governor, chest heaving slightly from the exertions of the double journey, marched up the aisle with Elizabeth on his arm.

The scabbards of his staff officers clanked haughtily along the stone floor. Their mirror-like boots creaked, their aiguilettes rustled as they knelt in prayer. The little orphan girls in the choir sang a few verses of a hymn, deafeningly accompanied by bandsmen bent upon earning their customary reward of new shoes.

Perhaps slim, mathematical Mr Cowper preached, and then it would be one of Barnes's sermons; if Mr Fulton, then one of Blair's. If Mr Marsden were there, they would have fulminations against the Colony's vice and iniquity, rumblings about the merciless wrath of God. Marsden's preaching was a blast from the lower regions of religion, containing "a little spark of piety in a vast heap of worldly rubbish".

Everybody usually hoped that the preacher would be Mr Cowper, and when it was there was a goodly if sheepish surge afterwards behind the Governor and his lady and the Brigade-Major (in that order) to the Communion Table.

It was noted with anger in some quarters by the more righteous and exclusive members of the congregation that they were compelled to rub shoulders with some decidedly immoral and upstart persons in the process of partaking of the Body of their Lord in the wake of Governor Macquarie.

* * * * *

The humanity and kindness of intention behind the Governor's proceedings did not save him. His convict policy remained always the main point at issue between himself and the "higher ranks" of the community.

But as he closed his dispatches about the Select Committee's report in July 1813 he could still look forward to three years of rule during which his Minister and the Colonial Office would be firmly upon his side whenever the general question of emancipists was raised.

CHAPTER XVIII

"Very Lively"

I

THE heat of December was not conducive to good temper at the end of the year 1812. Lord Liverpool's dispatches had left the Governor suffering a mood of irate innocence. The hospital contractors were urgent with their monthly pleas for more concessions to save themselves from bankruptcy. The Blaxlands plagued him for land and labour. He himself was ill. So was poor Elizabeth.

The ancient sloop H.M.S. *Samarang*, when she limped leaking through the Heads bearing £10,000 in Spanish dollars which were to provide the Colony with silver currency, had proved no argosy of peace and quietude. Rotting and waterlogged, she bore an appropriate naval complement which, from her commander, Captain Case, R.N., downward to the powder monkeys, lived life with the manners of men who knew that any day might be their last.[1]

Thus, though the Christmas season was cheery enough and displayed all the usual features of illuminated window panes, verandas decorated with palms and flowering bush, bands, waits, and drunken soldiers and their trulls, there was a general restlessness in the air.

That of the convictry was heightened by the example of a large, recent influx of new recruits skilled in the techniques of the London underworld.[2]

The *Samarang*'s sailormen raised their voices above the rest of the revellers, filling the nights with loud balladry and the crash and tinkle of breaking glass. Fence palings, the handy and inevitable weapons of every Botany Bay brawl, frequently were found by angry householders to be missing of a morning. The watch, as often as not, had cracked crowns to show.

This time the New Year addresses to the Governor struck a bolder note and were openly demanding upon matters which a year ago had been dealt with only in grandiloquent hintings. The settlers pressed home their points with some vigour, though they were not less than usual lost in admiration of the energy with which the Governor braved "all personal danger, and dispensed with every comfort in visiting the most remote parts of our settlement".[3]

They voiced their appreciation of his "not less dangerous and irksome confinement" to his office when in Sydney. They trumpeted their approval of his assiduity and high moral principles. But all this they did with an abstracted air, for some of them were wondering what effect the import of Spanish dollars would have on their little deals in usury, and what on earth they would be able to do with all the swelling bulk of produce which unusually good seasons had given them.

This was the real activating element behind their theme as they spoke with pride of "land brought to a state of high fertility"; of wool sent to England recently, "little inferior to that of Spain" and "soon to become an article of commercial importance"; of wheat so abundant and cheap that it appeared as if it would pay to pack it for export at eight shillings a bushel; of meat so plentiful that it could be casked in native woods to feed the Royal Navy; of whales whose oil could light the universe if there were colonial ships to carry it; of timber especially for ships' knees; of coal, iron, dyewoods, tanning bark, potash—indeed, of "all the articles worthy of the speculator". All of which ..ded up to "a great surplus over and above what is required for the support of the population in this infant country; which surplus for want of a market is being wasted".[4]

There was little pleasure for the Governor in their expressions of aspiration. His candles must have burned low as he leaned over his portable desk, planning his replies in such a way as to convey his sympathy without too far transgressing his firm instructions on policy from home or antagonizing superiors too seriously. The situation was the more awkward because of the tenor of Lord Liverpool's recent dispatches and of his own earlier support of the colonists' views.

It was, of course, safe to look forward to "the continuance of that cordiality which hitherto has existed between the Executive and the people", even though there were signs that he thus might exhibit visionary confidence. It was quite politic, also, to admit that, no matter how arduous his duties, they "had been eased by the cheerful readiness on the part of the people to second my measures". It would cause self-satisfaction in some of his lieges at least to be told that the population was "more peaceable, and more easily governed than could have been expected, or than will be readily believed by persons who have not been in this country".

From this point onward his tone must be *diminuendo*.

The eloquent framers of the addresses rhapsodized about "the daily increasing beauty and improvement of our metropolis—beauty justly exciting the admiration of strangers, an improvement, to those capable of judging the contrast, truly astonishing". But about that he must not be too prideful. He must keep in mind the Colonial Office's admonition that civic improvement must be dependent on the community's ability to pay for it. He was soon to learn that, for all their rhapsodies and appreciations, even the spurs of a subvention of £500 from the colonial funds and his own gift of £60 could not drive the inhabitants to subscribe the remainder of the £4000 needed to build a joint town hall and court-house for Sydney. They did not, it seemed, feel ready to give such practical proof of "the propriety and honour of their principally owing so proud an ornament and noble memorial of the liberal spirit of the inhabitants, to their own honourable and unanimous exertions and voluntary contributions".[5]

And in some other matters, also, they had failed him.

Their rejoicing, for instance, that through his exertions "the mid-night

robber was now scarce seen in our streets" had a hollow ring when everybody
knew that it daily became less safe to roam the Parramatta Road at night.
Also, the indications that they appreciated his "humane and philanthropic
exertions to banish the narrow, illiberal policy of invidious distinctions
so long the bane of this Colony" were in some quarters more apparent,
than real.

"The wisdom that planned, and the vigour that carried into effect
such various regulations, so truly calculated to contribute to our comfort,
happiness and future prosperity" was, he well knew, to some of the sponsors
of the sentiment, a mere oratorical fiction. Even the Judge-Advocate,
who had drafted most of those regulations, was already engaged in contemplation of their supposed illegality and of plans in his own interest to nullify
their operations.

All these things, however, the Governor could afford to treat either
with a friendly wariness or with a due show of modesty. It was only when
the meat in the coconut appeared that his problems should have knotted
his brow.

London and East India traders would shudder at these words: "Yet
amidst these our public acknowledgments of the benefits we have derived
from Your Excellency's just, wise and liberal administration of the Government of this Territory, we cannot but lament that such have been the
limitations of your Excellency's power, as hitherto to preclude the possibility
of your providing a market for our surplus grain, and other articles of
export?"[6]

London would disapprove an acquiescent response to an expression
of the community's "consciousness that Your Excellency beholds with
deepest regret the distressing embarrassments under which we labour
from these limitations, and from the want of a staple commodity, by the
exportation of which we may be enabled to procure such articles of import
as are absolutely indispensable to civilised life".[7]

But even these phrases should have been less embarrassing than that
shattering, though professedly obsequious, intimation which followed,
that "we intend with your permission, in a short time to suggest to Your
Excellency in a memorial, of which we humbly solicit your recommendation
to His Majesty's Government, the propriety of granting us such indulgences
and encouragements as appear to us most likely to remedy the many
difficulties which the inhabitants of this Territory have at present to contend
against".[8]

To recommend, with any appearance of conviction, such a programme
as the petitioners had in mind would have been dangerous to any administrator of a British colony. But the colonists spoke the truth when they
declared that it was the Governor's own attitude which had emboldened
them to look to him for protection and support.

A colonial export trade must compete with the British merchant and
could scarcely be pleasing as an ideal to a Colonial Office whose Minister was
beginning to consider, under the parsimonious influence of the Treasury,
whether it would not be cheaper to feed the Botany Bay population

regularly on wheat imported from India, rather than to support local agriculture by buying grain grown in New South Wales on the spot.[9] A local shipping industry must infringe the cast-iron monopoly of the East India Company in the waters of the South Seas.

In short, the whole of the main aims of the colonists were enough to send cold shivers down the spines of the Lords of the Council of Trade and Plantations, gentlemen with the taste of the consequences of American colonial secessions still in their hot mouths.

The Governor, however, like all Scots, was an incorrigible empire-builder, though naturally cautious. He could not tempt himself to refrain from admitting that some of their suggestions, particularly that regarding the building of a distillery, had long engrossed his attention. He declared that he believed that a few of their objects could be carried out "without interference with the interests of the Mother Country". And, to sweeten the pill for his Minister, he professed to look forward "to an increased exertion on their [the settlers'] part, by regularity of conduct and industry to render the Colony less burthensome to the British taxpayers", and themselves worthy of the great benefit conferred on them by the formation of the Colony.[10]

II

There seems to have been a considerable surge of hopeful activity following this pronouncement. A committee representative of all classes of property owners, under the presidency of Mr Simeon Lord, the eminent emancipist magistrate, was formed to draw up the much-talked-of memorial to the Home Government.[11]

There seems, too, to have been much conscious effort on the part of antagonistic factions to cling together long enough in brotherly love to achieve their common objectives. The visible epitome of the supposed triumph of national over sectional interests was the grand *"fête-champêtre"* held in a large marquee in the garden of Mr Robert Jenkins on 29 January 1813 "in celebration of the anniversary of His Excellency assuming command in this Colony".[12]

It was an inspiring scene. The British colours streamed above in the north-easterly. The festive board, over which the Provost-Marshal presided, with Mr William Cox of the Hawkesbury as his "Mr Vice", was decorated with native shrubs and boughs. The banqueters placed themselves "promiscuously without respect of rank or differences of condition". They bore with fortitude Mr Robinson's recital of a new ode, called "Effusions of Gratitude". Hob and nob, they drank together in a copious manner which did the greatest credit both to the salutary effects of the climate upon human thirst and to their iron constitutions.

They drank, bottoms up, to several members of the Royal Family; to "success to British Arms", to Lord Bathurst, to William Wilberforce, to all the Governors whose names they could remember, but more particularly to *"Governor Macquarie—a bumper—May the anniversary of his assuming command of the Colony be commemorated and reverenced by the latest posterity"*.

This last they quaffed with three-times-three, and in a softer mood they made libations to "Religion and Virtue", to the "intended library", to Lieutenant-Governor O'Connell, to the sentiment "May all Hearts be united for Mutual Benefit and General Good". But it was into the toast of "Prosperity to New South Wales and the speedy establishment of an Export Trade" that they really put their hearts and gullets.

Yet, at the end, they held enough internal space reserved to allow them to toss a glass to "Good night".

And good night it was to the whole episode.

The scheme for the memorial disappeared into thin air. The grand accord of exclusive and emancipist "for mutual benefit and general good" crumbled to dust.

When, later, there was inquiry as to what had become of the plan, it was merely for the purpose of damaging the Governor with his superiors; for the tale was produced by malicious persons, not without circumstantial corroboration, that Macquarie had objected to transmit the memorial, "because it was not signed by persons who had been convicts".[13]

The Governor declared the accusation "totally unfounded".[14] No petition from any description of people, he said, had ever been presented to him for transmission to England which he did not transmit. It had certainly been mentioned to him in a cursory manner, but not officially, that a few individuals intended to meet and discuss the interests of the colonists; and "the only observations which this had drawn from him were, that, as the grievances were general, so should the meeting be".

The Colony lapsed into its natural state of faction in which emancipists glared at exclusives and exclusives glared at emancipists and, daily ever with more fierceness, at their harassed Governor.

III

It was three months or a trifle more after the final public scene in the January festivities—the celebration of Macquarie's fifty-second birthday at the little Government House at Parramatta on 31 January 1813—that Mr Gregory Blaxland (according to his own tale) called at Government House, to discuss exploration.

In view of various contradictions in his own narrative at a later stage, it is not easy to accept Mr Blaxland's whole story of what took place, but there is one point in which it is easy to believe—that Mr Blaxland found in His Excellency's manner a certain reservedness. For this he professed to be unable to account.[15]

He would have found it easier to assign a cause of this restraint of mien had he himself suffered the painful experiences and distractions which had worried Macquarie during the previous six months.

There had been, for example, an affray with Captain Case of the *Samarang*, who had re-introduced the authentic naval choler and habits to which the Colony had been accustomed by Bligh. Though the Governor received Captain Case "with every degree of respect and attention due to the commander of one of His Majesty's ships of war", and continued "to treat him and his officers with hospitality and every civility", their "own improper and disrespectful conduct" had, in the end, forced him "to forego all further intercourse with them".[16]

Captain Case had put the Harbour Master, Mr Watson, in irons after a dispute over the loading of coals, and had referred to him outrageously as "an inebriated person".[17] He had argued angrily when the Governor had complained that "he could not for a moment allow that the Naval Articles of War are of such paramount authority as to supersede the British laws".[18] He had sailed away, after filching a few convicts for his crew, but had returned baffled by the Pacific Ocean, a stretch of water more arrogant and demanding than even the captain of a badly leaking naval sloop could be; and he had been derisive when asked by the Governor to submit his vessel to search for the missing captives.[19]

His men roamed the town swigging their flasks and bawling their ditties, while officers, no less rowdy, were guilty, only a fortnight after the Governor's birthday festivities, of "forcing and releasing a prisoner",—their servant—"confined in one of the watch houses from the Civil Power",[20] and "committing an assault on the premises of Thomas Clarkson",[21] a worthy citizen of Hunter Street. From Mr Clarkson's gateposts ornaments were riotously rolled, while a guard of naval revellers covered a discreet retreat with the customary armament of civilian palings, ripped from an adjacent fence.

These proceedings Captain Case condoned after "rigid inquiry" into what he designated "the trifling damage" done to Mr Clarkson's property in a "frolic".[22]

When the officers were hailed before the myrmidons of the civil law, they produced a wardroom colleague who proved upon his oath that *he* was the criminal, and that the whole of the witnesses for the prosecution, including his own landlady, had mistaken for himself—the deponent—an innocent colleague who had been outrageously arrested.[23]

So, at the time that the Governor communed with Mr Gregory Blaxland, he had rankling in his mind, among other things, a recent, prolonged correspondence in which outraged naval lieutenants impudently desired to "call upon Your Excellency to recall those charges, which from the fullest conviction you have found to be ungenerous, groundless and false";[24] and this was merely a fitting pendant to other gems of naval epistolary art from Captain Case himself, which a few weeks before had come to adorn the Government House files.

Captain William Case, R.N., to Macquarie

Sydney Cove, Port Jackson,
24 March, 1813.
Sir,

In reply to your letter of yesterday's date, in answer to mine of the 23rd Inst. which Your Excellency is pleased to style evasive and very unsatisfactory. I have only to remark that, as an Officer and Gentleman, I am incapable of practising evasion, either in my public or private correspondence. Very unsatisfactory it may have been, as my letter was certainly intended to clear the characters of deserving officers from unproved and unfounded allegations.

It remains with Your Excellency to institute such legal proceedings as you may deem necessary.

I have, etc.

Wm. Case, Captain.[25]

IV

Next, the problem of Van Diemen's Land had arisen almost contemporaneously with the first arrival of the *Samarang*.

The first convicts had been sent directly in October 1812 to the island (which had become a sub-colony of New South Wales in the previous June) and reinforced with a few hundred more of local types with whom the authorities at Port Jackson had felt that they themselves could well bear to part.[26]

The Devil looking after his own, they had arrived as, also, had their Lieutenant-Governor, Major Thomas Davey.[27] Him the Home Government, rejecting Macquarie's request that they appoint Foveaux or his brother Charles, had sent out to arrive in Sydney in time for the Christmas festivities of 1812.[28]

It was certainly not merit which had dictated that this relic of the First Fleet should be returned to the antipodes like a dog to his vomit, after being withdrawn from his curious incumbency as field officer to the Royal Marines at Cambridge.[29] He had been successful partly through flattery of a patron, partly through the hope of an avaricious Treasury that, by well-supervised service, he might repay the substantial peculations of his previous employments.

The flattery had been directed at Lord Harrowby, a peer so virtuous that even Miss Harriette Wilson had nought to tell of him, and so much in the ascendant in the inner circle of politics that conspirators soon would plan to assassinate a whole Cabinet round his dinner table.[30]

To him Major Davey had written, "I cannot help indulging a confidence and the proud consolation of securing the good opinion of a man whom all parties respect, and from whose integrity and honour even calumny withholds its whisper." Thus, and basing his own claim on his "practice and experience of the groundwork", the way had been paved for him to mar with his ribaldry the Christmas festivities of 1812 at Government House in Sydney and the Governor's birthday party the following January.[31]

Macquarie noted about Davey an "extraordinary degree of frivolity and low buffoonery in his manners",[32] and his worst fears of him were confirmed by a furtive letter of consignment from Goulburn, the Under Secretary to the Colonial Office, which accompanied the reveller, and which led Macquarie to ask him to assure Bathurst of his intention to take "every possible precaution to prevent his [Davey's] making any improper use of the authority with which he is invested as Lieutenant-Governor".[33]

The Governor had no hesitation in writing a promise that "the moment that I discover that he sanctions any peculation of the public property, applies any part thereof, or any Public Money he may be entrusted with, to his own use, I shall take immediate measures to prevent a repetition thereof".[34] He packed off his alcoholic deputy as quickly as possible.[35] The latter landed in Hobart in his shirt sleeves. He broke the course of his vice-regal progress to Government House to pause at a tavern and imbibe a draught of spirits, and entered upon a bibulous career which soon earned him among his worthy subjects the soubriquet of "Mad Tom".[36]

The Governor warned him well against his assistants:

Macquarie to Davey

The Lt. Governor ought to be very much on his guard on his arrival at the Derwent against some designing characters there, who will endeavour to impose upon him and mislead his judgment by artful insinuations and plausible but interested projects and speculations. Messrs. Knopwood, Fosbrook, Humphry, Loane, Bowden, and Kent, all come less or more under this description; and, having generally opposed the measures of the present commandant, the Lt. Govr. cannot be too much on his guard against their machinations. The Chaplain (Knopwood) is a man of very loose morals, by report, and ought to be severely admonished when guilty of any impropriety of conduct, and such reported to me. The Dy. Cmy. (Fosbrook) is, I fear, a corrupt man, and must therefore be very narrowly watched as long as he remains in office. His store-keeper and *confident*, Boothman, must also be narrowly watched as he is considered a bad and corrupt character.[37]

But these and others had little to teach Davey—whose salary was under garnishee to recoup his previous official depredations—unless it was the commandant, Geils,[38] who was discovered to have taken spirits for his own use from Government stores, who had plundered the Government's supplies of building materials and who, "in the exercise of his temporary power had displayed not only a sordid, mean and covetous disposition, but in many instances had shown himself venal and corrupt". His actions had generated such wrath in the Governor's mind that he had coldly returned a spy-glass with which the erring commandant had presented him.

Apart from Colonel Geils, Davey had worthy associates in Hobart in Fosbrook, the Deputy-Commissary,[39] who was next year dismissed the service after being tried for fraud, and P. G. Hogan, who succeeded Fosbrook and who soon was discovered to be over £2000 behindhand with the accounts of his minor office, apart from the fact that he was much given to drunkenness and intemperance of other kinds.[40]

No wonder the Governor was worried about Van Diemen's Land, more especially as many of Davey's charges had been prompt in recognizing in the rugged terrain of the island an ideal playground for successful bushrangers, over which they romped for many a riotous year.

V

Then there were the omnipresent hospital contractors whose enormous work was now filling the whole eastern horizon above the little town;

a doleful crew, for ever on the viceregal doorstep and for ever mourning their losses and their miserable prospects.

They were obstinately resistant about architecture. They viewed the prospect of selling their liquor in competition with the 120,000 gallons which seemed somehow to have got into the Colony,[41] apart from clandestine supplies, with the utmost pessimism. They railed at the Governor for paying workmen in liquor instead of in hard cash with which the toilers might buy from them.[42] And, their tempers becoming more frayed, they actually presumed to impute breach of agreement to their ruler, who responded with a blast of "surprise and displeasure" which momentarily silenced them, followed by an intimation that the whole subject had become most "irksome and disagreeable to his feelings"[43] and that he "could not allow his time to be encroached" upon by a correspondence "so very vexatious and apparently interminable".[44]

This ruling, however, it was soon clear, did not apply to the frequent statement of his own demands upon the wretched men, whose comfort from an increase in their permits to embrace the importation of 60,000 gallons of "Bengal", all told, and an extension of their term till May 1814 was shortlived.[45]

He was diligent in persuading the luckless three to put a hopper roof on the hospital—"regardless of the considerable expense it will cause us of upwards of £1000".[46] He was insistent that, in return for some cheapening modifications in the height of pediments and numbers of pillars on the veranda, they should compensate the Crown by building at once and free of cost in Macquarie Place a dwelling and offices for the chaplains.[47]

Meanwhile, he wrestled with dishonest commissariat clerks who showed favouritism in the issue of rations, whereby "the lower descriptions of colonists sometimes received an inferior sort of meat in their rations" and the prime cuts were distributed to the Upper Ten.[48] He promised a reward of one hundred lashes and an indeterminate sentence in the Newcastle coal-mines to those whom he should catch at such tricks.[49]

The bushrangers, his buildings, the need to patronize "the first public fair in the Colony by regular authority", when it was held in Parramatta, "numerously attended with a great show of cattle",[50] busied him from time to time. But it was a season particularly of improvements and widening vision in the outlands. He struggled to keep pace with the tide of eager seekers after land and labour.

Now he was in the Botanic Gardens at Sydney;[51] now, in April, at Woodriff's farm and across the Nepean on Emu Island. Now the natives beheld him west of the Hawkesbury on the first ridges of the mountains gazing with inquisitive eye upon the landscape from Grose's Head.[52] One day he might be found choosing a site for a school at Wilberforce in the northern marches of his settled domain;[53] the next, the dust cloud might advertise a ride of "forty-eight miles in one day"[54] as he reorganized the stockyards of East Creek and Rooty Hill. The following week again he might be selecting a spot on which to place Liverpool's new store and granary, far away in the south.[55]

His family life was none too happy. Young John Maclaine, about whom he had quarrelled with the Duke of York so long ago and who now was his aide-de-camp, had fallen from a mizzen mast, "in consequence of low drinking and intemperance",[56] but had survived precariously. Poor Elizabeth, in the first week in May, had another miscarriage—"the *sixth* she has had at home and in this country since the death of our darling little baby! ! !"[57]

VI

Certain it is that during this May of 1813, when Mr Gregory Blaxland declared that he went to see the Governor to discuss an attempt to cross the Blue Mountains, that ethereal barrier which looked so dreamlike from any vantage point in Sydney, and which hitherto had proved impassable, Macquarie had a mind overloaded with trouble and responsibility.

The very sight of Mr Blaxland would not have added to his gaiety. For Mr Blaxland had long since ceased to be the "pleasant facetious travelling companion"[58] the Governor had found him to be during his first journey to the Warragamba in 1810. He and his brother John, M'Arthur's first lieutenant in the raiding of Government House at the capture of Bligh, had in fact become two of the Colony's prime nuisances from the Governor's point of view.[59]

They demanded thousands of acres of land without producing the the *quid pro quo* of capital which they had agreed to bring to the Colony. They extorted "extraordinary concessions" and extensive convict labour which cost the Colony dear. And they had concerned themselves with trading "and with the lazy object of raising cattle" which called for no farm improvements, with the result that they were a heavy charge on the funds, without having added "one single bushel of grain of any kind whatever" to the common store.[60]

However, Mr Blaxland later declared that he had discussed his proposed expedition with Macquarie who himself had, "early after his arrival in the Colony, formed a resolution of encouraging the attempt to find a passage to the western country".[61] But much is uncertain about the adventure which now was pending and about Macquarie's share in the responsibility for it.

There are three separate versions, none contemporaneous with the events described. Two are written by Blaxland himself, the first dated 16 November 1816. In this one, complaining of his lack of reward, he wrote:

> I called on him (the Governor) a few days before I set out. I could not see him in the morning but was asked to dinner. I did not mention the subject to him nor did he mention it himself which I expected he would have done. When I took leave, I informed him that we intended setting out immediately. He wished us success but there was a reservedness in his manner I could not account for . . . . When I returned I called on the Governor, and informed him of our success. He did not doubt my statement, but appeared dissatisfied, since when I have reason to suppose that he neither expected nor wished us to succeed. That must remain in doubt.[62]

The second version also is from the pen of Mr Blaxland—a letter written to his nephew, John Oxley Parker, 10 February 1823, and reprinted in his public journal of the tour that year. "This expedition which had proved so completely successful," he wrote, "resulted from two previous attempts. One of these was made by water by His Excellency the Governor in person, whom I accompanied. We ascended the River Hawkesbury, or Nepean, from about Emu Island, to the mouth of the Warragomby or Great Western River where it emerges from the mountains."[63]

Blaxland wrote that the party had proceeded in a small boat as far as the river was navigable, but Macquarie certainly shows no consciousness in his diary that on that occasion he was assailing the Blue Mountains.

The second expedition, Blaxland wrote, was undertaken by himself and three servants and, apparently, did not reach the hills at all; but it confirmed him in his determination and:

> On inquiry, I found a person who had been accustomed to hunt the kangaroo on the Mountains, in the direction I wished to go, who undertook to take the horses to the top of the first ridge. Soon after I mentioned the circumstance to His Excellency the Governor, who thought it reasonable, and expressed a wish that I should make the attempt. Having made every requisite preparation, I applied to the two gentlemen who accompanied me, to join in the expedition, and was fortunate in obtaining their consent. Before we set out, we laid down the plan to be pursued, and the course to be attempted, namely, to ascend the ridge before-mentioned, taking the streams of water to the left which appeared to empty themselves into the Warragomby, as our guide. . . . To these gentlemen I have to express my thanks for their company, and to acknowledge, that without their assistance, I should have had but little chance of success.[64]

It was noticeable that when the *Gazette* mentioned the expedition it placed the name of Lieutenant William Lawson first among the participants, though in later official communications he was named last. A surveyor with experience of the inland on the Hunter, he appears a much more likely originator of the bushman-like scheme than Blaxland. And the third version, written anonymously in the *Australian* in March 1827, adopts this supposition.[65]

It says that Lawson, in London, had met Caley, the botanist, who had so far come nearest to crossing the mountains, and "frequently discussed with him the practicality of a mountain pass".

Immediately on his return to New South Wales, he "determined to set out to find a passage over the Blue Mountains. For this purpose he secured an agreeable companion in Mr Wentworth, and a persevering assistant in Mr Gregory Blaxland, and the party started, determined to succeed."

The significance of this statement is that, though anonymous, it was published in a paper controlled by Wentworth. And neither he nor Lawson nor any of Blaxland's representatives—Blaxland himself being in England—made any contradiction of the writer's assertions.

As recorded, the Governor had been at the expedition's starting point on Emu Island in April. He himself must have sanctioned the movements of the party, since on 11 April 1812 a Government order had directed that "no persons whatever (excepting the families of Messrs M'Arthur and Davidson, their shepherds and servants) shall pass or travel west of the Nepean River, unless with a written pass from His Excellency".

VII

Blaxland and his companions set out, with no cheering farewells, to dare the hills which had proved to the last previous adventurer who had essayed their passage "sufficiently terrific to deter any man of common perseverance from proceeding in his design".[66]

When their tiny cavalcade rode off from Blaxland's farm at South Creek, it would have been swallowed up entirely for a time by silence had it not been for a belatedly watchful editor of the *Gazette*:

> On Tuesday, the 18th Instant, a party consisting of Lieutenant William Lawson, of the Veteran Company; Mr. G. Blaxland, and Mr. W. C. Wentworth, attended by four servants, set out from Emu Island on an excursion of discovery, intending to proceed in a south-westerly direction on the north side of the Western River, which track had not before been attempted. Provided with every necessary for a six weeks journey, and prudentially taking with them four sumpter horses, they parted company with a gentleman at Emu Island early in the afternoon, in full spirits and with a determination to make every possible exertion in their power towards exploring the interior of this extensive country.[67]

The *Gazette* at any rate—and its censor the the Governor's secretary—hoped that "so spirited an undertaking would be productive of advantage to the Colony, and entitle the gentlemen employed in it to the thanks of the inhabitants".

It was a difficult undertaking, though not comparable in hardship, magnitude, danger or duration with many a later episode of Australian discovery. It pales before the achievements of Leichhardt, Eyre, Sturt, Forrest, and Gregory. But it filled the participants, at least, with a sense of awe, as their diaries attest.

Day after day they "forced a path through brake and briar",[68] at intervals stopped abruptly by "really terrific gullies . . . in some places nearly perpendicular for several hundred feet".[69] Now they were negotiating "one continued pass, in some places not exceeding fifteen yards in breadth, and no more than a mile in any".[70] They saw little life, heard naught but the crash of wind and waterfalls, the furtive rustling of observing blacks and the nocturnal howling of the dingoes.

At last the "boundless champaign" of the west burst upon their sight and

> . . . . . *nearer seen the beauteous landscape grew*
> *Op'ning like Canaan on rapt Israel's view.*[71]

Each had his opinion of the magnitude and nature of what they had discovered. Blaxland wrote with excited exaggeration that they had "descried all around, forest or grassland, sufficient in extent to support the stock of the Colony for the next thirty years".[72]

Lawson, the most experienced of them, the surveyor who had made their traverses, produced a document which might be used as a model in an explorers' school:

> *May* 31*st*: Encamped on the side of a fine stream of water, it raining very fast. Here is a great extent of fine forest land and the best watered country of any I have seen in this Colony. Went five miles to the westward. Our shoes worn and provisions nearly expended obliged us to return home the same course we came. This country will, I have no doubt, be a great acquisition to this Colony and no difficulty in making a good road to it, and take it in a political point of view if in case of invasion, it will be a safe retreat for the inhabitants with their families and stock, for this part of the country is so formed by nature that a few men would be able to defend the passes against a large body and I have every reason to think that the same ridge of mountains we travelled on will lead some distance into the interior of the country, and also, that a communication can be easily found from this to the head of the Coal River where to my knowledge is a large extent of fine grazing country, and it having water carriage from thence to Port Jackson which will be a great consideration.[73]

Lastly, young Wentworth, whose journal reverberated with grandeur and geology, had his say:

> Before it can be determined whether in this excursion we have actually passed the mountains, it will be necessary to ascertain whether the western boundary of the forest land which we discovered is similar to the eastern. But admitting that we have not traversed the mountains, we have at all events proved that they are traversable, and that, too, by cattle, a circumstance which by those who were allowed to possess some local knowledge of the country has been hitherto deemed impossible.[74]

This was the crux of the matter. In the uncertainty of Lawson and Wentworth—which Blaxland declared later, when rewards were in the air, that he did not share in the same degree—may be part of the explanation why, when Mr Blaxland once more called upon Macquarie to report their triumph, Macquarie—according to Blaxland's narrative written in 1816— "did not doubt" the flushed narrator's statements, "but appeared dissatisfied".[75]

Not that there were not other reasons why the ruler of Botany Bay might view with apprehension the public announcement of the existence of a land of milk and honey only a few miles over the western horizon. Those reasons could have been the same which led later administrators and governments to discourage the announcement of the finding of gold.

Indeed, in the very next year after the crossing, the Government was compelled to discourage the too adventurous eagerness of convicts to emulate their betters. Three villains, no doubt fired by the feat of Blaxland's party with ambition to escape, "formed the absurd idea of crossing the Blue Mountains, making for the western coast and there building a vessel to take them to the island of Timor".[76]

They crawled through the mountain fastnesses for seven days. They had eaten their dogs and then had gone three days hungry. They returned to captivity. Their reward was given to them almost as soon as that to

Blaxland and his companions—a set of chain-gang leg-irons and a grant of one hundred lashes apiece on their bare backs, along with a semi-official certificate that "the voice of pity is silent and the criminality of such desperate adventures becomes a subject of severe censure and reprehension".[77]

Authority had no burning desire to advise the flood of apprentice bushrangers then abroad that the mountains might provide them with lairs and refuges to which they might retreat before the law or drive stolen stock.[78]

It was not till November, five months after Blaxland's party had returned, that the Governor unobtrusively paid the party's guide, Mr Byrne, £10 for his services to the explorers. Publicity at the time of their return was limited, especially in the press.[79]

Next to a paragraph about a cockfight, the *Gazette* had pleasure to relate soberly their re-appearance, "without the slightest injury either from fatigue or accident".[80]

"They report", the *Gazette* announced, "a prodigious extent of fine level country lying in the direction they pursued, which time may render of importance and utility; but no further particulars of the expedition have as yet reached us".[81]

Perhaps the explorers intended that no further particulars should reach anybody until they had planned how best to benefit by their knowledge. Their correspondence and their public conversation seem to have been alike restricted until they made another discovery—that the spoils would not be theirs. But that was later in the drama.

VIII

Meantime, Macquarie, like most of the colonists, was content to leave the explorers' secrets with them. During the month of their return from the wilderness he was wrapped up in the writing of voluminous dispatches, the most important which he had penned while in the Colony.[82]

They concerned the findings of the Select Committee of the House of Commons (1812) which had reported on his policies. They involved representations on which all his main plans for the future turned. They dealt, also, with the tragic events which had just taken place as the result of the misbehaviour of officers of the 73rd Regiment.[83]

The hanging of Private John Gould in a hollow square fifteen months before had had little permanent effect on the morals of the soldiery. The officers, or some of them, had shown small disposition to covet the "honour of being called the defenders of peace and good order in New South Wales".[84]

The evidence of this was provided on 13 June, at the instant the ragged cavalcade of explorers had limped home out of the west, by Lieutenant Archibald M'Naughton, who once had risen in indignation from the Governor's table when asked to break bread with emancipists, and his boon companion, Lieutenant Philip Connor.[85]

The occasion was a bright June evening upon which these merry companions arrayed themselves in "coloured clothes" and repaired to

Pitt Street to seek the romantic society of a damsel, Miss Elizabeth Winch, whom they found upon the pavement with her beau, who was a "poor working man".[86]

They approached the lady with what seemed to them to be an alluring suggestion. Before the impact of this proposal she retired hurriedly behind the closed shutters of her dwelling, the home of Mr William Holness.

So precipitate a retreat naturally was insulting to officers and gentlemen who, while they were most reluctant to mingle with convicts at Government House, were perfectly ready to associate with them and even embrace them elsewhere, if they happened to be of the female gender.

An attempt to batter in the shutters of the maiden's refuge quickly brought Mr Holness on the scene—"a mild, inoffensive but healthy man", said a string of eager witnesses.[87] He resisted the entry of the visitors, barring their way. And from that moment onwards the reports of what took place were highly conflicting. Some onlookers believed that they plainly saw Lieutenant M'Naughton, mad with drunken fury, drag a paling from an adjacent fence and, with the aid of the heroic Mr Connor, belabour the impertinent defender of his home upon the back of his unprotected neck, so that he fell down.[88]

"Then," said the poor victim's wife, taking up the tale, "I put my hand to my husband's wrist and felt no pulse beat, I put my hand to his heart and felt no pulse beat, and says I, he's dead".[89]

With that the poor lady retired, weeping copiously, to make way for military witnesses much more vague of observation than the civilians who had gone before them. They testified that the supposedly inoffensive victim of a brutal and murderous assault had, in fact, destroyed himself. They swore that he had attacked the poor officers with a ferocity against which no defence was possible, before disobligingly expiring in the dust from the very violence of his own choler.

Messrs M'Naughton and Connor were committed for trial by the Coroner. The trial was held before the type of military court normal to the Colony—the Judge-Advocate and six regimental colleagues of the accused, including some of their closest friends. The Bench even included Lieutenant William Lawson, fresh home from the mountains.

The same curious nebulousness was noticeable in the medical diagnoses as in the testimony to the facts. Though many onlookers were clear in their statements that they had seen Mr Holness struck with a paling, military medical searchers could find no mark.

Dr Wentworth admitted that the victim's lungs were full of blood, but said there had been cases of persons dying suddenly from excessive agitation of mind, though he would not venture to say it was possible for death to proceed from a blow without leaving an external mark.[90]

The military and naval surgeons thought it probable that the choleric scoundrel had died of a spasmodic cardiac affection, produced by violent passion.[91]

The Court's members were just men. The Judge-Advocate convinced them, though with some difficulty, that Messrs M'Naughton and Connor were guilty at least of manslaughter. Each was sentenced to pay a fine of one shilling and to be imprisoned for six months.[92]

The Governor had less difficulty in coming to a decision than the Court. He vouched that the dead householder was "a very peaceable and unoffending man in the lower ranks of life". He attacked "the intemperate and disgraceful conduct" of the officers. He showed their behaviour forth as a beacon set up to guard fellow-soldiers "against the fatal consequences attendant on a life of drunkenness, debauchery, and riot, which inevitably tends to the debasement and degradation of the upright and manly character of a British soldier, and necessarily induces the contempt and indignation of all brave and honourable men".[93]

He made no bones about it that, to his mind, despite the verdict, the affair involved "murder". He considered that it would "remain on the records of the Criminal Court to the lasting disgrace of the perpetrators of that foul deed".

He wrote to Bathurst:

> This sentence being in direct variance with what was generally expected, and particularly by several of those who had been eye witnesses of the disgraceful scene, but were not called on in the prosecution, owing to the full and clear case made out by those who were brought forward, excited a public sensation of strong surprize and much indignation. Neither could the popular sentiment be suppressed or restrained that "*little justice could be expected towards the poor, whilst the Court consists of brother officers to the prisoners at the Bar.*" In fact, My Lord, the present construction of our Criminal Court is such as must necessarily induce *a popular*, if not *a just, feeling* against its decisions; especially when as in the present case, some of the members, who constitute that Court, were intimate friends of the prisoners.[94]

Gross irregularity of behaviour, he wrote, and an alarming degree of licentiousness had for a long time marked the general conduct of the officers and privates of the 73rd Regiment; and the circumstances of the recent incident had been so disgraceful that he felt he would be deficient in his duty if he did not give expression to his strongest reprobation.

He asked that the Minister recommend to the Commander-in-Chief the removal of the 73rd Regiment complete,[95] suggesting that in future no regiment remain in New South Wales more than three years. He stressed the need for this as a measure to guard the soldiers from forming too close connections with the women of the settlements, and thus losing sight of their military duty and becoming too intimately identified with the lowest classes of inhabitants.

He had other reasons, also, for wishing the Regiment away. A good deal of party spirit still existed, principally accruing from the circumstances of Lieutenant-Colonel O'Connell's having married the daughter of Bligh. She, naturally enough, "exhibited strong feelings of hatred and resentment against those persons and their families who were in the least inimical to her father's government". O'Connell, "though naturally a well disposed man, allowed himself to be a good deal influenced by his wife's strong-rooted prejudices".

The War Office had made up its mind about the future of the 73rd Regiment before it received the recommendation. Thus, in a few months, the paymaster of the Regiment, Mr Birch, was writing sadly from Colombo, "Sir Robert and Lady Brownrigg keep it up pretty well on the ball scale but not so much as in those pleasant family dinners which the General and Mrs Macquarie used to make every one so happy in".[96]

The incident did not add to the Governor's popularity with the regiments which succeeded the 73rd Regiment in New South Wales, though there was a chorus of approval from the lower orders of the New South Wales population.

Before the Governor could recover his breath, Captain Case was once more in action. Preparing to depart, he had fired a broadside—in Sydney Cove by the Government Stores—upon the small trading vessel *Governor Macquarie*, while the assistant Naval Officer, Mr Watson—he whom the captain earlier had ironed and described as an "inebriated person"—was aboard her. Her offence was that she had not dipped her colours when passing Captain Case's sloop. Several shots had been fired from *Samarang*, one of which had passed through the *Governor Macquarie's* main topgallant within a yard of a seaman. An enthusiastic marine, left ashore, joined in the fray. When the *Governor Macquarie* hove to, Captain Case had her boarded with cutlasses and impressed six out of her crew of ten into the Navy.[97]

He was righteously indignant at the Governor's protest; astonished indeed that the shore batteries had not fired a salvo or two by way of aid to him in performing his "indispensible duty to assure respect for the British Flag". And when Macquarie demanded that the firers of the shots and particularly the shore-based marine be handed over to the Civil Power, he expressed surprise and made charges that the Governor had obstructed the fitting out of his sloop, drawing the response that the "accusation was unjust and illiberal"; that it was too much to expect that a stop should be put to public works in the interests of "the repair of an old and decayed sloop of war, which had been several months ago condemned as unfit for H.M. Service, by your own authority".[98]

After that the quarrel was buried in the archives of Whitehall. The Governor was no doubt glad to see Captain Case's topsails fade into the blue of the Pacific. He turned to deal with a monopoly of speculators which was trying to take the control of currency out of his hands by a series of manoeuvres which called for instant repression, an operation which he carried out with a decisive swoop reminiscent of his campaign against the Pyché Rajah.

IX

On the whole, 1813 must have been a year of which Macquarie was heartily glad to see the end, though there had as usual been progress. There were again more buildings in the settlements, more roads leading out of them. Mr Lord, with the aid of an exile from Yorkshire, Mr John Hutchinson, had founded the glass industry with the production of a run of half-pint tumblers. He had founded, too, a fulling industry, though neither of these businesses was very successful.[99]

Macquarie's personal life was not without its bright moments. The late mails of the year carried the opinion of old David Baird that "Bonaparte is going as fast to the D—l as his greatest enemy could wish", and that Europe seemed to be—after almost interminable years of struggle—"at last aroused". He himself had been promoted major-general.[100]

His brother Charles was happily married to a highly accomplished young lady of Edinburgh with a fortune of £12,000. Thus he put an end to a busy campaign which his viceregal brother had been waging to induce him to come out to "this charming and delightful country" with a bride. "You are not to be permitted to land without a wife," Lachlan had written. "That is a *sine qua non*." But with a spouse he had hoped to see him in Sydney as lieutenant-governor, collector of customs, or free settler.

Murdoch Maclaine of Lochbuy had espoused a daughter of Maclean of Drimnin, and Flora Maclaine, Murdoch's sister, another Maclaine. Mrs Campbell of Corwhin, Elizabeth's aunt, was dead.[101] John Abercromby—he who had been present when young Lachlan Macquarie, hollow-eyed and back in Bombay from Tippoo's campaigns, had met his "Dulcinea"—had captured Mauritius.[102]

But the greatest domestic triumph was his own:

> *Nov.* 3: This being the anniversary of my marriage with my dearest Elizabeth—six years ago—we had a small party of friends to dine with us to celebrate the auspicious day. Mr and Mrs Riley, Dr and Mrs Redfern, Dr Wentworth, Dr Mileham, Major Cameron, and our own family. Our happiness is greatly increased in keeping this day by the gratifying reflection that my dear Elizabeth is now certainly pregnant and God grant that her pregnancy may come to maturity and prove fortunate.[103]

Elizabeth's child had "quickened *for the first time*" on 21 October.[104] Its proud father was able to write in his memoranda book, on the year's last day, that "it has ever since continued *very* lively! ! !"[105]

"Very lively", too, was the colony of New South Wales. Much that was organic in and vital to its splendid future lay concealed and in embryo there, apart from the first and only sprig of the Jarvisfield posterity.

CHAPTER XIX

Noontide in Botany Bay

I

Young Lachlan continued "very lively" until he was born on 28 March 1814.[1] His parents awaited his coming with trepidation. After so many failures to produce him and so much suffering for poor Elizabeth, he seemed almost too good to be true. But he came as he lived throughout his short and feverish life.

At three o'clock in the afternoon, as Macquarie (who had celebrated his fifty-third birthday two months earlier) and Elizabeth were taking soup in the drawing-room, he began to give intimations that he was about to broach the wicked world. Elizabeth retired to the new Great Bedroom and suffered.

Dr Redfern and Mrs Reynolds, the midwife, did what they could.

There began a very trying suspense for poor Macquarie. His young posterity could not have chosen a more inconvenient evening on which to make his bow to the Colony. For it happened to be the occasion of "a large dinner party" at Government House in honour of the new Lieutenant-Governor, George Molle, the Governor's "old, much-liked friend" of Bombay and Egyptian days, who had been sworn in that day. Colonel O'Connell and Bligh's daughter were there upon their last viceregal occasion. Mrs Ovens had done her best in the kitchen. But the guests knew all was not as usual; the sounds of the groanings of the palace fabric — not abnormal in that dilapidated edifice—were drowned by other strange noises whispering through the corridors.

The Governor must have passed the evening with a distracted, listening air, and those ladies among the thirty-eight guests present who did not know what was afoot and find their minds drawn as with a magnet to the new bedroom upstairs were more than human.

Any dowager or matron who departed except under the compulsion of etiquette before the verdict must have been of iron will.

However, they were all got away by half past eleven, except O'Connell and Bligh's daughter, who retired to the guest-room. An ominous silence fell over the saloon where the Governor paced.

The delay was brief. At two minutes before midnight there burst upon the air "the most joyful sound I had ever heard", a sound which made the Governor "the happiest of all human beings", the voice of Dr Redfern, excitedly affirming "that it was a boy".

When he compared notes with Elizabeth the "doating" pair agreed, over the newly-washed realization of their ambitions, "A finer child could not be, being perfection in all his parts and limbs, a good size, a sweet countenance and surprizingly strong and healthy . . . our happiness on earth being now complete, to which this joyful event was the only thing that was wanting."

The O'Connells heard an excited knocking on their door. . . .

Before breakfast next morning the joyful parent was busy writing the news to all his friends[2]; and for the next few months there was no event which could not be driven into the background by the urgencies of his son. That Young Jarvisfield "had a fine suck, milk having flowed freely from his dear mother's breasts" transcended the most glorious news from the Peninsula. And when Young Jarvisfield fell ill and "struggled for breath in spasms" emancipists and exclusives could have torn each other limb from limb without distracting the Governor from his anxieties.

It looked for a time, in the early stages of his life, as if the boy would die. He was so ill that they had him christened privately, but by May Day he had so far recovered that they took him and the latest sprig of the house of Molle and had them blessed anew in the font of St Philip's, with a christening dinner to follow and £5 each for the two midwives. By 24 May Elizabeth was back in the communal bed, churched, and "Thank God, perfectly recovered and quite well".[3] On King's Birthday she was able to entertain the "principal ladies"—and there were now many of them—for tea and coffee.[4]

The Heir was launched on the sea of life, his father's first idol. Yellowed with continual bouts of fever, pursued by bowel troubles largely due to the long courses of weird medicines which he had endured, his teeth fast leaving him, his cheeks beginning to sag, Macquarie could always find respite now by absorbing himself in the doings of Elizabeth and "my dearest boy . . . my darling". His diary at the beginning of every absence from them contained his regrets that they were left behind. His journeys were marred by his anxieties for them. The approach of every express rider filled him with joy because it was certain to mean letters from them. Without them he could not, in fact, have survived the trials which were to come.

II

These trials were increasing even before young Lachlan was born, in the anxious months while they awaited him.

December 1812 had been a "tempestuous" month.[5] But the Governor, during his tour of the inland at that time, had been happy to find that there was an abundant harvest.

The reapings of 1812-13 produced "a redundance of grain more than sufficient for a year's subsistence of double the present population, if well husbanded".[6] The output was so bountiful that Macquarie had been able to reduce the price of wheat taken into the King's Stores from ten to eight shillings a bushel.

Soon the Government could not deal with the amounts offered even at that price. The blight of plenty afflicted the wheat farmer, as it has done throughout history, with the customary effects. "A very serious check" was placed upon the industry of the settlers. This was "one of the strongest inducements to the immediate establishment of a distillery on a large scale, which I have already recommended to Your Lordship's consideration".[7]

However, since they could not sell or distil, the growers became indifferent about their produce and even began to "waste it in the most shameful manner".

By August 1813 the Governor was thoroughly alarmed. He wrote that

> . . . through the lazy negligence of the lower orders of the settlers, and their inexcusable and profuse waste of grain, in their feeding not only their horses and cows with it but also their pigs and dogs; there is now a great scarcity induced, and I am concerned to add that the quantity in the country will with great difficulty subsist the inhabitants until the next harvest.[8]

In fact, he felt forced to "guard against the calamity of famine . . . by restraining further waste".

The normal March rains had not fallen. The winter just past had proved a dry and brittle season. The Governor had been stern in his scoldings of squanderers of good food, vigorous in his promises of retribution for future transgressors, exacting in his design of new measures. He loudly condemned those who were accentuating the shortages by "spurning the blessings that Providence has thrown in the way of the Colony".[9] He ordered that all grain must be conserved for humans. Settlers must thatch their stacks. They must thresh quickly to defeat vermin. Owners of pigs must lose no time in killing and curing them so as to dispose of greedy mouths. Useless and unnecessary dogs which had been eating the staff of life must be destroyed. Persons with small holdings he strongly recommended to plant potatoes, turnips, and French beans; and he even thought it would be worth while to preserve cabbage stalks in the ground to send up a succession of shoots for the table.

Rations henceforward were to be issued half in wheat and half in maize. Heads of families were adjured to put their households on a weekly allowance of as much bread per person as could be made from a gallon of wheat and a gallon of Indian corn.

August came in hot and with heavy dews, but still rainless. The harvest obviously was going to fail. They could look forward next year to no more than eight bushels to the acre against a customary average of twenty-four. Even ponds and rivers were drying up. A few days of rain at last relieved the famished cattle, but produced only vain hope. The sun soon killed the slight spring of young grass.[10]

The speculator appeared, deluding the editor of the *Gazette* with tales of hopeful showers in the inland to bring produce into the market at low prices. The voice of the Governor was raised once more in September threatening those graziers who burned off their land and sometimes—inadvertently, it was hoped—that of their unfortunate neighbours, without waiting for the approach of a customary autumn break in the weather.

Early in October the outland paddocks were seeded with dead lambs; more than five thousand sheep and three thousand cattle had died.

Next month the Governor wrote to Bengal for wheat—"Two hundred and fifty tons . . . to be shipped with the greatest expedition".[11] There was a bare chance that this would arrive within five or six months. The consignee consoled the Colonial Office that it would probably cost less than local grain, of which he had now raised the price to nine shillings a bushel, though the advantage would be counter-balanced by the inferior quality of the Bengal product, which was always full of weevils. He again increased the price of local grain from nine to ten shillings a bushel and he was very much afraid that he would have to increase it further before Bengal supplies arrived.

Against the hope of this some base fellows were holding on to their supplies, as the height of summer was reached in a "total inversion of the natural order of the seasons", with all vegetation at a standstill, ponds and streams once more exhausted, cattle sickening and dying from want of food and water and "actual famine" well in sight.[12]

Their ruler's appeals to those with hidden supplies met with little response. Over the Christmas season matters became worse. In February 1814 Macquarie was seen writing in a proclamation which he ordered to be read in all churches, so that none might fail to know of it, and that all defaulters might be shamed before their fellows:

> Settlers of a different description, and especially those who are in opulent circumstances, principally owing to assistance they have received from the bounty of the Government in originally granting them lands, stock, provisions and Government men to cultivate their grounds, ought to have been the first to come forward at such a season to supply Government with such grain as they could conveniently spare, at a reasonable and moderate price.[13]

He warned them that unless they offered grain to the Commissariat, he would resort and trust entirely to foreign markets to fill the King's Stores. From foreign parts, he announced threateningly, grain could be landed at half the price now paid in the Colony. He told those who owed produce by way of Crown debts that they must supply or be sued at the next sitting of the Civil Court.

On the "lower classes" he enjoined closer habits of industry to enable them to fill their own needs.

The shortages were all the more galling because, ever since he had felt his feet in the Colony, more and more settlers had been thrust, and still were being thrust, upon the parched land. The number of farms directed to be measured in the three years before April 1814 had been 145 annually.[14]

But his lieges had him at their mercy and it was not till he had raised the price of wheat to fifteen shillings a bushel—nearly twice what it had been less than a year ago—and maize to nine shillings, that he scraped together a sufficient supply to feed the population for six months, and give himself a little breathing time.[15]

III

Meanwhile, he had been forced to face the problem of the Colony's dwindling flocks and herds.

The dreadful mortality of October, the columns of smoke which rose from the blazing pastures, the flames which afar at night could be seen licking their way from tree to tree against the horizon, the clean smell of smouldering eucalypts which scented the early morning air — all these things had given warning that the graziers were faring no better than the farmers at the hands of Fate.

These were the portents which urged the Governor to the project upon which he entered—to send George Evans to explore the country west of the Blue Mountains.

As he stated the position in a dispatch the following January, the influences which formed the need of this venture in his mind were "the drought and the consequent deficiency in grass and water for the cattle". It was only later when he himself had been to the new land that he claimed other objects—"if possible the discovery of some new tract of country fit for cultivation"; what he looked for was "some area where Nature was more bountiful than within the circumscribed limits of the Colony".[16]

He had been glad, he wrote when it was all done, to acknowledge the merit, the extraordinary patience and fatigue with which Blaxland, Wentworth, and Lawson had effected the passage of the most rugged and difficult part of the hills, as a starter for his more official enterprise. He had "willingly availed himself of the facilities which the discoveries of these three gentlemen afforded him".[17]

On 19 November 1813 Evans wrote in his tiny, placid hand, from Emu Island that he had "everything across the river and packed up, therefore shall take my departure early in the morning. We are amply supplied with every comfort and necessary for our use."

He had with him in his party the ebullient Mr Burns or Byrne who had been with Blaxland's party and who possibly was the kangaroo shooter who had guided it up the first ridge. There were, also, Richard Lewis, a free man, and James Cooghan, John Grover, and John Tygh, prisoners.[18]

Their guide, Byrne, failed them in the beginning and had trouble in finding the first camp of Blaxland's party. It seemed as if they were disappearing into another world, for fog hid the lowlands which they were leaving behind. It began to rain, drenching them to the skin.

On the fifth day they had crossed the first range and rested on the bank of a rapidly running rivulet. All around them were small meadows clear of trees, and good soil, watered by chains of waterholes. They saw flats clear of timber, and a few honeysuckles on the banks of the ridges. They found a rock resembling white marble with yellow veins in it. The "lockett bird singing and the seed of the wild Burnett sticking to our legs" were phenomena not known on the east side of the mountains.

Here, at the terminal point of Blaxland's expedition, Evans called a handsome mountain, at the foot of which they camped, Mount Blaxland;

and two others, on either side of the purling stream, Lawson's and Went-worth's Sugarloaves. He was at a loss to describe the pleasant appearance of the scene. The grass, quite green and good, made a delightful picture after the burned-out paddocks of Cumberland County; but the place was not to be reached, he thought, from east of the range without much toil and fatigue—"as the present track is, no person in the Colony on the choicest horse could reach this spot and return to the Nepean in four days"; for the mountains were covered with sharp granite over which it would be dangerous to push a horse beyond a walk.

Four days later he had passed over the main dividing range which marks the true boundary between the eastern and western watersheds of the region. He looked out over full forty miles of open country as he worked down the Fish River from near Waterfall Creek through Sidmouth Valley to its junction with the Campbell. He saw, enchanted, "the finest grass mixed with the white daisy as in England"; he saw the wattle—the "memosa"—growing in clusters on the river margins. The rain still poured down on them. Their horses were failing. It thundered as if they were at the gates of the Inferno. But there seems to have been a sort of exaltation on them all. The now roaring Campbell became no obstacle to them. Perhaps they sang a little as they heaved the fresh-cut logs across to build the first bridge in the west, for all around them the land seemed like an ordered paradise.

Soon, as they followed down the Campbell's nether bank, it led them to the point where it joined with still another river to form a single glorious stream which they named the Macquarie.

On 9 December they camped on its banks on the site of Bathurst. ("It requires a clever person to describe this country properly.") Theirs were the first white feet to tread the rich soil of the Bathurst Plains; then they were on the road to Ophir, not knowing of the gold that lay there.

Six days again onward, out by Billiwillinga towards Chambers's Creek, they turned about and began their journey home. They reached Sydney on 20 January 1814, having penetrated into the country one hundred and fifty miles, ninety-eight and a half miles further from the Nepean than the earlier explorers.

There was no doubt that they had crossed the mountains which divided east and west—nor that the earlier party had not completed the crossing. There was no question that beyond the hills lay "a beautiful and champain country of very considerable extent and great fertility, thro' which a river of large size, abounding in large and very fine fish, takes a westward course".[19]

Macquarie was at once fully persuaded that "this hitherto unexplored region will at no distant period prove a source of infinite benefit to this Colony. The land was much superior to any in N.S. Wales or Van Diemen's Land".

IV

Autumn was not a pleasant season that year. Westerlies blew clouds of dust from the interior. In place of the more normal floods the drought pursued its withering course. Rain still monotonously threatened and went away without falling. Early in March sulphurous thunderclouds appeared in the south-west and blew up in cataclysmic fury.[20] For a quarter of an hour a violent gale hurled three-inch hailstones against the settlement till Sydney was an almost glassless town. It would be months before the shattered panes could be replaced.

The dispatches which went homeward in April told of the completion of the road to Windsor; of the Sydney-Liverpool turnpike nearly finished; of Macquarie's intention to push a further highway out to the Nepean and the ford which gave access to the Blue Mountains pass, then to extend it into the newly discovered west.[21]

He was nervous about the expense of these works, though he gave the assurance that in time they would be paid for by the tolls, which in the interval would provide the interest on the cost. He was intent on his plans for new churches and barracks for the convicts. He was disputing with Mr Francis Greenway about plans for a town hall and court-house. He was plagued by the trading habits of military officers and officials, some of whom were tried and convicted. He had sent one hundred and fifty-four tons of coal—"from *our Newcastle*"[22]—for the use of the forges in Calcutta, thus initiating the regular staple export trade of the newly-opened northern port, and being paid in Bengal rum for the use of the Government.

He was establishing Mr Dickson, who proposed to introduce steam power. He was worried about the seizure of the *Unity* by convicts at Hobart Town and the *Speedwell* at Newcastle,[23] and by quarrels with Edward Lord—he who had so lavishly buried Lieutenant-Governor Collins in Hobart[24], and who had been rewarded for his extravagance and improprieties (and for having a brother in the House of Commons) with three thousand acres of land, with which he was far from satisfied

There were all the usual disturbances incident to the farewells of the 73rd Regiment and the welcomes to the substituted 46th Regiment.[25] Old Lochbuy's son, John, recovered from the effects of his fall off a mizzen mast in the Harbour, was going to India.

Norfolk Island had been evacuated. His emissaries, on orders, had made the birthplace of young William Wentworth and Phillip Parker King a desert; the population removed, the stock slaughtered. The few remaining wild goats and hogs were left at the mercy of a dozen dogs, male and female, the only living things willingly abandoned amid the charred desolation. All buildings had gone up in one sulphurous bonfire.[26]

Of course, as ever, Sydney was full of suppliants; persons who wished for land, or for compensation for lost ships, for redress of some wildly-stated grievance or for rewards. Mr Oxley, the Surveyor-General, importuned him for "all the fees, perquisites, profits and advantages"[27] of right belonging to his situation. And when nobody else had a favour to ask at that time, there was always Mr Hutchinson, an ingenious person[28] in whom a trustful Society of Arts had shown more confidence than his country's Assize Judge who had arranged his exile.

Mr Hutchinson professed scientific knowledge of almost everything under the sun. He pursued the Governor with his observations of "small shrubs of a reptile kind", from which he proposed to produce oil on a magnificent scale. He forged never-ending tales about the growing of tobacco with leaves four feet long on the Hawkesbury. He wrote essays on the production of thousands of tons of "mineral alkilie or soda" from blady grass. He urged the manufacture of coarse woollens with the aid of "a machine called a devil, 24 inches over, with fancy rollers, 1 billy, 36 spindles, 2 jennies, 60 spindles". He threw specifications for wire-drawing tools at Government House, plans for producing fuller's earth, schemes for making paint and paper, recipes for dyes and printing inks.

In his own phrases, "Nature bounteous nature furnished an inexhaustible source that no demand could run short". Especially, it appeared, was she productive of words and appeals for chemicals and experimental equipment which made heads at Government House reel and Mr Simeon Lord, who had been tempted to engage Mr Hutchinson as a partner, almost frantic.

Experiment after experiment failed to produce anything more definite than the Governor's conviction that the genius was "so unsteady in all his pursuits, that I can scarcely believe his researches of any subject will be of the least importance to the world".[29]

There were the inquiries into the deaths on the *General Hewitt* and other convict ships which led in the end to vast reforms in the supervision of convict voyages.[30]

One of them, the *Three Bees*, closed her history in Sydney Cove by catching fire and, solemnly firing, one by one, her twenty-four guns into the heart of the settlement while she burned to the waterline, with no more sensation than a ball thrown squarely through the Naval Officer's open window, to come sedately to rest upon his writing desk.[31]

Added to every other worry, there was the turbulence of the outlands.

The drought had ruined the small farmers. The more adventurous of their convict servants, whom they could no longer keep, had no wish to be thrown back upon the Government's hands. The influx of travellers upon the turnpike roads had increased the current chances of bushrangers many-fold. In Van Diemen's Land, where Macquarie was having all the plague of inducting and controlling the officers of the new Government—a sorry lot, in keeping with the drunken Davey, and fit companions for an unpleasant crew of free settlers—bushranging had almost reached the scale of a rebellion. In June in the bush round Sydney the blacks were troublesome.[32]

Violent trends called for the most vigorous measures—posses controlled by the dreaded Mr Samuel Marsden, the institution of chain-gangs in which, in magpie black and white, the members formed an awful warning as they swung their ponderous sledges along the roads[33]; ceremonious farewells from cart-tails out at the Sand Hills, accompanied by the most terrible viceregal denunciations:

At such an awful moment all *artifice*, all disguise is supposed to cease as being no further useful in *this world*, and the unfortunate criminal is expected to think, then, only of making his peace with his offended *Creator*, by an open confession of his guilt, accompanied with a fervent prayer, to the Throne of Grace, for mercy . . . *this malefactor* (shocking to relate) went out of life protesting in the most solemn manner his total innocence. . . . . In this manner did *Dennis Donovan*, with his latest breath, and without other apparent motive than the most detestable malignity to his fellow creatures, and to human nature itself, endeavour to deprive two innocent men of their lives by a murder perpetrated by himself in conjunction with John White who yesterday suffered the sentence of the law, on his own confession, and the clear evidence of others.[34]

Thanks were indeed due to Mr D'Arcy Wentworth for his "humane zealous and indefatigable exertions and . . . praiseworthy and well-directed measures" which whittled down the evil.[35]

Days had come reminiscent of an earlier time when "the implacable Pemulway" and his mischievous son, Tedbury, had roamed the tracks.[36] The editor of the *Gazette* warned nocturnal travellers from Sydney to Parramatta to fix rendezvous and associate in bands like Canterbury Pilgrims to protect each other from the villains.[37]

"It is incumbent on me," wrote the Governor, "to observe that had the inhabitants of the country been at those pains to apprehend runaways and bushrangers, which their duty as good subjects required, the chief part if not *all* the murders now brought to notice would have been avoided and thus four men and one woman, peaceful and inoffending persons, saved from deplorable and untimely ends, and possibly their murderers reserved for a better fate."[38]

Earnestly he entreated his subjects to work for the apprehension of bushrangers, threatening them with the direst penalties should they be found harbouring any of these scoundrels.[39]

If things became much worse, it was difficult to know what he could do. The police were sorry reeds to lean on—mostly they themselves had worn leg-irons. And this was at a moment when the military garrison had been reduced from 1000 men to 373, including drummers. He had only 167 men available to defend Sydney should he be called upon to keep a heady promise, against rumoured Napoleonic ships' adventurings southward, that he would "give any covey of the kind a warm reception and not allow it to exist longer than the time necessary to root it out".[40]

He longed for a full regiment, for a half-company of Royal Artillery, with heavy ordnance, and for a thousand stand of small arms to equip a militia, in case of sudden emergency.[41]

V

The turn of the winter brought the *Broxbornebury* from England with hundreds more convicts, male and female, to add to the larger batches which had landed earlier in the year. Many were old and infirm and a painful responsibility in present circumstances.[42]

The ship also brought the new Charter of Justice, the new Judge, Mr Jeffèry Bent, Sir John Jamison, son of the old-time surgeon who had sailed away to death after the rebellion. It brought intelligence of all the governmental changes due to victories in Europe. It carried refusals of many requests and other bitter news and comments from Downing Street—remarks far from pleasant about the Colonial Hospital project and its linkage with the spirit trade, an order to establish the unrestricted importation of spirits at a higher duty.

A wail went up in Sydney as it was learned that military officers were to have their servants withdrawn and civil servants were to lose the ration allowances for their own families and staffs. There were some nagging hints about the extravagance of colonial expenses and about convict policy.

Still the drought did not break. The price of wheat rose to £2 a bushel.

Long before the *General Browne* and the *Betsy* arrived from Calcutta[43] with their succour of grain in October, it was assured that the "ensuing harvest will be a very scanty one, although a greater quantity of land is under grain than has been any season since my arrival here. The seasons appear to have undergone a complete change in this climate within the last 3 years."[44] All vegetation was now nearly at an end. Springs were exhausted. Even settlers, once Micawber-like in their optimism, at last understood what they were facing. Among the superior orders of them, a "spirit of cultivation" had developed. They now devoted a share of their attention to agriculture "instead of confining themselves as heretofore to the grazing system only".[45]

From the beginning of 1814, as the outlook had grown steadily blacker after George Evans had returned from the west, the Governor had begun to think about carrying out a plan to open up the country which his envoy had explored, together with the Cowpastures along the southern Nepean headwaters. At present this last area was occupied only by the Government herds of "wild" cattle and the wandering sheep of M'Arthur and others who sent their shepherds down that way.

Macquarie had formed the plan to mark out Evans's westward course with a road. And as soon as this road should be "completed to admit of a provision cart passing over it",[46] he meant to traverse it, taking with him the Surveyor-General "and two or three intelligent persons who will enable me to appreciate the true value of the discovery more fully than could be expected from Mr Evans in his first hurried view of it". Thus, he expected to be able to give Lord Bathurst a "faithful report".[47]

He had found in Evans a soul of high courage to dare the void; so now he found in William Cox of Clarendon, late paymaster of the New South Wales Corps and the Magistrate at the Hawkesbury, a sturdy and suitable agent to undertake the second part of his western project.

He had frequently expressed to Cox his intention to build the road to the new country, mentioning tentatively that he had no person in whom he had confidence to carry out "such a hazardous and laborious undertaking".[48]

That it was laborious went without saying. That it was dangerous, apart from the bushrangers, was proved by the lu-luing of the natives in the corn along the marches of the outer settlement.[49]

Dusky plunderers that winter had been killed in the fields. In the first week in June the men of Airds and Appin had waited in the starlit and pellucid evening in their place of rendezvous, while they listened to the unearthly screams of the tribes which had come down from the hills as thick as locusts, and whose attack was expected at the full moon.[50]

The M'Arthurs had lost their shepherd, Joseph Ward, in the Cow-pastures. The brown mountain men had swooped from the very fastnesses which the road to the west must penetrate, ransacked Hannibal M'Arthur's Bringelly farm and speared his overseer. The Coxes themselves had been compelled to meet an attack at Mulgoa not far from where the road would begin at Emu Ford, driving off the marauders with musket-fire.

Nevertheless, Cox, who had just finished building the Castlereagh Glebe House, became a volunteer for the task. On 14 July 1814 the Governor wrote to him, " . . . I now most readily avail myself of your very liberal and handsome offer . . . and do hereby invest you with full power and authority to carry this important design into complete effect; Government furnishing you with the necessary means to enable you to do so."[51]

It would have been difficult to find a better man. Cox had the reputation both among the friendly natives and among the convicts of being humane and generous. On his great self-contained estates he managed all the activities which made life possible, breeding his own sheep and cattle, weaving and tailoring his own fine wool and flax and grinding his own corn, doing his own blacksmithing and wheelwright work with the aid of a princely retinue of convicts. He was a friend of the Governor's closer settlement policy. He often placed a deserving servant on a farm of his own; but there were those who thought him over-lenient and a menace to the general policy of strict order.[52]

His freely-issued leave passes were notorious among landowners. These feared, sometimes with good reason, the effect upon public morals of "Cox's Liberty". But while some of his beneficiaries repaid his leniency by devoting their freedom to cattle-stealing and moon-shining, others established dynasties which still persist in the middle of the twentieth century upon their original farms.

When his task was done there were many who loved to dwell on Cox's unsuitability for it and to tell their audiences how much better and—for the ear of a carping British Treasury—how much more cheaply they could have built the road themselves.

Macquarie himself had no doubt but that his hardy volunteer was "particularly well adapted for such a business, being active and very intelligent in the conduct of such affairs".[53]

Cox lost no time when he received his orders. He took Lieutenant Hobby, another retired veteran of the New South Wales Corps, once a doughty writer of "pipes" against Governor King, as aide-de-camp and helper. As "guide", he engaged the mysterious Mr Byrne who had been with both the previous expeditions—a man of irascible temper and a high-stomached outlook and a lover of his own freedom.

He marched up the first ridge.[54]

VI

Evans had thought the road could be built in three months, but Evans was no road-builder. The highway must climb more than four thousand feet, and wind for more than seventy miles among sandstone cliffs. It must squeeze its way between giant hardwoods, over immemorial and untrodden ranges on which the detritus of all the ages mingled with a tumbled and weather-worn chaos of rock and shrub.

The builders must plough a path through a region in which whirling tempests sometimes ripped the gnarled forests to pieces and flung huge tree-trunks to the ground to rot. Even the blacks and the game gave the summit region of the Blue Mountains a wide berth for much of the year.

When they began their task winter was at its height. It waned while all the County of Cumberland visible from the first range still lay drought-stricken beneath them, beyond the winding and constricted ribbon of the Nepean.

They had little need for surveying skill. Their instruction was to follow the track laid down on Evans's map. The natural course of the country left them small choice of route, and the excellent plotting of Lawson virtually marked their way for them.

The Governor himself drew the specifications of the road. He ordered that they should cleave through the forest to the "fine tract of open country to the westward lately discovered" a tunnel twenty feet wide, on which carriages could pass each other with ease. They were to grub the stumps in forest country and fill in the holes, so that a four-wheeled vehicle could negotiate the surface without difficulty or danger.

In brush country the grubbed way was to be only twelve feet broad, since the Governor conceived this to be sufficient, though he would prefer sixteen feet.[55]

Cox had a fitted caravan to live in, and Macquarie had assembled equipment for the party—thirty "well inclined handy men who had been some years in the Colony and accustomed to field labour", with eight soldiers.

From the Colony's very slender stock, they were given one precious horse, six bullocks, two carts (one harnessed for yoke and one for draught), ten felling axes, two cross-cut saws, ten grub hoes, six common hoes, six pick or grub axes, four sledge-hammers, two crowbars, six tomahawks, a dozen cross-cut and a dozen hand saw files, an iron maul and a spokeshave, tether ropes, scales for weighing provisions, two boards for making bread on, four buckets and four five-gallon kegs for water, carpenters' tools, twelve iron spoons, twelve knives and forks, a small anvil, a bellows.

They had all of two complete sets of blasting tools and twenty-five pounds of powder, for all purposes!

And their fittings were completed with four good muskets, forty rounds of ball cartridge, buckshot, duck shot, flints and six spades and six shovels, and—luxury of luxuries in that wilderness—"1 bag or 100 lbs of Bengal Soap".[56]

These meagre and primitive tools and supplies the Governor appeared to consider ample. *He* should have known. Had he not, full twenty-three years ago, built a track for Robert Abercromby's guns into the foothills of the Ghauts below Mysore, at the rate of a mile in five hours?

VII

The little band of convicts, with their red-coated guard to protect them against the mountain natives, pushed through sleet and fog into the massed and tangled timber of the plateaux and down the steep western pass. There, at first, footholds had had to be cut for expedition horses with a hoe.

By the end of September twenty-eight miles of highway was completed, and the Governor felt able to whet the anticipations of his Minister in London with the news that Mr Cox "expects to have it completed to *Bathurst Plains* (a distance of 154 miles from the commencement at the Nepean) by the month of March next".[57]

The expense, he wrote, would be trifling since the labourers employed were "convicts, who volunteered their services . . . on the condition of receiving emancipation for their extra labour at the conclusion of it". This, outside their rations, was the only reward they were to receive. All the way the highway was esteemed "a safe carriage road".

Actually, the work was finished on 21 January 1815.

Presently, on the site of Bathurst, 101½ miles from Emu Plains and 141 miles from Sydney, they set up the first British flagstaff west of the ranges; and there Cox carried on the affairs of the new settlements of the interior, until Lawson crowned his earlier experience by becoming the first commandant and magistrate at Bathurst in 1819.[58]

Macquarie felt that "the road, thus constructed by Mr Cox, does him and the party, who worked under his direction, infinite credit, due consideration being given to the extraordinary difficulties they had to surmount, and to the short period of time in which they completed it, six months only being employed upon it from the commencement".[59]

For his work Cox received no other reward than £300,[60] the price of the road, some extra sums for building depots, and permission to graze stock on the new plains. Macquarie recommended a salary for him to recompense him for his duties after the road was finished. Bathurst left the recommendation unnoticed. Macquarie paid him generously in cattle[61] and gave him the first grant of land beyond the ranges.

VIII

While Cox had been at his road-building, it had rained—seasonable falls.[62] The new harvest, which had been but a short time ago in a very unpromising state, gave a fair prospect of being abundant and the pasturage was so far recovered that herds and flocks were rapidly improving in condition, following losses which had run to 1200 cattle, 12,350 sheep, 500 goats, and 1000 hogs in a year, without counting the loss of natural increases.[63]

By the autumn of 1815, however, all that had been experienced that year was enough of the seasonable showers to benefit crops in the ground. The current harvest, for the lack of more steady falls at the right time, could "not be retrieved at this late stage by any moisture". It seemed likely that Macquarie would need to order more wheat from Bengal.[64]

This was the condition of affairs when in April 1815 the Governor, with a retinue of thirty-seven followers, his wife, Antill, his staff, his Surveyor-General (Oxley), his botanist (Lewin), and his explorers, came to inspect the highway which entered the mountains by the Macquarie Pass and terminated on the banks of the Macquarie River.

At that stream they arrived after many bivouacs. They had held divine service and walked in the wild woods on a Sunday. Mr Lewin had sketched the mountain scenery for them for the first time. Major Antill had philosophized by firelight. Macquarie had whiled away the evenings with Elizabeth playing cards in his tent and his pleasant days in giving names to the features of the everlasting hills.

He felt that the favourable reports of the country had done it only justice.

On 7 May 1815, with Oxley's help, he chose the position suitable for the erection, at some future period, of the first far-inland town, to which he gave the name of Bathurst.[65]

The site lay on the south bank of the Macquarie River, beyond the reach of floods, in a spot in which settlers would have the advantage .of "a rich and fertile soil", with a beautiful stream flowing through it, "for all the advantages of man".[66]

The Governor had wandered off twenty-two miles on an expedition of his own to the south-west, among "valleys and plains, separated occasionally by ranges of low hills, the soils throughout being generally fertile and well circumstanced for the purpose of agriculture and grazing".

He sent Evans to push another one hundred and fifteen miles west[67] into country which was discovered to be rich and densely populated with game. The reliable surveyor returned ready to add the Lachlan River, which he had discovered between the sites of North Logan and Cowra, along with Mount Lachlan, Maclaine's Peak and the Oxley Plains, to the map. He had been the first white man in history to look upon the Canoblas, blue and chilly upon the world's rim.

Much edified by the sight of natives clothed in skins, and convinced that the difficulties which presented themselves on the journey from Sydney must remain "great and inevitable, and that settlers in the west would have to content themselves with visiting the coast but rarely", the Governor returned to Sydney. He spread his enthusiasm for the "County of Westmore-land",[68] as he called the new-found region, over a whole page of the *Gazette*. The favourable reports which he had received on the country west of the Blue Mountains, he said, were "not exaggerated".[69] Within a distance of ten miles from the site of Bathurst he believed that there was no less than fifty thousand acres of land clear of timber and one half of this might be considered "excellent soil, well calculated for cultivation".

Natural food was abundant. Fish had been caught in the rivers up to twenty-five pounds in weight. The game seemed endless in quantity and variety—kangaroos, emus, black swans, wild geese, wild turkeys, bustards, ducks, quail, bronzewing and other pigeons were plentiful. The quaint, sleek, duck-billed "water-mole or paradox" abounded in every river and pond.[70]

He envisaged settlement beyond the ranges of small farmers on one-hundred-and-fifty-acre blocks—at first fifty of them, "particularly selected, sober, industrious men, with small families, from the middling class of free people". But pending instructions from London he made no grants of land, though he issued permits to tourists to visit the west and gave a few permissions for grazing to deserving persons.[71]

IX

Lawson crossed the Nepean,[72] moving westward with one hundred head of cattle on 21 July 1815. Rowland Hassall, shivering in a hut on the mountains, as the drover came through, was affrighted to behold him, an apparition whose meagre face was wet and frozen, his quaking shoulders and starving frame sheltered by a blanket. He had crossed the range in snow and bitter cold and on a boggy road and had, he said, never in his life before undergone such hardship. Cox and the Government stockman earlier had driven a few beasts to Bathurst. In October 1815 the first draft of fat cattle[73] threaded the Macquarie Gorge to the coast.

Macquarie had ordered the new superintendent who presided over the little group of huts at Bathurst, Richard Lewis, one of Evans's exploring band, and one of the two free men that Cox had employed in building the road, to sow seven or eight acres of wheat and a small vegetable garden.[74]

The yields exceeded even his "most sanguine expectations".[75] The small plots of ground produced "most abundant and excellent crops of wheat and vegetables without the ground being manured excepting in a very trifling degree". The western wheat was "pronounced by the best judges to be of a very superior quality to that grown on the east side of the Mountains". The cattle that were sent there became "wonderfully improved both in size and appearance owing to the abundance of rich grass and water to be met with in all parts of that country".

Cox's waggons lumbered over the dangerous track. Mr Antoine Joseph Rodriguez, lately of Portugal and prison, soon was sinking the first post-holes for the fences of the west. Mr John Wathen, a guest of his country, was hammering out the first inland hurdle nails from superfluous leg-irons.[76]

Blaxland, Wentworth, and Lawson, as well as Evans, blushed under the thrust of the Governor's virile encomiums and set about selecting the thousand acres of land which he gave each of them. Only one, Lawson, chose to have his plot beyond the ranges.[77]

The road itself, so quickly finished, "to the great surprise of all", was replete with the first essentials of civilization—guard-houses and military depots, geographical names and, all too soon, a large oversupply of savage blacks and eager bushrangers.

The Great West was even dowered with all the specifics of modern therapy, thoughtfully sent out by its enthusiastic ruler—"some Turner's Cerate; some yellow basilicon, some Epsom Salts, a little aqua fortis and a pint of turpentine".[78]

Cox added to the knowledge of the country through the exploration of much of the Lachlan River region.

Shepherds trod unheeding over the gold of Ophir. They were still unaware of the riches which lay embedded in translucent white treasure houses in the prosaic-looking hills of Lucknow and at Lambing Flat.

And Bathurst was amazed when he heard of the discovery of the Macquarie River. He was little prepared "after the fruitless attempt made by Captain Flinders to discover, on the west coast of New Holland, the embouchure of any considerable river", to expect that such a river would be found in the interior of the continent flowing for so far westward.[79]

He ordered at once—to find his order already anticipated—the dispatch of an expedition to explore the stream. Local opinion was that a few hundred miles beyond the present penetration of the continent, the Lachlan and Macquarie rivers ran into the western sea.

X

The Governor's homecoming to Sydney should have been triumphant. Not only had he been able to confirm from his personal observations the discovery of a rich territory which had been found and opened entirely on his own initiative, but he could authenticate a revelation of which his first report had excited surprise and that rare emotion, gratification, at the Colonial Office.

Though he had inaugurated a new world in the west, he was coming back, also, to a new and rather unhappy one in Sydney.

Despite the drought, he had written in October 1814 that all was "going on as quietly as I would expect, considering the heterogeneous materials of which the inhabitants are composed, who are daily improving, however, in consequence of the regulations I have introduced".

Just before he had planned his journey, on 31 December 1814, the old order of the Colony had died and the age of rum currency was over.[80]

The fretfulness caused by the changes this involved was manifest upon his return. The hospital contractors, for instance, were finishing their contract in such a testy spirit that he was pleased to be able to record that the business was "the *first*, and shall be also *the last* of that nature which I shall enter into".[81] Bathurst was even more glad than he, and had not even shared with him his "proud satisfaction that, in erecting this spacious, ornamental and most useful building, I have conferred a lasting benefit on the Colony without any departure from public duty, or violation of the revenue of the Crown".

His Minister admitted that he was quite aware that a public building of considerable convenience had been obtained and that a lasting benefit had thus been conferred on the Colony; but he had considered the price paid for the convenience had been beyond its value, and secured in a manner, "at once inconvenient and oppressive". He felt considerable satisfaction that the transaction would be the last of the kind, but he added kindly, "But at the same time that I speak thus strongly of the measure itself, I beg to assure you that the clamour against you on this or any other ground has no influence whatever upon my judgement."[82]

With rum currency out of the way, from 1 January 1815 Macquarie had been able to allow the free importation of spirits, raising the import duty to seven shillings a gallon because liquor could well bear so high an impost in a country "where there is so great a consumption, and so strong an avidity to this article".[83]

On the same day general free trade in all commodities with all ports in countries in amity with Britain was established; and this naturally had a very marked effect on trade and exchange and had unsettled the tempers of would-be monopolists.[84]

XI

One historic event marked the Governor's return from the interior and put the seal on the Colony's economic revolution.

Since he had arrived in the *Earl Spencer* in 1813, Mr John Dickson had been zealously occupied in setting up the queer monster, all wheels and gears and soot, which he had shipped from Maid Lane in Shakspere's Southwark.[85] The site the Governor had granted him was "a most convenient and eligible situation in the Town of Sydney having a run of fresh water thro' it, for him to erect his mills, steam engine and machinery on".[86]

Mr Dickson had brought considerable capital with him and was of "enterprizing spirit and persevering industry".[87] On his fifteen-acre grant on the borders of Dr Harris's deer park, bounded on the north by Liverpool Street and on the east by George Street, he was able, on 29 May, 1815, to receive the Governor with a whistle and a puff of fleecy vapour when the latter came to inaugurate the mills, which were now ready for "grinding grain and sawing timber on a large scale".[88]

The steam engine gave employment to a single industrialist and a very small one at that—far too small to form a union—but the political ancestor nevertheless of all the thousands of more or less horny-handed toilers who, through later generations, would wrangle about the millenium in a dingy trades hall upon an adjacent site.

Well smeared with charcoal dust, the grimy little minion stoked Mr Dickson's fiery prodigy. With a single set of stones, it could grind ten bushels of wheat in an hour irrespective of wind and weather. In its spare moments it could pulverize tanning bark and saw wood.

In all, then, June 1815 should have been a red-letter month for Macquarie and for the Colony, which never again would be in real danger of starvation. But this was not so.

The Governor had returned from Bathurst to find a bitter class war in full blast. In the same bags with his glowing dispatches about the opening of the west, about his improvements, about general tranquillity, other letters were going to London.

He was recommending the immediate recall of two judges and of Davey. He was dealing with the dishonesties of Allan, the Deputy Commissary, and others. He was face to face with open war declared by the Reverend Samuel Marsden. He had a hostile regiment in barracks doing its utmost to thwart his plans. John M'Arthur and others became more and more active against his policies in London, as they scented greater potential gains from the changing of his governmental system.

The echoes of the guns of the last phase of a generation of war were rolling across Belgium on the eve of Waterloo. The stirrings of world-wide social and industrial revolutions which had begun to affect Europe, as soldiers came home during the Hundred Days, were already making themselves felt in Botany Bay.

The inevitable expansions which must take place in New South Wales, as the result of the unlocking of the mountain gates to the interior and the south, and the growing pains which rapid development must generate, were not yet realized.

The noonday of the age of Botany Bay had just struck.

And the shadows of Messrs Ellis and Jeffery Bent, which the Governor found lying grimly across his path when he returned from Bathurst, were the portents of the coming of the afternoon of the reign of the autocratic governors.

Had he known what was brewing to discomfort him in the next two or three years he would not have cared very much.

His plans were made. He intended, early in 1818, "after having been *eight complete years Governor of this Colony*", to make his way home; for then he would "be entitled to a pension agreeably to Lord Castlereagh's promise to me when I received from him the first notification" of his appointment.

He hoped that they would not offer him less than £500 a year after his long period in office.

BOOK FOUR

*

1815 – 17

*

Very Strange Tales

'Tis strange to live a year or two in Sydney
And get acquaint with all its Nonpareils;
To dine with people of a certain kidney
And bask all in the sunshine of their smiles.
They don't live quiet as they might and did—Nay
Proud of expulsion from the British Isles
Some glory in their shame. Very strange tales
Are told of gentlemen of New South Wales.

—JOHN DUNMORE LANG, on *Mr Justice Barron Field*,
in "A Voyage to New South Wales."

CHAPTER XX

The Dangerous Contagion

I

THREE years before he had made his journey to Bathurst Plains Macquarie would have laughed to scorn any suggestion that his mild and delicate friend, Mr Ellis Bent, Judge-Advocate of New South Wales, would become his adversary in a bitter struggle.

Mr Bent had made the voyage from England in the *Dromedary* with the Governor, the first freely-come practising barrister to reach the colony. He had been twenty-six years old[1] when the Colonial Office had discovered him, an erstwhile Fellow Commoner of St Peter's College, Cambridge, a Master of Arts of the University. He had been called to the Bar in 1805 as a member of Lincoln's Inn. He described himself as one of the senior counsel of the Cumberland Circuit[2]. Lord Castlereagh conceded that he was "a barrister of eminence". He claimed to be "well known to Viscount Northland, the Bishop of Derry, Sir Harry Bruce and others" in Ireland; and to "the Judge Advocate General and Lord G. H. Cavendish in England".[3] His father had had some association with Charles James Fox.

His acceptance of so remote a situation as that which he crossed the world to occupy was attributed to "family misfortunes of the severest nature"; and severe indeed must they have been for he was scarcely the stuff of which pioneers are made. Any fortitude which might have enabled him to face the rigours of colonial life seems to have been severely sapped by attacks of pleurisy and rheumatic fever, which nearly destroyed him during the later part of his voyage to Sydney.

He was one of those men whose flesh is too abundant for a moderately strong spirit to carry. His frame was large and unwieldy, too heavy for his uncertain knees. He was prematurely bald. The sight of an amplitude of food raised protests in his ailing interior.

He had a sprightly little wife who was always having babies and falling off her horses. Though he often professed his love for her, she was clearly sometimes too much for him to manage. Now and then he complained of his sufferings from ophthalmia, and more frequently of the dullness of Botany Bay existence.

His happier past haunted him. He longed to link with it again. His one ambition was to return as early as possible to his brother, Jeffery, and to the young men of the Church and Bar who were his friends and intimates. Even during the voyage out he had suffered from fits of dejection and was forced to fight against the intense melancholy which afflicted him as he looked back on his parting with his family. Tears came into his eyes as he remembered "getting into the chaise at Moulsey, father and Bessie weeping at the door of it, and seeing you and Storks mounting in the mail coach at Portsmouth".

Sometimes young men of such a temperament as his find solace in brandy and water, which his stomach rejected and which his reason accepted only as a means of reaping profit. He very soon joined the rum-traders of the colony.

He landed in Sydney with "such a mixture of anxiety, of fear, of hope, of joy" as he had never felt before. Like most ailing men of his type, introspective and self-centred, he was always acutely aware of his own sufferings and discomforts, but little sensitive to those of others. This he showed in his personal account of the first criminal trials over which he presided in New South Wales:

Ellis Bent to Jeffery Hart Bent

I sat in my silk gown and wig and sentences of death are pronounced with my cap on. I must say the prisoners took it as coolly as I *did*, for notwithstanding I find in the papers that my *brother Bayley* when pronouncing the sentence of the law burst into tears and was obliged to turn his head aside, the Devil a tear could Mr Justice Bent squeeze out. This has proved to me an observation I have often felt on these occasions that it is very much more easy for a judge to cry, when he has on his left hand a fine, smart fellow, with a silk coat, bag wig, sword and white wand, on his right a jury box, a good many Big Wigs below him, and a crowd of ladies above him, a fine court to sit in, and a good salary, than it is for me who am obliged to sit in a bit of a hovel with no one to remark how extremely agitated I am, no High Sheriff, etc., etc. Give me all the above appendages and as good a salary, and I will cry with e'er a Judge on the Bench. But good God, if you could see, my dear fellow, the Court I sit in and the *crowd* I am surrounded by you would split yourself with laughing.[4]

He preened himself, three months after his arrival, on his feeling "that I am respected here by everybody, everybody looks up to me, and that I have already gained a character for abilities and integrity".

His uncharity towards vessels which he considered weaker than himself and his contemptuous air of disapproval of everything colonial fits well with his revelation that at college his nickname had been "Father" Bent.

Upon his first entry into the Colony, he was proud of his association with the Governor. He recorded that his Excellency lived very well and was very hospitable, and that "we are upon the best of terms with him and have dined there several times". He rejoiced that the viceregal pair made a great favourite of his little son. At the same time he was radiant with the expectation that, within a couple of years, earning more from his salary and fees than the Governor himself, he should be a rich man.

It was not long before discontent and irritation began to darken his mind. Government House dinners soon appeared to him "stupid" in their profusion. The viands under which the tables groaned were "much too much". Mrs Macquarie, he thought, "has not the art of making people feel happy and comfortable around her".

In December 1810, after the birth of his second son, he was obviously ill. He wrote of the "relapse of his complaint", which made him "infirm and lame"—not able to walk more than half a mile at a time.

From then onward matters began to drift for the worse.

II

Relationships between Governor and Judge-Advocate at first were the best possible. They competed in praising each other to the Colonial Office. Macquarie found in Bent "the mildest and gentlest disposition" blended with "the most conciliating manners, great good sense and accurate legal knowledge".[5] The Judge-Advocate was, at first, "one in whose sound sense and professional knowledge I have the fullest confidence". On matters affecting the proposed reorganization of the legal system His Excellency was happy to add that Mr Bent's opinion "perfectly coincides with mine". He told Mr Bent (so Mr Bent said) that he would do nothing without his judge-advocate's advice and that he should confide in him on all occasions.

Mr Bent's view of the Governor mirrored the Governor's view of him. He wrote to Cooke, the Under Secretary to the Colonial Office, in May 1810, "that His Excellency . . . has most readily and zealously offered to adopt any improvement I was able to suggest".[6]

He had the splendid advantage of being able to see the courts of New South Wales, as it were, emerge from the egg.

The court system, when he came, was rudimentary[7]—six military officers, with a Judge-Advocate president, to form criminal courts; the Judge-Advocate and two colonists selected by the Governor to sit as the civil courts.

The criminal courts were courts of record and were so constructed, some believed, "as to become the instruments of oppression". The civil courts—gifted with the power to hear and determine causes in a summary way—flourished under the banner of "justice and right"; though "whether the standard of justice and right was taken from Jewish or English laws, no direction is given".[8]

The Governor, in criminal law, was Lord-in-Appeal. He could do everything except pardon in capital cases, in which he might reprieve and hear the royal pleasure.[9]

In civil law, there was right of appeal to the Privy Council in every case involving more than £3000. Since there were no fat counsel's fees to pay in the Colony, and the Privy Council was twelve thousand miles away and unlikely to be able to hear any appeal for several years, defendants naturally appealed with embarrassing frequency. In effect, no verdict given for any sum over £3000 was ever likely to be enforced.

Judicial conveniences were primitive. The "only place appointed for the meeting of the Civil and Criminal Courts, for the Bench of Magistrates, and for the Judge-Advocate's Office",[10] was "a small low room about fifteen feet in length and of proportionate breadth, which does not possess one single accommodation for the purposes of justice".

A judge had nowhere he might lay his wig—"no places whatsoever for the custody of the Records of the Court, nor any desk or box where a paper can be deposited with safety". Once "the publick business of the office was entirely at a standstill from the total want of stationery".[11]

III

When he had landed Mr Bent had been bitterly disappointed with the Judge-Advocate's dilapidated dwelling, its yard a ruin, its windows dirty, and its doors painted alternately blue and white, all bordered with "low and vulgar caricatures", in keeping with the poor and grimy furniture. It was a "perfect pigstye". First the Governor secured Mr Thompson's house for him. Then, "having nothing so much at heart" as his Judge-Advocate's comfort, he determined to build him "a new dwelling house with more suitable accommodations, and an office for the assembly of the Civil and Criminal Courts".

Mr Bent "made a proposal" to the Governor to "contract in his own person" to erect these buildings, in order "to plan and execute them more effectually according to his own ideals of taste and convenience".[12]

He asked as payment one thousand gallons of spirits and £300 sterling.

The Governor granted him "a further sum of £550 in money and 200 gallons of spirits to enable him to finish the buildings agreeably to his original plan".

The "market price of spirits at that time was 35s. per gallon (tho' these spirits were paid by Mr Bent to the workmen at a much higher rate), at which price the whole of Mr Bent's buildings amounted to £2950 sterling, independent of the value of the materials of the old house and offices, and of various articles which he received either *gratis* or at a very reduced price from the Government Stores".

In June 1812 Mr Bent completed the curious edifice and Macquarie "received a very polite note from him expressive of his obligation to me for the extension I had made to the terms of his contract".[13]

Most of the heavy expenditure had been upon the private dwelling of Mr Bent, who had attached to it, for court accommodation, merely "one small room . . . totally inadequate in size".

This scarcely accorded with Mr Bent's undertaking to build the house with "necessary attached and detached offices". The court-room which he provided was only twenty feet square.

Mr Bent also importuned the Governor for an estate; and soon after arrival Macquarie, "as a mark of my attention to his comfort and welfare", had conferred on him "a very liberal and favourably circumstanced grant of land"—1265 acres. The deed was issued on 1 January 1811. The land was on the right bank of the Nepean River—"Moulsey", beside a little creek which he named the Mole.[14]

The grant carried conditions that he should not sell for five years, and without carrying out the clearing of the soil and certain specified improvements. Ignoring the covenants, he sold the land and went even so far, Macquarie discovered, "as to sell also the grant, which I had made to him for the benefit of his two sons, altho, he had not even got the Deed of Grant from the Office".[15]

Next, since a regularized-looking civil and small debts court had been established, the new Judge wished for equally regularized fees in accordance with British civil practice.

His fees were at once put on "a clear and equitable footing" and confirmed by the Governor's sanction.[16]

Every time His Honour issued a writ concerning a sum above £10 and below £30, a grateful applicant handed a small recompense of 3s. to him, via his clerk. The clerk received 2s., the court crier, 1s. On entry for trial, the Judge pocketed 5s., the clerk, 1s. 8d.; for hearing each cause and recording a verdict, another crown came his way, another 1s. 8d. for his clerk. The scale rose with the amount of the claim.[17]

Right through to the execution of the verdict, fees for affidavits, bail bonds, writs of execution and attested copies of proceedings fell steadily into the young Judge-Advocate's pockets. Every legal service from the copying of a document to the issue of letters of administration was accompanied by the ceremony of crossing the judicial and other palms with silver.

IV

Up to this point, all had been friendship and amity between the heads of the Executive and Judiciary of New South Wales, despite Mr Bent's growing ill-health and irritation of mind. When the new streets of Sydney were named, Mr Bent was honoured by being the only individual, other than kings, queens, princes and viceregal persons, whose name was attached to a thoroughfare—to one which, prophetically, descended hurriedly and tortuously from the carefree heights of the eastern hill to oblivion in the stinking Tank Stream.[18]

At the end of 1811 Bent had written to the Colonial Secretary in London that "the courtesy and conduct of Colonel Macquarie bespeak so strongly his uniform wish to promote the happiness of all, that I cannot but feel it a pleasure to serve under him".[19]

At the end of 1812 the Governor wrote to Mr Thomas Coutts, the banker, that Mr Ellis Bent continued to give the greatest satisfaction to all ranks of persons. "He has a great deal of trouble. The people are extremely litigious." Mr Bent was still "very truly yours".[20]

And when, as late as June 1813, the Governor penned a duplicate dispatch to Bathurst advocating the establishment of a new court system, he hoped that his Lordship "would not overlook the great legal abilities and services of Mr Bent, the present Judge Advocate, and that in Your Lordship's choice of a chief justice, it will fall upon him, as I do not know of any man more deserving of it, or fitter for that very high and important office".[21]

He recommended for appointment, as assistant judge, Mr Jeffery Hart Bent, Mr Ellis Bent's brother, "a barrister-at-law of Lincoln's Inn of seven years standing", bred to the Chancery Bar, a pupil of Mr Leach.[22] He wrote that he did this readily. He believed this younger Mr Bent to be "in every way qualified for this situation", a man of "considerable eminence as a lawyer, of good sense and conciliatory manners", who would be "a great acquisition to the Colony".[23]

Since it was desirable that unanimity should prevail in the courts, he felt that the appointment "could not fail of producing so desirable an object, when united with the mild and conciliatory manners of his brother, Mr Ellis Bent".[24]

The laughter of the gods, unfortunately, is rarely heard by mortals, except as an echo after the event.

V

Before long Mr Ellis Bent, beside the £800 salary of which his grateful country took £120 in income tax, was receiving in fees an average of £2300 per annum.[25] The Governor spoke the truth when he branded the colonists of Botany Bay as very litigious.

The Civil Court heard 1008 causes during the first four terms after Macquarie's arrival. From 1 January to 19 March 1810 between 350 and 400 writs were issued, one of which was for £20,000; another for £30,000 in an action for false imprisonment; and still another for £10,000 in a similar action. Actually 240 actions were tried in the Civil Court alone during the period.[26]

Court business increased at such a rate that no sooner had he completed his temple of justice than Bent asked for the erection of a new building on a more lavish scale. Macquarie showed every disposition to oblige. He proposed to build "a respectable court house and town hall" under one roof.[27]

Mr Bent would have been hard to please had he not been satisfied with this proposed edifice, the dream of the gifted free settler, Mr Daniel Dering Mathew—"one hundred and forty feet in length . . . thirty-six feet in height to the top of the parapet . . . galleries, one over each jury box for ladies or gentlemen of the higher order . . . a Grecian Doric portico at the main entrance copied from the Temple of Theseus at Athens".

Unluckily, a public subscription had failed to realize its quota towards this palace. And Bathurst had shown no disposition to build it at imperial expense. This was the year in which the Lords of the Admiralty were counting their clerks' candles.

Mr Bent, however, did not blame either Bathurst or the general public. He indicted the Governor and shouted in passionate terms that he thought it just that workmen should be withdrawn from other public buildings in favour of his court-house.

He ceased to visit the Macquarie household in "his usual familiar way". When Macquarie sent for him to discuss public business, he "assumed a very marked degree of coolness and reserve in his manner".

Macquarie, feeling conscious that he had not intentionally offered Mr Bent any offence, on 16 December 1813 asked him the reason for his frigidity, only a day or two after the judge had sent him a friendly report.[28]

He described what took place: "Then to my utter surprize and astonishment . . . he told me, for the first time, the cause of his reserve and dissatis-faction, observing that he had great reason to be offended and hurt at my conduct towards him, as '*I had shewn a great want of feeling for his situation and personal comfort, as Judge Advocate, in not sooner having a suitable and comfortable court house erected at Sydney for his accommodation.*'"

This accusation being "not less unjust than it was harsh and disrespectful", the Governor could not avoid expressing his amazement at the young man's unreasonableness and at the illiberality of his reflections.

However, having noticed that Mr Bent's chest was becoming more dropsical, he took no notice of his manner, invited him and his family to Government House as if nothing had happened, hoping that on cooler reflection, Mr Bent would "become sensible of the impropriety of his conduct towards me, and willing to bury it in oblivion". He trusted that "such an advance to reconciliation would not have been rejected".[29]

Mr Bent declined the invitation with pointed rudeness.

He ignored the Governor publicly. He did not afterwards "consider it necessary to preserve even the external appearance of respect" for His Excellency's rank.[30]

When congregations rose in church to do honour to the Governor's position as "the representative of Majesty", Mr Bent sat surly in his pew.[31]

Officers at the head of public departments had formed the "habit of going frequently into the country to their farms, or in pursuit of amuse-ment". An order signed by the Brigade-Major, Antill, proclaimed that no officer on the military or civil staff at Headquarters should absent himself for a whole day or night without the Governor's permission. This measure "had the desired effect with every officer in the Colony with the single exception of Mr Ellis Bent".[32]

Mr Bent, instead of setting an example as the senior court servant, became haughty and showed indignation that he should be treated "merely as a subaltern officer, a mere cypher, a person sent out simply for his [the Governor's] convenience and merely to execute his commands as one of his staff"[33]—which, in point of fact, he was.

He presumed to tell Macquarie in very plain terms, that "he did not consider himself bound to obey any such order", adding "that he was not subject to military discipline". He felt that the restraint which it was proposed to impose on him would "reduce me to a worse and more depen-dent situation than that of my clerk".[34]

He was clearly in the wrong. He was Crown Law Officer as well as Judge. His commission as Judge-Advocate placed him under viceregal discipline and adjured him, "And you are to observe and follow such orders and directions from time to time as you shall receive from our Governor . . . or any other your superior officer."[35]

The Governor felt compelled unequivocally to inform Mr Bent that he considered him an officer on the civil staff and that he expected him to attend at Government House every morning.

This, also, was reasonable in theory. He was the Government's only legal adviser. The only way to deal with the routine work of the Executive was to give summary decisions. Legal questions cropped up every day. The worst that can be said of Macquarie is that he perhaps did not realize, or make sufficient allowance for, the state of Mr Bent's health. He drove himself harder than he drove others, however, and made little allowance for even his own ailments.

Mr Bent ignored the Governor's acknowledgment of his civil status.

"It is the favourite maxim at Government House," he wrote, "that Sydney is a garrison and that the Government is a strictly military Government, and according to that maxim the Colony is governed".[36] Actually, the Minister regarded the Judge-Advocate as a military officer.

VI

Since the foundations of the courts it had been the invariable custom of the Judge-Advocate to preside every Saturday as chief magistrate of the Sydney Bench. On 31 December 1814 Mr Bent suddenly ceased to perform this duty without previously notifying the Governor, whose first knowledge of the move reached him when he came to initial the Bench Book, as was customary, and read a minute by Mr Bent that out of "a due attention to his leisure, his health, and the other functions of his office", he must decline to preside over the Bench in future.[37]

The young man said roughly that it was improper that a principal judge should perform the duty; that the new Charter of Justice which had just arrived in his brother's care placed the matter in his discretion.

Macquarie, some months before this happening, had decided to revise the Colony's port regulations to bring them into line with the new policy of free trade in liquor and the opening of ports other than Port Jackson.

The original regulations had been made by Bligh in March 1807. Bent had read and approved Macquarie's first re-enacted draft, which had been issued on 1 October 1810. The courts had heard cases involving breaches of various clauses without drawing a single cry of deprecation from Mr Bent upon the Bench. And the regulations had been "sanctioned with only two exceptions"[38] by the British Government.

Macquarie asked Bent to put his revisions of the regulations into legal language. Bent kept the draft a year,[39] despite frequent reminders.

Now, at the end of 1814, he returned it, with the brusque verdict that, save for one or two matters of special local necessity, such as measures to prevent the escape of convicts and the regulation of the liquor traffic, the British law seemed to cover everything.

He had, however, produced a lengthy rigmarole of criticism. He "saw no reason why the Colony should not be on the same footing as H.M.'s other Dominions". He knew of no Act of Legislature which provided otherwise. He felt that it highly concerned him as a judge to know whether the Governor "under the pretence of local circumstances requiring it, can abrogate Acts of Parliament which he is sworn to enforce, and establish (not measures meant to meet a pressing and temporary emergency but) a permanent system, affecting the general trade and commerce of the Colony, in many respects totally adverse to the spirit of the Plantation Laws".[40]

Macquarie was "much chagrined". Mr Bent had not hitherto shown tender regard for Acts of Parliament in giving decisions based on local "law".

He wrote that he must call on Mr Bent, as the only law officer in the Colony, to give his comments and redraft any regulations of which he disapproved, to give them legal status.

Mr Bent replied in insubordinate language that he did "not consider it to be part of my official duty to draw up *the Regulations or bye-laws* of the Colony, as such an occupation is incompatible with my various judicial duties, and more properly belongs to Your Excellency's Secretary".[41]

He hoped his situation was "sufficiently laborious to excuse my declining other labours not distinctly attached to my office, and which I never did or could imagine would be required of me".[42]

He had been performing similar duties unwillingly for five years, but this he attributed to "motives of courtesy to Your Excellency".[43] He had been hesitant and under a grievance about it from the first.

He now had become conscious of "his duty to his Sovereign" and "to his conscience", which forbade him to give form to something illegal. He found that the regulations contained powers which "set the Governor of New South Wales above the Legislature of Great Britain and at once resolved the rule of action in the Colony into the will of the Governor". He flatly refused to obey.

It was difficult to believe that this Ellis Bent was the same who had made the Governor only two years before "feel fortunate in having so capable and respectable an adviser", who "gave full and perfect satisfaction"; who had "sound sense and professional knowledge". It was difficult, indeed, to believe that it was the same Mr Bent who for years had been enforcing regulations made by the Governor, in conflict with British—even with constitutional—law; the same who had agreed in 1811 that "this Court should be guided in its decisions by the common and statute law of Gt. Britain, except in cases where that law is altered by the bye laws of this Territory, or is inapplicable to the local circumstances of the country".[44]

But the mainsprings of the changes in Mr Bent are apparent.

Firstly, he was overworked and ailing, perhaps more seriously than he realized, with "incipient dropsy of the chest", though he was not so concerned by the state of his health as to be unprepared to brave the climate of the East Indies if Bathurst would secure for him a judicial position there.[45]

Secondly, high earnings—higher than those of the Governor himself— had not brought Mr Bent either affluence or a clear conscience.[46] His pecuniary embarrassments had grown great. He had found that it was not so easy as he had at first thought to become rich enough to retire in a few years. He had become interested in the system of colonial currency speculation and had connected himself with others even more deeply concerned in it. Earlier, before temptation had assailed him, he had spoken of this sort of traffic with unbridled scorn: "Every blackguard though he cannot write issues them [currency notes] and they are in great discredit and at a very great discount."

The method by which speculation was carried on was not very creditable to anybody engaged in it, much less the Colony's only judge. Brown issued a note or notes of hand which Jones accepted. Brown's agent then went abroad whispering that Brown was on the verge of bankruptcy. Jones rushed to dispose of Brown's notes as quickly as possible, and at any price, before the sad news became public property. His disposal of them raised the alarm. Everybody who had Brown's paper engaged in a frantic endeavour to be rid of it, with the result that its value quickly depreciated. When his paper was worth only a small fraction of the value which he originally had received for it, Brown sent out another agent who bought it all up for next to nothing on behalf of his principal, who then was discovered to be— a broad grin on his honest countenance—as solvent as the Bank of England.

Also, promissory notes were in many cases "the mere impositions of unprincipled persons, possessed of no just means to discharge them"; even worse, they emanated "not infrequently" from "those who are not in law bound to discharge them, even if they had the means, as is the case with all those who are convicts by the sentence of the law". These included ticket-of-leave men.[47]

In trying to deal with currency abuses, the Governor had issued "a strong proclamation", framed by Mr Bent, declaring illegal notes other than those expressed in specific terms and payable in sterling. Mr Bent's views on the matter appeared to "coincide perfectly" with the Governor's own. Currency notes themselves were henceforth to have no status at law. But there were many citizens, friends of Mr Bent, apart from his own concern in the matter, who were likely to be ruined for a variety of reasons, if the new-made law was not speedily rendered a dead letter. A careful study of dates shows that Mr Bent began to be surly towards the Governor immediately the currency regulations were given force in the spring of 1813[48]; and that his first attacks on Macquarie took place a few days before silver was issued at the end of the year. Mr Bent, in his desperate condition of mind, had little hesitation in proceeding as if the regulations, which he had himself framed in full accord with his own specific advice to the Governor, had no existence.

Actions on illegally drawn promissory notes were admitted to his court and treated as if the notes were perfectly legal.[49]

The Governor later reported, "By these means, the old and base system of fraud, as exercised in the issue of *Currency Notes*, had returned upon the country, and at the time of Mr Judge-Advocate Wylde's arrival it was overflowing with the currency circulation, which by means of Mr Bent's irregular and inconsistent conduct had again grown into use."[50]

Thirdly, the reform of the law which had been accorded the Colony did not please the Judge-Advocate.

Both Ellis Bent and Macquarie had strongly recommended the adoption of a civilian legal establishment, both criminal and civil, based on the British system.

The "military tyrant" of New South Wales and Mr Bent had jointly pressed on Lord Bathurst a suggestion that there should be one court with two justices, of whom the senior was to be Mr Bent.[51] Macquarie had recommended that Ellis Bent's salary should be increased to £1500[52]; that Mr Bent's brother, Mr Jeffery Hart Bent, as junior judge, should receive £1200.

Lord Bathurst summed up the reasons for varying the plan by saying that His Majesty's Government did not think the Colony "sufficiently advanced to admit of withdrawing that appearance of military restraint, which had been found necessary on its first formation, and which the composition of its population had rendered it indispensable subsequently to maintain".[53] Thus, it was proposed to place a judicial officer with an exclusively military commission above the Civil Judge.[54]

There was sense in this. Martial law was actually at the moment a possibility in Van Diemen's Land.[55] Even Mr Bent canvassed that thought. It was only five years since a rebellious interregnum had ended; only seven since Bligh, and little more since King, had been arming the population against the possibility of an insurrection of Irish prisoners.[56]

The courts were, therefore, reorganized, but only on the civil side. The Judge-Advocate retained his old military commission and sat in criminal trials with a roster of military officers.[57] He became the senior judge, presiding in the Criminal Court, the legal adviser to the Government and to the Governor when the latter exercised his authority on appeal, the judge of the Governor's Court, which was composed of himself and two respectable inhabitants, and beyond appeal. This court was to clean up the crumbs of civil litigation in which sums of £50 or less were involved.

Mr Jeffery Bent was to become civil judge at a salary of £800 a year. Mr Judge-Advocate Bent was to have his salary increased to £1200 per year.[58]

VII

When the new Charter of Justice reached the Colony in the hands of his brother on 28 July 1814, Mr Ellis Bent was bitterly disappointed.

His handsome increment of salary spelt disaster for him, since reform was sweeping £2300 a year in fees out of his pocket into his brother's pocket. Neither the Governor nor Bathurst seems to have deduced the full extent of his income. And explicit explanation was risky for him.

The most that could be done was to mutter something about a "material diminution of my emoluments, as there have been several fees taken by the Judge-Advocate since the foundation of the Colony, amounting in the whole to something considerable to one in my circumstances"[59]; to remark on the circumstances of being "no longer provided with fuel; the issue of rations to my family is discontinued, and, although I have acted as principal magistrate of the Colony . . . I am no longer allowed the indulgence of having any servants victualled".[60]

These latter deprivations were his own doing through his retirement from the magisterial Bench. The indulgences which he complained that he had lost were rightly designed as the recompenses of an unpaid magistrate.

The last influences which had affected Mr Bent's health and judgment were mischief-making companions. He had fallen in with Mr Oxley, the Surveyor-General, one of M'Arthur's faction.[61]

Macquarie had complained to Bathurst a month after the Judge-Advocate's refusal to redraft the Port Office regulations.

Now he gave a general history of his relations with his adversary.

As for himself, he wrote, the dearest wish of his heart was to "discharge my public duty in every situation with the strictest honour and integrity; and I can with confidence declare that my best endeavours have been uniformly and strenuously exerted in the administration of this Government to produce the welfare and prosperity of its inhabitants, without favour or prejudice, and to conciliate the goodwill of every class of the community as far as I found consistent with my public duty".[62]

Moreover, he declared, he was "ever studious to avoid controversy on those subjects which might tend to produce party spirit or litigation".

However, he felt that Mr Ellis Bent's refractory and disrespectful conduct towards him might be fraught with the most dangerous consequences in a colony so remote from home; and that the Judge-Advocate's rank "must necessarily, in the exercise of such hostility and opposition, have a degree of weight in drawing popular odium on the executive power, the example of which, being once shewn, may be likely to spread a dangerous contagion among all those persons, whose natural disposition leads them to be discontented or dissatisfied with the measures of government; numbers of whom are to be found under all forms of government".[63]

Had such conduct proceeded from any other officer, the Governor said, he should have deemed it his indispensable duty to have sent him home; or, at least, to have suspended him. But if Bent went, there would be no legal mind available. He asked that Bent be instructed how far, by virtue of his office, he was subject to the Governor's orders and control and how far his assistance to the Executive should go.

And since Mr Bent had made a "presumptuous threat"[64] to him in their last conversation, "in a very insolent tone", that "he would complain of me to Your Lordship", Macquarie wrote that he felt it all the more necessary to speedily possess the Colonial Office of the facts, although he at all times felt reluctance to make a personal complaint against any officer under his Government.

He also believed himself bound to notice Bent's attitude to the emancipists:

> He acts as if he conceived that no degree of merit, however connected with birth, education, or former pursuits, should ever plead in behalf of him, who has fallen under the sentence of the law, so as to restore him to any degree of that rank in society, which he had formerly held. This illiberal principle he has never deviated from, except in a few particular instances where he found his own pecuniary interest or other personal accomodation concerned, and on such

occasions he is not at all scrupulous in associating with those, who had been convicts, which conduct shews most clearly that his motives in the one case or the other are not those arising from a strict sense of propriety.[65]

VIII

The Governor could not have written to the Minister anything which could have better pleased Ellis Bent and his newly-arrived brother, who became Ellis's fierce and obstreperous ally.

Jeffery Bent naturally had discussed the convicts before he left England. It would be surprising if he had not learned, during his many visits to the Colonial Office, of the exchange of letters on convict policy at the moment in progress between Macquarie and Bathurst. Particularly he well might have heard Macquarie's commentaries on the dispatches covering the findings of the Select Committee of 1812.[66]

Bathurst's letter on this subject was actually carried in the ship in which this second Bent travelled to Sydney.

Bathurst had given his considered view of Macquarie's policy and of the latter's arguments in favour of it.

Nothing could be more unjust to individuals themselves, wrote the Minister, nor more impolitic with a view to the tranquillity of the Colony, and the effects which it was the object of transportation to produce, than to lay down a general rule of perpetual exclusion against the convict class, and thus to deprive it of that feeling of honourable ambition, which was the best incentive to virtuous exertion.[67]

This principle, however, might in his opinion be carried too far; and he confessed that he was not as yet prepared to say that it would be judicious, unless under very peculiar circumstances, to select convicts for the office of magistrates.

The Minister considered that the illiberal, though not unnatural, prejudices which the Governor had had to encounter in his endeavour to restore meritorious convicts to their former rank in society would be still more violently excited by their elevation to the magistracy; and the hostile spirit which prevailed between the two classes of settlers and convicts, if it did not influence the conduct of the magistrate himself, would at least diminish the respect and deference which ought to be paid to his decision.

A failure, also, in an experiment of this kind would, he thought, not only render it difficult to recur to it again, but would confirm those prejudices against associating with convicts which, he trusted, time and a proper exercise of discretion on the Governor's part would ultimately overcome.

As those who had been desirous of counteracting Macquarie's measures had selected the admission of convicts to society as their main point of resistance, the Minister was sure than his agent would see the necessity of not compromising his authority by exerting it on a subject, where resistance might be so well cloaked under a rigid sense of virtue or a refinement of moral feeling.

It would be but a useless, if indeed it were a practicable task, he continued, to compel persons to associate with those whom they might dislike or despise; and he should certainly disapprove any measure which had for its object to force an association with convicts, however meritorious or respectable, or to punish those who refused it. He added, "Among the respectable part of the community, your example must have great weight, and I have to recommend that you should trust to the gradual effect of that example as the surest, if not the most expeditious mode, of procuring to the convicts the benefits to which I conceive them so justly entitled."[68]

There was little divergence in principles between Minister and Governor, but their views on procedure obviously varied. Much depended on whether Bathurst's terminology had exactitude; for it was to be noted that he wrote throughout not of emancipists or released convicts but of "convicts", a very different matter altogether. The Governor appears from his responses to have taken him literally and to have acted accordingly. There was possibly—even probably—confusion between them which was the seed of much future irritation and misunderstanding, due to a lack of precision on the part of the Minister of which the Governor was only too eager to take advantage.

IX

The vital aim of Ellis Bent, it was obvious, was to destroy the currency regulations by securing an official admission that all such regulations made by a Governor, and which had not express parliamentary sanction, were *ultra vires*. At the same time, the less said about currency regulations the better.

What was required was, firstly, a dispute about a set of regulations, other than the currency regulations, to test the validity of all such legislation. There could be little fear about the result. Parliament is a jealous god.

To succeed in their prime object would be easier, the factious brothers knew, if also they could discredit the Governor on some issue on which—in the words of Bathurst—"resistance might be so well cloaked under a rigid sense of virtue or a refinement of moral feeling". This would take his defences in the rear.

There could be no better basis ready-made for such an attack than the emancipist question, to which Bathurst referred. Their fight would conciliate both righteousness and self-interest. The spectacle of two incorruptible young judges heroically standing firm against the Scottish tyrant who proposed to contaminate their benches with vice, would appeal to all true virtue and especially to the British press. And they could depend on the Governor, as soon as emancipist policy was raised, to become frantically and fanatically angry, obstinate and—one hoped—very indiscreet.

Knowledge of Macquarie's reply to Bathurst regarding convicts would have filled the conspirators' cup of happiness to the brim. Perhaps they had knowledge. All sorts of people might have received access to the Governor's dispatch—the disloyal Molle, on intimate terms with the two judges and deadly jealous of Macquarie; Michael Robinson, the "poet laureate".

Macquarie himself may even have shown it to Ellis or Jeffery Bent in some early moment of unguarded intercourse.

Macquarie to Bathurst

On this subject, Your Lordship may rest fully assured of my paying the most respectful attention to the humane and wise line of conduct which you have suggested for my guidance.

To the high and important duties of the magistracy I shall be particularly cautious not to advance any person, who shall not appear to me fully and respectably qualified.

On this principle I have heretofore acted, and whilst I have the honour of administering this Government, I shall not deviate from it, being fully sensible of the necessity for the making of these appointments as respectable as the Colony and the population will admit.

Some illiberal men there certainly are in this country, who would destine a fellow creature, who once had deflected from the path of virtue, to an eternal badge of infamy, and however a subsequent conduct of rectitude might be expected to throw a veil over past errors, yet in the eyes of such persons no reform, no amendment however sincere, will be admitted as sufficient for this purpose. I am happy in feeling a spirit of charity in me, which shall ever make me despise such unjust and illiberal sentiments. I am happy to add that the illiberality of sentiment . . . is confined to a few; tho' I am sorry to be obliged to avow that they are to be found in the higher class, where more enlightened and liberal sentiments might have been reasonably expected to be cherished.[69]

X

By the time Macquarie and Ellis Bent had come firmly to grips, Mr Jeffery Hart Bent was well established in the Colony.

This second Mr Bent was a year younger than his brother, the Judge-Advocate. His chest and—more particularly—his lungs were sound. He was "a barrister of near ten years standing". During his Botany Bay career he rarely failed to force that impressive fact upon his readers.[70]

It is probable that Macquarie had met him in 1808 or the next year, if it was he that was selected to examine the papers of the Colony along with the Reverend Mr Marsden.[71]

Before he had left England he had reproved the Colonial Office for the affront offered to his dignity in not securing an audience for him with the Prince Regent.[72]

Major Abbott, of the New South Wales Corps, a good-natured fellow but deficient in the qualifications of his office, had been chosen as Judge-Advocate of Van Diemen's Land.[73] And he had christened Mr J. H. Bent "Sir Jeffery", because Mr Bent was deeply ruffled that he had not been knighted on appointment.[74] As "the honour has been conferred on persons going to India as Advocate General to the Company", Mr Bent had declared that he could "scarcely suppose that it could be refused to one holding a commission of importance under the Prince Regent though in a minor settlement".[75] This "occasioned much laughter".[76]

Afterwards, especially since he had been in the company of Mr M'Arthur, there might have seemed to be some hidden significance in Mr Abbott's final verdict, written to Captain Piper, "He is, however, a nice young man and wishes, I know, to do what is right. *Keep this to yourself.*"[77]

When the nice young man arrived in the *Broxbornebury* on 28 July 1814 the guns of the Port saluted him lustily.

He had brought with him a copy of the new Court Charter and Mr William Moore, a son of a London under-sheriff. The latter had been an attorney for four years and was one of two honest and unconvicted solicitors whom, on the Governor's advice, Bathurst had decided to send out, each with an official salary of £300 a year, to overcome previous difficulties regarding attorneys.[78]

Bent had asked at the Colonial Office what the attitude of the court should be towards the convicted attorneys and agents who hitherto had held the whole legal practice in Sydney. He was told to ask the Governor, who had full instructions. But, during his early months in Sydney, he had seemed too busy with personal issues affecting his own comfort and dignity to concern himself with any others.[79]

He was, it would appear, purposefully avoiding the issue for his own reasons. Surprise is a vital element in war. And publicity is especially the handmaiden of the evildoer. He was anxious to strike the foe with as little warning as possible and in full view of the world.

He haughtily demanded that, as a natural appanage of his eminence as "one of His Majesty's Judges", he should have a house. He scorned the offer that he should have lodgings till the Colonial Office should decide— Bathurst approved Macquarie's attitude.[80]

He and his brother refused a virgin half of the hospital building as courts—this had been Bathurst's suggestion after discussion with Mr Jeffery Bent himself!

The editor of the *Gazette* viewed this accommodation and wrote of massive pillars, wide verandas and windows placed at a proper distance, "in proportion so well adapted as at once to gratify the eye of taste and science". He felt that "did his limits permit him to extend his rhapsody he would fall short in conveying an adequate idea of the beauties of the place or of the solemn impression which the mind received on entering this stately building".

To the Bents it was but a "common hospital ward". "The room . . . was in a most disgraceful state from dirt and vermin". Their hearts were set on a separate court, no less than one of the "palaces for his [the Governor's] favourites", the home of Dr D'Arcy Wentworth.[81]

Mr Jeffery Bent was outraged that the personal convenience of such a person should be placed before his own: to his highly judicial mind the supposed fact that Mr Wentworth had been *acquitted* on charges of committing boyish acts of knightly acquisition upon the Highgate Road constituted him a notorious highwayman "charged . . . by Sir Henry Russell, late Chief Justice of Bengal, with robbing him of his watch on Hounslow Heath".[82]

His ire was still aflame when he turned his attention to the affairs of the Supreme Court.

Of this simple institution he was to be president, sitting with at least one, or normally two, magistrates nominated by the Governor under precept.

The Charter of Justice gave the Governor power to veto verdicts, on appeal by the judge, should the latter dissent from both magistrates. The Governor also became an absolute judge in civil appeal, save where the sum involved in the suit amounted to £3000 or more. In such cases, appeal to the Privy Council was provided for.

Mr Bent considered that his situation raised him to the status and dignity of a Justice of the King's Bench—his salary was £800 a year and even in its own internal management his court was subject to the Governor's control.

The Charter declared:

> And We do hereby authorize the said Supreme Court to administer Oaths and to frame such Rules of Practice, and nominate and appoint such Clerks and officers, and to do all such other Things as shall be found necessary for the Administration of Justice and the due Execution of all or any of the Powers, granted to them by these Presents, subject to the Approbation of our said Governor.[83]

The Court could not even settle its own table of fees, including those of attorneys, without "the Consent and Approbation of the Governor".

Macquarie had not desired the powers which the Charter vested in him to determine civil appeals previously remitted to the Privy Council. He had suggested that, with a proper civil court in being, "appeals to the Governor might possibly be then dispensed with". But, against his own will, the new system undoubtedly had given him very full powers of supervision over the courts.[84]

XI

Before the days of the new Charter, there being no unconvicted attorneys, both the Court of Appeal, presided over by all recent Governors, and Mr Ellis Bent's court had followed the practice of licensing convict or emancipated legal agents, who were not admitted solicitors, though they claimed to act as "attorneys and solicitors". They functioned in and outside the courts under generalized powers-of-attorney from their clients.[85] Apart from this, Mr Ellis Bent had not excluded convicts or emancipists from court offices. His own Clerk of the Court was James Foster, who had arrived in the Colony as a convict only in 1812.[86] Before him he had employed in the same office Mr Fleming, one of the applicants who was now appealing for admission to Supreme Court practice, an Irish attorney transported for passing a forged note, who was "very honest in his dealings" with Mr Bent, but sometimes was "drunk and indecorous in the street". Bent had sat on the magisterial Bench time and time again with Simeon Lord, who had actually been elected chairman of the committee to raise money to build the town hall and court-house.

The legal agents now asked the right to practise in the new court.

The first applicant, Mr George Crossley, had been struck off the rolls of King's Bench after conviction for perjury.[87] He had robbed various citizens during his outward voyage to Australia by dint of making purchases worth several thousand pounds on valueless notes of hand, drawn on a London citizen who proved so self-effacing that no note-holder could find him.[88]

Upon Crossley's arrival in the Colony, other honest citizens, including some who held every convict odious, had fallen into his clutches. Governor King, under the delusion that no convict was subject to prosecution in a civil court, had released him in order to make him open to the onslaughts of his many creditors. The same Governor had admitted him to legal agency practice in 1803—two years after his arrival.

Rebels had done their best to associate Crossley as a "worthy colleague" with Bligh during the rebellion, since it was a fetish that to be associated with Mr Crossley was synonymous with being vile. But Mr Crossley was the only private resident in the Colony who had any real pretension to experience of legal practice. He had been one of the first successful litigants before Mr Ellis Bent, who had awarded him £500 damages against some of the rebels of Bligh's time, for false imprisonment.[89]

Next to him came Mr Edward Eagar, an erstwhile "member of King's Inn, Dublin". He had been discovered in a Cork dungeon by the Reverend Boyle Davies, fearfully holding his throat and regretting his past life. For he had, in his youth, "been a complete Deist, never read the scriptures save to cavil at them and ridicule them". With the rope almost round his neck as the wages of forgery, he was weeping in desperation at the Throne of Grace. His "fervent prayers for mercy" secured the Heavenly pardon, which "came with power to the afflicted suppliant"—through the joint influence of a merciful Providence and "his connection with Judge Day who had tried him".[90]

"All in an instant was love, joy, peace," wrote Mr Davies, and Eagar soon was on his way to Sydney, consigned to the care of Mr Marsden. Mr Davies had no doubt but that he would "proclaim the glad tidings" in the Colony.

Five years later wayward Providence had looked down on him with such good effect that he was linked, in Mr Marsden's view, in contumacy and ingratitude with the Wesleyan missionaries.[91]

He was so far in Government favour that he had a ticket of leave. A year afterwards only the fact that his sentence was not concluded prevented his being elected to the first Board of Directors of the Bank of New South Wales, of which he became the largest original shareholder.[92]

Mr Eagar had, for a "considerable time", been "employed as law agent by the majority of the gentlemen and settlers of the Colony, as well as by some of the first mercantile houses at Calcutta, the Cape of Good Hope and London and now holds above one hundred and fifty powers of attorney from these persons and houses".[93]

He also professed to hold powers of attorney, some for persons absent from the Colony, whose business he alone could transact. He had brought one hundred suits to judgment in the old court, on which there had been as yet no execution, and was acting in twenty-five causes instituted but untried, which had been continued from the old court to the new.[94]

In all these causes, brought to judgment or untried, he had, he declared —and none denied it—"paid of his own proper monies all the fees of the Judge-Advocate and Provost-Marshal, as well as the other fees and expences attending the same"; and in respect of these payments and his own fees for work done and accepted, was due "nearly one thousand pounds".[95]

The other applicants who appeared were Mr Michael Robinson, poet laureate and Chief Clerk to the Government, also Mr Fleming, and a Mr Chartres, who kept a boozing den and shop in extra-legal hours.

XII

After Jeffery Bent had been in the Colony five months without holding a trial, the Governor began to press upon him "the propriety and expediency of opening the Supreme Court".

Mr Bent replied that there being only one free attorney[96] in the Colony —Mr Moore, whose immigration had been arranged by the Colonial Office—he declined to open the Court before the arrival of Mr Garling, a second solicitor who was on the water.

The Governor thought the excuse "frivolous and ridiculous". He thought it possible that Mr Garling might never arrive at all, since there was reason to believe that he had been captured by an American privateer.[97]

He urged that, as those agents who had practised in the old courts might be allowed with equal reason to practise, at least temporarily, in the new ones, there was no excuse for delay.

Early in April 1815, meeting Jeffery Bent, he told him he had received petitions from three of the agents—Crossley, Eagar, and Chartres. He asked whether he had done right in receiving them. Bent told him that if they were "properly addressed" he could not refuse to receive them.

Macquarie asked him if he had any objections to reading them.[98] Bent said that he would do so, but he could do nothing with them, "the proper place of application being to the respective Courts, as every Court had an exclusive power as to whom they thought fit and proper to be admitted to practise".

The Governor sent the petitions to Bent, covering them with a letter in which he summarized the situation in general, saying that he "could not but concur with the memorialists in the consequences, which must attend their being excluded from practising . . . both as they apply to their constituents and to themselves". Conceiving it would be "a very severe measure to debar persons of a respectable profession, whose only means of subsistence arise from the exercise of it, from practising", he declared himself "decidedly of opinion that it would be fair and reasonable to admit those attornies, who have practised heretofore in the Civil Court in this Colony to continue their professional practice in the new courts", adding:

I have only to call your attention to the consideration of the injury, which constituents, resident in distant places and countries, must suffer by their law agents here being prevented from following up their different causes and suits already entrusted to the management of the memorialists, and I trust, on a fair review of the subject, you will see the propriety of their being at least permitted to plead in the causes already on hands . . . I cannot but approve of their being admitted . . . and I therefore recommend to the favourable consideration of the Court that the indulgence they have solicited should be extended to them.[99]

It seemed that he knew little of the men themselves. He could not have looked with any personal favour on Mr Eagar, who, though a professional man, was not among those admitted to Government House. And he held the common-sense opinion that forgery, of which most of them had been convicted, was a crime meriting peculiar abhorrence.

He was aware that the senior judge—the Judge-Advocate, Mr Ellis Bent—had consistently permitted two of these men to appear; that Mr Bent had, without demur, presided regularly over magisterial benches on which Mr Simeon Lord had sat.

In advocating the establishment of trial by jury, the Judge-Advocate in May 1810 had written that "if the selection of jurymen were confined to that class of persons which has come out free, many would be excluded who are now among the most useful and opulent members of the society here". Thus Mr Ellis Bent had shown no official aversion to emancipist jurymen.[100]

There was little to cavil at in the Governor's course of action. He was, by virtue of his position, actually the Chief Justice in the military hierarchy, in which, by consent of the Crown, he was being even tacitly permitted to revise the English law to suit local conditions.

The Colonial Office view of his standing and rights in respect to admissions of attorneys was shown by its ruling on the matter to Mr T. S. Amos.[101] The Under Secretary told Mr Amos that he might emigrate to Sydney, but that "the question of your practising as an attorney there must be left entirely to Governor Macquarie, who can alone judge of the expediency or necessity of granting such permission".[102]

For that matter the Governor was not only, in the Colonial Office view, the chief judge—he was a military commander-in-chief, virtually on a sort of active service, able instantly, without recourse to other authority to abrogate all the civil law and institute martial law with a stroke of the pen, if he felt that special circumstances of lawlessness justified such a course.

He was no mere viceregal figurehead functioning as the formal part of a parliament like modern governors-general. He was vice-king, commander and parliament all in one piece; and he was expected by the Colonial Office to act up to his role.

But, when the question came later to be debated, he said that so far from wishing to exercise any influence over the court, he was prepared to leave the matter to the free decision of the Bench.[103] He merely meant to have it understood that, in the event of the applicants being admitted by the court, he should, for reasons given in his letter, confirm the appointments—a necessary legal preliminary to the applicants practising. He was doubly justified in writing his opinion since he was on the eve of his journey across the Blue Mountains to found the town of Bathurst, of which his mind was full. Thus he would not be present when the Court met; and for the courts to know his views might obviate delay.

Mr Jeffery Bent saw things in a very different light.[104] He wrote that he could not avoid expressing his "poignant regret that your Excellency should have thought proper to interfere on behalf of the petitioners"; that the Governor's letter placed him in an unpleasant and delicate situation. The Court was being subjected to an influence which never should be applied to it and which was inconsistent with the independent deliberation of British courts of justice . . . the open, avowed and direct communication of the opinion of the Executive on a point under judicial discussion. The petitioners had been convicted of crimes of an infamous nature. He would have it known—and this of course was contrary to the provisions of the Charter of Justice—"that the Court had full discretion to admit or strike off the roll of attorneys such persons as they thought worthy or unworthy".[105]

He considered that to comply with the applications would be "contrary to the express sense of the Legislature, to the recorded opinion of all the judges of England, injurious to the dignity of a court of justice, to my own feelings" and those of other solicitors. And in these sentiments Mr Ellis Bent concurred.

The Governor could not have realized what was afoot. He himself had pressed the Colonial Office to send out free barristers and solicitors to assist the courts.[106] If he had thought that any important controversy was likely to arise, he would not have left on the long journey across the Blue Mountains, which occupied several weeks, at a time when the question was about to be argued.

If he did have any qualms about whether the Colonial Office would support him in resisting the general exclusion of all emancipists from practice—as opposed to the exclusion of particular unsavoury individuals—he had the Charter to set his fears at rest.

Be that as it might, the incidents which had taken place had already spread the "dangerous contagion" which the Governor had so much feared to every powerful malcontent in the Colony.

L

CHAPTER XXI

Sir Jeffery in the Lists

I

THE Supreme Court had been convened for 1 May 1815,[1] for the first time in Australian history, and sat for business on 5 May. Its members were Jeffery Bent, Alexander Riley, and William Broughton. of the Commissary Department, who had come to the Colony with the First Fleet. Broughton, a steadfast servant to all governments, had sat on the magisterial Bench since 1808. He also had sat often in the old Civil Court and had "never once differed in opinion from the Judge-Advocate". Riley, son of a London freeman bookseller, had come to the Colony twelve years before with a warm recommendation from Lord Hobart. He was a well-educated, thoughtful, and politic man, save when his pocket was directly touched. Then he became false, and his good principles were stifled by his shrewd Londoner's acquisitive sense. Jeffery Bent considered both magistrates ignorant of law and of the common forms of proceeding in a court of justice.

Crossley and Eagar were present when the Court opened. Eagar presented a petition. Bent highly reproved him for underscoring particular parts of it and including in it arguments in favour of his admission. A magistrate interposed to say that this was established custom in the Colony. But Bent angrily brushed aside the interruption and dismissed the paper without consulting his colleagues, who formed the majority of the Court, and whose votes had the same status as his own, subject to his special right of appeal to the Governor on legal differences. In sullen temper, the Court adjourned till 11 May to allow the Bench to consider the situation in private.[2]

In chambers Bent offered resistance to the admission of the men on the ground of an Act of George I which excluded from practice attorneys convicted of perjury or forgery. He said that "the judges in general had decided that a man having been once convicted of felony was a sufficient plea for his not being ever again permitted to practise in any of their courts as an attorney". He said also that the admissions would be particularly injurious to his own feelings.[3]

The magistrates, with many assurances of their respect for him, pointed out that this law had been framed before the Colony was founded; that it appeared from its own text to apply only "within that part of Great Britain, called England". Bent flared up at them for refusing to take his legal advice; then argued that admission of convicts or former convicts would be unfair to the two free solicitors appointed from England, because they had been assured that they would have a monopoly of practice.

This assurance had certainly not been given by the Colonial Office, though Bent himself, who had helped to choose the two solicitors, may have volunteered it of his own authority. In any case, the very next minute he laid down a contradictory policy by avowing his determination to admit all qualified attorneys and articled clerks—irrespective of numbers—who produced certificates of good behaviour and who had not been transported as felons.

The magistrates acknowledged the benefit conferred on the Colony by the dispatch to it of men like Messrs Moore and Garling. They not merely agreed, but demanded, that every applicant for admission as an attorney of the Court should be strictly examined as to his current character and as to his qualifications. They cared not, in effect, how high the standard set, how severe the test, but they were firm that a decision by the Court that "no persons transported to New South Wales should ever be admitted, however reputable", would in their view "of its tendency have such harmful consequences, and be so contrary to the first principles of justice, that they could never assent to it".

They were prepared to agree that convicted persons considered fit should be allowed to act only temporarily as agents to meet existing difficulties. In other words, they suggested an extension, but not a permanent continuance, of the old system. Both men considered that the philanthropy of the British Government had established the Colony "more under a benevolent hope of effecting reformation in the principles of the unfortunate characters who were sent to it, than to render it a place solely of perpetual punishment and degradation". They pointed out that but for chance Mr Lord might have been a member of the Court. They emphasized that four-fifths of the population had been convicted.[4]

The Court met again. Crossley, Eagar, and Chartres then rose to make petitions. Bent stopped Crossley at once and told him to sit down. Crossley attempted to persist. Bent said he would commit him.

Broughton, the magistrate, from the Bench, said that he thought it understood that the petitioners should be heard and asked Riley his opinion. Riley, forming the majority, said that he considered that the applicants should "have an opportunity of *viva voce* supporting their petitions; that it was the sense he saw it in". Bent remarked politely, "If that was the sense you saw it in, you are destitute of common sense." Riley replied that he was "sorry Mr Bent had so little sense as to tell him thus publicly so".[5]

Broughton was brusquely prevented from speaking. Riley was asked whether he was in favour of admitting Crossley. He started to speak, when Bent interrupted him, shouting, "I want no Ifs, sir. It appears you cannot say Yes or No."

Riley replied that "he could express those monosyllables with as much facility as Mr Bent", but that he had informed Mr Bent before coming to Court that he was only prepared to speak on the general point, whether no persons who had been prisoners should be allowed to practise.[6]

Bent, now very angry, said the most insidious and improper means had been exercised to accomplish the forcing of the petitioners on the

Court.[7] He accused Broughton and Riley—they denied it—of being influenced by the Governor's letter. Otherwise, he said, it was impossible that "two men, who have declared that they would not allow their wives and daughters to be contaminated by associating with such people, should attempt to offer such an insult to my feelings and the dignity of this Court, as to assert that any of them are fit to be admitted as practitioners in it". He solemnly and loudly pledged himself that the Court would never be disgraced by the practice of such men as the petitioners. If they attempted it, he would severely punish them. If any attempt were made to obtrude them on him either by members of the Court or any other power, he now repeated it was his most solemn determination to adjourn the Court till the opinion of His Majesty's Ministers was known. And he informed them publicly that he should take special care to adjoin the names of the two members of the Bench who had differed from him in the proceedings that day and transmit the same to the Home Government, that a lasting stigma might attach to them for their conduct.

After thus publicly threatening his fellow judges, while a roomful of gaping convictry looked on, and without consulting the other members, he said, "The Court is adjourned."

Next day the two magistrates wrote the Judge a letter. Having allowed sufficient time to elapse so as not to be accused of inconsiderately acting under the hasty impulse of irritation, they declared that they considered Mr Bent had in "a most wanton, unnecessary and unprovoked manner, publicly insulted their feelings"; that he had unwarrantably charged them in open court with despicable conduct; that he had misrepresented the statements which they had made in private conference; that the threats denounced to them for their differences of opinion with him, the alarming, violent tenor of his conduct and his disrespectful demeanour to them as magistrates and members of the Court, had produced an impression which could not be effaced; and that until they could assure themselves that they ran no risk of suffering a repetition of similar indignities, or of being again the victims of a similar violation of the common rules of decency, they would refuse to sit with him.

Bent professed to be astonished. He told them in a lengthy letter that from his "office as Judge of the Supreme Court and a barrister of near 10 years standing", he had a right to expect from them a regard for his professional feelings and character, and a deference on points of law and practice, more especially on such a point as that which had occasioned their differences.

He denied threatening them. He asked for what purpose Macquarie's letter had been written if not to bias the Court? He asked them whether, for the sake of Mr George Crossley alone, they would altogether cause a suspension of judicial proceedings. And he added:

> I do not wish to preside as judge in any court where transported felons are admitted to practise, or where the members shew a determination to thwart me on points exclusively of law and practice, points on which you cannot possess the requisite information to enable you to decide. . . . I should wish to

ask . . . whether a barrister of near ten years standing is to learn law from you or you from him. You seem to have thought that you had only to out vote me, and what you pleased would then be law; I consider myself sent here to point out the law to the members of the Court, and supposing them to act with a sound discretion, I should imagine they would feel themselves bound to attend to my opinion on a point of law, as much as a conscientious British jury. . . . Your intentions seem to have been to establish a disgraceful distinction between Courts of Justice in New South Wales, and every other Court of Justice in His Majesty's dominions.[8]

Bent's magisterial opponents answered in turn that his letter was not only "ill calculated to restore the cordiality so desirable in three men placed in public action together on so important an occasion",[9] but designed to mislead those authorities interested to whom the case must go. Bent offered to continue sitting if they would agree not to admit the felons till the matter was referred to England.

Broughton put his opinions in writing, including the argument that the royal pardon, which some of the obnoxious applicants held, "expressly declares that they are restored to all the rights and privileges of free British subjects in this Colony; to deprive them of the benefit of their professions would destroy the effect of the pardon".[10]

II

The Governor returned in the middle of the mêlée. The magistrates asked that he replace them on the Bench by others. He refused.

On the eve of the next meeting of the Court there was another private conference of the Bench. Broughton asked what Bent's attitude would be if Ministers should sanction the admission of the emancipists. Bent said that he would "feel it a disgrace to sit in court with such men. And that he would not."

Broughton said that in that case it was useless to compromise, and that he intended to take his seat in court and deliver his sentiments with unrestrained freedom. This, as a member of the Court, he insisted, he had the right to do. Bent said he would not sit in court to hear comments on what he had said that day. Broughton remarked that he considered that the judge had no power to adjourn the Court without the consent of the other members. He said that he himself would take his own seat, and that Bent could secede from the Bench, if he wished to do so.

The magistrates entered the court-room. They took their seats. The petitioners sat in a row. The open-mouthed public waited. Jeffery Bent did not come; he sent a message when approached in his chambers by the provost-marshal that "there could be no court without him", and that he would not receive any message.

Next day, Bent announced that he would "not again preside in the Court, if those petitioners are admitted as attorneys".[11] The magistrates remained adamant. Each case, they said, must be treated on its merits. They could not say whether they were prepared to admit or reject any applicant till they had heard him. They would establish no general principle that an ex-convict, because of his conviction, must be automatically excluded.

Jeffery Bent did not re-open the Supreme Court. Closed also was the Governor's Court, over which Mr Ellis Bent presided.

Old criminals afterwards looked back on the next year, during which the well of civil justice remained battened down, as a golden age.

Jeffery Bent's action caused huge losses to the more steady merchants, and brought nearer to fruition Macquarie's plan for the establishment of a bank in New South Wales.

III

The contest between the Supreme Court Judge and the magistrates now turned into one between the Governor and the Judge, and every moment the exchange of discourtesies assumed a ruder note.

Macquarie asked Jeffery Bent firmly, but politely enough, for a report on the Supreme Court proceedings. To this he was legally entitled. Bent made it clear, however, that he did not think the Governor entitled to either obedience or courtesy. He inveighed against "the unprecedented disrespect and indignity"[12] with which, as one of His Majesty's judges, he had been treated. He wrote:

> My functions are entirely distinct from those of Your Excellency, and in the exercise of them I am not accountable to any but those to whom Your Excellency is also accountable; I am not placed under Your Excellency's command, either by the tenor of my commission, by His Majesty's Charter, or by any official instructions from His Majesty's Ministers.[13]

It pained him to observe, he declared, that though courtesy and custom universally gave to the Governor the title of "Excellency", the Governor had on no occasion extended the title of "Honourable" to the Judge. He continued:

> Feeling it to be inconsistent with my dignity and independence, as a judge, to submit to any interference or investigation into my judicial conduct on the part of the Executive Government of this Colony, I shall decline entering into any further discussion with Your Excellency on this subject, except we are understood to meet on terms of equality and independence of each other. . . .[14]

Macquarie answered:

> I have received the very extraordinary letter you have thought proper to address to me, under date the 31st of last month; the style of which is so highly disrespectful and offensive that I shall not trouble you with any further correspondence at present, as a continuation of it would probably subject me to further insult.[15]

The courts being now both adjourned, the Governor turned his attention to the operations of the senior judge, Judge-Advocate Ellis Bent asking for a copy of the Rules of Court of the Governor's Court, which to meet the provisions of the Charter of Justice, also must have viceregal approval.[16]

Ellis Bent graciously conceded a copy. At the same time, he begged "leave to be understood as by no means admitting the right on the part of your Excellency to control that Court in the adoption of such rules, as it may think proper to form as the basis of its practise".

There was no doubt about the view of the members of the Governor's Court on the convict attorney question. They had adopted a rule that "no person whatsoever" struck off the rolls in England or transported for any offence "shall on any account be admitted to practise as an attorney of this Court".

IV

Governor and judges retired from active dissension to put their cases to the Colonial Office.

Ellis Bent, seriously ill, renewed his demand for a purely civil law system on the British model. He represented that it was painful to his feelings to perform the functions of a civil judge under a military title. He protested against the convening of criminal courts with their military judges by the Major of Brigade. "The Governor because he is a military officer thinks he is a military governor. . . . I considered it highly necessary that these notions should be done away."[17] He, moreover, asked that all regulations and orders made in the Colony should be registered in the courts.

The Governor had, of course, already written to London about Ellis Bent's earlier conduct. He now wrote to Lord Bathurst of the alarm and indignation caused in the Colony by Jeffery Bent's behaviour. He mentioned the receipt of a request for permission to hold a meeting to protest against it, "but," said he, "delicacy towards Mr Bent and a greater regard for his dignity than he had shewn for mine, induced me to discountenance the measure." He referred to Bent's aspirations for the prefix of "honourable", and said that if he had been approached in a friendly and courteous way he should have attended to it.

However, it appeared that the Bents had "mutually determined to deny my possessing any powers whatever in regard to the internal regulation of their respective Courts, and that they have mutually resolved to resist me in any control that I might be disposed to exert under authority of the Patent, which specifically requires that all appointments in those Courts should be subservient to my approval".[18]

Macquarie considered that actions of the pair on the emancipist question were "in direct variance with the line of policy" of His Majesty's Government. He suggested "for your Lordship's humane consideration" a measure adopted from the ideas of Mr Wilberforce, M.P., the reformer, with whom he had been in friendly correspondence on the matter. He asked whether it would not be expedient to remove by statute any ambiguity which Crown advisers might discover in the civil status of emancipists. He believed it to be a point of primary importance, he asserted, that this should be done, "so as to prevent the recurrence of such differences in opinion hereafter on a point involving the dearest rights and privileges of British subjects". He pressed for a "speedy and serious" consideration of the matter.[19]

It had been, he declared, reserved for Mr J. H. Bent "to discover degradation and insult to his dignity in a measure, which I or my predecessors were not capable of discerning".

In a private letter to Bathurst, the Governor accused the two Bents of vindictive and unworthy motives, and delivered the following ultimatum:

> Under all these circumstances, it is utterly impossible that I can act with the Messieurs Bent, without a total abandonment of the principles, by which I have been actuated and have acted upon since my first taking charge of this Government; and consequently it now becomes absolutely necessary for the good of the Colony (which it is my ardent desire to leave flourishing and happy), that *they*, or *I*, should be removed from it.
>
> I therefore most respectfully take the liberty to solicit, that, in the event of the conduct of the Messieurs Bent being approved of (which of course will be virtually disapproving of mine) by His Majesty's Ministers, your Lordship will do me the favour to move His Royal Highness the Prince Regent to be graciously pleased to accept of my resignation as Governor of the Territory . . .[20]

Jeffery Bent naturally had his say. The rule and principle of Macquarie, he declared, had been "that *Quod gubernatori placent, legis habet vigorem*"; he said this principle had been carried in the Colony to the greatest extent.[21] He could not conceive, he wrote, upon what other reason Governor Macquarie should have adopted his line of conduct, except from a levelling principle, and a desire to impress on the Colony that, compared with him, the judge and the convict were at the same distance.

V

Everybody concerned now settled down to wait a year or so till the Prince Regent should indicate his commands; and Jeffery Bent decided to enliven the interval with a private rebellion against the Colonial Regulations. One of these prescribed that all must pay toll on the Governor's fine new turnpike road to Parramatta, the first highway of its kind in the Colony. Only the Governor and his immediate suite were excluded from this rule. When the toll regulations had been drafted in far-off and happier days, Ellis Bent had framed them. The Governor had offered to give the Judge-Advocate freedom from toll. Bent had refused the concession, because he could find "no reasonable ground for claiming the exemption". If he set the precedent, he declared, it might lead every magistrate and officer of the Crown to demand the same rights.[22]

His quarrelsome brother, however, had no such qualms. He now asserted that, as the equal of the Governor, he should travel the roads toll-free. He remarked in a lengthy epistle that

> notwithstanding your Excellency has made so mortifying a distinction between the Lieutenant Governor and His Majesty's Judges, and notwithstanding . . . your

Excellency possesses no legal power or authority whatever to levy taxes upon the subject, I am so much alive to the advantage arising from good roads that I should have most willingly contributed my quota towards their maintenance, had I not from the neglected state of the road sustained considerable personal risque.

His highway happened to be the Governor's pride. It had been completed only two or three years; it was his own conception, the delight of his eye. Never was he so happy as when spanking up or down it in his carriage, Joseph Big on the box, the dragoon outriders creaking in their saddles. And in any case Bent's law was bad. Tolls were not a tax, but a royal duty, and as such leviable without parliamentary authority.

No wonder the interchange of notes between Governor and judge acquired the staccato quality of gunfire. Macquarie wrote of insolence and disrespect,[23] of gross misrepresentation, of calumnies which merited no other answer than an expression of contempt for the weak and ineffectual efforts of the writer to disturb the peace of the Colony. Bent answered that he would restrain himself to observing that no judge in any part of his Majesty's Dominions was ever before treated with such indignity; also, "that your Excellency appears in the ebullitions of your violence to have lost sight of your own high station and to have totally forgotten the rank and office".[24]

Macquarie then wrote that, except on points of public duty, he must "decline all further epistolary correspondence"[25] with his adversary, who at once rejoined that he *never* had had any kind of commerce with the Governor which was not official; and that he had to express his sincere regret that most of his letters should have been principally confined to a resistance of Governor Macquarie's improper interference with him as a judge, and to a remonstrance against measures trenching on the liberty of the subject.[26]

He announced, in the third person, that he had never "as a private individual had any knowledge, acquaintance or correspondence with Governor Macquarie, and from the mortification he has in his public station experienced from his Excellency should by no means think such private knowledge or acquaintance desirable, or feel himself much honoured by such correspondence".[27]

Jeffery Bent now fell into the habit of riding through the George Street toll-gates without paying fee. The harried toll-keepers would peep out. There, between a pair of wheels or upon a prancing steed, and usually accompanied by Mr J. L. Nicholas, a holy intimate, would be Mr Justice Bent. Bent would shout, "I'll pay no toll, I am Judge of this Colony. I'll pay no toll whilst I am in it, and if you don't let me pass, I'll send you to jail." He threatened to "have the gate cut down and burned"[28] and shook it violently until it flew open.

The Governor publicly lamented that any person should be found in the Colony so wanting in public spirit as to wish to "evade contributing his mite towards the support of so useful and beneficial an establishment".[29] He felt it incumbent upon him to support the toll-keepers.

If any person attempted to use force or violence to pass the toll-gates, the toll-keepers were specifically enjoined to send for the police to enforce the regulations, preserve public peace and prevent the Government being insulted in the just exercise of its authority. Although he forbore "from motives of delicacy and out of respect for the high Office he holds" to name Bent, the Governor wrote that he could not "help expressing thus publickly his astonishment and regret that he should be the first and only person in this Colony, who has openly and avowedly attempted to break thro' and counteract the regulations the Governor has deemed it necessary to establish for the benefit and improvement of the country".

D'Arcy Wentworth issued a summons against Bent, not only for breaking through toll-bars without paying toll, but for having "declared . . . that you never would pay the said dues and threatened that you would commit . . . Michael Wyer and Patrick Cullen to gaol for attempting to demand the same".

It is surely the only time in British history that so original a charge has been lodged against one of His Majesty's judges.

Bent's response was to complain that Wentworth had "omitted my designation as Judge of the Supreme Court and you seem entirely to have forgotten that I have the honour to hold that office". He wrote, "As Judge of the Supreme Court, I am by no means amenable to any criminal juris-diction in this territory, and you must not expect any attention will be paid by me to your summons, a proceeding of great indignity towards myself and exceeding the bounds of your duty".[30]

Wentworth went calmly on to the magisterial Bench and fined Bent "forty shillings in the lawful money of Great Britain".

Ellis Bent broke down under the strain of the argument, and in October Macquarie gave him leave to travel to Europe to restore his health. He refused the offer of Jeffery to act as Judge-Advocate during his brother's absence, on the ground of his misbehaviour.[31] Mr Garling, rescued from the clutches of the privateer, and now arrived in the Colony, filled the gap. Bent protested. He called the Governor's appointee "so inferior a person in the profession to me, who am a barrister of ten years standing and to whom the high office of Judge has been confided by the *Crown*".[32]

Poor Ellis Bent did not live to see Europe again. On 10 November 1815 he died, leaving his vengeful brother to carry on the fracas alone and to plead with Lord Bathurst for consideration for the starving widow of a faithful servant, whose emolument from his situation had been "little more than sufficient to maintain a respectable appearance . . . only £720 pr. annum net money and the fees attached to the office were by no means great . . . a life of labour, anxiety and public duty (and I may say sacrificed from a continued attention to it)".[33]

Jeffery Bent remarked that "my brother declared to me . . . that he had contracted a disease (tho' he was mistaken in its nature) that would carry him to his grave" in sitting in "so miserable a place" as the court-room which the deceased had, of course, built for himself, but for the weaknesses of which the Governor was now blamed.

Macquarie added his plea. Ellis Bent's conduct as a judge, he said, had always given full and perfect satisfaction to him. Poor Bent had, he wrote, become unaccountably "my bitterest enemy", and his death had been "no loss to me". At the same time the Governor at that stage was prepared to admit that Mr Bent had been "certainly a great lawyer and an upright judge on the Bench", though this opinion seemingly was expressed upon the principle of *de mortuis nil nisi bonum*. He blamed others rather than the Judge-Advocate for what had taken place; for he was well aware that "factious, discontented and turbulent men" had been busy sowing the seeds of discontent between himself and Mr Bent, "who I have reason to believe", he declared, "lived long enough severely to repent his allowing himself to be divided from me, who had ever been to him a *true friend*".[34]

Though the poor, dead young man had shown no contrition or regret, he forgave him completely. And, as he had left a widow "in an advanced state of pregnancy, and four children the eldest of whom was now under eight years of age", the Governor feared they must be in a very destitute state; so he believed that the situation called for his lordship's humane consideration. Always, afterwards, there was a lingering note of affection when he or Mrs Macquarie thought of "poor Mr Bent".

But for the brother the Governor exhibited far different feelings.

"Having thus paid a just tribute to the meritorious services of the deceased," he wrote, "I shall now proceed to a much less pleasant duty, which is the recital of acts, most daring and insulting to me and my Government", by Mr Jeffery Bent. That hero he considered "an upstart and insolent puppy, who is at this moment doing all he can to excite a rebellion or insurrection in the Colony". This man, he said, could not be allowed to remain in New South Wales any longer. "If they do not recall him, I must go home immediately".

VI

Late in 1815 Lord Bathurst, fresh from the exertions of cleaning up after Waterloo, received the flood of dispatches which described the progress of the other Napoleonic war raging in Sydney.

His lordship wrote tartly that he could assure Mr Ellis Bent that "the title of Judge Advocate was not continued to you without due consideration". He wrote that "the continuance of a judicial officer who bore a commission exclusively military, and who, tho' a military officer, was by the Charter placed above the Civil Judge appeared to have many advantages with a view to the maintenance of that due subordination in the settlement upon which its welfare depends".[35]

His lordship showed astonishment that an issue had been made of the Port Regulations. He had "only to observe that the power of the Governor to issue Government and General Orders, in the absence of all other authority and the necessity of obeying them, rests now on the same foundation on which it has ever stood since the first formation of the Colony; for to these subjects the new Charter has no reference and can with respect to them

have made no alteration". As for relations with the Governor, he wrote
to Ellis Bent:

> Filling as you do the situation of Judge Advocate in the Colony, it is more
> particularly incumbent upon you to uphold the Governor's authority and to set
> an example of due obedience to it: for there could not exist a greater mis-
> fortune to a settlement, of so peculiar a description as New So. Wales, than a
> spirit of resistance, or any thing more calculated to produce such a calamity
> than an appearance of misunderstanding between the Governor and yourself,
> or a suspicion that you were disposed to question or disobey his orders.[36]

Lord Bathurst rejected the suggestion that Government Orders should
be registered in the courts, as a measure likely to create an impression that
the sanction of the courts was necessary to give validity to the Governor's
acts and orders.

Jeffery Bent also was rapped over the knuckles. The Colonial Secretary
thought the court accommodation offered by Macquarie deserving of
approbation. He would have nothing to do with civil law systems or anything which would savour of the withdrawing of military restraint. Furthermore, he fully approved of Macquarie's refusal to provide a house for
Jeffery Bent, which certainly, he said, had not been promised him.[37]

Macquarie's ultimatum giving the Government a choice between
dismissal of himself or the Bents brought matters to a crisis when it arrived
some time later with the rest of the flurry of angry correspondence. There
was not a moment's hesitation. The Government wanted no more rebellion
in Botany Bay. Bathurst's replies were instant and decisive. They not
merely were meant to put the Bents in their proper places—though poor
Ellis Bent was to be transferred to another situation—but they made it
plain to the Colony how much an autocrat his masters expected the Governor
to be.

To Ellis Bent, long dead before the letter reached the Colony, Bathurst
wrote:

> . . . I am utterly at a loss to discover how you could have made those Port
> Regulations (which I believe with only two exceptions have already been
> sanctioned from this country, and acted upon for a considerable length of time)
> the ground of a serious difference with the Governor . . . you will no doubt have
> easily deduced . . . the opinions entertained [by the Home Government] with
> respect to the continuance of that system of restriction, to which the population
> of the Colony has up to the present moment been subjected, and to which it
> appears you have now formed decided objections. Under all these circumstances,
> you must at once see that His Majesty's Government have no other alternative
> than that of relieving you from the performance of a duty, which is at variance
> with your own feelings, and which indeed, if it were not so, your disputes with
> the Governor would prevent your performing any longer with advantage. I
> have therefore been under the necessity of appointing Mr. Wylde to be Judge-
> Advocate of New South Wales. . . .[38]

Jeffery Bent also received a letter announcing that he had been removed
from office, Bathurst addressing him thus:

... I was little prepared to anticipate such a commencement of your judicial labours. It is not necessary that I should enter into the question, on which your difference with Governor Macquarie appears to have originated; for whether convicts be or be not authorized to practise is a question of little importance, when compared with the consequences arising out of its agitation, the closing of the Supreme Court of the Colony for at least twelve months. With every disposition to make allowance for your feelings in resisting the introduction of such persons into your Court, I cannot find any apology for your refusal to accede to the qualified admission, recommended by Governor Macquarie. You could not have been ignorant that the persons in question had before been admitted to conduct causes before the Judge Advocate, as agents for parties, and the same reasons, which induced him to overlook the deficiency of their qualifications for such an office, ought to have equally operated upon you, at least until you received instructions from home. You ought moreover to have considered that there being, from the unfortunate detention of Mr. Garling, only one regular attorney in the Colony to whom, if your regulation took immediate effect, cases could be confided, one party in every suit must be reduced to the alternative of conducting his cause in person, or entrusting it to his adversary's solicitor. But you ought above all never to have forgotten that the evil of a suspension of justice ... was one of too serious a nature to admit of any justification. It is to this measure above all that the disapprobation of His Majesty's Government is directed. . . .[39]

And Mr Jeffery Bent, also, was told that he might leave the Colony at his convenience.

VII

Macquarie regarded Bathurst's letter to himself as "conveying the delightful tidings of the Prince Regent's entire approbation of every part of the line of conduct pursued by me". It included the following passages:

After the transactions which have taken place and the communications which have passed between yourself and the Messrs. Bent, it was impossible for His Royal Highness to indulge the hope of ensuring to the Colony in future your joint cordial co-operation. Under these circumstances, His Royal Highness had no hesitation in recalling these gentlemen. . . . With respect to your own conduct on this occasion, His Royal Highness has every reason to be satisfied, and with no part of it more particularly than with your forbearance to exercise in the case of Messrs. Bent the power, with which you are vested, of immediately suspending in extreme cases the officers under your command. I cannot, indeed, avoid this opportunity of approving your discretion in not inflicting upon the Colony the suspension of all judicial proceedings, on account of any real or supposed misconduct on the part of the judges, and I derive much satisfaction from the additional assurance which this conduct has given me of your disposition, even under circumstances of a most irritating nature, to prefer the public service to your own private convenience.[40]

Of course, the Minister did not know the full measure of the pressure which had been put upon the Governor's temper—for the Bents were only one discordant element among many. His Lordship continued:

I deem it unnecessary to enter at length into the cause in dispute between yourself and Messrs. Bent. It is not against the opinions entertained by them, but against the manner in which they were brought forward and acted upon, that the displeasure of His Royal Highness is directed. It was certainly competent to the Judge Advocate to express any legal doubts which he might entertain as to the propriety of the new Port Regulations; feeling those doubts, it was his duty to make them known to you, but it was equally his duty to have lent his assistance in rendering the regulations finally determined on by you, as free from objection as possible. The remonstrances of Mr. J. Hart Bent against the employment of convicts in the confidential situation of attornies was equally proper, nor am I disposed to sanction their employment in the Colony under any other circumstances than those which existed at the time, namely there being but one other attorney in the Colony. Both gentlemen had clearly a right to protest against any act of yours which they conceived as illegal or improper, and to transmit that protest to His Majesty's Government; but they were not authorized on the ground of a difference of opinion, either to withhold from you the legal assistance which you required, or to interrupt the course of judicial proceedings.

VIII

Bathurst called attention to the importance of assimilating all regulations dealing with trade, which the local government might make, to the enactments of British statutes. Deviations from these he wrote, "must derive their justification from the necessity of the case, from their expediency with a view to the security of the convicts, or the maintenance of public tranquillity". The internal government of the Colony "must equally be guided by the English laws modified by the usages which have always subsisted there". He could not "perceive the necessity of applying to the present state of the Colony any more restrictive measures of police than those which were adopted in its infancy". He added, "You will therefore regulate your future conduct as far as possible on this principle."[41]

It had been the fashion of writers on the period, perpetuating the libels concocted by the Governor's contemporary enemies, to read these sentences as a stern rebuke to Macquarie for his conduct towards the Bents and for the behaviour which supposedly justified their rebellion against him. Bathurst's expressions of view when read in conjunction with Macquarie's earlier dispatch on which they form a commentary negative this interpretation.[42]

Bathurst's essay was clearly intended to traverse Macquarie's tentative view of his powers, sometimes repeating his actual phrases in process of doing so; also to illuminate the details of Colonial Office policy and to define the limits within which the use of viceregal legislative authority should be confined.

The correspondence dealing with the Bent affair is very important since it goes far to prove that any autocracy of which Macquarie can be held guilty was the consequence of his instructions and position, and pressed upon him by his superiors.

Macquarie's requests for the establishment of civil law, and his preference for being described as "L. Macquarie, Esquire", instead of "Major-General Macquarie", show, in fact, that he himself was inclined to lean toward civilian methods of administration. His eagerness to establish a bank and other commercial institutions, and to free external trade from the bonds imposed upon it in the interest of the British manufacturer and the East India Company, point in the same direction.

Bent's personal feelings regarding convicted solicitors might have been pardoned in him as a man and as a newcomer to the Colony. Even Macquarie had at first felt distaste for associating with the convict classes.

But how different the Governor's attitude from that of his judge! Macquarie wrote later, explaining his attitude, that "in fulfilment of my duty I must lay aside personal feelings"; for, said he, "If we are so delicate in our moral sentiments as to be unapproachable to the general mass of the population of this Colony . . . it will be difficult, if not impossible, to form a just estimate of the merits or claims which all alike have upon us."[43]

In a judge, Bent's subordination of his sense of duty to his personal inclinations was inexcusable in the circumstances. His duty obviously was to keep the fountain of justice flowing, and to place the interests of litigants and the provision of speedy redresses for those legally aggrieved before and above all other considerations; also, to remember the status of precedent, which has played so great a part in the development of British legal machinery and practice.

There need have been no complications at all in the matter. Macquarie often had adapted himself to more distasteful situations, as when he continued the system of using spirits as currency rather than interfere with the normal tenor of economic life and the tranquillity of the Colony—tranquillity being with him and the Home Government a paramount consideration.

Wylde, the politic Judge-Advocate who succeeded Bent, a man of much greater standing than either of the Bents at the English Bar, found no difficulty in adjusting himself to necessities, without quarrelling with Macquarie. To the latter, he had been told at the Colonial Office, "full instructions" on convict advocate policy had already been sent. In the interest of litigants, he admitted former convicts to the courts to complete suits and other business which they had begun, in spite of the fact that by the time of his arrival there were two free and unconvicted solicitors in the Colony. After their business was completed, he in general ruled against emancipist "lawyers" or "agents" appearing, but sometimes exercised his judgment in their favour in particular cases. In this course of action Macquarie, whom he consulted, concurred.[44]

IX

The Colony had not done with Mr Jeffery Bent yet by a long way. But when Macquarie continued the story of the nice young man's evil doings, Lord Bathurst merely remarked that he trusted the characters and qualifications of Messrs Wylde and Barron Field, the new judges, would be a sufficient security against a recurrence of the unpleasant and irritating transactions which had arisen out of the conduct of Mr Jeffery Bent. As for that gentleman, if he forbore to enter into the details with respect to him which formed so large a portion of the Governor's correspondence for the year 1817, "it is from a disposition to avoid recurring to a series of transactions, so little creditable to Mr. Bent, and now that he was removed from the Colony, so undeserving of further notice".[45]

Presently, when Parliament was becoming too closely interested in New South Wales for the comfort of a much overworked minister, when some of the fire had died out of the judicial rebel, Lord Bathurst sent Mr Bent to the West Indies. Thirty-five years after his escapades in the antipodes, he died, still administering barbarous justice to the benighted natives of British Guiana. There again he had fallen foul of a Governor, at a cost to himself of three years' suspension from office and £3000 in salary.[46]

Delectable havens for a nice young man with influence in high places were British Guiana and the other West Indian Stations in which the sands of Mr Justice Bent's life ran out. A judge there might inhibit the natives' eloquence by boring cheeks with a hot iron, and yet not outrage the law.

The level-headed Judge-Advocate Wylde, arriving in 1816, saw the end of the judicial fray in New South Wales, and summed it up: "With regard also to the Messrs Bent, I cannot but state my belief that the Governor has acted towards them altogether with a great generosity, consideration and forbearance."[47]

Mr Jeffery Bent's view was that his "perseverance, in not abandoning what was right in principle and right in law, has been exclusively punished, while the obstinacy of Governor Macquarie and his creatures, who were confessedly in the wrong, and to whom alone ought to be imputed the consequence of the dispute, has been scarcely, if at all, reprimanded, and has never been visited with the severity shewn to me".[48]

And he chided the Colonial Office that "if the Colony, as you have stated, is considered a mere penitentiary, I should have had it explicitly stated to me that I was going to a condemned spot, and must reduce myself to the level and practices and an association with those transported there".[49]

Macquarie's private contemporary view is on record:

Macquarie to Charles Macquarie

These two illiberal men wish to exclude them [the petitioners], and I wish them to be admitted. On this point, therefore we are at issue, and the business is referred home to the decision of His Majesty's Ministers. In the meantime the Courts of Civil Judicature are suspended and no law proceedings can go on, owing to the pride, arrogance, and illiberality of these two brothers, who have made a most ungrateful return to me for all the kindness and favours I have heaped upon them. I should not mind the mere objection to allowing men who had been convicts officiating in the Courts as attorneys, but these two upstart fellows of judges wish to exclude all persons of this description from all places of trust and consequence, as well as from society altogether. As I have however been all along the patron and champion of all meritorious persons who have been convicts, I cannot now desert them, and I am resolved to support their cause both at home and abroad. The subject will probably be laid before Parliament by Ministry, and if so I am sure of a complete victory. Perhaps, however this question may possibly be given against me, and if so you will see us in Mull eighteen months sooner than we intended being there. You will therefore lose not a moment in commencing to plant every hill or nob in Gruline where you think trees will grow at all.[50]

His future life might have been easier had the brothers succeeded in their objective.

Some time later Mr Justice Field, whose views had been as firm as his predecessor's on the subject of convict attorneys, was compelled by circumstances to empower Crossley, "one of the most obnoxious" of the convict applicants for the right to practise, to carry on the causes entrusted to him in the days of Mr Bent.

CHAPTER XXII

Holy War at Parramatta

I

ONE enemy of the Governor whom the example of the brothers Bent encouraged to hostile action was the Reverend Samuel Marsden, the Principal Chaplain.

He was a dour, uncouth Yorkshire apostle who played the part of an old fashioned squire-in-orders at Parramatta. In his past he had been an apprentice blacksmith. His roaring protestations of piety had impressed his simple neighbours and they had sent him to Magdalene College, Cambridge. Fate and the influence of William Wilberforce had transferred him, before he had taken a degree, to shine as a "beacon for the godly" in "Satan's Kingdom" amid the "depravity and vice" of Port Jackson.[1]

During his first Sabbath in Sydney in March 1794 he saw several persons at work as he went along, and warned them of the evils of Sabbath-breaking. "His mind was deeply affected with the wickedness he beheld going on"; and he spoke words from the sixth chapter of Revelations, "Behold the great day of wrath is come, and who shall be able to stand."[2]

He momentarily longed to retire from such scenes of "ungodliness and wrong".

In England, largely on the basis of his own narratives, he had become material for the legend of a toiling saint, sacrificing himself in a cesspit of iniquity; one who had "entered the Colony when it was in a state of nature and had been obliged to plant and sow or starve".[3] He was loud in his protestations that he and his colleague had not "taken to the axe, the spade and the hoe from inclination", though thinking it "no disgrace to labour". He cried out, "St Paul's own hands ministered to his wants in a cultivated nation; and our hands ministered to our wants in an uncultivated one. If this is cast upon me as a shame and a reproach I cheerfully bear it . . ."[4]

Impartial observers who enjoyed a near view of Mr Marsden's sufferings did not agree that his labours were nearly so onerous, or his anguish at the sight of evil around him so deep, as his letters to friends in England persistently suggested.

Even only four years after his arrival he was one of the most prosperous men in the Colony and could write in a moment of vainglory, "My goats and sheep, my cows and horses, continue to increase with rapidity . . . My servants the convicts are in number twenty-six."[5] Monsieur Péron, a visiting Frenchman, was entranced by the state kept up by the Chaplain, and by his opulent equipage.

When Macquarie reached Port Jackson, Marsden held 2855 acres of land and, next to John M'Arthur, was the largest owner of stock in New South Wales.[6] He earned the Colony's third highest official salary and gloated to his personal friends of his bulls "fit for any nobleman", of his mare, "the best for the road we ever had in this country", of his English cow, bought from the officers of the 73rd Regiment for £40, of his English grasses, and of the Spanish rams which King George had given him when he had visited his sovereign garbed in cloth made from his own wool, the pioneer clip sent to England on the *Admiral Gambier*, of which he accurately prophesied,[7] "This will be the beginning of the commerce of this new world."[8]

As a prophet of the fleece he ranked as early as, though not as high as, John M'Arthur. He had clear vision. He "expected to see immense national wealth spring from the great service of commerce". The ant, he wrote

> though it is a small creature, yet we see their numbers uniting together raising large hillocks, particularly here. The bee can carry but a little honey, but in time the hive is filled. When I consider that we have not much less than 50,000 sheep in the settlement, and that these 50,000 sheep will produce while I sleep or wake as many fleeces of wool, it is a national object to attend to them. . . . The man who introduced the potatoe into Ireland and England merited more from those nations than any general who may have slain thousands of their enemies.[9]

Innocent low-church zealots in London, however, agreed that Mr Marsden suffered in a situation which was "disgusting and painful", and that he was a "bright light in a brothel of felons".[10] Assertions that he was one of those clergy who would "sell a bottle of spirits or oblige some of those very persons to whom they have been preaching the virtues of temperance" merely filled them with indignant disbelief.[11]

Marsden had called on Macquarie in London in 1808, when asked to read over the Colony's papers in conjunction with Jeffery Bent. He had been received on a friendly and confidential footing, and "so far as I know," he wrote, "with real cordiality".[12]

He had returned to New South Wales from his visit to Britain, made almost entirely in the interests of his own commercial affairs, on 27 February 1810, and the Governor later had granted his request that he be allowed to retire to Parramatta, which was nearer to his farm at Mamre, near the modern St Mary's, than Sydney.

He felt sorely displeased from the first at Macquarie's appointment as Governor. He believed that the Colony would "never rise to a state of independence until a civil governor is sent out". He wrote that "a naval gentleman is partial to a ship; a military one to a grand barrack or parade; while neither have any relish for the labour and produce of the field; for this reason they are not proper for the government of a Colony which is to depend on agriculture".[13]

When it came to the test, however, it might be surmised that Macquarie's knowledge of the land and his personal attention to the technique of the Colony's agriculture proved to be a main grievance with Mr Marsden.

He had occupied a position of influence as "principal adviser" to naval Governors sent to Coventry by their officers and civil servants, and had been consulted by them on every important occasion, and particularly about agricultural matters. Macquarie, a farmer who loved the land, an administrator trained under one of the most experienced governors in the Empire and supported by a shrewd and capable secretary, had no need of advice. He himself came to believe that it was from this fact that much of the Holy Man's choler arose.

Marsden's antagonism to the Governor showed itself when he found himself appointed with the emancipist magistrates, Simeon Lord and Andrew Thompson, to manage the new turnpike road from Sydney to Parramatta. "From that day the wound never healed."[14]

He retired to his farms professing himself "happy to be free of politics" and content to live a quiet life and gratify his inclinations. This course, he trusted, would injure no person.[15] Diligently he used his extensive convict labour to fence a further hundred acres of his land.

The Governor later remembered his Principal Chaplain, during the early period of his rule, as the most gay and cheerful person he had at first met in the Colony. He had received him at Government House, he declared, "with that open hospitality which bespoke a disposition to consider him as rather a part of his own family than as a distant visitor". He had made him a magistrate and had given him considerable grants of land, "whereby he was enabled to become posessed of several large flocks of sheep, perhaps not less extensive than those of any person in the Colony".[16]

Even now, one might have imagined for a time that Marsden's rancour was ephemeral. At the end of 1810 he wrote to Governor King's widow that she would learn from the public papers how gay they had become in New South Wales. "It is not like the same place it was when you were amongst us."[17]

In June 1813 he wrote of the wonderful change that had taken place in the moral situation of the Colony, remarking that the Governor was very attentive to the Sabbath Day; that his superior was a very moral man; that a good understanding had existed between them for some time past; that the Governor "very readily meets all my wishes with respect to the good order and moral improvement of the inhabitants".

His daughter, Ann, described Macquarie at that time as "a great friend to the Gospel". She wrote, "Tho not pious, yet he is what the world calls a moral man, which is much more than any of his predecessors; he has also made great improvements in the Colony particularly at Sydney".[18]

II

In February 1814 there was open sacerdotal rebellion at Parramatta. The vicar refused to read from the pulpit a secular order eulogizing one Gilber-thorpe,[19] "the first to come forward in the present season of scarcity with the lowest and most reasonable tender to supply Government with all the wheat and maize he could spare"; in fact, the only settler who delivered into store the complete quantity for which he had tendered at the stipulated rate, although grain had advanced considerably in price since he had sent in his original tender.

Publication of orders in church assured that a majority of the inhabitants would hear them, which was all to the good from a magistrate's point of view. Mr Marsden hitherto had never resisted or raised the slightest objection. He now even read this particular order for the first time.[20] But meditation seemed to assure him that such a proceeding was "irregular and improper".[21] Mr Marsden was a farmer, who, unlike Mr Gilberthorpe, was *not* "entitled", as the order put it, "to the Governor's present commendation and an assurance that such meritorious conduct should not go unrewarded". And he had his feelings, as had many of his congregation. He refused to read the Governor's order a second time.

Macquarie cautioned him to beware of "resisting my commands in this way for the future as he shall answer for it to his peril"; but he directed him, should he feel any real conscientious objections, to appeal to the Archbishop of Canterbury, though he considered the objections raised by his disobedient churchman "illfounded and arising from illiberal sentiments and bigotted principles, which on all occasions pervade and strongly mark his conduct on political and religious subjects". The Archbishop remarked, "The practice of reading civil orders in church is established at home. . . . I don't see how he can object." But he did not see anything derogatory in Mr Marsden's display of conscience.[22]

Next there arose the matter of the Public Library. Mr Marsden while he had been in London had appealed publicly for the makings of "a lending library for the general benefit of the inhabitants of New South Wales".[23] He said that in the Colony books of any kind were very scarce and that it was "highly desirable that a public library should be founded . . . containing books suited to the poor settlers employed in agriculture, the soldiers and the convicts".[24] He appealed for books on history and morals, divinity, agriculture in all its branches, mineralogy and practical mechanics, through the use of which "the vicious and the wicked . . . should be led to serious thoughtfulness and a reformation of life by a perusal of good precepts and examples". "Donations for the above institution", his notice said, "in small tracts, books or money will be thankfully received by the Reverend S. Marsden, Chaplain to the Colony, at Mr William Wilson's, No. 150, Fenchurch Street, London."

Mr Joseph Butterworth and several friends subscribed,[25] and a goodly number of books chosen by the visiting chaplain were secured. The Bible Society furnished Bibles and Testaments in tolerable quantity. The list of four hundred and fifty-five volumes included an *Encyclopaedia Britannica*, six sermons on original sin, twelve sermons on the torments of hell, a hundred each of several tracts for unhappy women, drunkards, swearers and Sabbath-breakers; another long and comprehensive list of various sermons and a few works of a general nature. In fact, it was just such a public library as might assist a reverend public-of-one who needed to preach the wrath of God over a period of years. It was also appropriate for a "public" who found it vital to know how to deal with the ailments of Spanish rams and to have some tracts to donate to those who were given to that species of light reading.[26]

Though he had collected it for the "inhabitants of the Colony", Mr Marsden housed it "at the back of his house" at Parramatta, fifteen miles from the main centre of population.[27] There were people who knew it existed, but "very few individuals felt the benefit of it". Mr Eyre, the schoolmaster, and Mr Pasco Crook, the missionary, went thither and borrowed some tracts and Whitfield's sermons, and then interviewed the pious librarian, whom they discovered, with a naval surgeon in attendance, "in an old ragged coat . . . actively engaged in trimming and anointing his sheep."[28]

By September 1813 Mr Butterworth, the chief donor of books, had become restless. He wrote from Dublin to Mr Bowden, a schoolmaster newly arrived in Parramatta, that he was very sorry the books were not in action. "My respects to Mr Marsden and ask whether he has yet been able to organise a plan for a circulating library, that I may induce my friends to send out more books if necessary."[29]

Then some person who signed himself "A Free Settler" wrote a letter to the Sydney Gazette.[30] He had "lately arrived", he said, and had "learned with much satisfaction that a good library . . . had been established for the use and benefit of the public, and for the more easy instruction of the rising generation".

He mentioned the "various liberal donations of books made by pious and charitable persons for this express purpose" and characterized his information as "so unquestionable, that I feel it a duty to the public to call upon you, or any of the readers of the Sydney Gazette who may be acquainted with the circumstances of this to me mysterious case, to state them with equal publicity", in order that friends at home who might be coming to the Colony should be warned to bring their own books; for he now knew that no library ever had existed here.

"Another Free Settler"[31] presumed to reply to "Free Settler" and to mention Mr Marsden's name and the fact that he probably had not advertised the library because "so notorious a circumstance as the collection of books in England" did not need advertising. The right of possession in trust, he wrote, naturally belonged to him to whom the books were confided by the English public; to him, in fact, who had been at the pains and trouble of making so many appeals to the philanthropy of the donors.

"Free Settler" answered that Mr Marsden should have given the fullest publicity to the matter,[32] called a public meeting to express the thanks of the inhabitants to the donors, and established the library in Sydney where the population was sixfold that of Parramatta.

Mr Marsden himself now entered the fray. There was "no public library", he wrote to the Gazette, nor ever had been; nor were there any funds to support one. He himself while in England had collected from his friends a few books on religion and agriculture to "lend to settlers, soldiers and prisoners at my discretion; but I am not accountable to the writer of the last letter or to the public, for the distribution of these books, though they have not been withheld from any one that has applied for them".[33]

Certain school-books which he had disposed of were his "*sole private property* and sent out by Mr Murray, that I might have the satisfaction of furnishing the rising generation with means of instruction at a moderate expence". Not half the original cost of £200 had been repaid him.

"Free Settler" responded in sarcastic vein. Mr Marsden indited a memorial to the Governor, asking that the editor of the *Gazette* be forced to disclose the name of the author of the letters.[34]

He "humbly conceived that it was not intended that the Sydney *Gazette* which is published by Authority should be used as a vehicle thro which the envious and malicious should assassinate the reputation of any of His Majesty's subjects, and more especially those who have arduous and painful duties to perform in this settlement".[35]

He considered his public situation, he declared, of infinite importance. The eternal happiness of thousands was committed to his care. And, he continued:

> Whosoever holds up the clergy and magistrates to public contempt stabs at the very vitals of that Government which supports and protects him. The Throne and Altar generally fall together. The smallest act that tends to lessen the respect due to the sacred situation of the clergy and that of the magistrates tends in a tenfold degree to increase the idleness and insubordination of the lower class and to clog the wheels of Government. It is well known that many a valuable crop of grain has been totally consumed in this Colony by a single spark from a pipe.[36]

Macquarie replied that the series of letters certainly did "not appear to me of that offensive personal nature which you consider them else I should have made the Editor answerable for their insertion". He pointed out that, if libelled, the irate clergyman could ask the courts for redress.

"For other motives than those of justice", he wrote, " it does not appear reasonable to require a surrender of the author's name. And I would not feel myself acting with that impartiality which my situation demands, and my own conscience dictates, were I to require an exposure in a case where criminality does not attach *in my view* of the publications in question."[37]

Certain "unpleasant words arose". Mr Marsden accused the Governor's Secretary of being the author of the attack, but his charge was never proved.

And the missionaries decided to form a circulating library of their own in Sydney, to which they hoped Mr Marsden might present a few of the books which he had "so long concealed within the walls of his own library, although designed for public benefit". Eventually a reading-room was opened in Sydney in August 1820.[38]

III

Anon, there was issued, to fan the flame of the Chaplain's anger, the Governor's general order of 10 September 1814. Magistrates henceforward must muster convicts, save stockmen and those specially exempted, every Sunday morning.[39] The mustered, "to the true intent of good order", must undergo inspection by the district constable and—punctual, clean, decent, and sober—proceed to the nearest church. If there were no church, they might be dismissed after roll-call and questioning. This was a measure against Sabbath Day violence and robbery.

To avoid, as much as possible, "the necessity for resorting to corporal punishment", the Governor established limited jail gangs of major offenders in the settlements of the interior, of which the uniform was to be a parti-coloured dress, black on one side, white on the other. Magistrates were to transmit to him, through the office of the secretary, lists of fines and punishments of every description inflicted by them within their districts.

His order added:

> . . . and the Governor recommends in the strongest manner to the Magistrates, to inflict corporal punishment as seldom as possible; but to substitute in its stead, confinement in the stocks for petty crimes, and either solitary confinement, or hard labour in the gaol gangs, according to their judgment of the degrees of offence; still keeping in view the general conduct and character of the delinquents.[40]

Moreover, he forbade any magistrate sitting alone to inflict more than fifty lashes.[41] The order was to be read in church on two Sundays.

Governor and preacher were soon at loggerheads over the decree, which was issued at a moment when the Colony was unusually restless. The Colonial Office was trying to cut off civil servants' family rations. It saw "no reason for continuing them in the present state of the Colony". The drought continued. The wheatfields, including those of magistrates, were in "a state of universal languor", and much frequented by the grub and the caterpillar. The half-yearly sales at Parramatta were thinly attended and cattle brought poor prices. The Government ration of grain was ordered to be one-third maize henceforth. The *Broxbornebury* had come in, bringing Mr Jeffery Bent, the Reverend Mr Vale, Sir John Jamison, and other strange characters.[42]

The Charter of Justice[43] was read. The *Somersetshire*, only five months, five days out from London, brought the glorious news that "the name of Buonaparte was already expunged from the list of European potentates though his life was spared".

Nightingall had become a near neighbour, having taken Bali. Trincomalee had become a great British naval depot. Russia and France had offered the King 100,000 men to "assist in the reduction of the American continent".

The Parramattans, celebrating these distant events and "wishing to partake of the true old English fare", roasted an ox whole, "the first specimen we have had of the noble animal being so dressed".

Mrs Marsden had a serious stroke. Mr Marsden was in an exceedingly bad temper at the moment when news of the Governor's edict against excessive flogging reached him. He was indignant at the limitations placed upon him.

To him, fifty lashes was nothing. He knew one bold rogue, he declared, who, when that quantity each was meted out to him and five associates, turned with the greatest contempt and, with a horrid oath, sneered at the "retail" nature of the punishments and suggested that one of the party "should take the lot".[44]

He was averse, also, to Sunday musters of convicts. Among all the magistrates in the Colony he was alone at that time in deprecating this salutary measure. His resistance to the order was curious, since the scheme would have secured him a congregation of evil men who otherwise would have been indulging in fleshly vices.

And it did not placate him that the Governor mentioned the active exertions of himself and Mr Cox, which had so much discouraged the plunderers of Government cattle.[45]

His fury at the new order mounted as fresh issues rose to torment his mind and tease his fragile patience.

IV

Parramatta was full of missionaries and former missionaries, many of them waxing fat from barter. They had a simple desire to meet together in their own houses and privately take Communion in their own way. Mr Marsden told one of them that "the Lord's Supper was administered three times a year in church which was often enough".[46] He had in person led Mr Crook, one of the missionaries, before the Lieutenant-Governor for daring to administer the Sacrament. Mr Crook assured him that he was licensed under the Toleration Act; Mr Marsden said that the Act was "not in force in this country".[47]

Then, apparently feeling the pressure of competition, the reverend gentleman himself had begun to resort to Methodistical practices.

Early in 1814 he "imported, or received from a missionary", Dr Goode's version of the Psalms. Without communicating with His Excellency, he caused them to be sung in his churches to the exclusion of those attached by authority to the Bible and Book of Common Prayer.[48]

This was, to the local representative of His Majesty, "a very unwarrantable violation of the service of the Established Church, and one which would probably lead to still further and greater innovations on its sacred ceremonies".[49]

The Governor ordered that Dr Goode and all his works be banished till "reference could be made to the Supreme Authority of the Church and the commands of the Prince Regent communicated".

Macquarie to Bathurst

My apprehension of the consequences, which might attend the submitting to, or in any degree sanctioning, changes of this kind, are not a little heightened by the consideration that Mr. Marsden and some of the assistant chaplains are originally of low rank, and not qualified by liberal educations *in the usual way* for the sacred functions entrusted to them, and are also much tinctured by Methodistical and other sectarian principles, which dispose them to a hasty adoption of new systems or at least of *new forms*, to the exclusion of the old Establishment of the Church of England.[50]

If latitude were given, he was fully convinced that "various sectaries would spring up in this young and unschooled Colony, much to the injury of that established uniformity of worship" which he conceived it to be of the utmost importance to the peace and harmony of the Colony to preserve inviolate.[51]

Bathurst replied that His Royal Highness the Prince Regent gave the Governor's action his "entire approbation" and desired that "where a similar innovation may be proposed, you would enforce a strict adherence to those forms and services which are prescribed by the competent Authority".[52] But, again, in 1816 Macquarie was forced to warn the parson about his musical irregularities.

The Governor, in his private life, was not an intolerant man in religion; in his official life, little so.

He had, actually, in ordering the affairs of the South Sea Islands, decreed that shipmasters should leave the natives of the islands to the "free uninterrupted and undisturbed enjoyment of their religious ceremonies, rights and observances".[53]

Toward missionaries as a class he was not severe. He helped them to secure pensions. He told them that they might worship as they liked in their own homes, but the conduct in public of the services of the Established Church seemed to him to be his official concern.[54]

The missionaries of Eimeo in 1812 went out of their way to notice "that His Excellency the Governor, treated Brother Nott while in the Colony, with much kindness and respect, and manifested himself to be a real friend of the Mission. He sent us by Brother Nott, a very kind letter".[55]

To the tall and awkward young Wesleyan missionary, Mr Leigh, who came to the Colony without the necessary passport of a letter of introduction, he said, "It is of no importance what we may be called, if we are sincere in our profession. I believe your intentions are good, and therefore you may expect from me every encouragement you desire, and I wish you the same success in your mission as you wish for yourself."[56]

Then he gave Mr Leigh advice which that earnest young man felt that he "could not expect from any person less than a father".

Mr Leigh[57] could report that "a poor man walked fourteen miles to converse with me about salvation"; and his efforts produced the "pleasing sight of people flocking to the house of prayer, some with chairs and some with stools on their shoulders". Obviously, he was a very different type of apostle from Mr Marsden, and could expect far different official treatment from that accorded the latter, who thundered forth in his funeral oration on Mr Ellis Bent:

Nay, the very prayers of the wicked are an abomination unto him [God]. We may see the divine displeasure against sin wherever we turn our eyes. This truth is so evident it needs no confirmation.

What lamentable depravity pervades every part of society. There is no sin, however serious wh. is not practised without remorse amongst us. Lying and perjury and theft, and whoredom, and blasphemy and drunkenness are daily committed amongst us . . . The effects of the divine displeasure is felt by almost every individual in this Colony. And some are pining and languishing and wasting away . . . an awful period . . . it disarms death of its terrors.[58]

V

One of Macquarie's most engaging characteristics was his affection for the Australian aborigines.[59]

He became their champion from the moment he set eyes on some of them. And his anxiety to Christianize and civilize them soon brought him into conflict again with Marsden, who believed that "Commerce promotes industry—industry civilisation and civilisation opens up the way for the Gospel".[60]

The lu-luing denizen of the Nepean fastnesses had no commerce, no industry but goanna and wallaby catching.

Mr Marsden therefore answered at all times, when approached on the subject, that it was impracticable to civilize these natives, that they were little above the rank of beasts of the field and that all attempts to ameliorate their condition and improve their minds would be totally useless.[61]

Therefore he was not present to say grace at the Governor's bivouacs. He did not hand out the rewarding moral works at the prize distributions of the Native Institution which the Governor founded at the end of 1814, and which was the pride of the viceregal heart.

Instead, the eyes of Parramatta's lusty "Christian Mahomet" were cast afar upon the Maoris. *They* were far removed from the beasts. They had the materials of commerce—spars for the Navy, flax and industry which might be combined to weave a carpet with which to clothe the floor of the Kingdom of God. They had greenstone and perhaps gold.

They were men of reason and dignity who erected crosses on which to hang their thieves. With them the instrument for their conversion "sat down and conversed as a man with his friend and then laid down amongst them and slept in safety", even though he had disquieting thoughts about the *Boyd* massacre.[62]

Gentler shepherds the Maoris were apt to regard objectively as purely comestible.

Marsden to Hardcastle

So, commerce must be built for a start: None of these objects can be accomplished without a vessel. Myself and friends would willingly meet your efforts should anything of this nature be determined on. We would do it independent of our friends in Europe if it was in our power, but it is not . . . I would answer for myself and friends in this Colony to the amount of £1800 sterling and take a share in the vessel to that amount . . . I think the sale of the cargo would in a short period indemnify all concerned for any money they may advance. . . . [The vessel sent out] must be owned in some part by some persons here or held under such conditions as the proprietors think *proper.*[63]

Mr Marsden bought the *Active*, "which came to more than I could well command", though by 1816 he had "hopes that I shall be able to call the vessel my own, by paying the remainder of the money I was compelled to borrow". He announced, "I intend her to fly over these seas like the dove with the olive branch to carry the glad tidings of salvation to these poor heathen"—who, he believed, were "without hope and without God". On 28 November 1814 he sailed on an enterprise which, whatever his ethics and motives, was the first real step towards the colonizing of New Zealand.[64]

As the Church of England then would have refused to allow Mr Marsden to sing, "God moves in a mysterious way His wonders to perform"; and He has a curious habit of diverting the actions of vessels of wrath toward the most salutary ends.

Macquarie received the pious emissary on his return in friendly manner. He sent home and commended his report, which was indeed highly commendable, if somewhat imaginative in such of its implications as were more personal to Mr Marsden's own achievement and standing with the Maoris.

All Marsden's satisfaction at this praise was ruined by the fact that the Governor favoured a purely secular group of traders,[65] among whom the appearance of Mr Simeon Lord was an especial outrage, in its effort to form a New Zealand Company. This cut squarely across his plans. For he had taken it complacently for granted that if the Maoris were in need of iron, it would be provided by the missionary societies or by his more godly and favoured friends, selected by himself.[66]

From that time onward, Marsden left his parish to the tender mercies of the Devil and the missionaries and whenever the *Active* was in port (as his daughter reported) was "almost always in Sydney preparing things to send to New Zealand or else employed with the New Zealanders who are at our house".[67]

He did not "get so much encouragement from the *great folk* as he hoped he should".[68] Nevertheless, the Governor appointed his chosen agent as New Zealand's first justice of the peace—a reverend gentleman who allegedly indulged in a graduate course in practical Maori pornography, to the great scandal of the missionary world.

And the *Active* went forth to the Bay of Islands, to Fiji, to Otaheite, loaded down with goods, returning with the products of her barter; carrying missionaries, sometimes simple and godly, sometimes not.

The vessel became, indeed, a transport of Mr Marsden's "soldiers of God", who presently in still further isles than New Zealand "landed again in Satan's dark dominions".[69]

They "surrounded Pomare's city, blew their ram's horns, and the walls of the Otaheitan Jericho fell down".[70]

But the Australian aborigines on Mr Marsden's doorstep remained among the sons of darkness, their ways unlighted by their official pastor, who ignored them until a sterner policy was adopted towards them.

VI

By June 1815, in the midst of the dispute with the judges, the war between Church and State was reaching a crisis. Macquarie, however, still treated his senior religious officer with courtesy and consideration, even though he might reprove him.

He maintained him in his offices. He lavishly renovated his old parsonage and prepared to build him a new one. Parrramatta church he had earlier repaired. He would soon add its Reculvers steeples.[71]

He had officially praised Marsden's magisterial activity against footpads and cattle-thieves before September 1814, and had publicly given him a lavish reward—a large grant of land.

In his new towns almost the Governor's first thought was for an ample church, a commodious parsonage. He and Mr Marsden and Mr Cartwright had gone together in 1812 to a spot in George Street in Sydney next the burying ground on the southern limit of the town, and, opposite where the first milestone later stood, they chose a plot for a new great church or cathedral—near the site of modern St Andrew's.[72]

Certainly there was no warrant for Mr Marsden to say that he had been "persecuted" in the early period of Macquarie's reign, as he emphatically implied in a letter he wrote in 1821.[73]

Whatever his real excuses, however, the holy man decided to cross swords with the Governor.

The battle which ensued was no mere tussle between a country parson and his viceregal master.

The Governor's adversary had powerful friends. Wilberforce was his patron. The King had received him and given him Spanish rams. The personalities behind the British Government, caring little for his religion, looked upon him as a useful man in an age when their eyes were beginning to turn southward in search of raw materials—wool, flax, dye-stuffs and oils. The powerful missionary societies supported him, and their influence over Bathurst was mesmeric.

Wilberforce, when he heard that differences were arising, wrote to Macquarie in a peacemaking vein. He mentioned his pleasure that the Governor had been able to set his government on foot so quietly. He said that he could not doubt but that Macquarie's system would cause the Colony in a few years to exhibit a degree of improvement which men would now scarcely anticipate.

About Marsden he was soothing:

> I hope you will find my friend Mr. Marsden an able assistant in forwarding your excellent views. He is, I assure you (for I have received-accounts of him *ab ovo*, as I may say, from ye very egg) . . . a man of solid sense, of great good temper tho not refined in his notions and manners, capable of being made eminently useful. I was greatly struck with finding, how greatly he had advanced in the esteem and favour of the Great Men both in Church and State, tho he had never before been accustomed to such high society. If there be any way in which you conceive I can be useful to you during your stay in N.S.W., I beg you will frankly tell me so.[74]

And later, in March 1814, he wrote concerning the emancipist question:

> I am sorry Mr. Marsden differs from us on this subject. He is a very worthy man and has a sound understanding and in general good principles. Still like other men he is liable to error and I have frankly told him, tho he had not mentioned the topic to me for a long time before, that I think his opinions erroneous in this instance, stating however that I thought some guard ought if practicable to be found against the abuse of the principle.
>
> I will take as early an opportunity as I can of pleading the cause of the colony with His Majesty's Minrs. They are always apt to be too pinching, especially in these days of great expenditure.[75]

To Marsden, writing a week later, he made it clear that after the Governor's having recently consulted him "on the important and delicate topic of the admission into society (even occasionally into office), of persons, who, originally, came out as convicts", he had talked the matter over with several friends "whose understanding and principles appeared to render them good counsellors", adding:

> And the result is that we all, without a single exception are of opinion that persons who came out as convicts, should *after giving sufficient proofs of their having amended their ways*, be admissible into office, but then we all agree in conceiving that in order to preserve the principle from abuse and to prevent the practice from becoming injurious instead of being beneficial, some previous recognition of their reformation should precede their return into society.[76]

He concluded:

> P.S. Let me suggest what, however, would I am sure occur to you, that in all your proceedings you should cultivate the Governor's favour, so far as you can . . . as to particulars all must be left to your judgment.

Macquarie had been thinking along the same lines as Wilberforce regarding certificates of reform. He had actually suggested legislation on the subject to Bathurst.[77]

Marsden received his letter from Wilberforce at the moment when the Governor was engaged in his quarrel with the Bent brothers. He saw his opportunity. Mr Jeffery Bent was already his frequent visitor. It is not too much to believe that Marsden it was who supercharged Ellis Bent's discontent, as he fanned that of many another colonist.

There was something still and secret about the face of the crafty clergyman in his earlier and middle years. The flushed covering of that calabash dome of a head betrays ungovernable temper. And however "good his principles", however Christian his intentions, he had much of the ruthlessness of true greatness, if not its constructiveness.

"Worthy man" though he might be, he was not fastidious in his methods when he sought to strike down a mortal enemy.

Sometimes, however, his own internal fires seemed almost too much for their mortal container to hold. In such a condition he wrote, "Had I known the warfare I should have had to maintain in the beginning of the Christian life, I should have chosen strangling or death rather than have entered upon it. However, one contest gets over and another comes, but by-and-by they will all have an end".[78]

CHAPTER XXIII

The New Balbus

I

MR MARSDEN, that "Christian Mahomet of Botany Bay", as Mr J. T. Campbell, the Governor's Secretary, called him, chose his moment for hostile action against Macquarie with care and fought with advantage on his side.[1]

Unwittingly the Governor had done much to strengthen his foe's prestige and power to strike. He had made him a magistrate. He had given his voyage to New Zealand official recognition and praise. He had repaired and extended his church and parsonage. And, only five weeks before Mr Marsden had opened his campaign in the viceregal war, he had granted him a thousand acres of land as a reward for his magisterial activities against cattle-thieves.[2]

Marsden was at the time in high favour in England and was to be even more revered in a year or so when Mr Nicholas, his *fidus Achates* on his recent voyages, and Mr Jeffery Bent's companion in some of his toll-breaking exploits, should have written his book on his antipodean experiences. Mr Grey Bennet, M.P., considered Mr Marsden as "one of those who, praise be to God, are daily reared up amongst us, whose employment of life, is to carry the blessings of the Gospel to distant countries".[3] Dr Good had sent him a copy of his original translation of the Book of Job,[4] Mr Olinthus Gregory a copy of his *Evidences of the Truth of Christian Religion*.[5] He had the ear of Lord Calthorpe and of William Wilberforce.

Marsden knew that one question on which the Governor seriously differed from the Colonial Office and the Parliamentary Select Committee of 1812 was that of women convicts. He knew, too, that nothing would be more likely to excite public sympathy than a heart-rending tale of young girls plunged in vice and woe through the brutal neglect of an administrator.[6]

Macquarie was averse to more women transports coming to the Colony. So some of his remarks might be construed by sensitive religious hearers, even Mr Wilberforce, as a show of heartlessness toward these forlorn sisters. That must be capitalized.

II

Before Macquarie's day female convicts had been "very improperly disposed of", but one of his first resolutions made in the Colony was "to take care to keep [them] separate till they can be properly distributed in such manner

as they may best derive the advantage of industry and good character".
Those not sent at once to approved families went to Parramatta.

There the capable ones were soon indented for by settlers eager for
servants, of whom there was always a dearth. The rest were put to work
in the woollen factory under supervision of the magistrates, Messrs Marsden
and Hannibal M'Arthur.

They had the option of lodging in the town, since there were no barracks
to accommodate all of them. The good-looking ones had a free and hearty
welcome. The less attractive, for a small lodging fee, at least found beds.[7]

But the women with children, the pregnant girls who had fallen victims
to villains on their voyage from England, were unwanted by the outside
world. They had perforce to lodge in the remains of the beautiful factory
which Mr Marsden had had built at official expense in the good old days
—part of it had been burnt down.

Their accommodation consisted of a room eighty feet by twenty feet[8]
without any amenities of household life whatever. The whole place was
"only sufficient to contain about sixty women, whilst there are sometimes
not fewer than two hundred employed there".[9]

It contained the looms and spinning-wheels at which the women worked
by day. There was a fireplace in which the inmates stored their food.

The floor, covered with the filth and grease of a decade, showed wide
cracks between the boards, so that it could not be scrubbed without deluging
the male prisoners, who lived below and were for ever shouting lewd jests
towards the upper story.[10]

At one end were store-rooms for greasy wool and yarn, which filled
the whole place in summer with their almost insupportable smells. The
women dragged odorous pads of fleece from the store-room at night and
slept upon them with their babies and attendant vermin.

Those whose crime was no worse than pregnancy or motherhood shared
this den with the clanking victims of Mr Marsden's reforming measures.
Rarely a week went by that he did not—with or without the help of Mr
Hannibal M'Arthur—send some poor runaway to add horror to this prison
with the jangling of her irons: "Hannah C. and Eleanor H., making use of
infamous language, to be chained together for a month; . . . May M.,
stealing government goods, two months imprisonment in the factory and
to have a log chained to her leg" . . .[11]

It was significant that when Marsden acted he was involved in a plan
to tempt Macquarie into an indiscreet piece of cruelty and injustice. He
sought to have an old convict, William Refraine, recently acquitted on a
criminal charge, sent off to Newcastle, the Colony's equivalent of Devil's
Island. But Campbell, the Governor's Secretary, saw through the plot.
A "base trick", he thought, "one which would have afforded the little
genius of intrigue, the hopefulls of the midnight cabal, the kennel rakers of
slander . . . something to fasten the envenomed teeth of their malice upon".
He referred Mr Marsden to the eighth chapter of St John's Gospel; and
he wrote angrily of his regret that the Principal Chaplain should "step
singly forward and solicit the banishment of a poor, old cripple, struggling

THE REVEREND SAMUEL MARSDEN

From the original portrait by Richard Read the Elder in the possession of the Trustees of the Mitchell Library, Sydney

and tottering through life on a wooden leg, and ill-prepared to meet sudden and unexpected, because unmerited severities from him whose duty it was to administer justice with mercy". Had Mr Marsden's suggestion succeeded, Campbell declared, his associates, "their pens dipped in gall", might have given the Governor's cruel act "an honourable place in the chronicle of grievances". All this must have added heat to Marsden's anger.[12]

III

By way of launching his attack on his ruler, Marsden wrote a memorial to him on the state of crime in Parramatta.[13]

Writing as Principal Chaplain and Resident Magistrate, he informed the Governor that during his twenty years of residence he could not remember a period when so many offences had been committed. Nearly all his time, he averred, was given up to hearing complaints about housebreakings, highway robberies, and other daring crimes, which had increased to an alarming degree.[14]

This he attributed to the fact that convicts employed on public works were scattered all over the town with the free lower orders, and were compelled to steal for their lodgings. The magistrate's feelings, he said, had become imperceptibly interested in the prisoners' behalf, and his mind was greatly perplexed how to act. He knew the law "admitted to no plea for stealing, yet he often could not punish".

Hence the guilty "sought relief on the divine rule of justice, 'Do unto others as ye would that they should do unto you' ". He added, "Thus the guilty pass with impunity, who under other circumstances would meet with that punishment their crimes justly merit."

He pleaded for the erection of barracks to house convicts, well knowing that Macquarie long ago had asked the Colonial Office to permit him to introduce the barrack system.

The kind of "impunity" which evil-doers were enjoying in Parramatta at that time is clear from a reference to the Bench Book.

Out of 243 persons charged in succession before Mr Marsden and a co-magistrate, seven only were released. Among the rest, the Bench divided 11,321 lashes and a couple of centuries in the jail gang, the women's factory or the coal-mines, apart from some small helpings of solitary confinement.[15] Two poor wretches each received one hundred lashes for no worse crimes than "stealing a fowl" and "stealing a leg of pork and insolence".[16]

All Marsden's preliminaries merely led up to the fact that the women convicts had no official barracks to retire to, no means save prostitution to earn the four shillings a week necessary to pay for their lodgings and fire. He suggested that male convicts plundered and murdered to meet the urgent wants of these females. This, he wrote, produced "a condition of affairs destructive to all religion, morality, and good order", which "destroyed at once the most distant hope of any reformation"[17] being produced in either man or woman. He declared that when he was called in the hour

M

of sickness and want to visit these wretches in hospital or in their hovels, his mind was oppressed beyond measure by the sight of their sufferings:

> As their minister, and one who must account ere long at the bar of Divine Justice for my duty to these objects of vice and woe, I see how they live and how they die! and often feel inexpressible anguish of spirit in the moments of their approaching dissolution on my own and their account, and follow them to the grave with awful forebodings, lest I should be found at last to have neglected any part of my public duty as their minister and magistrate, and by so doing, contributed to their eternal ruin.
>
> So powerful are these reflections at times, that I envy the situation of the most menial servant who is free from this solemn and sacred responsibility; namely the care of immortal souls.[18]

He complained that, though he had made representations as early as 1808, "your Excellency is well aware that no provision has yet been made for the female convicts to this very day".

No clergyman, he averred, was ever placed in such a situation as he; and he asked the Governor to say whether, under such circumstances, any man of common feelings, possessed of the least spark of humanity or religion, who was spiritual pastor and magistrate to these people, "could enjoy one happy moment from the beginning to the end of the week".

Marsden had for long shown little interest in the plight of the females. He had not attended at the factory for over five years.

About the time Macquarie had written to Castlereagh of the Female Factory in October 1814, the parson had told his English friends how he was roofing his orphanage—"a noble building".[19]

Within a period during which, he now averred, he had been going through untold anguish for the sufferings of his wards of the factory, he had spent £1400 of his own money and some borrowed funds[20] on purchasing the *Active*, to keep him in touch with the heathen Maoris, to bring cargoes from New Zealand, and to sell trousers, soap, and comestibles to the missionary communities of the Pacific. He might have delayed this project and diverted the funds which he personally applied to it to assuage the agony of the girls of Parramatta and the torments of his bleeding heart.

A letter which he wrote about that time seemed to prove that he had only one real interest. The reverend writer told his friend Mrs Stokes, of Hull, that his mind was so strongly vexed by the wickedness of the people of the Colony, that he was tempted to leave it altogether.

Every time he thought of this course, he related, his wife would dissuade him, saying, "What will New Zealand do? What will the missionaries of Otaheite do?"[21]

No qualm of pity for the homeless mothers and prostitutes for whom he was pleading with the Governor shows in his letter to Mrs Stokes.

It is significant that he was moved to write the memorial, of which a copy was available in London early in the following year, only a few days before the departure of an English mail.

IV

Macquarie seemingly did not measure Marsden's missive at its true value. He acknowledged it, in his usual business-like fashion, the day after he received it, expressing his thanks "for the information and suggestions . . . respecting the immorality and profligate abandoned conduct of the male and female convicts at present employed by Government at Parramatta". He added that he had observed that in the last three years greater crimes and more serious offences had been committed in Parramatta and its vicinity than elsewhere in New South Wales.[22]

He agreed about the need for convict barracks which, he had no doubt, would prevent many robberies and other crimes. He pointed out that he had written "three years ago to His Majesty's Ministers, soliciting their permission to have buildings of this description erected immediately"; but that he had received no answer.[23]

"Though I am as sensible as you can possibly be of the utility and necessity of such buildings," he wrote, "I cannot take upon myself so serious a responsibility as to have these erected, incurring a great expense, without permission from the Ministry."

He recommended a more energetic policing of the district, with regular and more frequent patrols by an increased number of constables.

Marsden kept the subject alive in London with his letters to Wilberforce and to Grey Bennet, who deduced from his correspondent's description that New South Wales was "little better than the deposit of all the vices and crimes which have been, and are, the scourge of the more civilised inhabitants of the Mother Country".[24]

It was not till 22 July 1816 that Bathurst's dispatch arrived advising that Bligh's grant had become available as a site for the Female Factory, but that the building of a barrack for the male convicts must be dependent on the Colony's ability to provide the cost.[25]

And while the poison was sinking into the minds of politicians and zealots at home, all Marsden's memorial signified to Macquarie was that the holy man seemed to have drawn it up "with a view to acquiring a great name for himself, by detracting from the claims and merits of other persons".[26]

He reflected that it was to be lamented that "where so wide a field was open for this Gentleman's exertions, he did not devote his pursuits to the acquisition of popularity by some other more laudable means".

Meanwhile, Ellis Bent had died and Marsden preached his funeral sermon. Mark Antony could have done no better.

He took for his text 2 Chronicles, xxix, 10-11: "Now it is in mine heart to make a covenant with the Lord God of Israel, that his fierce wrath may turn away from us. My sons, be not now negligent: for the Lord hath chosen you to stand before him, to serve him, and that ye should minister unto him, and burn incense."

All enlightened members of the society (in which, as Mr Marsden presently assured them in his sermon,[27] no sin however serious—blasphemy, drunkenness, whoredom, perjury, theft—was not practised) had merely to turn to the Bible and they could not fail to see the allusions.

There was no doubt about the identity of the New South Wales counterpart of the virtuous young Hezekiah who began to reign when he was twenty-five years old, who did that which was right in the sight of the Lord, and who, in his first month upon the throne, opened the doors of the house of the Lord and assembled the priests and the Levites in the east street—Macquarie Street was the most easterly in Sydney. Hezekiah was obviously Ellis Bent.

From Mr Marsden's point of view the rest of the tale was very apt, especially the picture of Hezekiah adjuring his Levites and priests to "carry forth the filthiness out of the holy place"—the filthiness presumably being Messrs Crossley and Eagar. Some of the congregation possibly felt how apposite was the verse in the previous chapter which said, "Ye shall not bring in the captives hither."

All the implications were clear, especially when he mentioned poor Mr Ellis Bent by name and thundered that "God had taken from the Israelites an upright judge".

Another sermon was soon heard. The Colony's Ahaz, Governor Macquarie, paused in his "evil reign" to deliver it in person. Major Antill, the Brigade-Major, and the Reverend Mr Cowper were the only two members of the congregation save Mr Marsden who sat on the penitent stool while the Governor read him a "severe lecture".

According to Mr Marsden, he said that it was "blasphemous to speak too highly of any man".[28] And Marsden told Mrs Stokes that "we have some very profane and wicked men here in power and it is impossible either to conciliate their favour or to avoid the shafts of their hatred".

> I have felt myself aggrieved and I have appealed unto Caesar again and again. Men in power like religion so far as it agrees with their political measures; and tends to support their dignity and consequence, but no further. Ahab will never die so long as there is an Elijah on earth, and Elijah will always be considered as one that troubleth Israel.[29]

Before the new year of 1816 was very old he was confessing to Mrs Stokes that he had gone over the Governor's head to the Colonial Office, and that his campaign to regiment English public opinion against his enemy had begun in earnest: "I have made another application to Lord Bathurst and if I cannot obtain this necessary building for these poor exiles (these objects of vice and woe) I have determined to lay their situation before the British nation, and then I am sure it will be done."[30]

V

New Year's Day 1816 marked a record. Macquarie had survived in office longer than any predecessor. But this brought him little satisfaction.

The head of the Commissary Department, the representative of the British Treasury, had been added to his growing list of adversaries.

On his arrival in Port Jackson on 11 June 1813 the Deputy Commissary-General, Mr David Allan, proposed that he should issue his own promissory notes in payment for all purchases made on behalf of the Government. He proposed to consolidate the issue every two months by drawing bills on the British Treasury. The Governor gave permission.[31]

But before long Mr Allan was issuing negotiable paper far beyond the limits of colonial expenses and applying his surplus issues "to various private speculations, in making very considerable purchases of horned cattle and sheep, for which he paid in his own notes thus issued". The public in general, Macquarie heard, laboured under the dangerous delusion that all Mr Allan's notes were guaranteed by the Government, and considered them of equal value to a Treasury bill. He ordered that where dollars were not available the old system of store receipts should be reverted to.

Mr Allan's letter of protest bristled with quotations from the regulations of the Commissariat. Macquarie stood firm. Bad feeling developed. Mr Allan joined the underminers, and put a busy pen to work to apprise the Treasury of the Governor's extravagance and particularly of his price-fixing methods.[32]

As 1816 was born Mr Bent sulked in his lodgings. Mr Marsden was composing vituperative letters to Lord Calthorpe. Mr Nicholas Bayly was studying the methods of reform practised by the Acting Judge-Advocate, Mr Garling—for whom Mr Bent had been passed over—as applied in Parramatta Jail. And Mr Allan was giving substance to his wrath.

Then there sailed into Port Jackson, just as the Governor was about to leave for a tour of the interior, the American ship, *Traveller*.[33]

The American war had ceased. The British forces had long since gloriously burnt Washington when this vessel arrived in Port Jackson on 19 February 1816. No American merchantman had entered the harbour since 1812, but until that year forty-one of them had been admitted to trade in the port, including three in 1810, two in 1811, and two in 1812.[34]

The Governor had not yet received a dispatch—it came on the *Atlas* on 22 July 1816, five months after the *Traveller* incident—informing him that American vessels were barred from British colonial commerce. This ship had come from Canton. She had been cleared there by the authorities at the British East India Company's factory and she had a pass from the East India Company to visit Port Jackson.[35] She carried goods consigned to a Sydney merchant. She had on board tea and sugar, which were scarce in the Colony. The Governor granted entry "with the fullest publicity"[36]; then retired to the country to admonish settlers and inspect the progress of his towns.

As soon as he had left Sydney, the Reverend Benjamin Vale, chaplain to the 46th Regiment, who had now been in the Colony a little over a year, and Mr Moore, the solicitor, who was receiving a salary from the Government, proceeded straight from Mr Jeffery Bent's house, with all papers made out, and arrested the ship as a lawful prize under the Navigation Act.[37]

Her capturers made their prayer that an Admiralty Court be convened.

The Bent faction was familiar with the fact that Molle, the Lieutenant-Governor, the intimate friend of some of its members, was in bitter and clandestine opposition to Macquarie. They, perhaps, hoped that he would call the Court together in the Governor's absence. But, foolish as he was in some matters, Molle had a sense of caution and refused to act.[38]

VI

The mind of anybody who had observed the actions of Vale and Moore could have held no doubt about the malignity of their intentions toward the Governor.

Moore was Jeffery Bent's own nominee for the post of Crown Solicitor and still full of gratitude to him for "having been greatly instrumental in obtaining for me the situation I have the honour to fill".[39] Self-interest had made him very much a partisan spectator of Bent's rejection of the emancipist attorneys to whose lucrative practices he was the heir—one, indeed, who believed that there was "no doubt that the whole respectable part of the inhabitants of this territory will feel fully compensated by any further delay (in the opening of the Supreme Court) in having the question properly determined".[40]

The Reverend Benjamin Vale, also, was a close associate of Mr Bent and had come to the Colony with him on the *Broxbornebury* in July 1814.[41]

If prophets are reincarnated in the forms of army chaplains, Mr Vale most certainly was one of the later manifestations of the entity of Jeremiah. His life was one long course of misery; he suffered a cankerous discontent with his lot.

On arriving in the Colony he had waited on Macquarie full of demands. He had been told at the Secretary of State's Office, he said, that in Sydney he "should have a separate parish and church assigned to himself, and that he would be provided with a cultivated glebe, and a well-furnished parsonage house, with an allowance of Government servants, rations, fuel, etc."[42]

When all these rare luxuries did not at once begin to appear—there were then three churches, including the chapel at Ebenezer, in existence—he showed himself "discontented and miserable". Macquarie assigned him as assistant to the gentle Cowper at St Philip's, pending the completion of the church and a "comfortable house" for him at Liverpool. He gave him rations, a servant, and fuel and lodging money on a captain's scale, and even promised him a grant of land when he should "chuse to select a situation".[43]

But nothing seemed to please Mr Vale, in spite of the Governor's anxiety to do everything in his power to "reconcile this poor man to his situation . . . to render him as comfortable as his own temper and my ability will admit".

Mr Vale's only response was to "continue to be discontented". Long before the arrest of the *Traveller*, Macquarie had given him permission to return with his sickly wife and children to England.

There could, therefore, be little question as to what influences had infused into that doleful and slightly unbalanced clerical mind the patriotic urge to fend off American trade and to discomfort Macquarie. Vale's will to action, once engaged, was intensified by his indignation that after nineteen months of leisure (on a Government salary) in the Colony, he had not received his grant of land, his ideas of its just size and position being more than ambitious.

When the Governor returned to Sydney he was naturally angry and easily drew his conclusions as to who were the real prime movers in the *Traveller* affair. Mr Bent, however, blandly denied that he had had anything at all to do with the matter, except that he had expressed doubts to the Naval Officer about the ship's right to enter the port, and had advised him to consult the Governor.[44] His motive in doing this obviously would have been to see that the full responsibility for the entry lay on Macquarie's shoulders and on none other.

The Governor, considering that Mr Vale's action had been taken on "factious and illiberal principles" and that the clergyman's conduct had been "insolent and highly insubordinate", ordered him to be court-martialled; but when the court martial found that Vale's conduct had been derogatory to his office as Assistant Chaplain, and sentenced him to be publicly and severely reprimanded, the Governor softened the sentence and admonished the miserable fellow in private.[45]

Vale then, on 16 June 1816, brushed the ungrateful soil of New South Wales off his soles, sailing away in the *Alexander*.

And in the immediately subsequent proceedings Macquarie had more than a glimpse of the passion which his quarrels with the judges had unleashed. He was soon well assured that he had contravened the law—though he had not at the time known it and was following the "uninterrupted usage of the port" in admitting the *Traveller*.

He was moved to express to Lord Bathurst his "reliance on your Lordship for protection on this occasion", if he had done anything not conformable to the law or any existing treaties.

> The obstinacy and contumely with which Mr. Vale and his abettors persevere on this occasion leave me no room to doubt that he and they will prosecute the business elsewhere against me with all possible virulence, and thence I beg to submit to your Lordship's superior wisdom and kind consideration, the expediency of obtaining *an Act of Indemnity for me*, in the event of the Navigation Act having been thus unknowingly violated, my motives having been altogether pure and disinterested.[46]

The preparations for Mr Vale's departure had included the clandestine circulation by Moore the solicitor, who was dismissed from his situation to mark the Governor's sense of his "insolence and insubordination", of a petition attacking the Governor.

Moore, faced with the loss of £300 a year and perquisities, raised the anguished defence that he had only acted as Vale's legal agent, which was a somewhat lame excuse in view of the fact that he was Crown Solicitor, in reality if not in title. Macquarie ridiculing this viewpoint, his victim at once began to "tread in the steps of his preceptor and patron, Mr. J. H. Bent, in rendering indiscriminate opposition to all the measures of my Government, as far as a weak head and a bad heart could impel him".[47] Thus it came about that he lent himself so far to the "mischievous and mean faction as to become the chief mover and promoter of a memorial addressed to the House of Commons". And this, though ostensibly it was concerned with trade and the relief of certain imaginary grievances, was, Macquarie averred, actually designed "to convey charges of the most false and malicious nature against me".

The petition in its original form was shown to Mr Bent, who perused it without enthusiasm.

"Ho," said Mr Bent, "This is a niminy-piminy petition. *I'll* write a petition."[48]

Write it he did, and subsequent details of subject matter which leaked out showed conclusively that he was as good as his word. The document seemed to the Governor, when he heard its representations, to be "infamous, false and factious"; and he was under no illusions about the authorship.[49]

He had "good reason to believe (tho' no direct proof)" that Mr Moore was only a tool employed by Mr Justice Bent, who was the grand mover of this vile libel and cautiously kept in the background.[50]

Mr Moore secured signatures to his petition from "a few discontented wretches here, of the lowest and most infamous description", standing at his door and importuning passers-by, sending to public houses for "thirty or forty common low drunken fellows" to put their names upon the screed while "quite drunk".[51]

There were many who could not remember signing at all; but the discovery of this came later.

VII

The strain had begun to tell on the Governor, and his temper seemed to be failing him. Jungle wallahs beyond the age of two score years and ten were apt to be choleric persons. Illness with him became annual and seasonal. In his public relationships he became more irascible and more inclined to be stubborn.

A strong symptom of the change was noticeable in a matter which concerned one of Sydney's many walls.

Walls were an institution in Botany Bay. No new building's advantages ever were canvassed without reference to its fine, high wall. That round the new military barracks was ten feet high, though the Hospital wall was only nine feet in recognition of the feebler propensity of invalids as climbers.[52] The little orphan girls had a wall round their haven. The Dockyard wall was twelve feet high and the Lumberyard wall had had to be raised to the same level to prevent kindly workers inside from handing out their tools and materials to friends. The Jail paid a tribute to the vigour of the local criminal with a fourteen-foot barrier—and a "strong" one at that. And even the Government Domain, part of which Macquarie, and particularly his wife, visioned as the flowering garden into which it grew from their none-too-modest beginnings, was protected on the southern side, remote from the main gates and the guard, by ten feet of stone, "dividing it from the town across the neck of land between Sydney Cove and Wooloomooloo Bay".[53]

Strangely enough it was through this obstacle that inhabitants chose to enter the park, which provided a convenient refuge "for persons going thither for vicious and disorderly purposes, namely secreting stolen goods, which have been found there frequently, and for which many parts of it are well calculated, being wild rocky shrubbery, which had remained undisturbed by the hand of civilised man". This shrubbery was "also much frequented by lewd, disorderly men and women for most indecent improper purposes".[54]

Well might Commissioner Bigge, only three years later, deprecate the fact that the wall round the new convict barracks was only ten feet high.

Access to the Domain was easy. Mrs Macquarie's Road round it was almost complete. Anyone wishing to enter the enclosed area had merely to cross the Bent Street stile or go through the main gate—"always open to allow honest men and women the use of the grounds for recreation and amusement". This, indeed, was a matter in which the Governor was easy and undiscriminating rather than otherwise. Three years after he had left the Colony and another had assumed his office and made stricter rules, a poet sang:

> And even the green walks, which the late Autocrat
> Threw open to all, who were sober and decent,
> May be viewed, *thro the rails*; but must not be laid flat
> By unhallowed feet—see an order that's recent.
>
> To be sure 'twere profane that vile convicts should tread
> With long skirts and stiff collars, and cambric for trimming,
> Where Generals and Judges, and Freemen have led;
> Or should swim on the *spot*, where the Great have been swimming![55]

However, the legal method of access to the Domain had disadvantages for one carrying stolen washing or retiring for a *tête-à-tête* with the village hussy at three o'clock on a sunny afternoon. And in any case, with a mere ten-foot wall a foot thick between those outside and the shrubbery, the walk to the main gates was scarce worth while. Botany Bay made light of such impediments. Those who desired to frequent the park unobtrusively merely tore a hole in the wall.

The Governor determined to stop this reasonable and energetic practice —"if possible". He was the more firmly set upon it after he found that his "new shrubbery and young forest trees" were being broken down, to the annoyance of Antill and himself.[56]

He sent constables to secrete themselves in the Domain with orders to arrest offenders against his rules.

After several persons had been caught and mildly reprimanded he decided that he would punish those caught henceforward "in a summary manner to deter others from committing such indecencies in future".[57]

He considered he was "fully warranted in my magisterial capacity in ordering this slight summary punishment to be inflicted for a breach of the Government Orders and Regulations and trespass on Government enclosed grounds".[58]

Constable Willbow and a comrade pounced on an idling nursegirl, strolling with her charge and another maiden. And even the powerful influence of the nursemaid's employer, Mrs Robert Campbell, could not save the weeping pair from spending a night in jail.

Then on 18 and 19 April 1816, three citizens named Blake, Henshall, and Read were captured.

They were taken to the Jail. The Governor was advised of their arrest. Promptly, "in his magisterial functions and on the evidence of the Chief and other constables", he ordered that they be given twenty-five lashes each, without calling them before him. And not only were they given twenty-five lashes each, "so lightly laid on that it was hardly felt", but they were asked for three shillings each as a flogging fee.

Dr D'Arcy Wentworth, head of the police, "had the strongest inclination to suppress the order and greatly regretted to see it".[59] For few free men ever had been flogged before in New South Wales—if you *could* call twenty-five light lashes flogging, according to New South Wales standards.

Governor King had had a young prize master of a Spanish vessel marked with a hundred stripes. Afterwards King had made the *amende honorable* by creating him a pilot—"it was understood for preventing a prosecution".[60] The Reverend Samuel Marsden, during the floods of 1806, had ordered a freeman to be flogged, and had been applauded by King.[61]

Macquarie made no *amende honorable*; he had acted "not hastily or in anger or passion". He conceded that the "manner of my doing so may be considered *somewhat illegal*",[62] but said that "from a moral point of view I considered it an act of necessity and can never admit it to be either an act of cruelty or tyranny". He even rejoiced that "this summary example had the desired effect of preventing the recurrence of the evil and disgraceful assignations of persons which had so long before been carried on with impunity".

Further offenders were promised imprisonment and "most summary and exemplary punishment". And exclusive Sydney naturally was shocked.

On Tuesday it would be perfectly permissible for a couple of magistrates, or even one magistrate, to dole out fifty lashes to a convict resident. He might even be punished without trial on warrant from the Governor—who unfortunately always "leaned to the side of mercy too much considering the description of persons that have come before him".

If on Wednesday, however, the culprit's sentence were to have run out and he were free, and then were whipped, it would be a matter for the greatest "indignation and alarm". New South Wales was still a British possession. It had its game laws.

History barely glanced at two convicts flogged for the same "crimes" and at the same time as Blake, Henshall, and Read. But the flagellation of those three "free" worthies was accounted an outrageous infringement of British liberty. In their cases, the probability is that the Governor failed to take the trouble to discover whether the men were free or not. But it seemed that they were, and highly respectable citizens to boot.

Mr Henshall was Australia's first mint master. Sent from his native land, convicted of coining, he had been asked in 1813 to apply his talents to the conversion of the *Samarang's* cargo of Spanish dollars into "holey" dollars and dumps.[63]

He had gone to the Domain, he said, to find a little white sand to assist him in his profession as a silversmith.

Mr Blake, one of his companions, was a blacksmith turned businessman. He had immigrated as a free settler with his wife, who was a prisoner, the previous year. He was head of a flourishing concern which functioned opposite the hospital gates—"a notorious receiver", to wit. Some goods "had been found in his house" belonging to the *Traveller*, and "he would have been prosecuted, had the ship remained".[64]

The third victim was a Mr Daniel Read, who had come out a prisoner in 1803. He was reputed to possess more ingenuity than virtue, but he was the caretaker of Mr Marsden's Sydney cottage. A robbery charge against him recently had failed by a hairbreadth.[65]

Macquarie considered the three to be "depraved low vicious characters, and consequently proper objects to be made examples of".[66] And no doubt, left to themselves, his outraged victims might have retired as quietly as possible from the scene of their sufferings, lest worse befall. They were not, however, allowed the luxury of obscurity.

In no time, following agitation by various lovers of liberty and justice, the sheepish trio found themselves rushed into the presence of Mr Jeffery Bent.

Mr Blake described the proceedings: "I made affidavit at the request or suggestion of a considerable number of people who expressed their alarm at what had happened. . . . People were always laughing at me and urging me to go".[67] The "facts" were added to the petition of Mr Bent, who gave the three deponents a promise to put their cases to Lord Bathurst.

Then Mr Bent turned away to take up the cause of that "unfortunate gentleman", Mr Connor, one of the two murderers of the wretched Holness, who had been cashiered from his regiment and who now wished to return to the Colony to marry. Mr Bent was deeply shocked at the lack of feeling which the Governor displayed in refusing to have him in the Colony long enough to consummate his nuptials.[68] But, having found that he could make no headway, he at once thought of another issue on which he hoped to discomfort very greatly one of the magistrates who had opposed his anti-emancipist policy on the Bench. The scheme had long been maturing in his twisted mind.

VIII

Mr Bent's sister-in-law, Mrs Ellis Bent, had continued to occupy the Judge-Advocate's house after her husband's death, and Mr Jeffery Bent lodged with her. They turned loose at the end of 1815 one Harvey, a convict servant.

This man went straight to Broughton, one of the two magistrates who had been involved in the quarrel with the judge, and offered his services. A cook, he was tempting bait. Broughton consulted the superintendent of convicts to make sure that the man was regularly at large, then engaged him.[69]

Six months later Mr Broughton was suddenly required to return the convict to Mrs Bent, and warrants of attachment were issued to seize the servant and his effects and to bring the amazed magistrate before the Supreme Court Judge. Broughton ignored the writs.

Bent had him arrested and, using grossly insulting and most ungentlemanly language, interned him "like a traitor or murderer" in the common jail for contempt for "as long as I preside over the Supreme Court of this Colony".[70] Broughton was refused bail.

Flushed with anger, the Governor rescued his justice the same day. The Sydney Bench met, presided over by the Lieutenant-Governor, with the Acting Judge-Advocate, Mr Garling, present.[71] It took depositions from the witnesses who had been in court when Bent had dealt with Broughton, including the Provost-Marshal.

It then ruled that Broughton had been "indisputably entitled" to the services of Harvey;[72] that the proceedings brought against their brother magistrate had no relevancy to anything in the Supreme Court; that the servant had been transferred with Mrs Bent's knowledge and with that of the proper Government authorities; that such a committal without trial and without allowing the prisoner to give evidence, hear his accusers on oath, or secure bail, was "contrary to the spirit of the British Constitution", "repugnant to all the feelings of a gentleman", "highly disrespectful to the Governor and the Government", and "tending to produce distrust and alarm in the minds of His Majesty's subjects" residing in the Colony.

They forwarded the depositions and their findings to every magistrate in the Territory for perusal and comment on the affront which had been put upon one of their number.

Unanimously every magistrate in the Colony, except the Reverend Samuel Marsden, who had constituted himself Mr Bent's very Christian ally, endorsed their conclusions. Mr Marsden refused to form a judgment on the ground that he had not been present when the Bench inquiry was held.[73]

Mr Bent was not abashed. Uttering a mocking laugh, he retired to concoct a new villainy.

He could afford to wait and Macquarie had too many troubles on his hands to give his major adversaries need to waste ammunition. The demand for skilled workers and mechanics expanded among the employer classes. Crime continued in the outlands and the natives turned up again out of the forests that autumn and winter so that troops at last had to be sent out to harry them off.

It was about this time that Macquarie first was given some inkling of the contents of Mr Bent's petition, and, perhaps, even of the fact that there was a petition in existence. And this knowledge certainly was enough to startle any governor, if only for the reason that circulation of such a document contravened the regulations and practice of the convict Colony, in which there was no charter of liberty.

That the petition was addressed to Parliament meant nothing to the Governor; his contacts with that excellent but arbitrary institution so far had been slight. The clear assurance that the paper was being clandestinely circulated was enough to provoke his official wrath, but knowledge of the catalogue of wrongdoing alleged against him raised his anger beyond bounds.

The document has long since disappeared into oblivion; but Mr Bent assuredly had not drafted a "niminy-piminy" plea.

The outraged victim of his libellous aspersions lost no time in acting. "All those persons I knew had signed it, I struck off the list of names for whom lands had previously been designed."[74]

There were plenty of victims. There was Mr George Williams, who had travelled out on the *Broxbornebury* with Mr Jeffery Bent—a mysterious individual who had left the position of Government Printer at the Cape of Good Hope, and was now employed as a compositor in the office of the *Gazette*; there was a Mr Horsley, another boon companion *en voyage* of Mr Bent.[75]

There was a publican named Rose,[76] who had been "very nearly executed". He not merely lost any chance of further land grants and favours. Dr D'Arcy Wentworth, whose signature as Sydney magistrate was necessary, refused to sign his application for a renewal of his liquor license, and earnestly urged the Governor to refuse it. He felt that, since the Governor had given both Mr Rose and his wife's father free pardons and considerable land grants, the miscreant's conduct showed "such a degree of baseness and ingratitude that I could not sign his petition".[77]

And Mr Rose was in the same case with Mr Tompson, "a respectable man",[78] who afterwards admitted that he had been duped—he was the father of one of the first poets born on the Australian continent. Mr Armytage, "a person of little consideration . . . the first person who ever received a free pardon from the Governor",[79] also was blasted at one stroke out of the liquor business.

The embarrassments of the petition's circulators accumulated when it appeared that there was a veritable rush of honest gentlemen—holders, most of them, of valuable spirit licences—such as Mr Samuel Terry,[80] all eager to swear that they never had signed any petition. One or two offered rewards for the discovery of the scoundrel who had compromised them by forgery of their stainless signatures.

Mr Moore, the solicitor, was now, in particular, in a difficult position; for when the Governor resolved that his and his brother's names should be struck off the land-grant list, Mr Moore unwisely attempted to save his brother's portion by confessing that he himself had forged the latter's name during his absence.[81] Uttering a fresh cry of rage, Macquarie, on a sick bed, "suffering from a severe and alarming complaint of my bowels", sent for his secretary, and scarified the luckless man anew.

IX

What fresh mischief would have been worked in New South Wales had Mr Bent remained to organize it, no man knows. But his days in the antipodes fortunately were numbered.

On 5 October 1816 the tall masts of the *Elizabeth* were seen sweeping up past the Sow and Pigs and, peering over her rail, the dryly interested countenance of Mr John Wylde,[82] the new Judge-Advocate; in the rear his father, Thomas Wylde, who was to be clerk of the peace; also his wife and child, and his sessional clerk, Joshua Moore—his brother-in-law—late of the 14th Foot, whose house at Acton, in the early twentieth century was the oldest dwelling in the Australian capital of Canberra.

Mr Wylde was an entirely different kind of man from Mr Jeffery Bent. He was a brother of Lord Chancellor Truro, an uncle of Lord Penzance.[83] He was shrewd and sensible, if sometimes verbose.

After five months' experience of him, Macquarie declared that his conduct was "upright, manly and dignified" and had afforded "universal satisfaction", and that he had evinced "every possible desire to support this Government and to assist me with his advice and counsel".[84] He suggested that the new judge be knighted. He gave him and his train land grants, servants, and cows.

Wylde was strong-minded and self-reliant. He understood the peculiar circumstances of the Colony and did his best to balance British statute law with local expediency.[85]

Toward the Governor's emancipist policy he showed understanding tolerance. He spoke of New South Wales as "this land of royal mercy".[86]

He noticed that the Governor exhibited a "very strong and cordial" attention to emancipists on public occasions, but this seemingly did not offend him, though he sometimes feared the effect of his superior's humanity. He attributed the latter's general social attitude "in a great degree to urbanity on his part towards individuals who seemed not to gain an equal freedom of attention from and communication with the rest of the company".[87]

In general, his aim was "that no one under the Government should be more duly subject than myself, provided I stood independent in my judicial character, over which (he could write later) "no shade of influence ever passed".

He was certainly the ablest and most useful adviser ever vouchsafed Macquarie during his period of office, the more salutary since he was not afraid of dispute with Government House. But he always acknowledged the principle that the ultimate responsibility rested on the Governor, and that he himself was merely an adviser. He would push his opinion till the Governor became determined. Then he would "withdraw from the discussion",[88] and if, then, there seemed to be conflict of authority, one or other of the pair was always soon prepared to recant in the most handsome manner. And at the end of all the differences, Wylde would invariably be ready to admit that he had known all along that his adversary in the dispute had been "moved by erroneous judgment but not by any personal feelings or interest".

Mr Bent's welcome to Mr Wylde was far from hospitable. He clung to the judge's chambers; he clung to the set of Statutes which he had brought from England, and he clung to the official copy of the Charter of Justice.

Meanwhile, he and Ellis Bent's widow also clung to the Judge-Advocate's house like limpets; and as the minor skirmishes raged for its possession, involving Mr Wylde, who was seeking to secure a roof for his small family and at least a few sticks of furniture from poor Ellis Bent's home, Mr Jeffery Bent struck a final blow, aimed both at the Governor and the new Chief Judge.

Dismissed though he had been seven months before, he called Alexander Riley, one of the magistrates with whom he had quarrelled, to join him in constituting the Supreme Court once more. Riley ignored the summons. He issued warrants for the arrest of Riley, and of Gore, the Provost-Marshal, who had failed to acknowledge his judicial authority.[89]

Macquarie's patience was at an end. Mr Bent was ejected from his chambers.[90] The Governor issued a precept releasing Broughton and Riley from court service. He published a Government Order declaring Bent to be "positively and absolutely removed from the said appointment, and has no authority or jurisdiction whatever in this Territory". The order forbade the lawless young man to assume the functions of a Supreme Court judge "at his peril" and indemnified all who should disobey him.

Mrs Ellis Bent joined in the fray, adding to her brother-in-law's pompous phrases her own sprightly titbits of abuse, as she fought to retain almost everything connected with the Judge's house except the walls and the roof.[91]

In the end, Macquarie seems to have been relieved to be rid of Mrs Bent at any cost.

He bought her grates and her three fire irons for £47 5s. He bought her outside Venetian blinds for £60. He paid her £28 for her green doors. He bought her kitchen stove and oven door, her stew-holes and her corn bin, her roasting jack and her bell-ropes, her stone sink and her fenders and pantry fittings.

His frugal and agonized secretary, Mr Campbell, sought to lend some semblance of justification for a total bill of £238, while the lady alternately jeered at her husband's successor—"I should scarcely have thought the office of bidder at public auction would have been given to the Honble. Premier Judge"—and meditated as to whether she should hold out to enforce a Government purchase of the morticed doorlocks of her departed husband's official residence.

Threatened at last with eviction, she remarked to the indignant Campbell that he had "shown a pettishness which would hardly be excusable in one of my own sex", then flounced out of the argument.

Mr Jeffery Bent rose once more, hovering, as it were, beside his brother's grave. Ellis Bent had been buried in the Sydney Burying Ground in a spot chosen by himself, near his friend, Ferguson. But Jeffery Bent averred that his dignity demanded that he should lie in the chancel of St Philip's Church.

Mr Bent even threatened to cause his own request for a removal of the coffin to St Philip's and Macquarie's refusal to be inscribed on the present tomb, so that when those who knew his brother should chance to read the inscription,"The sigh they would breathe over departed worth may bear a silent malediction upon what I shall be authorised to call and ever shall consider your despicable conduct".

Joining hands, he and his sister-in-law finally saluted Government House with a chorus of demand and protest, as their creditors descended on them and served detainers to prevent them from leaving the Colony.

The Governor, however, seems to have had the last word, using as a weapon the very document which had been Mr Ellis Bent's first pretext for revolt—the Port Regulations:

Madam: *J. T. Campbell to Mrs Bent*

The Laws of the Colony and the Port Regulations, which constitute a part of them, are and must be the same to you as to every other member of the community; to them, Madam, His Excellency the Governor desires to refer you in reply to your letter of the present date.[92]

So, in a whirl of threats, the Bents sailed away with congenial spirits on 18 May 1817 in the *Sir William Bensley*, on a voyage during which Mr Bent devoted most of his talents for dissension to a rousing quarrel with the captain of his ship, who turned out to be a "great rascal." They all narrowly escaped drowning on the shoals of Biscay.

Eight years later the lady looked back on her antipodean sojourn: "I met Sir Charles Brisbane, (a gay old man). He asked me what sort of place was New South Wales. I told him a much better place than St Vincents."[93]

X

The Colony's discontented exiles in Britain were still stirring. Mr John M'Arthur was coming home. Young Mr William Wentworth, on his way to England, heard definitely at the Cape of Good Hope that Sir J. S. Maxwell had been appointed Governor in Macquarie's place and wrote hurriedly to his father, D'Arcy Wentworth, urging him to put his affairs in order before the coming of the new man, who might not be inclined to wink at some of his father's present activities.[94]

No news so pleasant to the ears of the rebellious was confirmed in the ensuing mails brought by the *Fortune*.

It actually seemed, at times, as if the Colonial Office had forgotten altogether that New South Wales had a governor or a government.

As His Majesty's Captain-General·in the Colony looked through his files in May 1817 he noted that he had received no replies from London

JOHN WYLDE
Judge-Advocate of New South Wales, 1816-24

From the original portrait in the possession of the Parliament of the Union of South Africa

to his dispatches about his right to pardon (1812), his circulation of his new "holey dollar" coinage (1813), his need for additional chaplains, the payment of William Cox for building the western road, and the latter's appointment as commandant at Bathurst.[95]

His intimate thoughts, at that stage, were not directed towards Downing Street. They were far away in Mull, whence he had received news that his brother Charles had succeeded in buying for him a delightful slice of the Duke of Argyll's disintegrating estate along the shores of Loch-na-Keale and near Laggan Ulva.

There had been a fight for the property, "mean collusion", disingenuousness on the part of rival bidders, but, to the Governor's intense joy, Charles, aided by Charles Forbes, had won the battle. Though the new owner of the land knew that his purchase would call for the use of every penny of his liquid assets of £22,000, he "would not have taken a £5000 profit on it".[96]

He instructed his brother to look to the leases of his farms, so that they could be taken over at short notice. For he still hoped that ere long he would be once more dwelling in Mull, in a dream palace which he described as "Jarvisfield-Castle", enjoying the opulence produced by anticipated rises in the prices of consols, sheep, wool, and cattle.

He could thus feel tranquil in the assurance that in two years or so he would be where Marsdens and Bents could no longer disturb his peace of mind.

His easygoing mood did not last very long.

CHAPTER XXIV

The Red-spattered Tartans

I

MERE Sassenachs found some of the Governor's procedures quite beyond their comprehension whenever he dealt with those problems in which dire circumstances had, long centuries ago, compelled the sons of Scotia to become expert. These mainly affected lawlessness and finance.

But on such issues, with their special appeal to the native talents of the north, there was not a Scot alive who would not have been proud to applaud both his technique and his style.

Who but a Scot, when faced with the problem of keeping a new silver coinage in the Colony, would have solved it by ordering a capable criminal to remove the centre from each coin, labelling it 1s. 3d., while foisting the outer residual ring upon the public at the original value of the whole, thus obtaining, from five shillings' worth of Spanish dollar, six-and-three-pence worth of local coinage?[1]

And who but a hardy son of the territory of Argyll would have carried through the Rum Hospital contract? In that affair the Governor had agreed with three hard-headed business men that they should donate the building under the delusion that in payment they were to have a virtual monopoly of the import of spirits into the Colony for a number of years.[2] The awe-inspiring edifice and its attendant buildings provided the Government not merely with a vast infirmary but later with a Parliament House, a Mint, for a time, Courts of Justice, and two chaplains' houses. The Governor had found only labour and bullocks to the value of £4200 but had taken from the unfortunate contractors £9000 in spirit duties.

Thus the Government had been paid £5000 for the privilege of allowing three citizens to present it with an enormous building for nothing, at a cost of about £40,000. And the originally eager entrepreneurs of the enterprise had found that they had had no monopoly at all in the spirit trade, nor anything like one. All the spirits which the Colony needed and more was imported outside the deliveries of the luckless builders, so that no duty was lost otherwise.

Even at that, the Governor and his architect-inspector had canvassed the advisability of fining the builders for delay in completing the work and for omissions; this, despite the fact that the poor fellows—malicious gossip about their "enormous" profits notwithstanding—all professed to be on the brink of ruin.[3]

Mr Garnham Blaxcell[4] was obliged to flee the Colony and his creditors to die in exile in Java. Poor Dr Wentworth was heard apologizing to his son William that he was behindhand with the young man's frugal allowance.[5] And Mr Riley became the Governor's mortal enemy.[6]

No observer, indeed, could have failed to hold a very strong suspicion that the Colony's ruler had succeeded in grafting upon its system something very like the organization of the Highland clan.

His paternalism might have emanated from the headquarters of a Duart or a Lochiel. His spasmodic bursts of punishment given straight from headquarters, as in the case of the men caught in the Domain, seemed like an echo of the behaviour of his ancient relative, John Maclaine of Lochbuy, who had been fined, within a half-century past, for putting one of his clansmen in a pit, without legal trial and against the laws of the Scottish Realm.

The great dinners at Government House (at the Governor's personal expense), at which a hundred and fifty hungry guests often sat down, were in the "true old Highland stile". The Governor's continual agitation for a distillery would have been accepted as evidence against him in any court. And even Mr Robinson, the poet laureate, was a relevant exhibit, since one of the most necessary appanages of a chieftain was a bard or *sennachie*. Certainly Mr Robinson's Oxford accent might have been judged incongruous by the unknowledgeable; but had not Dr Johnson inveighed against the anglicized habits and accents of the MacDonalds, as much as forty years ago?[7]

II

In his contacts with the wild native and the Van Diemen's Land bushranger, Macquarie's national characteristics displayed themselves most clearly and puzzlingly to the English.

His outlook on banditry and freebooting was apt to be influenced by his immediate origins. His ancestors in a late generation had been esteemed "bad soldiers but good plunderers".[8] In the environment of his earliest boyhood years the bagpipe had not lost its illegal flavour as a prohibited instrument of war.[9] His own generation was so little removed from lawlessness that, only twenty-five years before his birth, his neighbour-relatives on Coll had gladly sheltered a fleeing Cameron who had left his own haunts because he had been "so unfortunate as to kill a M'Martin".[10]

It was in the years 1814-17 that Macquarie exhibited the best examples of the Scottish flavour of his administration. In New South Wales the blacks in particular were troublesome in those years, even within an easy day's ride of Sydney; the bushrangers in the very environs of Hobart itself.

In their habits the aborigines were uncommonly like the lower order of Highlander of the sixteenth and seventeenth centuries, though in some ways less impish in their mischiefs.

They had the same hunger for other people's barley as seventeenth century Maclean and Macquarie raiders of Ardchattan and Iona;[11] the same appetite for raw cow-beef as the pristine Ulvan. Their *didgeridoo*, their only musical instrument, would have entranced a primitive Macintyre.[12] Their taste for scarlet vied with that of the Highlandmen "redshank" whose drooping forms so often had dangled from Crieff gallows. And, as with the Hebrideans, their songs and dances became extraordinary and exuberant under the influence of a gulletful of *usquebagh*. The gibberish battle-yell of the Cammerays was not less outlandish to English ears than the Macquarie clansman's "*An-t-arm breac dearg*".[13]

Even the districts in which the native dwelt now had Highland names!

In fact, altogether the primitive aboriginal had so Scottish an air about him that it was only natural that the Governor should revert to the methods and diction of the eloquent James VI and of the Edinburgh Privy Council in dealing with him. Thus, the Macquaries of James's day, accustomed to being denounced as "wicket thieves and lymmaris" for their "barbarous cruelties and daylie heirscappes",[14] would have been quite at home with one of their more civilized descendant's comminations against those "violent and atrocious banditti",[15] the Australian blackfellows fleeing before the consequences of their own "atrocious and wanton barbarities . . . murders, robberies and depredations".[16] Homesick indeed would a Stuart-period Ulvan—"rude, barbarous, uncivil . . . a wild savage, devoid of God's feare"—have felt as he read upon the official parchments of New South Wales the proclamations authorizing all and sundry to "kill and utterly destroy those wild, rude people",[17] his outlawed Australian imitators.

When Macquarie wished to take counsel with the natives about their own reformation, he used the same bait as King James to lure them to discussion—beef and good liquor—and proposed a paraphrase of James's methods to them.[18]

III

During his early years in the Colony Macquarie had discovered the simple savage to have "scarcely emerged from the remotest state of rude and uncivilized nature",[19] though appearing to possess qualities which, "if properly cultivated and encouraged might render them not only less wretched and destitute by reason of their wild wandering and unsettled habits, but progressively useful to the country according to their capabilities, either as labourers in agricultural employ or among the lower class of mechanics".

The principal part of their lives, he saw, was "wasted in wandering thro' their native woods, in small tribes of between 20 and 50, in quest of the immediate means of subsistence, making opossums, kangaroos, grub worms, and such animals and fish, as the country and its coasts afford, the objects of their fare".[20]

He conceded that, like other savages, they were subject to "great indolence" and indifference about the future;[21] but he found them "of free open and favourable dispositions, honestly inclined, and perfectly devoid of the designing trick and treachery, which characterize the natives of New Zealand and those of the generality of the Islands in the South Seas".

They never had been cannibals; in fact, they had almost "as great an abhorrence of practices of that kind as if they had been reared in a civilized state". Those near or in Sydney, when he had arrived, and for some time afterwards, were in "a state of perfect peace, friendliness, and sociality"[22] with the settlers and ready to help them with their labour. It seemed only to require "the fostering hand of time, gentle means, and conciliatory manners to turn those poor un-enlightened people into an important degree of civilization",[23] and to imbue them with a sense of duty, as the first and happiest advance towards a state of comfort and security. But the usual influences which disturb relations between white and black operated.

Idle and ill-disposed Europeans interfered all too often with native women. The tribes which came down on "walkabout" to Appin and Airds in April-May 1814 could not understand that the new corn, which had sprung up in the fresh-ploughed fields along Bunburry-Curran Creek, did not belong to all. They swept joyously into the fields, lu-luing in praise of their bountiful gods, and eagerly plucked the juicy ears of grain. They were deeply puzzled and insulted when those who should have been their willing hosts, according to all pristine Australian tradition, turned them out with guns.[24]

From "the tranquillity and good understanding that had existed for the last five or six years" had arisen a flattering expectation that native violences were not again likely to occur. But many a shepherd was killed; many a native laid low. Buckshot flew about like rain in the wind. At the rising of the full moon in Appin in June bloodcurdling shrieks in the night seemed to the gathered settlers who clutched their blunderbusses to suggest the possibility of open battle with the tribes.[25]

Luckily it did not come. But there was soon more blood upon the corn and the Governor, after holding a magisterial inquiry, lamented that any cause should have been given on either side for "the sanguinary and cruel acts which had been reciprocally perpetrated by each party".[26]

He mourned for the number of lives sacrificed by the settlers as by the natives in retaliation for real or supposed grievances. He said that his investigation had shown that, though the evidence was not clear and satisfactory enough to warrant criminal prosecution, it was sufficient to convince any unprejudiced man that the *first* personal attacks were made by the settlers and of their servants.

He acknowledged that the natives had shown a disposition to help themselves in the unfenced fields of maize in a manner very different from their former habits, and that the settlers had just ground for complaint about the depredations committed. But he declared that, whilst it was to be regretted that the natives had thus violated property, it had not appeared to him that they had carried on their robberies to any alarming extent or even to the serious prejudice of any individual settler.

He admonished settlers not to take the law into their own hands and to beware of wanton acts of cruelty and oppression. He said that the natives, while law-abiding, were as much entitled to legal protection as the whites. He promised to punish in an exemplary manner future aggressiveness by either whites or blacks.[27]

Also, he pointed out that the absence of acts of hostility by the natives for several years and the free and kindly intercourse that had existed between the Australians and the invaders of their country, with few interruptions, since Governor Phillip's day proved that existing hostilities arose only from casual circumstances.

Lastly, he counselled patience and forbearance as highly becoming in the whites, a conciliatory line of conduct which would reflect credit upon those adopting it and most effectively secure their own personal safety.

He took much personal pains to warn the dusky heathen of the Cow-pastures and interior regions that they must desist from acts of robbery and violence, asserting that they had strongly assured him that, unless they were wantonly shot at or attacked, "as in the case which occurred lately in Appin, wherein a native woman and two children were, in the dead hour of night, whilst sleeping, inhumanly put to death", they would conduct themselves "in the same peaceable manner as they had done previously to the present conflict".[28]

He set about trying to make the peace permanent. In December 1814 he established at Parramatta, under the contemptuous eye of Mr Marsden, an institution in which Mr Shelley, formerly a missionary and "a very moral man", was charged with the task of "educating and bringing up to habits of industry and decency, the [native] youth of both sexes, commencing at the outset with six boys and six girls".[29]

Whilst it was well known, he wrote—making a shrewd pass at Mr Marsden—that considerable sums had been expended by the Missionary Societies of London and other parts of England "in attempting to evangelize the nations of *New Zealand and Otaheite*", it might be allowed to be an objective favourable to the interests of humanity to see an attempt of the kind he proposed made on a frugal and prudent scale in New South Wales, the natives of which appeared to him to have "peculiar and strong claims to the philanthropic protection of a British Government".

He proposed, also, to give the natives some lands of their own on Port Jackson and in the interior, where they might fish or farm.

The natives showed eagerness to hand over their children to Mr Shelley, no doubt especially tempted by the news that each pupil of the new college would receive a weekly ration which included three and a half pounds of meat, two pounds of rice, ten pounds of cornflour, two pounds of wheat, half a pound of sugar, and pepper, salt and soap.[30]

IV

In December the Governor himself met the native tribes. The children were selected and washed and cleaned, as he and Jane had cleaned their little Cochin slaveboys twenty years before. Their stomachs showed the evidences of extreme distension. Their elders went off happily, well filled with beef and rum. On Port Jackson sixteen small plots were laid out, the chosen holders of them furnished with tools, a communal boat and other facilities, and adjured to set good examples to other aborigines in the vicinity.[31]

But all at first did not go well. Some parents almost at once began to show "unaccountable caprice" in decoying their offspring from the seminary into the bush.[32] Settlers who had had their sheds burned, their sheep stolen, their crops torn to pieces and their shepherds killed, refused to share the Governor's tenderness for the native. They met the latter's happy grin—he was a forgetful fellow to whom last week's murder or depredation was well over and done with—with a blast of buckshot. Even though the Governor received for his schemes "the cordial approbation of the Prince Regent",[33] provided the money for them were raised from the colonial funds and by public subscription, the blood sown on the corn in 1814 and 1815 produced its crop.

The native had not been known to act in such a ferocious and sanguinary manner for many years past as in the autumn and winter of 1816. It was enough to sap one's optimism momentarily. "I begin to entertain a fear that I shall find this a more arduous task than I first imagined, tho' I am still determined to persevere in my original plan of endeavouring to domesticate and civilize these wild rude people."[34]

The marauders were to see another side of the Highland Chieftain in very short order. He felt it soon "absolutely necessary to inflict exemplary and severe punishments on the mountain tribes",[35] before their next walkabout. Letters of fire and sword were issued when their raidings continued lustily. Captain Schaw[36] went north-west to scour the Evan lands and the Grose along the Nepean marches. Lieutenant Dawe marched down to the Cowpastures; Captain Wallis took the sector where the invaders were most numerous and troublesome, the new country of Airds and Appin. All were to converge in the end on Woodhouse's farm upon the Appin road. Their orders were explicit. Every native met after they left base was to be taken prisoner of war, whether man, woman or child. Men who fled were to be shot down and their bodies hung "on the highest trees and in the clearest parts of the forest".[37]

The tribes were to be driven to a safe distance from settlement. Blacks who resisted were to be killed, but a few were to be brought home "in order that they may be punished for their late atrocious conduct, so as to strike them with terror against committing similar acts of violence in future". Women and children were to be spared, "if possible"; a few children taken for the Native Institution.

If the measures were stern, so was the need. Many settlers had "entirely abandoned their farms", and the Governor felt that "nothing short of some signal and severe examples being made" would prevent the frequent occurrence of trouble.[38] However painful to himself, the remedy was absolutely necessary.

At dawn on 17 April 1816 Captain Wallis crept upon the natives in camp near Broughton's farm in Appin.[39] The dogs gave the alarm. In the moonlight, "men could not be told from women as they dashed from rock to rock". Fourteen blacks were killed, including "two of the most ferocious and sanguinary leaders of the perpetrators of the recent murders". A few were taken prisoner. And how many women and children met their deaths, as they rushed shrieking and terrified over adjacent precipices, nobody knew for certain.

The expeditionaries had their "prizemoney" in slop clothing and rum (fifteen gallons for captains, half a pint for native guides) after twenty-three days of campaigning. The Governor issued his later famous proclamation to the illiterate natives, which ever since has amused historians. He knew full well what he was about. His own Erse nature told him what those ghostly and mysterious broadsheets would mean to the superstitious savage. While those eerie talismans were to be seen among the timber of their grounds, the terrible eye of Macquarie of Ulva would be upon them.

The remote settler did not share the historical derision about these sheets, for they contained his bill of rights, his chartered authorization to protect his wife and children and his property with his musket.

The documents set out that, whereas the natives had been recently guilty of most atrocious and wanton barbarities in indiscriminatingly murdering men, women and children, it was necessary to take steps to "reclaim them from their barbarous practices and to conciliate them to the British Government".[40] Again the Governor used the dialect of King James's *Acta Penes*.

From and after the fourth day of June 1816—"the Birth Day of His Most Gracious Majesty King George the Third"—no black native or body of natives must appear within one mile of any town, village or farm occupied by British subjects, while armed with weapons of any description, even nulla-nullas or waddies, on pain of being "considered in a state of aggression and hostility, and treated accordingly".

No more than six aborigines, whether armed or not, must loiter round any farm in the interior. The practice of large bodies assembling or fighting on the plea of inflicting punishment under their own customs was abolished, as being "barbarous . . . repugnant to the British laws".

Natives who transgressed these regulations might be first of all "desired in a civil manner to depart", but if they persisted in remaining armed, within civilized limits, or showed any tendency to rob or plunder, they might be driven off with force of arms by settlers banded together or by the military detachments.

On the other hand, natives who desired the protection of the Crown and who were prepared to conduct themselves in a peaceful, honest and inoffensive manner might be furnished with "passports or Certificates to that effect, signed by the Governor, on their making application for the same at the Secretary's Office at Sydney, on the first Monday of every succeeding month; which certificates they will find will protect them from being injured or molested, so long as they conduct themselves and do not carry offensive weapons."

The Governor promised to use such means as were within his power to enable them to obtain an honest and comfortable living by their own labour. He notified them that he was always willing to grant them small portions of land as farms, to victual them and their families from the Government Stores for six months, to give them tools. Wheat, maize, and potatoes for seed, and one suit of slop clothing and one colonial blanket for each person in the family were theirs for the asking. He reserved a block of land twenty-one miles from Sydney for their use—it bears still the name of Blacktown.[41]

He further advised them that "on Saturday the twenty-eighth of December next at twelve o'clock noon at the Public Market Place" at Parramatta he proposed to meet such of the tribes as cared to attend "for the purpose of more fully explaining and pointing out to them the objects of the [Native] Institution . . . as well as for consulting with them on the best means of improving their present condition. On this occasion . . . the Governor will feel happy to reward such of them as have given proofs of industry, and an inclination to be civilised."[42]

He proposed to repeat this *jirga*, he told them, on 28 December in each succeeding year, "unless that day fall upon a Sunday".[43]

There was but one more outrage in his time, like a retreating rumble of thunder after a storm.

That winter ten "most violent and atrocious" fellows tried their old tricks. They were promptly proclaimed to be "in a state of outlawry, and open and avowed enemies to the peace and good order of Society and therefore unworthy to receive any longer the protection of that Government, which they have so flagrantly revolted against and abused". Rewards were offered for their utter destruction. Their names—Murrah, Myles, Wallah, Narrang, Kurringy, Bunduck[44]—sounded no more outlandish to English ears than those of "M'Cloud, M'Kynnowne, M'Clane of Coll, Donald Gorme of Sleat and Gillespoc MacQuarie of Ullowa" who had been put to the horn in other proclamations of outlawry not two hundred years ago.

But it all ended amicably. The villains kept out of harm's way until the Governor, threatened with the failure of his Christmas native gathering, summoned the "principal chiefs to come in at the heads of their respective tribes to sue for peace and deliver up their arms all in due form".[45] The last of them, Narrang Jacky, surrendered.

Strange to tell, the Governor's methods were soon "attended with the desired effect." By April 1817 all general hostility on both sides had long since ceased. The black native, he told Bathurst, was now "living peaceably and quietly in every part of the Colony".[46]

V

The meeting in December 1816 attracted one hundred and seventy-nine blacks. They were all very happy together. It must have been a pleasing sight as they left for the bush, full of laughter. Later, they were given a uniform which the Governor had designed for them—"a frock or loose jacket, a pair of pantaloons or trowsers" of a "red colour", with a common leather cap, for the men: for the women, a red jacket and petticoat; for the piccaninnies each a shirt.[47] All received blankets. And some of the capering elders would be wearing brass gorgets like Dian's moon, bearing their names and hung upon their manly chests; or perhaps the insignia of the Order of

Merit which the Governor had invented for them. But their pace was not as fast as usual, for they bulged with a "plentiful treat of meat and drink".[48]

The children at the Native Institution made "very great progress"; they evinced "a good natural understanding and an aptitude for learning whatever it was proposed to teach them":

> There are now eighteen healthy boys and girls in this Institution, well clothed, well-fed and well instructed in the common branches of education, including needle work for the girls, and knowledge of agriculture for the boys, there being a large field and garden attached to the school house for them to work in. Nothing has yet been done in this Colony that has so much conciliated the adult natives to the interests of the British Government generally, as the establishment of this Institution, as they appear to be highly gratified and delighted beyond description with the contented and happy appearance of their children.[49]

By the time he left the Colony he had seen some of the native youth top the examination lists among Europeans. Girls from the Institution had married. Boys from it had been settled on small farms in the Blacktown centre, where there were neat huts, and "cornfields waved in undulating green".[50] Three tribes were settled on their own lands—one on the shores of Port Jackson at George's Head, the other two inland. All sometimes disappeared on "walkabout".

As settlement pushed the native further out, Macquarie had proposed to form a reservation in the heart of the rich country on the outer Cow-pastures fringes on the southern tableland, recently discovered by Charles Throsby, building a native village and setting aside 10,000 acres of land for native use. The Reverend Mr Cartwright, who did not share Mr Marsden's contempt for the aboriginal, offered himself as supervisor of this retreat, which he proposed to name Macquarie City.[51]

Macquarie was sure Bathurst would "approve this measure, as one worthy of British feelings to a harmless race, who have been without struggle driven by the progress of British industry from their ancient places of inhabitation". The Minister did not respond.

To the end, his native festivals continued to delight the Governor. At them chieftains were received in levee, confirmed in office, decorated: "Coogee, King of George's River, and Norwong, King of Botany Bay, Gorgets, and the Order of Merit to Tindall of the Cowpastures and Pulpin of the Hawkesbury".

Little ones from the Institution read aloud, while warrigals leapt high, yelling, "Governor! That one good settler! He *my* piccanninny!" Dusky mothers were observed to weep with pride. The scene always aroused emotions "grateful to the bosom of sensibility".

VI

In Macquarie's dealings with the bushrangers of Van Diemen's Land, Scottish-Australian parallels come just as readily to the mind as in his dealings with the natives.

The conditions in Tasmania were, in fact, very much like those of the M'Gregor country in its palmiest days. The drunken Davey, then in office, was himself not unlike a bushranger. The community of interest between the bushranger and the kind of settler with which the island was blessed was intimate.

Mr Peter Mills, a deputy-commissary,[52] took to the bush and became a leader of the villains. Military posses were sometimes nearly as predatory and undisciplined as those they professed to hunt, their members deserting to join in the search for booty.

Such was the position that the Government could take seriously some evidence that the Colonial Chaplain, Knopwood,[53] had been harbouring a notorious murderer and associating with despoilers. The settlement's surgeons were not above suspicion.[54] But all this did not seem out of place where the senior Royal Naval officer was discovered one day boarding a customs boat by force, slashing at the customs man with his cutlass and dragging him by the scruff of the neck into his own ship, shouting that he proposed to iron and flog him.[55]

Familiar with rock and glen from their training as hunters of the nimble marsupial, in the skins of which some of them went clothed entirely, bushrangers in Van Diemen's Land, three or four years after the island had acquired sub-colonial status, were as hard to extirpate as any tribe of "redshanks" that ever raided Crieff. Farms were so lonely that descent upon them was easy. The administration was so slothful that escape afterwards was a foregone conclusion. At the approach of authority, a ruffian might lead his band into the bosky shelter of the "wild woods", with which the rugged surface of the island was almost entirely clothed.

Even a Governor might feel a sporting sympathy for them; for what Highlander of the age of Walter Scott could resist the sentimental appeal of the leader of the wretches, Mr Michael Howe, who lived as if in his person Rob Roy and Robin Hood together had been reincarnated?

Mr Howe's career,[56] despite the fact that he hailed from Pontefract, might have been invented by Sir Walter himself. Linked in romance with a dusky maiden—Mary, a name ever dear to Scottish ears—he roamed the wild wood with his gang, plundering all with assets worthy of his touch. Anon, he paused to inscribe with his own blood, upon white kangaroo hide in his "journal of dreams", his longings to retire for ever to a secluded dell. And in his wake there trailed perpetually that inexorable black-tracker and experienced murderer, Musquito.

Legend hallowed Mr Howe. He glorified himself as "Lieutenant-Governor of the Woods". Past experience led even magistrates to fear him like the black plague. He and his band seemed more like an enemy than criminals, a force whose case called rather for negotiation than attrition. Even Mr Ellis Bent agreed about that.[57]

The Governor at first called for "the number and names of these depredators", so that he might take measures to apprehend and destroy them. However, they continued to steal chattels and drive off cattle and sheep, till in May 1814 he recognized their special status by inviting twenty-nine of them, by name, "peaceably and upon their allegiance as subjects of His Majesty, to return to the settlement of Hobart Town"[58] and there receive pardons.

This proclamation followed two similar ones by Davey. The bush-rangers interpreted it to mean that they had been granted a licence for seven months, free of all penalties, during which they could rob and murder to their hearts' content. They became insolent as well as predatory. They sent a message to Davey, through a waylaid corporal's guard, that when chance offered, they would "send some buck shot through his old paunch",[59] and they jeeringly added that they did not intend to take advantage of their proclaimed pardons, "since they had not done half mischief enough".

Then fourteen of them, led by Howe and all well armed, robbed Ingle's farm twelve miles from Hobart, stripped it of seven hundred pounds worth of plunder and "cruelly abused the person of a female".[60]

The Hobart Bench of Justices by this time was in such a flurry of fear that it felt that all lenity towards such villains was ill-applied and that, unless the military were ordered out in force and "a speedy stop is put to the system of bushranging, on the approach of summer the greater part of the prisoners of both the settlements on this island will join the lawless band now in the woods, and many valuable lives will be lost 'ere they are subdued".[61] It was apprehended, even, that the inhabitants in general would soon make compacts with their despoilers and treat them as if they were in authority. The unhappy justices submitted "the disgrace that must fall on every part of the Police of this Settlement, should the actors of these unprecedented depredations be allowed to escape with impunity."

The haughty actors themselves merely laughed loudly. Issuing from the woods on the evening of 23 October 1814, a few weeks before the last day for pardoning was due, they were involved in fresh pranks on the farm of Mr Denis M'Carty of New Norfolk, one of the foremost among the framers of the eloquent addresses which the Governor had received during his visit to Hobart in 1811. Macquarie actually had spent a night in Mr M'Carty's house during that memorable tour.[62]

Mr M'Carty, on this new occasion, was absent—he was in Sydney in jail. His lonely grass-widow sat in the parlour with Mrs Hibbins, who had an infant in her arms, and Mr William Holsgrove. After preliminary "noises off", which were at first attributed to "the servants playing," a gentleman with a musket, his "face blacked with sut", came into the parlour, followed by others, one of whom was "in complete kangaroo dress, constantly wearing his cap over his eyes". They made Mr Holsgrove lie down. Then they retrieved the nimble Mrs M'Carty from under the table and tied her hands, roundly meditating aloud in rude, four-letter Anglo-Saxon on what they might do to her.

Only judicious revelation of the whereabouts of the family treasures saved her from her prospective fate, and the remainder of the night was spent round the tea-table in light conversation.

The visitors discussed Macquarie's proclamation irreverently and with derision. They observed that the "Old Gentleman's proposal was a very favourable one for them if they wished to embrace it"; for if they returned to Hobart by 1 December next, "what they were doing would be done away with, unless they were secured and taken to camp, which they had little fear of".

In fact, they said, "the Old Gentleman had given them a fine chance to do just as they liked";[63] and they were damned if they would give themselves up, since they were going out of the country with £4000 sterling worth of booty.

Then the cocks crew. The sun began to rise over the lovely Derwent River, revealing a piteous scene—Mrs M'Carty weeping in the hollow shell of her family mansion, while down the scrub tracks the feet of the freebooters bit deep into the ground as they staggered under mountains of spoil accumulated by Mr M'Carty's zealous years of self-sacrificing reformation:

> Three silk dresses, £26 . . . three silk pelisses, £26 . . . seven yards of pink silk . . . forty yards of black and white silk, £32 . . . twelve cambric muslin dresses, £37 . . . five muslin dresses, £25 . . . eight chemises, two pair of gold earrings . . . jewels . . . one scarlet Spencer . . . twelve silver spoons . . . fifty-six pounds of powder, twenty-eight pounds of shot.[64]

Thus the list unfolded into dozens of items which Mrs M'Carty would never see again. The robbers even removed all Mr M'Carty's six pairs of pantaloons.

It read more like the inventory of a ravished Spanish galleon carrying a viceroy's daughter than of the bush dwelling of an Irish emancipist whom the Hobart authorities (in vain) were begging the Governor to prevent from returning to the Derwent after his sojourn in Sydney.

VII

Macquarie was very reluctant to abandon civil for martial law administered by the dissipated Davey. He urged more energy by the civil authorities. But the bushrangers continued to behave as "detestable monsters", stealing and murdering.

Mr Howe and his band stripped the farm of one Triffit on 8 April 1815 and again menaced the demesne of Mr M'Carty,[65] who now was at home burning for revenge. Word of their approach sent him shouting for his horse and volunteers. He mustered but five fowling-pieces and three pistols, against nine desperate men with twelve muskets, two double-barrelled guns, and several pistols; yet he charged the miscreants (as they sat at lunch) with a hurroo. His fleet lieutenant, Mr John ("Kitchme") Brown, was in a moment with his cutlass among the foe, who left *en masse* for the timber. Thence they opened a heavy fire. Soon all Mr M'Carty's followers, save Mr Brown, lay round him bleeding.

"Surrender!" shouted the Foe.

"Never!" cried Mr M'Carty. "I'll take another shot and see who runs fastest." One of his men died of wounds. The wretches fled. But Mr M'Carty had reason to live in terror for months.[66]

Davey declared martial law.[67] Macquarie averred that he must ever consider such a proceeding "not only illegal and irregular, but also as highly derogatory of my authority as Governor in Chief of this Territory". He promised to report this "strong and extraordinary step" to the Colonial Office.[68] But he allowed matters to remain as they were for six months, though he refused to sanction the court martial of Howe.

It did little good. The bushrangers wrote to Davey vaunting their power to destroy all the parties he might send. Eighteen months later, at the end of 1816, they were flourishing like the banyan-tree, sending out clutching roots everywhere. There seemed no longer any colour of romance about Mr Michael Howe. A conviction had grown luxuriantly in the Governor's mind that the braggart "lieutenant-governor of the woods", if "ever taken alive . . . will be a proper object to make a public and awful example of".[69]

Of the chances of this, his vivid correspondent, Mr Broughton, who was in Hobart unravelling the villainies of the Commissariat Office, could hold out little hope.

Things had come to such a pass in the Settlement, he reported, that "if its safety, like Sodom and Gomorrah, depended on finding six honest men . . . it would be swallowed up in all its iniquity".[70] It was quite evident that depredators were assisted by many settlers. He even thought they were "encouraged by those who wished to justify the necessity there was of establishing martial law", of the operation of which he gave an affecting description:

> Soon after I came here, a report came in that the bush rangers were at the Coal River; it was laughable to see the hurry scurry it caused, soldiers running ready to break their necks! where to! Why to the stores, to get rigged out with blue jackets and shoes, and which by the by never answer but for one expedition; for the next, another supply is required. The whole place was in an uproar, and, as may be immagined [sic], the bush rangers had information of our movements before the soldiers were out of town. Such is our system of policy, not even villainy is kept a secret, for there are some who boast of their iniquity and glory in their misdeeds. . . . I sincerely hope that the report of a Lieut. Governor coming to relieve Colonel Davy [sic] is correct, though, when he is spoken to on the subject, he bawls out "Ponticherry."[71]

That this "unusual picture" did not much exaggerate the facts was proved by the affidavit of Mr John Peachey,[72] overseer of Lieutenant-Governor Davey's own country mansion, Carrington Park, Coal River, on events which had taken place only a month earlier, on the evening of 8 September 1816. This was just two months after Mr Howe had written to Davey that if the latter's "bloodhunters" came to his territory he "would feed them with forcemeat balls".[73]

On the eventful evening Mr George Jones, a bushranger, opened Colonel Davey's front door, peered into the lamp-lit front room, and to a servant reading there ventured courteously, "How do you do, Wood?"

Mr Peachey, who was in bed with Mrs Peachey, hastened into the front room where he found not only Bushranger Jones but also the romantic Mr Howe and three others, all armed to the teeth with muskets and pistols.

"Well, my lads," said Mr Peachey heartily, "what do you want?"

"Oh, we just called to see you," chorused the polite freebooters.

"I suppose you want something to eat?" queried Mr Peachey. "I have some fresh pork dressed."

But bushranger Chapman cried out, "No. I must have some of the ham that hangs up. Let Manchester get the pan and begin to fry."

Obviously the viceregal tradition for hospitality would have been dishonoured had Mr Peachey refused. The ham was taken to the kitchen. The great Mr Howe himself did not disdain to raid the pantry for eggs or to do the menial task of beating them up with cream and spirits.

Soon all the freebooters were full of ham and eggs, and, with the best of goodwill, they assured their host that they would not take his wearing apparel, but only such things as they needed—powder and ball, some pounds of the best green tea, thread, needles, six bottles of wine.

They visited the servants' quarters and came back with pitiful mien to requisition grog for a sick convict they had found there.

Then, putting the residue of the ham and three loaves of bread in their knapsacks, they departed, though not before they had expressed regret at Colonel Davey's absence and their yearning for "some private conversation" with him. Mr Howe's last request was for a dictionary; and when Peachey said he hoped he would return it when he had done with it, Howe said that he would.

In the lightening dawn the band stole silently off into the woods.[74]

VIII

Macquarie long since had been satisfied that Davey could not remain in office. He was in a "constant state of intemperance" rendering him totally indifferent to orders.[75] There were "strong reports abroad" that he was not merely dissipated and profligate in his private life, but that he was extremely venal and corrupt in his public life—"privy to and sanctioning a great deal of clandestine trade and smuggling of spirits". He was drawing fraudulent bills for his garnisheed salary. A great deal of the bushranging was due to his lethargy. But the Governor regretted, "both on your own account and that of your amiable family", that he should be the cause of the removal of the drunken fellow from "a situation of so much respectability and comfort".

As a result of his reports he was authorized at length by Bathurst to dismiss Davey "in the way least hurtful to his feelings and those of his family".[76] His deputy-governor resigned his office with another grant of land to console him.

The retiring marine's feelings were deeply outraged. He wrote a pathetic appeal[77] to his patron, Lord Harrowby. He said that he had served the Crown for forty-four years in situations equally perilous and important in other parts of the world, without the smallest reproach or blemish; that the loss of his baggage in the armed brig, *Emu*, which had been captured by the Americans, had cost him several thousand pounds; that he had earned a "distinguished reputation"; that he felt it a pleasure to refute "the dark and invidious insinuations"[78] against him in Macquarie's vile reports of him.

Lord Harrowby did not fail his sodden follower. The three thousand acres of land which had been given him on appointment was increased to six thousand acres—two thousand of it in the richest part of the Illawarra district of New South Wales.[79]

And so soon as he was relieved of office he made his way to Sydney. There, till late on in 1818, he remained a festering thorn in the Governor's side.[80]

In his place, the Colonial Office sent Lieutenant-Colonel Sorell, whom Elizabeth had "liked the best"[81] of those whom they had met at Capetown on their outward voyage. He reached Sydney on 27 March, re-embarked the same day, and was at the Derwent on 8 April 1817.

He was a man of Macquarie's own calibre and they soon were friends. His coming lifted a great weight off the Governor's shoulders. His measures were "vigorous, energetic and judicious".[82] Within a month Macquarie was able to offer him sincere congratulation.

His excellence, of course, was not the reason for his appointment. He was a man made for bigger things. He was, in a sense, himself "transported" for his indiscretions, because he had deserted his own and eloped with somebody else's wife, whom he brought with him to the Colony.[83] He had been a defendant in *Crim. Con.* proceedings, but the facts suggest that he was a fit object for at least some sympathy.[84] Nevertheless, the "respectables" of the Colony looked upon him as a shocking example.

His predecessor, Davey, wrote his sorrow at Sorell's "disregard of all moral restraint, and even timid attention to principle".[85] He described how, in his own decent day, Government House at Hobart had "been throng'd on the birthdays of our Gracious Queen with the most respectable females, married and unmarried", but how "now, alas not a female appears at Government House", and "thus unhappily circumstanced, Society sinks into oblivion".

Captain Anthony Fenn Kemp, erstwhile of the New South Wales Corps, whose cloistered existence in Botany Bay seemed to have sheltered him from consciousness of human naughtiness, cried out in protest "as a married man . . . with a family of six children".[86] He called attention to "the dreadful example of the Highest Authority living in a public state of concubinage" with Mrs Kent at Government House and publicly parading the lady about the garrison in an equipage bought at Government expense. This he thought so insulting to public decency that it could not be forgiven. But it occurred to Mr Kemp to make his protest only after Colonel Sorell had acquired the same bad habit which had afflicted all previous Governors who had come into contact with him—that of "oppressing" him.

Sorell had dismissed him from the magistracy, it seemed, for "wishing to preserve the *bonos mores* of this Colony and reprobating vice".[87]

By all this the Governor was unperturbed. Two years later Sorell could still rejoice that he had "acquired the confidence and the repeatedly expressed approbation of Governor Macquarie".

IX

How swift the change the pair began to effect! The velvet glove was in evidence only for a moment more, after the first smashing blow. With Macquarie's approval the new man sent an emissary to Howe, whom he considered "of the first importance, both with a view to taking the rest and to discoveries respecting their abettors".[88] The wretch was offered a conditional pardon for all offences, murder excepted; and even on murder the Governor was prepared to intercede for him for the royal clemency, provided Mr Howe would make full confession and expose his confederates. Thus it was intended "to sift this train of infamy to the bottom and root it out".[89]

Howe surrendered and made a deposition—the Government already had laid hands upon his lady-love. Macquarie promised to plead for a full King's pardon for him.[90] But the villain, thinking upon the discomfort of the gallows should the appeal fail, was soon loose again after an attempt to escape by sea.

Then what a coil and how uncomfortable the profession of freebooting became. Letters of fire and sword, ringing proclamations of outlawry and promises of rewards stirred the whole place to activity.

The once light-hearted "Lieutenant-Governor of the Woods" soon came to know how woman's perfidy and the human hunter's zeal can wreck a bright career.

But a month after Sorell's arrival the dusky Mary of Mr Howe's romance had pursued him like a bloodhound from fire to fire, guided by her remarkable facility for "tracking footmarks". To her Pontefract lover, as his merry men were taken one by one, it must have been sad news indeed that "to her assistance success is chiefly owing".[91]

At last even the bold idealist was himself destroyed.

He did not suffer the anguish of discovery by his former inamorata. It was the implacable Musquito who led the minions of the "Old Gentleman" to his lair to knock him on the head like vermin and rob his body of the little white book of kangaroo hide in which his romances were written in gore.[92]

Even in this fate he was fortunate; for the Governor, in his requiem sermon, described him as a "daring and atrocious villain and outlaw", and meditated that he himself would have been "better pleased if he had been taken alive, so as to be made a public example of on a gibbet".[93]

Other culprits were quickly laid by the heels.

The inexorable Musquito, it is sad to relate, himself embraced the profession of freebooting in the end; and in due time he was hanged.[94]

X

Within two years after the bushrangers and most honest men had been shaking their sides with laughter over the Governor's "futile" measures, within about the same period after Hobart itself seemed threatened with

N

invasion, "perfect peace and tranquillity" reigned, according to Macquarie, "by virtue of the vigorous, energetic and judicious measures of Lieut. Governor Sorell".[95]

When ambitious imitators of the Howes and Millses arose, a year or two afterwards, the measures which the Governor took against them were as energetic as those against the blacks who attempted to break his pacification. He had no intention ever again to allow the conditions of 1814-17 to develop.

He himself went to the scene of action, taking Judge-Advocate Wylde with him. The ghostly war-cry of the Macquarie Clan—"*Here come the red-spattered tartans*"—seemed to ring through every copse and glen.

Kirke's Lambs and Jeffreys could not have been more thorough. Stair and Glenlyon would have approved the way in which he set out to make "signal examples among these depraved wretches".[96] Without a qualm he "yielded up his feelings of humanity to his sense of public exigency". Within four days of his arrival, ten out of twenty-six marauders caught were strung up in one horrible exhibition of the consequences of depending too implicitly on the apparent genial weakness and long-suffering good-nature of a Highland chieftain.

Then, another batch of desperate characters having been apprehended in the north,[97] he personally journeyed thither to decree the prompt suspension of five of them in Launceston and four in Georgetown, though by now his resolution faltered and Wylde and Sorell had needed to use some persuasion to induce him to complete a task of immolation so little palatable to his nature. He wrote to Bathurst: "Now that these dreadful examples have been made, I am enabled to report that there is every reasonable prospect of the bushranging system being completely at an end, most probably for many years to come."[98]

For the time being only two marauders remained skulking in the woods, though the respite was only temporary.

In payment for the extra duty of sentencing so many scoundrels in so short a time, the Governor voted Judge-Advocate Wylde £100 from the Police Fund.

CHAPTER XXV

The Lads in Black

I

As 1816 ended a host of uneasy letters, telling of doubt and even of consternation at the nature of the operations of the Reverend Samuel Marsden, flowed homeward from the devoted brethren who were blowing their rams' horns before Pomare's Jericho.

There had been a stir three years earlier when rumours had connected the Pacific Islands missionaries with the spirit trade in the islands; and, despite the indignant denials which rang out both in Parramatta and London, the Reverend Pasco Crook[1] had admitted that some evangelists did produce —to Macquarie's annoyance—a little poteen.

But now the complaints concerned the saucy *Active*.

The crew of Mr Marsden's vessel were no bright exemplars of righteousness, it seemed, but a "desperate set . . . a sad example before the eyes of the natives".[2] And Mr Marsden's methods gave his customers cause for worry, since they were "assured on clear grounds" that, though the ship was largely owned privately, and the cargoes even more so, "private, public and ship accounts were all blended together" and charged to the London Missionary Society; so it seemed that "the owners of the vessel, some of whom are not in connection with us, are like to have the use of a great deal of the Society's money to the manifest disadvantage of myself and others who may join with us".[3] Thus the matter was put to Mr Rowland Hassall, whose son wed Mr Marsden's daughter, by Mr Crook. He asked Mr Hassall to ask Mr Marsden about the facts.[4]

But all Mr Hassall could dredge from Mr Marsden was that he could not send the missionaries particulars of their personal accounts, and that "if they wished it he must refer them to the directors as he always sent home an account with the bills to show what they were drawn for". Mr Hassall added, "There can be little doubt that all accounts are added together as you refer to in yours."[5]

While the matter was under debate a vigorous agitation was in progress in the missionary world of New South Wales; and, as ever with agitations which take place in small ponds, it brought to the surface much sour-smelling matter unrelated directly to the main causes of the disturbance.

One corpse which floated upwards was that of the Philanthropic Society,[6] a body formed in 1813 to assist the poor Polynesians when visiting Sydney —they usually were the guests of Mr Marsden, who saw to their maintenance.

Mr Marsden had been secretary, Mr Robert Jenkins, collector. The Governor had headed the subscription list; his secretary, Mr J. T. Campbell, had been upon the committee. But the institution had died with only a single palpitation of its kindly heart.

Now, on 4 January 1817, appeared a letter to the *Gazette* signed by one Philo Free, a "settler at Bradley's Head". His epistle he described as "written in my cabin without the aid of books (for my little collection went on a pilgrimage, I have been told, to the Friendly and Society Islands)". It throughout exhibited that mordant type of humour which is a hallmark of crusading Christianity as practised more particularly in Ulster, the home land of Mr Campbell, the Governor's secretary. The writer recalled the happily conceived formation of the society, referred genially to the South Sea Bubble, and remarked that "although the circumstances will not perhaps warrant its [the Philanthropic Society's] being *also termed a bubble* yet there are some features in the two schemes so much alike that I think, an able hand could make no bad parallel between them—*si fas est magnis componere parva*".[7]

The South Sea scheme, he wrote, held out the bait or lure of extravagant profits in the way of trade; but "the South Sea Islands philanthropists in 1813, without the temptation of the gilded pill of wealth uncountable . . . cheerfully subscribed their money under the assurance that they would have the spiritual consolation at least of having performed charitable acts, and rendered human services to the natives of the South Sea Islands!"

In 1817, he continued, they knew all too well what profits the scheme had realized. They had received no report on the application of their funds. "Like the bubbletonian of 1720, after having come *down with our dumps*, we have had no return, either to our purse or to the stock of our benevolence." And—for aught that he could learn or read—they did not seem likely to be gratified in the future.

After referring to "the active and enterprising spirit of the Jesuits," the word "active"—the name of Mr Marsden's ship—being seemingly very much upon his mind, the author proceeded:

> *Now* a missionary spirit of a somewhat more humble cast has pervaded the Islands in the South Seas, introducing with it the art of distillation and that tiny race of animals, which on being boiled, do not prove to be lobsters! An ardent thirst for the influence *of this spirit*, at this time pervades the inhabitants of all the Islands of the Pacific, with which we have any intercourse; and pigs, and pine trees, New Zealand flax, etc., are the return made in full tale for the comforts of the spirit instilled into them, and by which they are inspired. The active exertions of him who is the worthy head of these sectarian visionaries or missionaries (whichever you please, Mr. Editor), in propagating the Gospel by such means, and the transmission from time to time of muskets and cutlasses, will, no doubt, redound much and highly to the honour of the Christian Mahomet and the church so planted, whilst the pecuniary advantage of the chosen-few will not be altogether overlooked.

There was more in the same strain leading to the conclusion that "those who bolt the pork and the profits should . . . unbolt their coffers and bear also the expences of their Gospel venders and their bacon curers". And the writer candidly concluded that he did not wish to see men in any garb, or under any mask or pretence, "arrogate to themselves such consequential airs of importance for acts of public beneficence which they have never exhibited in their private lives . . . and still less, if possible, in their public character towards the abject natives of New South Wales".

The history of the Philanthropic Society, on the face of it, looked very much like that of Mr Marsden's "public" library, all over again.[8]

II

Mr Marsden at once demanded that Wylde, the Judge-Advocate, should indict the editor of the *Gazette* for criminal libel. Mr Jenkins, the Philanthropic Society's collector, rushed to declare that he still had all the funds—in four years nobody had asked him for them! Wylde advised Macquarie to repudiate the letter.

The Governor withdrew all presumed "Government sanction, authority or concurrence" from the missive—this "in justice to his own feelings, as also to the highly respectable and benevolent persons and societies engaged in missionary labours which have ever received his public support and sanction". He expressed his "disapprobation" of the document, and his "regret that it should inadvertently from the great pressure of Government business in the Secretary's Office have got admission into the *Gazette*".[9]

Mr Campbell, the Governor's secretary, at this stage, accepted personal responsibility for publication, saying that the letter had come late to his office on publication day[10] and that he had found time to read only the beginning and the end. Mr Marsden's eyes gleamed. Mr Campbell was almost closer than a brother to the Governor, who described him as "an inmate of my family on most confidential and friendly terms", one gifted with "assiduity, zeal, firmness, honour and incorruptible integrity"; in fact, "a particular friend of mine".[11]

Marsden now demanded that a criminal indictment be prepared against Campbell.[12] Wylde tried to soothe, offered himself as an intermediary, suggested civil action. But the holy man's virtues did not include the will to loose his clutch upon the throat of an enemy. He was in an ungovernable rage. When Wylde, saying he would accept an indictment if it were supported by affidavits, gave the salutary warning that those who made the affidavits should first "pause", he treated it angrily as an improper judicial threat.[13]

Mr Moore who was, naturally, the cleric's attorney and counsel, hastened his preparations for trial; but Mr Garling, who appeared for Mr Campbell, won the right to "traverse" and secured a long adjournment to prevent the case being heard before a bench of officers from the 46th Regiment, whose mess by this time was so much at loggerheads with the Governor that its members probably would have taken delight in consigning the defendant in irons to the chain gang.

Macquarie appears at first to have given little thought to the matter after he had officially disavowed the letter in the *Gazette*. He was in good spirits as, three days afterwards at Parramatta, he gazed with pride on the

"Beautiful Temple of Hymen with transparent lights, erected under the taste and direction of Mrs Macquarie on the lawn in front of Government House, which was lighted up after dark in honour of the marriage of Princess Charlotte to the Prince of Saxe-Coburg-Gotha".[14]

III

When, near the year's end, this first criminal libel action heard in the Colony, and one of the most curious ever heard in any British country, did come before the court, members of the newly-arrived 48th Regiment formed the tribunal.

The Judge-Advocate presided with three officers in scarlet on either side of him. Mr Moore, for Marsden, would have been supported by Mr Amos, one of the other two free solicitors in the Colony apart from the Clerk of the Peace, but Mr Amos mysteriously had deserted him the evening before the trial.[15]

The charge against Mr Campbell was that, holding the official situation of Secretary to His Excellency the Governor,

> against the Peace, he designed and intended, as much as in him lay, to defame and vilify the good character and reputation of Samuel Marsden and to insinuate and cause it to be believed that the said Samuel Marsden was of a sordid and avaricious disposition, and had, under a false pretext of religious motives, introduced amongst the ignorant and uncivilised inhabitants of certain islands of the South Seas and Southern Pacific Ocean the art of distilling a pernicious and spirituous liquor, and also introduced a certain loathsome, offensive and uncleanly species of vermin; that the said Samuel Marsden . . . had from time to time transmitted to the said Islands certain dangerous and destructive weapons; and that he was a religious imposter and not a preacher and believer of the Christian religion, according to the usages and ceremonies of the Church of England.[16]

And that the defendant had set out to accomplish all this by composing, making, writing, publishing and causing and procuring to be published the letter of Philo Free. There were some other counts.

Mr George Williams, the *Gazette's* erstwhile compositor, who had travelled to the Colony with Mr Jeffery Bent in the *Broxbornebury*, had worked in the *Gazette* office till a few weeks after the publication of the letter. He had then extended his partisan spirit and support of the Bent faction to his employment, turning away an advertisement in which Mr Samuel Terry offered a reward for the conviction of the person who had forged his name upon the Vale-Bent petition.[17]

Macquarie had learned of his action and of his presence in the Government Printing Office. Mr Howe, the printer, promptly had heard from Government House: "Now it being my determination that no such infamous incendiary shall be employed in any department under Government in this Colony, I hereby command and direct you at your peril not to retain the said George Williams in your employ after one month from the date hereof."[18]

Mr Howe had hastened to be rid of Mr Williams.

So Mr Williams came to the trial as an enthusiastic witness to swear that Campbell had brought Philo Free's letter into the composing room and delivered it to Howe in his presence; also that he "thought"—from other specimens he had seen on notes which had come from Campbell's house—it was in the latter's handwriting.

Mr Marsden swore that the *Active* had been purchased for the promotion of the Church Missionary Society and that he was authorized to draw expenses on the Society by Bills which were always honoured; that the ship was "wholly and solely occupied by the Missions in the South Seas, without any trade except with a view to lessen the expences of the Society". The ship was "wholly at his disposal for the concerns of the missions" and the London Missionary Society and Church Missionary Society. He did not point out that in 1816 he had secured subsidies of £250 a year each from the London Missionary and Church Missionary Societies to help maintain the *Active*.

Eventually it was elicited:

> I gave £1400 for this ship. I paid £500 in money, and £900 in sheep out of my own stock; they were sold for £2 a head at that time. . . . I have never drawn upon the Society for a single shilling of the purchase money. I am entitled to draw for it any day; the ship is my property and I am the registered owner. . . . I purchased the ship without any instructions particularly from the Society on my own responsibility.

This was October 1817; the ship had been purchased in 1813. He admitted having had a few muskets repaired for Maori chiefs. The Sandwich Islanders were blamed for teaching the Tahitians how to distil liquor. And by a sort of tacit common consent the indelicate subject of the tiny race of animals which when boiled were not lobsters universally ignored.

Mr Howe, the printer of the *Gazette*, swore that the letter had been handed to him by Campbell, not in Williams's presence, but in his own office. He could not swear to the handwriting, since it was so much like that of other people—even like that of Mr Marsden, it seemed. He named three witnesses who could swear in support of his statement of the case. These witnesses were not called.

Next day Mr Richard Jones, Sydney commercial agent for Mr Marsden, and supplier of £8000 worth of the merchandise which went in the *Active* to Otaheite and New Zealand, swore that Howe had told him that Williams had been dismissed from the Government Printing Office because he had revealed the authorship of Philo Free's letter.

He was allowed to swear to the opinion that he would *not* now believe Mr Howe on oath. And neither would Mr Riley, his partner. Dr Harris, of Ultimo, was called to swear that he *would* believe Mr Howe on oath.

The day ended with Mr Jones returning to the witness-box to admit that he recollected that "Howe told me that Williams was discharged, not as I have before stated, for making disclosures as to the letter of 'Philo Free,' but on account of having signed a petition that went to the House of Commons". The Judge-Advocate made some caustic reference to Mr Jones and his testimony.[19] The unfortunate Court retired in an utterly confused state to consider its verdict.

Nobody discovered what had happened to the Philanthropic Society's funds. Mr Marsden declared that he was merely the secretary, that he knew nothing of funds. He revealed a mind above such matters. Mr Eagar swore that £130 had been subscribed and none of it paid back.

And a notable absentee from the trial was Mr Robert Jenkins, the collector of the Society, who could have salvaged completely the reputations of that body, of Mr Marsden, and of himself, by presenting a straightforward financial statement. Mr Jenkins had, at first, burned to help initiate the suit; but on hearing Mr Wylde's injunction to the makers of affidavits to pause, he had said, "I think I'll pause", and had been seen no more.[20]

In such an atmosphere it was comforting to hear an approving note creep into the oratory of Mr Marsden's solicitor when he spoke of the Governor's part in the affair, especially since Mr J. H. Bent had advised him and had seen his address before its delivery.

"I cannot forbear offering my humble mite to the general feeling which the handsome, liberal, most honourable and most manly manner, in which his Excellency was pleased to express himself on the subject [of the letter] . . . Nothing could be more liberal, more handsome or more honourable to His Excellency than his conduct on this occasion."[21]

And he wished that a similar disposition had been shown by the defendant.

IV

The impression left by the confused testimony and the lawyers' wrangling on the military minds of the captains and subalterns of the newly-arrived 48th Regiment, who had not been accustomed to this sort of judicial proceeding, was exactly what might have been expected. All they could make of it was that some wretched civilian at Government House was there to be convicted of something, and they were determined not to be remiss in their duty.

The Judge-Advocate informed them firmly that they certainly could not convict Mr Campbell of composing, printing, and publishing the libel, because there was no evidence of it.[22] They debated the matter. They resolved to find the culprit "guilty of having permitted a public letter to be printed in the Sydney Gazette, which tends to vilify the public conduct of the Prosecutor, as the Agent of the Missionary Societies for propagating the Gospel in the South Seas, which it was in the power of the Defendant in his official capacity of Secretary to His Excellency the Governor of the Territory to have prevented publication of."[23]

Mr Moore knew better than to call for sentence on such a verdict, which was tantamount to "not guilty".

Instead, Mr Marsden rushed off to prosecute a civil action, instructing his solicitor to make the damages high—£3000, at least—so that he could appeal to the Privy Council if he failed.[24]

There were other advantages in civil proceedings, not the least of them that Mr Justice Barron Field, Jeffery Bent's successor, would preside. For Mr Field was one whose sympathies were not likely to be with the Governor's friends or with the traducers of holy men.

A barrister, now thirty-one years old, and of two years' standing[25] when he was transferred to the Botany Bay Bench from the chair of a dramatic critic of *The Times*, Mr Field had arrived the previous February sniffing disgustedly at the Colony's "barren wood"[26]—in it he found no virtue and no *Times*.

The natural expressions of his youthful countenance were appropriate to a boon-companionship with Leigh Hunt ("Jennie kissed me") and to a "distant correspondence" with Charles Lamb;[27] but they were mitigated, after his elevation, by a severe look of piety, emblem of his willingness to read scripture to naughty convict girls, and enamelled over with a judicial composure which evaporated rapidly in the presence of a tort or a convict attorney.

Macquarie already was ceasing to be "very much prejudiced in his favour by his mild, modest and conciliating manners",[28] though the day had not yet come when Sir Thomas Brisbane would describe him as "guided by no moral restraints", or Disraeli rate him "a bore and vulgar, a Storks without breeding . . . a noisy, obtrusive, jargonic judge, ever illustrating the obvious, explaining the evident and expatiating on the commonplace".[29]

A critic wrote in his envy:

> Thy poems, Barron Field, I've read,
> And thus adjudge their meed,
> So poor a crop proclaims thy head
> A barren field indeed.[30]

But none dare be so derisive of his court proceedings, as fat Mr Amos learned, later, when he entered into a secret compact with the villain Crossley, and was struck from the court rolls without being allowed to say one word in his own defence.[31]

Following Mr Field through one of his judgments was somewhat like running in the wake of an exuberant boy in pursuit of an agile goanna. The hunt was always some lengths ahead of the full comprehension of the audience; but, through a scrub of words, one heard the hunter's challenging view-halloos, the crash of dog-Latin precedent and of solid hunks of Blackstone upon the hide of fleeing Error. Then all would be silence for a moment, till the breathless follower of the chase burst into a clearing flowered with allusive asterisks.

And there Mr Field would be discovered whistling as he sat resting upon a Horatian tag, his quarry twitching at his feet.

All Sydney was agog to hear how Mr Field's piety and lore would react to the *cause célèbre, Marsden* v. *Campbell*, but it offered him little scope and his talents were more in evidence later in a stay-of-costs motion.

Despite Mr Moore's assurances at the first hearing, it was whispered by Mr Marsden that the Governor had been party to the libellous letter;

that the defection of Amos, Mr Marsden's second solicitor, from the criminal trial, had been due to fear of consequences which might have ensued had he dared to support the prosecutor; that relevant witnesses had been afraid to come forward because of their dread of what Macquarie might do to them.[32]

However, the civil trial unearthed one witness who apparently did not fear the wrath either of the Governor or his secretary. When the trial opened no less a personage than the poet laureate, Mr Michael Massey Robinson, the famous writer of threatening letters, who in his unpoetic moments was chief clerk at Government House and Mr Campbell's assistant, adorned the witness-box.

Mr Robinson calmly took an oath and swore deliberately that he had seen the Philo Free letter in Campbell's hand,[33] that it was in Campbell's handwriting, and that Campbell had told him that he had copied it from a document he had received that morning and which was so illegible that he had been obliged to write it out anew.

Garling, Campbell's solicitor, already seems to have known how the land lay. He pleaded not guilty, throwing away all chance to prove justification or to cross-examine effectively, and called no witnesses. Mr Robinson completely settled the matter.

Mr Field found a verdict for Marsden and gave £200 damages. Mr Campbell's witty resentment had cost him, including legal expenses, a matter of £476.[34]

The damages were indeed modest. One might have thought that the association of Mr Marsden's name with the "tiny race of animals" alone would have been worth more than such a trivial sum, which was very far from the £3000 claimed.

Mr Campbell in any case had little cause to care, for a time at least. He went about gleefully admitting authorship; and when, two years later, the Governor gave him a grant of land, he christened it Mount Philo.[35]

The *Gazette* already had published a presumed report of the criminal trial, which was almost as offensive as the original libel. It averred that "several witnesses failed in establishing any of the points, or meeting the allegations set forth in the information".[36]

Mr Howe added a long personal statement about his own position. And though the Judge-Advocate was wroth, he did not mention the matter to the Governor, because he had discovered that reminder of the affair was apt to produce in Macquarie's breast the most "disagreeable feelings".[37] He refrained from bringing the printer before the Court for contempt, only because "the statement formed what is termed the leader of the paper and did not purport to be a formal report of the trial".

Two months afterwards, while the Marsden faction was raging in a flood of angry correspondence which sought to pin responsibility on the Governor, Macquarie showed that his feelings were not so deep as to prevent him from giving Mr Robinson his customary annual reward of two cows for his services as poet laureate.[38]

V

Missionary society in London was deeply shocked that so vile an assault should have been made on so great a saint as its idol, the Reverend Samuel Marsden, whose adventures in New Zealand had proved a profitable advertisement for its evangelizing activities. Its view of the evidence was based upon Mr Marsden's sketchy version of it.

Mr Wilberforce wrote to the good man:

> I am sorry to see that you still experience so much low hostility; but besides the support of your own conscience it will be justly gratifying to you to know that your character is held in due estimation by all I trust in this country for whose approbation you would be at all solicitous. Let me beg you always to write me with the utmost openness and put me in the way of receiving all authentic information . . .[39]

Mr Jeffery Bent told the wronged cleric that he was "greatly rejoiced to hear of your success in bringing the shameless author of Philo Free to his well-merited punishment; I was the first person who gave the news to Mr Pratt [Secretary of the London Missionary Society]. . . . He is much delighted that Philo Free had been so completely mortified".

> You must have enough upon your hands to contend against Wylde and the higher powers, and it is certainly a great thing to say you were able to succeed. . . . I understand also that Governor Macquarie at last is about to be removed. . . . You need not be under any alarm, as to yourself it isn't in the power of Wylde or the Governor to effect your removal. Indeed, Mr. Pratt and other friends were surprised that you should think it necessary to vindicate yourself. I said to him they might impute wrong motives to your pursuit of Philo Free, but it was necessary you should pursue him to the utmost, in order to secure future freedom from attack.[40]

Mr Bent averred that "the Governor knew and saw the libel before it was published". It was "almost incredible" to him "that Macquarie should persist in a line of conduct which he cannot boast of when he returns". He believed, he wrote, that the Governor's spirit was "that of an arbitrary and cruel man; and in other times he would have been more intolerably despotic".

Bathurst heard of the Campbell trial, and especially of the *Gazette's* vindictive report of it, and called for the papers. He ordered Campbell to be censured, but Marsden was also censured by the Colonial Office for his "equally derogatory" attack on Wylde.[41]

Campbell apologized to Macquarie for the publication of his "hasty and inconsiderate letter" and explained that:

> as character and motives must be ever dear to me, I beg to offer as a slight extenuation that the letter in question was written in the midst of much hurry and with little previous reflection, being altogether dictated by a feeling, which I trust I shall have some credit for, namely of indignation at the marked disrespect shewn by Mr. Marsden to Your Excellency's orders and establishments in his

not attending the meeting of the natives at Parramatta, which had been convened by Your Excellency a very few days before that letter appeared, altho'
I knew him to be sitting in a house within a few yards of where that meeting
was held.
. . . I had it also in recollection that the former year's Native Meeting had
experienced the same marked disinclination on Mr. Marsden's part to countenance efforts towards the civilisation of the natives of this country.[42]

There was an aftermath two years later. As Mr Marsden left for New
Zealand, in the *Dromedary*, muskets were found among the missionary
supplies in the ship. Mr Marsden "could not deny the facts, nor could he
explain them";[43] but he rushed to the Governor and Mr Commissioner
Bigge, who was then in the country, to sheet the guilt home to his missionary
colleagues. Those wretched men he berated in subsequent correspondence
for their alleged part in the "nefarious traffic". None of them, however,
appeared anxious to accept the guilt of what had occurred. They "refused
to exculpate" Mr Marsden. They jeered at his pretension that he had not
been involved in supplying the natives with arms; charged that he had
exchanged an axe for a human head. Wrote the Reverend Mr Butler to
Mr Marsden:

> Did you not pay Mr. Hall for two muskets 26 lb. of powder at one time and 50 lb.
> another? . . . Did you not purchase a lot of flax and potatoes . . . with muskets? Did
> you not afterwards send down 51 bayonets at one time? . . . Has not the *Active's*
> cargo been bought with these forbidden things? . . . I believe these things can be
> very easily proved. . . . Did you not say to me with your own mouth that a
> gentleman of one of the universities had applied to you for a skull without hair?
> Did you not signify your intentions to obtain it if possible? Did you not employ
> Mr. Hall to go to the village of Rangeo Aloo and see if he could obtain such a
> thing? Did you not receive a native head from Jackey, and give him an axe?
> I am sure I saw him with one and he afterwards assured me he had given it to you
> and that you gave him an axe which he showed me. Have you not sold the
> supplies sent out to administer comfort to the poor naked New Zealanders?
> You say for want of an invoice alone? Granted. But do the Society or the Christ-
> ian world expect to be repaid by the wretched, distressed heathen? Have you not
> sold the *Active's* crew the slops intended to clothe the native servants? And further
> have you not even sent away the Society's slops to Van Diemen's Land, to be
> bartered away for food for the crew of the *Active*, instead of forwarding them to
> New Zealand in order to afford comfort to the destitute?[44]

VI

When Mr Campbell's libel action was over, Macquarie must have thanked
Providence that the outcome had been no worse.

In the interval between the adjournment and the trial, he had been
vouchsafed unpleasant glimpses of the capacity of the officers of the 46th
Regiment, which was supposedly at the Governor's disposal, to thwart
his policies and promote his discomfiture.

Commanded by Macquarie's "old and much liked friend" of David
Baird's staff during the Egyptian Expedition of 1801,[45] Lieutenant-Colonel

George Molle, the Regiment's officers constituted about as insolent a moiety of the British Army as ever was sent abroad.

The Governor had, as usual with strangers, welcomed them all with open arms when they reached the Colony early in 1814.

He received Molle "with the freedom and cordiality of ingenuous friendship". All his public measures seemed for a time in perfect unison with Molle's own public sentiments and views of political expediency.[46]

Macquarie was ready to oblige him and the Regiment in every possible way. The Government House table was even more open to the officers of the 46th Regiment than it had been to their predecessors of the 73rd Regiment. For the rank and file there would be—"in the interests of sobriety!"—a regular daily tot of spirits, a privilege which no regiment had hitherto enjoyed in New South Wales.[47]

The officers discovered "considerable difficulty and embarrassment in supporting and keeping up the respectability of the regimental mess, as well as defraying the other necessary expences attending their living and in supplying their uniforms".[48] Oilmen's stores were dear. Scarlet cloth was never under five guineas a yard. And the purchase of wines was attended with so enormous an expense, "as almost to deprive them of so beneficial an indulgence (even in a moderate degree) in a climate, where *such indulgence is salutary & requisite*".[49]

The Governor rushed to recommend their succour by the War Office, so that they might live in "respectable decent style in this very expensive distant Colony".[50]

Little thanks he had for his trouble. It was soon plain that he did not, as he had thought, possess Molle's reciprocal regard. It came out that, on Molle's recommendation, members of the mess, even before arrival in New South Wales, had passed a resolution not to associate with convicts or emancipists.[51] Some of them had been in close contact with John M'Arthur before leaving London.[52]

Despite this resolution they for a time did consort with emancipists. Colonel Molle expressed himself "in terms of admiration" of the principles on which the Governor was acting towards them and even entertained some at his own table. But they had made up for a brief lapse into tolerance by a gentlemanly disregard of all interests save their own and by frequent displays of insufferable arrogance.[53]

Mr Campbell would have shown hardihood indeed had he trusted his liberty to a court formed of members of the 46th Regiment. Led by Captain Edward Sanderson, they had burst into a campaign of opposition to the Governor contemporaneously with Bent and Marsden.

At the mess table before servants they jeered at Macquarie. They insulted his emancipist guests in his own drawing-room. A number, enrolling under the seditious banner of Captain Sanderson, more than once refused invitations to Government House.[54]

Macquarie "knew the mutinous licentiousness" of this faction, but held it "suitable to his dignity to let such efforts pass unnoticed", till "the spirit of annoyance even descended so low, and became so vulgar, that in July,

1816, Ensign Bullivant, when on duty in command of the Main Guard at Sydney, had the audacity to draw with chalk or charcoal on the wall of the guard room a full length caricature of myself in a position of ignominy, with indecent scurrilous labels underneath it".

The original friezemaker had been a beardless boy, but senior officers had added the labels. The horror had remained on the wall for several days for all to see.

The Governor was very angry. Bullivant apologized. He said that he "meant no insult or disrespect to nor contempt of His Excellency", and that he "only drew or sketched the said figure for amusement in a moment of thoughtless levity".[55]

His Excellency "very willingly" abandoned his intention to have him court-martialled, he being "very young and inexperienced". But he would have dealt with the seniors, save that there was only their own mess to form a court to try them.[56]

The 46th Regiment, in truth, by the beginning of 1817 had come to be a very centre of rebellion, and its discontented officers possessed a facility which enabled them to cover intrigue and arrange discussions among those opposed to the Governor, under the cloak of a peculiar privilege not available to others in that rigidly controlled community.

Some of its members were custodians of the warrant of the movable military Masonic Lodge, No. 227, Social and Military Virtues.[57]

Macquarie was, of course, an old-standing member of the Craft; but, with this crew of disreputables, that counted for nothing.[58]

The Right Worshipful Master was Captain Sanderson. Colonel Molle was a brother. The other members included John Drummond, the naval (customs) officer at Hobart Town, who presently was charged with his unmarried sister-in-law with murdering their illegitimate infant; Jeffery Bent; John Horsley, Bent's fellow-traveller from England and boon companion; David Allan, the outraged and dishonest commissary; Oxley, John M'Arthur's friend and near neighbour and fellow intriguer; Riley, the now disgruntled hospital contractor, and his friend, J. R. O'Connor; W. H. Moore, the dispossessed solicitor; and Surgeon John Harris.[59]

VII

In 1816 a brother Mason, that queer character, Captain John Piper, the man who appeared able to keep the confidence of both sides in every quarrel, was about to build himself a mansion at Point Piper—Eliza Point, to the Macquarie era.[60]

The Lodge decided to lay the foundation stone in true Masonic fashion, but the brethren were somewhat in a quandary, since the demand for aprons and scarves had outrun the ability of the Colony to provide them.

In their extremity, the brethren turned to Mr Francis Howard Greenway, the Government Architect, for help. He was one who would himself have rushed gladly to build King Solomon's Temple, and he apparently had some knowledge of Masonic symbols and lore.[61]

He even showed a fraternal disposition to do the work for nothing, quite forgetting that he was a convicted felon. The officers insisted on paying him.

So great was the demand upon him, however, that he found himself short of important colours. There was delay. The Worshipful Master, Captain Sanderson, a "powerful and athletic man", reproved him. Mr Greenway, again forgetting his captive state, retorted. As a letter-writer, he wielded a bitter pen.[62]

Then he apparently realized his position and sent a letter of apology, which seems only to have added fuel to the captain's wrath.

Meanwhile, the foundation stone of Captain Piper's house was laid with full Masonic rites. A battery fired a seven-gun salute. A vessel in the Harbour flew a Masonic emblem at the mast head. The Lodge was constituted in a glade. The members marched in solemn procession to the scene of the ceremony, armed with all the implements necessary to so grand an occasion. They were marshalled by Brother Grant, of the Regiment, and led by Sanderson.

Corn was scattered, wine and oil poured. The Worshipful Master struck the foundation stone three strokes of his mallet. The regimental band burst into "Pleyel's German Hymn" followed by "God Save the King". The sum of £6 14s. was laid on the stone for the poor and needy, and the Reverend Samuel Marsden, who was not of the Craft, stepped forward, as a spectator, to praise the Lodge.

At the Barracks another brotherly (but far from Masonic) ceremony soon was enacted. Mr Greenway, painter of aprons, was passing through the barrack yard. He went smiling to meet the request of Captain Sanderson to come to the Orderly Room. He felt that Sanderson intended to accept his apology; but it seemed that his host merely proposed to "attend to Mr Greenway's spirit of English independence".

Captain Sanderson's "powerful and athletic" form seemed to be shaking with rage. He took up a large riding whip, flogged Mr Greenway and beat him with his fists, part of the assault being in the presence of several onlookers.[63]

Poor Greenway could offer no defence beyond crying, "Mr Sanderson, sir, recollect! Consider my situation, sir. I dare not run the risk of resisting, were I able. You know how I am circumstanced."

As a convict, had he resisted physically, he would have been in danger of being ordered to the triangles by a court of which even Sanderson might easily have been a member. And, as this was the kind of experience which every prudent artist avoids, he could only take his beating.

Captain Sanderson laid on with a will, which was the greater, no doubt, because Mr Greenway was at the moment one of the Governor's most trusted servants.

VIII

The victim of the brutal assault complained to the Governor and the Judge-Advocate. A criminal charge was laid against Sanderson. The Judge-

Advocate, Wylde, in "the most polite and delicate manner communicated to him the necessity for taking his trial at the next criminal court".[64]

The captain said he was much offended and outraged at the suggestion and promised to horsewhip Mr Greenway again, whenever and wherever he met him. Mr Greenway had him bound over by the magistrates.

At the trial Judge-Advocate Wylde was the only member of the Bench of seven judges who was not a brother officer of the accused.

Two of the judges had gone bail for Sanderson. When Mr Garling, Greenway's solicitor, attempted to open his case, the Court abruptly ordered him to desist from criticizing the prisoner.

The Judge-Advocate insisted that Garling should be allowed to proceed. There was a riotous scene while members of the Court threatened the solicitor with personal consequences if he continued his attack.

Calm was restored. A judge, who proved a most unsatisfactory witness, left the Bench to give evidence for the defence. Later he asked the Judge-Advocate to tell him whether the tenor of his oath bound him to reveal what he considered to be a friendly and confidential communication from a brother officer.

The Judge-Advocate said it did. The young man then reversed his evidence and swore to a conversation which previously he had sworn had never taken place.

The Judge-Advocate expressed his views with candour. The Court hastily fined Captain Sanderson £5 and added a majority rider "that the Judge-Advocate had acted with unnecessary and ungentlemanly harshness in compelling Captain Sanderson to give sureties and in allowing the prosecutor's solicitor to pursue the course he did"; that the conduct of the solicitor, Mr Garling, was "exceedingly ungentlemanly and exceedingly improper"; that, "although they were bound in strictness of the law to find Captain Sanderson guilty, yet his conduct was that which, as an officer and a gentleman, he was fully justifiable in".

Far different was the Court's treatment of free-born, sixteen-year-old George Reiby, who whipped an exclusive sprig for calling him "convict bastard" before his sweetheart. Him it fined £100, exacting fearsome peace sureties.

Mr Greenway now went to a civil court and secured damages of £20 in a trial at which Sanderson flagrantly insulted the Bench.[65] The Governor felt compelled to admonish Captain Sanderson severely in "as private and delicate a manner as possible" for rudeness to the magistrates.[66]

Lieutenant-Colonel Molle professed to be indignant at the general behaviour of the mess. He reported that he had "found it at length necessary to lecture several of them on the bold licence which they gave their tongues".

However, all knew that Molle was in close league with the exclusive party; also that intrigue already was afoot in London to have Sir Thomas Brisbane, who was on the verge of marrying one of Molle's relatives, appointed Governor in Macquarie's stead.

The Governor was polite to Molle in public, but in a letter to Bathurst in May 1817 his theme was the futility of Lieutenant-Governors,[67] who seemed to him to fill "one of those inefficient and altogether useless departments which could be well dispensed with".

In fact, he claimed, useless was a "gentler appellation" than he considered the office deserved, since the title seemed to be favourable to the cherishing of principles of opposition to a superior's plans; also to the growth of "a jealousy of power of a Superior" which, when excited, led to the harbourer of it gathering round him "all the dissatisfied and disaffected in the inferior classes". These "would be glad to associate themselves under a leader of the nominally high rank of Lieutenant-Governor".

There was, however, now more than the incentive of jealousy to spur Molle to war against the Governor.

Something had happened at the beginning of 1816 which had almost destroyed Colonel Molle's sense of proportion and developed a disturbance which still raged a year later.

In Sydney Barrack Yard someone had discovered a "pipe", the contents directed against the bold commander of the Regiment.[68]

IX

The use of pipes was a not uncommon feature of the social hostilities of New South Wales.

Damped overnight by dew, in a conspicuous place, somebody would discover a neat roll or "pipe" of paper. Inside it a few doggerel verses, such as small boys write on fences or on less cleanly places, would be found inscribed. These would reflect on the honour and integrity, perhaps even on the beauty and chastity, of a distinguished victim.

Twentieth-century minds find it difficult to believe that any adult person ever took a pipe seriously; but pipes appeared to drive those in colonial authority in Regency days into a very insanity of alarm and rage. The anguished cries of "sedition" which Governor King raised when made the subject of a pipe have echoed down through a hundred and forty years of history.[69]

And the pipes which Governor King suffered were a trifle beside that directed against Colonel Molle.

The surviving copy of the effusion is in a small neat hand on four tough pages of elephant cartridge paper. It would, indeed, have been just to refer to it as a sewer or a *cloaca*, rather than as a pipe, having regard to its immensity and to the odorous record of Colonel Molle's supposed falsities and failings which flowed smoothly through its interior.

It was no wonder that Colonel Molle turned pale and purple by turns under his scarlet thatch as he unfurled the enduring-looking parchment. The verses[70] were introduced by a Latin tag. The scene was laid in Botany Bay—where "Vice and Folly reign in every place". The poet's "sickening Muse", seeking a focus of attack upon antipodean turpitudes, was discovered "irresolute of choice" amidst the numerous votaries of Vice:

> Till thou, G . . . rg M.ll., high oer the rest art seen,
> Thou of the stately port and haughty mien.

Who, asked the poet, would not say

> *. . . that such a portly gait*
> *Reveal'd a mind aspiring noble great?*
> *Who would imagine that contemptuous smile,*
> *Which seems so keenly others to revile,*
> *Conceals a Soul, attached to filthy pelf,*
> *One undivided, mercenary self.*

The wretched commander was pictured "clothed in humble guise, pacing the streets with modest down-cast eyes". The eager chronicler of his habits threw a glance at his boon companions:

> *Oft have the lads in black, thy chosen crew,*
> *The canting, preaching tribe assailed my view.*

Then, after a few more indirect but contemptuous reflections on the Lieutenant-Governor's associates, Mr Marsden and the others, he flashed his light upon Molle's perfidy to Macquarie:

> *See him, on days of state, with joyful haste*
> *Attend the Ruler's summons to the feast;*
> *Hear him with three times three in bumper toast*
> *Propose "the Health of our Illustrious Host"*
> *Then, in oration ready cut and dried,*
> *"Wish that the helm of State he long may guide."*
> *"And oer these happy regions long preside."*
> *Look at his open, unembarrassed air,*
> *With what effrontery he makes the pray'r.*
> *And can it be that he is not sincere?*
> *Yes. While he feigns with friendship's warmth to glow,*
> *He is His Greatest, bitterest, deadliest foe;*
> *He seeks his pow'r and influence to thwart,*
> *By ev'ry dirty, sly, insidious art,*
> *And seems averse in factions toils to fall,*
> *Himself the secret spring propelling all.*

A derisive expedition into the breach at Seringapatam with the gallant Molle followed; his Egyptian medals were cast aside as dross, "the feats he did, the enemies he slew" were appraised; and readers were ushered into Elizabeth's drawing-room:

> *And now the Gents, their quantum drunk of wine,*
> *The ladies in the drawing room rejoin:*
> *And while their tea they sip, some in their ear*
> *Whisper soft nonsense, others stand and jeer,*
> *And with their neighbours kind assistance soon*
> *Rake up the current scandal of the town.*
> *George to the Governess his due respects*
> *First having paid, a chosen group collects;*
> *And on by Bacchus' mantling bowl inspir'd,*
> *Or by his own heroic actions fir'd,*
> *He very soon prodigious witty grows,*
> *And now in puns he deals, now in bons mots.*

Which he, Joe Miller's *pages scanning o'er,*
Or staler wits', has added to his store:
Or, if to aught that's novel and his own
His Brains give Birth, tis some quaint lifeless pun,
Of all the mongrels, that to wit lay claim,
The basest bred, that e'er prophan'd the name!
And should some luckless Butt, perchance, draw near,
He marks his coming with a wink and sneer.
And when approach'd, his man begins to quiz,
Thinking himself prodigiously wise.
And should the ass, to scape his scoffs sneak off
From all the circle bursts a hoarse horse-laugh
Which draws the eyes of all to his retreat,
And serves the fool's confusion to complete.

The spectator saw Colonel Molle leading the long, intricate, mazy movement of the dance irrespective of everybody else's convenience, only pausing to discomfort the rustics, as:

With grin triumphant, and malicious sneer,
His joy he whispers in his partners ear.

There was a threat to tell a tale "which better were untold, a tale, which only to a few is known, yet of that few *thy enemy* is one".
The poet left the now apoplectic officer with the injunction:

And now, farewell, thou dirty, grov'lling M-ll-
Go with thy namesake, burrow in thy hole!

After the word "namesake" was a minute asterisk which looked like a drawing of a disgraceful insect.

X

According to the Governor's retrospect Molle, instead of suffering this anonymous and scurrilous document "by silent contempt to be altogether harmless", began an inquiry which "excited a general curiosity about the contents of the lampoon and copies were quickly multiplied, so as to gratify every person desirous of seeing it".[71]

There is some suspicion that the colonel's proceedings at first were not purely and solely the emanations of fury. He was aware that popular rumour credited the Governor's secretary with the libel on his Christian friend, Mr Marsden. Why, then, might not some of the Governor's friends have dropped the pipe in the Barrack Yard?

Not all the mess of the South Devons were of the "faction". A full third of them were prepared to accept the Governor as the arbiter of society and to follow his views. Some of them were actually on his staff. And it was surely at them and not at loyalists like Captain Sanderson and Lieutenant Grant that Molle aimed when he asked all the officers of the regiment to render up their keys so that he might go through their desks.[72]

If the colonel's eyes were turned to Government House, however, it must surely have been for lack of reading.

> *"Vice and Folly reign in every place!"*

Where had one heard that?

> *Or hail at once the patron and the pile*
> *Of vice and folly, Greville and Argyle!*[73]

Whoever would have accused any Scot of adopting echoes from the lines of an "English Bard" so polluted by recent usage?

Colonel Molle, if he had any hopes that his inquiry would lead him to exalted spheres, was doomed to failure. When he had finished with his task, there was probably none in his whole life which he more regretted.

The Governor, when shown the pipe, immediately had denounced it as reflecting in "unjust and malicious" terms upon its victim.[74] He offered freedom as a prize to whatever convict might name the author.

The outraged mess of the 46th Regiment, to save their own faces, offered a reward of £200 for the detection of the scoundrel who had dared asperse the courage, habits, and principles of their beloved commander. But all these temptations produced was more pipes.[75]

The officers had their pill:

> *If then you mean Boys what you say*
> *And really have the pow'r to pay*
> *Down with your Dumps and let me see*
> *That you possess th' ability.*
> *For altho I might take a kick*
> *For payment, I will not on tick.*[76]

There was a derisive pipe for the Governor chiding him by his Christian name:

> *But, L-chl-n, have I injured thee?*
> *Why then art thou my enemy?*
> *To whom have I e'er given pain,*
> *But to those hostile to thy reign?*[77]

Then came a long pause while the verses circulated ever more widely, with additions in the shape of a dialogue "poem" in which "Janufacies" Molle conversed at length with "Cacomanus" Riley, the disgruntled hospital contractor, *alias* the Count.[78]

"If possible more severe and scurrilous than the former", Macquarie pronounced it as he surveyed new aspersions on Molle's military career and recognized his viceregal self gently lampooned as "poor Sandy".

XI

Suspicion of the authorship of these last efforts fell on Captain Robert Lathrop Murray who had, perforce, abandoned the uniform of the Royals to wear a convict garb. He was an employee of D'Arcy Wentworth, and a clerk and constable to the Sydney Bench.[79]

Molle and Riley demanded that the magistrates, with the Judge-Advocate presiding, should inquire into the guilt or otherwise of Murray.[80] The Bench sat in June 1817, sixteen months at least after the discovery of the original pipe. Sensation followed sensation. Dr Wentworth was called as a witness, so that the whole judicial task fell on the shoulders of Wylde and Simeon Lord. Dr Wentworth appeared dramatically and confessed that he had discovered some time ago that his son William, who had sailed for England in March 1816, had been the author of the original libel.[81]

The effect on Molle was electric. He seized Wentworth's hand and trumpeted his thanks for the clearing up of the mystery.[82] He disappeared into a lengthy retreat with Murray and emerged to cry that he wanted no more of the proceedings of the Bench. He seemed like a man from whose mind a great weight had been lifted. He could not conceal his transports of joy. And Riley joined him in asking that the proceedings be closed.[83]

The regimental officers were no less delighted that all officers and gentlemen had been cleared of suspicion. They declared that the recent disclosure of the author afforded them so proud a triumph that they hailed the opportunity to give publicity to those sentiments which so unanimously prevailed among them:

> Publications, of such a nature as those alluded to, are at best the secret weapons to which the mean and timid filchers of good name resort for the gratification of personal resentment, and by which they covertly strive to wound integrity.
> These we perceive issuing from the pen of Men so much our inferiors in rank and situation, that we know them not but among that promiscuous class, which (with pride we speak it) have been ever excluded from intercourse with us.[84]

They furthermore requested that their Commander "allow us still more to approve and applaud that system of exclusion, which even prior to our arrival in a colony of this description was wisely adopted, the benefits of which we have reaped with advantage to ourselves as Officers and Gentlemen, and which, altho' it may have prompted the malignity of those whom we have kept aloof, has established the name of the 46th Regiment on a most respectable basis".

They felt, they announced, that by their exclusiveness they had caused their mess table "to be regarded as the standard of society in this Colony" and that they had "established a salutary rule" for succeeding regiments. They conceded that, had the effusion been the work of respectable men, the consideration would have been more grievous; but "*Here* it is enough to know the *men, their origin* and history, and the venom of their libellous pens becomes absorbed in the contemplation of each contemptible mœvius in satire".[85]

They professed towards Colonel Molle "an inviolable friendship, a generous reciprocality of feeling and interest".

The manifestation of their elation was signed on behalf of the regiment by the Right Worshipful Captain Sanderson and two other of Mr Greenway's customers for aprons.

Colonel Molle, on his side, felt that the discovery of the authorship of the pipes represented "one of the happiest moments of my life", and he deeply regretted having held suspicions for a single moment "in regard to those, under whose garb I should have well known the dagger of the midnight assassin or the pen of the anonymous libeller never was concealed." He averred that it would ever be a joyful reflection to him and his that "during the whole period of my labouring under the *Demon of Suspicion*, I never conducted myself towards you in any manner painful to your feelings, as gentlemen, or derogatory to my own character as Commanding Officer of the Regiment". And he held the warmest hope and confidence that surrounded by them, his brother officers, their "*hearts and hands*" would "ever be united in friendship, esteem, and emulation, equally cordial in the hours of private and social intercourse, as distinguished in *that* field, which our speedy removal from the Colony may afford us an opportunity of enjoying".[86]

XII

Members of the mess considered that two such documents as their letter to their Lieutenant-Colonel and his handsome and manly reply, containing as they did so many mutual encomiums upon themselves and so many salutary insults to the Wentworth faction, to four-fifths of the free community and to the Governor himself, should be published in handbills which they circulated "very generally".[87]

They professed to be astonished at Macquarie's belief that such things should not even be written, much less printed in a public document.

The Governor opined that persons who, beside being military officers sent to keep the peace in a convict colony, were His Majesty's criminal judges, should set an example in moderation and subordination.[88]

Their attitude to himself he thought insulting—particularly so their assumption that they had brought the mess table of the 46th Regiment "to be regarded as the standard of society in this Colony" and their disposition "to treat with supercilious insolence every rule of my conduct as well in private life, as in my public administration of this Government".

They were treating him, their supreme Commander, he wrote, "with insolence and contempt", inferring that *his* table was not only inferior to their own, but something "improper and discreditable". He proposed to report the whole matter to the Duke of York.

Colonel Molle rushed to the defence of his officers.

On the eve of Marsden's criminal action against Campbell, the argument between Governor and Regiment reached its greatest fury, and the officers of the 46th Regiment were undoubtedly emboldened in their noisy insolence by the reflection that within a few days or weeks they would be on the high seas out of Macquarie's reach. All the hubbub of trial and the military quarrel mingled while the poor, ailing Governor conned the angry set of dispatches from the Colonial Office, transmitting the latest libels and inventions loosed against him in London.

The loudest voice of all was still Molle's. Egged on by the mess he suddenly demanded the court martial of D'Arcy Wentworth averring that he had not before realized that the latter was a commissioned officer and amenable to such proceedings.[89] He made the demand in language far different from "those unbounded expressions of respect and regard with which he had extorted an unwilling shake of the hand" from Dr Wentworth after the magisterial inquiry about the pipes.[90]

Dr Wentworth's voice also rose in anger to point out that he had "held His Majesty's commission at home long before the Lieutenant-Governor was ever known in the Service", and to promise that, if charged, he would "overwhelm my accusers with confusion and disgrace".[91]

The gallant Captain Murray rushed up supports for the defence in an affidavit. He swore that when the emancipist "attorney", Chartres, had shown Wentworth the pipes, the latter had reprimanded him and forbidden his employees "either to listen to, inspect, read, or even be present when such . . . extremely improper and reprehensible productions were read or spoken of in public or private".[92]

Molle's retort was to send the Governor a supposed "true copy" of a letter to Colonel Foveaux from Major Grose, a former Acting-Governor, and commanding the New South Wales Corps, written in 1799 from Ireland. Major Grose warned the officers of the impeccable corps that if the Duke of York should hear by accident that any of them had disgraced himself by associating with "a person named Wentworth", His Royal Highness "would be sure to turn him out of the Service".[93] Colonel Molle added that it would appear from Grose's letter "that Mr. D'Arcy Wentworth's claim to the character of an officer and a gentleman is not of so old a date as he arrogates to himself, *viz*. since his arrival in the Colony". Macquarie wrote to Wentworth affirming Foveaux's high opinion of him; Wentworth cried out that Grose's supposed letter was "a singular enclosure . . . anonymous without any authority of any sort . . . shown [by Molle] to divers persons whom he doesn't even name, but who he states to have admitted its originality".[94]

It was "a vile and infamous forgery", wrote Dr Wentworth, who continued in burning and indignant sentences:

> The Lieutenant-Governor is *himself the libeller* for he publishes a libel against me which I defy him or any other person to establish. . . . Did *he*, then, or does the Lieutenant-Governor now know of any act I had committed from the moment of my putting my foot on shore in this colony that deserves such an anathema? Did I not arrive here as free and uncontrouled as either Major Grose, or any of his officers, or the Lieutenant-Governor himself, and have I ever been otherwise; why therefore am I to be subjected to such a libel as this, after 30 years faithful and unblemished service in some of the highest and most important situations in this Colony?[95]

On 9 September 1817 Macquarie sent this letter to Molle.[96] In a few hours Dr Wentworth found himself opening the angriest looking document in all the annals of the Macquarie age. Its words gallop, out of control, across the page on a course like that of a demented camel:

You have *grossly insulted* and *threatened* me, *His Majesty's Lieutenant-Governor of this Colony and your superior in office*:—I . . . therefore . . . hereby through Lieutenant Madigan, the adjutant of the 46th Regt place you *under close arrest* until the pleasure of his Excellency is known to whom I shall report this proceeding and apply for a General Courtmartial to be immediately assembled for your trial.[97]

The 48th Regiment now was on the spot. The court martial was summoned. Wentworth's defence promised to be buttressed with counter-charges against Molle of "a false and scandalous libel . . . with intent to debase, degrade and villify myself". Molle's remarks covering the Grose-Foveaux letter, his victim interpreted as "disgraceful to Colonel Molle as an officer and a gentleman and subversive to all discipline", beside being calculated "to bring contempt upon the Royal Authority" which had declared Dr Wentworth "right trusty" in his commission.[98]

All attempts at conciliation by Macquarie, by Erskine, the new Lieutenant-Governor, and by the politic and sedulous Wylde, who even, in vain, devoted a holy Sabbath to the task, were "frustrated through the indelicate and unreasonable propositions of Colonel Molle".[99]

The Governor, though he thought the charges against Wentworth "frivolous and ridiculous", was now as anxious as Wentworth himself that the proceedings should be carried to a finding. But at the last moment the trial fell through. Wylde ruled that Wentworth, as surgeon to the settlement, was not liable, by the tenor of his commission, to court martial for the offence alleged against him.[100]

XIII

Macquarie cancelled the court martial. The same day he ordered Molle aboard the *Matilda*. The 46th Regiment sailed for Ceylon and Madras. There, six years later, Molle died in his bed.

After his departure from New South Wales several postscripts were written to the furious drama.

One was from the Governor to Dr Wentworth, and was set aside for the eyes of Lord Fitzwilliam, who must be warned to still the storm which was certainly due to break in England:

Macquarie to D'Arcy Wentworth

Being now relieved from the severe pressure of public business, which I have been for the last fourteen days subject to, I can no longer defer offering you most cordially my sincere congratulations on the happy issue of your contest with Colonel Molle, over whom you have obtained, in my opinion at least, a most complete victory, and I think he will have no reason to boast of his malicious attempt to injure you, in the opinion of the world.[101]

I forwarded to Colonel Molle agreeably to your request, a copy of the charges you exhibited against him. I did not hear from him afterwards, and I therefore conclude he must have felt no small degree of mortification on receiving them.

He remained "with esteem, my dear sir, yours sincerely, L. Macquarie".

The officers of the 46th Regiment wrote a public letter of congratulation to Mr Marsden on his victory over Mr Campbell. Marsden replied in an epistle, vicious in every line, in which he dwelt at length on the services of his gallant correspondents in setting an example of virtue under conditions in which "every barrier against licentiousness and immorality was broken down, every fence swept away".

Young Mr Wentworth, outwardly uncouth like the colonial "butts" at whom Molle had "loved to jeer", wrote pensively to Colonel Johnston's son. The latter had come to the conclusion that the writing of pipes "certainly was not a manly way of attacking another man", but he agreed with the Governor that young Mr Wentworth's father had scored "a complete victory" in his part of the affair.[102]

As for some buried pipe against the M'Arthurs, young Johnston agreed with the poet that he would feel "as much uneasiness as yourself should they be able to trace the production".

The author himself, thinking it all over, decided that if it were in his power to secure a revision of his conduct in the matter he would do so, "not because I can ever entertain any respect for Colonel Molle, but because I have at present considerable doubts in my mind as to how far such anonymous attacks are under any circumstances justifiable".[103]

XIV

There was one more aftermath. A young duellist, Dr William Bland, became infected with the pipe-making virus in the following year. He aimed at the highest kind of game with two poisonous barrels, which went off—apparently by accident—on the Parramatta Road.

So terrible were his aspersions, the *Gazette's* editor felt, that "to recapitulate any part of the libellous matter would be to distress our readers". Dr Bland's effusion was "conceived in malignity, brought forth in the blackest ingratitude".[104]

Mr Wylde fined the perpetrator of it £50, sent him to jail for a year, and ordered him to find fearsome sureties for his good behaviour.

Dr Bland went off to prison to weigh his sentence against the satisfaction of having written such lines as:

> *Thy puerile, weak ambition there I see*
> *That prompted thee to mark thy name in stone*
> *And bids thee sigh and languish to be known*
> *Like some rude younker, that with charcoal scrawls*
> *And marks his name upon the school-room walls.*[105]

The incident proved that the Governor was no more capable than Colonel Molle or any other contemporary of "suffering an anonymous and scurrilous document by silent contempt to become altogether harmless"!

The impartial reader must feel that Mr Wylde's conscience might have told him to be kinder to Dr Bland. For he himself was not without guilt. When the clamour of Molle was at its height and Jeffery Bent was leaving the Colony, he had produced a pipe as crude as any of the rest, within which was enshrined the first recorded Australian judicial pun:[106]

> The bow is bent—but weak the bow—
> The envenomed arrow harmless now!
> Macquarie scorns the treach'rous foe.
> What dread can souls like his e'er know?
> Australia marks th' insidious aim
> And burning with indignant shame
> Receives the insult, feels the wound
> And strikes the ingrate to the ground!

"A pretty specimen, indeed, of poetic talent," wrote Mr Wylde gaily, "though I feel it might expose me to the suspicion of being a sort of printer's devil to the scrub pipe-maker of the Colony."

Fortunately, his effort delighted the eyes only of an audience of one or two—the Governor and, perhaps, his secretary, Mr Campbell.

CHAPTER XXVI

Farewell to Toorali-addity

I

THE real pressure of opposition to Macquarie's convict policies had begun in 1815.[1] Romilly and Henry Grey Bennet, the chosen mouthpiece of Botany Bay agitators, along with other supporters of the penitentiary system, had persuaded Parliament that transportation should be renewed for one year only. After that the matter was to come up for fresh consideration.

During that year great changes became imminent both in New South Wales and in the British Empire. Colonial policy had begun to alter as soon as some very small batches of free immigrants had reached New South Wales[2] after the end of the Napoleonic wars.

Many eyes were turned distractedly abroad seeking to light on some haven far from the insecurity of an almost exhausted Europe. In the United Kingdom dangerous popular aspirations were seething in the melting pot of the new industrialized civilization. The existing system of deterrent punishments had failed to cope either with the demagogue inspired by the French Revolution or with the soldier who had learnt in Spain not to respect other people's rabbits and loaves.

It was natural at this moment, just when the petition Mr Bent had declared to be not "niminy-piminy" had arrived in London, that penal colonies and their effect upon crime should be very much in the public mind.

It was to be expected, also, at such a juncture, that property owners should be suspicious of the policy which seemed to operate in New South Wales. Few would be ready to favour general leniency towards the convicts, especially if it were proved that it was accompanied by a contrasting failure to recognize true worth in free men.

All too well leading members of the Government understood the dangers of popular insubordination. Some of them[3], marooned in Paris three decades before in the earlier flurries of the Revolution, knew what "Ça ira" sounded like when sung by a fanatic mob. In fancy they heard anew, as the age of Waterloo merged swiftly into the age of Peterloo, the blood-drunk snarl of the crowds in the Place de la Concorde.

As the groundwork of their fears they noticed a malign and inflammatory tendency everywhere[4]. The dangerous intent of the times was crystallized in the Spa Fields Assembly[5] at which there had been talk of plunder and forcible division of property; of pikes and coloured flags. Parliament heard of "insurrection" planned in Derbyshire,[6] of a "general rising" proposed in Yorkshire, of incipient "rebellion" in Lancashire—of such doings, in short, that the report of them could be presented to the House of Lords only in a "sealed bag".[7]

All this disturbance the Ministry, in a state of diligent panic, was seeking to strangle, though with each new measure of suppression the tumult rose higher. Stones rattled against shutters and carriage windows, right up to the portals of St James's and Portland Place. Royalty itself was pelted at the doors of Carlton House, though it was paradoxical that the fashionable poison had sunk so deeply into the body politic that even the Prince Regent seemed infected by the democratic virus. Was he not to be seen "driving in the Park every day in a tilbury, with his groom sitting by his side", a practice which shocked grave men?[8]

Between January and March 1817, while the heads of Botany Bay malcontents in London nodded approvingly over the humble prayer to Parliament which Mr Grey Bennet was preparing, the House of Commons was absorbed with its measures for the safety of the realm. Its proceedings took shape as a series of Bills appropriate only in a country which felt itself threatened with civil war. The Mutiny Bill, the Seditious Meetings Bill, the Prince Regent's Message on "dangerous meetings and combinations", the Soldiers' Seduction Bill—not to mention the Scotch madhouses—all had a turn upon the parliamentary stage.

Only a few days before Bennet appeared in the House with the Bent-Vale petition, the Habeas Corpus Act Suspension Act—amid outcry from the City—had been passed to "empower his Majesty to secure and detain such persons as his Majesty shall suspect of conspiracy against his person and Government".[9]

When in March 1817 young Mr William Wentworth went to the Colonial Office to inform Lord Bathurst's mind about the vileness of the signatories to the petition, he found "the pressure of business at all the public offices now so great from the alarming view which the Govt. have of the present distressed and turbulent state of the country . . . that all circumstances of minor importance were entirely overlooked or neglected". In such an atmosphere, with even the lives of Ministers threatened, he was compelled to "leave the petition to its natural course", contenting himself with observing its progress and "narrowly watching the manoeuvres of the Governor's enemies in the public newspapers".[10]

II

The exact terms of the petition are not known. The curious document has disappeared; but a letter from Macquarie to Goulburn, the Under Secretary to the Colonial Office, mentions some of its charges.[11]

The petitioners accused the Governor of selling pardons, an accusation which boiled down to the fact that he had given their freedom to some ticket-of-leave men who had helped to build the road to Bathurst[12] with the aid of their own horses and carts. They charged him with pulling down houses[13]—he had removed buildings erected on allotments which never had been granted to their "owners". He was alleged to have seized land; so he had, but with the approval of the Colonial Office, as in the case of Bligh's granted plots at Parramatta.[14]

It was told that he had prohibited the banns of marriage. That referred to the case of Lieutenant Connor, whom he had expelled from the Colony on his wedding eve, but Connor he considered a murderer.[15] He was charged with interfering with court proceedings. Actually all he had done was to instruct the Coroner to empanel a jury and inquire at once about the death of a child who had been killed accidentally by Elizabeth's carriage.[16] The question of foreign trade was raised with the cunning intent of stirring up the fears of the British manufacturers.

It was, in fact, a "catalogue of crimes . . . such a compound of villainy and falsehood . . . sent home by a low rabble . . . totally unworthy of regard or notice".[17] And the vindictive spirit in which it was framed can be gauged from a letter which Vale some time later wrote to Lord Bathurst. This document, though its author proclaimed that it "all admitted of the most lucid confirmation",[18] was actually a tissue of poison, falsehood and exaggeration—such charges as that the Governor "whips free persons without the formality of trial, imprisons others with little ceremony", tittle-tattle that he left a gap in the Domain wall "to catch people", and had young girls who went to the park to show children "the pretty daisies" flung into a foul jail with the vilest criminals.

There was even worse:

> Political traders whose interests it is to have the patronage of the executive Government, understanding the general maxim which is laid down, take care to bring an investment suited to the taste of the Governor, and invoiced at a price so low as to be a very considerable present. In this manner they insure a large praemium on their remaining investment and find it worth their while to come from America and India to pay their court to N.S. Wales while no one in the Colony is benefitted except the Governor. A more flagrant instance of this perhaps I need not point out than the trade to India for wheat, when the Colony is able to provide not only for home consumption but even for exportation.

The Governor had imported only three cargoes of wheat, one ordered the week he arrived in the Colony, when the population was likely to starve, two in the drought of 1814-16 under the imminent threat of famine. Vale wrote further:

> But the monopoly of the sale of spirits is allowed by the Governor to the Indian merchants to furnish a supply of wheat cheaper than it could be grown in the Colony, and this is said to be the foundation of all the misery which the poor settlers have ever since suffered, and, in one communication I have received on this head, it is said that the Governor had a present of ten thousand gallons of rum by the Governor General of India, as a return for two hundred tons of coals.

These, however, were not the main charges which would affect public opinion. With all subordination disappearing, all respect for law and order at a low ebb, what the ruling classes of England most cared about in the reports from Botany Bay was the allegation that life there was easy for the convict; that transportation, instead of being a punishment to be regarded with a shudder by the hardiest criminal, was now, through the misplaced humanity and laxity of the Governor, becoming an actual incentive to Britons to commit crimes.

It all would have been laughable had Macquarie been on the spot to answer allegations instantly when they were made. But he could not even hear of them for at least half a year; he could not publish his rebuttals in London till from eighteen months to two years after the launching of the libels. In the meantime, London would be full of vengeful Bents and Vales and Rileys, all swearing solemnly and indignantly that every word was true. And so, by the time the answers arrived, the damage would be done and public opinion firmly formed.

Even without the tall tales which were wafted up from the south with every ship from the antipodes, there was enough evidence in the United Kingdom to produce an ugly presumption in interested British breasts.

The court records showed clearly what was happening.

In 1814, the year before Waterloo, a mere 558 death sentences had been passed in England. Fifty-three persons had been sentenced to transportation for life, seventy-eight to fourteen years' transportation and 625 to seven years'—total penal punishments, 1314.

By 1816 the death sentences had grown to 890 a year. Sixty were sentenced to life-long transportation, 133 to exile for fourteen years, 861 for seven years—total, 1944.

In 1817 the number of death sentences was 1302; life sentences, 103; fourteen-year sentences, 157; and seven-year sentences, 1474—total, 3036. Out of those sentenced to death that year only 151 were executed. Their country sent the rest of its victims mainly to Port Jackson and Hobart Town.[19]

It must have appeared plain to the dullest mind that, over the whole range of wrongdoing, prospective felons felt that it was worth while to take the one-in-twenty risk of being hanged to obtain a berth to Botany Bay.

III

For two decades before 1810 the starving criminal had paused with uplifted hand before the tempting loaf or rabbit as he remembered the tales of the *Neptune* transport[20]; of how her complement had gone out, six months in the holds, ironed, some waist deep in water, while disease raged through the ship. He had heard how her dying and thirsty wretches had crawled her decks at sea, furtively searching the corpses of their comrades to steal the saliva-producing tobacco quids out of their dead cheeks. He had heard how the dead had been concealed so that others might draw their rations; and how, one awful morning in the drizzle, the residue of her shivering wretches had been flung, living, into the rain-filled boats, to be piled on the wet earth of Port Jackson foreshore, or dead and naked—

since their clothing was worth more than their corpses—into the waters of the harbour, to be washed up for days afterwards on the rocks round the coves.

Dreadful floggings, nakedness, hunger, and cruelty in those days were part of the legend of Botany Bay. Men begged then to be hanged rather than to be exiled to New Holland. But now the graduates of the trans-portation system sent back their encomiums on Macquarie's promised land, to add to his own accounts of the "luxurious" manner in which Port Jackson felons might live.

These "distant correspondents" urged their fellows not to dwell upon their coming, lest they arrive too late to enjoy a good thing.

In 1814 Macquarie, on Redfern's report, had discovered how barbarous were the conditions in some transports. Among three ships on which many had died, one instance had been unearthed which filled all who conned the story with horror—prisoners kept below decks for twenty-nine days before sailing from England, then for seven days in the sweaty heat of Madeira; lastly at Rio de Janeiro for ten days. All this confinement had happened in a nine-hundred-ton ship, the *General Hewitt*, in which there were five hundred and fifteen souls, most of them in irons made for the Guinea slave trade which prevented them from bending their bodies.[21]

The cleaning and shaving of the convicts once a week had been little attended to. The poor wretches had been allowed no water to wash their linens—they had three pints a day through the tropics for all purposes. Their wine and little luxuries had been "purchased" from them by the officers almost by force. They had been given no mustard to kill the taste of the maggots in their coarse ration. Fifty had perished; even the captain himself had died as the result of his own brutal neglect and misbehaviour.

Redfern's remedial scheme of supervision and hygiene, devised by Macquarie's orders, had been adopted swiftly.[22] The voyage to Botany Bay was thus "disarmed of half its terrors". The settlement there was "no longer a desert". All agreed that transportation was "no longer an object of dread". It had, in fact, generally "ceased to be a punishment". Voyages were regarded by the commoner denizens of any British city as the pious Grey Bennet or Mr William Wilberforce would have regarded a voyage to Heaven.

"*Toorali-addity!*" sang the prisoners assembled for exile in the Newgate Yard.

Cotton, the prison Ordinary, later heard them at it and informed the Police Committee of 1818 that "the generality of those who are transported consider it as a party of pleasure—as going out to see the world; they evince no penitence, no contrition, but seem to rejoice in the thing, many of them to court it".[23]

He had, he reported, heard prisoners when sentenced to transportation by the Recorder, return thanks for it, and seem overjoyed. Horrified, he had watched a party being put into a caravan to go to the convict ship. They shouted and huzza'd and were very joyous. Several of them called out to the keepers that "the first fine Sunday we will have a glorious kangaroo hunt at the Bay", seeming to anticipate a great deal of pleasure. Some even committed felonies in the deliberate hope of being transported.[24]

IV

Bennet rose in the House on 10 March 1817 to present Bent's petition. He put forward complaints on the mode of administering the laws in New South Wales, and particularly on the unjust and oppressive conduct of the Governor—oppressive, that is, of the free and exclusive population, but not of the emancipists and convicts.[25]

He said that he had been at some trouble to ascertain who the persons were who had signed the petition, and he found that they were not individuals sent out of their country for their crimes, but *bona fide* colonists.

Mr Wentworth, who knew the petitioners far better than Mr Bennet, begged to differ. He certified that the greater part of the signatories were "publicans and shopkeepers of the lowest description, who live by preying upon the very vitals of the settlers, whose name they have assumed".[26]

He spoke, of his own knowledge, of the untruthfulness of most of the allegations which the document contained and gave his opinion that the charges constituted "one of the grossest calumnies ever fabricated against the character of a public officer". This, as later knowledge has shown, was very near the truth.

For all his apparent confidence, even Mr Grey Bennet appeared to have some sneaking doubts. For he stated that all the persons of whom he had made inquiries respecting Macquarie's conduct had testified to his general humanity and moderation. He said he felt on that account by no means inclined to attach implicit belief to that part of the petition which complained of the Governor's tyrannical conduct. He spoke in "very cautious" terms.[27]

In this and in his other methods of procedure, Mr Wentworth suspected him of a *ruse de guerre*.[28]

Castlereagh vindicated the Governor "very warmly", hoping that the House would "not allow any of the statements in the petition to act unfavourably towards the character of the distinguished officer in whom was vested the Governorship of New South Wales".[29]

It was certainly, he asserted, due to him to state that he had filled the situation of governor respectably for many years. He had been appointed to the office when he (Lord Castlereagh) had held the Colonial Office seals. And the only recommendation which he had possessed had been his merit. From all that had since been heard of him, it seemed that he had completely fulfilled the sanguine expectations entertained of him.

"One thing is certain," reported young Mr Wentworth, "he [Macquarie] has warm friends in Lord Castlereagh and the Duke of York."[30]

But this could help the Governor very little. It did not matter that his enemies proffered a series of contradictions in their charges; of cruelty for the saints to ponder; of softness to stir the new manufacturing interests in the Commons to uneasiness.

The English never have been discriminating in these matters. There is little in them of the reasoning Gaul—they usually leave their articulate reasoning to the Scots and the Irish among them. Thus the effect upon them of diverse libels depends, not upon logic, but upon the cumulative impact of the charges on their well-developed sense of self-preservation. The tales which hinted that the criminal of New South Wales lived better than the honest man of Britain at once set their national instincts to work.

It was quite clear that the Government would be compelled to consider quickly what the future of New South Wales should be. And Bathurst seemed to feel that "for service most timely, for warning most wise" he could not choose a better counsellor than his noble relative, that wily "bird of to-day", Viscount Sidmouth, the Home Secretary, who had equal responsibilities with himself in respect of transportation.[31]

Five weeks after the petition had appeared in the House, therefore, Bathurst put his thoughts on paper for the benefit of his cautious colleague.

V

It was not long after the colonization of New Holland, he wrote, that the settlements were found to hold out to many individuals inducements to become cultivators. Thirty years' experience of the climate and fertility of the soil had, for some time past, rendered a permission to settle in New South Wales an object of anxious solicitude to all who were desirous of leaving their native country, and had capital to apply to the improvement of the land.[32]

This, together with the number of convicts who remained in the Colony with their families growing up under them, had so increased the population of free settlers, that the prosperity of the settlement as a colony had proportionately advanced; and hopes might be reasonably entertained of its becoming, perhaps, at no distant period, a valuable possession of the Crown.

It was this very circumstance, Bathurst declared, which appeared to him to render the settlement less fit for the object of its original institution.

The settlers felt a repugnance to submit to the enforcement of regulations which necessarily partook much of the nature of rules applicable to a penitentiary and interfered materially with the exercise of those rights which they had enjoyed in the United Kingdom, and to which, as British subjects, they conceived themselves entitled in every part of His Majesty's dominions.

The greatest objection, however, to the present system arose from a cause over which regulations in the settlement would not have an immediate control.

He dwelt on the "increases beyond all calculations" of the convict population. This continued influx, he thought, must annually increase the difficulty of enforcing on the convicts a strict discipline. Also:

> The difficulty of finding regular employment for them has been such, that it has been the practice of late years to grant tickets of leave, almost without

o

exception, to those who had any prospects of obtaining a livelihood by their own exertions; and also to place a greater proportion of servants in the families of free settlers. In the former case, the convicts could be subjected to little more than nominal restraint and, in the latter, it is obvious that with less regular labour, they must enjoy a freedom inconsistent with the object proposed in transporting them.[33]

He mentioned especially the inadequacy of penal buildings, which resulted in the convicts having to find their own lodgings, thus making superintendence difficult.

He concluded, "I propose, should it meet with your concurrence, to recommend to His Royal Highness the Prince Regent, the appointment of commissioners who shall forthwith proceed to the settlement with full powers to investigate all the complaints which have been made, both with respect to the treatment of the convicts, and the general administration of the government."[34]

VI

The dispatches which reached the Governor[35] in the *Almorah* on 31 August 1817 and the *Dick* on 3 September seemed to admit of only one conclusion and to provide an illuminating picture of Bathurst's mind in process of transition between support of the old policies and of the new during the first four months of 1817. It seemed to be a very uneven instrument. Now it hewed out his customary equable and friendly letters, now brusque, unjust and almost savage censures, on the basis of complaints which earlier he could have been trusted to treat with the contempt which they deserved. The day had passed when he could declare truthfully to his satrap, "Clamour against you has no influence whatever on my judgment."[36]

If his letters bewildered their recipient it is not astonishing. The Governor must have been puzzled to square their tone with the praise he had received in Parliament from Castlereagh.

Among the matters with which Bathurst dealt was the case of Mr Vale. He wrote that it was not without considerable surprise that he had learned of the Governor's having brought the reverend gentleman to trial over the *Traveller* affair. Admitting that his position as a chaplain might make the melancholy parson fit food for a court martial, under appropriate circumstances, his Lordship thought the Governor would have found, had he referred to the Mutiny Act and the Articles of War, that military chaplains could only be brought to trial for "absence from duty, drunkenness or scandalous and vicious behaviour, derogatory from the sacred character with which a chaplain is invested". That Vale had been guilty of such offences could not, Bathurst thought, be pretended; it was "not even imputed in the charges that there was any vice or turpitude, reflecting on his moral character, in the act which he had committed, and the decision of the Court had negatived any such supposition".[37]

True, the Colonial Secretary admitted, Vale's conduct in seizing the *Traveller* was in many ways extremely reprehensible and he would willingly have interfered with a view to its correction. Nevertheless it was, he said, out of his power to give the Governor's conduct in the matter "any sanction or approbation".

He could only lament "that you should, in a moment of irritation, have been betrayed into an act which, at the same time that it exposes you personally to considerable risk, cannot fail to diminish your influence among the more respectable part of the community, who justly look upon the law as the only true foundation of authority".[38]

This was a new outlook with a vengeance. No minister hitherto had shown any tendency to give a single button for the law or for the more respectable part of the community, where the interests of either interfered with the colonial government or with the tranquillity of the Colony. How different this from the Bathurst of 1812-13 who had flatly refused to agree to the establishment of a Governor's Council because he felt it imperative to "leave the Governor unfettered", and who had realized the "danger of weakening the higher authorities in a society composed of such discordant materials".[39] Far different also from the Bathurst who had written to Ellis Bent not much more than a year ago, "It is natural that the Governor . . . should incline to the opinion that the convenience of those who have freely placed themselves in a Colony of such a description, should be a secondary object, when compared with the control which he considers necessary for the security and the proper government of the convicts."[40]

The Minister's strictures were unjust. Not merely a legal but a judicial opinion had supported the Governor. Vale had pleaded that the proceedings against him were illegal, but the Court, including the acting senior judge of the Colony, had rejected his plea. Perhaps public opinion worked on Bathurst. Vale had issued a pamphlet in which he claimed that Macquarie had said the Yankee captain should have flogged him.

Whatever his fright when first threatened with reprisals, Macquarie now showed no signs of it. In a cold fury, he refused to admit that his charges against Vale were either illegal or irregular. The Articles of War, he believed, entirely warranted his action; for he considered the wretched parson's "conduct in seizing the American vessel in the capacity of the meanest excise officer, not only insolent under the particular circumstances to me, but also derogatory to the sacred character *with which he was invested as a chaplain*', and consequently *scandalous and vicious*". And, he said, "according to my construction of the *Mutiny Act* and the *Articles of War* founded thereon, which I have now studied upwards of forty years, the charges I gave in against Mr Vale were perfectly legal".[41]

He repudiated the idea that his action would diminish his influence among the respectable, since he believed that there was not a respectable person in the country who did not "highly disapprove and execrate the mutinous, seditious and insolent conduct pursued towards me by that depraved, hypocritical unprincipled man".

Your Lordship has mistaken my motives in supposing that, in my conduct to Mr. Vale, I acted under the influence of sentiments of irritation or passion, the very reverse being the case both before and after his trial. So very different was my conduct towards that worthless man that I gave him, tho' without effect, every opportunity and reasonable delay to explain away or apologize for his insolent, insubordinate conduct, before I proceeded to exhibit charges against him at a General Court Martial, as the last step for the support of my own public authority, and which, be the consequence what it may, I shall never allow to be trampled upon or set at defiance by any subordinate officer under my command.[42]

He flung back in the Minister's own teeth the very words the latter had used about the danger of weakening the Government in a community composed of such discordant materials as New South Wales:

I have been bred in the school of subordination too long, not to respect it; and your Lordship must be fully aware, how necessary it is to support it in a distant Colony like this, and composed of such discordant materials; assured at the same time that your Lordship would not wish to see me degraded by tamely submitting to the subversion of my authority as Governor in Chief of this Colony either by Mr. Vale or any other seditious and unprincipled person.[43]

VII

Next, the case of Moore, the solicitor, had received the consideration of the Minister. Macquarie had dismissed him from his office as a Crown solicitor, following his implication in the affair of the *Traveller*. He had withheld the land grants which were pending for him when his various peccadilloes and worse in relation to the petition were discovered.[44]

Bathurst concluded that Moore had merely acted as an innocent legal adviser in the *Traveller* case, and it was ordered that he should be reinstated in his office, though the dispatch was accompanied by a copy of a letter which the Under Secretary, Goulburn, had written to Moore. In this it was hoped that the Colonial Office could trust that his future conduct would prove him worthy of indulgence and that he would "not again become the willing instrument of acts done in opposition to the Governor". Since he had applied for more land—little knowing that he was about to lose that already in his grasp—Goulburn remarked tartly that he "had as much land as his rank justified".[45]

The fact was that Moore's early letters about the *Traveller* showed no traces of his being an agent. His first menaces to Molle were his own. Macquarie did not intend to allow him to enjoy any indulgences. "*This the Governor will never do*, as he considers it inconsistent with due support of the executive authority entrusted to him in this country."[46]

He informed Bathurst that he "respectfully declined to act on the instruction". He was, he said, interested more in Moore's private circulation of the petition to the House of Commons, by the manner in which Moore obtained signatures to it, and by the forgery of names upon it, than by his association with the *Traveller* affair.

He considered that "this Act is of too much importance (connected as it certainly was with a seditious and violent Cabal headed by Mr Justice

Bent and some other disaffected persons then here) to the respectability of this Government, and stands in too prominent a point of view in regard to the future tranquillity of this Colony, to be passed over unpunished".[47]

Therefore, he refused to be made an instrument to bestow favours on "persons, who have set themselves up in open defiance of the legal authorities of this Colony, and who have exerted themselves so earnestly to contaminate the minds of others to the disturbance of the public peace, and the violation of all decency of conduct".

He had fully expected, he wrote, that his lordship would have sent him a list of the persons who had signed Moore's false and slanderous document, to enable him to prosecute them for the libels which he could easily have proved their statements to be.

And, in any case, he professed himself sure that his Minister entertained too high a respect for the commission he had the honour to hold to sanction any act which tended to lessen his authority, or to degrade him in the public opinion of those over whom he ruled.[48]

It was a landmark in his career—the first and only time in forty years of public service that he had openly disobeyed a specific order from a superior. And his disobedience seemed to involve him in "an essential point of difference", which must mean the end of his career.

He had decided on a course of action on which he was prepared to stake his fate for good and all. But the Moore and Vale cases formed only part of the issues which determined his stand.

VIII

The factor which brought matters to a crisis between Macquarie and his Minister at the end of 1817 was a letter which some time during the previous year had been passed on to the Colonial Office by Sir Henry Bunbury, head of the Transport Department, under whose aegis all convicts were shipped to New South Wales.

Bathurst enclosed extracts from this document in his dispatches to Sydney by the *Almorah*, but without stating the writer's name or supplying anything from the text which would identify him.[49]

The letter began by stating that its signatory had learned that Mr Goulburn, the Under Secretary to the Colonial Office, had written to the Governor in his favour. But the Governor, the writer declared, had denied receiving any letter from Goulburn on the subject and had done nothing to promote the aims put forward, the appointment of the writer to "any eligible situation". He obviously needed the appointment since he proclaimed himself to be the parent of "eight children entirely unprovided for".[50]

This prologue the Governor was not shown. Neither was he allowed to read a panegyric on the late Ellis Bent, whom the writer described as "my most intimate friend", nor a suggestion that judges should be completely independent of the Governor and should draft the Colony's legislation. He was not made aware that the letter contained a charge, surely as serious as any of those which had impelled the Minister to action, that while the influence of the head of the police in Sydney was "incredible", that post was held by Dr Wentworth, described as "the greatest dealer of spirits in the Colony".

The anonymous correspondent attacked Sunday musters of convicts, so objectionable to Mr Marsden, as leading to depravity through providing convicts with a chance to associate. He dwelt on the lack of power vested in magistrates to prevent the ill-behaviour of convicts. He held up his hands in horrified shame at the condition of the poor women who were prostituted on convict ships and ill-treated in the Parramatta Factory.

And he described his experiences during a visit to Parramatta Jail. In company with Mr Marsden, "horrid to relate", he had seen "a prisoner who had nearly lost the use of his limbs and faculties by confinement on bread and water in the jail".[51]

In a cell, he asserted, he had seen also a prisoner, perfectly mad, chained to the wall. He had noticed four men confined under the "most dreadful sentence I hope ever heard of".

He wrote:

I understand it has been ascertained that human nature cannot exist without endangering the faculties the half of twelve months upon bread and water, but here is the additional sentence of two years imprisonment in the Gaol should they by any miracle survive the first twelve months confinement in a solitary cell upon bread and water; and after that transportation to New Castle for life.

Lastly, the writer announced that he would at all times feel much honoured in giving Sir Henry Bunbury information about the Colony. He added, "Should there be any native curiosities which you should think worth the trouble of naming, I shall be extremely happy in the pleasure of procuring them for you."[52]

IX

One could scarcely imagine a busy Minister of the Crown paying any attention whatever to such an obviously interested piece of slander. But it brought Bathurst sharply to attention.

He was particularly zealous to call attention to the charges of the prostitution of convict women on ships bound for New South Wales and afterwards in harbour. He also showed anxiety for details about the state of Parramatta Jail and the conditions under which the four men whom his informant declared that he had seen in solitary confinement, during his visit to the jail, were sentenced and punished.

He expressed himself confident that Macquarie would be anxious to afford him "the most explicit information as to all the circumstances therein stated". These were matters, "affecting as they do to a great degree your character and conduct in the administration of the Colony", to which he particularly called the Governor's attention. The last phrases stung the Governor to the quick.[53]

London surely needed no telling at that stage that Macquarie's way with the convict was humane. His indignation at the charges about the convict ships was perhaps the greater because the month before he had received Bathurst's ill-conditioned dispatch he had begun to deal with the case of the disorderly *Chapman*, in which a romantic and imaginative aggregation of Hibernians alleged that they had suffered almost every misfortune that could befall a felon at sea.[54]

They complained of being starved, deprived of money and clothing, shot, stabbed, flogged, beaten, abused, threatened with "smothering by brimstone and charcoal", barbarously hammered with the butt-end of a bayonet, chained to a cable, and "kicked and leapt upon". One gentleman had moaned that he had "got two dozen for coughing"; another that he had been "twice flogged for speaking Irish and making a noise". The captain and officers said they were a rebellious crew on whom it had been necessary to fire, and generally fit food for stern measures.[55]

It had taken the combined exertions of Wylde and D'Arcy Wentworth, the two men outside his immediate *ménage* who had most influence with him, to restrain the Governor from sending home under close arrest not merely the surgeon, three soldiers, and the officer of the guard, but everybody concerned. He had, in his fury of indignant humanity, become possessed of a fruitless longing to see all involved hanged, and the depth of his feeling in the matter had proved the climactic factor in producing the first serious breakdown in health which he had suffered in the Colony, though he had been ill the previous year.[56]

The tale in the letter about the distribution of female convicts was completely anachronistic. It might have been true in a less highly coloured form ten years before, when King, Marsden, and the Military were arbiters of such matters. And what happened to transported ladies on the high seas, in any case, was something the Governor could not control—the sea was outside his territory.

Vice there certainly was on convict ships. Even the damping influence of Mr Justice Field had not inhibited it on the *Lord Melville*, a vessel crammed with passengers, bond and free, though Mr Field harangued the ladies at intervals on moral and religious matters. Nay, the sinning took place under Mr Field's very nose; he was sure that, even had the hatches been battened down firmly every night, the best that could have been done would have been to "preserve a decent exterior".[57]

Once the females reached Sydney, however, none of them were left on board ship, Macquarie said, "either for purposes of prostitution or any other". The charge was so foul and slanderous that the Governor wondered that Bathurst should pay any attention to it.[58]

Before they left the ship, Mr J. T. Campbell mustered all the women. The usual questions were put to them about their treatment on the voyage. If they appeared healthy and did not complain, they were sent out at once as servants, or to Parramatta Factory. And if women were "really to be pitied", as Lord Bathurst's solf-hearted correspondent alleged, for the conditions under which they lived at Parramatta, he would point out that he had not suitable buildings for convict lodgings, that the evils rampant in Mr Marsden's town were "as old as the original foundation of the

Colony",[59] and that he himself had suggested a remedy in the erection of an adequate female factory five years ago—as far back as November 1812.[60]

X

The extracts which Bathurst sent from the anonymous letter were, of course, almost a year old when they left England. They had been written on 16 March 1816, and they reached the Governor on 31 August 1817. The letter apparently had been sent to England originally in the *Emu*, which had taken home the news of the trial of Vale, and all the mail containing the relation of the story of the *Traveller's* arrest. It was pardonable that the Governor should feel bitter. During his illness in December, Elizabeth made this manifest to his friends in the House of Commons.

She wrote to Drummond that Macquarie considered Bathurst's tone "very insulting", though this was "quite new from His Lordship who till now had expressed himself in the most agreeable manner on all subjects".[61]

She declared that it was still the custom for designing and truly wicked men in New South Wales to carry on an underhand correspondence with the clerks of the Colonial Office and everywhere they could think of, to propagate falsehoods and represent, in as unfortunate a light as they could, the conduct of different Governors, all of whom had been compelled or induced to relinquish the command by these false spies.

"We have long known," she wrote, "the exertions they were making to poison the minds of His Majesty's Ministers, but the Governor considered them too contemptible to take any notice of their cabals, nor did Lord Bathurst until now. He is unacquainted with the Governor personally and he does not know the despicable characters of these people who wish to vilify him."

If Lord Bathurst "encouraged every disaffected and unprincipled man in the Colony to set himself up in open opposition to the legal authorities of this place, he would soon have a fine commotion among the set of villains with which the Governors of this Colony had been surrounded". While the Governor held the government he would not suffer any disorderly proceedings. "Now that Lord Bathurst thinks it would be better to let every blackguard act as he pleases, it is full time he should find some Governor who will submit to his wishes."

Macquarie, therefore, saw all that was happening in England—or the little he knew of it—as the fruits of intrigue. He did not connect it with the British political situation. There is an article in the officially censored *Gazette* of 1 December 1817, reproducing the opinions of *The Times* newspaper,[62] in which the same sort of sympathy is shown for the British underdog as he himself had shown for the unfortunate convict in New South Wales. In that article the Poor Law was blamed for the troubles at home. It would scarcely have been published in Sydney had the Governor realized the trends of British official opinion.

Macquarie prepared carefully before he answered Bathurst's dispatch. Through replies to a circular letter, which his secretary sent out, he secured the agreement of all his eleven magistrates and chaplains, save two that, the results of the Sunday musters of convicts, which the anonymous writer condemned, were beneficial.[63]

It would be easy to guess the names of the dissenting justices. The Reverend Mr Marsden pretended that he had at first approved the musters —this was specifically untrue—but said that he had changed his mind when he had discovered that, after parades on the Sabbath morn, the convicts resorted "to such houses of ill-fame as were in their districts, and to such as sold spirits or cider without a licence, where they spend the remainder of the day in scenes of vice".

Complaints were made, he wrote, by some of the most respectable settlers including Messrs John and Gregory Blaxland and Nicholas Bayly, "of the misconduct of their servants when they attended this muster". He added, "And I recollect Mr. N. Bayley at the general muster in the year 1815, mentioned to his Excellency the misconduct of his servants."[64]

Mr Hannibal M'Arthur, Mr Marsden's colleague on the Parramatta Bench,[65] wrote that, as a justice, he had no complaint against the musters, but as a master, in common with most others, he had felt that serious evils arose from his servants mixing with other dissolute characters. The charge against the Government about solitary confinement, he wrote, was "totally unfounded".

Against the Parramatta magistrates Macquarie, in his comments for the Colonial Secretary, hurled himself with righteous fury. "They are the only ones to start any objection to the muster . . . calling in support of their opinion Messrs. John and Gregory Blaxland and Nicholas Bayley [sic] three gentlemen settlers who are notorious throughout the Colony for being very severe arbitrary masters and embroiled constantly in quarrels with their servants, whom they are frequently dismissing on the most frivolous pretences."[66]

XI

The story of the prisoners who supposedly had been subjected to unbearable solitary confinement in Parramatta Jail gradually unfolded of itself.

It mainly concerned a villainous convict soldier, Michael Hoare.[67] Garling, whom Jeffery Bent had called "so inferior a person to me", had sentenced him, with three others, early in 1816. The precious gang formed "a banditti, who marauded about in the woods, and are designated in this Colony bush rangers, men of the most alarming and dangerous description, who, lost to all sense of moral and social duties, live by plundering the honest settler".

They had been indicted in October 1815 for having stripped the schoolmaster at Kissing Point of the cream of his possessions, after threatening his life with clubs. Garling had sent each of them to jail for three years, the first year to be spent in solitary confinement upon bread and water.

And thirteen days after Hoare had been remitted to his cell, Mr Marsden and the sympathetic witness had discovered him bellowing in apparent insanity. Showing an unusual sympathy for him in his suffering, Marsden had ordered him to be taken in a cart to the asylum at Castle Hill.

Mr Oakes, the Parramatta jailer, disagreed with Mr Marsden. He had "never observed any symptoms of insanity" about Hoare "except his violence".

However, solicitously tended, the bushranger was carried grinning to Castle Hill, where his new keeper, Mr George Suttor, was no more convinced that his patient was unstable of mind than his colleague, Oakes, had been.

Mr Suttor reported that his prisoner was allowed his liberty in the yard because he showed no signs of insanity. Mr Marsden, however, who once again viewed the prisoner, declared that the reason he showed no signs of insanity was that he had been set free.[68]

But none could dispute that one day Mr Hoare had stolen silently out of the asylum with his bedding and another lunatic's clothes—which the unfortunate owner was never to see again—and that he had turned up whole in mind and body on—of all places—the farm of Mr Gregory Blaxland.

To cap the story, Hoare himself now came forward, "willingly and of his own accord", and swore upon the Holy Evangelist that he had "pretended insanity in the Jail for the purpose of getting out of the cell". He added cheerfully that after he had come back to Parramatta Jail, following his Arab-like retirement from Castle Hill, his sentence had been remitted by the Governor, along with the sentences of his associates, according to Macquarie's usual lenient habit.[70]

He had been, for some time before the complaints of his agonies drifted back from London into Botany Bay, "as much at liberty as any other convict in the Colony".

XII

On the most charitable reading of the facts possible, it was clear that Mr Marsden had become the subject of "a gross imposition".

It was not unnatural that the Governor should ascribe to him the worst and most uncharitable motives towards himself.

Had Marsden felt any real desire to relieve Hoare, or held any real belief in his insanity, an application to the Coroner in lunacy, or a short note to the Governor, would have seen the whole matter dealt with at once. Instead of taking these courses, Marsden had acted clandestinely on his own initiative. Then somebody had transmitted a malicious version of the whole matter to England to stab Macquarie in the back.

The Governor now thought that he knew full well the name of the writer of the anonymous letter who had so stirred the anger and suspicion of Bathurst:

> Altho' the name of the author of these gross calumnies is withheld, I have good reason to suppose it proceeded from the pen of the Revd. Samuel Marsden, as I firmly believe he is the only person, in *the character of a gentleman* in the whole colony, capable of writing and making such unfounded and malicious representations with a view to injure me in the opinion of His Majesty's Ministers.[72]

This opinion as to the authorship he continued to hold, despite the solemn assurances of Mr Justice Field, out of his literary experience as a dramatic critic of *The Times*, that the letter was not in Mr Marsden's diction.

Marsden undoubtedly had some association with the missive. But it smells strongly of other unpleasant people as well, and notably of Mr Jeffery Bent.

The actual claimant to authorship, the suppliant with the "eight young children entirely unprovided for", proved much later to be Mr Nicholas Bayly, brother of General Bayly[73]—he who, according to Mr Marsden, had complained to the Governor in person in October 1815.

He had in his early days been an officer of the Military. He had gone bail for M'Arthur when arrested by Bligh.[74] He had been an active participant in the Rebellion and had acted as Johnston's secretary[75] when the latter assumed office as "lieutenant-governor". He had been, as part of his letter which was not shown the Governor averred, in close touch with Ellis Bent. He had written to Captain Piper, two months before the date of his libellous letter, "Remember me to the Justice. I shall be always glad to see him *sans cérémonie*." The "justice" was Jeffery Bent.[76]

To add to the suspicion that that worthy was concerned was the fact, not momentarily observed, that this same Mr Bent had come to Port Jackson on one of the two convict ships carrying women to which Bayly's charges referred.

But in these matters Macquarie had no scent to follow.

<h1 style="text-align:center">XIII</h1>

For the accuracy and sincerity of Bayly's statements little could be said. His assurance that his eight children were entirely unprovided for needed qualification. He had been involved in rum-trading with some others of his regiment. He had two large farms, comprising 2100 acres of land. It was from him that Macquarie had recovered, at the end of 1810[77], the land on which Richmond township was laid out. The Governor had granted him two hundred acres in 1812, was about to grant him another two hundred acres at the very moment when his mind was wracked by these unworthy complaints. Bayly had a large number of convict servants, a fine herd of cattle, and eight hundred sheep. He was a prosperous gentleman settler.

His pity for the sufferings of a prisoner who was merely chained to a wall scarcely accorded with his record. His humanity, like that of Mr Marsden, seemed to be a new-born thing. In his days in the regiment, he had thrice been court-martialled[78] for illegally flogging servants.

Of Marsden, Dr Harris, a fellow magistrate, said, "I have known him to order 500 lashes."[79] The punishments inflicted by his authority were "much more severe than those of any other magistrate in the Colony".

In 1800 he had written of the flogging of a young Irishman *suspected* of conspiring to rebel, but convicted of no crime, who had fallen under his hand; and it was difficult to believe that the author of what happened to that felon could be moved to pity and action by the sight of a bushranger howling in solitary confinement. His own description of the flogging, administered by his own order, is certainly not so horrible as that of the rebel Irish "general", Holt, who witnessed it, but it serves to measure Mr Marsden's standards of pity:

Marsden to King

Mr. Atkins and I ordered him to be punished very severely in hopes of making him inform where the pikes were. Tho' a young man, he would have died upon the spot before he would tell a single sentence. He was taken down three times—punished upon his back, and also on his bottom when he could receive no more on his back. . . . He is not in a situation to be sent down to Sydney yet.[80]

The beating which the reverend gentleman had prescribed for the youth had laid bare his shoulder blades.[81] And the hypocrisy of his pretence at being horrified at the sight of a brutal thug in a solitary cell on bread and water was shown by letters which he wrote to Grey Bennet contemporaneously with his action in the interest of Hoare. Those he had expected to be kept from the light of day, since they were intended to be confidential. But Grey Bennet's zeal let them out.

In one Marsden said that there was scarcely a female convict in Parramatta who would go to service with a mistress; that all the women "in the most open and positive manner refuse to obey the order of the magistrates to that effect, preferring to live upon bread and water in a solitary cell till they wear out by length of time the patience of the magistrates".

A few months earlier Dr Arnold had heard him complain that he could not execute sentences of solitary confinement for want of cells. Yet he pretended to be convinced that one of the stoutest bushrangers in the country had gone insane after a mere thirteen days of lonely hardship.

His contrasting attitudes were scarcely less astonishing as a phenomenon than Bathurst's concern for the lady felons of New South Wales, some of them the dregs of humanity. For in that year in the United Kingdom itself, Parliament heard, little moved, the tale of a girl, free, "young and beautiful", who had been whipped, naked to the waist, through the streets of Inverness, while in a drunken stupor which she or her friends had achieved in preparation for her ordeal.

But most amazing of all was the fact that Marsden and Bayly with their trumped-up and easily-refutable charges came within an ace of clinching the grand objective which the Bents and the military officers and exclusives had worked for so ardently and for long. The pair had provided the last irritation needed to exhaust their adversary's patience.

XIV

Because of what had happened, though at this stage—despite previous resolutions to go home early in 1818—he wished to remain two or three years more in the Colony, Macquarie decided to resign his office.[82]

He wrote a bitter official commentary on the charges made against him, with a reproving peroration:

. . . I am free to indulge the hope that your Lordship will readily admit that my character and conduct, as Governor in Chief of this Colony, have been most malignantly, because most falsely aspersed in the assassin-like attacks, so covertly made on my administration of this Government by the anonymous libeller in question. And I am proud to be enabled, in concluding this letter, to add that, so far as precept and example go, I can defy the most envenomed malice to tax me justly with omitting any opportunity or means, within my power to restrain and repress vice and immorality thro' all the classes of this community, or of neglecting to encourage virtue and religion conformably to the high sentiments I entertain of their importance, both in my public station and private capacity.[83]

He wrote a public and official letter to Bathurst in which he regretted that "from the tone and manner of conveying your sentiments of disapprobation and censure, I have had the misfortune to lose that confidence which your Lordship has hitherto been kindly pleased to repose in me". And he asked that his successor's ship, or preferably the old *Dromedary*, on which he had made his voyage from England, should be allowed to take him home, "so as not to subject me to the mortification and serious expence of a protracted and circuitous voyage by way of India or China".[84]

In his private covering letter to Bathurst he was more expansive.

Foveaux, he said, had told him what to expect from Marsden and "many other deep designing men, whose delight it is to sow the seeds of discord and insubordination".[85] He had never found Foveaux wrong in his representations of these persons, but he himself was so far from acting on the information he gave that it had been his principle on all occasions to treat men according to their merits while under his command, without any retrospect of times past.

He had also invariably preserved and kept up amicable intercourse with the officers of Government—however ill disposed he knew they were towards him—while their conduct in their different offices was such as enabled him to comport himself towards them in an amicable manner.

He had all along known the never-failing exertions of those evil-minded men to vilify his conduct and the administration of the Government of the Colony; but, as long as his lordship did not notice these matters to him, he thought it unnecessary to make any effort to counteract them.

It had hitherto, he wrote, been a gratification to him to act under his lordship's administration, from the mild and reasonable as also perspicuous tenor of the Minister's orders.

That so great a reverse should so suddenly occur in their intercourse, he must consider "as one of those mortifying *trials* to which human nature is liable".

He did, he confessed, look forward to a period of repose at the termination of, perhaps, one of the most arduous, troublesome commands under the British Crown; but even this hope had been destroyed by the harsh tenor of his lordship's late letters. On this subject, therefore, he had only one source of comfort left to him, and this no man would take from him— namely that his lordship's strictures were unmerited on his part.

Every honest man in a public station, he continued, who studied the interests of his sovereign and his country in preference to gaining popularity at the expense of his conscience and integrity would have many foes and slanderers, and this he had experienced in the Colony in an eminent degree.

The very people on whom he had heaped many favours had become his greatest enemies and calumniators, mainly because he had declined, from a sense of justice, to gratify their further demands for unreasonable indulgences.

He named the list of persons "*in the rank of gentlemen*"[86] whom he looked upon as his "*secret* tho' not avowed *enemies*", and from whom he had "always experienced every opposition they could give with safety to themselves either publicly or privately".

There were a round dozen—Marsden, labelled as "discontented, intriguing and vindictive"; Dr Townson, Nicholas Bayly, John and Gregory Blaxland, Dr Throsby, John Horsley, as "discontented"; Sir John Jamison, David Allan the Commissary, John Oxley the Surveyor-General, as "intriguing and discontented"; and W. H. Moore the solicitor and his brother, Thomas Moore, as "seditious, intriguing and discontented".[87]

At the head of the list he placed the name of Marsden, to whom, personally, as well as to his family, he declared that he had always shown every civility, kindness and attention, having conferred several favours on them.

> His enmity is therefore the more unaccountable, and I can only ascribe it to a deep rooted malevolence and to his avidity for power and consequence, being extremely desirous of giving his advice on all occasions, and having the merit of every good measure ascribed to himself.
>
> He had been the principal adviser of some of my predecessors as Governors, and, I believe, his first illwill to me arose from my not consulting him on every occasion as they had done. Be that as it may, Mr. Marsden set out systematically, from the commencement of my government of the Colony, to oppose, both publicly and privately, every measure and regulation of mine however bene-ficial they may have been for the best interests of the Colony. I am grieved to be compelled to say so of any man of his sacred profession, but I do firmly believe that there is not a more malicious or a more vindictive unfeeling character in existence than the Revd. Mr. Marsden.[88]

His lordship, he believed, could not wonder at his deprecating a Minister's giving too easy credit to "the artful and insidious representations, clothed in the garb of humanity and hypocritical religious cant of this malevolent man, the effects of whose base misrepresentations I have already, with deep mortification, experienced and felt in recent official communications".

Finally, came another regretful conclusion:

> Had your Lordship reposed the same degree of confidence in my administration and integrity, that you appear to have done in his representations respecting the affairs of this Colony, I should not now have to lament the sudden change in your Lordship's sentiments towards me; and the consequent necessity I feel of tendering my resignation as Governor of this country, which I could not, on any principle of honour and justice, reconcile to myself to hold any longer after

forfeiting your Lordship's confidence. I must confess that, instead of censure, I looked forward with a confident hope for praise and approbation on the termination of my Government of this Country; for, I can safely venture to affirm that no Governor of His Majesty's Colonies has ever laboured harder in the discharge of his various, arduous public duties or has discharged those duties with more inflexible integrity than I have done; and certainly the most gratifying reward I could possibly receive or look for, was the approbation of my Sovereign and his Ministers on the termination of my Government of this Colony.

Having lost this, I lose all that I have been so long labouring for with so much anxiety, fatigue of body, and distress of mind, for I have certainly *not added to either my rank or fortune* by my eight years of hard service in New South Wales; consequently all that is now left to console me is an approving conscience!" [89]

XV

Whatever Macquarie might do, the fate of his distinctive plans had been sealed without his knowledge, from the moment Bathurst had written his letter to Sidmouth, the previous April, and had begun to fertilize Botany Bay economy with a policy which would presently make Australia within the nineteenth century a land of self-governing free people, and the convict era an almost forgotten, unpleasant episode buried in the dark ages of history.

It did not matter that the new conditions had been brought forth in the early Macquarie age largely by the Governor's unceasing drive and energy, applied to an increasing population against continual resistance. And it did not matter that they constituted the beginnings of the realization of his own aspirations for the Australian community.

The age of Toorali-addity lay dying. And the elated onlookers round its deathbed began to gird themselves for the new class-struggle which would decide whether, for the next couple of generations and more, the continent would make a home for a community of small, and chiefly emancipist, farmers, or be dominated by large landowners, organized aristocratically. In the political atmosphere of the era there could be but one answer.

For a time it seemed as if, very early, the posterity of the Governor, arch-champion of the little man, might be found marching with the big battalions.

Macquarie made two requests, apart from his supplication that he might be allowed to administer the Government after the arrival of a successor until the day of his own departure from the Colony. [90]

He pointed out the inadequacy of his salary—a mere £2000 a year, plus his allowances as a major-general on the Staff, [91]—for the support of his rank and the necessary expenses of his establishment and table in the increased state of the population and society. From his pay it had been impossible to save anything during his reign.

He asked for the customary indulgence of a pension [92] and that it should be extended to his family after his death. And he requested—"with a view to enabling me to make a suitable provision for my wife and child (having a son born to me in this Colony), after my death"—that the Minister move the Prince Regent to grant him "about fifteen thousand acres of land in some eligible part of the Colony".

As part of the grant he asked for "the unappropriated Government farm of Toongabbee",[93] which had been now for some years lying waste, and unoccupied, with the fertility and strength of the soil entirely exhausted through continual cultivation. He desired this plot "on account of the beauty of the situation and contiguity to the seat of Government, it being only 17 miles west of Sydney".

Those who had granted the drunken Davey six thousand acres and every lieutenant-governor for many years past at least three thousand acres, much of it before the beneficiaries assumed office, did not even acknowledge this request.

One of the greatest mistakes of the Governor's career was that he failed to flatter regularly some weighty patron in the peerage.

BOOK FIVE

★

1817 – 24

★

The Never-Erring Arm

O Thou who, unexpected, steal'st serene
Into the bosom of the fertile year,
Tell me of climates which I ne'er have seen,
And let me feel the fragrance thou dost bear!

For with thy presence, nature is adorned,
Clad in gay green, luxuriant and mild,
Erewhile the embryo blossom lay unformed,
In sweet profusion scattered o'er the wild;

Till, by degrees, it op'ning to the sun,
Now spreads, enamoured, to his warmer ray;
At length, by aged infirmity overcome,
'Twill, once more closing, droop and die away.

Thus in the midst of pleasures, man's cut off,
Struck by the never-erring arm of death,
Tho' some, above their fellows, rise aloft,
Yet fate, at length, will stop their vital breath.

—CHARLES TOMPSON, "Ode to Spring."
Written when he was "but twelve years" old,
in an "acacian grove" at Castlereagh, 1818.

CHAPTER XXVII

The Favourite Measure

I

A GLIMPSE at the records of the time proves that, though the Bayly letter was the match which fired the Governor's resolution to resign from office, his full reasons must have lain in a great accumulation of causes.

He was ill, though he insisted to his relatives in Scotland that he was not, and that his real anxiety was Elizabeth's failing health. It had been a wet and dreary year. In a few months, with great labour and anxiety, he had fought to success several firmly pursued projects. He had suffered his troubles with Moore and Vale and the men whom he had punished for trespassing in the Domain. He had been through the endless fatigue entailed in dealing with the charges against the officers in the convict ship *Chapman*. He was trying to compose the differences of the two judges, who had quarrelled over precedence.[1]

Ship after ship had arrived with more and more convicts, each to be greeted with a loud clamour from importunate settlers for mechanics and artisans, but for no other classes of prisoners. This threw a yearly greater burden on the Colony's power to feed the rationed population.

Van Diemen's Land in 1817 had seemed to reek with fraud and disobedience. In Sydney he had dealt with arrogant exclusive officers, greedy and fraudulent commissariat employees, blacks who till this year had become annually more savage and daring, irate clergy, whining remittance men; also he was now plagued by the new race of *poor settlers*, that come out *as such*[2]—mostly "decayed tradesmen and merchants and idle profligate adventurers".

The moment the Colony ceased to feed them and provide them with indulgences they managed, "in some underhand way to sell their farms and take to lawless pursuits, keeping low public houses, or becoming itinerant merchants, hawkers and pedlars". England seemed to send everything in the way of immigrants save the class most wanted—"respectable *monied men*, who would support themselves, set an example in industry" and take six to eight convicts off the shoulders of the commissariat, whereby "the expences of the Colony would be greatly reduced".

Experience of the operation of the new tentative free settlement policy of the Home Government had certainly done nothing to wean its representative from his conviction that the emancipists and their offspring formed by far the most industrious and desirable classes of poor settlers.

A fresh cross had been added to his burdens in the shape of Father Jeremiah O'Flynn[3], an Irish Catholic priest whom he felt moved to expel.

The priest had come to the Colony without Colonial Office sanction and was like to disturb the minds of the touchy Roman Catholic community, which had become so docile that some of its members had formed the habit of attending the Anglican Church upon the orders of the Government.

The Governor was deeply concerned lest the religious feelings of his conscripted followers of Rome "might be worked upon by a designing artful priest, so as to excite a spirit of resistance", which would bring back among the local Irish the old insurrectionary spirit of 1804, with all its attendant terrors.

It was lucky for him that the Prince Regent and his Minister saw eye to eye with him, since Mr Marsden, a Low-Church Protestant, had developed a deep sympathy for the Roman Catholic cause. But it turned out that when O'Flynn had applied to the Colonial Office for permission to go to Botany Bay "the orthography of his letter induced a suspicion of his fitness".[4] Reference had been made to "the heads of the Catholic Church", whose answer was "that the person in question was a most improper one to be entrusted with the cure of souls". So when O'Flynn reached Sydney "in a clandestine manner", after having been told by the Colonial Office that he would have no permission to visit the Colony, Macquarie's decision to send him back to Europe had "the entire approval" of the Prince Regent.

II

Heavy, drenching rain fell almost incessantly between the winters of 1816 and 1817. Farms, stock, and property of feckless settlers along the Hawkesbury and Nepean[5], who refused stubbornly to take advantage of the highland refuge homesteads which the Governor had granted them, were ravaged no less than three times during that period by the flood waters. The plight of the victims had flung back hundreds of convicts whom they could not feed upon the Government's hands. The roads and streets were torn up sadly by the deluge and the narrow tyres of the colonial waggons.

The isolation of outlying districts through the rains made bushranging easier. And in the towns robbery was always popular, to the great harassment of rulers. Plunder of the Government stores was continual, "from the description of persons who must necessarily be employed"[6] in them. Carriers of grain from the Hawkesbury by sea nearly always stole some of the cargo and drenched the rest with water[7] to replace lost weight, or stole the good grain which they carried for others and replaced it with their own weevily rubbish. In the Cowpastures, in spite of the military guard, Government cattle were fast melting away.[8]

The Governor's building programmes gave him a great deal of worry. His method of promoting them was systematic. He "did not shrink from the avowal that he had always been disposed to give preference to Public Works of Government[9] in regard to mechanics over the private accommodation of individuals".

He firmly maintained that the first call on labour must be to provide those stable bases to which, he had believed from the first, permanent settlement might attach itself. The central town and township and their amenities must take shape as the heart of everything; for he believed that without a conductive heart life could not survive in the outlands. With a centre in each district providing a local market, justice, medicine, religion, education, and fellowship, settlement would have something to which to anchor. But it was difficult to adhere to his plans when his ears were filled with the clamour of exclusives anxious for carpenters and masons to build them mansions on a ducal scale in the guise of "necessary improvements".

His schemes nevertheless went forward. Never had a British colony acquired such buildings in so short a space of time. Barracks for one thousand men and officers' quarters were finished—"the best and most compleat in any of His Majesty's foreign dominions"—the whole surrounded by a high wall. There were other barracks for Parramatta and Liverpool and Windsor. New churches were to be built at Sydney, Windsor, and Liverpool, and spires put on St John's at Parramatta. A fort was to be built at Benelong Point with seven guns to "prevent boats leaving . . . or being cut out of the Cove at night, a frequent occurrence".[10]

He had planned, on the site of the old bakehouse, Government House stables designed for transformation into a fort, should need arise. So "grand and magnificent"[11] was this edifice to be that his enemies believed that he would be forced to build "a very large and expensive Government House" to match it, though the Colonial Office hastily vetoed a move for its erection.

Even the convicts were to have a "large and commodious" home in Macquarie Street.[12] The female orphans shortly were to move into a "large elegant and commodious" house at Parramatta. "The new female factory" at the same centre was to be a very dream of comfort and convenience. Messrs Cowper and Marsden were acquiring "handsome dwellings and offices". But Government House continued a "decayed, mean, shabby" place.[13] In it the Governor was "worse accommodated than any private gentleman in the Colony". Its timbers were dissolving under the constant gnawing of the termites. Its rooms were miasmic from the springs which oozed out of the "abrupt declivity of a hill" behind it, except when rain sent a Niagara tumbling off the cliff into the kitchen area. Men walked softly in Government House; there seemed a chance that one day it might fall bodily round its occupants' ears.

Yet the Colonial Office, for the moment, showed no anxiety about his domestic comfort, and concern would have been too much to expect from a Government which quibbled about that "noble magnificent edifice" on the South Head of Port Jackson, Australia's first lighthouse, the apple of its promoter's eye:

> . . . yon tall Tow'r, that with aspiring Steep,
> Rears its proud Summit o'er the trackless Deep,
> The recent Care of His Paternal Hand
> That long has cherished this improving Land,
> Thro' the drear Perils of the Starless Night
> Shall shed the lustre of revolving light.[14]

III

All building labours were carried through, of course, in a turmoil of protest, obstruction and dishonesty.[15]

Bathurst demanded at first that local projects must be paid for out of Colonial funds; but when the funds were raised, the British Treasury turned a greedy eye upon them, "with a view to reducing the expenses of the Mother Country".[16] Then the Minister began to impress on the Governor the need to have plans and specifications of his proposed works approved by the Home Government before he proceeded with them. The exclusives railed at the extravagance involved in so much grandeur and adornment— especially the extravagance in cheap labour which would, they believed, have been better devoted to their own enrichment and the promotion of their own comfort. Mr Grey Bennet sneered loudly about the futility of "temples round pumps".[17]

With these sections the Governor must wrestle on the one hand. On the other he must subdue the fiery little Greenway, his architect, whom he sometimes seemed to fear as much as all of them put together. Mr Greenway's ambitions ran to a vast civic circus, a reminiscence of Wren's plans for the setting of St Paul's, centred in the Gothic mass of a cathedral, to castled palaces and towering ramparts, to Doric colonnades and town sewers. "Great as his talents were", he could never be induced to remember that he was a convict architect, whose salary of three shillings a day[18] was for ever threatened by the Colonial Office, and who was compelled to draw his plans piecemeal upon odd bits of masonry because upon paper they were sure to be plagiarized.[19] His mind dwelt perpetually, it seemed, in those happy days of yore when "his pursuits in England [were] on a scale of magnitude and decoration as yet unfit for and unknown in this Colony".[20]

IV

Despite his tribulations and all opposition, the Governor "felt both pride and exultation" at being able to provide the Colony in so short a time with so many useful and important buildings. He was not even contrite of heart about his minor adornments of his capital:

> The Turnpike gate may be unsuitable, the Obelisk not necessary, the Fountain absurd, the Tower, Lighthouse Railing, etc. all useless extravagant expenditure— but the Governor *did not* consider them so; nor does he think the little unadorned Obelisk, placed as it was, at a point from whence distances were to be measured, and rendered at a trifling expence, somewhat ornamental to the town, meriting any censure.[21]

It was galling to have to turn from the contemplation of works which the enlightened M. Arago thought fit to grace any European capital, at the agonized cry of Mr Greenway that bricks which should have gone into some church wall had gone instead into a contractor's mansion, so that the church was falling down of its own weight. It was harassing to have to join in the search for the coins which one had last week placed under a foundation stone, which had now been overturned by light-fingered marauders.[22]

But, when he looked back on the civilized places of the Colony, it was almost totally true to say, "I made them all." In this sense the description of him upon his mausoleum is true, "The Father of Australia".

When Macquarie left Port Jackson, he had entirely rebuilt Sydney's main public edifices, all upon a grand scale.[23] He had done the same at Parramatta, and he had created the townships or stations of Windsor, Liverpool, Richmond, Pitt Town, Wilberforce, Penrith, Emu Plains, Springwood, Bathurst, Campbelltown, Newcastle, and Port Macquarie, most of them out of wilderness. He had replanned and rebuilt Hobart and Launceston. He had put up something like two hundred main buildings, from cottages to grand barracks for a thousand men, and left New South Wales with three hundred miles of turnpike and carriage road, where before there had been none at all worthy of the name. He had given the antipodes their first paved streets, lighthouse, fountains, and obelisks.

No governor in any colony of similar size and remoteness has ever come near to his achievement as a constructor.

And his mellow red-brick buildings stood, a loveliness and an inspiration to all with the sense of beauty in their hearts, till the age of the twentieth-century vandals who began to pull them down with no more compunction than if they had been infected fowlhouses.

V

One piece of building to Macquarie's credit in 1817, however, was not of brick and stone; yet it gave him more pleasure than even his new lighthouse. In 1818 it fought for life and he waited to discover how the Colonial Office would react to its unauthorized foundation. He must have breathed more freely when that year it produced its first balance sheet.

From almost the moment of his arrival he had promoted his "favourite measure of a bank".[24] He had wished to found it upon the methods in vogue at the Bank of the Cape of Good Hope, which had drawn its inspiration from the Bank of Pennsylvania. His transports of enthusiasm about the scheme had been received coldly in England, especially by the Treasury and Lord Liverpool. And it was not till the end of 1816 that he could find a pretext upon which to take the initiative without asking permission from Whitehall.

His chance arose out of the actions of Ellis Bent and his riotous brother. The former's recognition in the courts of locally issued promissory notes which had become "illegal and irrecoverable" under the currency regulations had brought back "the old and base system" of currency frauds which had flourished five years before.[25]

The Colony was soon once more "overflowing with the [colonial] currency circulation, which by means of Mr Ellis Bent's irregular and inconsistent conduct has again grown into use".[26] All the Governor's measures to establish the silver sterling currency had been brought to naught.

The closing of the Supreme Court by Jeffery Bent had completed the chaos.[27] Indeed, a suspicious mind might be inclined to believe that the whole of the incidents leading to Bent's culminating action had been designed for Ellis Bent's protection. If the Court were closed, civil actions on currency could not come before it and he would not be under the painful necessity of giving illegal decisions to support his erring brother. Litigation, if the regulations were acknowledged, must ruin them and their friends.

Death had solved Ellis Bent's problem for him; but that did not mitigate the position. When Mr Wylde arrived in October 1816 he saw with surprise and dismay "that actions of an immense amount" on paper issued "in actual contravention" of the currency regulations were coming before him for adjudication.

If he strictly enforced the regulations, a vast mass of property must inevitably be lost by more or less honest citizens who had put their faith in Mr Ellis Bent's dishonest acceptance of the promissory note currency as legal.

The ramifications of what had happened were so vast as to affect the whole financial structure of the Colony. Governor and Judge-Advocate hurriedly consulted and acknowledged the position by suspending the regulations which made silver the basis of legal tender. An "amnesty for the past" in respect of breaches of the currency law was extended to all by proclamation.[28]

Now the way was open for the Governor to found his bank.

This, of course, required great courage in Botany Bay; but it was a measure which he believed afterwards to have been "the saving of the Colony from ruin",[29] and consequently the greatest benefit that could have been conferred on it.

The ambitious institution had been conceived at consultations[30] held between the Government and the commercial community on 22 November 1816 at John Wylde's chambers in Macquarie Street.

The ostensible purpose of the gathering was "to take into consideration the present state of the colonial currency and what would be the consequence of an immediate sterling circulation". "The Magistrates, Principal Merchants and Gentlemen of Sydney" attended, specially invited by the Governor's secretary, Mr Campbell, who had served in all departments of the Bank of Ireland[31] and taken a principal part in founding and conducting the Bank of the Cape of Good Hope.

Lieutenant-Governor Molle presided. All present were for sterling, though outside a large number of speculators violently opposed the abolition of "currency". Wylde and "a few other gentlemen inforced with much ability" the expediency of forming a bank. In truth, the benefits of such a move "stared every man so completely in the face as the only means whereby public distress could be fully averted, [that] it was embraced by the meeting at large", and resolutions to implement the suggestion were at once brought to discussion.

Wylde was satisfied that "no contributions could have been obtained for the necessary common stock, but on the strongest legal assurance of personal indemnity from all general liability or partnership risk". He thought the Governor had power to grant letters of incorporation for the constitution of a joint-stock company. There was nothing contrary to the statute,[32] he believed, in such a measure, nor anything in conflict with the principles on which such institutions were encouraged in the mother country. Why, he said, the Governor had, besides all sorts of fiscal powers, even authority to erect boroughs and *cities* which would have been impossible without the issues of charters. But he did not keep back from the meeting his opinion that the exercise of the Governor's authority was inferential from and upon the terms of his commission and dependent upon the Home Government's confirmation.

However, he expressed the strongest confidence that the Home Government would not deny sanction to a proposal that "came so much recommended both by the Governor and by the public opinion of the whole Colony".[33]

Resolutions were agreed to—*inter alia*:

> That the present Meeting is desirous that a Sterling Currency should take place in this Colony under such Regulations and Provisions as His Excellency the Governor may deem proper and applicable to a reduced price of Labour and rate of Sterling Charges, in every kind of Dealing and Trade within the Colony.
>
> That a sum of not less than Twenty Thousand Pounds, in Shares of not less than One Hundred Pounds each invested in a Public Colonial Bank, transferable by Assignment or otherwise in due course of Law, will be necessary for supplying a circulating medium for the uses of the Colony.
>
> That the general object and Business of the Bank be to advance upon due Interest, and the credit of the Bank, pecuniary assistance to the Colonial Trader, Agriculturalist, and Settler, as well as to afford a Safe Depository of Money Committed to its Security and Charge.[34]

After that, meeting followed meeting.

One on 29 November considered the relation of local currency to sterling and agreed to alter the exchange of local notes from fifty per cent of sterling value to 13s. 4d. in the pound sterling value. The Governor on 7 December proclaimed all wages and contracts to be expressed in sterling at the new rates. All copper—it had circulated at local rates—was called in and reissued in sterling terms.

On 5 December a general meeting discussed the question of subscriptions to the Bank. Applications came thick and fast after Wylde in the chair "expatiated in an eloquent strain upon the patriotism of the undertaking". Emancipists and respectables tumbled over each other to share in the good things which the proposal offered.[35]

Thus Eagar the Irish convict, not yet completely freed, became the largest shareholder and voter in the corporation; George Howe of the *Gazette*, *The Times's* contribution to reformed Botany Bay, the second largest; and Massey Robinson, the poet laureate (though he was harassed by "the little claims and requests incidental to the season"), George Crossley, the much esteemed but convicted attorney, S. Lord, J.P., William Hutchinson, and William Redfern, the Nore rebel, all figured in the share lists, along with judges and three members of the Governor's staff—J. T. Campbell, Captain Gill, and Antill—and later the Governor's wife. The names of the exclusives were conspicuous by their absence, save for Dr Harris.[36]

A committee of fifteen[37] was appointed to draft regulations and fix the basis for the choice of directors. The list of its members was headed by the name of the experienced J. T. Campbell and ended with that of S. Lord, and in between were those of Messrs Eagar and Howe, flanked on the one side by that of the Clerk of the Peace and on the other by that of Garling, former acting Judge-Advocate.

On 7 February 1817 the first board was elected,[38] "each member separately by ballot at a General Meeting", to be sworn in by the Judge-Advocate. The first directors were D'Arcy Wentworth, Robert Jenkins, William Redfern, Alexander Riley, Thomas Wylde, Dr John Harris, and John Thomas Campbell, the Governor's secretary, who then signed for the first time as chairman.

Mr Riley did not reach the point of being sworn in[39]; for he learned that when the Bank functioned it proposed to be so unreasonable as to refuse to accept his notes of hand as cash deposits. Mr Riley had never been so insulted in his life; so he resigned, and was succeeded by Mr William Gore, the Provost-Marshal, who shortly before had been thrown into a dungeon by the rebels of 1808 and who shortly after his election became mentally deranged and bankrupt.

There had been some trouble about the election and a number of "respectable" candidates said they would withhold their nominations if a conditionally pardoned convict were put up. Wylde had the task of informing the Governor of this position and found that the latter knew what had taken place and that it had engendered in him feelings and opinions so strong that his adviser "retired from all explanation".[40]

As usual Macquarie had taken a very determined stand on the emancipist question. Emancipists, he insisted, must be eligible as directors because they had the chief wealth of the Colony, and were entitled to every benefit which might be received in it. The Bank, he thought, could not be established without them. Everything eventually was settled more or less amicably.

Wylde in the meantime had drafted the charter to constitute Australia's first public company. When the Governor came to issue the parchment, he seemed, said the Judge-Advocate later, "to act entirely upon my opinions as to his power".

VI

On 25 March the Board was sworn in at the President's house,[41] he being ill. It addressed its grateful thanks for the charter to the Governor who responded, "Persevere, gentlemen, in your exertions to foster this infant establishment and be assured it shall ever have my warmest support and patronage—and that the time is not far distant when the Bank will on its own merits obtain a public confidence, and gradually flourish, to the credit and benefit of the proprietors and the country at large."[42]

The directors hired Entally House, No. 6 Macquarie Place,[43] at a rental of £150 a year, from Mrs Reiby—she who had come to the Colony through having borrowed a neighbour's pony in a frolic.

They ordered that all inlets through which the most slim and agile burglar might crawl should be sealed up, thus plunging the interior into perpetual gloom; and they accepted the responsibility of securing a cashier and other officers without increasing their expenses above £600 a year. For any management costs greater than that amount they must seek the authority of a shareholders' general meeting.

Then they took a fidelity bond of £1500 from the enterprising Mr E. S. Hall,[44] whom they chose as their first manager and cashier, though the fact that he had founded the Benevolent Society seemed to be his principal qualification. They advertised for "an iron chest or safe", ordered, by resolution, a cane-bottomed lounge for the board-room, and decided that the name of a mythical "J. Lee" should appear as acceptor on all their bank notes.[45] All was now ready. They met at the Bank on 8 April, which they had declared as foundation day. They established their meeting day as Tuesday—one hundred and thirty years later it still was.

Mr Hall sat behind an immense pile of new bank-notes.

There were 639 five-pound notes issued that year; 1794 single one-pound notes; 440 valued at 10s. each; 1192 at 5s.; and 809 at 2s. 6d. with bank tokens, £27 5s. 6d.—a total of £5635 8s.[46] And each note was inscribed with a piece of the highest idealism which augured a new era of honesty and stability:

> Let us possess the public confidence so long only as, by a faithful discharge of the honorable trust reposed in us, we may shew ourselves worthy of it. Whenever any one man can say with truth "the Bank has broken faith," be then OUR ruin, and ours only, the immediate consequences.[47]

As if this were not enough, Mr Hall had an opulent coinage for small change—8000 one-shilling tokens, 6000 one-and-sixpenny tokens and 4000 spotless two-shilling tokens, all inscribed by order of the Board with the date "eighth of April in printed characters".[48]

The first deposit had come earlier. Sergeant Murphy, of the 46th Regiment, who had been helping to guard the western road from bush-rangers and blacks, had on 5 April lodged £50 with the Bank.[49]

VII

Meanwhile Macquarie was attempting to transfer some of his own enthusiasm about the venture to the Colonial Office. Having given a charter for seven years, subject to the Minister's approval, he "certainly advised" that if the Bank were conducted for a year or two with discretion and success, the Colonial Government should either become a party to it, or "should at least make the Bank the depository and medium of all Government monies and payments".

Bathurst merely referred the project to His Majesty's law servants,[50] who coldly reported that the Governor was "not legally empowered either by his commission or instructions to grant such a charter and that it is consequently null and void".

Bathurst wrote, "I must confess, however, that [the charter] appeared to me to contain some provisions of so objectionable a nature that I cannot regret its want of legal validity".[51]

He could not see that "any public benefit was to be derived from the establishment of a bank under the proposed charter, which will not equally flow from its being conducted by private individuals at their own risk without any interference on the part of the Government, or any protection beyond what is afforded to all other traders".

So long as it was conducted on sound principles, the Bank would, of course, have a due degree of support from the Government; but the Governor must carefully avoid implicating the Colonial Government's faith in its pecuniary transactions.

After Macquarie had written his resignation, the Bank was fighting very successfully for its life upon the most advanced principles—in February 1818 it even acknowledged the right to votes of "female proprietors", perhaps out of deference to Elizabeth Macquarie, the first woman shareholder in an Australian public company.[52]

Before Bathurst's stiff disavowal of the charter had reached the Colony, the President, at the meeting held on 21 July 1819, had been able to report "a success perhaps unparalleled in the annals of banking being unabated by any losses whatever."[53]

When Bathurst's cold dispatch arrived Macquarie felt justified in refraining from suspending the charter, pending further instructions.[54]

While the matter was being argued with the Colonial Office, however, events which might have proved that Mr Campbell's presidential transports had been premature had come to light.

VIII

From the very first the inhabitants of New South Wales, particularly the more intimate directors and shareholders, heartily appreciated the benefits conferred upon them by the Bank. Some of them, of course, were disappointed in the bright prospects which seemed to loom for them.

Dr D'Arcy Wentworth, one of the directors, having observed the profit to be made out of discounting, decided to enter into the discount business himself, undercutting the Bank rate from two per cent to one-and-a-half per cent.[55] But that trouble was smoothed over before it caused any serious heart-burning.

Then a few directors were shrewdly suspected of taking notes away to sign and of putting them into circulation on their own accounts. This was never proved[56]. But the whole community saw cause to be convinced that this note-issue business made it apparently a fine thing to be a bank director. For the Secretary and Cashier some time later indignantly repudiated a suggestion that he might have cast a slur upon the honour of the directors by listing the numbers of the wads of notes which they had taken to sign and which seemed to have vanished.[57]

The Bank tried many cashiers and managers before it achieved stability. It tried Mr Hall, Mr Bayly (he of the eight children entirely unprovided for), and it tried Mr Francis Williams, former partner of Mr Simeon Lord, J.P.[58]

Even his enemies had been hopeful of Mr Williams, feeling that if he could cope with Mr Lord he could certainly cope with the intricacies of general finance.

Unfortunately, as soon as he appeared on the scene, an aura of generosity began to hang over Entally House. Hearty shareholders dropped in on Mr Williams and left him "a little wine and spirits[59] and a variety of small amounts of cash" at Christmastide, about £60 per year, which he considered as "the ordinary acknowledgment of a person in my situation". The son of Solicitor Amos came and gave him £25 for allowing him a loan[60]. Mr Robert Campbell, Junior, promised him an £800 banking house for himself in Bligh Street, as compensation for the risk he ran in occasionally handing Mr Campbell a casual pocketful of bank securities to pay for a cargo.

Also, if Mr Hankinson, the draper, had no money[61] to pay for an adventure, Mr Williams took his cheque, put it in his own pocket and handed his friend the cash out of the till. Then he sat down to wait till Mr Hankinson should have a sufficient balance to meet the cheque—a consummation which, alas, was never achieved.

One sad day the Bank proprietors discovered that there was a £12,000 deficiency in their cash account.[62] Sorrowfully Mr Williams explained how one of their number, Mr Robert Jenkins, a director, with Messrs Laurie, Armytage and Amos, to whom he had granted the loan for a consideration of £25, had taken him to a club where he met the persons who made him their victim. They put him up for membership. "I was induced to make promises overnight which I had not the resolution next day to refuse."[63]

But it takes more to ruin a good bank than the disappearance of an amount only £600 short of its current capital issue. This sum the Bank of New South Wales eventually lost by Mr Williams's generosities. Mr Williams retired to "durance vile" and Macquarie temporarily withdrew £3000 of Government deposits.[64]

The enterprise, even in the face of such disaster, was far from the edge of the grave. Before Macquarie's letter to Bathurst deferring the cancellation of the charter had been effectively dealt with in Downing Street, the crisis had been weathered and the owners of the Bank were able temporarily to contemplate the position of their institution with equanimity.

They had the household furniture of Mr Williams. Their books noted fifty-nine shareholders who represented £12,600 of invested capital. Their list of depositors formed a sort of current roll of Australian history. They held £1 8s. 6d. for Mr Daniel Cooper and £3 17s. 10d. for Mr Greenway, the architect, and £1139, the property of Captain Terence Murray; but they did not have any account of the Governor's unless in the name of one of his staff—Antill had £1766 on deposit. The poet laureate's balance was £356 10s. 9d.—eleven times that of the whole judiciary. Even Mr J. T. Bigge had an account—£217.[65]

On 30 December 1820 they had a balance to profit and loss account of £1038[66] and they had formed a commendable habit of paying regular and frequent dividends—12 per cent in August 1819; 9 per cent in February 1820; 6 per cent in August 1820; and another 6 per cent in December 1820.

Within the seven years of its probationary term, the concern, having gone ahead as if it were as legally chartered as the Realm itself, received its royal parchment.[67]

Macquarie's greatest ambitions usually fructified in time. His foundation of modern corporate financial enterprise in Australia proved more solid and enduring than it at first looked to be.

If it was not true in 1817 to say, as the Governor said in his enthusiasm, that the Bank rescued the Colony from bankruptcy, its solidity was comforting on many a later occasion. In 1893 and 1929-31, if the Bank of New South Wales had collapsed, the whole financial structure of the Commonwealth would have been in danger.[68]

In September 1956[69] the Bank's paid-up capital was £17,560,000, its reserve fund £12,000,000 and its net profit for the year £1,870,000, or more than fourteen times the British Government's expenditure on the Colony in the second year of the Bank's existence. Deposits had risen from £26,867 17s. 10d. in 1820 to £443,290,000. It boasted 974 branches and agencies, as well as thousands of foreign connections. Its total running cost in 1817 had been under £600; its salary bill in 1956 was above £10,000,000.

One of its agencies was seated at Ba, in Fiji, where (as in New Zealand) the merits of bank directors would have been decided purely on epicurean grounds when the Bank was founded. A branch was at 29 Threadneedle Street, London, E.C. The inhabitants of Taumarunui and Karangahape Road (New Zealand) and Wyalkatchem, Western Australia, have been blessed by the Bank with nice impartiality with the same facilities of deposit and loan as those in Berkeley Square, W.1., which supports a branch.

Whereas the loans during the unparalleled year of 1818-19 were quoted by Mr Campbell in his ecstacy as reaching £1280, loans and advances to customers at the end of 1956 totalled about £258,000,000. The Bank's assets were then valued at round half a billion pounds. And the number of its employees, 8600, equalled that of the whole civilian population of New South Wales in the year in which Macquarie began to govern. It sent to the wars of 1914-18 and 1939-45 a civilian force far greater than the military garrison of Australia in the year in which it was born.

It had lost some of its more adventurous features before the twentieth century. All chance had evaporated of a cashier being able to dispose of four-fifths of the capital without exposure till all was lost. It had ceased to be possible even for a director to take the general manager to a club and persuade him overnight to lend the bank's securities to a ruinous extent while in a state of exaltation. And though the modern bank had more money and was more wary with customers, it had, in 1945, less bank holidays than in 1820, when twenty-three were recognized.

In the twentieth century it had ceased even to celebrate *"Jan. 31: Governor Macquarie's Birthday—the Establisher and promoter of the Bank".*[70]

IX

There were two Macquaries after 1817. One was the grim administrator pushing his endless works to completeness with all possible drive against the approaching time when he must leave the Colony.

The other was a yellowed but genial fellow who glowed with pleasure as he laid the foundation stone in George Street of a church, naming it for St Andrew,[71] or as he and Young Lachlan dedicated the new church at Liverpool, which should have provided a tabernacle for the odious Mr Vale; or planned to make George Street that year the first paved street in the antipodes.[72]

His diaries began again to expand. His personal life became richer. His festivals seemed to take on a new significance for him. He clung with an almost desperate affection to his wife and child, his endearments written in many a page of his journals and letters. Lachlan, "our dear boy",—now safely "inoculated with the cowpock[73] from a very healthy child in the female orphan school" and also with Mauritian lymph—accompanied him everywhere, assisting in his ceremonies.

He saw that the boy had everything to be wished for[74]—a boat (the *Elizabeth*), a little harbour with a name ("Port Lachlan") to put it in, a curricle to drive in with John and Nancy Moore, or small Charlie Whalan, son of the sergeant of his Guard, bats and balls in abundance.

The booty of no voyage or expedition was complete without pets and presents for Young Lachlan. Settlers knew of this and the urge to give to the child seemed to infect everybody whom the Governor met on the roads, from lonely overseers who came bearing stuffed wild turkeys to Major Morisset, one of the Newcastle commandants, with a modest offering for his "young friend" of "four black swans, two emus, two kangaroos, (Foresters), one wild goose and one wanga-wanga pigeon".[75] Elizabeth's rooms and the nursery smelt hotly of "rare stuffed birds from the Hunter River".

Young Lachlan's birthday, too, became like no other for the method of its celebration:

Tuesday 28. March ! ! !

This being the anniversary of the birth-day of our beloved dear son, who completes his sixth year today, it was celebrated by every demonstration of joy we could manifest on such a happy interesting occasion;—but the joy and pleasures of the day were greatly clouded by the indisposition of his poor dear mother, who, on that account was unable to partake of the festivities of this, to us at least, most joyful day.— At half past 8 o'clock in the morning, Lachlan, being dressed as a Highlander for the first time in a suit of tartan and bonnet, proceeded with a number of his juvenile friends on a water excursion in the Govt. Barge, attended by his own little cutter, together with three boats full of the natives—and accompanied by myself and Lt. H. Macquarie. The *Fleet* rowed slowly from Port Lachlan, where we all embarked, round Garden Island, and from thence to the beautiful little Bay on the south side of the Harbour, next to Wooloomooloo Bay, and which on this occasion, I christened "*Elizabeth-Bay*" in honour of Mrs. Macquarie, it having no particular distinguishing name before—and intending soon to establish some native settlers there.— From Elizabeth Bay we returned home to breakfast after our very pleasant water excursion.[76]

Lachlan entertained 19 boys and girls at a sumptuous breakfast and the same number at dinner.— About sixty male and female natives were also entertained by him at a separate breakfast and dinner highly to their satisfaction.— Between breakfast and dinner Lachlan accompanied Major Druitt and myself to inspect the Tower and Light House, at the South Head.— The Russian ships, having sailed, and cleared the Heads early this morning, we saw them at a great distance in the offing.—

We got back just in time for Lachlan to sit down with his 19 juvenile friends to a sumptuous dinner.—We had a select party of our adult friends to dine with us today, in honour of Lachlan, and we sat down 26 at table to a very excellent dinner, the company consisting of the persons specified in a distinct memorandum.—

In the evening we had the band of the 48th., and gave a pretty little dance to the ladies.— Lachlan sat up as long as he was able, and was much amused with the dancing—and the company very much admired him in his Highland dress.— Lachlan went to bed at half past 9—and the whole company broke up at 11, o'clock after spending a very pleasant day.—

The only thing to be regretted was our dining at so late an hour, which threw back the sports of the evening for Lachlan and his juvenile friends.

These glimpses of the Governor's later private life give an insight into his intimate daily interests. But, though in the privacy of his home he might seek to exercise without restraint his passionate love of his isolated family and his Highland genius for hospitality, the sectional contentiousness of the Colony could not be banished.

Even Government House was not free from brawling, as when his faithful henchman, Mr Broughton, upon a royal occasion, looked too lovingly upon the wine-cup, and then too long upon his own and the Governor's mortal enemy, Mr David Allan, the Deputy Commissary-General,[77] who resented public descriptions of his countenance and being threatened and drafted off from a lady by an inferior as if he were one of Mr M'Arthur's merinos.

Mr Allan was, in fact, a great man. It was told that he wore "two epaulettes and a feather in his hat". He kept a carriage and had a wife and family. It was "very easy to know how he came to this great advancement and why he was formally introduced to the Prince Regent on his appointment", since Mrs Allan was "sister to Mrs Harry Johnston, and Mrs Harry Johnston was mistress to Colonel M'Mahon, and Colonel M'Mahon was private secretary to the Duke of York".

So it became necessary to have poor Mr Broughton court-martialled, with the direst and most dangerous results to himself and much embarrassment to the Governor, whose seat became daily more uneasy.

P

CHAPTER XXVIII

An Habitation and a Name

I

IN February 1818 the first ten free settlers, half of them Australian-born, were set upon their way across the Blue Mountains to the Bathurst Plains.

Their names were William Lee,[1] George Cheshire, James and John Blackman, Richard Mills, John Abbott, John Nevill, Thomas Thite, Thomas Swanbrooke, and John Godden. They went each endowed with a grant of fifty acres of wheat land, two acres of township land, a cow, rations from the King's store and four bushels of seed wheat for sowing. The names of half of them were to rank high in pastoral history, especially that of William Lee, whose great red shorthorns came to be known on every stock-route in Australia.

This settlement followed exploration in 1817, which had served to whet Macquarie's appetite for still wider discoveries. Apart from the fact that it advertised the opening of the attack upon the resources of the west, it set up a new milestone in the progress of the country and of those who looked upon it as a home and as the fit object of patriotic fervour.

Here was opening, in that eventful year, the infant age of the Australians, as opposed to the preceding one of the mere colonial exploiters, whose ultimate objective had been to return home with a fortune.

When on 26 January 1818 the Anniversary Day of the foundation of the Colony was for the first time officially celebrated by the Governor's order[2]—with a gun for each year of the settlement's thirty, reviews in Hyde Park, entertainments at Government House and the hoarsening notes of Mr Michael Robinson's lyre—these young men were about to set out, and the old estates of Botany Bay were in the melting-pot in which some of them eventually would be rendered down to nothingness.

Already the classes opposed to the old exclusives—and these included even a few exclusive chips—were blending through marriage, mutual interest, enforced communal activity, and the influence of sheer neighbourliness in lonely places. Birth, in particular, was beginning to do its work as a catalyst.

There was active a powerful and vigorous community of young natives of European blood, the "currency lads" and "currency lasses". They considered themselves as Australians and were ready to defend their rights (as Lieutenant-Colonel Molle had learned to his cost) against the haughtiest British regimental messes and the sons of immigrant sea-captains who chose to look down upon them. Each lad felt a bond with the other in having sprung from the same soil.

The Governor from the first had nurtured this young and virile group, some of its members destined to play so great a part in the history of the continent. The young Wentworths, Johnstons and others knew well the value of his steady patronage and interest.

He sought to persuade his only son to "cherish the warmest affection for his native land", and indeed, it seems that the emergence of the first generation of native-born Australians impressed itself deeply upon his mind.[3] In later days he always had one or two about him. It was at the point of their first maturing in noticeable numbers that he began to identify himself with the people, to speak inclusively of himself and the community as "we", to think of the Colony which he governed in continental and national terms; to develop so strong a national sense, in fact, that he could wish to see the story of the country upon record through his own agency. On 30 September 1816 he wrote in his *Journal*, "I talked to Secretary Campbell this day, *for the first time*, on the important subject of his collecting the necessary materials and information for writing a correct and impartial *History of New South Wales*, alias *Australia*, and he promised to take this subject into his serious consideration."

Only a few weeks before the settlers had been chosen to go to Bathurst, the Governor had been able to write, in a dispatch dated 21 December 1817, that Lieutenant P. P. King, R.N., had left in the *Mermaid* to survey the west coasts of the continent:

> I trust that in time [he] will be able to make important additions to the geographical knowledge already acquired of the coasts of the continent of *Australia*, which I hope will be the name given to this country in future, instead of the very erroneous and misapplied name hitherto given it, of "New Holland," which properly speaking only applies to a part of this immense continent.[4]

A few others had used the word "*Australia*", Flinders included—"*il reste à savoir si ce nom sera adopté par des géographes européens*".[5] The Governor himself frequently had used it in his correspondence, underlining it meaningfully. His emphasis seemed to rebuke Lord Bathurst's regular recognition of the name "New Holland". And one of the greatest significances of the event was, not the actual official naming of the country, but the fact that the occasion was the exploration of its coasts by one of its own native sons;[6] for King, Governor King's son, later the first Australian Fellow of the Royal Society, had, like W. C. Wentworth, been born on Norfolk Island.

Ever afterwards, the Governor impressed the sound of the country's name upon the Colonial Office and others by using it as frequently as possible. The *Sydney Gazette*, which his secretary controlled and censored, adopted it into the language of journalism at once. It was appropriate that the first monument upon which it should be inscribed was Macquarie's own tomb.[7]

II

The competition for land had started to grow as the free settlers, some new to the Colony, some strangely familiar, drifted in more frequently in the seasonal ships.[8] So far they were few enough to be named individually in the viceregal dispatches as they arrived, but they were a portent of what must come, an incentive to anxious preparation for a busy spread of settlement.

East of the mountains, north of the Cowpastures, and south of the Hawkesbury, all land was occupied, and most of it in any case was susceptible to drought and unsuitable for agriculture.

Not that the kind of free settlers coming out under the new policy were likely to call for much land. They tended to be "the ruin of the country." The Governor had begged Bathurst to send no more of them[9] for three years. But he was still zealous for expansion and still zealous for an emancipist policy; and luckily one of the subjects on which the enthusiasms of the Minister and the Governor were not always directed to opposite poles was exploration.

When the dispatch telling of the crossings of the Blue Mountains reached Bathurst, he could not conceal an almost boyish excitement. He conceded that Macquarie's extension of the original explorations of Evans had only anticipated his own instructions.

He salted his "sincere congratulations upon the feat" with warnings[10] of the need to practice a rigid policy of parsimony beyond the mountains and his hopes that, in the primitive interior, some of the settlers would be willing to subsist on a frugal diet of kangaroo-meat. But he showed his enthusiasm by suggesting measures whereby future exploration, whether by government effort or private individuals, should pay the fullest profit.

He demanded that private travellers should set down in their diaries daily observations upon flora and fauna, agrostology and water supply, ethnography and astronomy.

He cocked a snook at the competent George Evans, who, as a surveyor, was a highly practical observer of the countryside, and a landscape artist of considerable ability, remarking that "he did not appear from the style of his journal to be qualified by his education for the task of giving information respecting the new country which it is desirable to obtain". He did not wish imputed to him, he wrote, "any intention of disparaging Mr Evans's exertions"; but he wanted a man for the work "who unites to Mr Evans's perseverance and courage, some knowledge of those sciences which an intelligent travveller ought to possess".[11]

He suggested that Evans should have associated with him some person of more scientific information and general knowledge; or an officer or a medical officer competent in botany and mineralogy.[12]

He well knew what was coming. From now onward the Colonial Office—and, through its dispatches, the Governor—would be plagued with all sorts and sizes of scientific inquiry and requisition. And in truth it was not long before the New South Wales mails were fat with requests to smooth the paths of collectors fresh from Kew and the African jungle, and with demands for rare plants or specimens for an even rarer collection of personalities—"*Jassminum Occidentales*" and "*Paneraticum Macquaria*" for the Emperor of Austria, the organs of the female ornithoryncus for the Royal College of Surgeons.[13]

It would have been astonishing if such attention had not bred in Macquarie a stern pride in the very strangeness of the land he governed, as if he himself had something to do with its creation. He developed the habit of surprising personages beyond the seas with the most remarkable gifts. Even the Queen might become the unsoliciting recipient of "various shrubs and plants, one tub of Gigantic Lillies and one tub of Norfolk Pine plants . . . these curious productions . . . with my dutiful respects".[14]

III

Examination of the country remote from Sydney had never ceased since the opening of the west. Young Hamilton Hume had pushed over Stonequarry Creek beyond the Cowpastures down to Marulan and what later was named the Cookbundoon Range. Macquarie himself had followed in his tracks to view the stony Bargo. Meehan found Lake Bathurst. Others had come, along the trail blazed by Evans in 1812, from across the Shoalhaven, past the long beach near Gerringong, past shady Jamberoo, past Macquarie Lake and the high, coal-seamed bluffs and the luxuriant palm and cedar scrubs of the Bulli region. The Governor recommended a new settlement at Jervis Bay and began granting the rich Illawarra lands. Charles Throsby opened a track from Bathurst to the Cowpastures.

From every direction, from Evans's and Cox's tracks out to the Lachlan, from the coast, from the southern tablelands, the reports must have greatly astonished the gloomy fellows of the House of Commons Select Committee of 1812. There seemed to be new Canaans everywhere. And at each fresh revelation of pastoral riches Bathurst urged the Governor, who needed no spurring, to extending effort.

It seemed that under Bathurst's own eye discovery was about to become a profitable occupation, the assiduous practice of which would certainly be brought to the favourable notice of the Home Government. And it had taken next to no time for Mr Oxley, the Surveyor-General—who had been five years in office without showing the slightest inclination either to manage his department's detail or to indulge in exploring—to volunteer "in a very handsome manner" to probe the secrets of the continent.[15]

"In pursuance of His Lordship's commands" Macquarie early in 1817 appointed him to organize an expedition to explore further the course of the rivers discovered by Evans beyond Bathurst. For the management of this enterprise he considered Oxley "well qualified from his general knowledge and liberal education".

IV

The previous December Macquarie had sent William Cox to examine the Lachlan River,[16] on the banks of which a military post was established "not less than 240 miles from Sydney in a due west direction". Cox had gone as far as possible along its banks. He had, the Governor reported, "given me a most satisfactory and pleasing account of the river itself, and of the fine, rich, open country along its banks".

There was every reason to believe, from Cox's story, that the Lachlan would be found navigable for small boats. If so, the Governor surmised, it would "facilitate the progress and success of the expedition wonderfully". He hoped that Oxley would now be able to trace the river "to the south west coast of Australia",[17] and that the Macquarie River, on which the town of Bathurst stood, might be found to unite with the Lachlan at some point distant from the sea.

Cox took all the provisions, stores, and horses for the expedition to a depot on the Lachlan.[18] He built two boats. When all was ready, Oxley set out from Sydney on 3 April 1817. Evans went as second in command, "as an act of justice". This was the only association possible for him with his superior. Allan Cunningham was the party's botanist.

They went off equipped with the boats to take them down the river.

It soon became clear that Mr Oxley belonged to the dismal-swamp school of explorers.[19] He had an unfailing pessimism and an affinity for water in large quantities, all his previous experience having been upon the ocean as a naval lieutenant. His glimpses of dry land had been spasmodic until he had been chosen to hold a sinecure as Surveyor-General over the competent Mr Meehan's head, after he had taken a leading but underhand part in the Bligh rebellion.

A fortnight's journeying upon this initial expedition built the normal prototype for his subsequent explorings, the results of which were almost invariably the product of the experience of better men. He became mazed in the marshes of the Lachlan.

Hurriedly leaving his boats and making for his natural element, the sea, through "a barren and desolate country", he saw his path barred by morasses, turned back only two days' trek short of discovering the Murrumbidgee River; lost two of his horses; found once more the Lachlan River, wandering in places where it certainly had no right to be according to all the rules, and eventually, *via* the good country on the Macquarie River, fled to Sydney from more deeply involving swamps which threatened to swallow him up.

He informed the waiting world that "the interior of this vast country is marsh and south of 34 degrees latitude and west of the meridian of 147° 30' E. longitude is uninhabitable and useless for all purposes of civilized man".[20] He was sure that he had "demonstrated, beyond the shadow of a doubt, that no river whatever could fall into the sea between Cape Otway and Spencer Gulph, at least none deriving their waters from the east coast".

Thus Mr Oxley appraising, according to the "principles of science and general knowledge", a district which was to become one of the richest in the continent in the production of wool and wheat and, in an intermediate period, of gold. Long before a century had passed, it was dotted with thriving towns and criss-crossed with many roads and railways.

However, Macquarie took the great explorer at his face value. He thought Oxley's findings about the Lachlan River a matter of "great disappointment and mortification" but trusted that his journal would impress Bathurst "with as much satisfaction in contemplating his talent and ability as it has done me".[21] He thought his officer "justly entitled to a liberal pecuniary acknowledgment of the services which he had rendered to his country", say £200. As a symbol of the expedition's success he sent the Minister a specimen of the limestone from the banks of Macquarie River.

All this was a singular commentary on Macquarie's fairness of attitude— he later exhibited the same characteristics towards Charles Throsby. A fortnight before this letter of recommendation was written he had branded Oxley in his private dispatch to the Minister, as "intriguing and discontented"[22]; and Elizabeth, in her letter to Drummond, when Macquarie himself apparently was too ill to write, bracketed the new-fledged explorer with Marsden as one of the most "artful" of the Colony's "villains".[23] Yet the Governor could differentiate between Oxley's behaviour as a public servant and his conduct as a private citizen. As in the case of Marsden, he strengthened, by his fulsome praise, an implacable enemy's position with the Colonial Office.

V

In the winter of 1818, following the departure of the Bathurst settlers, the Governor sent Oxley away again, to explore the Macquarie stream which Oxley had described as "a noble river of the first magnitude". He was once more shepherded by Evans as his deputy. Science was strengthened and general knowledge reinforced in the party through the inclusion as botanist of Mr Charles Frazier, first curator of the Sydney Botanical Gardens,[24] and of—as a volunteer—that queer Doctor John Harris, late of the Old Corps, entrepreneur of guinea-fowl, confessedly the importer of the only spotted deer in the Colony, and recently returned from Britain blushing under the praises of two royal dukes.

The leader was ordered "to trace the Macquarie River to its embouchure".[25]

Oxley on 4 June 1818 set out from a depot in the Wellington Valley beyond the Blue Mountains.[26] He went down the river in boats. He was beset by floods. He became once more involved in the reeds. He concluded that in 30° 45' S. and 147° 10' E. the Macquarie ceased to have the form of a river at all.[27]

> To assert positively that we were on the margin of the lake or sea, into which this great body of water is discharged, might reasonably be deemed a conclusion that has nothing but conjecture for its basis; but if an opinion may be hazarded from actual appearances, which our subsequent route tended more

strongly to confirm, I feel confident we were in the immediate vicinity of an inland sea, most probably a shoal one, and gradually decreasing or being filled up by the immense depositions from the waters flowing into it from the higher lands, which, on this singular *continent*, seem not to extend beyond a few hundred miles from the sea coast . . .[28]

It was "sufficiently proved" to him that "the interior was covered with water"; but it was physically impossible, he found, to gain the edges of the inland sea since the approaches to it were discovered to be a "barren wet marsh, over-run with a species of polygonum, and not offering a single dry spot to which our course might be directed".[29]

Soon he was quite surrounded by waters, while Evans, having swept away to the north-east with the reserve members of the party, returned to report the discovery of the Castlereagh River.[30]

There seemed no alternative for Mr Oxley to his usual course—he "determined to attempt making the sea coast".[31] He paused for a moment to look back when he reached the ranges. "From the south by the west to north it was one vast level, resembling the ocean in extent, but yet without water being discerned".[32] Still as he drove north-easterly he was "in an entire marsh, interspersed with quick sands". Then, "surrounded by bogs", he swung abruptly eastwards.

Thus the first white men who had trod those prosperous regions which now bear musical aboriginal names—Gulargambone, Coonabarabran—turned their contemptuous backs upon the riches of the west and made pell-mell for the ocean.

They passed through a land of gentle hills, smiling valleys and full rivers—the Peel, the Cockburn, the Apsley—and over the rich, undulating Liverpool Plains. Finally, they looked down upon the Pacific from Seaview folded in the embraces of the shining Hastings. That was a great moment for Mr Oxley.[33]

"*Thalassa! Thalassa!*"

He had scarcely noticed the lush pastoral plains which he had traversed. In his report he dismissed them with a line or two—"a very different description of country,[34] forming a remarkable contrast to that which has so long occupied us . . . a rich and beautiful country." He notes it down with a preoccupied air, as he dares the "very lofty mountains" which embarrassed his progress to salt water.

But once he beholds the wide sea, out there beyond an "immense triangular valley",[35] he is himself again. "We had the further gratification to find that we were near the source of a very large stream running to the sea." They hurried breathless to the beach and, where the silver ribbon of the Hastings joined the ocean, they named Port Macquarie.[36] Even then, if Evans had not pushed ahead down the coast to secure succour for the main party, all might have perished.

The Governor, as the "original promoter of the expedition" was "happy in offering his most cordial congratulations on their safe return from this arduous undertaking". The result, he declared, was "no less honourable to Mr Oxley than conducive to the public service." He wished to express his "high sense and approbation of Mr Oxley's meritorious services on this occasion",[37] which he promised to report to the Home Government.

He was, however, again frustrated. Though he personally interrogated Oxley and other members of the expedition, he was "(tho' most reluctantly), forced upon the conclusion that no outlet whatever in *the character of a river* conveys the waters, once belonging to the Macquarie, to any embouchure on the coast of New South Wales".[38]

He was fully satisfied that Oxley's report "details with accuracy the circumstances of, and preceding the total dissipation of the waters of the Macquarie in the vast extent of swamps over which they diffuse themselves". And he was certain that Mr Oxley had made every exertion towards his objective, "short of what would most probably have terminated in the destruction of the whole party".

Thus impressed with the futility of sending any further expedition "to inspect all the boundaries of the vast Savanna" on which the explorer had abandoned his survey "in hopeless disappointment", he reported to Bathurst that he should not take any measures of discovery in the far west unless instructed.

The result of the efforts to find a way to the nterior by water had been "abortive", at which the Governor was "much mortified". He did not live to learn by what tortuous wanderings the waters of the Macquarie reached the distant southern ocean.[39]

For all Oxley's neglect of them, the districts which he had discovered on his way to the coast had been the most important to the Colony yet found. The efforts of others soon opened up the Bulga track and defined a land route from Sydney to the fat lands of the Hunter, the Paterson, and the Peel. Within a decade the whole prospects of the country thus were utterly transformed, with horizons widening southward, northward and westward in what seemed illimitable promise.[40]

On the Governor's order, Oxley and King surveyed the mouth of the Hastings and the surrounding country. Steps began to be taken, before Macquarie left the Colony, to tap the areas inland from the sea north of the Hawkesbury Ranges.

VI

Towards the opening of the outlands, the Governor's own exploring efforts must not be forgotten. They were becoming less rare. They were intensive and, if brief, they were always ceremonious and upon a grand scale.

See him now, in the last days of July 1818, bent upon such an enterprise in the district of Newcastle.[41]

His journey in its beginnings is normal to his method. It starts in a cockle-shell of a Government brig, the *Elizabeth Henrietta*, a vessel of one hundred and fifty tons which it had taken nineteen years to build and which, a year or so before, had capsized at her moorings, drowning the captain's wife. All the naval architects "say she is a very fine vessel and very judicious in plan and construction". Her name—his Elizabeth's name—certainly is a recommendation.

They sight Nobbys overnight, but it is some time before they can make the undoctored Hunter River mouth because of the rough land breezes and heavy sea. Elizabeth and their child are with him. They are rowed ashore in his official barge, which he has taken in the brig.

Captain Wallis has his company lined up to receive them. Guns sound off salutes. The Governor announces to the Commandant that he intends to explore the "three principal branches of the Hunter River".

They set off in appropriate strength. Let Oxley, if he will, start for the wet interior with a mere twelve men and eighteen horses. There can be no such skimping when the Governor is concerned. His barge leads the way, sinking under the weight of his staff. Five other boats follow in a string, "with 52 attendants of all descriptions, four of whom were musicians and formed our little band".

The leader glows with enthusiasm: "The sight of our six boats so well manned, with the band playing, and with the brigs *Elizabeth Henrietta* and *Lady Nelson* saluting, had a very fine and gratifying effect". The smoke of the guns blows out to sea.

They row twenty miles up river to Raymond Terrace. They camp round many fires. In the night there is a severe frost. The camp is that of an Indian nabob, for he cannot forget old habits. He sleeps upon a bedstead. The faithful Cochin boy, George Jarvis, is there to be his bearer and valet. At daylight he is awake. He is always up and doing with the dawn. By the time the night falls he will have explored in detail the whole of the farms higher up the river which some time ago he gave to "six well-behaved convicts and two free men"; he will have stridden seven miles through virgin country, partly forest land, partly thick, close brush, to the main stream, reaching it at three in the afternoon. He will have urged his rowers, against a powerful fresh in the river, three hours further up the stream to the Burying Ground, not camping till six o'clock, when it is quite dark.

It is 11 p.m. before they fall into bed; but they are off again at break of day. He exercises his passion for naming features—Macquarie Reach, Wallis's Plains. He sees a fig-tree twenty-four yards round the base, a gang cutting cedar. He hurries back to Raymond Terrace, where he makes another dash, searches out a large, tall bluegum-tree, "the one marked by our poor dear John (Maclaine) with the initials of my name L. M., 4 Janr, 1812, and his own initials J. M. on the other side".

"Trifling as this circumstance was," he writes, "I was deeply affected with the recollection of the activity, manliness and warm affection this noble youth displayed on all occasions, during the tour above alluded to".[42] He has forgotten altogether, in the face of the carver's death in battle, that once this unfortunate young man had "deserved little pity" when he fell off a mizzen mast, "in consequence of low drinking and intemperance", a few weeks after he had marked that tree.

Newcastle meantime has composed itself to sleep off the effects of the first vice-regal impact. But suddenly there is music on the river.

What? It cannot be? It is only seventy-five hours since *He* went away. But without doubt it is "He". The band plays him in. Gunfire reverberates against Nobbys. The weary rowers rest on their oars. The aides-de-camp feel their chafed insteps and mosquito bites.

Next day they are climbing Newcastle's hill—or rather it is Wallis's Hill. The Governor could not help christening it.

They are bent upon another piece of pioneering.

> Mr. Cowper . . . preached . . . the first regular clergyman who has ever performed Divine worship at Newcastle and of course the first in this Church which was only completed a few weeks ago. I have named it CHRISTCHURCH on the recommendation of Captain Wallis, the Founder thereof. The congregation on this occasion consisted of between 500 and 600 persons.[43]

It is all very decorous and solemn.[44] The day is perfect in sunshine, the event such as apostles might dream of. All round is nature. One observer thinks that no language can adequately exhibit to the mind the place on which the new tabernacle stands. On two sides are the ocean with its rolling waves; on another a calm haven dotted with islands; afar there are immense mountains. The air will not be thick with smoke for many a year.

Above them rise the clean red walls of the sacred edifice, itself adorned with a steeple and a spire; on top a ball and a "NEWS". Higher yet a flying angel with a trumpet soars in the breeze as if proclaiming to the four quarters of the earth, "Good tidings of great joy to all people . . . Let the captive exile hasten that he may be loosed".

The "captive exiles" however are anything but "loosed". With their vague eyes they view the remarkable piece of architecture into which they have been shepherded and in which simplicity, order and cleanliness are supposed to "excite in the pious mind the most heavenly and devout sensations and enrapture the human soul". Mr Cowper is preaching and beatified. The scene reminds him of the Hill of Zion, once the only place where the power and glory of his God were worshipped.

"'The hill of Zion,'" he intones, "'is a fair place . . . beautiful for situation; yea, the perfection of beauty, the joy of the whole earth is Mount Zion. . . . How amiable are thy tabernacles, O Lord of hosts!'"

But what else is it that the scriptures say, "As well the singers as the players on instruments shall be there"?

The players of instruments undoubtedly are there. They suddenly announce themselves with a loud, brassy noise. The captive exiles brighten.

Hark! Governor Macquarie's band![45]

VII

In the afternoon they worship again. All prisoners are mustered before service. But there are other things to think about. There are the twenty-one to twenty-four piratical convicts, largely Hibernian and partisans of the exiled Father O'Flynn, who have escaped to Port Stephens. The *Antelope* cannot find them. They have sworn to seize some small brig and range the seas under the Jolly Roger. Mr Campbell is worried in Sydney because he has heard rumours of a plot also to seize the Governor and his lady and offspring, since some of the escapees are none too pleased at the expulsion of their priest.

The Governor himself gives them little thought. He is overjoyed that on Monday Mr Cowper marries ten couples and baptizes thirty young Australians, "the first ceremony of the kind performed in Newcastle". He gives the soldiers rum and the convicts a holiday and fresh meat.

On Tuesday morning he is on Coal Island (Nobbys). He plans to fill up entirely the channel which divides it from South Head, "by constructing a strong mound or causeway between the island and the land for the purpose of deepening the main channel or entrance into the harbour". The island is inspected. The channel is inspected—he finds it "does not exceed seven feet in depth at low water and is only about a quarter of a mile in breadth".

Not an inch of red tape is needed to bind a decision. On the spot, "it was finally determined to commence forthwith filling it up by constructing a strong causeway 30 feet broad from South Head to Coal Island". And no resting on one's laurels. "After deciding on this important work, we went to visit the new Jail, the new Hospital, the new Guard-House, the Battery and Light House, and the several workshops. We did not return home till after 5 o'clock, soon after which we sat down to dinner."[46]

Next day, when he comes back from visiting (with band) the Government farm and the limeburners—one mile and six miles up the river—the first stone of the causeway and pier is cut and ready to be laid. Laid it is, "in all due form in the presence of artificers and Labourers" who are to build it. The name "Macquarie Pier"[47] is cut already upon the stone, with the date. The artificers have spirits to drink to their undertaking, which they do with three hearty cheers. While they begin work their ruler, in the next two breathless days, inspects the provision store, the watch-house on the shore, the fishermen seining the beach, and receives Burigon, King of the Newcastle tribe, who is come with a retinue to do "a carauberie in high stile" and receive his bounty of grog and maize.

And so homeward with the usual dead calm which holds them to the Newcastle coast like a strong cable and the equally usual gale which tosses them contemptuously into Port Jackson, to be greeted with the thunder of saluting guns and the cheers of a harbour full of shipping.

Mr Cowper has a pale, taut look. On the voyage homeward he has longed often for the Hill of Zion, as he has leaned over the scuppers, making most unclerical noises. For Mr Cowper, like most of the party, but not the Governor, has been "extremely ill from seasickness".

Nobody in the end is the worse for the adventure, and Newcastle is certainly much the better.

Apart from other miscellaneous services, it has had its streets regularized and its facilities plotted. Old hands would not recognize it at the end of 1818 as the hell-hole, with one hundred miserable convicts of the worst type and a grim company of sentries, which it had been in 1810, or even as the port which had been opened for shipping in 1813.

Under Wallis's command and the Governor's encouragement it has advanced in two years "from the appearance of an humble hamlet to the rank and capabilities of a well laid out, regular and clean town",[48] holding nearly seven hundred persons. It has its large church, (the walls prove all too thin), a stone hospital and a commodious jail. The Governor has endowed it with a school, "where the rising generation are taught and brought up in the pure principles of the Christian Religion".

But the greatest thing that has happened for the benefit of Newcastle is that the route from it to Windsor has "become familiar to several of those persons who have been transported thither, and who now find little difficulty in deserting from thence and returning to this place".[49]

VIII

Botany Bay after the various expeditions between May 1813 and November 1818 was no longer a lonely geographical phenomenon, a point poised unsupported in the nether vastness of nowhere. A rule had been run across the surrounding land surfaces and the settled focus of the continent had been related in distance and economy to other points in the same plane.

In terms of geography, New South Wales in 1817-18 ceased to be a settlement and began to become a country. Its community did not now cower upon a ledge between the opposing terrors and lonelinesses of ocean and impenetrable wilderness.

In practical acknowledgment of the fact, the Governor on 20 October 1818 paid an advance to Edward Cureton to enable him to complete an obelisk in Macquarie Place[50] near Government House gates, to mark the starting-point of all roads into the interior of the newly named Australia. The little monument, in rosily tinted sandstone, but very dirty and neglected, is still a slightly submerged landmark amid the bustle of the twentieth century.

It was, when it rose, the tangible symbol of the fact that Australia had acquired a wide surface and, in young Wentworth's adopted phrase, "an habitation and a name".[51]

The country had gained, too, a native-born white race. They were proving what D. D. Mann had said of them seven or eight years before, that they were "very robust, comely and well made . . . remarkably quick of apprehension . . . promising to become a fine race of people", though they did not always realize the ideal of John M'Arthur that "when educated in the right way they were exceedingly modest and disposed to be properly obedient".[52]

At the end of 1818, as he toured the outlands making his musters,[53] the Governor's subject of inquiry was the Colony's facilities for their education, of which he could claim to be the real father, despite the shortage of schoolmasters and the lassitude of the Colonial Office in the face of his pleas.[54]

He strove hard to give them teaching. In 1817, on King's Birthday, he had reviewed two hundred and sixty boys and girls from the military and free schools. His great Georgian School would be a central feature of Sydney. Before his departure, one fifth of all local official spending would be on education.

And already the youth of the Colony had begun to show the result.

It was in the year 1818, out by the shining Nepean, that one of the younger native-born[55] skipped through the "Zean fields" of maize, past "fair Castlereagh",[56] the only one among the Governor's townships which had failed in its purpose.

The boy passed from the cornfields into an "acacian grove". There he laid himself down on the sun-dappled earth among the trees. He was "but twelve years old", born in the Colony in 1806, of an emancipist father. He was already rich with the treasures which the Reverend Mr Fulton had helped him to cull from the storehouses of Greece and Rome.

He took out a stub of pencil and began to write.

His simple verses, with their fresh pastoral flavour and their gropings after thought and allegory, might have come from the heart of some great Elizabethan in his boyhood years. They seemed to symbolize alike the stirrings of the new and eager spirit of Australian youth, striving to pierce the exciting future, and the decay of the Macquarie age:

> O Thou who, unexpected, steal'st serene
> Into the bosom of the fertile year,
> Tell me of climates which I ne'er have seen,
> And let me feel the fragrance thou dost bear![57]

Thus Young Australia, in the person of Charles Tompson, an Adam among native poets, began to weave its odes. The country had added to its annals a picture, the like of which had never before perhaps been recorded in any land—of a continent's earliest literate singer, exclusive product of its soil and teaching, giving forth his first "native wood notes".

He himself it was who later told the story. He it was who handed on the torch to Charles Harpur.

CHAPTER XXIX

The Return of the Exile

I

By the time Macquarie had sent his resignation to England there was at work in the Colony a new adversary whose roots sank deep into Botany Bay's history. His return had been heralded early in 1817 by a brief sentence or two in a letter from young William Wentworth.

John M'Arthur, Mr Wentworth wrote, had "at length completely triumphed over the Government"[1]; a government which young Mr Wentworth, himself a consistent Whig, was pleased to describe as "so corrupt as the present one".

This, happening almost at the moment when Bennet presented the Bent-Vale petition, was an event of great significance. For the Colonial Office, however much it might have changed its views about other matters, was firm about the necessity of continuing Mr M'Arthur's exile.

For seven years "the Botany Bay Perturbator" had been nursing his rheumatic gout and frail digestion in London.[2]

Having met Macquarie in 1804 at the house of his own namesake and distant relative, he at first hoped that the change from naval to military government would be to his advantage. But he was soon disillusioned. His nephew Hannibal, returning to the colony in 1812, hastened to warn him of the unhappy trend of affairs:

> The Governor told me, that if any man, even the Lt-Governor was to set himself up in opposition to any of his public measures he would ship him off, in the first vessel leaving the colony either for India or England. This he told me in a private conversation in which he warned me to avoid a Party which he conceives is existing among some of the older school. Whether there is such a party or not I am at a loss to know. The introduction of those people who have been convicts is certainly disliked by many, but I see no opposition either to that or any other public measure.

Young Hannibal "could not but think the present governor as arbitrary as Bligh only that he has a manner of reconciling people to his measures". He complained that there was so much whispering to His Excellency by a set of favourites delighting in the annoyance of respectable characters that to live at Sydney and be on terms with Macquarie was next to impossible; for the latter's "spies were in all companies and nothing passed without their knowledge".

From his nephew the exile learned now, how the Governor could not spare men from his parades to deal with murdering blacks; now, how settlers, "after the example of His Excellency", had fled from the burning *Three Bees* in terror.[3] And under the impact of such news his dejection seemed often about to crush his spirit within the self which he had called his "storm-tossed bark".

Despite the bad times and the heavy hand of the Government his pastoral ventures made money for him, but not enough to satisfy him. And he could not bear to sit helpless ten thousand miles away while others managed his estates. Letter after letter is full of his complaints that he has not been told the details of his own affairs by his wife and his nephew who managed them in the colony. He yearned to be in Sydney, though afraid to go there.

That many of his colleagues of the N. S. Wales Corps were in the Colony, living unobtrusive, more or less fatted lives, unmolested by authority, did not encourage him to join them.

His own case, he felt, was different from that of the others. Through the "favour of a friend" he had obtained clandestinely a copy of an extract from Macquarie's instructions. It enjoined the Governor that "as Governor Bligh has represented that Mr. McArthur has been the leading promoter and instigator of the mutinous measures . . . against His Majesty's Government you will if examinations be sworn against him charging him with criminal acts against the Governor and his authority have him arrested thereupon and brought to trial before the Criminal Court of the Colony".[4]

The "perturbator" knew all too well how many eager applicants there might be to charge him; for he was not loved for his doings during his short and prosperous period as bogus Colonial Secretary.

With such instructions in existence, he wrote to his wife, there was "much cause to fear that Governor Macquarie might even now consider himself obliged to act upon them if I were within the grasp of his authority".[5] The Governor would certainly be borne out, he thought, if he decided to resort to such a method to get rid of him. He had been told that His Excellency had referred to him in exceedingly hostile language.

Mr M'Arthur felt that it would surely be imprudent to return to the Colony "with such a drawn sword suspended over his head, as it were by a single hair". He wrote, "Nothing could in my judgment sanction such an experiment either in regard to my personal security or the peace and welfare of you my beloved wife and dear children—in this opinion I am strengthened by that of several sensible and dispassionate friends who have advised me to try to accomodate with Government."[6]

He related that his friend Mr Brogden had seen Mr Goulburn, the Under Secretary to the Colonial Office, but had found him ready to do no more than promise an "unprejudiced consideration" of his case.

From this M'Arthur had little comfort, since he knew "from good authority" that there was still a powerful influence exerted against him; and in "this melancholy state of things" he sometimes indulged the hope that his spouse might succeed better with the Governor:

> I think you might safely sound him or Mrs. Macquarie and if you discover anything like a favourable inclination *you* could candidly state the difficulties that you are informed are opposed to my return to my family. If he could be prevailed upon to recommend to the Secretary of State that the general amnesty should be extended to me it would I know be directly complied with. . . .[7]

His wife tried to reassure him; but he remained in terror "that a misplaced confidence might eventually overwhelm you, my children and myself in irretrievable ruin".[8]

There can be but one inference. Macquarie had been kind to M'Arthur's wife from the first moment he had arrived. He had called upon her immediately he landed. He had given her grants of land. He had sheltered her in every possible way and had asked her to his table. He had shown a lack of disposition to reopen old sores or to hold the past against rebels. There was no reason why the arch-rebel might not return as others had returned, if he were prepared to admit himself in the wrong and to retire to Parramatta or the Cowpastures and live the quiet life of a grazier.

The cause of M'Arthur's fears quite evidently lay in the fact that he had no intention of living a quiet life, that he nurtured many schemes which he had conceived of old to make great sums of money, and to acquire a wide expanse of land at the expense of the Government. He knew that the prosecution of these ideas was almost bound to bring him into conflict with the local ruler. So he must be free to agitate. Soon he wrote again to his wife:

> You assure me, that I have nothing to fear, and everything to hope from the benevolence and goodwill of the Governor. Perhaps it may be so, and I hope it is . . . unless the instructions of which I sent you copies be revoked the existence of *your* husband, and the fortunes of your children must depend on the forbearance of an individual—which numberless incidents over which I could have no control might transform into an active persecution. This is a fact I am persuaded Governor Macquarie has long been acquainted with . . . Could he have been persuaded to recommend me to the favourable notice of the Government nothing more would have been needed—they would have instantly complied.[9]

He wrote that in times like these the Government was anxious to avoid the discussion of the reasons for Bligh's dismissal — the "country is ruined".

He had gone off to the Continent in March 1815 to study the olive and the vine,[10] hoping to find in his new knowledge an offering which would bring him the favour of the Colonial Office. He saw Napoleon, fresh from Elba, but was not inspired to firmness by the sight.

By August next year he was in a seemingly abject condition.

John M'Arthur to Elizabeth M'Arthur

Your own good sense will point out to you that you ought on no consideration to suffer these papers to go out of your hands for if a copy of the private letters were to get abroad it would ruin me in the opinion of my friends and the world. I think indeed that it would be most prudent to show them to no one, but to Governor Macquarrie whose kindness to you entitles him to the fullest confidence, he will at once see how desirable it is I should procure a revocation of the hostile instructions he received from Lord Castlereagh; as he might if I were to return without that being effected find himself much embarrassed by new instructions in the same spirit altho' not to the same extent. I am convinced a man of his benevolent heart will be gratified to find himself unencumbered by official trammels and at perfect liberty to act towards me in the manner that my exertions for the advancement of the real interests of the Colony may appear to him to deserve. I wish to God it may be my fortune to live some years under his auspices, for from all you tell me, he is the man best calculated to promote my undertakings and the only man who has yet governed the Colony with a sufficient elevation of mind and depth of judgment to discover, that his own interest and honor would be improved by my ultimate success.[11]

Public opinion, however, was changing so quickly in England that he dared direct methods without waiting for news of Macquarie's reactions. Watson Taylor, Lord Camden's secretary, was his intermediary.

II

Bathurst at first proved grim. He agreed, through Goulburn, to authorize the return of the sly man to New South Wales only in view of "assurances that His Lordship has received from various quarters as well as from yourself *that you are fully sensible of the impropriety of conduct which led to your departure from the Colony*".[12] He was willing to transmit to the Governor the necessary instruction not to offer any molestation on account of the penitent's "past transactions", but merely to adopt towards him any measures which his future conduct might appear to require.

Watson Taylor pleaded that his client should not be humiliated by being publicly made to admit his guilt, having regard to an undertaking imposed by Bathurst and which M'Arthur was ready to give—that he should be prepared to apply himself exclusively to his important pursuits within the Colony.[13]

Bathurst "did not feel that he could go further than he had done", though there seemed to be "every disposition to comply with Mr M'Arthur's wish".[14] He even threatened to revoke his offer if the rebel were not penitent, as he at first appeared to be. He refused to sanction any measure which might "give a dangerous encouragement to those in the Colony who might feel a disposition to direct against the authority of the present Governor, a spirit of resistance which, under such circumstances, they would readily persuade themselves, was no longer discouraged at Home".

But at that stage the garbled barrage of querulous complaints about illegal floggings, extravagance, disorder, and tyranny began to arrive from New South Wales, while, paradoxically, the reformers in England shouted of the effects of Macquarie's leniency. Despite "a supposed total rupture" of his negotiations with Bathurst, the tone of the Government towards M'Arthur became more tender.[15] The old rebel, it was to be noted, no longer needed an intermediary at the Colonial Office. He now was received there by officials on friendly and confidential terms.

Ten days before Christmas 1816 he wrote that Goulburn had told him that the complaints against Macquarie "were as bad as those made against Bligh". He heard that Sir Thomas Brisbane might replace the Governor. If so, it was "extremely probable" that he himself would accompany the new man. He redoubled his efforts to secure indemnity, as he learned from Parramatta in "sorrowful style" that the Governor had become highly unpopular, and that young William Wentworth, fresh arrived from the Colony, had received news that Macquarie "had flogged a man of good character who came free to the country, for merely crossing the Domain, and that notwithstanding that a magistrate had previously refused to sanction the punishment".

> The Colony is reported to be in an absolute state of fermentation and matters had proceeded to such a length that a subscription was opened by staunch government men to raise a fund to prosecute the Governor whenever he may return to England. There is another version to the story in circulation which states that the Acting Judge Advocate had lent himself as a willing instrument to authorise the flogging but time will unfold the truth.[16]

Suddenly M'Arthur had "triumphed completely".[17] It was agreed, he reported, that "neither concession nor retraction be insisted on by either side". It had been done by the influence of Brogden, M.P., an old friend.

There is no dispatch in existence to suggest that Macquarie even was informed by his superior of the condition under which the "Botany Bay perturbator" returned to his family and his spoils—that he should take no part in the public affairs of the Colony. There is no evidence, indeed, that the Governor was told officially at all of the rebel's impending return.

Downing Street's new-found goodwill crystallized in the shape of free transport for M'Arthur, two sons, and vast supplies. Even a violent cold and "my old tormenting complaint, unsettled gout",[18] could not strangle his glee. He wrote that the Governor had "many secret enemies as well as open ones who innundate the Secretary of State with complaints". But the exile, it seemed, was constituting himself the Governor's gallant defender.

It was a new role. No Governor ever had been defended by Mr M'Arthur. But Mr M'Arthur no doubt knew that the calumnies which were issuing from Botany Bay included one that the Governor opened private mail, so he was playing safe with his correspondence.

III

He sailed in the *Lord Eldon*, due to reach Port Jackson in September 1817,[19] after more than eight years of absence. He carried only the ordinary permissive introduction of the Colonial Office, a necessity to all travellers who wished to settle in New South Wales. Macquarie merely notes his arrival in Sydney as "a settler in this Colony".

That he did not pay the immediate courtesy call upon the Governor which normally it was the custom of arriving gentlemen to make[20] is explained by the turgid and anguished letter which he sent ashore by one of his sons from the Heads. For his ailments had him in their grip and denied him for days even the felicity of reunion with the wife and daughters for whom his strange nature held such a passionate affection.[21]

When he did become fit to travel he retired to his farm till, appearing at Government House in due course, he had to admit that he was received with "marked attention", but seemingly not polite enough, though he was granted extra convict labour.[22]

The situation which he saw about him must have filled him with the strangest feelings, but these were not wholly unpleasant, for it was clear that trends both in England and in the Colony favoured his aspirations.

His friendly contacts with the clerks of the Colonial Office could not have failed to secure news for him of the dispatches which had just now censured the Governor and questioned his proceedings.

If not immediately, at least shortly after his superior took his decision to resign, he learned also "from those who are supposed to possess the Governor's confidence" that Macquarie had "written, by Mr Riley's ship, the *Harriet*, asking to be relieved".[23]

He still suffered from gout, was "seldom relieved from this dreadful gloom except by the return of acute pain". His "mental depression" grew, but could not stifle his ambition or impatience with current conditions.

Nevertheless he was careful to be ever circumspect. To see the Governor dealing with his enemies in his current mood was enough to make him so. They were feeling how hard the hand of authority could be once the velvet glove were cast aside, and the spectacle was somewhat frightening to one with a bad reputation as an agitator.

That Marsden was used as material for the first exhibition of viceregal wrath would have been secretly pleasing to his old Parramatta rival, for more than one reason. It would please M'Arthur as much to see the humiliation of the Christian Mahomet as it had delighted that "immaculate priest" to see him discomfited in England after the downfall of Bligh.[24]

M'Arthur, as he watched the quarrel between Macquarie and Marsden, knew that it held the seeds of destruction for both the parties. It was obvious that, once roused, Macquarie would show his adversary little quarter. And the returned exile knew all too well from bitter experience both the extent of the influence of his clerical enemy in the Palace of Westminster and the implacable vengefulness which opposition could engender in his bosom.

Much as M'Arthur hated Marsden, that angry man's wrath boded no good for the Governor; and this might be all to the advantage of the Perturbator's own plans, which certainly were not in line with an emancipist policy.

Nevertheless, the parson's downfall was a warning that caution must be exercised.

IV

Marsden, as well as M'Arthur, seems to have heard of the Governor's resignation. This news, and perhaps something which he discovered of the Governor's denunciations of himself, appears to have rendered him a little reckless.

The occasion which led to his immediate misfortunes was a visit to the store of Mr Robert Campbell, in Sydney.

There he proceeded to take down a deposition of Mr Hughes, the executioner,[25] who came to make oath about the supposed dreadful atrocity which the Governor had committed in flogging the three free men found in the Domain.

Mr Marsden professed afterwards to have led such a cloistered life that, though one of the victims had been the caretaker of his Sydney cottage, he had been perfectly ignorant of the affair for more than eighteen months, until now the conscience-stricken Mr Hughes asked for his services as a justice of the peace.[26]

In such circumstances, what could he do? True, his commission as a justice empowered him to administer oaths only in Parramatta. But Justice must be served. So he administered an entirely illegal oath to Mr Hughes, who swore to the facts in language remarkable in an illiterate executioner—language, in fact, remarkably like that of the Reverend Samuel Marsden, J.P.[27]

Mr Hughes had a different version of the story from Mr Marsden's.[28] His tale was that he had three times refused to see Mr Marsden when importuned by Marsden's injured employee, Read. But Read in the end, he declared, frightened him into going by pointing out that, since he was a prisoner, a magistrate could order him anywhere.[29]

So Mr Hughes called on Mr Marsden, who, he said, pointed out to him that the Government had "done nothing for him" and that "this will make them do something for you against their stomachs".

The record of what happened subsequently to Mr Marsden also exists in two versions. The Governor's is in his own bold and angry handwriting; Mr Marsden's is in cramped calligraphy, in a letter which he wrote to the hospital-contractor and merchant, Alexander Riley, in London.[30]

Mr Marsden was suddenly ordered to Government House. He came into the Governor's office. Though its furniture was as usual, there was something ominous in its atmosphere.

The eighteen chairs which graced it and its chests of drawers were in their normal neat arrangement. But the mien of His Excellency as he sat in state at his large table, his portable writing desk open before him, with papers displayed upon it, boded a "serious interview".[31]

This was the more plainly evident, because his dour and vengeful secretary, Campbell, Major Antill and the Reverend Mr Cowper of St Philip's sat sternly with the Governor.

Mr Marsden saw, as he occupied the lonely chair placed directly in front of his superior, "that he was in a pretty mess, though they were all honourable men".[32] For the Governor appeared "much agitated".

When Mr Marsden tried to interrupt his opening sentences to say that he objected to His Excellency making any observations upon his public conduct before the gentlemen now present, unless he had a friend to hear what was said, Macquarie became "extremely violent".

As Mr Marsden made a motion as if he would escape, he thundered, "I command you, as governor of this colony, to sit down and to hear me patiently."[33]

He asked Mr Marsden if Mr Cowper were not his friend. Marsden said, "Yes." Then the priest said he was not ashamed of attesting Hughes's deposition. "I had not drawn it up . . . I conceived it my duty as a magistrate to attest."[34]

At every excuse, the Governor, according to the interested victim of his discourse, became more flushed, and eventually took up a scroll. The contents of this he had indited in his own careful handwriting. Later it was initialled by each of his three witnesses.

After recording that these were present that they might "hear and bear witness", Macquarie began to read aloud the terrible document.[35]

He had long known, he announced, that his victim was his secret enemy; but so long as the enmity remained secret, he despised too much Marsden's malicious attempts to injure his character to take any notice of his treacherous conduct.

Now, however, that his reverend adversary had thrown off his mask, he could no longer, consistently with what he owed to his high station and the tranquillity of the country, "pass over unnoticed a recent most daring act of insolence and insubordination".

He demanded to be told on whose order and by what authority the factious parson, by examining Hughes, had "dared to investigate and take depositions, respecting my public measures and administration as Governor-in-Chief of the Colony".

The Governor was perfectly within his rights in this. Marsden was a civil servant under his orders. If subordinate employees of the Government were to go about undermining his authority in a community of several thousand convicts and former convicts and malcontents, by holding magisterial inquisitions into his conduct, it would be a poor look-out for discipline.

Marsden answered "that he did not consider that he had done anything wrong".

This merely seemed to enrage Macquarie, who continued that such conduct had been not merely insolent and impertinent to himself personally, but "insubordinate and seditious"—inasmuch as it tended to inflame the minds of the inhabitants, excite a clamour against the Government, and bring the administration into disrepute. It would, he said, be "highly criminal in any man", but still much more so in a magistrate and clergyman, who might be expected to set an example.

He had known what was going forward, he continued, but since up till now it concerned himself personally, he had not wished to interrupt his foe's "treacherous and insidious endeavours to injure my character", and thereby gratify a spirit of revenge.

"But now," he remarked with deadly coldness, "that I conclude you have fully completed your investigation, on the subject in question, and transmitted home the result thereof; I must thus publicly warn you, that if you ever dare or presume again to interfere with, or investigate any part of my conduct as Governor of this Colony, I shall consider it my indispensible duty—as a measure of necessary precaution alike due to my own high station, the support of my authority and the tranquillity of the country—immediately to suspend you from the exercise of your functions in your present offices, as a clergyman and a magistrate, until I report your conduct to His Royal Highness the Prince Regent."[36]

He paused to gain breath for his final outburst, then concluded:

> Viewing you *now*, sir, as the *head of a seditious low cabal* and consequently un-worthy of mixing in private society or intercourse with me, I beg to inform you, that I never wish to see you *excepting on public duty* and I cannot help deeply lamenting that any man of your *sacred profession* should be *so much* lost to every good feeling of justice generosity and gratitude, as to manifest such deep rooted malice, rancour, hostility and vindictive opposition towards one who has never injured you but has, on the contrary, conferred several acts of kindness on both yourself and your family.[37]

Mr Marsden said that His Excellency "might rest assured that he should be very particular in not violating his commands" conveyed in his perora-tion; but he informed Mr Riley that he was "conscious of his entire innocence", and that His Excellency "might as well have beat an anvil as to excite fear in my mind where no fear was".[38]

V

The Governor's reverend victim affected to take all that had happened to him "very callously".

He attempted to resign his commission as a magistrate. When the Governor refused to accept his resignation, he "resolved, the first insult I receive, to act no longer".[39]

He went boiling back to Parramatta, to write to Wilberforce fresh and horrible libels about the neglect of Parramatta Hospital. "I do not believe there is a more infamous brothel in the whole universe . . . drunkenness, whoredom, sickness and death . . . the dead lie in the room with the living patients . . . The hospital is a place I have seldom seen the Governor at . . . I met him there by accident . . ."[40]

The truth was that Marsden himself had not attended the hospital for six years.

Then he plunged into contention with Wylde, who, it appeared, had made an official judicial visit to Parramatta Jail, where "desperate fellows" complained about the local Bench of Justices.

Mr Marsden "saw at once what his objective was—to court the good opinion of the vilest of men, at the expense of the authority of the magis-trates".[41] Wylde was no mean adversary. He categorically proved his traducer's statements about an interview in the jail to be invention.

Marsden once more resigned from the Commission of the Peace. Macquarie again refused to accept his resignation; then dismissed him ignominiously by notice in the *Gazette*,[42] spurred by the knowledge that his enemy had secured the sentencing of his servant, David Hornby, to fifty lashes and twelve months in double irons in the chain-gang for being "insolent" to him.

The Christian Mahomet tried to leave for England, but the Governor kept him in New South Wales, and Bathurst supported his action.[43]

The angry parson wrote:

> I have used every means to get out of the Colony, but in vain . . . no sacrifice I could make would prevail with him [the Governor] to part with me. I am a man of too much consequence to be allowed to leave the Colony. . . . Here I am and here I must stay; I believe I shall stand a long siege before I surrender; at the same time I must be prepared for war. I expect some heavy shot will be fired upon me yet.[44]

He seemed to lose all restraint. He went so far as to establish communication with the Irish priest, O'Flynn, whom the Governor later expelled, since he had come clandestinely to New South Wales after being refused permission by the Colonial Office, and was likely to stir up disaffection among the lower orders.

Marsden wrote to Riley that the Catholics were much "enraged" and that "if they can meet with a leader, we must look out for broken heads.[45] I know not whether they will be able to find one or not. We are in a very uncertain state—I would not have advised the Governor to put the priest in gaol—some one must pay for this."

Ere long he was warmly denying a report—which Mr J. T. Campbell "could not doubt"—that he had "mentioned as a matter of notoriety" that thirty-seven convicts had left the harbour "to intercept the *Elizabeth Henrietta* with the Governor and all his family and staff on board"; that convicts at Newcastle were to join the conspiracy; and that "little doubt could remain that they would affect their purposes".[46]

When, presently, Macquarie offered him permission to go to England, it was discovered that he had lost all his zeal to make the perilous voyage to recruit clergy.[47] For there were now very good reasons why he wished to remain in New South Wales for some time to come. He took a six months' vacation in New Zealand, having offered his influence with the Maoris to secure timber for the Navy.

He was not present to see the last act in the drama which he had started by the writing of his memorial to the Governor about the conditions of the Parramatta Women's Factory.

On 9 July 1818 Macquarie recorded in his diary:

> After breakfast went to the place selected for building the Factory and Barracks for the female convicts on the left bank of the Parramatta River—where I met Mr. Greenway the Govt. Architect and the contractors Messrs. Watkins and Payten—and at 12 o'clock laid the foundation stone of this new building in the usual form; giving the workmen four gallons of spirits to drink success to the building.[48]

There had been stirring preliminaries before the tender for the building was accepted. Mr Marsden had attempted to secure the contract for a friend, Mr Smith, at £14,000; but, Mr Greenway, the civil architect, having reported that this was nearly three times a fair quotation and that Mr Smith had offered him a bribe of £500, the Governor was forced to deal with the whole matter in person. Afterwards every measure which obstructive brains could conceive was resorted to to ruin the successful tenderers and delay the construction of the factory which Mr Marsden had held to be so urgently needed.

VI

Now another event took place which boded good for M'Arthur's plans and evil for the Governor. Bathurst had succeeded in his search for an impartial mind to apply itself in his promised inquiry into the affairs of New South Wales.

His eye had lighted—or perhaps Goulburn's eye lighted—on Mr John Thomas Bigge, who of yore had been on circuit with Mr Ellis Bent, and who since then had spent three years as one of the large number of Chief Justices who maintained the King's Courts in the West Indies. He had filled his "high judicial situation" with "the entire approbation of His Royal Highness the Prince Regent".[49]

Why he had returned from that salubrious clime, and what qualifications he had to enable him to remould the policies of an antipodean colony, none knew. But he was given the job, with minute instructions.

His college at Oxford had been Christ Church—as was Mr Goulburn's —so that it was obvious that he must be a gentleman and that he had a sound heart. Young Mr Wentworth pronounced him "a relative of Mr Grey Bennet, who had been appointed through Mr Bennet's influence".[50]

He was thirty-nine years old. His salary in his new position was fixed at £3000 a year, a thousand pounds more than that of the Governor, whom he was given power, during his stay, to overrule in everything, subject to appeal to the Colonial Office.

He selected as his companion on the voyage his brother-in-law, Mr Scott, whose earlier career is veiled in mystery. He appears to have had some training as a wine merchant. However, he matriculated at Oxford at thirty years of age, presumably after the marriage of his second sister to the Earl of Oxford had rendered him qualified to lead a higher type of life.

Mr Scott was made official heir to Mr Bigge's commissionership, so that if the latter were to die on the voyage or be destroyed by enemies, Mr Scott would succeed to his mantle and hold the inquiry. He would, too, step out of his £500-a-year office, and become invested with the power to govern New South Wales in many matters, over the head of Governor Macquarie.

A small humiliation of that sort inflicted on a faithful governor need cause no qualms to so daring a government as Lord Liverpool's. Neither would it bother any official at the Colonial Office that Mr Bigge, the Commissioner, having been given a half more salary than the Governor and such authority over him that Bathurst felt that Macquarie would be incurring a "severe responsibility" even in resisting him, was by his commission designated as junior in precedence to the Lieutenant-Governor who received £400 a year plus military pay, and who was a nonentity even in the absence of the Governor, when he acted "under instructions which may rather be called restrictions".

The Minister had in mind the possibility of the abandonment of transportation.[51] He was beginning to fear that New South Wales was not serving its purpose as a "receptacle for offenders, in which crimes may be expiated, at a distance from home, by punishments sufficiently severe to deter others from the commission of crimes, and so regulated as to operate the reform of the persons by whom they had been committed".

So long as the Legislature continued convict settlements, he wrote, their growth as colonies must be a secondary matter[52]; and the leading duty of those to whom the administration was entrusted would be to keep up in them such a system of just discipline as might render transportation an object of serious apprehension, of "real terror", to evil-doers.

This, he was afraid, it was ceasing to be.

He thought it necessary to inquire how far it might be possible to enforce, in the colonies already established, a system of penal discipline, constant work, and vigorous superintendence, with complete separation of convict elements from the mass of population, and more or less personal confinement according to the magnitude of the offence.

If the present settlements were not suitable for such an object, he was prepared to consider the gradual abandonment of them altogether as convict settlements and the forming, in other parts of the coast or in the interior, of distinct establishments exclusively for the reception and proper employment of convicts.[53]

VII

All this suited M'Arthur's policy and ambitions.

His life in and out of the Colony had been a long contest with un-imaginative governors chained to the idea that New South Wales was a jail. He had been chronically ill and in pain.

Only under Grose, who had trusted him with the management of agriculture, public works and convict labour, had he been able to lead a peaceful life; and that, be it said, to the great advancement of settlement, production and his own interests.

Hunter, at first sight of him, had praised him, but he resigned in anger when the Governor permitted interference with his control of convict labour. He had then criticized Hunter's lack of plan in administration and muddled standards of civil discipline; and Hunter had responded with violent heat and furious charges that he was the head of the military clique and of all the forces of disorder—charges which unfortunately appear to have been adopted rather for their lethal effect than for their truth, which there was no substantive attempt to prove.

King, quarrelling with M'Arthur after Hunter had been recalled—but before the latter was observed acting as the friendly minister of M'Arthur's ambitions before the Privy Council in 1804—repeated them garnished with exaggeration and furious abuse.

M'Arthur had come back in 1805 from England,[55] whither Governor King, frustrated and angry, had sent him under arrest in 1801. He had arrived, to the astonishment of some contemporaries, in the guise of the hero of the Golden Fleece. He had brought with him such land grants, recommendations, and indulgences from the Government at home that King had fawned on him. He then had put forward a plan whereby he would have the sole right to kill wild Government cattle[56] for the stores, on such a scale that other private meat producers would have been in a bad way. King refused to countenance the scheme, which would have given M'Arthur a profit of nearly £3000 a year, besides releasing the Cowpastures lands for his sheep. Within a year King was glad to leave the Colony.[57]

And all knew what had happened to Bligh after he had interfered with M'Arthur; but that fight, like Waterloo, had been a "damned close-run thing" and had left him ageing, broken in health, disarmed. He was without initiative, unless he used it through some complacent ally. Only through some convenient agent could he hope to forward his dream of a rural policy based on grandee estates, convict served, under which he could benefit to the full from expansion of the sheep industry[58] and his own monopoly of sires. He had written: "Mine was the only flock in the Colony from which the pure merino rams could be obtained."[59]

Therefore, his idea was that the Government should settle the country with large-scale sheep-farmers for wool production.[60] Mr M'Arthur would supply *all* the rams, taking land in exchange. And, in any case, for the privilege of buying from him, the Government would deed him a premium of "50,000 acres to pasture my flocks".[61]

"Was not that reasonable," asked Mr M'Arthur, "when every clever active scoundrel in the Colony is becoming the proprietor of large estates?" And "must not all the small estates that are now bestowed upon the herd of prisoners finally centre upon such vile characters?"[62]

It was inevitable that Macquarie should differ vigorously from the proposer of such a plan; equally inevitable that he should, in consequence, join Hunter, King, and Bligh as an object of M'Arthur's bitter resistance.

M'Arthur's scheme was calculated to have a strong appeal in Downing Street. England, and indeed Europe, needed fine wool almost more than any other commodity. A market was assured for all that could be grown.

Wool, therefore, provided a medium through which the adventurous and acquisitive Briton of the colonizing classes—which were also the governing classes—could transfer effort to a new country now that the fountain of riches which had long spouted in India and the Americas had begun to run dry.

But Australia had no native population worth the name to provide cheap farm labour, and the principle of the African *asiento* was scarcely applicable, with the world growing fuller every day of Wilberforces and their like, and British ships already debarred by statute from carrying slaves.

It was necessary to secure the continuance of transportation, to supply the labour needs of the primitive continent's new ventures. Thus, it was toward the objective of the large corporate estate, patriotically growing wool for Britain with the aid of floods of convicts, that M'Arthur and his lieutenants now began to lead British public opinion, with a reasonable certainty that a Governor who opposed them would receive little sympathy in London.

Towards the end of 1818 M'Arthur had seen enough of what was going on in the Colony, and heard enough of what was going on in London, to show his hand and plan to his partner and London agent, Walter Davidson, nephew of the Royal physician, Sir Walter Farquhar:

> The regenerated few are in high court favour ... Governor Macquarie is certainly humane, liberal and of the most courteous and gentlemanly manners, but with what extent endowed with talents to govern this most singularly constructed society, the condition of the Colony will present you with a better criterion to form your own judgment than any opinion of mine. In fact, it is a subject I never speak nor write upon. Our chief, indeed, almost only export, is Bills upon the Treasury and I am not aware that any encouragement is given to create any other. I believe the Bills this year will amount to £150,000, and as convicts are continually arriving the amount must rapidly increase, and continue until ministers take alarm at its magnitude, or the nation become indignant at the enormous weight of the burthen ... I fear my flocks must remain static unless an unexpected change should be made in the system of managing prisoners.[63]

It was certain that that epitome of colonial affairs would permeate into the circles in which it would do most good. Farquhar, who long ago had incurred a debt of gratitude to M'Arthur, was close to the Duke of York and to the Throne.[64]

Events undoubtedly were shaping themselves to the pattern most desired by the exclusives.

VIII

At this fateful period, dating from early in 1817, there is a strong conjunction of action as well as policy between the Colonial Office and Botany Bay malcontents, after the thoughts and interests of both began to run in the same direction. There are endless evidences of this development.

M'Arthur is suddenly allowed to go home to New South Wales. With him on the same ship goes a naval surgeon, Dr Bowman, one day to be his son-in-law. Dr Bowman,[65] who on several voyages has had intimate communion with numerous exclusives, returns to England.

D'Arcy Wentworth, ageing, resigns as Principal Surgeon. Redfern, who has been his assistant for years, and who is heir to the position by Colonial Office policy and regulation; who, in fact, designed the whole naval surgeon transport supervision system under which Bowman works, is passed over for promotion.

Bowman is appointed in his stead. He travels out to Sydney on the same ship with Bigge, the Inquiry Commissioner.[66]

Campbell, the Governor's secretary, is in disgrace in England over the "Philo Free" letter. Gore, the Provost-Marshal, becomes insolvent. Campbell, to help Gore's indigent wife and children, fills Gore's office, but pays the return of £700 a year to that deranged man's family.[67]

The Colonial Office which, throughout history, has watched official after official in New South Wales holding two paid positions together—D'Arcy Wentworth had been Principal Surgeon, Metropolitan Magistrate, head of the Police, and Treasurer of the Police Fund for a decade—suddenly decides that it is against policy that there should be any holding of double offices.[68]

The Home Government removes Campbell, not from the subsidiary position which he has acquired to help a suffering woman and children, but from his office as secretary to the Governor, which he has filled faithfully and efficiently for many years. The salary and fees are £1200 a year.[69]

It sends out, in his place, Major Goulburn, brother to the Under Secretary to the Colonial Office, and bestows on him the title of Colonial Secretary, which Macquarie for so long has been anxious to see conferred on Campbell.

This new Goulburn[70], now the chief administrator of the New South Wales Civil Service under the Governor, is temporarily sympathetic to M'Arthur's policy, and acts as a private link between the malcontents and his brother at home. He is an arrogant, mutinous fellow.

Bigge, the Commissioner, in a highly formal age, is so friendly with the Under Secretary to the Colonial Office in London, that he addresses him as "My dear Goulburn",[71] even in semi-official correspondence.

J. H. Bent has made some progress with the Government. Not for nothing has he an influence deriving from a connection with the Holland-Fox family. Even by August 1818 he has been able to write to Captain Piper in Sydney that he has been engaged in a correspondence to some extent with the higher powers of the Colonial Office. If his own statements are true, he has once more acquired the ability to influence the Minister. "They have declared me not ineligible for another office and will provide for me whenever a proper time arrives. Great changes are about to take place in the Colony I understand, what they are likely to be, I do not exactly know. But the Governor is not of long continuance there and that you may rely upon."[72]

Presently the vindictive young man gives evidence before the House of Commons Select Committee on Jails. He is heard by the Committee, largely consisting of Mr Marsden's friends, with attention.[73]

Again he writes in November 1819:

J. H. Bent to Captain Piper

I have never received a line from you since I left N.S. Wales, and except from Mr. Marsden (whom I have been remiss in answering) [am] in the dark as to all that concerns the Colony; I have been fighting up the matter since my arrival, and have in some measure succeeded, for myself I am provided for by the Chief Justiceship of Grenada, the most healthy Island in the West Indies. I have had it since last April, and I have a great prospect of getting a higher and more lucrative situation. With regard to the colonial affairs the arrival of a Commissioner would shew you that Governor Mac had not got all his own way and the enquiry of a Committee of the House of Commons with the examination of Mr. Riley and myself before it, will shew that he has not succeeded in setting his conduct in the most favourable light but that he may expect hot water when he returns to England. Andrew Allan will I have little doubt get over his affairs with ease; but Broughton, is I think, likely to be removed, if he is not already so. He was too violent and intemperate, unnecessarily so and caught himself. He will be rightly served . . . It is here reported that the Commissioner is to be the new Governor, and that he has his Commission in his pocket to open when the Governor leaves; He knew my brother well, they were on the same circuit together.[74]

From this it seems that Bent received his new appointment while Mr Bigge was at the Colonial Office, reading the files of New South Wales to make himself familiar with antipodean conditions.[75] And be it remembered that Mr Bigge knew Mr Ellis Bent well and had been on circuit with him. Also, the office which Mr Bent had acquired so suddenly after his period of disgrace was one concerning which the advice of Mr Bigge, formerly a West Indian Chief Justice, assuredly would have counted.[76]

When Bent wrote his letter, Bigge actually had arrived in Sydney. Other people beside Bent had the news that he was to be the new Governor. Macquarie's old friend, Charles Forbes, made trouble about it in the House of Commons.[77] The rumour may have been true, but the Government may have changed its mind.

At any rate, there was no question that Macquarie's policy each day was receiving more attention in the highest quarters, in a manner favourable to Mr M'Arthur and the exclusive standpoint.[78]

IX

Parliament had begun to hold more frequent discussions on New South Wales. Henry Grey Bennet initiated one in February 1819 by moving for a Parliamentary inquiry into the management of the hulks, the general conduct of the convict transport system and the general government of New South Wales.[79]

The resolution was easily defeated after the Government had been forced to disclose that a month earlier Mr Bigge had been appointed Commissioner to inquire into the affairs of New South Wales, and to promise half-heartedly the appointment of a Select Committee on Jails.

Mr Bennet's supporting speech was a tribute rather to the ferocity which the Governor's public rebuke had generated in Mr Marsden, than to the speaker's passion for accuracy. There was an untrue tale about wheat imported in 1813 to ruin the colonists (when no wheat had actually been imported).[80] There was a legend of "two attorneys named Laud and Johnson" (born apparently of Mr Marsden's execrable handwriting), transported to the Colony and appointed magistrates by Macquarie; of how Mr Laud, "as soon as he came down from the seat of justice . . . got into a cart and sold blankets . . . one of the most indecent acts that could possibly be exhibited".

There was a wild, baseless story of how "the Governor conceived it his right to inflict up to five hundred lashes",[81] a matter in which Mr Grey

Bennet thought it was "the duty of the House to interfere". And lastly there was the Low-Church Christian Mahomet's affecting picture of the brutal Scottish satrap casting out the Reverend Jeremiah O'Flynn, and of the poor Irish weeping on his departure with eyes that "appeared to be following some beloved friend to the grave".

Castlereagh was perfectly correct in surmising, as he did in the subsequent debate, that Mr Grey Bennet, in his well-meant zeal, "reposed, not unfrequently, more confidence in communications which were made to him than they merited".[82] But Wilberforce rushed in to lend authority to the holy witness of Parramatta—one who had "acquired the admiration of all who knew him and was entitled to assume as high a station in the moral world as any individual who had ever lived".

However, the hackneyed charges brought forward were not the main issue, which was the future of the Colony and the choice of channels into which its destiny must now be guided.

The state of British thought on that question was shown by the fact that even Castlereagh now doubted whether New South Wales had "not acquired a character more colonial than should belong to a gaol".[83]

The subsequent warm defence of the Governor by his friends mattered little. This was only a curtain-raiser. In the next month, the heavier guns of the attackers of the Colonial Office administration were brought up.

Brougham this time led the assault, presenting petitions from the dismissed *Gazette* compositor, Williams—that eager witness in *Marsden* v. *Campbell*—and the flayed receiver of stolen goods, Blake, who must have blushed as he listened to his Parliamentary spokesman's assurance that both the petitioners were "good characters and not likely to mislead the House".[84]

Mr Blake was there because Messrs Marsden, Bent, and "other equally amiable councellors" had "joined in making a subscription to pay his expences".

The petition, in the hands of Brougham, raised issues which the Government could not evade, those of parliamentary rights; for it was alleged that "taxes to the amount of £24,000 a year were imposed by the Governor without his having any warrant in his Commission to authorise such an act".[85]

X

All Governors of New South Wales had imposed small taxes apart from levying duties and market dues, which were the King's prerogative. In this they had enjoyed the connivance of the Colonial Office; but, until now, no Governor had ever dared attempt to enforce payment if the taxpayers resisted. The most that could be done was to "report the defaulters home".[86]

Times, however, had changed. With the increase in population and in the development of the settlement both the needs and the taxes had ceased to be microscopic and had become worthy of parliamentary attention. Macquarie, in the previous February, had put a new complexion on the whole fiscal situation by ordering the Judge-Advocate to issue process in the Supreme Court against some resisters of taxation.

Mr Justice Field, when he heard what was afoot, lost no time in persuading his superior to withdraw actions in which he felt it certain that—for want of an authorizing statute—he must give judgment against the Government.[87] He wrote:

> I have privately communicated to Mr. Wylde this my opinion, founded as it is upon one of the first principles of the British Constitution, which declares that "no subject of England can be constrained to pay any aids or taxes, but such as are imposed by his own consent, or that of his representatives in Parliament." And also upon a recognition of this principle by the legal advisers of the Crown in the year 1772 . . . that no tax could be imposed upon the Colonies but by their several legislative assemblies, or (if they had none) by an Act of Parliament; and your Excellency will recollect that the great contest of the Americans (during the war) was that the Colonies could be taxed only by their legislative assemblies, and that all the Crown then contended for and enforced was that the British *legislature* (not the King alone) could also tax them. But here it is the King *alone* (through the medium of your Excellency) that imposes duties, which by the British Constitution and law cannot be.[88]

For the Governor's comfort, Mr Field added that he "could not cherish the least doubt that we must (and as I understand that we soon shall) have an Act of Parliament for the purpose of legalising those duties which Your Excellency has thought it expedient to impose".[89]

This, so far from discouraging him in his designs, had seemed to spur the Governor to fresh projects.

With a view to lightening the burthen of this Colony to the Mother Country, he wrote eagerly to Bathurst, and to restraining the immoderate consumption of spirituous liquors, he had proclaimed an increase in the import duty on spirits from seven shillings to ten shillings per gallon. That possibly would prove a protective measure for the local distillery when established.[90]

Next, he had put a duty on tobacco, sixpence a pound, "so small as not to produce any sensible effect on the minds of the consumers", but calculated to stimulate farmers to cultivate the tobacco plant, "which at present grows here most luxuriantly and only requires the hand of care and attention to render it fully equal to our internal consumption at least". Also, he had his eye on various articles which could bear, without being oppressive to consumers, an addition to the present trifling *ad valorem* rates, to increase resources to a very great degree "and consequently go in aid of the necessary expences of the Government . . . and to the relief of the weighty drafts made at present on the Mother Country . . . On Green Tea, five pence, on Black Tea, three pence. . ."[91]

Green Tea, five pence; *Black Tea*, three pence! Shades of Lexington and Bunker Hill!

The Government hastened to take legal advice.

The King's law servants more than agreed with Mr Field. Even though they supported him in a belief that the Governor had power to levy King's

VIEW OF PORT JACKSON, 1821

From a print of a drawing by Major Taylor, in the possession of the Trustees of the Mitchell Library, Sydney

port and market dues, they warned the Minister[92] that imposition of even these royal imposts should be under close supervision.

Now here was Brougham, not only in possession of the facts, but of allegations, born partly of Jeffery Bent's toll-breaking days, that the Governor "grants [tax] exemptions amongst his favourites to his household and connections"; that he had dismissed a public servant for exercising his inalienable right to petition Parliament and that he had indulged in general oppression.[93]

What was worse, Brougham was not hunting governors; his quarry was the Home Government.

If Macquarie were guilty he was disposed to consider such conduct rather a fault of the system than of the man.[94] The Governor was placed, he said, in a station of high and uncontrolled authority in a distant settlement, under very peculiar circumstances, and he was sure the House would deal leniently in judging any act, even if it exceeded the bounds that sound discretion and a moderate temper would prescribe. He meditated:

> The Colony is extremely important and might very soon become the most so of all our foreign colonies. This was the very time for inquiry when the Governor appeared to be entering upon a wrong course, and might therefore be the more easily set right. He thought that any charges which might justify a Parliamentary inquiry into his conduct might also justify his recall. His Majesty's subjects in that distant colony had an indefeasible, and till now, an unquestioned right to ask Parliament to redress their wrongs.[95]

It might be argued that the individual of whom they complained was absent. That was his misfortune unless, against the misfortune, he chose to set off his being governor of the settlement. While he continued to exercise his functions as Governor, the petitioners could not enter actions against him. If he quitted the Government, but did not come home, they were still incapacitated, because no process could be served on him, said Brougham.

Here again was a matter of which the Government believed itself accurately cognisant, and on which, in the case of Moore and Vale, the originators of the petition of 1817, it already had roundly rebuked its viceroy.

Bathurst had professed himself astounded to learn that the Governor had "seemed to have no hesitation in considering the signature of a petition to Parliament as an act of sedition and deserving of such punishment as it was in your power to apply . . . and a ground for witholding indulgences".[96] He had declared it his duty to apprize his erring agent that "in thus attempting to interfere with the right which all His Majesty's Subjects possess of addressing their petitions upon every subject to the House of Commons, by making the exercise of that right prejudicial to their interests, you have been guilty of a serious offence". Of this conduct, he signified "His Royal Highness the Prince Regent's entire disapprobation", coupled with a caution that any future proceedings of the same kind would be likely to "call from His Royal Highness the strongest marks of displeasure".

Q

The Ministry left as much of the debate as possible to the Governor's friends and enemies.

The friends were very much in evidence.[97] Macquarie's old Bombay acquaintance, W. T. Money, could only say that "Governor Macquarie must have completely and essentially abandoned all his principles if he were guilty of the charges against him". General Hart, from "long experience", declared that "he had never known a man of more unquestionable character or one who appeared to be less capable of any unjust or harsh proceeding". Charles Forbes added to his belief that the Governor would court inquiry, that "if he was not mistaken, Governor Macquarie had long ago expressed a wish to return home". Sir James Mackintosh was "bound to say that the Governor was a man of high honour and humanity and he did not think it likely that he would depart from his principles". But Wilberforce obviously had difficulty in reconciling his own judgment with tales from Parramatta.

He had personally "formed a favorable opinion of the goodness" of the Governor, but he warned the House that possession of absolute power was at all times one of the most dangerous gifts that could be intrusted to an individual, and that, with all respect to Governor Macquarie, he should think him something more than human if, vested with almost uncontrolled authority, his conduct had not been in some degree affected by that circumstance.[98] It commonly, he said, had the dangerous effect of shutting up, or of corrupting, the channels of information to him who was so unhappy as to possess it.

Lastly there was Goulburn, who spoke for the Ministry. With the Opposition he scarcely improved the case. He said that "if it was necessary to discipline with severity those who were sent to the Colony for crime, it was necessary that the free part of the inhabitants should be placed under great restraint, with a view to enforcing the regulations against the convict community".[99] And the fact was, he pointed out, that when an insurrection had broken out in the Colony, the greater part of those by whom it was instigated and conducted were free settlers.

Corporal punishment, he said, was applied to offenders to whom it did not apply in the United Kingdom.

Even the Select Committee of 1812 had not objected to that position and that made it natural that the Governor should conclude that there was no objection.

He had, however, he said, repeatedly inquired of settlers and by them he generally was told that "if error existed, it was that punishments were too mild".

Local taxes were illegal; but he had only just heard it!

The Government hastened to take control of New South Wales taxation through legislation[100]; but something more important in itself to Macquarie was the fact that this debate and others of the period gave Mr Bigge a very clear indication of the trends of parliamentary thought, guided all malcontents in their courses of action and showed Mr M'Arthur that he had not returned from his exile in vain.

XI

The most curious thing about Parliament's discussions is that no ironic laughter was heard in the galleries.

Surely some citizen must have smiled at the scene: a Parliament which recently had suspended the Habeas Corpus Act[101], which was contemplating the suppression of the right of public assembly, which in six months would use the Cheshire Yeomanry, armed with swords, against a half-starved, unarmed mob of all ages and sexes at Peterloo, looking solemn when faced with the spectacle of a colonial governor who was accused of becoming a little of an autocrat and of suppressing a few of the civil rights of a convict territory in the interests of discipline.

Convict colony though it was esteemed to be, New South Wales was far better off than the Mother Country, and far more tranquil.

There the ear was not frequently assailed with the mournful chorus of "got no work to do". Convicts in New South Wales[102], in the main, worked from six in the morning till three in the afternoon, and the remainder of their day was spent in amusement or profitable labour. They were clothed and fed at public cost.

In New South Wales Sir Robert Peel could not justly have told the House that it was impossible to hear a working men's deputation and see its plight without shedding tears of pity. In New South Wales there could be no complaints, as there had been frequently in the House of Commons, about the selling of young orphan children for labour, and of babies, from six years old upwards, being compelled to work from fifteen to sixteen hours a day in ill-ventilated and overheated rooms, with scarce time to take their food.

In the antipodes none went hungry. A convict's weekly ration would have kept most English textile operatives fat, by Manchester or Nottingham standards, for a month.[103]

And education and health among the working classes had grown to be, in the past decade, of a standard more than a generation ahead of the Mother Country.

Indeed there was room for a little ironical laughter; but neither the Ministry nor the people of England were in a laughing mood.

The day when the Cato Street conspirators would be rounded up—some to be sent to New South Wales—was less than a year away.

CHAPTER XXX

John M'Arthur Holds Trumps

I

It was at the time of Grey Bennet's motion in Parliament, or a little later, that the Governor began to watch eagerly for Bathurst's answers to his official communications about the complaints in Bayly's letter and to his request to be allowed to retire from the governorship.

Bathurst had replied with unusual promptitude,[1] and apparently in some alarm. With a Commissioner about to visit the Colony, the last thing he wanted was that the Governor should leave Australia, even if they could find as good a servant to replace him, which would be doubtful.

Such a move might defeat all the Government's purposes, leaving Mr Bigge to operate in a sort of vacuum.

Apart from that, Macquarie in his present mood, and with the defences which he obviously could make to the kind of charges which formed the occasion of his resignation, could be a very awkward customer in London. Bathurst's reply to the Governor's torrent of words, therefore, was a model of conciliation, calculated to smooth down the hackles of even a ruffled Highlander:

> . . . I gladly avail myself of the less official mode of communication, to which you have resorted, in order to explain to you the reasons which have induced me to defer submitting your resignation to The Prince Regent, until you shall have had an opportunity of reconsidering a determination, which I cannot but consider to have been hastily adopted.
>
> In the first place, I must express my regret that you should have so far misunderstood the tenor of my communications, as to consider them as conveying any imputation upon your character and the uprightness of your intentions. I am happy to assure you that of these I never entertained a doubt; nor upon a review of the dispatches, in which you consider such imputations to have been conveyed, can I see any ground for the inference, which you have drawn. I have certainly in your case, as in that of many other officers holding similar situations abroad, felt myself obliged in some instances to differ from you in opinion, and in others to disapprove the conduct which you have adopted. But however your conduct might have appeared to require disapprobation or censure, I have nevertheless always given you full credit for the motives by which your conduct, however erroneous, has been influenced. So far indeed from admitting that you have in any one case had occasion to complain of want of support on the part of His Majesty's Government, or of an undue regard to the statements of your adversaries, I am convinced that the whole tenor of my communications on the subject of the Colony has been to uphold your proper authority, and to discountenance those attacks to which in common with other public men, you

have undoubtedly been subjected. But I must at the same time confess that I should have thought myself guilty of a great dereliction of public duty, If I had abstained from pointing out to you those cases in which you have either transgressed the laws, or adopted an erroneous line of conduct. You would in my opinion have had just reason to complain if, by omitting to mark my disapprobation, I had given encouragement to a repetition of what was either illegal in itself or beyond the limits of your authority, nor can I doubt but that you will on reflection admit that, in so expressing my sentiments to you, I have done what was most consistent with a discharge of my duty without any impeachment of your authority.

I have certainly never been insensible of the difficulties, to which every person placed in the administration of a Colony like New South Wales must of necessity be exposed; and I have much satisfaction in recurring to the occasions, on which I have approved the manner in which they have been surmounted, and I cannot give a better proof of the confidence which notwithstanding some errors of administrations to which all those in such situations are liable, is still reposed in you, than by withholding to take any measure for appointing a successor, until I shall learn that you still persist in your determination to return to England.[2]

This politic document was dispatched in the *Hibernia*,[3] which reached Sydney, after being held for a month in Hobart, on 18 June 1819, well in advance of Mr Bigge. The ship brought other dispatches for the Governor. The mail bag was sent on from the Derwent in the *Mary* by Sorell. But this vital letter and the *London Gazette* announcing the Queen's death disappeared. About their fate there is plenty of room for surmise connected with the facts that Hobart Town was full of exclusives, and that Captain John Lennon, of the *Hibernia*, was a lawless fellow, who later sailed from Sydney "without clearance in a piratical manner".

Bathurst, no doubt, was much influenced for a time by the Governor's seeming boorishness in ignoring so handsome an overture. Macquarie, on his part, felt "injured" that Bathurst had "never condescended even to notice or acknowledge the receipt of my letter . . . which I think is very rude and uncivil of his Lordship". All he received, in fact, was a letter out of the blue at about the time Bathurst's reply might have come to hand, informing him that Bigge had been appointed to inquire into the Territory's affairs; and this came only five days before Bigge reached Sydney in person on 26 September 1819.

Another letter which reached the Governor gave cold comfort in an assurance that he had "entirely misunderstood the tenor of His Lordship's despatch", the one in which Bathurst had censured Macquarie for having court-martialled the Reverend Benjamin Vale.

II

Bathurst wrote on 30 January 1819 his dispatch announcing Bigge's appointment as Commissioner to inquire into the circumstances of the Colony under Macquarie's government, and more particularly to ascertain "how far in its present improved and increasing state" the settlement was "susceptible of being made adequate to the object of its original institution".[4]

He informed Macquarie that Bigge had "had free access to all the correspondence connected with the Colony, and has been put perfectly in possession of the views of His Majesty's Government". He announced that Bigge had been instructed to "recommend to your immediate adoption any alteration or improvement of the system at present in force in the Colony, which he may consider necessary either for the remedy of existing evils, or for the prevention of causes of complaint in future. . ." The Minister added:

> . . . I have only to desire that you would give to his recommendations in this particular the weight due to them by an early, if not an immediate, adoption of them. Should, however, any case occur, in which you may deem it adviseable to take upon yourself the heavy responsibility of declining to adopt his suggestions, you will communicate to me without delay the reasons of your refusal for the special consideration and decision of His Royal Highness.[5]

Mr Bigge's commission instructed him to

> examine into all the laws, regulations and usages of the settlements . . . and its dependencies, and into every other matter or thing in any way connected with the administration of the Civil Government, the superintendance and reform of the convicts, the state of judicial, civil and ecclesiastical establishments, revenues, trade and internal resources thereof.[6]

The results of his initial researches at the Colonial Office led him to believe that it "becomes a matter of much importance both to myself, and to the objects connected with the enquiry, that the principal place of my residence should at all times be under more effectual protection, than that of the ordinary police".[7] He was granted an armed sentry to guard him continually.

III

At last all was ready for Bigge to begin his voyage to Port Jackson in the *John Barry*.

While he journeyed southward, a document of importance, drafted in ignorance that he had been appointed, was drifting towards Whitehall. At the very period of the year when Mr Bigge had been searching the Colonial Office archives, a fresh and historic conjunction of nearly all exclusive and emancipist interests had been achieved in New South Wales, under pressure of economic circumstances, following some interferences with the smaller trade with the Colony in English goods.

With the Governor's consent, in March 1819 Sir John Jamison had presided over an assembly of "free settlers, merchants, land- and householders".[8] The pious Irish emancipist and financier, Mr Eagar, was appointed secretary, and the meeting proceeded to draft an anxious plea to the Home Government to establish civil law in the Colony, including "that great and valued inheritance of our ancestors, trial by jury"; a blessing already available to the coloured native of India, to the Hottentot of South Africa and the negro slave of the West Indian possessions.

The settlers humbly hoped that "We . . . Englishmen, the sons of Englishmen, with all the habits and feelings of Englishmen, will not be deemed unworthy of that great blessing and suffered to remain the solitary exception within the wide range of British rule and Dominion to the enjoyment of that great safeguard of British rights and British subjects".[9]

They feelingly asked the Minister to allow a distillery, which the Governor had consistently advocated, to be built. They pleaded for the repeal of the statutory limits upon commerce which forbade the sailing of ships of less than three hundred and fifty tons between the Cape of Good Hope and Cape Horn, thus limiting the trade between Britain and New South Wales to East India Company ships. They asked earnestly for the removal of the British import duty of 6s. 8d. a hundredweight upon wool, which hampered their export.

As the Governor remarked in his covering dispatch, he had, almost from his first entry into the Colony, importuned the Home Government for nearly every measure for which the petitioners asked.[10] And he declared himself to be in complete accord with the 1260 signatories, who embraced, "with the exception of very few persons, most of whom holding official situations did not consider themselves warranted, all the men of wealth, rank or intelligence throughout the Colony".

This was sober fact. About the only accessible prominent citizen whose name was not high on the petition was John M'Arthur.

However, the moment for the dispatch of the paper was well chosen. It undoubtedly influenced Government policy which already was in a state of flux when it arrived. When Bathurst replied, almost exactly a year later, he informed the colonists that the antipodean ports had been opened in 1819 to ships of every size and that he, as Colonial Secretary, was able to reflect with satisfaction that the Legislature had already "in so many instances anticipated the earnest wishes of the memorialists" by the removal of duties and the decision to allow distilling in New South Wales.[11]

There was no promise of the institution of civil government and kindred measures. The Minister felt that he had already sufficiently stated his reasons for refusing such requests, and he apologized for the delay in considering others which, he said, was due to the necessity of receiving Mr Bigge's report on the Colony before coming to a decision.

IV

The memorial had arrived in London at a period when the Governor's enemies there were reaching for their weapons, against the day when Macquarie should return to England. The malicious commissary clerk, Andrew Allan, was writing:

> The Man of Mull will have enough to do when he returns to this country. I will give you a list of actions ready against him on his arrival. Bent 2, Vale 2. The men he flogged 2. The owners of the *Chapman* 1, Captain Eddis of the *Triad* 1,

Busteed 1, Drake 1, Dr. Dewar 1 [these were all convict ship misdemean-
ants]—and a number of others which I at this moment do not recollect. I suppose
the Great Man did not much admire a Commissioner going out to inquire into
his conduct. Sir Thomas Brisbane has positive promise of the appointment
[as Governor of New South Wales] and as I have interest with him . . . I may
make a trip to Scotland to see him.[12]

Mr Allan was the son of David Allan, the now retired commissary,
whose successor, Mr Frederick Drennan, was as dishonest and as factious as
himself and almost as much a burden to the Governor.

The Select Committee, a sop to the advocates of the penitentiary
system, rushed to take up its task of considering the state of the jails, not
only with zeal on the part of all, but with enthusiasm on the part of some
of its members.[13]

Its impartiality may be judged by a letter of one of its presumptively
inquisitive members, Sir Thomas Fowell Buxton, M.P., who wrote to Mr
Marsden that "tho' personally unknown to you, your character and conduct with regard to Botany Bay and New Zealand and the hardships you
have endured from persons in authority, are very familiar to me, and have
excited in my mind a lively interest and desire to rescue you from the
oppression of those, who hate you and the cause in which you are
engaged".[14]

Providence, the writer averred, had happily given him "the chance
to relieve your mind from that deep anxiety which your letters to our
excellent friend Pratt so feelingly disclose".

He asked Mr Marsden to

be assured of this—you have friends in the Committee who will guard your
reputation as if it were their own—Mr. Wilberforce—Mr. Bennett [sic] and
myself all feel that it is with us a matter of sacred duty to protect you from that
gross injustice to which you have hitherto been exposed. I value my situation as
a member of that Committee upon many grounds—but upon none more, than
that it has enabled me in some small measure, to befriend and to console a
worthy man who has almost been weighed down by arrogant oppressors.[15]

The Committee heard the depositions of Messrs Bent, Riley, and
Jones, that agent of Mr Marsden who had found his memory so untrust-
worthy in the trial of the libel action *Marsden* v. *Campbell*.

What it did hear made its members too wary to carry out the purpose
which some of them had had in mind. Its findings did not amount to much
more than a summary of the evidence of half a dozen biased persons with
grievances, some of whom—even Mr Jeffery Bent—did not baulk at a
little perjury.

The supporters of Macquarie were conspicuously absent, no doubt
sensing the atmosphere.

V

Macquarie, when he heard of Bigge's appointment, professed to hope that
the inquisitive fellow would "render the most important benefits to the

Colony, by making a fair, impartial report *of the then real state of* it, without showing favour or partiality for any party or individual in it".[16]

He wrote to his brother:

> Commissioner Bigge arrived here on the 26th ultimo with full powers to investigate and inquire into everything connected with the Government of this Colony, which is a most fortunate thing for me, as it will place my conduct at Home on an eminence beyond the reach of faction malevolence and gross envious misrepresentation . . . I certainly feel much obliged to H. M's Ministers for sending out a Commissioner as his report *must* be favourable to my administration of the Colony and highly honourable to my character.

He regretted that Mr Bigge's arrival would "remove still further the prospect of seeing our native land as soon as we had hoped", a delay of possibly two years which involved his "paying very dear for this *boon*". However, he felt that he must submit with the best grace possible. The only real distress he felt was at the "declining health of my poor dear Elizabeth" and he "trusted to God she will not get worse".

He had the mistaken notion that Mr Bigge would view his transformation of the wilderness in the same light as other visitors. M. Arago, when he came, was enchanted as he gazed on the settlement's "magnificent public buildings, majestic mansions" and "fountains ornamented with sculptures worthy of the chisels of France's best artists". It set him wondering whether he had not been transported to "one of Europe's finest cities".

Only a few days before Bigge's arrival, the Governor laid the foundation stone of the Church of St Andrew[17] on Australia's first cathedral site, in what had been the yard of a poor cowherd who one night had disappeared mysteriously into the waters of Cockle Bay. He was engrossed, at the moment, with his heady visions of the soaring Gothic towers which Mr Greenway hoped to build there.

With pride he opened the new convict barracks in Macquarie Street, drinking "health and prosperity" to the inmates as they ate plum pudding. Well might he look forward to Mr Bigge's approval.

Mr Bigge, however, gazed with a jaundiced eye upon the "useless magnificence," the "sumptuous" splendours which he beheld, as he sailed up the harbour to the reverberation of saluting guns, to read the letter which the Governor had left behind to welcome him. Then he followed the Governor to Windsor, where the annual muster was in progress.

Macquarie viewed Bigge with his usual friendly unwariness. From the latter's "very gentlemanly manners and polite address", he was "much prepossessed in his favour".[18] He "had the pleasure of receiving him at the Government Cottage with every possible mark of attention, respect and kindness". He remarked, "I am also much pleased with Mr Scott's manners, and mild address."[19]

In person, he took the strangers to the Macquarie Arms and arranged for their rooms. But in a chariot with four horses the Commissioner soon returned to Sydney, squired by young Hector Macquarie. A house, "at once roomy and chearful from situation . . . a spacious and respectable residence",[20] protected by the perpetual armed sentry, awaited him. He spent little time there at first; he lingered instead at Parramatta, observing the muster and imbibing the doctrine that convicts were dangerous save when scattered in the country on private estates.

M. Freycinet, with the observant M. Arago[21], arrived in the *Uranie* to lend an air of Gallic lightness to the atmosphere. On 7 October the Governor laid another foundation stone—that of the new court-house, which was to be adorned by Mr Greenway's Greek portico.

There was social amusement. Bigge was sworn in and his commission was read.[22] He declared that he was "determined to observe the strictest impartiality" in his inquiries relative to the Colony, which inspired everyone with confidence in his honour and rectitude.[23]

"Certainly," wrote the Governor, "none more than myself."

Before a month had passed good relations had begun to deteriorate, and this was only natural, in view of the different planes upon which Governor and Commissioner reacted to circumstances.

Macquarie was fifty-nine years of age, Bigge thirty-nine. Bigge came fresh from the centre of a gay world of fashion, from contact with many men who were his superiors or equals. Macquarie had not seen, even as a passing guest, any man whom he could treat as an official equal since he had come to the Colony ten years before.

The London which he knew was not merely a decade away in time but changed in habit, thought, and principles beyond recognition. A great victory and the destruction of Napoleon's power lay between him and his English experience. And while he had acquired the habit of autocratic command as the result of his peculiar situation and the insistence of the Home Government on the military nature of his office, there must have been a touch of the bushwhacker about him to anyone fresh from Pall Mall. Imperceptibly he had grown "colonial". He wrote of New South Wales as if it, and not Mull, were his permanent home.

He did not personally know Bathurst. He had never seen Goulburn, the Under Secretary with whom he dealt, and unluckily for him there were in the Colony factious and ambitious men, such as John M'Arthur, who shared with Bigge an acquaintanceship with Ministers, and to whom exile had given interests, memories, and friends in common between them and the Commissioner.

These troublesome exclusives were not slow to capitalize their advantages. Nor was Mr Bigge loath that they should do so. His early sojourn at Parramatta had brought him into fruitful contact with these men whose experience and outlook were so much like his own. From the first he courted their advice, though all concerned were careful to see to it that his association with them was as unobtrusive as could be managed.

Mr M'Arthur told his son John, his agent in London, in a letter written four months after the Commissioner reached the Colony, that as yet he had had very little conversation with Bigge on business except on his own immediate subject; indeed, he did not think he had seen him more than half a dozen times, owing to several causes.[24]

The Commissioner's fixed residence was, he wrote, at Sydney, to which place he himself seldom went; and the prejudices which Bigge knew existed against him in Downing Street and the jealousy (he feared he must say dislike) which prevailed at Government House, had made the Commissioner, he thought, consider it necessary to avoid even the appearance of being biased by his opinion or counsel.[25]

The wary correspondent's son must not, however, imagine from this that Mr Bigge had been cold or disregardful when they met—"quite the contrary not only to me but to every individual of the family". Mr M'Arthur knew that Bigge had on several occasions said that he considered him a public benefactor and the example set by the whole of his family most praiseworthy.

> Immediately after his arrival, Mr. Scott (the Secretary) who brought a particular introduction to me from Dr. Warren (you will recollect he attended me in South Audley Street) said we are aware Mr. M'Arthur of the importance of your friendship and the value of the information you possess, but we are very particularly circumstanced. There is so strong a prejudice against you in a certain quarter at home that we are unwilling to ask you any questions but shall nevertheless be thankful and feel always disposed to receive with the greatest attention anything you may be inclined to impart.[26]

M'Arthur remarked that he hoped his reserve and forbearance to obtrude himself would enable Mr Bigge to bear evidence how little he was disposed to meddle in the affairs of the Colony.[27]

Then, observing that this startled and surprised Mr Scott, he added that the silence imposed on him regarding public affairs would not extend to private ones, and that nothing would give him greater pleasure than an opportunity to make the visitors' stay amongst them agreeable.

This overture was "of course politely replied to", and "several little accommodations" which M'Arthur immediately offered were "frankly accepted and have been gratefully spoken of since":—

"For instance the Commissioner and the Secretary have constantly rode two beautiful valuable horses that I lent them—two such as could not be equalled in the Colony. . . . The Commissioner, as you must have observed is not inattentive to externals and 'tis evident for he is an accomplished horseman that he bestrides his prancing Arab with no little satisfaction."[28]

Moreover, on the few times that Mr Bigge had touched on the affairs of the Colony in conversation with him, Mr M'Arthur could easily discover that the opinions he expressed were "in conformity with my own though he affected to think differently, evidently with the design of drawing me on".

From then onward the way had become clear for a conspiracy, the main objective of which was one of self-interest; one designed, in fact, to transfer the convict skill and labour employed on public works and the promotion of small settlement to the task of extending and developing the Colony's great privately-owned estates.

Macquarie was not slow to note what was happening. Though he was aware that the principal malcontents had been well known to Bigge before he left England, he had thought it only justice to furnish him with the names of them when he arrived.

Yet, to his surprise, those disturbers of the peace had become the Commissioner's "intimate associates and most frequent visitors".

VI

Dissension arose out of Bigge's very first steps towards beginning the inquiry. Bathurst had ordered the Governor:

> As it may be necessary for him in the course of his enquiry to have the power of administering an oath to the persons, whose testimony he may require, it is the pleasure of His Royal Highness that you should immediately on his arrival in the Colony appoint him a Justice of the Peace and Magistrate for the Territory; you will further give him every facility of access to official documents, and every other assistance in your power in the prosecution of the objects of his Commission.[29]

Bigge's novel explanation, given much later, of his refusal to be made a magistrate was "that being in expectation of getting more full information without the solemnity, it was unnecessary to invest him with that authority"[30]; but this seemed "incomprehensible" to the Governor.

It, indeed, produced a strange state of affairs. Nearly the whole of the evidence heard by Bigge was given unsworn and mostly behind closed doors, by happy witnesses, free of the penalties accruing to those who broke oaths taken upon the Holy Evangelist. There was little or no cross-examination, and examination was without method, save when somebody had an axe to grind.

No scandal of the hospital kitchen, no vengeful complaint by a furtive convict that his overseer had stolen a little stone, no tale of petty pilfering in an outback store escaped the attention of Bigge while he roamed the countryside.

The Governor noted:

> The course pursued by Commissioner Bigge in his various inquiries, and the constant disapprobation he expressed of my system of Government, of the general management of convicts, and the public buildings I had erected, indicated as it appeared to me, that the principal object of his investigation was to affix to me, if possible, neglect and mismanagement as Governor of the Colony, and misrepresentation in my communications to your Lordship. I was confirmed in this opinion, on finding that one of his first questions to most of the people whom he examined, was, *Have you any complaint to make against Governor Macquarie?*[31]

Open warfare between Governor and Commissioner began about a month after Bigge's arrival.

D'Arcy Wentworth retired from his position of Principal Surgeon. His long-recognized heir apparent was the faithful Redfern,[32] who had popularized vaccination and had been a tower of strength to Macquarie in reforming conditions of transportation on convict ships.

The Government, in its contemporary ungrateful mood, had preferred Dr Bowman. And Redfern, with the best grace possible in the circumstances, proposed to retire to his estate in Airds.

There being no magistrate at Airds, Macquarie decided to appoint Redfern a justice of the peace, though he made his commission not merely applicable to that district, but to the whole Colony, a proceeding which played into the hands of his critics.

Redfern was an emancipist. He had been transported on a reprieve from a death sentence for the awful crime of having, when nineteen years old, advised the crew of H.M.S. *Standard* to "be more united among themselves", during that tame, if not bloodless, affair which history knows as the Mutiny of the Nore.

Even Mr Jeffery Bent, who disliked Redfern, admitted that the latter's offence had been "strictly against the Crown, the King's person and dignity",[33] and that his case was not analogous to cases of moral turpitude, especially since the King had pardoned him and granted him a commission in his service.[34]

He was brother-in-law to Antill, the Governor's brigade-major.

By the irony of fate, he had been called upon to act as medical officer for Bligh, whose stern presence had been one of the features of the Nore affair. Showing no resentment, the surgeon had, during another rebellion—that of 1808—exerted himself "in preserving an existence most dear to him [Bligh], that of his own daughter, the Governor's only companion in that hour of horror and misery".[35] He had brought Macquarie's son into the world.

He, also, in earlier years, had saved the life of M'Arthur's favourite daughter, Elizabeth, and M'Arthur had momentarily wished that he had as much power as he had inclination to make the reward as great as the skill manifested in discovering and applying an efficacious remedy to his daughter's "extraordinary disease".[36]

This generous attitude suffered a sharp change at the thought that Mr Redfern, a friend of the Governor, was about to become a justice of the peace on the fringes of the demesnes ruled by Messrs M'Arthur and Oxley, especially since Redfern's supplanter, Dr Bowman, who had adopted an arrogant and insulting attitude both to him and to Wentworth from the moment of his arrival, was not only Mr Bigge's "obsequious, intimate and humble friend and protégé", but was well on the way to becoming Mr John M'Arthur's son-in-law.

All the opposition to Redfern's elevation to the Bench, however, did not come from the Bigge faction. Wylde, "in strong terms", begged the Governor to "pause"[37] before at such a time he made an appointment, "which, as it regarded the class of persons, I had reason to know had not been approved at home". But Macquarie had given his word. His soul cried out with indignation at the thought that a long-employed and faithful officer should be supplanted without receiving some mark of honour to signify the Government's gratitude for his services.

The most that could be got from him was that he would ask Bigge whether he objected to the appointment, with no understanding that he would be guided by Bigge's views. And it was in the course of nature that Bigge should disapprove very violently.

He wrote heatedly of "the serious responsibility" involved in thwarting his will,[38] in defiance of the authority and commands of His Majesty's Ministers. He urged the Governor to reflect that, by sacrificing Redfern, "instead of affording a triumph to your enemies, you will at once silence and disarm their malignity by setting a noble example of devotion to the higher interests of the Government you serve, and by making a magnanimous sacrifice of your personal feelings to your public duty". Macquarie expressed the view that Redfern was "singled out for persecution", and pleaded his cause as that of "a man, who for the last seventeen years has been actively employed for the benefit of his fellow creatures; who has during that time been one of the most loyal and useful subjects to the Government in this country".[39] He represented that "however unjustifiable Mr Redfern's juvenile dereliction from duty and the allegiance he owed to his King and Country", he had "amply atoned for that much to be lamented single indiscretion by subsequent good conduct and unimpeachable loyalty".[40]

Bigge, however, would have none of it. He held that Redfern had been transported for "the most foul and unnatural conspiracy that ever disgraced the page of English history". He declared, "I say, that Mr Redfearn's crime is unparallelled, even amongst those of his unfortunate brethren; and that altho' his crime may be forgiven by Englishmen, it never can be forgotten by them; and if so, his exclusion from office of trust and dignity in an English Colony must either be perpetual or those offices must be contaminated by his admission.[41]

Every remonstrance or entreaty seemed to move him to a fresh outburst of anger. Nobody seems to have had the wit to point out to Mr Bigge that his expressions cast a serious reflection upon the judgment of his Sovereign, who had "contaminated" the office of Assistant Surgeon by commissioning Redfern to it, at the same time declaring him "trusty and well-beloved" and certifying him to be a "gentleman".[42]

When Macquarie proposed that Redfern's magisterial jurisdiction should extend to the whole Colony, instead of to Airds only, and described Bigge's protest as "this fresh attack from you",[43] it drove Bigge into a paroxysm of rage.

"*Attack*", indeed!

He esteemed that noun "an intemperate if not indecent expression". He hastened to complain to Bathurst and to the astonished user, who hastily withdrew his phrase in mild apology.

From now on Redfern was the core of Bigge's antipathies. He missed no chance to strike at him and, through him, at the Governor, and at those of the latter's policies which were especially anathema to the exclusives of the M'Arthur faction.

An excellent picture of the atmosphere is to be found in Redfern's description of the scene, when Bigge sent for him to give evidence "at nine o'clock at night, on June 26, 1820, in the depth of winter":

> The appearance of the room, the piles of books, the demeanour of yourself and secretary, the gravity of your countenance, the awful solemnity with which you made your opening speech, the threatenings you denounced, the dreadful charges you had exhibited against me, not forgetting the stale trick in imitation of Banquo's ghost, forcibly impressed on my mind [the similarity of the scene to] the introduction of some unhappy victim clothed in his San Benito, with his own picture portrayed thereon surrounded by figures of flames and devils, to the inquisitorial hall at Madrid preparatory to the *auto-de-fé*.[44]

The quiver of Mr Bigge's lip, the curl of his nose, the expression of his eye and, "in short, his *tout ensemble*", revealed his thoughts, which seemed such that Dr Redfern was only prevented by his respect for the King's Commission from "making a low bow and instantly retiring".[45]

That he seems to have had the better of the encounter did not help him. For it merely provided Bigge and his supporters with one more evidence of the state of insolence to which the criminal classes of New South Wales had been brought by the Governor's extraordinary policies of reform and rehabilitation. These policies formed the main target for the exclusives' arrows, and for the discussion of them the case of Redfern provided the most useful kind of concrete instance.

Macquarie had no illusions about the issues. He was fighting for every tenet of reforming method which he had laid down, for every concept of the growth of settlement which he had adopted and applied. He called all his fervour and eloquence to the defence.

Macquarie to J. T. Bigge

> The mal-contents, who, since Governor Phillip's time to the present moment, have been the burthen and turmoil of this Colony, have free access to you; they have the refinement of manners, deep dissimulation with much apparent good-nature, and in the sun shine of prosperity make their way good in possessing themselves of the favourable opinions of all strangers, on whom they seize the moment of their arrival with all their blandishments, and generally, if not always, lead to their own way of thinking. This is of little consequence to persons making a short stay, or who have not a duty to perform to the whole population of this Colony, be they bond or free, black or white. But You and I, who have voluntarily undertaken a duty, which combines us equally with all, must in the just fulfilment of those duties, lay aside our own personal feelings; for, if we are so delicate in our moral sentiments as to be unapproachable by the general mass of the population of this Colony, or so refined in our senses as to be unable to bear the approach of a naked and generally filthy native, it will be difficult, if not impossible, to form a just estimate of the merits or claims which all alike have upon us.[46]

He admitted that all free settlers were not necessarily factious, discontented and turbulent. Some there were than whom he could not wish to meet better. But upon the mischief-makers with whom the Commissioner had become so intimate he poured his scorn:

Compare them with the convicts, on whose labours they have fattened; when you will find that they have been bad subjects; that they have been unfaithful even in their engagements to each other; that they have raised themselves by the labour and the extension of their dealings with the convicts, whom it is their grand and first principle to keep in a state of depression, except when any individual among them is found capable of promoting their interests, and whose services can only be obtained by personal intercourse on terms of equality; such persons are singled out, and not only admitted, but solicited to the most intimate intercourse . . .

Let not the disposition, with which Nature seems to have endowed you for doing good, be overwhelmed by an over strained delicacy, or too refined a sense of moral feeling; for such I consider the preference given to a bad man, who has perhaps narrowly escaped the stigma of having once been a convict, to one who is *now* good, but who has been proved to have not been always so.[47]

He besought the Commissioner:

Avert the blow you appear to be too much inclined to inflict on these unhappy beings (if you make them so!); and let the souls now in being as well as millions yet unborn, bless the day on which you landed on their shores, and gave them (when they deserve it) what you so much admire, Freedom![48]

VII

Just before Mr Bigge had arrived M'Arthur had propounded one of his schemes for his own enrichment—that for a huge land grant and a monopoly right to supply rams to the Government and to settlers.

He put the matter to Macquarie, endeavouring "to excite him to decided steps by hopes that he might procure the favourable opinion and interest of the commercial and manufacturing gentlemen at home to oppose to that of his inveterate foes the saints".[49] The Governor "declined taking any steps, but offered to recommend it to home". He suggested that M'Arthur put his proposal in writing.[50]

On mature reflection, Mr M'Arthur had declined to follow the Governor's advice, for he "had no faith in his excellency", and he was of opinion that any project from him would receive little favourable notice, unless supported by the Commissioner.[51]

He left it to his son's discretion to mention the matter in Downing Street, adding, "If you do speak of it the chief points to enforce are that the Colony must continue an increasing burthen until exports are found, for without exports what have we to pay for our supplies but the money expended by Government?" And he feared that no move would be made by the Commissioner without a favourable lead from Downing Street, though if his son spoke of this, "it must be done with the greatest circumspection, for the communication was made to me under an understanding of strict secrecy".[52]

He had proposed, also, that the Government buy sires from him to establish the sheep industry on an improved basis in Van Diemen's Land. True, Lieutenant-Governor Sorell thought the settlers so reluctant to improve their sheep that they would need special financial temptation to

"THE OLD VICEROY"

From the original portrait of Major-General Macquarie, "finished from life" by Richard Read the Elder 11 February 1822, now in the possession of the Trustees of the Mitchell Library, Sydney

be induced to buy pure-bred rams,[53] but the author of the plan averred that, so great was the demand, settlers were rushing for his stock at twenty guineas a head. As a philanthropist, however, he was prepared to sell to the Government for the good of the community at £5 5s. a head and take land reckoned at 5s. an acre in payment.[54]

He was, of course, "fully sensible that my advancement always has been and continues to be a fearful object at Government House and to the creatures that surround it"; but when he "thought His Excellency was disposed to be a little friendly", he proposed this charitable scheme.[55]

According to M'Arthur, the Governor agreed to a price of £5 5s. a ram, taken in land at 5s. an acre; then became thoughtful. He insisted suddenly that the rams should be young. He declared that land at 5s. an acre was too cheap a reckoning. He forced a rate of 7s. 6d. upon the philanthropist. Finally, he put forward the revolutionary proposal that the Government should have the option of paying for the rams in money.[56]

What better evidence than this could Mr M'Arthur have had that the Governor was a deadly enemy to all his best interests?

He went to Bigge. "The Commissioner had always been acquainted with my intentions and as soon as I had completed the bargain with the Governor I waited upon him and told him the particulars."[57]

In time, the rams were supplied—"culls" said some buyers. Half died on the voyage across the Tasman Sea. All early pastoral history is noisy with the indignation of customers whom Mr M'Arthur supplied with his culls.[58]

All that Mr M'Arthur received as the price of 300 sheep, of which 185 survived the voyage, was 4368 acres of land in the best part of the Cowpastures district, forty miles from Sydney, near where Camden stands![59]

There was still another cause for grudging hatred of Government House. The Old Rebel had revived, apart from his ram-monopoly scheme, the plan on which Governor King had rebuffed him and which was designed to give him a contract for killing the wild cattle[60] of the Cowpastures.

It had captivated Macquarie less even than King. The Governor, in fact, hastened "at a trifling cost" to reclaim the 872 head of wild cattle remaining in the vicinity of the Cowpastures before they vanished. He estimated their value at £7266 13s. 4d.[61]

Mr M'Arthur was moved to record:

> I find James has told you of the Governor's conduct respecting the wild cattle—it was not my intention to speak of it on this occasion—nothing could be more ungentlemanly and faithless—first he cajoled me out of my plan—approved of it and promised to leave its execution to me—then made some absurd alterations of his own and employed another person without saying a word to me—the truth is—he attaches no value to consistency on his word.[62]

Macquarie credited M'Arthur with the plan, but young George Johnston with its successful execution. Had M'Arthur carried it out, his would have been the profit. As it was, the Government profited.

VIII

M'Arthur had had a little trouble in persuading Bigge that his fifty-thousand-acre land-and-ram monopoly scheme was sound. The Commissioner "seemed convinced at last and said he really saw no objections". But into their debate he had injected the thought, "Consider the prejudice the (British) Government entertain against you. I own it is not a deserved one, but 'tis an obstacle."[63]

Mr M'Arthur replied that Mr Bigge's "late communication encouraged him to hope that the prejudice to which he alluded no longer exists". And Mr Bigge had responded, "Well I wish it may be so, but I fear."

Mr M'Arthur then threatened that if the Government did not bow to him, he would keep his monopoly of the pure merino, and that no settler would be allowed to buy his stud sheep.

I must endeavour to take care of myself—and it will not be expected that holding some trumps in my hand, I shall resign them to others to play."[64]

Mr Bigge conceded the logic of this—though had he looked round he would have found, certainly in Cox's flocks, and probably in Riley's, a few fine-woolled sheep as good as M'Arthur's.[65] But the Commissioner had no wish to seek inconvenient evidence. His casual glances could see no good in M'Arthur's rivals.

The next and last step was easy. Mr Bigge already had cast off his aloof, judicial air. He had said frankly, the wary grazier testified:

> When I left England I was certainly prepared to encounter great difficulties in the execution of the business I had undertaken but I find them much greater than I had contemplated, in short, they so thicken upon me that I cannot at present form any opinion of the period when I shall get through them all, we have much to say to you so much indeed that I cannot think myself at liberty to request your attendance at Sydney or to withdraw you so much from your own affairs. Your examination will be a work of many days perhaps of weeks. We have therefore determined . . . to come to Parramatta.
>
> I want evidence to show that the Government may be relieved from the heavy expense which this Colony creates and at present I have received none. If I do not, I shall be under the necessity of reporting unfavourably and recommending that no more convicts be sent here.[66]

That, of course, was something that could not be allowed to happen if the M'Arthur interests were to survive.

Mr M'Arthur meekly replied that the Commissioner would always find him ready to answer questions and give his opinion in the most unreserved manner, that he saw no reason to despair of reducing the expenses of the Colony or in fact of adopting a system of management which would ultimately enable the colonists to provide for themselves; and he drew a rapid sketch of his plan.

Mr Bigge listened attentively and, said Mr M'Arthur,

> often when I paused in the midst of a sentence eagerly finished it (to shew that he entered into my views) and concluded by declaring that he concurred in the opinion that the Colony might be made productive instead of continuing an

increasing burthen but that the more he waded into the follies and abuses now practised the more he became disgusted. "There is but one excuse to be offered for your Governor which is his total incapacity, but that of course Government have long known."

If the Commissioner did say it—and there is every reason to believe from his conduct that he might have done so—his statement was open to serious challenge. Bathurst, a little more than a year before, had expressed his confidence in the Governor.

IX

There is an air of insincerity about the paragraphs of M'Arthur's narrative letter in which he tells his son that he is "sorry to say that the Governor and Commissioner had parted on very distant terms", when the latter left for Van Diemen's Land early in 1820.

The Governor, the writer learned, had made a foolish "attempt to smuggle from the magistrates and clergy a favourable report of the morals, virtue, religion and improving agriculture, flourishing commerce, pure administration of justice, strict discipline maintained among the convicts and surprising advances of the Colony in every respect from the commencement of his command".

And M'Arthur wrote that after he had taken leave of Mr Bigge, Mr Scott had followed him to his cottage and had told him that they looked to his evidence "as the key or touchstone of the truth of all they had heard".

The same thing, he declared, was said to Dr Bowman, who was "of course on intimate terms and enjoys their confidence". M'Arthur noted that the doctor had frequently repeated many handsome things which the Commissioner had said—"though perhaps they were said with an expectation that they would reach me".

"The Commissioner," he remarked, "is a man of the world and knows a little flattery well applied seldom does mischief."

Mr John M'Arthur henceforth was Mr Bigge's constant counsellor; while young Mr John M'Arthur, in the Temple in London, heard how much gratified his father was at his success in "forming a friendly connection at Downing Street". He was advised, "You cannot cultivate that too assiduously".[67]

Every effort must be made to bring the day when they were to be "regenerated entirely" by Mr Bigge's mission, with the help of a little urging upon the Colonial Office of the awful facts about the existing condition of the Colony.

John M'Arthur to John M'Arthur, Junior

In our present state Governor Macquarie's distinguished convict friends are the majority and their voices preponderate on every public question. They depend altogether upon the continuance of Government expenditure and when that becomes seriously diminished they will be involved together in a mass of ruin and bankruptcy. . . .

You have no idea of these people my dear John, nor have I any desire that you should—the only places to acquire it out of this Colony are at St. Giles' and the flash houses to which the gentlemen of the fancy clubs resort—Good God! What labours has the new Governor whoever he may be to perform. I maintain it would be easier to found five colonies than to reform this. He must have unlimited authority and power to cleanse out the Augean Stables.

Dr. Bowman has performed miracles already at the Hospital considering that he is entirely unsupported (except by the countenance he receives from the Commissioner). At Government House he is an object of aversion which they take little pains to conceal. Between ourselves the Law Department is a complete pest—but I am at present in their hands and must preserve a prudent silence. It was not inaptly remarked by a shrewd man "when these people came here they represented themselves as Pillars of the Colony. I think they prove Catterpillars." . . .

I observe what you say of the probability of Mr. Bigges being offered the Government, I do not know a fitter man, or so fit, when it is considered that he will have the advantage of so much sound information of the real state of things. But I do not think he would accept it unless it were made more lucrative than it is at present, that is to say by all honourable means. Nor am I quite sure that he would not be appalled by the difficulties of the task—difficulties that, as I before said, are increasing every hour—what can Government be thinking of?—do not the increasing expenses alarm them? If that do not the increasing confusion vice and immorality of all the settlements ought. But they will hear enough of this from Mr. Bigge when he makes his report.[68]

It is important that M'Arthur should have been at great pains to prevent the Governor from learning that he held such views. So successful was he that when Macquarie left the Colony he assured his successor, Brisbane, that the "perturbator" had "always conducted himself with the utmost propriety". Who would have dreamt that, before long, he would go to the unsuspecting Governor, to warn him privily that Bigge's first question to most people he examined was, "Have you any complaint to make against Governor Macquarie?" He told the keeper of the Augean Stable that the Commissioner—his own "particular intimate"—"had *twice, if not thrice*, put this question to him, notwithstanding that he had answered it in the negative the first time".[69] He obviously had no stomach for further exile.

X

While this situation was developing, the Governor received from London a copy of a letter which Mr Grey Bennet, M.P., had written[70] to Lord Sidmouth and which then had been printed in pamphlet form.

The stay of Macquarie, Mr Bennet vowed, had been prolonged beyond his term of years; and if he could satisfy his masters at home that a necessary connection existed between the improvements in the Colony and his continuance in office he might retain his situation for the remainder of his life.[71]

Testimony, however, was to be met with, drawn from parliamentary documents, which, though meagre and incomplete, when added to that obtained orally and from official papers established a case which to Mr Bennet's mind was conclusive.

He was depending for facts, he made it clear, on Mr Marsden—"this respectable minister of the Gospel . . . one of those distinguished persons whom, praise be to God, are daily raised up among us, whose employment of life is to carry the blessings of the Gospel to distant countries, to relieve the spiritual wants of their fellow-creatures, and to spread far and wide the doctrines of good-will; one who in the midst of despair has performed all the tasks of hope."[72]

Though, continued Mr Bennet, he was agonized at the life he was compelled to lead, at sights and scenes he was doomed to witness; though his lot was cast among thieves and felons, murderers and incendiaries, in a community in which an experiment of reform was ripening into such a school of vice and crime as the world never saw[73]— nor had the heart of man conceived it—yet Mr Marsden resolutely and firmly was clinging to his post. Neglect had not slackened his zeal nor failure his exertions.

He did not propose to lessen the value of Mr Marsden's heartrending statement by attempting to use other words than those of the writer in describing the details of misery and neglect which he enumerated; for Mr Marsden's letter was ample evidence of the state of moral reformation which the friends of this Colony of felons vaunted as having taken place.

His theme was the old one—the Women's Factory.

There was naturally no addendum to tell that, when Mr Bennet's letter was published three and a half years after Mr Marsden wrote, the new Factory at Parramatta had almost been completed.

And when Mr Marsden had sent to Mr Bennet his copy of his memorial to the Governor, it was perfectly evident that he had been in one of his more imaginative moods. He had supplemented the document with a few vivid details which he certainly would not have dared to allege within visiting distance of Parramatta, and which were not in his original letter of complaint to the Governor. He told how the

> male convicts nightly *rob or plunder, either Government or private individuals,* to supply the urgent wants of the females. On this account, there is not a bushel of wheat or maize in the farmer's barn, nor a sheep in his field, nor a hog in his yard, nor even a potatoe, turnip or cabbage in his garden, but what he is liable to be robbed of every night he lies down in his bed, *either by his own or his neighbour's servants.*[74]

Such, wrote Mr Bennet, were the results of the orders of Lord Castlereagh in 1809, and the engagement entered into by the Governor to obey them in 1810.

Would it not have been better, he asked, to have built a home for the reception of these poor women, than a palace for the Surgeon-General, D'Arcy Wentworth, and two other similar edifices for two assistant surgeons? "Would it not have been better than the construction of temples round pumps, and all the fopperies and follies which have been recently erected?"

He drew pictures of the convict women arriving in Port Jackson. Newly dressed and cleaned, he said, they were turned out upon decks to be chosen like slaves in the bazaar or cattle at Smithfield. Though the most respectable and best dressed were taken as domestic servants, the greater part of those who were well-looking were carried off as prostitutes by the officers of the Colony, or by those who had an interest with the Government in priority of selection.[75]

Such a system had not been in vogue since the days when the Colony had been at the mercy of the Exclusive faction and Mr Marsden, before Macquarie's coming.[76]

Time and period, however, were nothing to Mr Grey Bennet. He continued in the same state of anachronism and falsity, to write of the public houses which now abounded in every street, as the result of the awful conditions of immorality permitted to exist by the Governor.

Actually, the number of licensed houses had been reduced more than fifty per cent[77] in proportion to population in ten years.

Next, Britons heard of "graveyards like ploughed fields"[78]—the mortality rate was considerably lower than in Britain.

And, the reformer asked, what was the lot of the survivors of this plague of death? What must be the sum of vice, misery, disease, want, prostitution, sufferings of children, robberies and murders, that had resulted from the hospital contract? If it could be reckoned up, let his readers judge if he were erroneous in thinking the slaughter of so many of their fellow creatures the least part of the evil.

He ranted against the extravagance, the "flagrant examples of mis-government", the failure of the Colony as a place of reform, the selection of improper persons for offices, the appointment of convicts to officiate as magistrates—no *convict* ever had been so appointed—the "open and avowed encouragement shown to men whose characters were far from being even problematical".[79]

All these things, he wrote, had "filled to the brim the cup of abominations of the felon settlement". To think of commerce under these impediments and obstructions was as wild a speculation as to expect reformation of convicts among their fellow-settlers in this New Newgate.

Read the history of British commerce, he adjured the Home Secretary; look at the formation of their British colonies. *They* had been made by Moravians and Quakers, by conscientious men, who fled from persecution and slavery at home; in fact, by sober, religious, patient, industrious beings who laboured hard and suffered cheerfully under the greatest privations.

These were the men who had built flourishing colonies and great empires— fellows who had sown in sorrow and reaped in joy, as contrasted with the villains of Botany Bay. "The Buccaneers, who are alone to be compared to this colony of felons, though enriched by pillage and piracy, have disappeared, and have left no trace of their existence but the record of their crimes."[80]

But, he concluded, it was by no means his intention to advise the abandonment of Botany Bay and Van Diemen's Land, those ill-fated projects which had cost about £3,000,000 sterling; for about 20,000 Europeans were settled there.

The colonies themselves were in a state of improving cultivation, and though he was less sanguine than others of the future of such a nursery of English villains, he wished to suggest the propriety of limiting the convict accretions to 500 or 600 a year from among those who had been sentenced to death or transportation for life.

He sealed his malice with charges of ignorance, inattention, and misrule.

XI

Who could wonder that the poor Governor was hurt and furious? He raged at the foul document:

Macquarie to Bathurst

Your Lordship is no doubt fully aware how cruelly my public and private character, as Governor of this Territory, has been attacked, censured and calumniated by certain members of the House of Commons in their public speeches in that House, grounded on reports and informations flowing from the most polluted sources and false communications of unprincipled individuals. . . . [81]

Your Lordship . . . must have observed how severely my conduct is animadverted on by Mr. Bennet, and how insultingly he treats my public and private character. A man must therefore be devoid of all feeling, who could tamely submit to have his character thus cruelly slandered and calumniated without making some attempt to repel and refute such false accusations, when perfectly conscious of his own innocence and rectitude of conduct, both in his public and private life, which I can proudly and with confidence assert I am.[82]

He told his lordship that his feelings had been "severely wounded", and that he proposed either to publish an answer or to solicit a public inquiry on his return to London, to enable him to clear his character and "to refute satisfactorily all the vile and slanderous accusations brought against me by my enemies in this country and in England".

Bigge was already showing himself in his true colours. His attitude on matters now arising seemed to justify young Mr Wentworth's claim that the Commissioner had come to the Colony "predetermined to support all the charges which his relative, Mr. Bennet, had made against the Governor".[83]

This seemed to be the last straw and to shake poor Macquarie to his foundations.

He had, in the words of young Mr Wentworth, "fought every species of calumny to which unbridled and vituperative ingenuity could give birth". And "in the teeth of all discouragements and obloquy, which the indefatigable and rancorous malignity of his enemies continued to throw in his way". he had "continued his course with the undeviating inflexibility of a man who knew that he was pursuing the path of honour and duty".

Now, it seemed, they proposed to hold his wrists while the thugs battered him; to rob him of his legitimate defences.

The pamphlet of Bennet had barely arrived before illness struck him down. On 27 December 1819 he wrote in his Journal:

I have been for the last four weeks confined to the house and principally to
my bed-room until the last 4 or 5 days—when I ventured below—and have
rode out a little on horseback for the last three days.—My disease is now
removed—but I still continue extremely weak, reduced in flesh and very much
debilitated.—Doctors Wentworth and Redfern both attended me during my
severe and dangerous illness and were assiduous and kind in their attentions.—
But had it not been for the extraordinary exertions, unwearied solicitude, and
most affectionate attentions and exertions of my good beloved Mrs. M. I think I
should have fallen a sacrifice to my disease.

To her therefore—under God—I may chiefly ascribe my recovery.[84]

XII

Bigge and Scott were about to leave for Van Diemen's Land, when in
January 1820 the Governor, recovering from his illness, decided to attempt
to refute Bennet's libels. To secure material he sent a circular questionnaire[85]
to his magistrates and chaplains throughout the Colony, asking their
opinions of the progresses of his reign.

No pressure was brought to bear. The Governor's proceeding seems
to have been legitimate enough, even had he wished to use such material
for preparing a case for his Government before the Commissioner. It was
more legitimate than some of the devices of the Commissioner. But the
Commissioner pretended to be outraged, though he at once issued his own
questionnaire—to exclusives only.

Such a battery of commendation as His Excellency was bound to reap
from his inquiries might prove awkward for some people, in view of the
game which was being played, and this was soon shown by the answers
received.

Bigge, when he heard of the circular, rushed to Government House. He
said that the Governor's procedure was an improper interference with the
objects of his commission. He considered, he declared, that the Governor
had treated him with the greatest indignity and that in support of his own
authority he must decline all private intercourse with His Excellency. They
parted "not friends".[86]

Macquarie disclaimed all intention to give offence. He thought the
Commissioner unreasonable, but he was uneasy at the idea of coolness
subsisting between them, as it might not only disturb the harmony of the
Colony but prove injurious to the public service.[87]

He assured Bigge, through Scott, that he was prepared to make any
sacrifice consistent with his dignity rather than remain on distant terms.
Eventually Bigge consented to renew their intercourse, providing the
offending documents were not used till he had made his report. He had
flared up again, after the interview with John M'Arthur, on the verge of
leaving for Van Diemen's Land, and protested violently.

Macquarie considered his protest "a very unreasonable one and of too
dictatorial a nature, and therefore returned him an answer in terms such
as his letter merited".

Bigge came back, still in an autocratic temper, after a regal voyage which cost the Government £250 in fares.[88] He had, while in the south, decided to extinguish the Governor's settlement at Georgetown and he returned feeling that Van Diemen's Land had been neglected. Its population had grown fivefold in ten years and it was ripe for separation. At the same time, he was seized with the "impropriety of anywhere continuing any ornamental work",[89] a matter on which there had been angry correspondence during his absence.

This time it was five months before there was reconciliation.

XIII

In January 1820 Macquarie had reached his sixtieth year. He never had known leisure in the Colony, had never been out of sight of convicts; had never been free for a week together in more than a decade from importunity and abuse.

He had written as early as 31 March 1819[90] a reminder of his resignation. His note had been ignored. He had continued to complain privately throughout the year and into the next at the very "annoying conduct" of the "great folks in Downing Street" who had not given him "the least hint of the time they intend keeping me here". He now wrote again in the mail which carried the account of his illness and of his disputes with Bigge, expressing his regret and mortification "that after two years and two months" Bathurst had not even condescended to notice his letter.

He wrote, "I must confess, my lord, I am now heartily tired of my situation here, and anxiously wish to retire from public life as soon as possible."[91]

He told his brother on 1 March 1820 that he had written "very strongly" and that he had insisted that Bathurst should relieve him immediately, since he was "most anxious to quit the Colony and get home" for new reasons—"for the purpose of clearing and vindicating my character from the foul calumnies and false, slanderous and infamous attacks made upon it by Mr Bennet and some of the demagogues in the House of Commons".

The new Colonial Secretary, Major Goulburn, brought the reply at the end of 1820, in a ship ironically named *Hebe*, after the Goddess of Youth. Bathurst's response had been instant. He had written:

> I regret to find that you had not, at the date of your former dispatch, received my communication of October 1818, in reply to your original application, as it would have fully explained the reasons, on which alone I had thought it my duty to decline submitting your resignation to the King, until you had an opportunity of reconsidering the grounds, upon which it was then tendered. Finding, however, that your anxiety to resign your command has no longer any reference to the circumstances stated in your dispatch of 1st December, 1817, I have thought it incumbent upon me to submit your request to the King, and have the honour to acquaint you that His Majesty has been graciously pleased to accept your resignation.[92]

The letter arrived just as the poor old Governor had come to the conclusion that, despite all his efforts to convince them, Ministers "thought he was not in earnest in asking to be relieved and that 3 or 4 years was of no consequence".

A surge of relief must have risen up in his aching mind, especially since Elizabeth's state of health had become such that he seemed now to be obsessed with the fear that he might have to leave her poor corpse, like Jane's, behind him in foreign earth. "Her state alarms me and at this moment I would sacrifice half my little fortune to see her once more safe in England."

Moreover, the coming of Major Goulburn as Colonial Secretary showed the way matters were trending. And among those numerous other dispatches which the mail carried—"all of a very unpleasant and mortifying nature"—was one which proved beyond doubt how far the twilight of his age had advanced; how little usefully he could remain longer.

Bathurst told him that it was "on many grounds unadvisable to enter into a consideration of those general measures" which he had proposed "for the improvement of the Colony, or the better government and employment of the convict part of the population . . . until the Commissioner should have made his report".[93]

It was little consolation to Macquarie to have his Minister's "approbation of the attention, with which you received the Commissioner . . . and the readiness, with which you made the most advantageous arrangements for his accommodation", even though Mr Bigge bore "ample testimony" to these services.

For there was a bitter sting in the knowledge that Bathurst felt he "could not but augur from it that, whatever misunderstandings may arise on points of public duty, which may come into discussion between you, you will nevertheless continue to be animated by a cordial desire to promote the objects of his commission and to co-operate in the measures, which he may be disposed to recommend".

The Governor's power was gone; his authority fatally impaired. It was not even sure that he could finish the works begun. His fate was completely in the hands of the M'Arthur faction, which now held all the cards in the game.

He was unnaturally subdued as he thanked Bathurst for his assurance that he would "lose no time" in sending his successor to New South Wales. This instance of his lordship's condescension he found "very gratifying".[94] He told his superior he might "rest well assured that, after the many indignities and mortifications I have experienced *for the last eighteen months*, the early arrival of my successor here will be a source of sincere pleasure".

He showed only one flash of his old combative spirit, at that time, though it revived later. He had triumphed in the fight which he had carried on for four years against the solicitor Moore. He had at last exacted from Bathurst an admission that Jeffery Bent's malicious satellite, in forging signatures to the Vale-Bent petition, had committed "an offence more particularly deserving of animadversion in one of his profession".[95] His defiance had secured the Minister's assurance that he "had no hesitation in approving the discretion you have exercised" in confirming Moore's removal from the office of solicitor.

Mr Moore at last had been forced, after bitter negotiations, to apologize publicly to the Governor and in the presence of several of "the principal officers of Government", for his transgressions.

After this humiliating ceremony was over, Macquarie took up his pen to describe its aftermath to Goulburn. "I then shook hands with Mr. Moore, and ordered the arrears of his salary to be paid to him; which measure I indulge a hope Lord Bathurst will be kindly pleased to approve of. Thus one of my bitterest enemies is disposed of; but I find I have *a great many at home* still to subdue."[96]

Out at Elizabeth Farm, John M'Arthur sat conning his mail, from which he must have learned that his intended victim had thrown in his hand,[97] without waiting for Mr M'Arthur to trump him.

CHAPTER XXXI

Sic Semper Tyrannis

I

WHILE Mr Bigge and Mr Scott roamed the countryside, sometimes bestriding John M'Arthur's mettlesome horses, the Governor sat down with his quill to confound Mr Grey Bennet.

Had it been possible for him to use the responses of his magistrates to his questionnaire, it might have been a sufficient answer to his critic. But this avenue of defence was barred to him through the attitude of Mr Bigge.

Even most of those whom he had on his list of "factious and dissatisfied" persons replied favourably, though two or three delayed and balked. Sir John Jamison's answer was typical, and he was of the faction:

> Crimes are less frequent in proportion to the increased population . . . I seldom or never see any one intoxicated. Punishment, though merciful, seems to me to follow more promptly on perpetration of crimes. . . . The youth are the most promisingly sober race under the British Crown . . . I have reason to believe the measures of the present Government to have been less arbitrary, and that persons and property throughout all the gradations of society are protected more consonant with the principles of the British Constitution, than heretofore.[1]

Lieutenant-Colonel Erskine, the Lieutenant-Governor, declared that the conduct of the lower classes, "viewing them as they ought to be, was more circumspect and their personal appearance decent and cleanly". He found it "really surprising to see the influence the police have, particularly in Sydney. I have not yet heard of an instance where their authority has been resisted. . ."[2]

Lieutenant Bell, an enemy of the practice of admitting emancipists to society, deposed that public exhibitions of immorality had nearly ceased to exist and that the general habits of all classes were more correct than formerly. Captain Coane, he declared, had enlisted young Australians in the 73rd Regiment and, to his great surprise, could not get them to take a glass of spirits; and it was his own experience that this was by no means an extraordinary incident.[3]

The Reverend Samuel Marsden, the cause of much of the trouble, had his say, too. He was in a quandary. There were matters in his own conduct which he could not have wished to see investigated. He did not dare to revive in 1820 the pictures of depravity and wrong which he had painted in 1815, and again in 1817 and 1818, and which even at that very moment were the main weapons used in London against Macquarie and his system by Bennet.

In 1815 many hands had been against the Governor—the judges were the hostile Bents, the Lieutenant-Governor was Molle, most officers were enemies. Now there were respectable magistrates scattered through the Colony who would raise their voices if he impugned the orderliness of their districts. The two contemporary judges were very different types from the Bents. There was a commissioner in the Colony with access to facts and figures, and of whose attitude he was not yet certain. So the Christian Mahomet recorded:

> Some crimes more frequent than formerly: forgeries and highway robberies; they may be partly accounted for by the inhabitants travelling with more money or property than formerly and from the circulating medium being principally paper. . . . Within 20 years there have been 732 marriages in Parramatta, 500 within the last ten years. . . . The Police Establishments have tended to secure public tranquillity.

Evidently, there was no longer widespread "immorality and profligacy and abandoned conduct" in Parramatta. But he grumbled about the state of agriculture, about commercial conditions, and false prosperity.

> There is an increased appearance of opulence, which will be very liable to captivate the eye of a stranger; but I believe that there are few resident in the Colony but who consider these appearances as very fallacious; it is a fact but too well known to many, that the Colonists are burdened with such a load of debts to foreign merchants, as they are not likely ever to liquidate. The system of agriculture is wretched; and it is not possible that persons and property can be protected as well as formerly, when the convicts were kept more under the eye of the police.[4]

There had been no effective police until Macquarie's time. He had established them at the end of 1810..

II

Macquarie, in default of power to make use of these magisterial witnesses publicly, was thrown back on his own resources.

He dipped his pen in gall. It seemed to Mr Grey Bennet's victim that his persecutor had coolly and deliberately "made the Press, that powerful engine of evil and of good, the vehicle for circulating, far and wide, his unfounded attacks, and he was compelled to adopt the same medium of repelling them".[5]

After three and forty years' service to his King and Country, the Governor wrote, "with, at least, an untarnished reputation; while engaged at the distance of half the Globe in discharging the duties of the least grateful and most arduous government in the King's Dominions", he was called on to uphold what was dearer to him than life, "his character for humanity, for justice, and even for veracity against charges which, if true, would justly expose him to the execration of mankind".

He trusted, he declared, that the golden maxim, *Audi alteram partem*— though lost sight of by Mr Bennet, in the blindness and intemperance of

his zeal for the convict at the expense of the Governor—was not now forgotten by the people of England. And he could not entertain a doubt but
that he should be "fully acquitted at the Bar of that Public, before which
Mr Bennet had ventured on *ex parte* statements, the most suspicious of all
testimony, to arraign and vilify his conduct. . . ."

So far from having been guilty of "ignorance, inattention and misrule",
he said, he had ever considered it his duty to see that humane attention
was given to, and ample provision made for, the most degraded subjects—
a proceeding which implemented one of the brightest characteristics of
the policy of the British Empire.

> I cannot but feel it to be one of the many trials attendant upon the office
> I have the honour to hold, that my conduct should be stigmatized with every
> epithet of abuse which the tongue or pen of malice could employ, previously
> to an investigation, and upon authority unworthy of belief; the charges,
> too, being promulgated by a man I have never seen, and with whom I have
> never had any intercourse. The incitement to this unprovoked attack I have yet
> to learn.
> It is an unpleasant task for a man to be under the necessity of sounding his own
> praise; but I can with truth assure your Lordship, that the utmost efforts of my
> mind, and my most unremitting personal exertions, have ever been devoted to the
> service in which I happen to be employed; and most certainly the time and
> attention I have devoted to the improvement of this Colony, have not been
> bestowed in vain.[6]

Marsden he assailed in bitter words as one "himself accustomed to
traffic in spirits", who must "necessarily feel displeased at having so many
public-houses licensed in his neighbourhood".[7]

He wrote that the holy man's statement, on which Mr Bennet's opinion
was founded, appeared to have been drawn up "with the view of acquiring
a great name for himself, by detracting from the claims or merits of other
persons";[8] and he lamented that where there was as wide a field open for
his exertions, he did not devote his pursuits to the acquisition of popularity
by more laudable means.

As to his reverend adversary's troubles of mind, and pathetic display
of sensibility and humanity, *they*, he thought, must be so deeply seated and
so far removed from the surface, as to escape all possible observation; for
his habits were those of a man for ever engaged in some active, animated
pursuit. No man travelled more from town to town, or from house to
house. His deportment was at all times that of a person most gay and
happy.

> When I was honoured with his society, he was by far the most cheerful person I
> met in the Colony. Where his hours of sorrow were spent it is hard to divine;
> for the variety of his pursuits, both in his own concerns and in those of others, is
> so extensive, in farming, grazing, manufactories, public and private agencies,
> and bartering transactions, that, with his clerical duties, he seems, to use a
> common phrase, to have his hands full of work; and the particular subject to
> which he imputes his extreme depression of mind is, besides, one for which few
> people here will give him much credit.[9]

Then he rushed to his defence of his convict policy:

> It is true, indeed, that you do send us from the Mother Country men, who are stained by 'vice and crime' of every description, but happily for them and us, many who come out vicious, do not remain so; and some few have taken up their voluntary abode with us, who would be an honour and a credit in any country.
>
> As to those base and restless spirits, who have ever eaten the bread of unthankfulness; who have never been satisfied with any administration here during its existence; who being themselves bad 'are always for evil and never for good' who gaining the ear of all strangers by *offers of civilities*, which they liberally bestow for the purpose of obtaining a free and familiar intercourse with them; employ all their means and abilities to poison the minds of such persons, by representing everything as wrong; and above all by impressing them with that which is to themselves the grand *sine qua non*, the shutting of the door of advancement for ever against men who had . . . been . . . convicts, let their present character and circumstances be what it might; though at the same time availing themselves, with glaring inconsistency, of an intimacy with such individuals of this class as they find suited to their purpose:—if these discontented and factious men had been removed, or even promoted, by being transplanted to some other Colony, happy it would have been for this Settlement; and their removal would have relieved it, and those concerned in its management, of one of the greatest evils, and perhaps the only insurmountable malady, with which it has had to grapple.[10]

He admitted that the expense to Britain of governing the Colony was high, and that there was little local revenue.[11] But let them take the restrictions off commerce and see what Australian resources could do. He mentioned wool as "the staple commodity of this colony"—its development as an article of commerce[12] was still a dream when he had come. He felt that he had solid reason to hope "that a few years will add progressively to the increase in the quantity produced, as the climate has already contributed to the improvement of its quality".

He emphasized that if expenses were increasing, it was because of the increase in the influx of convicts which must always determine its level:

> The increased population must demand an increase of all the accommodations of civilised life. For I cannot suppose that it is the wish of the British people, that this their Colony should be allowed to remain in the state of nature in which it was found, and her settlers and convicts turned adrift into the woods, without churches, schools, courts, barracks, hospitals and all the other accommodations of civilised nations.
>
> Now it requires little explanation to prove, that such buildings and other improvements, are not to be procured without much labour of man and beast; and this labour must occasion a large expenditure of money; for although Government commands the labour of convicts without pecuniary reward, yet they must be fed, clothed and lodged, or allowed time to work for themselves to obtain lodgings. The expence of feeding draught cattle is also very great; for in the neighbourhood of Sydney, where the principal works are carried on, the ground is so barren and unproductive, as to afford little nourishment for cattle.[13]

III

So, gradually, he worked through all Mr Bennet's themes, categorically justifying his actions and his appointments of emancipists to office, till he had reached, in due course, a remarkable passage in which he associated himself with his charges:

Mr. Bennet reproaches us for the materials of which our Colony is composed. That we are not all Moravians and Quakers is indeed to be lamented; but he should recollect, that this settlement was formed, not for the purpose of depriving England of her virtuous subjects, but to relieve her of her vicious population. In condemning us all in the lump, as the most dreadful description of persons collected together in modern times, he seems to lose sight of one small matter of fact which it is rather surprizing should escape his observation. Suppose that we, the old inhabitants and offenders of New South Wales, should all feel disposed to mend our manners; yet, Mr. Bennet should have recollected, that we receive numerous annual importations from the other side of the water, of persons who are not considered the most correct in the world, as to their principles and behaviour, and that it will be impossible for us all to become a reformed people, unless time be given us to breathe, contemplate and amend, before those new supplies of delinquency and guilt are sent out to us, which we are condemned by this gentleman for possessing; for even allowing that the old stock has been improved by a change of clime, yet while new grafts continue to be added to it from Newgate, and other similar nurseries, however these may in time be benefitted by the change of situation, some fruit of a bad, and even of the worst quality, must be perpetually produced, and perhaps the former contaminated, in every successive period, after each successive importation . . . I cannot avoid saying that this country should be made the home AND A HAPPY HOME to every emancipated convict WHO DESERVES IT. HERE, according to my system, they feel themselves encouraged and protected, if they deserve it, and are on a footing of equality with the general population . . . Let (punishment) be as severe as may be necessary to effect the grand object, but when that which the Law has ordained has been fulfilled, for the sake of mercy and justice there let it terminate. "This is the whole of his sentence and ought therefore to be the whole of his suffering. No one could desire to visit many different degrees of guilt with the same measure of punishment. Nor would anyone, I hope, venture to do evil, that good may come."

"*A merciful and enlightened jurisprudence, like the Author of all that is merciful and wise, does not rejoice in the death of a sinner, but rather that he should turn from his wickedness and live.*" But how is he to live if he is for ever doomed to feel the weight of punishment, even after that portion which has been awarded him by the law has been suffered? For if a man's crime and sentence, long since past and expiated, are to be had recourse to in contradiction of his present acquirements and fitness for any situation; is not that trying and condemning him, time after time, during his whole life?

It would be better not to hold out hope to a man, by pronouncing a short sentence, or by giving him a free pardon, if he is ever after to be treated as infamous.[14]

Punishments, he cried, were inflicted that crime might be prevented, and crime was prevented "by the reformation of the criminal and that 'he, being amerced of one period of his life,' may be enabled to spend the remainder more respectably".[15]

He seemed to take a firmer grip of his pen:

My principle is, that when once a man is free, his former state should no longer be remembered, or allowed to act against him: let him then feel himself eligible for any situation which he has, by a long term of upright conduct, proved himself worthy of filling.

What can be so great a stimulus to a man of respectable family and education, who has fallen to the lowest state of degradation, as to know, that it is still in his power to recover what he has lost, and not only to become a worthy member of society, but to be treated as such?

I trust the British people will not adopt a principle, which every liberal man must disclaim and banish from his breast, namely that of never forgiving an injury; but on the contrary that they will continue to cherish the more generous one upon which they have hitherto acted, of tempering Justice with Mercy.[16]

IV

The letter was published in London in pamphlet form. But in the meantime, Mr Bigge and his secretary beat a pathway to Mr M'Arthur's house. He was the only man called upon by the Commissioner for constructive suggestions. The Governor certainly was not.

He was not even examined, save upon the complaints and petty tittle-tattle of his foes. He was, indeed, denied privileges accorded to the meanest and lowest convict in the Colony.

Daily the door of Mr Bigge's confessional box was seen closing behind the scum and riff-raff of New South Wales. The furtive convict pimped upon the storekeeper in charge of him. The Marsdens, the M'Arthurs told their unsworn tales.[17]

When it was all over, Mr Bigge, after he had left the Colony, wrote out a matter of sixty-four charges for the Governor to answer.

Most of them concerned the kind of affairs of which every jail might provide a crop, whispered against the warders. Matters dead and gone these seven or eight years were raked up; accusations which had been explained and forgotten, of which the explanations for years had lain unregarded in the dusty files of the dispatch room at the Colonial Office . . . personalities.

No less then fourteen of the charges concerned the petty affairs of the hospitals, the grievances of Dr Bowman, the friend of M'Arthur and of Bigge himself:

Treatment of Dr. Bowman after his arrival and continued refusal of the smallest accommodation to him, especially the loan of a carpenter to put up fixtures in his house, when such indulgences were granted individuals among whom was Dr. Redfern . . . Denial of a man to put up shelves in the hospital store room . . . No

R

notice taken of Mr. Redfern's insolent letter to Mr. Bowman tho' shown the Governor by him . . . A verbal permission granted to Mr. D'Arcy Wentworth to sell some cases and apply the proceeds without accounting . . . Major Druitt's refusal to allow men to draw water for the use of the Hospital in March and April 1821 . . . Countenancy of a circular letter dated 26th April 1820, addressed to a Board of Medical Officers, in which a reflection was cast upon the medical management of the hospital before any inquiry was made into the causes of the deaths that occurred . . . refusal of convicts to settlers except favoured individuals. . . .[18]

It should have been sufficient answer to the last charge that even Nicholas Bayly—he of the eight young children entirely unprovided for—had thirty-two of the villains on his books, M'Arthur considerably more.

There followed "Sanction of all Mr Cox's payments and expenses at Bathurst by Governor Macquarie".[19] The reply was that the expenses were passed as correct and legitimate and sanctioned therefore as a matter of course.

Then came "Refusal to pay Mr Moore's salary, tho twice ordered by Lord Bathurst, with deprivation of lands, etc.,[20] until Mr Moore consented to make a degrading apology". Lord Bathurst had approved *that* action two and a half years before. The stream of the Governor's correspondence with Mr Moore had flowed through the Colonial Office for two years as enclosures with dispatches.

"Grant of a tract of land to Mr J. T. Campbell[21] dated 17th August, 1819, and called *Philo Mount* in apparent ridicule and allusion to the letters of *Philo Free* for the purpose of perpetuating the remembrance of a subject irritating to the feelings of Mr Marsden and reflecting disgrace upon the Government." The Governor could not be responsible for Mr Campbell's choice of a name.

The clumsily phrased inquisition rolled on through page after page of foolscap. It does not seem even to have been submitted to Macquarie until Bigge was about to leave the Colony.

V

How different the treatment to which M'Arthur was subjected! Mr Bigge asked him to draft a scheme for the settlement of New South Wales, and Mr M'Arthur did not fail him.

He already had given evidence twice before the Commission.[22] He had told his untruthful tale of the foundation of the wool industry through his own unaided efforts. He had planned the future on an ample scale.

John M'Arthur, Senior, to J. T. Bigge

If His Majesty's Government propose to retain this Colony, as a dependency of Great Britain, there is no time to be lost, in establishing a body of really respectable settlers—men of real capital—not needy adventurers. They should have estates of at least 10,000 acres, with reserves contiguous of equal extent.—Such a body of Proprietors would in a few years become wealthy and with the support of the Government powerful as an aristocracy.— The democratic multitude would look upon their large possessions with envy, and upon the proprietors with hatred—as this democratic feeling has already taken deep root in the Colony, in consequence of the absurd and mischievous policy, pursued by Governor Macquarie — and as there is already a strong combination amongst that class of persons, it cannot be too soon opposed with vigour.— If forty or fifty proprietors, such as I have described, were settled in the country, they would soon discover that there could be no secure enjoyment of their estates but from the protection of Government. As the population increases, the aristocratic body should be augmented; and as fine woolled sheep will increase, in a few years, with surprising rapidity the new settlers, with capital, would find no difficulty to stock their estates.[23]

It was evident from Mr M'Arthur's proposal that this was to be done with some of the merino sheep. However, reaching this happy state:

They would maintain a large body of domestic servants and labourers; and from their numerous flocks supply Great Britain, so abundantly with wool of the finest quality that the price must considerably diminish.—This point once attained what nation could export a yard of fine cloth at the price the English manufacturer could produce it aided as he would be by cheap wool, machinery, capital, and skill.— In return for the wool exported from hence British manufactures to an immense amount would be consumed in the Colony, and as the carcase of the sheep will be of no value off the estate in which it is produced the proprietors would be desirous to take as many convicts as possible. These men would produce bread for themselves and their surplus labour would be directed to clearing, fencing and draining, so that every year the estates would become capable of supporting more sheep and the proprietors in circumstances to provide for more labourers to carry on his improvements.[24]

The cultivation of Indian corn appealed to him as a sideline, with the growth of tobacco, bark, hemp, flax, and, further north, sugar, coffee and cotton; though there would be no success "unless the convicts were restrained from their present bad habits". There could be no change for the better, "whilst the practice was followed of indiscriminately granting lands to convicts".

Surely, [wrote Mr M'Arthur] these are points entitled to the most serious attention of the Government—they present the double advantage of giving Great Britain the most extensive monopoly that any nation ever enjoyed and that upon the most unexceptionable principles namely supplying other peoples cheaper than they can be supplied elsewhere, and there is a certainty of an increasing demand for the labour of any number of convicts or paupers Great Britain and Ireland may send forth. Effectual means must be adopted to compel the grantees of large estates to fulfil the conditions; if it be made a job of, it will disappoint the Government and embarrass the Colony.[25]

When men are engaged in rural occupations, he said, "their days are chiefly spent in solitude . . . they have more time for reflection and self examination—and they are less tempted to the perpetration of crimes than when herded together in towns amidst a mass of disorders and vices".[26]

He proposed to give the new class of aristocrats magisterial powers—

authority to punish disorders, to compel their servants to execute a due
quantity of work, to determine the amount of rewards and to make the
quality, and in some measure the quantity, of the convicts' food depend
upon their industry and good behaviour. Thus the prisoners were to "then
discover that honesty and diligence, vice and idleness were differently
estimated and that nothing but desert could establish claim to a month's
indulgence". "A thief's most vulnerable part," he wrote, "is his belly."
And he believed punitive food stoppages would amount to enough to pay
for the cost of rural police.

He knew, the artful fellow continued, that Mr Bigge must have
remarked "the pernicious and demoralising operation of the general regulations which placed the good and bad servant, the honest man and the
thief on an equal footing". If the Colony was to be maintained as a
receptacle for convicts, they must be kept in subjection.

And he could think of no means by which these objects could be
obtained but by confiding to intelligent and honourable men extensive
powers, though they should be subjected to the control of a vigilant
government, prompt to correct abuses, and ever ready to distinguish and
reward merit.

This, then, was "the key and touchstone of the truth" of all that Mr
Bigge and Mr Scott heard. It was a scheme to captivate any justice who
had received his colonial education among the slave-owning estates of the
West Indies.[27]

The Macquarie plan of things was doomed, since the ideas of Mr
M'Arthur and his kind fully accorded with the staple of public opinion
among the great sugar kings and Indian nabobs of England.

Sadly the Governor watched his world falling about his ears, watched
his principles of reform repudiated, his schemes of ornament disallowed,
his work on his cathedral church placed in abeyance, his court-house
turned into a church (he named it for St James), his Georgian school to
become a court-house.

VI

The year of Peterloo was just over, and at its end, as the Cato Street
conspirators plotted, young Mr Wentworth sat in his chambers near Tom
Pinch's Fountain in Middle Temple to write to his father.

Mr Wentworth was in a bitter mood, though it was softened by the
fact that he had marked the changes in the Australian scene by publishing
and selling out his first edition of the *Statistical Account of New South Wales*
at a profit of £150, which he badly needed to mitigate the state of "constant
self denial"[28] in which he was living.

But anybody might have been pessimistic about such conditions,
especially if he were a Whig and educated in politics by Lord Fitzwilliam
and his friends.

He did not know whether the Government would succeed in carrying
through the Manchester business with a high hand, but it seemed to him

"evident from the tenor of the Prince Regent's speech that the most vigorous measures would be proposed for repressing that spirit of reform which was universally prevalent among the manufacturing population, and, indeed, among the lower orders generally throughout the country".

It was confidently rumoured, he wrote, that serious encroachments were to be made on the Bill of Rights; and that instead of the Habeas Corpus Act's being suspended for a time as had been the custom on similar occasions, the right of assembling to discuss public grievances and petition for the redress of them was to be materially abridged.

> . . . If these reports be, as I fear they are, well founded, there is no doubt that a military despotism will before long be the recompense for all the sacrifices which the nation has made for many years in defence of what has been considered to be the cause of liberty and independence. A civil war in this case will be the only resource left for that portion of the people who are desirous of bequeathing to their children that freedom which they themselves inherited from their ancestors—for in the present constitution of the House of Commons it is absurd to hope for any resistance from that quarter. The Methodist Party, at the head of which is the Old Woman, Wilberforce, certainly promised to support the Ministry through thick and thin . . .[29]

Judging from this and other accounts of British conditions drifting into the Colony, Mr Bigge, if he happened to make up his mind in the wrong direction so far as to recommend the Macquarie policy of leniency and emancipist colonization, would find himself very much in the position of a Daniel bearding the lions, with the smell of blood about him.

At the same time, the Government was not anxious, apparently, to have a zealot Governor on its doorstep in London, implicating his Minister in a policy of weakness by recalling the immediate past of an administration which had approved or framed his policies and plan of convict redemption.

Under Ministers' eyes every day was the conclusive evidence that the tide towards the settlement of Australia by free peoples, which had already begun to flow when Bathurst wrote to Sidmouth in 1817 and decided to appoint a Commission, was beginning to flood.

Late in 1820 came another letter from the observant and active Wentworth whose own campaigning life had begun:

W. C. Wentworth to D'Arcy Wentworth

The favourable accounts received from the Colony by the *Foxhound* have excited a considerable feeling of partiality towards it in this country; and I have little doubt that the number of respectable persons emigrating to it will be much greater during the ensuing year than at any other former period. . . . Colonists [designed for the Cape of Good Hope] are anxious beyond measure to be sent to Port Jackson.[30]

Baillie, secretary to the Commissioner on Claims between England and France, had been using all his influence to induce the Government to give preference in settlement to New Holland. The Government had determined not to send any more emigrants to the Cape of Good Hope till it should hear favourable reports from the present party.

He heard that the report of the Committee on Jails recommended the establishment of distillation and the abolition of duties on oil procured in colonial ships; these things he thought would be at once conceded (as they were), but a legislative council would not be appointed till the arrival from Sydney of Mr Bigge's Report.[31]

The Government was very averse to the measure, but it was believed that ultimately it would be induced to give way.

He added:

> I hear no rumours whatever of Governor Macquarie's removal.— I have been informed that there are several applications for his situation, but that it is not the intention of Govt. to recall him at present; and they are only fearful lest he should take offence at the appointment of Mr. Bigge to inquire into the State of the Colony, and resign the Government in consequence. I sincerely hope that he may not take that hasty step, but I assure you it is the general opinion here that such will be his conduct.[32]

So saying, Mr Wentworth turned to a private war with an old enemy. For Mr Jeffery Bent, among his perjuries before the Committee on Prisons, had related how Sir William Garrow, Attorney-General, had been in the Old Bailey when D'Arcy Wentworth had been tried, and remembered that the old surgeon had been graduated as Mr Bent's "notorious highwayman" by leaving a stolen watch on his seat when he left the Court in which he had just been acquitted in respect of it.[33]

Sir William Garrow now flatly denied that he had had any recollection of any such affair; so Mr Wentworth found Mr Bent "vile" and promised his parent "that I will either wipe out the stain which he has endeavoured to cast on your character with his blood or shed the last drop of my own in the effort".[34]

Mr Bent was impervious to insult. At the moment, he preferred a bench in Grenada to a couch in Valhalla and was keeping out of his indignant adversary's way.

Bennet had "changed colour several times"[35] as he swallowed the large quantities of leek which young Mr Wentworth was making him eat as the result of his parliamentary assertion that D'Arcy Wentworth had been a convict — Mr Bennet had professed to quote Lord Erskine as his authority.

And the Colonial Office soon hastily assured D'Arcy Wentworth's son that its voucher in favour of his father's sterling character would consist of a pension of £200 per annum.[36]

VII

There was, without a doubt, a clearly marked change in the tides as they affected New South Wales. Mr Wentworth exhibited it in his letters, Lord Bathurst in the sterner and harder note with which he adverted to the disputes between the Governor and the Commissioner, and reprimanded the former for his appointment of Redfern,[37] mentioning the serious regret of His Majesty "that any circumstance should have arisen to interrupt the harmony, which had previously existed between His Majesty's Commissioner and yourself, and from the continuance of which the most beneficial consequences might justly be anticipated".

His Majesty, it seemed, readily acquitted his satrap of having intentionally violated his public duty, and was willing to believe that, in rejecting Mr Bigge's suggestion that he suspend Mr Redfern's appointment until a reference to England might take place, the Governor had been actuated by the feeling that he could not honestly retract an engagement into which he had previously entered.[38]

But, while His Majesty thus did "full credit to your intentions and motives", he was "nevertheless compelled to disapprove of the course you have thought it advisable to pursue".

The dispatch continued:

> I should but ill execute His Majesty's commands, if I were to imply that persons, who have been convicts, should be for ever altogether excluded from all situations of trust and profit in the Colony. If subsequent good conduct was not to atone in some degree for previous offences, the great inducement to reformation of character would be altogether withdrawn; and although the situation of magistrate is that to which the admission of convicts is evidently most objectionable, His Majesty is not prepared to state that a case of pressing necessity might not arise to render even such an appointment justifiable.
>
> The case however in the present instance has no necessity to plead in its justification. The appointment appears to have been originally promised to Mr. Redfern as a compensation for the disappointment of not succeeding Dr. Wentworth as Surgeon, and to have been carried into effect, not on any plea that his services as a magistrate were indispensible, but in consideration of the previous promise which he had received.[39]

All this was bewildering in view of the pronouncements of the Colonial Office as late as the date of Bigge's departure from England. In the instructions issued to him, Bathurst had written:

> I allude to the propriety of admitting into society persons, who originally came to the settlement as convicts. The opinion, entertained by the Governor and sanctioned by the Prince Regent, has certainly been with some exceptions, in favour of their reception at the expiration of their several sentences upon terms of perfect equality with the free settlers. But I am aware that the conduct of the Governor in this respect, however approved by the Government at home, has drawn down upon him the hostility of many persons, who hold association with convicts under any circumstances to be a degradation. Feelings of this kind are not easily overcome, but I should be unwilling to forego the possibility of reconciling the conflicting opinions on this subject by not adverting to it as a proper question for your consideration.[40]

That being Downing Street's outlook, it might have seemed reasonable to believe that a home administration which had backed its statements of policy by tolerating for years the presence of Simeon Lord, a reputed pickpocket, on the Bench, would have shown no antagonism towards the elevation of the Colony's most eminent surgeon, guilty only of a youthful indiscretion, who had given long and loyal service to the Government, and in whom the public had just shown confidence by electing him a director of the country's first bank of issue. But home policy was clearly altering rapidly.

VIII

To all the changes prejudicial to their interests taking place in England in colonial policy the emancipists as a whole certainly could not be insensitive. They were soon made aware of how great was the peril in which they stood.

Edward Eagar, the noted Irish convict, one of the Colony's most pious residents and one of those local emancipist attorneys whom Mr Jeffery Bent had refused to have in his court, had occasion on New Year's Day 1820 at Parramatta to come before a Bench of magistrates presided over by Mr Justice Field.[41] Mr Eagar was not the same cringing person who had arrived in the *Providence* in 1811, praying volubly and occasionally feeling his spinal column to make sure that it was still unfractured.

He had become a rich, substantial, and somewhat litigious citizen. He was the largest shareholder in the Bank of New South Wales; he was a pillar of those churches which worshipped according to the purer dectrines of Wesley. But when he had gone before the Parramatta Bench, Mr Justice Field had seen fit to shout at him, "You have made seditious speeches. You have raised up the standard of disaffection and party. You are a revolutionist!"[42]

These were frightening words. It was no light thing in the year of Cato Street to be called a revolutionist, especially if one had been a convict.

Mr Eagar, who had received an unconditional pardon from the Governor two years before, developed a vendetta against Mr Justice Field. He sued him in the Governor's Court, which was presided over by the Judge-Advocate, and otherwise consisted of two settlers, for £50 damages for slander and for the repayment of some of Mr Justice Field's very high fees.[43]

It was beside the point that the Court thought the actions "vexatious, malicious and brought forward only with a view at least of casting an odium on the Judge in his public character and office".[44] It was scarcely relevant to what occurred that for years Mr Eagar without a murmur had paid similar fees to those which he sought to reclaim.

Mr Field chose to raise an issue which he knew would affect disastrously the affairs of every freed man in New South Wales.

There were two forms of pardon in vogue in the Colony apart from the expiry of a sentence of transportation which, under the relevant Act of Parliament, had the effect of a pardon under the Great Seal.[45]

A convict who had not completed the full term of his sentence might either receive a full pardon by the King himself under the Great Seal. Or he might, under the Act of 1791, receive fron the Governor a certificate under the seal of the Colony which purported to "remit either absolutely or conditionally the whole or any part of the remainder of the term or time" unexpired of the original sentence or order of transportation.

Mr Justice Field now rested his resistance to Mr Eagar's claims on a decision in the case of *Bullock* v. *Dodd*,[46] which recently had been heard in England and in which it had been decided that a governor's pardon, as distinct from a royal pardon, did not restore a convict to any civil rights whatever, save the right to remain on the earth.

Until his name appeared in a general pardon sealed with the Great Seal of England a felon was minus rights at law. In vain Mr Eagar pleaded previous cases in which the courts had recognized the right of locally pardoned —even conditionally pardoned—convicts to sue and be sued. In vain, he cried out that "this defence is as odious as that of slavery".[47]

The Court granted Field's prayer that he be allowed "twelve months time to procure such evidence from Ireland, as will maintain his rightful (and in this case) equitable plea to convict attaint." The Court further felt that this delay would give the Home Government a chance to review the situation.[48]

Meantime, the results to the poor emancipists were devastating, for the judgment at home and the attitude of the New South Wales courts and particularly of Mr Justice Field, who ruled the Supreme Court and primarily decided the legal validity of every action within its ambit, applied to every one of them in some degree, if not so severely and widely as they at first thought.

Macquarie himself, between 1 January 1810 and 31 December 1819, had granted 352 free pardons and 1164 conditional pardons. And not only all those pardoned but those who had dealt with them had taken it for granted that they had been, by their pardons, restored to all the civil rights under which they might buy or sell, sue and be sued, hold official appointments, make oaths in the ordinary form and acquire and transmit property by the ordinary legal instruments of commerce, by agreements and by their wills and testaments.[49]

It seemed to the emancipists—on the basis of the local judicial attitude —that the effect of the decision in *Bullock* v. *Dodd* was as follows: The former convict pardoned by the Governor who sued would be non-suited. The decisions of coroner's juries, on which sat pardoned convicts who had not the King's Pardon under seal, were of no effect. Free men who had bought from or sold to convicts under local pardon would find their contracts not worth the paper they were written upon; free children who had inherited from a convict parent would be without title, and those to whom they had sold their legacies of land or houses or rights of any description would be in the same position. It was later proved that they had been misled and that their perils were considerably mitigated by the Transportation Act of 1815.

The emancipists rushed to protect themselves. They drafted a petition to the King. It was signed by 1368 of "those persons, by whose labour and industry this your Majesty's Colony has been cleared and cultivated, its towns built, its woods felled, its agriculture and commerce carried on".[50]

It pointed out that nine-tenths of the population were either convicts or emancipists. It quoted figures to show the power and consequence which the emancipist interest had attained.

Of the land in cultivation in New South Wales former convicts owned 29,028 acres, the freely-come immigrants, rich and poor, only 10,787 acres; their pasture lands covered 212,335 acres, those of the originally free only 198,369 acres. They had 1200 houses in towns, against 300 owned by completely free men. They possessed 42,900 horned cattle and 174,179 sheep. The freemen, including great holders like the M'Arthurs, Coxes, Jamison, Oxley, and Marsden boasted only 28,582 cattle and 87,391 sheep. They sailed the seas with fifteen colonial vessels, while the exclusives and freemen had but eight. Their total wealth was valued at £1,123,600— nearly double that of those who had never known the feel of a leg-iron.[51]

Now, despite the generation of "good conduct and industry, whereby they had attained to wealth, character and rank in society", they were, they declared, all to be "thrown back at once and for ever to that state of degradation from which they had . . . they hoped not undeservedly arisen":

> Notwithstanding that the system prevailing in this Colony has been established by the Sovereign . . . sanctioned by Parliament, carried into effect by the Government of the Colony, and in good faith trusted to and relied upon by your petitioners. Yet that your petitioners, retrospectively and prospectively, are to be considered as convicts attaint, without personal liberty, without property, without character or credit, without any one right or priviledge belonging to free subjects.[52]

The results of the judgment, they said, would "go near to defeat, unsettle and subvert the foundation and title of almost all the property in the Colony"; it would "have the effect of introducing and perpetuating party distinctions, unpleasant discussions, irritable feelings and jealousies, heats, animosities and diversions, between your Majesty's free subjects in these territories, not only for the present generations, but for generations to come".[53]

Industry, they declared, could not flourish where there was no security for the enjoyment of its fruits, and the position which had arisen would take away all encouragement and stimulus to good conduct and reformation of manners among convicted persons. In fact, they believed that if the new theories of law were allowed to prevail, the Colony would be thrown back to a state of poverty, immorality and distress; the whole of the results of the hitherto maintained humane and benevolent policy destroyed.

Mr Eagar himself was deputed to carry home the petition. The Governor gave it his warm support. He further showed that he did not believe Mr Eagar to be the "revolutionist" which Mr Justice Field had proclaimed him to be, by introducing him to Bathurst as "a man of strong sound good sense and superior understanding[54] . . . extremely well informed as to the resources of the Colony". Redfern, who was bound for England, also carried a friendly viceregal letter in which the Minister was informed that his unimpeachable loyalty and service had long since blotted out his "single juvenile dereliction".[55]

IX

Macquarie's last two years in Australia were the busiest of his reign, though his overriding wish was to get away from it all; from the heavy expense of his fortnightly public dinners at which a hundred and fifty guests, largely foes, ate and drank his larder bare; from the interminable quarrels; from the increasingly carping complaints from Whitehall; from the obstruction of the new race of officials, headed by Major Goulburn, in league with the exclusives.

Every day there was less to hold him. All his more faithful servants, like himself, were growing old. Some were already dead or had left their offices. Wentworth and Campbell had retired. Broughton, his loyal friend and confidant, to whom he had given hurried orders to stave off starvation in January 1810, perished; so did Lewin, his artist, and young George Johnston, whom he called "the most rising and promising young man, to which this country has given birth". Even King George III, whose reign had spanned almost exactly the Governor's whole life, had disappeared from earth, and the news came just as the thirteen guns roared across the harbour to welcome Bigge back to Port Jackson from Van Diemen's Land.

In July 1820 the colonists had mourned their Sovereign in a procession from the Domain to St Philip's behind a band playing "The Dead March in Saul", the colours and drums covered in black.

The Governor wrote, "Our dear Lachlan made one of the procession dressed in deep mourning and looked remarkably well."[56]

That day he and Mr Bigge buried their long-standing feud before they honoured the memory of the old King while eighty-two minute-guns exploded. They ushered in George IV with royal salutes and ceremonies. The Governor, the Commissioner, the Judges, and the Provost-Marshal signed the accession proclamation.

The colours rose to full mast and the troops fired three volleys. At Government House, there was wine to drink the health of the new monarch, and rum for the convicts at the Hyde Park Barracks.

An edified population watched Mr J. T. Campbell in the unusual role of a herald, staff of office under arm, scroll held high, as he rode on horseback with magistrates in his train and read the proclamation in a loud and appropriate tone of voice at crowded wharf and market-place, just as if New South Wales had been Merrie England.

X

The Governor laid the foundation stone of the Roman Catholic Mother Church where St Mary's Cathedral Basilica came to stand and ushered in the priesthood with a kindly lecture.

There had been edifying preliminaries. That stern Orangeman, Mr

J. T. Campbell, had been treasurer of a committee to raise funds for the popish work, which received the financial patronage of a number of staunch Protestants, who were lured from their prejudices by the Governor's dispensation and example. To him or to Elizabeth, a noted Roman Catholic historian believed, was due "the amazing proportions of the building", in which Mr Campbell's investment was represented by a gift of £20.[57]

The Roman Catholics of the Colony, many of whom had enjoyed Elizabeth's St Patrick's Day dinners, subscribed to present the Governor with a trowel with which to perform the ceremony of foundation-stone laying; and an observant altar boy preserved a memory of the scene when the first corner of the building, on which a Cardinal's basilica would stand in little more than a century, had been bedded in the earth.

"The Governor wiped the trowel with his handkerchief, and put it in his bosom, saying 'You must know, Mr. Therry, that, although I never laid the first stone of a Catholic church before, I am a very old Mason; and I shall keep this trowel as long as I live, in remembrance of this day, and I wish you and your flock every success in your pious undertaking.' "[58]

Church and State exchanged flattering addresses. And, on leaving for England, Macquarie promised to move Bathurst to assist in completing the church. As a result, the Government decided to enter its "name for a sum equal to the total of all such additional donations" as might be given privately to the building fund.[59]

Other works, of course, were going ahead apace. The Governor's records were full of memoranda of inspections of buildings which rose throughout Colony in 1820-1, and all of which he personally supervised. He opened the first antipodean poorhouse, the first blind institute. He presided over the annual school examinations of the orphans and gave out medals, created St James's parish, sat as president of the Benevolent Society and the Bible Society, both founded in his time, also of the meeting to found the Savings Bank which had sprung into being under the impulsive hand of Mr Justice Field. He disposed of the new immigrants and convicts who arrived on every ship—Macleod of Talisker and groups of English and Scottish freemen, five Cato Street conspirators, and the Reverend Mr Reddall, sent out at his request to open a school on the system of the excellent Bell.[60]

In November 1820 he ranged widely through the Colony to see all its parts before he left it. He travelled southward to the new-settled Toombong country, and to Lake Bathurst and Lake George, the first Governor to set foot in that region, one of the first little group of whites to ride down the eastern side of Lake George. His story, full of records of vicissitudes, of exposure, of lost horses, and of the jolting travail of a journey for which the road was being cut just ahead of him, show the strain of such expeditions upon a sick and ageing constitution. But he slept in the first bed set up on the borders of Canberra Federal Territory, he drank the first toast drunk on the shores of Lake George. He heard the Reverend Mr Cartwright preach the word of God there for the first time[61]—a plea for kindness to the aborigines. Yet he was all oblivious that a century hence a shining white capital would rise only a few miles south-westerly across the low range of hills which he could see, with a national parliament, and with a royal duke, son and brother of a king, sitting there in state as his own successor.

He returned to hear that Government House at Parramatta had been struck by lightning and Elizabeth shocked into illness.[62]

In December he marked out and named Campbelltown in Airds after his wife's family,[63] but in that month Elizabeth was still not stout enough to go to divine service at the new Church of St Luke in Liverpool.[64] The rains all over the Colony were savage and severe. They marked the passing of "my poor, dear little godson Macquarie Whalan, son of our faithful Sergeant Whalan".[65]

XI

Bigge sailed away in February 1821, after having been almost wrecked near the harbour mouth on the shoals of the Sow and Pigs, where the old *Dromedary* bumped round for days. He left Lachlan a "very pretty little present", and made "a very handsome complimentary and gratifying speech to me on my drinking his health".[66]

In March Captain Allman was sent off to found the settlement of Port Macquarie, two hundred and fifty miles or so to the north of Sydney,[67] a month after Throsby reported completing the southward road for seventy-five miles from Stonequarry Creek over the Cookbundoon Range.[68]

The Governor began his final tours. His was an arduous though triumphal progress. Van Diemen's Land gave him a rousing welcome, except for the bushrangers, among whom there was a busy epidemic of executions. He crossed the island, often wet through, sometimes "more fatigued than in all his life", and scarcely in the mood to enjoy the illuminations with which Sydney welcomed his return, especially since he landed to hear of the death of Broughton.

They sent Young Lachlan to school with Dr Reddall, who had been established in Meehan's "castle" at Macquarie Fields. He and young Sorell, son of the Lieutenant-Governor of Van Diemen's Land, whom the Governor had brought back from Hobart with him, were the first boys to arrive at that nursery of good colonists.

The Government carriage horses began to work overtime, for the Governor filled in all his spare hours posting down to Castle Meehan to see his wife and son. And whenever he arrived there, Lachlan fired a salute for him with his little battery.

He had made in the Lumberyard "for Master Macquarie a small box containing four small spades, four small hoes, two rakes, twelve cricket bats and six cricket balls" which were to be considered as belonging to his son so long as he remained at the school, but afterwards to be left for the school as a gift from the Crown"— the first sporting equipment with which a public school in Australia was endowed.

His last journey as Governor was made to Port Macquarie.[69] The expedition was one of the most arduous of all. It involved a two-hundred-and-fifty-mile voyage up the coast in the little *Elizabeth Henrietta*, which Elizabeth prepared for him with anxious care. He was compelled by the weather to roll up past Smoky Cape, beyond his destination. He remembered to drink a bumper to his wife and his boy upon the anniversary of his wedding day, which he had never failed to commemorate. There were the vicissitudes involved in crossing the dangerous bar on which his old ship of 1811, the tiny. eighty-ton *Lady Nelson*, lay piled upon the sands. There was the usual feverish planning of the new settlement, the journeyings into the dark scrubs fifteen miles up the Hastings where only a few days before the blacks had been throwing spears at whites in "a hostile spirit". There was the landing of four cows and calves, "all well and in high condition", the bovine pioneers of a dairying district which in later generations was to be among the richest in the whole British Commonwealth, a district from which hundreds of thousands of tons of dairy produce were shipped to feed a hungry United Kingdom in and out of war times.

Finally came the quite normal difficult departure, nearly ending in a wreck, the contest with towering seas that stove in the bulwarks, the four days' struggle against the tempests before the ship could tear herself away from the shore and make her course southward—with a pause to say good-bye to Newcastle and the Hunter—to what the Governor now thought of as "home".

It was home no longer. On 21 November he was "agreeably surprised" to find his successor, Sir Thomas Brisbane, walking in the Domain.[70] It had fallen to the lot of Elizabeth to welcome him.

The pair greeted each other cordially, but for the first time in his life Macquarie failed to approve the conciliating manners of a new acquaintance.

He did his last official duty on 30 November 1821, sitting as a judge in appeal. He went next day to hear the new Governor's Commission read by his old friend and servant, J. T. Campbell, in Hyde Park. . . .

Save Fulton, there were no emancipists in the list of justices issued on 1 December.

XII

There were two last journeys, one in December 1821 to Bathurst, one in January 1822 southwards.[71] The latter took him through the Cowpastures on an arduous inspection, during which he was sometimes called to spend seven and a half hours in the day in the saddle. He seemed at times to forget that he was no longer Governor, and so did the colonists as he drifted from Hassall's Macquarie Grove to "Bradbury's", fixed the site for the new burying ground and parsonage at Campbelltown and inspected the new church there which was ready to receive its roof on walls which had risen in the heart of a "rich populous centre". The countryside had been a desolation haunted by blacks when he had come to the Colony.

Then he made his way to the edges of the Bulli downfall, peered, as thousands of tourists since have done, at "the very grand and magnificent bird's eye view of the ocean and 5 Islands and the greater part of the low country of the Illawarra as far as Red Port", slipped down "the horrid, deep descent" with his packhorses—it had first been negotiated in 1815 by Charles Throsby. He saw the sparse pioneer farms of Allan, Jenkins, Brooks, and Brown, under the guidance of the versatile Mr O'Brien, after whom he named the pass by which they returned to the plateau and in which his cicerone had built a road "frightful to look at but perfectly safe for cattle and persons on horseback".

On his way to Illawarra he had placed upon a vale near Appin one of the very last geographical names which he was to give in the antipodes. He called it David's Valley, after young David Johnston, whose dead brother he had loved, whose father, the rebel George Johnston, had given the turn to fate which had brought him to the Colony.

The rebel, incidentally, marked the end of the Macquarie era, as he had heralded its beginning, by falling out of his gig on the way home from dinner.

XIII

Macquarie feted three hundred and forty blacks at his last native gathering introducing the chiefs to the new Governor.

On his birthday the emancipists gave him a dinner. Mr Robinson's laureate muse "sang for the last time with her accustomed grace" of the "benignant hand" which had "nurtured first her infant land".

The colonists at a meeting in the Court House, voted to present their late ruler with a piece of plate valued at £500—it took two years to collect the money. Windsor envisioned a fund to paint his portrait to be hung in the court-house. Every district sent its delegation with fulsome addresses. He had a fierce quarrel with Mr Francis Greenway, the only emancipist whom he had befriended who showed him ingratitude.

And then it was all over.

On 11 February 1822 he performed his final service in New South Wales:

Sir Thomas Brisbane came down to Sydney . . . and having taken early breakfast with us at Government House, he was so good as to accompany Mrs. M., Lachlan and myself, immediately afterwards on a water excursion in the Government Barge to "George's Head" for the purpose of witnessing our settling *Boongaree* and his tribe of the "Pittwater" Tribe of black natives for the second time in that pretty place, Barney Williams having put the farm in very neat order for them, built good huts for their residence, and made a most excellent and romantic road from the landing place to the village.

Mrs. M. had ordered a plentiful feast . . . for Boongaree and his tribe . . . 15 men and women, and I gave him an old suit of general's uniform to dress him out as a chief. We strongly recommended Boongaree and his tribe to the kind protection and good offices of Sir Thomas Brisbane, which he has promised to extend to them. He has, also, at my request, promised to give

Boongaree for himself and his tribe a fishing boat with a nett. Having stayed at George's Head for almost an hour, we took leave of our sable friends and returned to Sydney.[72]

On the following Wednesday, he "got up at day break to pack up and prepare for our embarkation". At eleven o'clock, he handed over to his successor the balance of his books and official papers.[73]

All the town was out and about, and there was "an immense concourse manifesting by their melancholy looks their severe and undisguised regret at our separation from the Colony".

The small boys of Dr Laurence Halloran's school were lined up, their medals hung round their necks, with young Master Halloran breathing hard, preparatory to his speech of farewell.

Soldiers stood in line all through Lachlan's Garden. On the harbour which had been so completely empty when he had sailed into it twelve years ago, a man in the full vigour of his life, was another great gathering— launches, barges, cutters, pinnaces, and wherries, of which the complements appeared determined on "catching a glimpse of the *object* of their profound veneration and fondest regard".

The continent's first native-born newspaper reporter was there. Stirring sights were no novelty to him. He had seen the search for Governor Bligh, and Lieutenant Laycock falling out of the printing house attic on his "principal joint", but he was profoundly moved. Only two items took precedence in the paper over his descriptive report—the "assize of bread" and a cryptic two-line paragraph which read, "We regret that 'Casca' came after 1 o'clock, it was then too late."

"Never did Sydney look so attractive and gay," wrote young Mr Robert Howe. "The shores were lined with spectators innumerable but on each countenance was an indication of feeling too big, too sincere for utterance."

> Australia [the *Gazette* used the word habitually now] saw her benefactor for the last time treading her once uncivilised unsocial shores and *felt it too*. The parent and the child must endure the parting pang and Australia can not repine at the varied events time brings about, for time has wrought vast and beneficial changes in her midst.

As the *Surry* passed slowly down harbour, pursued by the launches and "large boats loaded with respectability and opulence", the scribe reflected that "he whose chief principal aim and chief happiness had been the colonists' good has no longer a place among them, (the heart excepted)".

But during that slow progress, the Governor and Elizabeth "occasionally gratified the anxious eye, and departing cheers were consequent upon every glance".[74]

XIV

Weather kept them in the harbour for days. They lay anchored under the shadow of Belle Vue Hill, where the Governor, of yore, had been "wont to take his evening drive". Antill and Sergeant Whalan and his boys stayed with them for the night. Wylde came off to see them.[75]

Antill stole away without saying good-bye. The sensitive fellow, who had wept at leaving Glasgow in 1809, had scarcely been out of sight of his superior for thirteen years. He had been on every journey with him in the Colony. Both had been at Seringapatam. Antill had named his estate at Stonequarry Creek after the Governor's Jarvisfield in Mull, the final monument for poor Jane. He could not bear the parting.

Thus it came about that the last Australians to bid good-bye to Governor Macquarie and his family were humble people:

> Our good affectionate Sergeant Whalan and his two sons, James and Charley, remained with us on board till the last moment and after I had delivered him his letters we took an affectionate leave of them, all of us being deeply affected and poor dear Lachlan particularly so, suffering great distress at leaving (most likely for ever) his dear good Sergeant and his favourite young friend, Charley.[76]

There was but one more entry to write about his Australia: "At 4 p.m. we lost sight of the Light House and Heads of Port Jackson."

The "Man of Mull" had ceased to be the ruler over half a continent. He had become one of Britain's hundreds of burnt-out viceroys who are ever returning home to be forgotten in the press and excitement of younger, more exuberant viceroys going away.

CHAPTER XXXII

The Old Viceroy

I

THERE was not much more to tell.

The voyage was like a hundred other voyages. They rounded the Horn. Their ship, the *Surry*, was a stout vessel of 443 tons burden. They had with them Hector Macquarie, a casual major, John and Nancy Moore, the faithful George, their servants, a stockman, a poulterer and a groom.[1]

They carried the Governor's Sultan, dun-coloured, fifteen and a half hands, nearly nine years old, and their favourite cow, Fortune, a quadruped which was observed being coddled in the Mull equivalent of satined ease a year later.

They had sheep and ducks, turkeys and geese, and one hundred and six fowls. They had aboard their seven pet kangaroos, five emus and seven black swans, Cape Barren geese, native companions, white cockatoos, bronze-wing pigeons, wonga-wongas, and several parrots and lowries. Death played havoc among these simple Australians.

They celebrated Young Lachlan's birthday with a dinner for the captain and the officers. They drank a bumper to Seringapatam's conquerors on its battle anniversary, reminded by their servant George, a combatant who was not forgotten in the toasts. They saw birth and death—George's wife presented him with a daughter—called at San Salvador in Brazil and acquired a monkey and a parrot; celebrated Elizabeth's birthday on 13 June with a sight of whales and turtles.

At 2.30 a.m. one morning the captain woke them to say that they were in the chops of the Channel.

It was all over on 4 July, when they were at Woolwich and could see St Paul's. They sailed up-river to Deptford, admiring the seats of noblemen and gentlemen on either hand. The old Governor was going through the process by which England deflates her autocrats to their normal state: "Landed at Tower Stairs and took a hackney coach, called at Coutts's Bank for £50, and so to Osborn's Hotel in the Adelphi".[2]

A year ago, almost to the day, Sydney had been illuminated for his return from his tour in Van Diemen's Land. Now, with his family, he was in lodgings in Westminster for which he paid £5 5s. a week, and Lord Bathurst found himself able to spare almost half an hour to discuss with him the momentous subject of a twelve years of autocracy over a continent. His lordship's was a "kind and gracious welcome".

Something was said about a pension, but it looked, for long, as if Castlereagh's promise to him when he took office would not be kept. In the end they arranged to pay him £1000 passage money, and Castlereagh, now Marquis of Londonderry, only three or four days before committing suicide, took him to Carlton House to see the King.[3]

He met all his old friends—General Balfour, under whose command he had gone out to India; Charles Forbes; his executor, Drummond, soon to be Lord Strathallan.

He submitted his report to the Colonial Office:

> I found the Colony barely emerging from an infantile imbecility and suffering from various privations and disabilities, the country impenetrable, agriculture in a yet languishing state; commerce in its early dawn; public buildings in a state of dilapidation and mouldering to decay; the few roads and bridges formerly constructed almost impassable; the population in general depressed by poverty; no public credit, no private confidence; the morals of the great mass of the people in the lowest state of debasement and religious worship almost totally neglected. . . .[4]

The population when he had arrived had been but 11,590 souls, including the two regiments; it had grown to 38,778. Horned cattle had increased from 12,442 to 103,000; sheep from 25,900 to 290,000; and land under tillage from 7600 to 32,270 acres. He had found a settlement; he had left a widespread colony. Where there had been but two townships on the mainland when he came, there now were several and nearly 300 miles of roads. It needed nearly seventeen closely printed octavo pages to catalogue his works—churches, public buildings, highways, bridges, gardens. The penetrated area on the mainland had risen from 2500 to 100,000 square miles in his time.[5]

But his greatest satisfaction lay in the knowledge that his policy had been based on humanity; that, as he declared in answer to a flattering address from the inhabitants of the Colony, he could look back upon his proceedings and reflect on his motives with serenity.

Bathurst wrote a month later:

> I have lost no time in submitting to His Majesty, according to your desire, the report of the proceedings of your administration of the Government of New South Wales . . .
>
> I have great satisfaction in being able to assure you of the sense, which His Majesty is graciously pleased to entertain, of the assiduity and integrity with which you have administered the Colonial interests of that settlement. Its great increase of population and the advances, which it has made in agriculture, trade and wealth of every kind, cannot but be highly creditable to your administration.
>
> If, as a place of punishment, it has not answered all the purposes for which it was intended, this is certainly not owing to any deficiency of zeal or solicitude on your part, but is mainly to be attributed to the many difficulties, with which the rapid and unprecedented succession of convicts, transported of late years to New South Wales, appear to have embarassed your Government, and which progressively required a change of system, which you could not have contemplated in the earlier periods of it, the necessity for which, however, continued to increase by such slow and imperceptible degrees, as not necessarily to force itself upon your attention.[6]

II

With this gratifying, if somewhat ambiguous document to comfort him, Macquarie retired to the land of his fathers.

In August 1822 he had heard news of the death of the husband of his sister, Betty, "as good and honest a man as ever spelt the name of Maclaine".

Times in the Highlands, and especially in Mull, were now so bad that no rents at all could be collected there and he must give up for the present the idea of building the castle which he originally had planned, or even a cottage at Gruline, though they were prepared to regard their deprivations philosophically.

Macquarie to Charles Macquarie

We shall be so very short a time at Gruline that we don't care a farthing about the dilapidated state of it, so it has doors and windows and is *water tight.*—you must not, on any account, paint any part of the house, as poor Elizabeth cannot stand painted houses—Don't do anything to it beyond making the house water-tight and glazing the windows. We shall carry with us beds and all the furniture we shall have occasion for during our few days stay at Gruline. Your sister is very anxious about our poor old useful cow, and begs she may not be removed from Gruline in case she arrives there. She requires to be kept *at night under cover,* and in case there is no suitable place at Gruline for her, perhaps our worthy friend Donald Knock would give her quarter on his farm till our arrival.

Elizabeth fell ill through the bitterness of the cold of the north and, in November, they set out to make the tour of the Continent[7] which they had planned exactly seventeen years before.

They returned to London on 31 July 1823 to find Bigge's reports issued, three hundred pages solid with ominous words. If Grey Bennet's letter had stung the old Governor to the quick, this crushed him.

As a picture of the more jealous and factious minds of the period, the reports form an invaluable record. Twenty-eight large boxes are needed to hold the transcripts of the detail of what was said to Mr Bigge behind closed doors in New South Wales and mostly in a sort of secret confessional. In them the minds of thieves, of thwarted monopolists, of land-grabbers, and particularly of skilled and unscrupulous prevaricators with an axe to grind, are laid bare for the centuries to view. Mr Bigge himself contrived the epitome, aided, apparently, by M'Arthur's triumphant son.

It was a strange set of documents, full of inaccuracy and prejudice. No petty scandal had been forgotten by Mr Bigge. Incidents long since lost in the mists of time rose up at his bidding like ghosts of the forgotten dead.

Added to the testimony of John M'Arthur (whom he praised in glowing terms), of the Marsdenites, the Bentites, and the flotsam of the New South Wales Corps, were Mr Brigge's own impressions, formed upon the most singular and unjudicial grounds.

He was "informed on good authority"; he had "heard from trusted people at Windsor"; he had even turned to Andrew Thompson's tomb-stone to read from it what he represented as Macquarie's true view of a living man, though all had been written of him dead.[8]

Macquarie felt that no chance was missed to impugn his policy and methods and the technique used was an old one. There was the air of deliberation in approach, the Antonian display of impartiality, the setting out of all the little good that could be said, the balanced moment of hesitation and weighing of the facts as Mr Bigge appeared to be making up his highly judicial mind. Then the sudden, swift stab to the rib.

Sometimes the diction resembles that of John M'Arthur. And he was not the only witness whose words were embodied as accepted fact, and served up as Mr Bigge's own weighty conclusions. Both in the recording of "evidence" and of findings there is slovenliness. The reports teem with error from end to end.

Often where the Commissioner has gone to endless trouble to elucidate the details of some old scandal with an array of damning facts, the "facts" prove to be mere gossip. He was not even accurate in stating the crimes for which many of the victims of his comments were sent to the Colony.

Mr Greenway, for instance, he branded as a bankrupt who had concealed his assets,[9] whereas his crime was forgery of an indorsement. He wrongly described D'Arcy Wentworth as having been a convict.

He devoted some pages—in a report written in 1822—to the question whether the Governor in January 1810 should have appointed Andrew Thompson, who died in October 1810, a justice of the peace at Windsor. He reached the conclusion that there had been no need for the appointment of an emancipist, since Mr George Palmer or Lieutenant Bell could have been commissioned.[10]

Actually George Palmer was not in the country then or for some time afterwards. He did not live in the Hawkesbury district till six years after the event. And when the appointment of Thompson had been made, Lieutenant Bell was under orders to leave for England.[11]

But it was his acts, more than his statements, which condemned Bigge. He had insisted that Macquarie's court-house at Hyde Park should be transformed into the Church of St James. He had shown a mysterious and irritable haste in forcing the reconstruction. Now the reason became apparent. He advised his brother-in-law and secretary, the former wine-merchant, Scott, to take Holy orders. His henchman was at once ordained and equipped with a fine advowson. Bigge then secured him immediate appointment to St James's as Archdeacon of Sydney, at the same salary which Macquarie had received as Governor, £2000 per annum.[12] Mr Marsden was not amused.

To Macquarie, the reports were "lying malicious and infamous", "of a very insidious and hostile nature"; yet he would have excused Bigge's "invective", had it not been that he himself stood accused of having deceived the Colonial Office.

He pronounced the charge just as slanderous and unfounded as the accusation that he had had three emancipated convicts—who were named—as his confidential advisers. To that statement he gave a "most positive contradiction".[13]

But he might just as well have saved his breath. His long letter to the

Minister remained secreted in the archives. He saw Charles Forbes; he importuned Royalty, but all to no purpose. The libels persisted, even in the *Edinburgh Review*, which he thought at one time of suing for libel. He could only content himself with the reflection "that a clean conscience may defy the whole world".

It was, indeed, only after he lay dead in 1824 that he found a ready, articulate defender in young William Charles Wentworth. That young man's own righteous wrath at calumnies against his father spurred him to do justice to Mr Bigge's "nauseous oleo . . . that chaotic and discordant jumble which Mr Bigge calls his report", in his inimitable idiom:

> Instead of confining his report to public objects, and public interests, he [Bigge] has polluted almost every page of it with private scandal and vituperation, as if these had been the exclusive ends of his appointment.
>
> This nauseous trash, the insertion of which could conduce to no one object of public utility, and could only, indeed, have been meant to inflict a gratuitous wound on individual feeling, he has not scrupled to promulgate to the world on the faith of mere ex-parte evidence collected with mischievous industry from the very dregs and refuse of the people—from the whores, and rogues and vaga-bonds of Sydney; on evidence, too, not even taken under the sanction of an oath, because forsooth his high mightiness could not brook the indignity of receiving a commission of the peace from His Majesty's representative.
>
> On such vague and contemptible authority as this, like a public scavenger, as he was most appropriately termed by an honourable member of the House of Commons, he has raked together all the dirt and filth, all the scandal, calumnies and lies, that were ever circulated in the Colony, with a good share of traditionary embellishment besides, and has thus given, as it were, "a local habitation and a name," to circumstances and rumours, which every consideration of public policy required to be forgotten, and which nothing but the most pitiful spirit, the most despicable curiosity, could ever have dragged forth from the oblivion into which they had happily subsided.[14]

It was full four years before Macquarie's friends could induce the Government to publish, as a Parliamentary paper, Macquarie's vigorous answer to Bigge.[15] Meantime, Mr Bigge's report appeared so large and imposing that Britons regarded him with something like awe.

III

In November, broken-hearted, Macquarie and Elizabeth returned to Mull.[16] They were now so poor that they had travelled in a Leith smack, "not being able to afford going by land". It was necessary to ward off the impor-tunities of his brother Charles with an unaccustomed burst of impatience:

> I greatly fear, my dear Charles, that you, *like* all the world, think I have an immense *fortune* concealed and that I have only to open my money bags and take out thousands of thousands. The real truth however, at present is, that I am no less than £500 in debt to Messrs. Coutts and Co. . . .

In Mull they found the winter storms in progress, the little island so lashed with the fury of the elements that the small vessels which carried their coals and their stores and belongings could not leave port.

For sixty days they were compelled to be the guests of a friendly Campbell. It was 19 January 1824 before they could go home.

They must have thought many a time of New South Wales with longing, and the greater portion of the colonial population had similar longings for their own return.

Already the main recommendations of the Bigge report were being implemented.

Orders had been sent in September 1822 to "discontinue any ornamental work" until plans of more immediate utility were completed. The importance of restoring transportation to its original character, so that it might be properly dreaded by wrongdoers and become once more "a salutary prevention of crime" was stressed vigorously in the Home Government's dispatches. The emancipist policy of settlement was thrown overboard, and one more in line with M'Arthur's aspirations replaced it.

IV

That summer a new song, sung for the first time at the emancipists' celebration of Foundation Day, pervaded New South Wales. Exclusives scowled as they heard the chorus rolling up from the tavern and the workshops:

> *Macquarie was the Prince of men!*
> *Australia's pride and joy!*
> *We ne'er shall see his like again;*
> *Bring back the OLD VICEROY!*[17]

The hero of the musical demonstration knew nothing of it. When eventually he and his wife were able to move into their own temporary home at Gruline, it was so small that the old Governor had no room to call his own, but was compelled to sit in the dining-room, while the wind and rain blew continuously through the doorway, and sometimes snatched the fire from the grate. There was "not one dry room."[18]

But though he had not the privacy in which to write a letter, he was never heard to complain, not even when he went on a four days' ride, during which he was soaked to the skin, on a sad visit to see his Uncle Lochbuy's widow, who lay ill in a house no better than his own.

Shaking with ague, he went about his estate, planning his new mansion house, setting out his plantations. Every day he rode his horse three miles over the slippery tracks of Mull to do duty as a village justice in the tiny settlement of Salen, where, upon the Bench, he employed himself, for whole days at a time, just as assiduously as he had formerly employed himself with his greater affairs in New South Wales.[19]

He seemed to be failing and often in pain as the rain-soaked spring unfolded. And on young Lachlan's birthday he rowed his wife and the boy out on the lake to a distant point.

There, leaning on his oars, he said, to his son, with a sweep of his hand,

"My reason for bringing you thus far is to show you the extent of *your estate*."

This Elizabeth thought very odd, but she said nothing, though she was very sad when he went to visit his sister Betty and a lady who had been kind to him, farther off, and was ten nights absent.

By this time it was plain what were his forebodings about the future. He went to Tobermory to pay his debts. He cleared himself of every obligation, performed every visit of civility or kindness which he felt due to make, settled all his business. Next he laid all the plans for the immediate future of Jarvisfield and made them so concisely clear to everyone that none could misunderstand his intentions.

In March his connections had begun to urge him to come up to London, for there was much to be done to his interest. He said he would go alone, since the weather was dreadful, Elizabeth had a bad cough, and young Lachlan had begun work with a tutor and must not be disturbed.

Elizabeth, at first, was not loath to be left behind, for she intended to use his absence to enlarge and improve the house, a project which he did not approve, since he hoped to build a mansion and would not throw away money on the leaking dwelling they were in. She settled that George, that faithful relic of his past, would go to be, as always, a "comfort without alloy" to his master.

The day before he was due to leave, though it was showery, Macquarie took his wife and son out upon the horses, showing them every line he had fixed for roads and enclosures and plantations round the estate.

He seemed determined to impress everything upon their memories. It was then that Elizabeth began to be a little frightened and said that she could not bear the thought of his going without her.

"Well, come!" said the old general.

But Elizabeth said that she could not help dress him as George did. He answered tartly, "I can dress myself."

They returned to the house. He cleaned out his writing desk, acting like a person who was going away and had no intention of returning. And presently he handed to Elizabeth a little box which she never before had seen, and which he had always kept to himself in a trunk with his particular and private papers.

When she opened it, she found that it contained trinkets, pocket-books, and different little things which had belonged to his long-lost Jane in the happy days of thirty years agone.

He said, "I give you this because there are things in it which might be useful to you and Lachlan."

But Elizabeth was astonished and alarmed.

"My God, you terrify me!" she said.

Without warning, the old man suddenly burst into tears as he said farewell, a thing those around him could not remember his ever having done before.

Young Lachlan watched him, from the top of a hill which gives a view of Mull and Loch-na-Keale, ride away from home for the last time.

V

Of all the unpleasant voyages of his days this was the worst. He was fatigued when he reached Edinburgh. His experience on the Leith packet made him "most heartily sick of all steamboats".[20] Nothing but necessity, he wrote, would ever induce him to take his family or go himself in one of them. His berth was so small he could scarce get into it.

But he reached London safely on 24 April and took lodgings at 49 Duke Street, a little street in St James's which runs from the Royal Academy to Willis's Rooms, a stone's-throw from St James's Palace.[21] He was giddy with a sick headache, stayed next day in bed, then went abroad. His old friends received him joyously, for he was a popular figure with them. There was no rest; he had never been so social since the happy days when he had been on Harrington's staff in the early summer of his life.

Yet in his contacts and movements there again seemed to be that sort of fatality which had guided his actions in Mull, as if he were discharging his obligations rather than promoting his own enjoyment. Everybody who meant anything in his past he saw, some of them so old as to seem like ghosts. He visited Balfour, the Morley family, Drummond, Dunlop, Nightingall, David Baird, Money, Charles Forbes and many more. He dined out again and again. He went to a rout given by his old Bombay friend, Mrs Carnac, and came home wet at half past two in the morning.[22]

He did not forget to drink his usual bumper on the anniversary of the capture of Seringapatam.

In between these activities he sandwiched the main business which had brought him southward, and negotiated for the opening of a church in his village of Salen.[23]

A day or two after he reached London he saw Wilmot Horton at the Colonial Office, and was told that his pension would be £1000 a year, paid from the day of his return to England.[24]

He had a friendly interview with Bathurst and wrote to Elizabeth:

> It is true the pension is granted and the official notification thereof from Lord Bathurst is as gratifying and complete as anything of that kind can be; but the world does not know this, and of course, I cannot publish it, or make it known except to my private friends; whereas this vile insidious Bigge Report is everywhere in the hands of everyone, and has gone all over the world. It must no doubt have made a very unfavourable impression even in the minds of His Majesty's Ministers against me.[25]

He urged the Colonial Secretary to clear him. Even after his death, the Colonial Office held that his pension "sufficiently shows the estimation in which his services to the public were held without additional steps being taken on the part of His Majesty's Government with a view to that object".[26]

He suggested that he might be given some mark of his sovereign's approval. The refusal reached him within seven days.[27]

May had come. London had responded to its magic as usual, and up in Mull, where Elizabeth was as busy as ever in her life, the weather suddenly became fine. The birches began to show their leaves and the ground was enamelled with primroses.[28]

Elizabeth lost her cough. She went to see her sister-in-law and her sister, Lochbuy's widow, for the first time since she had returned from New South Wales, this upon Oak Apple Day. That little Hugh Maclaine whom Macquarie had first set upon a military career when he was almost an infant in arms, during the days after Jane had died, was with his mother, Betty Maclaine, Macquarie's sister. He was a lieutentant-colonel now, commanding his patron's old regiment, the 77th.

Elizabeth had hardly returned home when she was called back once more with the news that her sister was dying. In all the distractions of her painful death-watch she lost some of her sense of what might be happening in the south. Then forebodings began to flood her mind.

She did not wait for her sister's end. She expected her man to come home, but after riding all the way to her house over the mountains—"no roads and in some places the paths very terrific"—she was disquieted to find only friends at Gruline, and not the figure she longed to see.

VI

At the end of the month there seemed no point to Macquarie in his remaining longer in London.

He was almost merry towards the end of his visit. He was able, even, to laugh a little at Lady Londonderry, Castlereagh's widow, when he called on her. "She does not appear to suffer from affliction from the death of her good amiable Lord. She has grown amazingly fat and appears very gay".[29]

On June 1 he took leave of Bathurst and of the Duke of York, who talked to him of Mull and his improvements and employments there. He went to see the King at Carlton House a few days later and received from him a kind farewell.[30]

But within 48 hours he was in bed and had written the final entry in his journal:

> *June* 11: Between 2 and 3 o'clock I awoke very ill. . . . I sent immediately for Dr. Andrews. . . .[31]

Next day he took a drive in the park in the glass-coach which he "had become so extravagant" as to hire; then wrote to Elizabeth of his intention to remain quiet for a week or so. The first two pages of his long letter were about her sister's illness.[32]

Mr Meiklejohn, the tutor, calmed her fears when the epistle arrived, and advised her to await the next post, which brought another letter:

> 49 Duke Street, St. James,
> London, 14th June, 1824.
> My dearest Love—I wrote to you on Saturday evening last, and in half an hour afterwards, your letter of the 17th instant, from Lochbuy, reached me.

This letter put me in high spirits, and feeling myself then in very good bodily health I ventured out to dine where I had been a fortnight engaged. I came home early, but this did not suffice, for I felt myself quite in a fever when I awoke the next morning. I kept my bed all day yesterday, and also all this day having merely got up to write this hurried scrawl to you, to keep my promise. I have the happiness of assuring you, however, that the two main points in this attack have been overcome, namely, the attack in my bowels and the strangary, the first by constant hot fomentation and the second by passing a catheter into the bladder, which gave me instant relief. I certainly suffered much pain, and now feel extremely weak in consequence; but you may assure yourself I am not in the smallest danger whatever. I shall write you again to-morrow to report the state of myself in point of health. I have not been able to get a frank, from having been all day confined to the house and, chiefly to my bed. With my love to yourself and Lachlan, and kind regards to Mr. Meiklejohn, I remain, my dear love, your affectionate husband, L.M. *Mrs. Macquarie.*

A week later he wrote to Charles telling of his representation to the Marquis of Huntley, to whom Charles had applied for help in becoming Governor of Dumbarton and of some negotiations about land with Sir Fitzroy McLean, whom he esteemed "a great Jew".

Elizabeth knew at once that "all was lost".[33] She flew as hastily as possible to London with her boy and his tutor and found her husband not pleased at her coming. He was thin and worn and fatigued, but he laughed when Lachlan indulged in childish narrative about events in the Highlands.

Next morning he got up early to write letters of introduction for some young friend going out to India, and this brought on a relapse. His old ague came back. The hand of death seemed at last actually upon him, and after that Elizabeth never left him save to find some lodgings. While she was away he wrote more letters and it made him worse. Now, those who watched over him, lived between hope and fear, sensing all the time that the end was near.

It came on 1 July 1824. Elizabeth knew of its approach. She sent for Lachlan and Sir Charles Forbes to come at once. Lachlan came first, full speed in Forbes's carriage, and they heard his lamentable crying on the stairs. It was some time before he could be calmed sufficiently to come to his father's pillow.

Elizabeth said. "My love, here's Lachlan come to see you", on which father and son kissed each other.

Sir Charles Forbes came about that time and agreed readily to do what Elizabeth knew would have to be done.

Elizabeth herself has described what followed:

I took Sir Charles into the small room to see my love, who fixed his eyes upon him with an expression so extremely tender, benevolent and kind, that I never saw anything so benign and beautiful in my life but once, and that was when our darling daughter regarded me with intelligence; her eyes were exactly like his.

After a little time Sir Charles left the room. I saw our love looking for him. I called him back.

The same extraordinary expression was renewed, and I observed him to say, "Fine fellow! fine fellow!" Those were his last words.

This was the way he always mentioned Sir Charles, who stroked our love on the face, and said, "I am obliged to leave you for a little time, but I shall soon be back, and I hope to find you better."

Our love shook his head with an intelligence which it was impossible not to understand. Time goes at such moments—one does not know how.

I think it was but a few minutes after my beloved looked earnestly, as George thought, for me.

Unhappily, I was not in the room, not apprehending the event so near.

He gave a heavy sigh before I entered. At that moment his eyes were turned up to heaven; he continued to breathe gently for some time; ceased without a groan or struggle of any kind.

I was on my knees beside him, and had hold of his shoulder. Every one was perfectly tranquil.

He was certainly undisturbed at the last, which is all that I can say in commendation of my services.

The only persons present were myself, his faithful servant George, and a manservant of Sir Charles Forbes's, who I had got to assist us for several days.

The moment of his departure was to me the most sublime in my life.

His countenance remained the same as usual, but strongly expressive of exhaustion and resignation.

Thus he died, in a thirty-four-shilling-a-week lodging in St James's.

Elizabeth's thought was that had Dr Wentworth and Dr Redfern been there they might have saved him.

Wellington and Bathurst spared empty carriages to follow him to the Hermitage Wharf. This was the realm's whole official tribute. The Duke of Argyll, Breadalbane, also Sir Alured Clarke and many Indian friends, were present to see him off.

Elizabeth took him back to Mull. On the way she retrieved, at Perth, the coffin which contained the remains of her little daughter.

They laid Macquarie in the new room which Elizabeth had built for him, his daughter's coffin on his breast, and the great vase which the colonists had given him and which he himself had chosen two months before in London at his head. A few Mull tenants and friends walked behind him to his grave.

Later he was buried with all his family in a granite tomb with a florid inscription which calls him "The Father of Australia".[34]

VII

In the mail which brought the tidings of his death to Sydney, young William Wentworth, now returned to the Colony, received "a private letter". It seems to have been one of those missives, the writing of which according to Elizabeth, had caused her husband's fatal relapse:

I have had two interviews with Mr. Peel. I found him most polite and a man of business. He has acceded to all my wishes; and the [Transportation Continuance] Act, in which there is a clause restoring the emancipists to all substantial rights and privileges, not only in New South Wales, but in all His Majesty's Dominions, has passed both Houses of Parliament and will receive the Royal Assent this week!!!

Mr Wentworth did not reveal the signature; but none was needed. The characteristic three exclamation marks identified the jubilation of the Old Viceroy at the success of his final battle for his beloved colonists.

The great bulk of the Sydney population put up its shutters when the news of his passing came, on a hot summer day. The *Gazette* draped its pages in black. The church bells tolled over many days at dawn and dusk.[35]

> *Hark! O'er the waves the plaints of mourning rise,*
> *And Grief's black ministers pervade the skies,*
> *And a sad voice proclaims from yonder shore:*
> *"Weep, Nation, weep! Macquarie is no more."*[36]

A sombre procession marched, in the November sunlight, through the shuttered town.

Two mutes . . . three mutes . . . two mutes; then all his chief associates, who had survived his time: Cowper, who had glorified him as the Young David when he had preached him into office; Antill and Campbell, who had come to the Colony with him and remained his staunch apostles throughout and who now stayed behind in New South Wales to keep his memory green; Redfern, and all the estates of the Colony; finally two more mutes, sad convict fellows.

Of all New South Wales the Government alone, now in the hands mainly of the M'Arthur faction, was not represented.

Cowper preached one more sermon for his old friend—this time upon a text from Isaiah "Arise, shine, for thy light is come, and the glory of the Lord is risen upon thee".[37]

The Colony behaved, in all things, in fact, as if the dead man were a king.

Inhabitants even held a meeting at Campbell's house to secure funds for a monument to him, a thing never before known in Australasia; yet in later years there were times when he was almost forgotten in New South Wales, and there was in Mull, for long, no public earnest that he had ever existed, save for the tombstone which Elizabeth raised for him on his lonely estate, and an institution which survived all his world and the prosperity which he had so coveted.

This was called the Macquarie Trust.[38] Elizabeth endowed it in 1829 to provide for ever for the future of the descendants of George, the little black Cochin boy whom he and Jane Jarvis had bought so many years before for eighty-five rupees, whom they had so gaily washed at Staffa Lodge in Calicut, who had been his constant companion all the rest of his life.

VIII

Charles Forbes presently moved to secure for Elizabeth a pension[39] such as other Governors' wives, though dowered with land grants and the products of their husbands' colonial indulgences, had rushed to secure for themselves. Her part of her husband's estate was a mere £300 a year and

Macquarie, of course, had never drawn his pension. But Elizabeth was noted writing tartly that "no necessity whatever exists on my part for requiring pecuniary assistance from any quarter whatever".[40] As Forbes apologized to Wilmot Horton, "You know the independence of the Highland character".[41] In the end the pension was paid— £400 a year, only twice that which the remarried Mrs Ellis Bent received after her husband had served five rebellious years in the Colony.

Later, Elizabeth appears in some negotiations between the colonists and their friends, an intermediary in the fight for trial by jury.

She seems in 1829 to have written the final postscript to the Macquarie age, in her last preserved letter to "My dear William", that young Mr Wentworth who was a very great man now out there in Sydney with all the emancipists and the smaller settlers rallying to his banner and Governors quailing before his glance and his oratory.

He did not awe Elizabeth. She remembered when the colonial world had looked askance as her husband honoured William, in his new-born manhood, with the first commission to fill a senior civil office granted to an Australian born.

Young D'Arcy, his brother, who through Macquarie also had come to be the first Australian native to hold a commission in the King's Army, was going to Port Jackson. So Elizabeth wrote to William, "I have given D'Arcy a commission to get your hair cut and in short, to make your appearance from top to toe so much a dandy as to be like other people, which I understand you have not been much since your return to Australia".[42]

Six years later Elizabeth died.[43] In a few years more young Lachlan was dead at thirty-two and, while the sons of his Uncle Charles fought with his executors for his estate, old Lachlan's grave lay forgotten in Mull.[44]

The Old Viceroy did not have reared for him in Australia the monument of bronze and stone dreamed of by his friends.

The commemorative urge of those who projected the idea of a memorial soon wilted. The staunch William Wentworth did his best to keep it alive, but soon before the general apathy even his stout heart quailed. His effort had produced only lists of promised subscriptions unpaid and of committee meetings lapsed for want of quorums.

Nevertheless, the name of Macquarie was not forgotten in the continent which he named. The curious, strongly persisting ancestral memory of the people, which throughout the ages has acted as the best embalming fluid for the remembrance of men who have touched the imagination of the oppressed and suffering, acted as a preservative. In fact, to some strangers, parts of Australia seemed in themselves one vast memorial:

Macquarie Street, Macquarie Hills, Macquarie River, Macquarie Island, Macquarie Pass, Macquarie Plains, Macquarie Electorate, Macquarie Ward, Macquarie Grove Aerodrome (built and named by the descendants of John M'Arthur), Mount Macquarie, Macquarie Falls, Macquarie Fields, Macquarie Hall, Garage, Teashop, Galleries; Fort Macquarie, Port Macquarie, Macquarie University . . .

The strange word came in time to permeate even the antipodean stratosphere.

Hundreds of thousands of Australians, descendants of the long-blended factions of the Macquarie age and of vast later human infusions, came to hear it spoken nightly as the name of a great broadcasting network, the voices of which reach the remotest corners of the Australian continent.

APPENDIX I

The Portraits of Macquarie

THE EARLIEST KNOWN PORTRAIT OF MACQUARIE was that painted by John Opie, "one of the most eminent artists now in London", in 1805. The subject was forty-four years of age when he gave sittings for the picture, and serving on the staff of the Earl of Harrington, as Assistant Adjutant-General of the London Military District.

Macquarie noted in his Journals that the picture was "reckoned by all who saw it to be very like me". For it he paid twenty-eight guineas.

In November 1821, a little before the Governor's departure from New South Wales, a project was put forward in the Hawkesbury district to have a portrait of Macquarie painted by one of the two Reads then painting in the Colony.

There exists a letter from William Cox (*Mitchell Library MSS., Am.* 17), dated in December 1821, in which he says: "On Saturday evening I received a letter from Major-General Macquarie. . . . The General expresses the strongest feelings of pleasure and satisfaction for our offering to have his portrait taken, but as it cannot be done in the country and the length of time and other circumstances that may occur in getting it done in England, he very politely wishes his friends not to persevere in it, and will no doubt thank them personally for their offer when he meets them here to receive the address."

On 4 January 1822 the Hawkesbury settlers suggested that Macquarie might have his portrait painted in England at their expense. To this offer he replied, "I with sincere pleasure and pride acquiesce in your request by agreeing to sit for my portrait on my arrival in England, and I shall ever bear in mind a lively recollection of the honour thus conferred on me."

In the *Sydney Gazette*, 8 February 1822, p. 3, a notice states that "the last likeness of our late revered Governor, which was taken by Mr. Reed, Senr., at the instance of the Honourable the Judge Advocate, is pronounced to be the best performance yet to come forth from the pencil of that artist, and will afford every beholder as faithful a delineation of feature and expression as could possibly be exhibited on canvas. We are informed that Mr. Reed is engaged to paint the picture of Major-General Macquarie intended to be placed in the Town Hall at Windsor, and we anticipate with pleasure to ourselves and posterity an additional reputation to the artist in the able accomplishment of this very gratifying subject."

On 15 May 1823 Read, Senior, advertised that "he has just finished some portraits [of Governor Macquarie]. The likeness is a most striking one, being finished from life."

The Mitchell Library now possesses a portrait in mixed media (reproduced in this book). This bears on its face the words in the handwriting of Richard Read, Senior, (who professed to have been a pupil of Reynolds): "Finished from Life by Read Senr., Feby. 11, 1822."

On the back of the picture—also in Read's handwriting—appears this inscription: "*Sydney*, 1822. *Take notice that none are original pictures of Governor Macquarie but what has got the name of Read marked in Latin on the seal annexed. Governor Macquarie never sat to any artist in the Colony but to Read Senr. Lego artist.*" The seal, a male head facing dexter, is intact.

S

This inscription seems to suggest clearly that there were imposters abroad in the land.

There is only one other picture signed with the "*Lego*" signature in existence—a portrait of a boy which, has been proved on comparison with an authenticated portrait to be that of Lachlan Macquarie, the younger. It bears the date 1823. The writer discovered it in the collection of Mr E. A. Crome, of Sydney, who has since lent it to the Mitchell Library for exhibition.

It is to be noted that, in referring to the authenticated (1822) portrait of Macquarie in the Mitchell Library, on which the inscription is in Read's own handwriting, Read mentions that it was "finished from life". He uses exactly the same phrase in his advertisement in the *Gazette* in May 1823. In the *Gazette* notice of February 1822 the faithfulness of the likeness in Read's painting is mentioned; Read in his 1823 advertisement makes a point of the same quality in the picture. It seems almost certain that the original from which the copies were made in 1823 was that now in the possession of the Mitchell Library Trustees, or that it is a certified copy of that original.

There is no evidence that Read or anybody else ever painted a later portrait of Macquarie, but a very fine likeness of an officer hangs in the court-house at Windsor and is pointed out to visitors as a portrait of Macquarie painted by Read, Senior.

On the evidence of the two striking and authenticated portraits by Opie and Read, Senior, and of some others which are not so excellent but sufficiently like to be adduced as evidence, the Windsor portrait is not one of Macquarie and bears no resemblance to him. It is difficult to believe even that it was intended to be a likeness, for so excellent a painter could scarcely have failed to capture some of the semblance of that unusual countenance. As it is, he has produced a portrait full of character of somebody entirely unlike the subject of the two authenticated portraits of Macquarie in anatomical conformation, expression, texture of skin, texture, colour and set of hair, and general characteristics. And it certainly is not the likeness of an ailing man more than sixty years old. Moreover, as has been confirmed by the experts of the Royal United Service Institution, the uniform worn by the officer in the portrait is that of a *Lieutenant*-Governor of the period of 1822 when Macquarie was a full Governor.

Mr Norman Lindsay agrees that the Windsor painting is not by Read, Senior, and that it is not a work of the period in which it was supposed to have been painted. In this he is certainly borne out by comparison with another painting in oils of Macquarie which hangs in the Dixson Gallery of the Mitchell Library.

This fourth portrait is easily identifiable from the 1822 watercolour as a likeness of Macquarie.

Though it is labelled as being by R. Read, Senior, Sir William Dixson, more frank than the New South Wales Justice Department, and more careful about his authentications, informs me that there is no signature on it. He writes: "When I purchased it, over 30 years ago, I gathered, for some reason or other, that it had come from Tasmania, but heard no further particulars. As both those who had to do with buying and selling it to me have been dead for some years, it is now impossible for me to obtain further particulars."

It is taken at a period earlier than the 1822 likeness which is authenticated by Read himself. It is, moreover, the only acceptable portrait in oils of the Governor which seems to have been painted during his period in Australia.

The Under-Secretary of the New South Wales Justice Department was asked for authorities to establish the identity of the sitter for the Windsor portrait and of its artist. His officer went to considerable trouble, but could produce no vestige of proof, or of matter seriously contributory to proof, that the painting was of Macquarie. The

Department has no record of how, when, and by whom it was placed in the court-house. It was stated that some person at the Art Gallery had said that the signature of Read appeared on the painting, but this witness was not produced. And a request to be allowed to examine the signature, and, in the alternative, that the painting be brought to the Mitchell Library or Sydney Art Gallery for expert examination was met with a terse refusal.

On the evidence which the Justice Department has to produce—none—no jury would, after comparison of the painting with other portraits, convict the Windsor portrait of being a likeness of Macquarie, especially of him in old age, and it would be difficult for the Department to prove it a Read by any means short of producing a well-authenticated signature, which it does not seem to be able to do.

The portrait looks as if it might have been produced later than Macquarie's time by some historically-minded artist who had been told that the Governor was an autocrat and who was determined not to fail in making him look like one. Or it may be a portrait of Lieutenant-Colonel Erskine, who was Lieutenant-Governor in 1822.

Sir William Dixson owns two small sketches which look as if they might have been experimental notes for the Windsor portrait. They differ from each other and from the Windsor portrait itself in some details. One is of the subject, showing him with light-coloured hair and a somewhat youthful face; the other of an old, sick man, darker of hair. This version differs in the length of torso painted from its fellow. Neither is very well painted. But about these there is nothing to show their origin or the name of the artist.

There is no evidence that Macquarie at any time sat for his portrait after returning to England. Had he done so he almost certainly would have mentioned the matter in his Journals.

Only one other creditable portrait of Macquarie exists—a charming little minia-ture in the possession of the Hobart Museum and Art Gallery, Tasmania, to which it was presented by Dr Giblin, along with the portrait on ivory of Elizabeth Macquarie, of which a copy appears in this volume. It purports to be signed by Read, Senior, and is dated 1819, but seems to represent a much younger, healthier and better-pre-served man than the Governor then could have been. Nevertheless, it corroborates the likeness and expression of the two authenticated pictures in the Mitchell Library and provides further condemnation of the Windsor portrait.

There is one other picture—a miniature presented to the Mitchell Library by the Lawson Family, which looks more like a portrait of the ghost of Macquarie than a portrayal of the man himself. Its resemblances tend to confirm the 1822 portrait and discredit the Windsor one.

Notes on Regiments in which Macquarie served

THE 84th REGIMENT (1776-81)

The regiment in which Macquarie first served was not the old 84th raised by Sir Eyre Coote which fought at Arcot, Wandewash, Villova, and Pondicherry, but the second corps of the name—the Royal Highland Emigrant Corps—which was raised in America by Colonel Allan Maclean, "out of the families of soldiers of the 42nd and the old 77th and 78th Highlanders who had settled in Canada in 1763". It defended Quebec against Arnold and afterwards saw frontier service. The second battalion was raised from settlers in Nova Scotia and served in Carolina and Virginia. Both battalions were disbanded in Canada and Nova Scotia in 1784.

THE 71st HIGHLANDERS (1781-4)

The 71st Regiment was raised for service in America by Major-General Simon Fraser, Master of Lovat, in December 1777. It was known as the Glasgow Highland Regiment of Foot. It served under Lord Cornwallis in the Carolinas and Virginia and the greater part was included in the surrender at Yorktown. This fate Macquarie escaped through being at that time in Jamaica. It is not to be confused with the 71st (Highland Light Infantry.)

THE 77th (EAST MIDDLESEX) REGIMENT (1787-1801)

The 77th Regiment in 1787 was the third of the number and the junior of four regiments raised in that year at the cost of the East India Company when England was threatened with involvement in European war. After the danger had evaporated the Company repudiated its obligations. The regiment had a narrow escape from disbandment, and Macquarie from being sent back to his farm. Mr Pitt, however, countered the Company's sally with the Declaratory Bill, which provided that "the expense of raising, maintaining and transporting such corps as may be deemed necessary for the security of the British Possessions and Territories in the East Indies shall be defrayed out of the revenues accruing from such possessions and territories". After its Indian wars, the regiment returned home in 1807, was retitled as the "East Middlesex" and later the "Duke of Cambridge's Own". It was at Walcheren and played a glorious part with Picton's division in the Peninsula. Its men were among the heroes of El Bodon and fought in the assaults of Ciudad Rodrigo and Badajoz, until its strength was so reduced by battle that it was no longer battleworthy. It was in the Crimean War under General Buller, served in Bulgaria, was through the Siege of Sebastopol fought at Alma, Inkerman on the two assaults on the Redan, and in June 1857 was sent to New South Wales, which it left to take part in the closing phases of the Indian Mutiny. Its battles and officers gave names to many Sydney streets. Shadforth Street, Mosman, was one.

THE 86th REGIMENT (SHROPSHIRES, ROYAL COUNTY DOWNS) (1801-5)

The 86th Regiment was originally the Shropshire Volunteers Regiment of Foot, later transmuted into the 2nd Battalion Royal Irish Rifles (Royal County Down Regiment). It bears on its helmet badge the words: "Egypt, India, Bourbon, Cape of Good Hope, Talavera, Busaco, Fuentes de Onoro, Ciudad Rodrigo, Badajoz, Salamanca, Vittoria, Nivelle, Orthcs, Toulouse, Peninsula, Central India, Egypt."

It was the third of the name raised in Shropshire, Lancashire, and West Riding by Colonel Cornelius Cuyler. It served first as a marine corps and most of its personnel escaped when H.M.S. *Boyne* blew up at the Nore in 1794. After many hazardous naval adventures, it was sent to Madras in 1799, "a splendid body of men, 1300 strong". It was part of Admiral Blankett's force in the Red Sea in 1801. It served in Guzerat in 1801-4 and joined Lord Lake in 1805 at Bhurtpore. It returned to England in 1806. Later it took part in the capture of the Cape of Good Hope.

THE 73rd REGIMENT (SECOND BLACK WATCH) (1805-10)

The 73rd (Perthshires) Regiment was originally the 2nd Battalion of the Black Watch (42nd Foot, Royal Highlanders). It was embodied at Perth in 1780, and landed in India under Colonel Norman Macleod on 21 January 1781. It served against Haidar Ali and Tippoo. It withstood investment by the whole of Tippoo's forces at Mangalore in 1783 and did not evacuate till February 1784, and then only on the most honourable terms. In 1786 it became a separate corps, numbered the 73rd Foot, and its facings were altered from blue to dark green. It fought against Tippoo in 1790-1 and took part in the Battle of Seringapatam in May 1799, having in the interval been employed against the Dutch in Ceylon and the Polygars. Leaving New South Wales (1810-14), for Ceylon, members of headquarters and flank companies became the first British soldiers to travel *via* New Guinea, New Britain, and the Moluccas. In 1881 it reverted to its old position as 2nd Battalion of the Black Watch.

At the period of Macquarie's command up to 1809 there was only one battalion of the regiment, but when this was sent to New South Wales a second was formed and fought with Halkett's Brigade and Baron Alten's division in the Peninsula. It was at Quatre Bras and Waterloo, where it had 22 out of 23 officers killed or wounded. It was disbanded at Chelmsford in May 1817.

BIBLIOGRAPHY

STATUTES, OFFICIAL DOCUMENTS, RECORDS, REPORTS AND PARLIAMENTARY PAPERS, MANUSCRIPTS, JOURNALS AND PRINTED BOOKS CONSULTED DURING THE PREPARATION OF THIS WORK.

Lettered numbers are catalogue numbers of the items listed in the Mitchell Library, Sydney, Australia. In referring to printed books and pamphlets, full titles are not always given, but Australian works published before 1838 carry their reference numbers in Mr Justice J. A. Ferguson's excellent *Bibliography of Australia*, 1784-1838, in square brackets, thus: [1000]. In the Ferguson *Bibliography*, under these numbers, the student will usually find a full and scholarly collation and description of the work mentioned. Books and documents, other than those herein mentioned, have been referred to by the author, but are not catalogued because he has made no use, or only a very cursory use, of them. There are, also, a few sets of papers and works which he has not had an opportunity to peruse satisfactorily.

SECTION I

(*Referring to India*)

MANUSCRIPTS

A768-A771. Macquarie, Lachlan, Journals, 1787-1807. 4 vols.
A769A.   Macquarie, Lachlan, Journal sent to Charles Forbes, giving details of the War against Tippoo Sahib in 1799, 14 April to 4 May 1799.
A787-A796. Macquarie, Lachlan, Original Letterbooks, 1793-1809. 10 vols.

PRINTED BOOKS AND JOURNALS

Annual Register, 1787-1808.
Biddulph, Colonel John, *The Nineteenth and Their Times*. London, 1899.
Bowring, Lewin B., *Haidar Ali and Tipu Sultan*. Oxford, 1893.
Busteed, H. E., *Echoes of Old Calcutta*. 1908.
Capper, J., *The Three Presidencies of India*.
Cornwallis, Marquis, *Despatches*.
Dalrymple, A., *Oriental Repertory*. 2 vols, London, 1793-1808.
Dirom, Major, *Narrative of the War with Tippoo Sahib*. 1793.
Douglas, James, *Bombay and Western India*. London, 1893.
Elers, George, *Memoirs*. Monson and Gower Edition, 1903.
Fay, Mrs Eliza, *Letters from India*. E. M. Forster's Edition, 1925.
Forbes, J., *Oriental Memoirs*. 2 vols., London, 1813.
Fortescue, Sir John, *History of the British Army*.
Hickey, William, *Memoirs*. Spencer Edition, 1923.
Hook, Theodore, *Life of Sir David Baird*. 2 vols, London, 1832.
Hunter, Sir Martin and Lady, *Journal*.
Innes, Lieut.-Col. P. R., *History of the Bengal European Regiment*. 1885.
Lushington, S. R., *The Life of General Lord Harris*. London, 1840.

Mackenzie, Lieut. Roderick, *Sketch of the War with Tippo Sultaun*. 2 vols, Calcutta, 1793-4.
Moor, Edward, *Narrative of Captain Little's Detachment Serving with Purseram Bhow*.
Munro, Captain Innes, *Narrative of the Operations on the Coromandel Coast in 1789*.
Norie, J. W., *The Country Trade or Free Mariner's Pilot*.
Scurry, James, *The Captivity, Sufferings and Escape of James Scurry*. 1824.
Teignmouth, Lord, *Life and Letters*. 2 vols, London, 1843.
Thornton, Lieut.-Col. L. H., *Light and Shade in Bygone India*. London, 1927.
Tilley, A. W., *The English People Overseas*.
Wellesley, Marquis, *Despatches and Correspondence*. 1858.
Wellington, The Duke of, *Despatches from India*.
Wheeler, J. T., *Early Records of British India*. London, 1878.
Wright, Arnold, *Annesley of Surat and His Times*. London, 1918.

REGIMENTAL HISTORIES

Cannon, Richard, *Historical Records of the Seventy-third Regiment*.
Chichester, H. M., and Burges-Short, Geo., *Records and Badges of the British Army*. London, 1900.
Lawrence-Archer, Major J. H., *The British Army: Its Regimental Records, Badges, Devices, etc*. London, 1888.

SECTION II

(*Referring to New South Wales*)

MANUSCRIPTS AND COLLECTIONS OF FAMILY PAPERS IN THE MITCHELL LIBRARY, SYDNEY

THE MACQUARIE PAPERS

C126.	Macquarie, Elizabeth, Journal of Voyage to Australia.
	Lachlan Macquarie's Papers:
A772.	Memoranda, 1808-21.
A773.	Journal, 1816-18.
A774.	Journal, 1818-22. 3 vols.
A775.	Journal of a Voyage to England from New South Wales, 1822.
A776¹	Journal of a Tour of the Continent of Europe, 1822-3.
A776²	Journal of a Visit to London in 1824.
A777.	Journal of a Tour in Van Diemen's Land and to Port Stephens and Newcastle, 1811.
A778.	Journal of a Tour in the Interior of New South Wales, 1810.
A779-A780.	Journal of a Tour to the Western Districts of New South Wales, 1815. 2 vols.
A781.	Journal of a Tour to Newcastle and the Hunter River, 1818.
A782.	Journal of a Tour to the Western and Southern Districts of New South Wales, 1820.
A783.	Journal of a Visit to Bathurst, 1821.
A784.	Journal of a Visit to Van Diemen's Land, 1821.
A785.	Journal of a Visit to the Northern Settlements, 1821.
A786.	Journal of a Tour of the Cowpastures and Illawarra, 1822.
A796-A797.	Letterbooks of Lachlan Macquarie 1809-20.

A798.	Commission as Governor of Colonel Macquarie.
A799.	Commission and Instructions as Governor of Colonel Macquarie.
A800.	Settlers' Address to Governor Macquarie, 1821.
A800[1]	Certified Copies of the Letters of Governor Lachlan Macquarie to Earl Bathurst, Colonial Secretary, in Answer to Mr J. T. Bigge, July 1822 and October 1823.
Safe, 15, No. 6.	Letters to Charles Forbes (1809-10) and Miscellaneous Correspondence and Documents.
Safe, 15.	Letters to Governor King, Bligh, etc.
Am 2.	Various Newspaper Cuttings and Correspondence.
Am 15.	Copies of Correspondence Relative to the Granting of a Pension to Elizabeth Macquarie (1927) and other Documents.
Am 17.	Various Documents and Correspondence, Newspaper Cuttings, etc., including Letter to Thomas Coutts, 10 November 1812.
A423.	Correspondence of Lachlan Macquarie with the Rev. T. Reddall.
A1749.	Correspondence of Allan Cunningham with Governor Macquarie, 1817-21.
	A large collection of original letters and holograph copies in the Colonial Secretary's In-letters and other collections of Government and private papers in the Mitchell Library, Sydney.

The Official Papers of Governor Macquarie:

A1190-A1193.	The Governor's Dispatches, 1813-23.
A339.	Proclamations, 1810-18.
D145-D146.	Government and General Orders, 1810-18.
A1932.	Copies of Letters to the Governor, 28 December 1809 to 3 February 1810.

OTHER MITCHELL LIBRARY MANUSCRIPTS AND COLLECTIONS

Safe, 9.	Antill, H. C., Journal of a Voyage to Australia and of Tour to the Interior to Bathurst, 1815.
C720.	Arnold, Dr Joseph, Journals, 27 August 1810 to 15 December 1815.
A1849[2]	Arnold, Dr Joseph, Correspondence, Sydney, 1810.
A329.	Bank of New South Wales, Manuscript Records, 1818-39.
D168.	Mss. Copy of the Charter granted to the Bank of New South Wales by Governor Brisbane 31 October 1823.
A80[4]-A85.	The Banks Papers.

Brabourne Collection:

A78-[4].	Papers Dealing with Australia. 1801-20.
A78-[5].	Bligh Correspondence, vol. VI. 1805-11.
A79-[1].	Caley Correspondence, vol. VIII. 1795-1808.

The Banks Papers:

C181.	Miscellaneous Correspondence. 1778-1819.
C196.	Blaxland Family Papers. 1793-1923.

C129.   Blaxland, Gregory, Journal of a Tour of Discovery Across the Blue
                   Mountains. 1813.

                   Collections Relating to Governor Bligh:

D144.   Bligh Papers on the Military Rebellion, January 1808 and
                   Afterwards.
Safe, 19.   Bligh, William, Letters, 1803-10.
A1982.   Documents Relating to the Arrest of Governor Bligh.

                   The Bonwick Transcripts:

A2000-1-2-3-4.   Selections of Biographical Extracts.
                   The Inquiry into the Affairs of New South Wales by Mr J.
                   T. Bigge. 1819-22, Appendices, Boxes 1-28.
                   Selections from the Papers of Missionaries in the South Pacific,
                   Boxes 49-51.
A2130-A2131.   Statistics and other Papers from the Bigge Appendix.
A314.   The Papers of William Broughton and His Successors. 25 May
                   1815 to 3 May 1831.
A589-A605.   The Papers of James Erskine Calder.
                   The Colonial Secretary, In-Letters. 1810-23.
C708.   Cox, William, Narrative of Proceedings . . . in Constructing a
                   Road from Captain Woodriff's Farm, on the Nepean River . . .
                   to Bathurst Plains. 1814.

                   Papers of Allan Cunningham:

A1744.   Journal.
A1749.   Correspondence with the Colonial Government 1817-31.
A362.   Description of the Country North of Bathurst.

                   Ellis Papers:

Am. 17.   Correspondence re Details of Lachlan Macquarie's Life.

                   Evans, Geo. William:

A1190.   Report on Discoveries Near Bathurst (G.D. I. 9, of 1815, pp.
                   593-4, 596-7).
C709.   Journal of an Expedition Overland from Jervis Bay to Mr
                   Broughton's Farm, Near Appin, 20 March-7 April 1812.
B795.   Notebook Containing Notes taken during Tour beyond the
                   Blue Mountains, 26 November 1813 to 8 January 1814.
B156.   Sketch of Tour of Van Diemen's Land.
A144, A1451.   The Papers of Francis Howard Greenway and His Successors.
C225-C226.   Harris, S. L., Report and Estimates of the Value of Improvements
                   . . . Buildings of Sydney, Parramatta, Windsor, Liverpool and
                   Campbelltown, 25 December 1822 to 24 December 1823, etc.
A859-A860.   The Papers of Rowland Hassall.
A1677-1-2-3-4.   The Samuel Hassall Correspondence.
A1976.   The Papers of the King Family.

                   Papers of William Lawson:

A1952.   The Lawson Papers, 1784-1822, including holograph letters from
                   Governor Macquarie (6 July 1815, 15 April and 9 November
                   1819, 6 March 1820) relative to affairs in the Bathurst District.
C120-1.   Journal of Journey Through Country to the North of Bathurst.

C120-².   Journal of Tour from Bathurst to the Liverpool Plains, January 1822.

C123.   Journal of a Tour of Discovery Across the Blue Mountains, 1813.

A2897-A2967.   M'Arthur Family Papers.

M'Garvie Papers:

C254.   Narrative of the Last Days of General Macquarie.

The Marsden Papers:

A1992.   Letters to the Rev. Samuel Marsden. 1810-37.

A1993.   Letters and Reports of the Rev. Samuel Marsden. 1810-37.

A1995-A1996.   Letters of the Rev. Samuel Marsden, the London Missionary Society, 1802-36 and South Sea Missionaries, 1810-26.

A1997.   Journals of the Rev. Samuel Marsden, 1814-23.

A1998.   The Rev. Samuel Marsden's Replies to Accusations, 1825-8.

A1999.   The Rev. Samuel Marsden, Essays and Sermons, 1810-13.

C244.   A Collection of Holograph Letters to and from S. Marsden, with Newspaper Cuttings and other Documents, 1793-1928.

D167.   Miscellaneous Documents Connected with the Rev. Samuel Marsden, 1793-1828.

James Meehan's Papers:

C90.   Memorandum of a Tour from Sydney to Jervis Bay, 3 March to 14 April 1818.

C330.   Field Book of Journey from Windsor to the Hunter River.

I128.   Original Sketch Map of Journey into the Interior, showing Lake George.

A334.   Military Papers of New South Wales, 1789-1923.

A254-A256.   The Piper Family Papers, vols I, II, and III.

A423.   The Reddall Papers.

A106-A111.   The Riley Family Papers.

Safe, 15, No. 3.   Letters from Edward Riley (1811-14), mainly concerned with the import of spirits.

A1940-A1941.   The Papers of Charles Throsby, 1818-24.

A751-A763.   The Wentworth Family Papers.

C122.   Wentworth, W. C., Journal of a Tour of Discovery Across the Blue Mountains.

D88.   The Wentworth Accounts.

B196.   Medical Notebook and Receipts of Dr Wentworth.

PAPERS IN THE NATIONAL LIBRARY, CANBERRA

A141.   Bent, Ellis, Letters, 1809-12.

PAPERS IN POSSESSION OF THE BANK OF NEW SOUTH WALES

Minute Books of the Bank of New South Wales, No. 1.

BRITISH STATUTES DEALING WITH NEW SOUTH WALES

27 Geo. III, c. 2 (1787): To enable His Majesty to establish a Court of Criminal Jurisdiction on the East Coast of New South Wales.

46 Geo. III, c. 28 (1806): Extends Transportation till 1813.

53 Geo. III, c. 39 (1813): Extends Act above for one year.

54 Geo. III, c. 15 (1813): An Act for the more easy recovery of debts in New South Wales.

54 Geo. III, c. 30 (1813): Extends Transportation Act for two years.

54 Geo. III, c. 145: Removes the effects of corruption of blood and forfeiture of real property save from those convicted of treason and murder, as from 27 July 1814.

55 Geo. III, c. 156 (1815): Amends Transportation Act and continues it for one year.

56 Geo. III, c. 27 (1816): Extends Transportation Act to 1821.

59 Geo. III, c. 60: To permit the Archbishops of Canterbury and York and the Bishop of London to admit persons into Holy Orders specially for the colonies. (22 July 1819.)

59 Geo. III, c. 101 (1819): Amendment to the Transportation Act Amendment Act of 1816, to continue it with increased Royal powers to May 1821.

59 Geo. III, c. 114 (1819): To stay proceedings against the Governor or other persons concerned in the levy in New South Wales of duties not authorized by Parliament. The duties were given legislative authority and the Governor was authorized to impose a duty on spirits.

59 Geo. III, c. 122 (1819): To authorize vessels under 350 tons to carry on trade and commerce between the United Kingdom and New South Wales.

1 & 2 Geo. IV, c. 62 (1820): Extends the period of protection in the New South Wales Duties Act until 1 January 1822.

1 & 2 Geo. IV, c. 6 (1821): Extends Transportation Acts for two years.

1 & 2 Geo. IV, c. 8 (1821): Extends New South Wales Duties Act to January 1823. (24 March 1821.)

3 Geo. IV, c. 96 (1822): An Act to extend the Duties Validation Act to 1 January 1824, and to empower the Governor to levy duty up to 10s. on British and West Indian spirits, and up to 15s. on spirits from other sources; and on all other goods not the produce of the United Kingdom, duty not exceeding 15 per cent *ad valorem*; also, empowering the Governor to make regulations and punish breaches of them.

HOUSE OF COMMONS PAPERS

A Return of the Number of Persons, Male or Female, who have been Transported as Criminals to New South Wales since the first establishment of the Colony. 15 February 1810 [496].

Twenty-eighth Report from the Select Committee on Police and Convict Establishments. Reprinted, 7 June 1810 [497].

Report from the Select Committee on Transportation, with Minutes of Evidence and other Documents. 10 July 1812 [543].

Letters and Enclosures of Earl Bathurst to Governor Macquarie and of Governor Macquarie to Earl Bathurst, concerning the Report of the Committee on Transportation, 1812. 11 June 1816 [646].

Report from, and Minutes of Evidence taken before, the Select Committee on Jails and Prisons. 12 July 1819 [747].

Report of the Commissioner of Inquiry into the State of the Colony of New South Wales and its Government, Management of Convicts, their Character and Habits. 5 August 1822 [854].

(Q991/B., Mitchell Library, Manuscript Index to Names in Report.)

Report of the Commissioner of Inquiry, on the Judicial Establishments of New South Wales, and Van Diemen's Land. 21 February 1823 [891].

Report of the Commissioner of Inquiry, on the State of Agriculture and Trade in the Colony of New South Wales. 13 March 1823 [892].

Return to an Address of the Honourable the House of Commons, to His Majesty, dated the 3rd of July 1823;—for a Copy of the Instructions Given by Earl Bathurst to Mr Bigge, etc. Letters from Bathurst to Bigge, 6 January 1819; and from Bathurst to Viscount Sidmouth, 23 April 1817. 7 July 1823 [893].

No. 1: Copy of a Report by the late Major-General Macquarie on the Colony of New South Wales, to Earl Bathurst, in July 1822. No. 2: Extract of a Letter from Major-General Macquarie to Earl Bathurst, in October 1823, in Answer to certain part of the Report of Mr Commissioner Bigge, on the State of the said Colony. 25 June 1828 [1192].

HOUSE OF COMMONS DEBATES

Relevant Debates on Transportation and the Affairs of New South Wales, 1810-22

1810: 4 and 9 May and 5 June.
1811: 13 February and 4 March.
1812: 4 February and 12 February (Committee on Transportation).
1813: 8 January.
1815: 22 June, Bill to extend the duration of Transportation Acts.
1816: 20 February, First and Second Readings of Transportation Bill.
    3 April, Tierney's Address.
1817: 10 March, Bennet's Petition.
1819: 18 February, Bennet moves for the appointment of Committee on Jails.
    1 March, Castlereagh's Motion—agreed to—for Appointment of Committee on Jails and Prisons.
    23 March, Brougham presents petition of Blake and Williams.
    7 April, Bennet's Motion (lost) to prevent departure of female convict ship.
    29 June, New South Wales Duties Bill (59 Geo. III, c. 114), First Reading.
    2 July, Committee Stages.

BRITISH DEPARTMENTAL PAPERS

C.O. 201. Colonial Office: Original Correspondence, 1784-1823.
H.O. 10. Home Office: Convict Papers, New South Wales, 1788-1823.
A1267. Missing Dispatches, Mitchell Library Transcripts.
P.C. Privy Council Registers: Orders in Council concerning Australia.

HISTORICAL RECORDS AND JOURNALS

Historical Records of Australia, Series I, vols 1-2; Series III, vols 1-4; Series IV, vol. 1.
Historical Records of New South Wales, vols I-VII.
Royal Australian Historical Society of New South Wales, Journal and Proceedings, vols I-XXXII.

CONTEMPORARY NEWSPAPERS AND PERIODICALS

Annual Register, 1805-23.
Australasian Pocket Almanac, 1822.
Australian. 1825-30 [931].

New South Wales Pocket Almanac, 1811-21.

Derwent Star and Van Diemen's Land Intelligencer, No. 7, 3 April 1810; 20 November 1811 to 7 February 1812 [494, 535].

Van Diemen's Land Gazette and General Advertiser, Nos 2-9 1814 [596].

Hobart Town Gazette and Southern Reporter, 1816-25 [649].

Sydney Gazette and New South Wales Advertiser, 1810-22 [383].

BOOKS AND OTHER ITEMS ON EXPLORATION

Blaxland, Gregory, *A Journal of a Tour of Discovery Across the Blue Mountains in New South Wales.* B. J. Holdsworth, London, 1823 [894]; reprinted, Sydney, 1870 Edinburgh, 1893, and Sydney, 1904 and 1913.

Field, Barron, (Editor), *Geographical Memoirs on New South Wales . . . and Van Diemen's Land.* John Murray, London, 1825 [1009].

King, Phillip P., *Narrative of a Survey of the Intertropical and Western Coasts of Australia. Performed between the years* 1818 *and* 1822. John Murray, London, 1826 [1084]; 1827 [1130].

Oxley, J., *Journals of Two Expeditions into the Interior of New South Wales . . . in the Years* 1817-18. John Murray, London, 1820 [796].

Reid, Thomas, *Two Voyages to New South Wales and Van Diemen's Land.* London, 1822 [876].

SOME OTHER AUTHORITIES CONSULTED

Abbott, J. H. M., and others, *The Macquarie Book: The Life and Times of Governor Lachlan Macquarie (Art in Australia).* Sydney, 1921.

Arago, J. E. V., *Promenade autour du Monde, pendant les années* 1817, 1818, 1819 *et* 1820 *sur les corvettes du Roi L'Uranie et La Physicienne, Commandées par M. Freycinet.* 2 vols. Leblanc, Paris, 1822 [850].

Atkinson, James, *An Account of the State of Agriculture and Grazing in New South Wales, including Observations on the Soils, etc.* London, 1826 [1054].

Bank of New South Wales, *Rules and Regulations for the Conduct and Management of the Bank of New South Wales. Framed by a Committee appointed for that purpose.* G. Howe, Sydney, 1817 [669].

Beattie, J. W., *Glimpses of the Lives and Times of the Early Tasmanian Governors.* Hobart, 1905.

Bennet, Hon. Henry Grey, *Letter to Viscount Sidmouth, Secretary of State for the Home Department, on the Transportation Laws, the State of the Hulks, and of the Colonies in New South Wales.* J. Ridgway, London. 1st Edition, 1819, dated 27 December 1818; 2nd Edition, with pp. 110-12—which described D'Arcy Wentworth as having been a convict—rewritten. Mitchell Library, 991B [731].

Bennet, Hon. Henry Grey, *A Letter to Earl Bathurst, Secretary of State for the Colonial Department, on the Condition of the Colonies in New South Wales and Vandieman's Land, as set forth in the evidence taken before the Prison Committee in* 1819. J. Ridgway, London, 1820 [777].

Bentham, Jeremy, *Panopticon versus New South Wales: or, The Panopticon Penitentiary System, and the Penal Colonization System, compared. Containing* 1. *Two Letters to Lord Pelham . . .* 2. *Plea for the Constitution, etc.* London, 1812 [531].

Bonwick, James, *The First Twenty Years of Australia.* Sampson Low, London; George Robertson, Melbourne and Sydney, 1882.

Cowper, William Macquarie, *The Autobiography and Reminiscences of William Macquarie Cowper, Dean of Sydney.* Angus and Robertson, Sydney, 1902.

Cramp, K. R., and Mackaness, George, *History of the United Grand Lodge of Ancient, Free, and Accepted Masons of New South Wales.*

Dixon, James, *Narrative of a Voyage to New South Wales, and Van Diemen's Land in The Ship Skelton, during the year* 1820. Edinburgh and London, 1822 [858].

Eagar, Edward, *Letters to The Rt. Hon. Robert Peel . . . on the Advantages of New South Wales and Van Diemen's Land, etc.* London, 1824 [939].

Ferguson, John Alexander, *Bibliography of Australia.* Angus and Robertson, Sydney, 1941, vol. I: 1784-1830; 1945, vol. II: 1831-1838.

Field, Barron, *First Fruits of Australian Poetry.* G. Howe, Sydney, 1819 [738].

Hassall, Rev. J. S., *In Old Australia.* Brisbane, 1902.

Holford, George, *Substance of the Speech of George Holford, Esq. in the House of Commons, on Thursday, the 22nd of June, 1815, on the bill to Amend the Transportation Laws.* London, 1815 [608].

Holford, George, *The Convict's Complaint in 1815 and the Thanks of the Convict in 1825.* London, 1825 [1025].

Holt, Joseph, *Memoirs of Joseph Holt, General of the Irish Rebels in 1798.* Edited from the original manuscripts in the possession of Sir William Bentham. 2 vols. H. Colburn, London, 1838 [2521].

Houison, A., *A Short History of St Philip's Church.* Sydney, 1906.

Howe, Michael, *Michael Howe, The Last and Worst of the Bush Rangers of Van Diemen's Land. Narrative of the chief atrocities committed by this great murderer and his associates during a period of six years in Van Diemen's Land. From authentic sources of information.* Andrew Bent, Hobart Town, 1818 [716].

Johnston, George, *Letter to the Right Honourable the Earl of Liverpool.* 16 November 1810. London, 1810 [498].

Johnston, George, *Proceedings of a General Court-Martial held at Chelsea Hospital . . . for the Trial of Lieut.-Col. George Johnston . . . on a charge of Mutiny.* London, 1811 [514].

Kenny, Very Rev. Dean, *A History of the Commencement and Progress of Catholicity in Australia up to the Year* 1840. Sydney, 1886.

Lang, John Dunmore, *An Historical and Statistical Account of New South Wales, both as a Penal Settlement and as a British Colony.* 1st Edition, Cochran and M'Crone, London, 1834 [1806].

Lang, John Dunmore, *Poems, Sacred and Secular, Written Chiefly at Sea.* Maddocks, Sydney, 1873.

Lee, Ida, *Logbooks of the Lady Nelson.* London, 1915.

Lowe, Robert, *Letter to the Honourable J. T. Bigge, Commissioner of Inquiry, Sydney, in Reply to Four Questions on Convict Discipline and Agriculture,* 15 July 1820. Sydney Mail, 1890.

M'Arthur, John, *Letter to . . . Viscount Castlereagh.* London, 1808 (Mitchell Library, C475). The authorship is attributed on surmise to M'Arthur by the Mitchell Library catalogue, but the pamphlet actually appears to have been the work of Plummer.

Mackaness, George, *The Life of Vice-Admiral William Bligh, R.N., F.R.S.* 2 vols. Angus and Robertson, 1931.

Macquarie, Lachlan, *Letter to The Rev. Philip Conolly, and John Joseph Therry, Roman Catholic Chaplains.* 14 October 1820 [793].

Macquarie, Lachlan, *A Letter to the Right Honourable Viscount Sidmouth in Refutation of Statements made by the Hon. Henry Grey Bennet, M.P., in a Pamphlet "On the Transportation Laws, the State of the Hulks, and of the Colonies in New South Wales."* London, 1821 [830].

Mann, D. D., *The Present Picture of New South Wales*. Illustrated with four large coloured views. London, 1811 [518].

Marsden, J. B., *Life and Work of Samuel Marsden*. 1857.

Marsden, Rev. Samuel, *An Answer to certain calumnies in the late Governor Macquarie's Pamphlet and the third edition of Mr Wentworth's Account of Australasia*. London, 1826, [1086].

Marsden, Samuel, *Some Private Correspondence of the Rev. Samuel Marsden and Family 1794-1824*, edited by George Mackaness. Sydney, 1942.

Mellish, *A Convict's Recollections of New South Wales*. London, 1825.

Mudie, James, *The Felonry of New South Wales: being a faithful picture of the real romance of life in Botany Bay. With Anecdotes of Botany Bay Society, and a Plan of Sydney*. London, 1837 [2312].

Nicholas, J. L., *Narrative of a Voyage to New Zealand performed in the years 1814 and 1815, in company with the Rev. Samuel Marsden*. 2 vols. London, 1817 [690].

O'Brien, Eris, *The Dawn of Catholicism in Australia*. 2 vols. Sydney, 1928.

O'Brien, Eris, *Life and Letters of Archpriest John Joseph Therry, Founder of the Catholic Church in Australia*. Angus and Robertson, Sydney, 1922.

O'Brien, Eris, *The Foundation of Australia*. 2nd Edition, Sydney, 1950

O'Hara, James, *The History of New South Wales*. London, 1817 [691].

Onslow, S. Macarthur, *Some Early Records of the Macarthurs of Camden*. Angus and Robertson, Sydney, 1914.

Paterson, G., *The History of New South Wales from its First Discovery to the Present Time*. Newcastle-upon-Tyne, 1811 [523].

Péron, F. A., and Freycinet, Louis De, *Voyage de Découvertes aux Terres Australes . . . pendant les années 1800, 1801, 1802, 1803 et 1804*. 4 vols. 2nd Edition, Paris, 1824 [978].

Phillips, Marion, *A Colonial Autocracy—New South Wales under Governor Macquarie, 1810-21*. 1909.

Roberts, S. H., *History of Australian Land Settlement*. Melbourne, 1924.

Shann, E. O. G., *An Economic History of Australia*. Cambridge, 1930.

Slater, John, *A Description of Sydney, Parramatta, Newcastle, etc. Settlements in New South Wales, with some account of the manners and employment of the Convicts*. Sutton and Son, Nottingham, 1819 [768].

Tompson, Charles, *Wild Notes, from the Lyre of a Native Minstrel*. R. Howe, Sydney, 1826 [1093].

Vale, Rev. Benjamin, *A Pastoral Letter, to the Congregation Assembling at St. Philip's Sydney*. G. Howe, Sydney, 1815 [629].

Wallis, James, *An Historical Account of The Colony of New South Wales and its Dependent Settlements*. London, 1821 [842].

Wentworth, W. C., *A Statistical, Historical, and Political Description of the Colony of New South Wales and its Dependent Settlements in Van Diemen's Land*. 1st Edition, London, 1819 [771]; 2nd Edition, 1820 [802]; 3rd Edition, 2 vols, 1824 [990]. Reviewed in *Farmers' Magazine*, Edinburgh, 13 November 1820.

Wentworth, W. C., *Australasia. A Poem Written for The Chancellor's Medal at the Cambridge Commencement, July 1823*. London, 1823 [924].

West, Absolom, *Views of New South Wales*. First Series, Sydney, 1813 [570a]; Additional Series, 1814 [596a].

Windeyer, W. J. V., *Lectures on Legal History*. 2nd Edition, Sydney, 1949.

Wood, G. A., *The Discovery of Australia*. London, 1922.

REFERENCE NOTES

ABBREVIATIONS

Bigge Appendix: Appendix containing the evidence given before Mr John Thomas Bigge, sitting as Commissioner of Inquiry into the Affairs of New South Wales, in the years 1819-21.

Bonwick Transcripts: Transcripts from official and other documents made in London for the Government of New South Wales. (Mitchell Library.)

CSIL: Colonial Secretary In-Letters. (Mitchell Library.)

G. and G.O.: Government and General Orders.

HRA: Historical Records of Australia, quoted according to series and volume Numbers, for example, HRA, I. 9, means *Historical Records of Australia*, series I, volume 9. H. of C.: House of Commons.

Journals: The Journals of Lachlan Macquarie, original copies preserved in the Mitchell Library, A768-776, 1787-1824.

Letterbooks: The Letterbooks of Lachlan Macquarie, A787-797, original copies preserved in the Mitchell Library.

NSWHR: *The Historical Records of New South Wales*, 1787-1811, vols I-VII.

RAHSJ: *Journal of the Royal Australian Historical Society*.

Figures preceded by a capital letter refer to the number of the item—manuscript, book or pamphlet—in the catalogue of the Mitchell Library, of which it is the property.

INTRODUCTION: THE PAST OF ULVA

1. Macquarie spelt his name in the modern way and not in the forms current in his time, "MacQuarrie" and "Macquarrie", the latter accepted by Scottish genealogists as the proper form. In referring to his chieftain, Ulva, Macquarie nearly always uses the form "MacQuarie" which is not in accordance with the Gaelic rule. In a name derived from a proper name the capital is used, for example, MacArthur, son of Arthur; MacDonald, son of Donald; but where the name derives from a quality, or trade or calling, a small letter is employed, e.g., Macintyre (*Mac-an-t-saoir*) son of the carpenter; Macnab, offspring of the abbot; Macquarie, descendant of a *guaire*, noble (race).

2. For the details of the Macquarie coat of arms, see Adam, *Clans, Septs and Regiments o, the Scottish Highlands*, p. 388.

3. *Reg. Seg. Concilii*, vol. 1563-7, fo. 274. The miscreant was Lachlan Maclean of Duart; the bishopric that of Icolmkill (Iona).

4. Boswell, *Life of Johnson* (Birkbeck Hill Ed., 1887), vol. III, pp. 126-7, Johnson asked (15 July, 22 July, and 9 September 1777), "What is become of poor Macquarrie?" Boswell replied that his estates, "Staffa and all", had been sold up to a Campbell the previous day. The rents of the Ulva and Ormaig estates together totalled only £239 17s. 4d. per annum. Johnson commented, "Every eye must look with pain on a Campbell turning the Macquarries out of their *sedes avitae*, their hereditary island." Lachlan Macquarie described his aged relative in a letter to General Abercromby on 1 January 1794 as "now reduced to extreme indigence".

5. Boswell, *Tour of the Hebrides*. Johnson calls MacQuarie's house "the hut of a gentleman".

6. He lived at Glenforsa, under the care of Lachlan Macquarie's brother Charles.

7. Letterbook, A790, p. 44: to Charles Macquarie, 24 August 1797.

BOOK ONE

CHAPTER I: THE DASHING LIEUTENANT

1. Some military documents give the date of his birth as 29 January, but he celebrated 31 January, and there is no real question about the date.

2. *Annual Register*, 1761, Chronicle, p. 68.

3. He died suddenly on 25 October 1760 from a rupture of the right ventricle of the heart. *Dictionary of National Biography*, XXI, p. 170.

4. Mrs Mary Hume Greenfield, to *Oban Times*, 2 December 1917: "General Macquarie's Territorial designation was of Ormaig, not of Ulva." See Douglas, *Baronage of Scotland*; Burke, *Landed Gentry of Great Britain*, 1846 Ed., vol. II, Macquarie of Ulva, and of Ormaig. (*Oban Times*, 9 November 1918; 22 June 1940; and 20 November 1940.) Macquarie Papers, National Library, 19 October 1811: to Charles Macquarie. There is a tradition in Mull that Macquarie's father was "a carpenter and miller by trade" (Burnett).

5. "Here, in the hope of a glorious resurrection, Lie the Remains of the late MAJOR-GENERAL LACHLAN MACQUARIE, of Jarvisfield, who was born 31st January, 1761, and died at London, on the 1st of July, 1824.

"The private virtues and amiable disposition, with which he was endowed, rendered him at once a most beloved husband, Father, and Master, and a most endearing Friend. He entered the Army at the age of 15, and throughout the period of 47 years, spent in the public service, was uniformly characterised by animated zeal for his profession, active benevolence, and generosity, which knew no bounds.

"He was appointed Governor of New South Wales, A.D. 1809, and for 12 years fulfilled the duties of that situation, with eminent ability and success. His services in that capacity have justly attached a lasting honour to his name.

"The wisdom, liberality and benevolence of all the measures of his Administration, his respect for the ordinances of Religion, And the ready assistance which he gave to every charitable institution, the unwearied assiduity with which he sought to promote the welfare of all classes of the community, the rapid improvement of the Colony under his auspices, and the high estimation in which both his Character and Government were held, rendered him truly deserving the appellation by which he has been distinguished—*The Father of Australia*." (Memoranda A772, p. 222, Copy in Mrs Macquarie's handwriting. Other versions differ slightly.)

6. Douglas; *Baronage of Scotland*; Burke, *Landed Gentry of Great Britain*, 1846 Ed., vol. II, Macquarie of Ulva and of Ormaig.

7. Letterbooks A787, p. 104, and several other references in the Journals.

8. Letterbooks, A787, p. 47: to Lochbuy, 1 January 1794.

9. Letterbooks, A787, p. 85: to John Abercromby, 12 January 1794.

10. Banks climbed Hecla in August 1772. *Dictionary of National Biography*, III, p. 131.

11. Journals, A768, I, p. 59; Bonwick Transcripts, A2000 (vol. IV), War Office, 833; Cannon, *History of the 73rd Regiment*, Appendix. Small is a prominent figure in Trumbull's painting of the Bunker Hill fight. Macquarie joined the 71st Regiment on 18 January 1781 and went on half-pay on 4 June 1784.

12. Journals, A768, I, p. 1.

13. *Ibid.*, Title Page.

14. Letterbooks, A787, p. 162: to Mrs Morley, 12 August 1794.

15. Journals, A768, I, p. 2, 15 December 1787. The remainder of the story of his adventures, to the end of the chapter, is told in his Journals, A768, I, pp. 1-67, 15 December 1787 to 27 March 1788.

Chapter II: A PASSAGE TO INDIA

1. The whole of the material for this chapter is taken from the Journals, A768, I, pp. 67-132, 27 March - 14 September 1788.

2. Journals, A768, I, pp. 86-7, 12-13 June 1788.

3. *Ibid.*, p. 104, 18 June 1788.

4. *Ibid.*, p. 132, 14 September 1788.

Chapter III: THE THRESHOLD OF GLORY

1. Douglas, *Western India and Bombay*. This was the population within the walls.

2. Generally, the description is taken from the Journals, A768, p. 117, *et seq.* Some of the houses were floored with cowdung and earth, thus setting a fashion for Australian pioneers.

3. It was on the property of the Gandhi family. A second tower was not put up till Dadabhai—"Mr Dady"—secured permission to build his own tower in 1797.

4. Journals, A768, I, p. 116. Causeways actually linked the islands at this time, but later the channel was filled in completely as part of a scheme to extend the foreshores of Bombay.

5. In India—especially in the *mofussil*—the visitor calls attention, as he approaches a house, by clapping his hands and calling, "*Koi hai?*"—lit. "Is anybody there?" The same method is adopted by the old-fashioned in calling servants. The usage corresponds to the medieval usage of "What, ho, there!" or "What ho, within!" A *kvoee-hai*, therefore, was an irascible old gentleman who was for ever calling servants and keeping his underlings on the jump.

6. Sir James Mackintosh; but his standards were high. He was accustomed to the company of Burke and Fox.

7. "When you were in Bengal, the business was transacted between the hours of nine and two. At present, the interval of occupation, in almost every department, is between seven and four; and I doubt if there is more regularity in any Government in the world . . ." Teignmouth, *Life and Letters*: to Inglis, 1794.

8. Journals, A768, I, p. 140, 1 October 1788.

9. 24 George III, c. 25.

10. It was signed 11 March 1784, and Article 1 provided that "peace and friendship shall immediately take place" between the Company and Tippoo Sultan and "their friends and allies, particularly including therein the Rajahs of Tanjore and Travancore, friends and allies of the English and the Carnatic Pyenghaut".

11. Mackenzie, *War with Tippoo Sultaun*, I, p. 14 *et seq.* George Powney to John Holland, 4 January 1790, gives details of Tippoo's injury and discomfiture.

12. Journals, A768, I, p. 170, 13 January 1790.

13. *Ibid.*, p. 171.

14. Mackenzie, *War with Tippoo Sultaun*, I, pp. 59-60, where the correspondence between Tippoo and Medows is quoted. All the hesitation lay at the door of Macquarie's old Commander-in-Chief in the West Indies, Sir Archibald Campbell. Actually, as early as March 1790 Cornwallis considered that "the Government of Fort George was guilty of a most criminal disobedience of the clear and explicit orders of this Government dated August 29 and Nov. 13, by not considering themselves to be at war with Tippoo from the moment they heard of his attack on the Lines of Travancore".

15. *Ibid.*, p. 141 *et seq.*

16. Journals, A768, pp. 184-5, 20 September 1790.

17. The fight between Floyd and Tippoo took place near Satiamungalan on 13-14 Sept.

18. Minute of Speke and Cowper to Council of Fort William, 6 November 1790: "The presence of the Governor-General in the scene of action would have been considered by our Allies, as a pledge of sincerity and of confident hopes of success against the common enemy." The General Order to augment the forces was issued on 8 November two days before Macquarie heard that he was to go on service.

19. Journals, A768, I, pp. 189-190, 10 November 1790.

20. For description of embarkation and voyage to Tellicherry, Journals, A768, I, pp. 193 (24 November) to 199 (6 December).

Chapter IV: MOVING DAY IN CANAAN

1. The narrative of events in this chapter closely follow the account in Macquarie's Journal A768, I, pp. 207-86, 14 December 1790, to 25 May 1791.

2. Journal, A768, I, pp. 211-12.

3. *Ibid.* p. 213.

4. *Ibid.* p. 221, 17 December 1790.

5. *Ibid.* pp. 256-7, 12 May 1791.

6. Innes Munro, in *A Narrative of the Military Operations on the Coromandel Coast*, Chapter XIII, gives an amusing account of the manner in which the Major Mangos of that period went to war.

7. Mackenzie divides an army of 76,000 into 17,000 fighting men, 59,000 camp followers, with 3000 horses, 210 elephants, 20,289 grain bullocks, and 9211 ordnance bullocks. See also Dirom, *Narrative of the War with Tipu Sultan*, p. 242; Moors, *Narrative of Captain Little's Detachment with Purseram Bhow* (1794), p. 84.

8. In Journals, A768, I, pp. 234, 257, and elsewhere, Macquarie describes the kind of load a soldier carried.

9. Journals, A768, I, pp. 260-1, 15 May 1791.

10. *Ibid.*, pp. 266-7. The Bombay Army celebrated the victory on 20 May.

11. *Ibid.*, pp. 269-71, 23 May 1791.

Chapter V: THE SPOILS OF MYSORE

(Note. *The numbering of the pages of the Journal and Letterbooks to the end of Book III, Chapter I, is erratic, sometimes duplicated and sometimes non-existent. Dates, therefore, are a better guide than page numbers. Page numbers marked with an asterisk are the second set of duplicate numbers in the same volume.*)

1. Again the Journal provides the main material of the narrative. Journals, A768, pp. 269 *et seq.*, 23 May 1791.

2. *Cornwallis Correspondence*, vol. II, p. 98: Cornwallis to the Bishop of Lichfield and Coventry: "You will have heard that, after beating Tipu's army, and driving him into the

Island of Seringapatam, I was obliged by the famine which prevailed amongst our followers, by the sudden and astonishing mortality among our cattle, and by the unexpected obstacles to my forming a junction with General Abercromby, in time to attempt the enterprise before the rising of the river, to destroy my battering guns and to relinquish the attack on Seringapatam until the conclusion of the rains. Had the numerous Mahratta Army which joined me on 26th May unexpectedly and without my having received the smallest previous notice, arrived a fortnight sooner, our success would have been complete and the destruction of Tipu's power would actually have taken place."

The facts were that Purseram Bhow materialized out of a dust cloud with 120,000 fighting men and over 300,000 camp-followers. The delay had been caused because he had felt impelled to await the full moon to indulge in purification ceremonies, since one of his staff had defiled them all by dallying with a friend's wife!

3. Journals, A768, I, pp. 278-9, 24 May 1791.
4. *Ibid.*, pp. 279-305, 24 May-7 June 1791.
5. *Ibid.*, p. 326, 9 November 1791.
6. *Ibid.*, pp. 315-16.
7. *Ibid.*, pp. 334-5, 5 December 1791. The cost is left blank in his journal.
8. *Ibid.*, pp. 359-60, 15 February 1792.
9. *Ibid.*, pp. 361-2, 15 February 1792.
10. *Ibid.*, pp. 362-3, 16 February 1792.
11. *Ibid.*, p. 365, 23 February 1792; Hook, T., *Life of Sir David Baird*, I, pp. 111-12.
12. *Ibid.*, pp. 366-7.
13. Journals, A768, I, p. 368, 3 March, to II, p. 382, 13-20 April 1792, conclude the narrative of the war.

CHAPTER VI: THE SOLDIER'S WEDDING

1. They usually arrived just before the break of the monsoon.
2. Speech from the Throne, 1792.
3. Letterbooks, A787, pp. 82-3: to John Abercromby, 12 January 1794.
4. Letterbooks, A787, p. 33: to Lochbuy, 1 January 1794; A789, p. 207: to Mrs Morley, 3 February 1797.
5. Letterbooks, A787, p. 36: to Lochbuy, 1 January 1794; also pp. 3-4: to General Allan Maclean, 31 August 1793. In this letter he wrote: "She is nineteen years of age . . . handsome in face and person, elegantly accomplished, a charming disposition, of most agreeable manners, and possessing a private fortune of six thousand pounds sterling." *Ibid.*, p. 78: to Allan Park, 8 January 1794.
6. Journals, A768, II, p. 434 *et seq.*, 2 August 1793.
7. *Ibid.*, p. 436, 3 August 1793.
8. *Ibid.*, pp. 440-2, 4 August 1793.
9. *Ibid.*, p. 446.
10. *Ibid.*, p. 449.
11. *Ibid.*, pp. 451-5, 5 August 1793.
12. *Ibid.*, pp. 468-9, 12 August 1793.
13. *Ibid.*, pp. 487-99.

CHAPTER VII: ESCAPE FROM FORTUNE

1. Journals, A768, II, p. 499 *et seq.*
2. Letterbooks, A787, p. 76: to Small, 8 January 1794; p. 77: to Park, 8 January 1794.
3. Letterbooks, A787, p. 5: to Mrs Jarvis, 28 September 1793.
4. Letterbooks, A788: to Tasker, 6 May 1795. Macquarie had written earlier to Mr Thomas Jarvis, "I have been made completely happy by a Matrimonial Union with your charming and amiable sister Jane."
5. Letterbooks, A787, p. 16: to Z. Hall, 4 December 1793.
6. Journals, A768, II, pp. 534-5, 20 December 1793.
7. *Ibid.*, p. 535, 21 December 1793.
8. *Ibid.*, p. 566, 25 March 1794.
9. Letterbooks, A787, p. 141: to Hall, 31 May 1794.
10. *Ibid.*, p. 17: to Hall, 4 December 1793.
11. *Ibid.*, pp. 22-3: to Hall, 18 December 1793.
12. *Ibid.*, pp. 34-6: to Lochbuy, 1 January 1794.
13. *Ibid.*, p. 43.
14. Letterbooks, A788: to Mrs Clephane, 1 January 1796.
15. Letterbooks, A787, p. 32: to Lochbuy, 1 January 1794.
16. Letterbooks, A788: to Lochbuy, 20 March 1795.

17. Letterbooks, A 787, p. 33: to Lochbuy, 1 January 1794; p. 85: to J. Abercromby, 12 January 1794.
18. *Ibid.*, pp. 44-5.
19. *Ibid.*, p. 38.
20. Journals, A768, II, p. 512, 24 October 1793.
21. Letterbooks, A788: to Lochbuy, 20 March 1795.
22. Journals, A768, II, p. 556, 31 January, 1794.
23. Letterbooks, A788: to Auchmuty, 1 March 1795; to Lochbuy, 20 March 1795.
24. Letterbooks, A787, p. 135: to Robertson, 17 May 1794.
25. Journals, A768, II, p. 546 *et seq.*, 16 January 1794.
26. Letterbooks, A787, p. 156 *et seq.*: to Mrs. Morley, 12 August 1794.
27. Journals, A768, II, pp. 560-604, 29 March-8 April 1794. (Macquarie's numbering, p. 198.)
28. Letterbooks, A787, p. 60: to Allan Maclean, 4 January 1794.
29. *Ibid.*, p. 84: to J. Abercromby, 12 January 1794.
30. *Ibid.*, pp. 78-9: to Park, 8 January 1794.
31. Letterbooks, A788: to Auchmuty, 1 March 1795: to Lochbuy, 20 March 1795.
32. A787, pp. 161-2: to Mrs Morley, 12 August 1794.
33. A787, pp. 162-3.
34. Journals, A768, II, pp. 619-27, 14-16 June 1794. She died on 14 January 1794.
35. *Ibid.*
36. *Ibid.*, pp. 635-6, 15 July 1794.
37. Letterbooks, A787, pp. 183-4: to C. Macquarie, 6 September 1794.
38. Journals, A768, II, pp. 684-705, 25 October-27 November 1794.
39. *Ibid.*, p. 720, 19 December 1794.
40. Letterbooks, A788: to Balfour, 20 January 1795.
41. *Ibid.*: to Dunlop, 1 January 1795.
42. *Ibid.*: to Geo. Jarvis 5 November 1794.
43. Letterbooks, A788: to Lochbuy, 20 March 1795.
44. Journals, A769, I, p. 4 *et seq.*
45. A788: to Z. Hall, 24 February 1795. It actually was Hall's own "old grey charger".
46. *Ibid.*: to Balfour, 20 January 1795.
47. Journals, A769, I, p. 20.
48. Letterbooks, A788: to Dr Ker, 1 May 1795.
49. *Ibid.*: to Mrs Maclaine Lochbuy, 21 January; to Lochbuy, 20 March 1795.
50. *Ibid.*: to John Murray, 17 March 1795.
51. *Ibid.*: to Dunlop, 1 and 19 January, 8 and 25 February, 3, 9 and 30 April, 16 May, 21 July 1795; to Hadjee Eesof, 23 July 1795.
52. *Ibid.*: to Dunlop, 19 January 1795.
53. *Ibid.*: to Forbes, 24 July 1795.
54. *Ibid.*: to Dunlop, 9 April 1795.
55. *Ibid.* He wrote to Dunlop a month later: "All has been peace and quietness over the Malabar Province, though its British residents know that Bombay not improbably was hearing that 'Twenty Thousand Nairs and Moplahs were up in Arms' against Calicut a few days ago ... the real fact being that a few thousand natives met for an annual Festival that the Zamorin celebrates."
56. *Ibid.*: to Stirling, 18 April 1795.
57. *Ibid.*: to Auchmuty, 18 April 1795.

Chapter VIII: THE GOVERNOR OF GALLE

1. Journals, A768, II, pp. 676-7, 10 October 1794.
2. *Annual Register*, 1792-5.
3. *Ibid.*, 1795, p. 49.
4. *Manifesto of the Revolutionary Committee of Amsterdam*, 19 January 1795.
5. Letterbooks, A788: to Lundin, 20 March 1795. The implications of the word democracy were somewhat different from those of modern times: "Those two odious appellations Aristocrat and Democrat, the former bestowed on all those who oppose all changes in the Constitution; the latter on all those who demand these, together with an immediate peace with France."
6. *Ibid.*: to Halkett, 25 January 1795.
7. *Ibid.*: to Stirling, 31 January 1795.
8. *Ibid.*: to Stirling, 18 April, 18 May, 20 June, 16 July, and 14 August 1795, in particular.
9. *Ibid.*: to Stirling, 9 March 1795.

10. Dundas had fought at St Malo and Cherbourg in 1758. The *Rules and Regulations for the Formation, Field Exercises, and Movements of His Majesty's Forces* were drawn up and issued by him under a Horse Guards Order in June 1792, so that it was three years before they reached India. They provided the recipes for drill as they were known to the British Army during the greater part of the Napoleonic wars. John Moore was the utterer of the "Damned Eighteen Manoeuvres" epithet.

11. Letterbooks, A788: to Stirling, 31 January 1795.
12. *Ibid.*, 11 February 1795.
13. *Ibid.*: to Stirling, 20 June 1795.
14. *Ibid.*: to Stirling, 18 May 1795, and 16 July 1795; to R. Gordon, 1 July 1795.
15. *Ibid.*: to Stirling, 18 May 1795.
16. *Ibid.*: to Gordon, 1 July 1795.
17. Journals, A769, III, p. 22, 5 July 1795.
18. Letterbooks, A788: to Dunlop, 24 July 1795.
19. *Ibid.*: to Geo. Mackenzie, 29 July 1795.
20. Journal, A769, III, p. 28, 23 July 1795; A788: to Gordon, 1 July 1795.
21. *Ibid.*: to Geo. Mackenzie, 29 July 1795.
22. The story of events at Cochin are told in Journals, A769, III, p. 29—from which page the narrative was written ten years later from notes—to p. 89. (15 August-30 October 1795.)
23. Journals, A769, III, p. 58. Wredé was the postmaster of Cochin. He was known as the Maecenas of Malabar. He financed the translation of the history of the Malabar Jews into Low Dutch. The Muttoncherry Jews traditionally were offshoots of the Tribe of Manasseh, sent to India during the captivity of Nebuchadnezzar. Their history was inscribed in their synagogue at Muttoncherry. Pennant, *The View of Hindostan*, vol. I (1798).
24. *Ibid.*, p. 70 et seq.
25. *Ibid.*, pp. 75-6.
26. *Ibid.*, p. 81.
27. *Ibid.*, pp. 89-112.
28. *Ibid.*, p. 127.
29. *Ibid.*, pp. 157-8.
30. *Ibid.*, p. 161.
31. *Ibid.*, pp. 162-9, for journey to Galle, (19-23 February 1796).
32. *Ibid.*, p. 170 et seq.
33. *Ibid.*, pp. 179-80.
34. Letterbooks, A788: to Colonel James Stuart, "Feb. 23, 1796, 6 o'clock P.M."
35. Journals, A769, III, p. 187, 24 February 1796.
36. Journals, A769, III, p. 193, 15 March.
37. Letterbooks, A788: to D. F. Fretz, 29 March 1796.
38. Journals, A769, III, p. 199.
39. *Ibid.*, pp. 199-200, 21 March 1796.
40. *Ibid.*, pp. 213-14, 15 April.
41. *Ibid.*, p. 220. Journals, A769, III, p. 224, recommence a year later on 3 May 1797.

BOOK TWO

Chapter IX: ALL FOR EVER FLED

(*In A789 the numbering goes to p. 200 and then begins again at p. 100 on the following page.*)

1. Guedalla, *The Duke*, p. 67.
2. Letterbooks, A788: to Dr Anderson, 7 and 8 May 1796.
3. *Ibid.*
4. Letterbooks, A789, pp. 6-11: to Auchmuty, 16 June 1796.
5. *Ibid.*, p. 7.
6. Letterbooks, A789, pp. 66-113: to Mrs Morley, 24 October 1796, give a full account of the adventures of Macquarie and Jane and of the latter's death.
7. Letterbooks, A789, p. 36: to George Jarvis, 24 August 1796.
8. *Ibid.*, p. 14: to Lestock Wilson, 10 July; p. 48: to Anderson, 24 August 1796. The story of his grief is poured out in the 48-page letter which he wrote to Mrs Morley (Letterbooks, A789, pp. 66-113, 24 October 1796), from which quotations which follow are taken.
9. Letterbooks, A789, p. 40: to G. Jarvis, 24 August 1796.
10. *Ibid.*, p. 107*: to Mrs Morley, 3 February 1797; p. 190: to George Jarvis, 21 January 1797; A790, p. 1: to Lestock Wilson, 3 August 1797.
11. Letterbooks, A793, pp. 71-2: to the Marquis of Breadalbane, 20 September 1805.

12. Letterbooks. A789, p. 194: to John Forbes, 22 January 1797.
13. *Ibid.*, p. 106*: to Cox and Greenwood, 31 January 1797.
14. Letterbooks, A789, p. 153*: to John Forbes, 25 April 1797; A790, p. 20: to Gosling and Sharpe, 18 August 1797; p. 53: to Jarvis, 10 December 1797.
15. Memoranda, A772, p. 220.
16. *Ibid.*
17. Letterbooks, A790, p. 53: to Jarvis, 10 December 1797.
18. Memoranda, A772, p. 217.
19. Letterbooks, A790, pp. 5-9 *et seq*: to Mrs Morley, 18 August 1797. Subsequent letters bearing on the matter include those to Mrs Morley, (p. 63) 13 February 1798, (p. 133), 25 June 1799, and (p. 49) to Morley and Tasker, 4 September 1797.
20. Letterbooks, A789, pp. 187-90: to Mrs Kerr, Mrs Coggan, etc., Kerr, Scott and others, January 1797.
21. Letterbooks, A790, p. 51: to G. Jarvis, 10 December 1797.
22. *Ibid.*, p. 63: to G. Jarvis, 12 February 1798.
23. Letterbooks, A789, p. 102*: to Charles Macquarie, 31 January 1797.
24. Letterbooks, A790, p. 64: to Mrs Morley, 13 February 1798.
25. Letterbooks, A789, p. 140*: to Mrs Morley, 31 March 1797.
26. Letterbooks, A790, pp. 91-2: to Lochbuy, 15 December 1798.
27. Letterbooks, A789, p. 112*: to Dunlop, 14 February; pp. 114* and 124*: to George Jarvis, 10 and 21 March; to Forbes, Smith and Co., p. 111*, 4 February and p. 150*: to John Forbes, 25 April; A790, p. 22: to Charles Macquarie, 24 August 1797. These letters are worth careful study.
28. A789, p. 130*: to Weston, 21 March 1797.
29. *Ibid.*, p. 120*: to Jarvis, 18 March 1797.
30. *Ibid.*, p. 152*: to John Forbes, 25 April 1797.
31. *Ibid.*, p. 160*: to Geo. Jarvis, 7 May 1797.
32. The account of the expedition is given in the letter to Jarvis and in Journals, A769, III, pp. 224-359.
33. Journals, A769, III, pp. 339-40.
34. *Ibid.*, pp. 344-5.
35. *Ibid.*, pp. 352-3.
36. Letterbooks, A789, p. 169*: to G. Jarvis, 1 June 1797.
37. Letterbooks, A790, p. 6: to Mrs Morley, 18 August 1797.
38. *Ibid.*, pp. 38-9: to Charles Macquarie, 24 August 1797.
39. *Ibid.*: to Mrs Maclaine Lochbuy, p. 257, 8 March 1802.
40. *Ibid.*, p. 40: to Charles Macquarie, 24 August 1797.
41. Letterbooks, A789, p. 148*: to Anderson, 25 April 1797.
42. *Ibid.*, p. 172* *et seq.*: to James Drummond, 13 July 1797.

Chapter X: CORN IN EGYPT

1. Letterbooks, A790, p. 83: to Mrs Maclaine Lochbuy, 15 December 1798.
2. *Ibid.*, pp. 105-10: to Mrs Maclaine, 27 January 1799.
3. *Ibid.*, p. 85: to Mrs Maclaine, 15 December 1798.
4. *Ibid.*, pp. 85-6.
5. *Ibid.*, pp. 108-9, 27 January 1799.
6. *Ibid.*
7. *Ibid.*, p. 255: to Mrs Maclaine, 8 March 1802. He accompanied the letter with a gift of £500, to help pay for the education of the girls.
8. *Ibid.*, p. 91, 15 December 1798.
9. *Ibid.*, p. 81: to Dr Alex Duncan, 13 December 1798.
10. *Ibid.*, p. 82.
11. *Ibid.*, p. 101: to Mrs Morley, 17 December 1798; p. 105: to Mrs Maclaine, 27 January 1799.
12. *Ibid.*, pp. 116-17: to Lestock Wilson, 8 February 1799.
13. Theodore Hook's, *Life of Sir David Baird* gives a detailed account of the proceedings both before and during the campaign; so does Lushington's *The Life of General Lord Harris.*
14. *Ibid.*, Malartic's Proclamation, 20 January 1797.
15. *Ibid.*
16. Letterbooks, A790, p. 122: to Charles Macquarie, 9 February 1799; Journals, A769A, 10 April-5 May 1799.

17. *Ibid.*, pp. 125-33: Macquarie's report from the Camp at Seedapore to Lieut.-Col. Cliffe, Adjutant-General, 15 March 1799.

18. One of Tippoo's most trusted generals. See Lushington's *Life of General Lord Harris*, p. 343.

19. *Ibid.*; also Wilks, *History of Mysore*, III, p. 436 *et seq.*

20. Journals, A769A, 10 April-5 May 1799.

21. *Ibid.*, 2 May 1799.

22. *Ibid.*, 4 May.

23. *Ibid.*, 4 May.

24. *Ibid.*; Letterbooks A790, p. 137: to Mrs Morley.

25. Journals, A769, III, pp. 124-5.

26. *Dictionary of National Biography*, XVI, p. 242.

27. Letterbooks, A788: to Murray, 30 December 1795; A769, III, p. 380 to IV, p. 408, 27 June-3 December 1799, for description of his visit to Bengal and Madras.

28. Letterbooks, A790, p. 199 *et seq.*: to Charles Macquarie, 12 October 1800.

29. Journals, A769, IV, pp. 413-47; 28 April-9 July, for account of expedition to Surat.

30. *Ibid.*, p. 458, 18 September 1800; p. 461, 16 October 1800.

31. Letterbooks, A790, p. 206 *et seq.*: to Lochbuy, 1 December 1800.

32. Journals, A769, IV, pp. 476-84, 21-31 March 1801.

33. *Ibid.*, pp. 485-90, *et seq.*, 31 March, 1 April 1801.

34. Wellington, *Supplementary Despatches*, II, p. 381: to Campbell, 10 May 1801.

35. *Ibid.*, p. 439: to Robertson, 12 June 1801.

36. Hook, *Life of Sir David Baird*, I, pp. 290-1.

37. Journals, A769, IV, pp. 590-1; Letterbook, A790, p. 232: to Lestock Wilson, 24 January 1802.

38. For description of Egyptian Campaign, Journals, A769, IV, p. 663 *et seq.*; A770, V, pp. 1-73, 2 July 1802; Letterbook, A790, pp. 226-36: to Lestock Wilson, 24 January 1802.

39. Journals, A769, IV, p. 693, 1 September 1801, to A770, V, p. 10, 5 October 1801.

40. *Ibid.*, IV, p. 719.

41. Journals, A770, p. 27.

42. Letterbooks, A790, p. 245: to Mrs Morley, 28 February 1802.

43. Journals, A770, V, pp. 34-5, 11 February 1802. His commission was dated 15 January 1801.

44. Journals, A770, V, pp. 39-413, 21 March 1802; to Charles Macquarie, 8 March 1802.

45. *Ibid.*, pp. 66-77. The *William* sailed from Suez—"a most miserable poor place"—on Saturday, 5 June 1802, and anchored at Bombay, 2 July 1802.

46. Letterbooks, A791, p. 6: to Wredé, 24 September 1802.

47. Journals, A770, V, October 1802; Letterbooks, A790, pp. 247-50: to Mrs Morley, 28 February 1802.

48. Letterbooks, A790, p. 239: to John Forbes, 12 February 1802.

49. Journals, A770, V, p. 97.

50. *Ibid.*, A770, V, p. 104.

CHAPTER XI: THE LAIRD OF JARVISFIELD

1. The account of the voyage to London is given in Journals, A770, V, pp. 103-61, 6 January-8 May 1803.

2. Guedalla, *The Duke*, p. 118.

3. Letterbooks, A792, pp. 31-3: to Mrs Morley, 5 May 1803.

4. *Ibid.*, pp. 33-5: to Lochbuy, 5 May 1803.

5. Journals, A770, V, pp. 161-320 *et seq.*, for his adventures in Britain, 8 May 1803-12 June 1804.

6. *Ibid.*, pp. 227-9, 11 July 1803.

7. *Ibid.*, p. 235, 13 July 1803.

8. *Ibid.*, p. 237, 14 July.

9. Letterbooks, A792, p. 53 *et seq.*

10. *Ibid.*, p. 56: to the Queen, 8 September 1803.

11. *Ibid.*, p. 71: to Reeve, 17 December 1803.

12. Journals, A770, p. 291 22 December 1803.

13. *Ibid.*, pp. 317-19, 31 May-9 June 1804.

14. *Ibid.*, pp. 321-2, 17-22 June 1804.

15. *Ibid.*, pp. 331-48, 27 June-5 July 1804.

16. *Ibid.*, p. 349 *et seq.*, 6 July 1804. They travelled over "Maum-Antrolan" by Rossall to old Ulva's house at Gribon; thence by the ferry of "Ballanahaird".

17. *Ibid.*, pp. 356-8, 10 July 1804.

18. *Ibid.*, VI, p. 365, 16 July 1804. The vow was "*never* to *marry* again in India—nor to bring a wife to India in the event of my ever again marrying". A793, pp. 71-2. He had taken Mrs Morley into his confidence before he left Egypt (A790, p. 250).
19. Journals, A770, VI, pp. 368-371, 16 July 1804.
20. Letterbooks, A793, p. 1: to Campbell, Edinburgh, 24 July 1804.
21. Journals, A770, VI, pp. 379-80.
22. Letterbooks, A793, p. 26: to Donald Maclaine, 27 November 1804.
23. Journals, A770, pp. 392-442, 28 July-12 August 1804. Account of his proceedings till his arrival in London, Journals, A770, pp. 451-500, 23 August-22 September 1804.
24. Letterbooks, A793, pp. 24-5: to Murdoch Maclaine, 16 November 1804.
25. *Ibid.*, pp. 14-15: to Lieut.-Gen. Sir Jas. Craig, 13 October 1804.
26. Letterbooks, A790, pp. 86-7: to Mrs Maclaine, 15 December 1798; *ibid.*, pp. 109-10, 27 January 1799.
27. Burke, *Landed Gentry of Great Britain*. He was so young that Elizabeth Campbell escorted him home from school to see his dying father three months later.
28. Journals, A770, V, pp. 306-7, 10-12 March 1804. Hector was on half-pay on the strength of the 40th; John, on that of the 9th. There is no question about the fact that the boy was Charles Macquarie's son, but it is a curious fact that there is no mention in the Macquarie papers of his mother or of his father's first marriage.
29. *Ibid.*, p. 306-7, 10 and 12 March 1804.
30. Letterbooks, A792, p. 60: to Clinton, 5 September 1803; p. 61, 13 September 1803.
31. Letterbooks, A793, p. 4: to Clinton, 3 March 1804.
32. *Ibid.*, p. 5. The Duke was Bishop of Osnaburgh. The position was a Hanoverian royal sinecure.
33. *Trial of the Duke of York* (1809), p. 237.
34. Letterbooks, A793, p. 4: to Clinton, 10 March 1804.
35. *Ibid.*, p. 61: to Charles Greenwood, 1 September 1805.
36. *Ibid.*, p. 37: Calvert to Macquarie, 11 February 1805.
37. Journals, A770, VI, p. 572, 16 April 1805; pp. 550-1, 15 March 1805.
38. Letterbooks, A793, p. 55: to Major George Cuyler, 16 August 1805.
39. Journals, A770, VI, p. 570, 14 April 1805.
40. *Ibid.*, pp. 545-6, 9-10 March 1805.
41. *Ibid.*, p. 591-2, 24 April 1805.
42. *Ibid.*, p. 606, 21 June 1805.
43. *Ibid.*, pp. 610-11, 11 August 1805.

CHAPTER XII: LORD ULLIN'S DAUGHTER

1. See Chapter I, p. 8.
2. Journals, A770, V, p. 323 *et seq.*, 22 June 1804.
3. Burke, *Landed Gentry of Great Britain*, Campbell of Ardnamurchan.
4. F986B, Mitchell Library, J. Beattie, *Historical Photographs Relating to Tasmania*.
5. Journals, A770, V, p. 329, 26 June 1804.
6. *Ibid.*, V, p. 334, 27 June 1804.
7. *Ibid.*, VI, p. 389, 27 July 1804.
8. *Ibid.*, VI, p. 444, 20 August 1804.
9. *Ibid.*, VI, pp. 461-2, 28 August 1804.
10. *Ibid.*, pp. 558-61, 26 March 1805.
11. *Ibid.*, pp. 559-60.
12. *Ibid.*, p. 578, 20 April 1805.
13. *Ibid.*, pp. 575-6, 20 April 1805. It is now in the Gallery of the Mitchell Library, Sydney.
14. Letterbooks, A793, pp. 71-2: to Breadalbane, 20 September 1805.
15. *Ibid.*, p. 73.
16. Journals, A770, VI, pp. 626-7, 25 October 1805. The item was in the Madras paper of 12 October 1805.
17. Letterbooks, A793: to Forbes, 6 November 1805; to Elizabeth Campbell, 4 November 1805.
18. Journals, A770, p. 622, 18 August 1805.
19. *Ibid.*, VI, pp. 634-5, 7 November 1805. Cornwallis died on 5 October; A793, note dated 7 November 1805.
20. Letterbooks, A793: to Forbes and Co., 6 November 1805. The account of events at Dohud, Journals, A770, VI, pp. 644-93, 19 November 1805-22 January 1806.
21. Letterbooks, A793: to Duncan, 14 July 1806.
22. *Ibid.*

23. *Ibid.*, p. 78: to Elizabeth Campbell, 28 September 1805.
24. *Ibid.*, p. 79: to Jane Stewart, 28 September 1805.
25. *Ibid.*: to Elizabeth Campbell, 2 November 1805; 12 July 1806.
26. *Ibid.*: to Elizabeth Campbell, letters, 22 February–12 July 1806.
27. *Ibid.*, 12 July 1806; also 12 August.
28. *Ibid.*, 18 October and 18 November 1806.
29. *Ibid.*: to Capt. C. C. M'Intosh, 22 May 1806.
30. *Ibid.*: to Samuel Manesty, 6 October 1806.
31. *Ibid.*, 18 November 1806; to Elizabeth Campbell, 16 January 1807.
32. Journals, A770, VI, pp. 719-20, 24 December 1806; p. 721, 1 January 1807.
33. Letterbooks, A793, p. 96½: to Charles Forbes, 1 January 1807. He notes: "Received a most kind, friendly and affectionate reply to the above." Forbes presented him with an Arab charger worth 1000 rupees.
34. Letterbooks, A793, p. 8: to Mrs Louisa Macquarie, Bombay, 26 March 1804.
35. Journals, A770, VI, p. 730, 18 February 1807.
36. *Ibid.*, pp. 723-4, 730, 15 January and 15 February 1807.
37. Letterbooks, A793, p. 97: to Elizabeth Campbell, 16 January 1807. See p. 50.
38. For the story of his journey as far as Astrakhan, Journals, A771, pp. 3-164, 8 March-14 August 1807.
39. *Ibid.*, pp. 168-225, 16 August-13 September 1807, for journey across Russia.
40. *Ibid.*, pp. 230-58, 24 September-12 October 1807, visit to Copenhagen and voyage to England
41. *Ibid.*, p. 263, 17 October 1807.
42. *Ibid.*, p. 264, 17 October 1807. His journey from Bombay to Yarmouth had totalled 6400 miles and had occupied six months and twenty-seven days. He had been absent from England two years five months and twenty-one days. (Mitchell Library MSS., Am. 17, Holograph Itinerary and Timetable.)
43. Letterbooks, A796, p. 21, Memorandum on p. 19: to Geo. Canning, 15 April 1809.
44. Letterbooks, A795, p. 3: to Wm. Page, 8 December 1807.
45. *Ibid.*, p. 9: to Duke of York, 10 March 1808.
46. Letterbooks, A794, p. 7: to Wallace, Poona, 21 February 1807.
47. Letterbooks, A795, p. 13: to General Harcourt, 6 September 1808.
48. Letterbooks, A796: to M'Tavish, 15 August 1808.

Interlude: THE BARREN WOOD

1. The corroboree grounds were on a site now enclosed by the Sydney Botanical Gardens.
2. Michael Massey Robinson.
3. *The New South Wales Calendar*, 1834, p. 1: Rev. C. Pleydell Wilton; National Library, A141, Bent, Ellis, Correspondence, 1810.
4. Ho. of C. Select Committee, 1812, Appendix, p. 36: Bligh's Evidence.
5. Mann, D. D., *The Present Picture of New South Wales*, p. 44.
6. Wentworth, W. C., *Statistical Account of the Colony of New South Wales* (1st ed.), p. 14.
7. HRA, I. 7, pp. 281-2: *General Return of Inhabitants*, Macquarie to Castlereagh, 30 April 1810.
8. The spelling of John M'Arthur's name is accurate to the times and in accordance with his signature. The modern form "Macarthur" was adopted, apparently by his sons in the first place, about 1823. It is not a correct Scottish form. See Chapter I, Note 1.
9. Mann, D. D., *Present Picture of New South Wales*, p. 44.
10. HRA, I. 7, p. 781: to Bathurst, 28 June 1813.
11. While the Irish sometimes gave more trouble than all the rest of the population put together, they included some of the most useful and docile men, for example, Meehan, the surveyor, and Rev. Henry Fulton.
12. Kay, *Original Portraits*, I, p. 169. It was Margarot, the Scottish martyr.
13. *Ibid.*, pp. 307-8, Thomas Muir.
14. *Williams's Justice*, II. 2, Hawk; Bennet, H.G., *Letter to Viscount Sidmouth*, p. 116; British Statutes, 4 George I, c. 2; and 19 George III, c. 74.
15. Bennet, H. G., *Letter to Viscount Sidmouth* (2nd ed.), p. 25. There are noted some sad examples of the way female prisoners were treated.
16. *Ibid.*, p. 10. Some of those included in these statistics were girls.
17. *Ibid.*, p. 29. Bennet gives, in a list of prisoners on the *Retribution*, the following proportions: Out of 552 prisoners, eight boys under 15 years for life, six for 14 years, 23 for seven years. Of the remainder, 81 were under 20 years old. Two of the "little infants" were nine years of age. (*Letter to Viscount Sidmouth*, 1st ed., p. 37.)

There are various descriptions of the clothing of convicts, *e.g.*, in the evidence before the Select Committee of 1812 and before Bigge. (Bigge Appendix, Box 1, p. 156: Wm. Hutchinson's Evidence.)

18. Ho. of C. Select Committee, 1812, App., p. 61: Jno. Palmer's Evidence.

19. Mann, D. D., *The Present Picture of N.S. Wales*, p. 53.

20. *Ibid.*, p. 54.

21. *Ibid.*, p. 61.

22. Bigge Appendix, Box 1, pp. 234-5: John M'Arthur's Evidence.

23. "In the year 1797 a combination-bond was entered into by them, by which they were neither to underbuy nor undersell the one from the other . . . it was offered to me to sign, and I refused it, and from thence began my persecution." (Ho. of C. Select Committee, 1812, Appendix, p. 53: Margarot's Evidence). *See also* NSWHR, III, pp. 636-9: Portland to Hunter, 26 February 1799; to Paterson, 6 March 1799.

24. NSWHR, VI, p. 250: Bligh to Windham, 7 February 1807.

25. *Ibid.*, p. 250; p. 622: Bligh's Account of the Rebellion.

26. Bigge Appendix, Box 12, pp. 62-115: "State of Agriculture in N.S. Wales in 1798; Complaints of Farmers, Causes of Agricultural Distress."

27. NSWHR, IV, pp. 500-1: King to King, 21 August 1801.

28. *Ibid.*, pp. 83, 85, 86, 201, 228, 419. Johnston had bought the fiery poison at 10s. a gallon and had forced the sergeant to take it as part of his subsistence allowance at 24s. a gallon.

29. *Ibid.*, p. 528 *et seq.*, pp. 604, 725.

30. Kemp, Bayly, Laycock, Sr., William Cox, Piper, Neil McKellar, D'Arcy Wentworth, Dr Harris.

31. HRA, I. 6, p. xi: Banks to Bligh, 15 March 1805.

32. NSWHR, VI, p. 685: Caley to Banks, 7 July 1808.

33. Banks Papers, A78-⁵, vol. 6, p. 11: Bligh to Charles Greville, 5 November 1807; NSWHR, VI, p. 378.

34. NSWHR, VI, pp. 588-92: Deposition of William Minchin, 30 September 1807; p. 312: J. Blaxland, 16 October 1807; pp. 336-42: Dr Harris to Governor King, 25 October 1807; p. 342: to Mrs King, same date.

35. It was Bligh who thus christened him. NSWHR, VI, pp. 607-9 *et seq.*, p. 610, par. 10, p. 612, pars 19-20: Bligh's Account of the Rebellion.

36. NSWHR, VI, pp. 395 *et seq.*, 411, 412, 413, 418, 419, 422 *et seq.*, 435, 438, 465 *et seq.* Report of the Trials of John M'Arthur.

37. *Ibid.*, p. 612, pars 20, 21: Bligh's Account of the Rebellion; IV, pp. 500-1: King to King, 21 August 1801.

38. NSWHR, VI, pp. 355, 422 *et seq.*; Onslow, S. Macarthur, *Early Records of the Macarthurs of Camden*, pp. 135-53.

39. NSWHR, VI, pp. 422 *et seq.*, 465 *et seq.*, p. 613, par. 23: Bligh's Account of the Rebellion.

40. *Ibid.*, p. 615, par. 33.

41. *Ibid.*, pp. 578-9: Johnston's Report on the Rebellion, 11 April 1808; p. 608: Bligh's Account of the Rebellion; pp. 681, 685: Caley to Banks, 30 June and 7 July 1808.

42. *Ibid.*, p. 608, par. 6 *et seq.*: Bligh's Account of the Rebellion.

43. *Ibid.*, p. 434: Johnston to Bligh, 26 January 1808.

44. *Ibid.*, p. 687: Caley to Banks (Open Letter to Johnston), 7 July 1808.

45. Foveaux arrived in the *Sinclair* 29 July 1808; Paterson on 1 January 1809. M'Arthur and Johnston sailed for England in the *Admiral Gambier* on 28 March 1809. (NSWHR, VI, pp. 710, 818.)

BOOK THREE

CHAPTER XIII: SOUTHWARD HO!

1. Onslow, S. M., *Early Records of the Macarthurs of Camden*, p. 168 *et seq.*: Ed. M'Arthur to John M'Arthur, Sen., 1 October 1808; p. 167: to Davidson, 30 September 1808.

2. NSWHR, VI, p. 692: Caley to Banks, 7 July 1808.

3. For Nightingall's biography, see *Dictionary of National Biography*, XLI, pp. 66-7; Memoranda, A772, p. 3.

4. Macquarie Papers, Mitchell Library, Safe, 15, No. 15: Macquarie to Charles Forbes, 13 February 1809.

5. *Ibid.*

6. Mitchell Library, Safe 9: Antill's Journal, p. 5.

7. NSWHR, VI, p. 816: Banks to Mrs Bligh, 24 December 1808, 16 April 1809; to Bligh, 13 May 1809. Nevertheless, Banks expressed his pleasure at Macquarie's appointment. (Banks

Papers, A78-⁵, Brabourne Collection, VI, p. 153; A83 pp. 323-5: Banks to Macquarie, 13 May 1809.)

8. Wellesley sailed from Portsmouth, 15 April 1809. Antill's Journal, p. 13.

9. *Ibid.*, pp. 14-15.

10. Letterbooks, A796, p. 15: Macquarie to Castlereagh, 11 April 1809.

11. Macquarie Papers, Mitchell Library, Safe, 15, No. 8: Macquarie to C. Forbes, 22 April 1809.

12. *London Gazette*, 1 May 1809; Letterbooks, A796, p. 23: Macquarie to Castlereagh, 1 May 1809; Memoranda, A772, p. 3, 27 April 1809. It was, perhaps, something which occurred during this function—some representation, possibly, by his old commander, Baird—which secured his sudden promotion within a few hours to the Governorship.

13. Letterbooks, A796, p. 35: Macquarie to Cooke, 12 August 1809.

14. Memoranda, A772, p. 4, 15 May 1809; his sailing, 19-22 May. They made a false start on 19 May.

15. E. Macquarie, Journal, C126, 12 June 1809.

16. *Ibid.*, 16 June 1809.

17. *Ibid.*, 3 August 1809.

18. *Ibid.*

19. Memoranda, A772, p. 6, 7 August 1809; E. Macquarie, Journal, C126, 7 August 1809.

20. *Ibid.*, A772, 8 August 1809, *et seq.*; E. Macquarie, Journal, C126, 8 August 1809.

21. *Ibid.*

22. *Ibid.*, 23 August 1809.

23. *Ibid.*

24. *Ibid.*

25. *Ibid.*

26. *Ibid.*

27. Memoranda, A772, p. 7, 23 September and 13 October 1809; E. Macquarie, Journal, C126, 24 September 1809.

28. *Ibid.*

29. *Ibid.*

30. *Ibid.*

31. *Ibid.*

32. E. Macquarie, Journal, C126, 27 November 1809.

33. *Ibid.*, 10 December 1809.

34. *Ibid.*

35. *Ibid.*, 15 December 1809.

36. *Ibid.*

37. *Ibid.*, 25 December 1809.

38. Memoranda, A772, p. 11, 28 December 1809; Mitchell Library, Large Safe, 15. Letters to Governor Macquarie to Paterson, 10 a.m. 28 December 1809. Macquarie reports his arrival in the Harbour "about ½ an hour ago".

39. *Ibid.*, p. 15, 31 December 1809; NSWHR, VII, pp. 247, 248, 263, 300.

CHAPTER XIV: "ARISE, ANOINT HIM"

1. HRA, I. 10, p. 671, *et seq.*: Macquarie to Bathurst, 27 July 1822.

2. Banks Papers, A78-⁵, No. 11: Bligh to Charles Greville, 5 November 1807, gives a graphic picture of how business was done at Government House before Bligh's time.

3. NSWHR, VII, p. 253: G. and G.O., 1 January 1810; p. 313-314; HRA, I. 7, p. 259: Macquarie to Castlereagh, 30 April 1810.

4. *Sydney Gazette*, p. 2, 7 January 1810.

5. Letterbooks, A797, p. 25: Cooke to Bligh, 15 May 1809. A "true copy" in Macquarie's handwriting.

6. *Sydney Gazette*, 7 January 1810, p. 2.

7. *Ibid.*, pp. 2-3.

8. Letterbooks, A788: to Lundin, 20 March 1795.

9. HRA, I. 7, p. 183 *et seq.*; Wentworth, *Statisical Account of New South Wales* (1st ed.), p. 165.

10. Banks Papers, A78-⁵: Bligh to Charles Greville, 5 November 1807.

11. HRA, I. 4, p. 167: King to Hobart, 9 May 1803, Enclosure entitled "*Epitaph*".

12. *Sydney Gazette*, 7 January 1810, p. 3. In the Macquarie period the church was normally described as "St Phillip's", in compliment to the settlement's founder.

13. *Ibid.*

14. *Ibid.*, 21 January 1810, pp. 1-2: Colonists' Address to Macquarie and Macquarie's Reply.

15. This kind of dinner was, of course, normal to the age wherever English was spoken. I owe Mr Ellis Bent a debt for recording the details of Mrs Macquarie's menu.

16. HRA, I. 7, p. 321. She brought 3500 bags of wheat and 500 bags of rice.
17. *Sydney Gazette*, 21 January 1810, p. 2.
18. NSWHR, VII, pp. 255, 263-5: Macquarie to Bligh, 6 January 1810.
19. Arnold Papers, A1849, II, Arnold's Letter, 25 February 1810, 18 March 1810; Bligh Correspondence, Mitchell Library, Safe, 19: Bligh to Mrs Bligh, 8 March 1810.
20. NSWHR, VII, pp. 255-7: Proclamation, 4 January 1810; HRA, I. 7, p. 220: Macquarie to Bathurst, 8 March 1810; p. 248.
21. Memoranda, A772, p. 18, 4 January 1810. Macquarie took with him on this visit Lieutenant-Governor O'Connell, who would not have been so welcome had Mrs M'Arthur known that a few months later he would marry Bligh's daughter. Macquarie told his brother Charles that the bride was a handsome, accomplished woman, about twenty-six years of age, but that she had very little money.
22. Memoranda, A772, p. 18, 12 January 1810; A1932, Broughton to Macquarie, 5 January 1810. The *Hindostan* and *Dromedary* actually contributed 6275 pounds of flour towards feeding the settlement.
23. Bligh Correspondence, Mitchell Library, Safe, 19: Bligh to Mrs Bligh, 8 March 1810.
24. NSWHR, VII, pp. 326-7.
25. Bligh Correspondence, Mitchell Library, Safe, 19: Bligh to Mrs Bligh, 8 March 1810.
26. *Ibid.*, postscript.
27. Arnold Papers, A1849, II, Letter, 18 March-10 May 1810, p. 4.
28. *Ibid.*, p. 10.
29. *Ibid.*
30. *Ibid.*, p. 12.
31. Bligh Correspondence, Mitchell Library, Safe, 19: Bligh to Mrs Bligh, from Rio de Janeiro, 11 August 1810.
32. *Ibid.*
33. *Sydney Gazette*, 26 May 1810, p. 2.
34. Arnold Papers, A1849, II, 18 March-10 May 1810, p. 4.
35. Macquarie Papers, Mitchell Library, Safe, 15, No. 6, Macquarie to Charles Forbes, 14 April 1810.
36. HRA, I. 7, p. 331.
37. RAHSJ, XVI, 1, p. 27: Macquarie to Charles Macquarie, 10 March 1810, quoted by C. H. Bertie, who received his copy from Mr F. W. Clark, owner of the Isle of Ulva, 19 July 1913.
38. Macquarie Papers, Mitchell Library, Safe, 15, No. 6: Macquarie to Charles Forbes, 14 April 1810; HRA, I. 7, p. 247: Macquarie to Castlereagh, 30 April 1810.
39. Macquarie Papers, Safe, 15, No. 5: Macquarie to C. Forbes, 18 June 1810; HRA, I. 7, p. 222: Macquarie to Castlereagh, 8 March 1810.
40. NSWHR, VII, p. 272: to Foveaux, 11 January 1810; CSIL (1810), No. 21.
41. *Sydney Gazette*, 14 April 1810, p. 2; Memoranda, A772, p. 23, 11 and 12 May.
42. HRA, I. 7, p. 128: Bligh to Castlereagh, 10 June 1809; *Derwent Star*, 3 April 1810.
43. NSWHR, VII, pp. 241, 399: John M'Arthur to Elizabeth M'Arthur, 28 November 1809 and 3 August 1810.
44. *Sydney Gazette*, 9 June 1810, p. 2.
45. Macquarie Papers, Mitchell Library, Safe, 15, No. 5: Macquarie to C. Forbes, 18 June 1810.

Chapter XV: THE WONDERFUL YEAR

1. NSWHR, V, p. 209 *et seq.*: Captain Colnett, R.N., to Nepean, 14 September 1803.
2. CSIL (1810), Bundle 4; NSWHR, VII, p. 267: G. & G.O., 8 January 1810; also *Sydney Gazette*, 14 January 1810.
3. NSWHR, VII, p. 280: G. & G.O., 27 January 1810.
4. *Ibid.*, p. 292 *et seq.*: Proclamation, 24 February 1810.
5. *Ibid.*
6. *Ibid.*, VII, p. 294: G. & G.O., 24 February 1810; CSIL (1810), No. 54: Agreement, 5 February 1810.
7. NSWHR, VII, p. 293.
8. *Ibid.*, pp. 135-6: Instructions, 9 May 1809.
9. *Ibid.*, p. 338: to Castlereagh, 30 April 1810; p. 289: G. & G.O., 16 February, 1810; p. 382: G. & G.O., 26 May; p. 385: G. & G.O., 7 June; CSIL (1810), p. 245: G. & G.O., 22 December 1810.
10. NSWHR, VII, p. 338: Macquarie to Castlereagh, 30 April 1810.
11. *Ibid.*, p. 341: to Castlereagh, 30 April 1810.
12. See Chapter XX; lsoa NSWHR, VII, p. 591: 24 September 1811, Contract with John O'Hearne.

13. CSIL (1810), No. 86, p. 149: Indenture of 21 April 1810; No. 97: Indenture of 1 June 1810.

14. NSWHR, VII, p. 306: Macquarie to Castlereagh, 8 March 1810; p. 605: to Liverpool, 18 October 1811.

15. Ibid., pp. 381-2; Sydney Gazette, Notice, 19 May 1810, p. 1; NSWHR, VII, pp. 449-53; Wentworth Papers, A761, p. 1 et seq.

16. Wentworth Papers, A761, p. 2: Indenture. For the reference to Dr Wentworth's "palace", see Bennet, Letter to Viscount Sidmouth (1st ed.), p. 77.

17. Bigge Appendix, Box 5, p. 359: Contractors to Macquarie, 25 July 1810.

18. Wentworth Papers, A761, Indenture, p. 1 et seq., 6 November 1810.

19. HRA, I. 7, p. 597: Macquarie to Liverpool, 17 November 1812.

20. NSWHR, VII, pp. 449-53; p. 427: G. & G.O., 4 October 1810.

21. Missionary Papers, Box 49, 73, p. 295: Wm. Hassall to Rev. Geo. Burder, 9 May 1810; H. of C. Select Committee (1812), Appendix, p. 53: Margarot's Evidence: "Sydney is a camp, not a town; it is under military discipline . . . there are centinels posted in different parts of the town."

22. NSWHR, VII, p. 512: Proclamation on Liquor, Section XII.

23. Ibid., p. 389: G. & G.O., 23 June 1810; pp. 384-6: G. & G.O., 2 June and 9 June 1810; p. 471: G. & G.O., 15 December 1810.

24. Ibid., p. 402: G. & G.O., 11 August 1810; pp. 428-9, 6 October 1810. George Street consisted of old, meandering "rows", formerly known as High Street, Spring Row or Sergeant Major's Row, on the western side of the Tank Stream. It stretched from Dawes Point to Brickfield Hill. (Sydney Gazette, 6 and 27 October 1810.)

25. NSWHR, VII, p. 430, and CSIL, No. 132, p. 223: G. & G.O., 20 October 1810.

26. NSWHR, VII, p. 402: G. & G.O., 11 August 1810.

27. Ibid., p. 429: G. & G.O., 6 October 1810.

28. Ibid., pp. 410-11: G. & G.O., 15 September 1810.

29. Ibid., p. 403, 11 August 1810.

30. Ibid., p. 438; HRA, I. 7, p. 343: Macquarie to Liverpool, 27 October 1810; NSWHR, VII, p. 594: G. & G.O., 5 October 1811.

31. NSWHR, VII, p. 427: G. & G.O., 6 October 1810.

32. Ibid., p. 550: G. & G.O., 29 June 1811.

33. Macquarie Papers, Mitchell Library, Safe, 15, No. 14: Macquarie to C. Forbes, 31 March 1810.

34. Ibid.

35. Ibid., No. 11, 27 July 1810.

36. HRA I. 4, p. 471: King to Hobart, 1 March 1804.

37. Sydney Gazette, 9 June 1810, p. 2.

38. NSWHR, VII, p. 423, par. 12: Instructions to Purcell, 1 October 1810.

39. HRA, I. 7, p. 388: to Liverpool, 18 October 1811.

40. Memoranda, A772, p. 22, 17 March 1810.

41. Sydney Gazette, 5 May 1810, p. 2.

42. Macquarie Papers, Mitchell Library, Safe, 15, No. 11: Macquarie to Forbes, 27 July 1810.

43. HRA, I. 7, p. 341 et seq.: Macquarie to Liverpool, 27 October 1810.

44. Ibid., p. 348. Schedule, dated 24 October 1810.

45. George Howe, alias "Happy". HRA, I. 4, p. 661, Note 39.

46. NSWHR, VII, p. 406; Sydney Gazette, 13 October, p. 1; 20 October, p. 2. An "emancipist" was a convict who had completed his or her sentence or who had been freed by pardon; an "exclusive" was a member of the class of free settlers which refused to mix socially with emancipists or to agree to the justice of their possessing civil rights.

47. Ibid., 20 October, p. 2.

48. Ibid.

49. Ibid.

50. Memoranda, A772, p. 25, 19 August 1810.

51. Journals, A778, pp. 1-2 et seq., 6-7 November 1810; CSIL (1810), No. 141, p. 237. The road was built under indenture between Wentworth, Lord, Thompson, and James Harrex, who agreed to proceed to make and complete a public turnpike from Check's corner in the town of Sydney to the Bridge at the Hawkesbury. It was to be two rods wide, with a ditch on each side, from three feet to eighteen inches deep, for keeping the road perfectly dry . . . stone or equally sound and lasting material covered with gravel to be used and the road raised not less than one foot in the centre and sloping to the ditch. Substantial bridges were to be built over every place necessary and timber was to be cut down for four rods on either side of the highway. The whole was to be completed before 1 January 1811; and inclusive in the

contract price of £2500 was an undertaking to keep the artery in repair for seven years. CSIL (1810), No. 95. The road became a turnpike, 11 April 1811. CSIL (1811), No. 18, 30 March 1811.

52. Onslow, S. M. I, *Early Records of the Macarthurs of Camden*, p. 205: John M'Arthur to Eliz. M'Arthur, 11 November 1810; NSWHR, VII, p. 454.

53. Journals, A778, p. 23, 20 November 1810.

54. *Ibid.*, pp. 38-40, 29 November 1810; quotation, pp. 39-40.

55. *Ibid.*, p. 53.

56. *Ibid.*, p. 60.

57. *Ibid.*, pp. 60-78.

58. *Ibid.*, p. 78.

59. NSWHR, VII, p. 468: G. & G.O., 15 December 1810. His tour ended on 13 December after 37 days.

60. *Ibid.*, pp. 468-9.

61. *Ibid.*, p. 469.

62. Memoranda, A772, p. 29; NSWHR, VII, pp. 479-85: G. & G.O. (Police Regulations), 1 January 1811; CSIL (1810), No. 146, p. 250.

Chapter XVI: A MOLEHILL RISES

1. Memoranda, A772, p. 29, 1 January 1811. The address was presented by Nicholas Bayly, Gregory Blaxland and Charles Hook.

2. NSWHR, VII, p. 600: Macquarie to Liverpool, 18 October 1811.

3. *Ibid.*, p. 471; p. 498, Government Public Notice, 23 February 1811. The District of Airds embraced the lands of Bunburry-Curran Creek, Minto and West Minto.

4. HRA, I. 7, pp. 434, 654-655.

5. It happened in Windsor in September, 1811. The lady was exhibited in Thompson Square and agreed to the transaction. Her husband, one Rattey, received £16 for her. She herself was sent to Newcastle, while her spouse received fifty lashes.

6. Memoranda, A772, pp. 31-2, 4 June 1811.

7. Letterbooks, A797, p. 49: Drummond to Macquarie, 16 April 1811.

8. *Ibid.*, p. 36: Wilberforce to Macquarie, 3 December 1810.

9. *Ibid.* Also, a little later, Sir David Baird.

10. *Ibid.*, pp. 36-7, 29 Sept 1811; Memoranda, A772, p. 41, 29 January 1812.

11. Memoranda, A772, pp. 36-7.

12. Journals, A777: Journal of Tour to and from Van Diemen's Land to Sydney in New South Wales, 4 November 1811-6 January 1812. The account follows the details in this Journal

13. *Ibid.*, p. 36, 2 December 1811.

14. *Ibid.*, pp. 38-47, 3-8 December 1811.

15. *Ibid.*, p. 48, 8 December 1811.

16. *Ibid.*, pp. 57-61, 16-19 December 1811.

17. *Ibid.*, pp. 72-3, 31 December 1811.

18. *Ibid.*, p. 73.

19. *Ibid.*, pp. 83-5, 6 January 1812.

20. *Sydney Gazette*, 18 January 1812, p. 2; Memoranda, A772, pp. 39-40, 7 and 18 January 1812.

21. Memoranda, A772, p. 40, 14 January 1821.

22. *Ibid.*, p. 41, 27 January 1812.

23. *Ibid.*; *Sydney Gazette*, 18 January 1912, p. 2.

24. *Sydney Gazette*, 18 January 1812, p. 2.

25. *Ibid.*

26. *Ibid.*, p. 3. "Ode for the Queen's Birthday, 1812".

27. *Ibid.*: Address of Merchants, Freeholders, Settlers and Traders, Inhabitants of the Town of Sydney. It was signed C. Hook, N. Bayly, G. Blaxcell, Alex Riley, and G. Blaxland.

28. *Ibid.*, p. 2: "His Excellency's Answer".

29. HRA, I. 7, p. 598: Macquarie to Liverpool, 17 November 1812.

30. *Ibid.*, p. 598.

31. *Ibid.*, pp. 597-8, 17 November 1812.

32. Bennet, Letter to Viscount Sidmouth (1st ed.), pp. 8-9.

33. *Ibid.*

34. *Ibid.*, pp. 15 et seq., 116-19.

35. Bigge Appendix, Box 1, p. 189: Wm. Cox's Evidence.

36. *Sydney Gazette*, 7 March 1812, p. 2.

37. *Ibid.*, 14 March 1812, p. 1: G. & G.O., 9 March 1812

38. *Ibid.*
39. HRA, I. 7, p. 176: Liverpool to Macquarie, 1 November 1809. The news reached New South Wales in the *Canada*, 10 September 1810.
40. *Ibid.*, p. 344: Macquarie to Liverpool, 27 October 1810.
41. *Ibid.*, p. 476: Liverpool to Macquarie, 4 May 1812.
42. *Ibid.*, p. 477.
43. *Ibid.*, pp. 477-8.
44. *Ibid.*, p. 479 *et seq.*
45. *Ibid.*
46. *Ibid.*, p. 481.
47. *Ibid.*, p. 384: Macquarie to Liverpool, 18 October 1811.
48. *Ibid.*, p. 486-7: Liverpool to Macquarie, 19 May 1812.
49. *Ibid.*, p. 488.
50. *Ibid.*, p. 525: Macquarie to Liverpool, 9 November 1812.
51. *Ibid.*, p. 526.
52. *Ibid.*, pp. 531-2.
53. *Ibid.*, pp. 595-6: to Liverpool, 17 November 1812.
54. Mitchell Library MSS., Am. 17: Macquarie to Thomas Coutts, 10 November 1812. The body of the letter is in the handwriting of Mrs Macquarie.
55. HRA, I. 7, p. 497: Bathurst to Macquarie, 11 June 1812.
56. HRA, I. 8, p. 638: Bathurst to Macquarie, 4 December 1815.
57. Memoranda, A772, 5 June, and p. 52, 25 October 1812 (His appointment dated from 25 November 1811); CSIL (1812), p. 125: Order of the Day, 31 October 1812.
58. Piper Papers, A254, p. 197: Eliz. Macquarie to John Piper, 2 December 1812.
59. Onslow, S. M., *Early Records of the Macarthurs of Camden*, p. 233: John M'Arthur to Eliz. M'Arthur, 9 December 1812.
60. Memoranda, A772, p. 53, 18 December 1812.

CHAPTER XVII: THE MOST MERITORIOUS MEN

1. Bennet, H. G., *Letter to Viscount Sidmouth*; Bigge Appendix, Box 1, p. 23: Major Druitt's Evidence: "Before the days of the [convict] barrack, newly arrived convicts were mustered in the Gaol yard, distributed to gangs in the Lumber Yard and told by the superintendent: 'You must go and provide yourselves with lodging where you can and come to your work in the morning when the bell rings'." Ho. of C. Select Committee (1812), p. 11.
2. H. of C. Select Committee (1812), Appendix, p. 40: Bligh's evidence: "In April, 1807 . . . there appeared to be . . . in the Colony . . . 166 free men who never had been convicts." Broughton and Riley in the middle of 1815 put the proportion at four-fifths, but estimates varied. HRA, I. 10, p. 549, the emancipists gave their own numbers in 1820 as 7556 (apart from their 5859 children), and those of persons who had arrived in the Colony free at 1558. To these undischarged convicts must be added.
3. HRA, I. 10, p. 222: to Bigge, 6 November 1819.
4. NSWHR, IV, p. 235: Marsden to King, 30 September 1800, gives an excellent example of the type of punishment in vogue. Though the power of magistrates sitting alone in Sydney to flog was limited, those in outlying districts could award 300 lashes or more, but "a heavy punishment was not executed without the previous approval of the Governor". Ho. of C. Select Committee (1812), p. 11.
5. H. of C. Select Committee (1812), Appendix, p. 36: Bligh's Evidence; Report, p. 13: Committee's comments.
6. His order CSIL (1811), No. 34, p. 62, 8 June 1811, made clear his "unalterable intention" to release "only such persons as have by a long and uninterrupted period of good conduct and sincere contrition for their past offences, evinced themselves worthy of such favours and indulgences". See also Bigge Appendix, Box 1, p. 91: Druitt's Evidence, for his merciful habits.
7. Bigge Report, Convicts, pp. 88, 149-54.
8. Macquarie, L., *Letter to Viscount Sidmouth*, p. 79.
9. *Gleaner*, 26 May 1827, p. 4, Ode addressed, on the opening of the New Year, 1820, to His Excellency Major-General Macquarie, etc., etc.; H. of C. Select Committee (1812), Report, pp. 12-13.
10. Mann, D. D., *Present Picture of New South Wales*, p. 70.
11. All the officers of the 102nd Regiment had left the Colony, together with several senior civil officials, including Palmer, the Commissary.
12. HRA, I. 10, pp. 222-3: to Bigge, 6 November 1819.
13. Mann, D. D., *Present Picture of New South Wales*, p. 53, enlarges on the subject of comparative virtue.

14. Wentworth, W. C., *Statistical Account of New South Wales* (1st ed.), p. 203.
15. Bigge Report, Convicts, p. 146. Macquarie, *Letter to Viscount Sidmouth*, p. 41, says that Fitzgerald also "was honoured by the personal friendship and intimacy of Ellis Bent and Lieutenant-Colonel O'Connell".
16. Wentworth, *Statistical Account of New South Wales*. See Note 14.
17. Bigge Appendix, Box 5, p. 2054.
18. *Ibid.*, Box 5, pp. 2047-9: Arch. Bell's Evidence.
19. *Ibid.*, Box 5, p. 2045.
20. *Ibid.*, Box 11, Points of Administration submitted by the Commissioner and answered by Governor Macquarie, Answer 5.
21. *Ibid.*
22. CSIL (1810), No. 68, Hayes's memorial, is an interesting document for the student of the times. NSWHR, VII, p. 316 *et seq.*
23. Marsden arrived on 22 February 1810. When he refused office, the Governor appointed Dr D'Arcy Wentworth in his stead.
24. Marsden, *Answer to Governor Macquarie's Pamphlet* (1826), A922-3M, p. 4 *et seq.* Marsden's account, pp. 4-6, is that he learned of his appointment with astonishment on reading the *Gazette.* Also, Bigge Appendix, Box 8, p. 3375 *et seq.*
25. *Ibid.*, p. 5; Bigge Appendix, p. 3380.
26. *Ibid.*, pp. 5-6.
27. *Missionary Papers*, Box 49 (B.T.), 72a, p. 293: Marsden to the Archbishop of Canterbury, 2 May 1810.
28. *Ibid.*, p. 82: Marsden to Wilberforce, 27 July 1810.
29. NSWHR, VII, p. 319: G. and G.O., 23 and 24 March 1810; p. 328: G. and G.O., 7 April 1810.
30. Macquarie, L., *Letter to Viscount Sidmouth*, p. 44 *et seq.*
31. Bigge Report, Convicts, pp. 81-2; H. of C. Papers (1828), XXI: Macquarie to Bathurst, 10 October 1823, pp. 31, 67, Appendix (C), "Communication from Mr Andrew Thompson to Mr Howe, Oct., 4, 1810".
32. *Ibid.*
33. Macquarie, L., *Letter to Viscount Sidmouth*, p. 45. Bigge's version is in his Report, Convicts, pp. 82-3.
34. Macquarie, L., *Letter to Viscount Sidmouth*, pp. 44-7.
35. NSWHR, VI, p. 434. The order of the signatures was: John M'Arthur, John Blaxland, (Dr) James Mileham, Simeon Lord, Gregory Blaxland, James Badgery, Nicholas Bayly. Bigge Report, Convicts, pp. 82-3.
36. Macquarie, L., *Letter to Viscount Sidmouth*, pp. 44-7.
37. Bigge Report, Convicts, p. 83; HRA, I. 10: Bigge to Macquarie, 10 November 1819, enclosure, Examination of John Harris, 7 November 1819 (p. 231).
38. Bigge Appendix, Box 8, p. 3376: Marsden's Evidence. The Bigge Report, Convicts, p. 82, meditates "upon several attempts, which on investigation appeared to have been made by him, to seduce two girls of the orphan school at Sydney . . . although these animadversions did not positively charge him with the crime."
39. Bigge Appendix, Box 5, 80B, p. 2055: Bell's Evidence.
40. *Ibid.*, Box 8, p. 3375: Marsden's Evidence. The Bigge Report, p. 82, says that Thompson's habits of domestic life were immoral. Macquarie Papers, A800-1: Macquarie to Bathurst, 10 October 1823. It was the Hawkesbury settlers, in an address upon Thompson's death, who described him as "the common friend and patron of all . . ."
41. Macquarie, L., *Letter to Viscount Sidmouth*, p. 35 *et seq.*; Bigge Report, Convicts, p. 82.
42. NSWHR, IV, pp. 5, 16.
43. NSWHR, VI, p. 827: Marsden to King, 26 March 1806.
44. NSWHR, VI, p. 450: Examination of Thompson by the Rebels:—Q.: Have you the management of the public business at the Hawkesbury? Ans.: I have, under Dr Arndell. HRA, I. 6, p. 373: Thompson to Bligh, 1 January 1808; NSWHR, VI, p. 262.
45. NSWHR, VI: G. & G.O., 22 February 1807.
46. NSWHR, VI, pp. 237, 257. Thompson's signature appears third among some hundreds on the addresses (p. 257), and directly after that of the Hawkesbury magistrate then in office and James Cox.
47. Bigge Appendix, Box 1, p. 268: Dr Harris's Evidence; Bigge Report, Convicts, p. 81.
48. Macquarie, L., *Letter to Viscount Sidmouth*, p. 37.
49. HRA, I. 7, p. 609: to Liverpool, 7 November 1812; Macquarie, L., *Letter to Viscount Sidmouth*, pp. 41-4; Bigge Report, Convicts, p. 145.
50. NSWHR, VII, pp. 444-5: Meehan to Lloyd, 28 October 1810.
51. *Ibid.*, p. 445: Meehan to Lloyd, 28 October 1810.

T

52. Bigge Report, Convicts, p. 84; Macquarie, L., *Letter to Viscount Sidmouth*, pp. 38-40.

53. The opening words of an Assistant-Surgeon's Commission were: "George the Third by the Grace of God ... to our Trusty and well-beloved [William Redfern], gent ... greeting."

54. Australian Encyclopaedia, II, p. 392.

55. Bigge Report, Convicts, p. 146. The conclusion of Bigge was based on a single instance.

56. *Ibid.*

57. *Ibid.*

58. HRA, I. 8, pp. 131, 190; Wentworth Papers, A752, pp. 29-31.

59. Wentworth Papers, A752, p. 9: D'Arcy Wentworth to Earl Fitzwilliam, an undated fragment, apparently written early in 1810, probably for the mail of 17 March 1810.

60. Wentworth Papers, A751, p. 27. Governor Hunter showed his regard for him in 1798 by asking him to Government House for Christmas dinner. (Wentworth Papers, A751, p. 33.) Other Governors praised him. King said that he "had never had a complaint from him or those under him, and, in fact, he is a real treasure here". Even Bigge, who did not like him and who erroneously described him as having been a former convict, apart from attacking his private life, declared that "no fault could be found with his official character" and that he was "much trusted by all classes". Macquarie later testified to Foveaux's high opinion of him.

61. Wentworth Papers, A753, p. 51: D'A. Wentworth to Macquarie, 6 September 1817.

62. Wentworth Papers, A756, p. 116: W. C. Wentworth to H. G. Bennet, 12 February 1819.

63. *Ibid.*, pp. 116-17.

64. HRA, IV. 1, p. 146: J. H. Bent to Bathurst, 1 July 1815, and Note 90; Bigge Appendix, Box 1, p. 269: Harris's Evidence. There is no doubt that Wentworth was a highwayman, but the Crown repeatedly failed to secure his conviction.

65. *Ibid.*

66. *Ibid.*, Bigge Appendix, Box 1, p. 271. For Earl Fitzwilliam's account of D'Arcy Wentworth's going to New South Wales, A757, 9 February 1821.

67. Portrait in Vaucluse House, Sydney.

68. In the 73rd Regiment.

69. NSWHR, VII, p. 630: G. and G.O., 26 October 1811. Information which has come to light since the first edition of this book was published makes it certain that W. C. Wentworth was born before 1793, very possibly on 26 October 1790.

70. Wentworth Papers, A756, p. 2: Cookney to D. Wentworth: "William is certainly a very fine boy, but 'tis the opinion of Mrs. Cookney and myself that a surgeon is a very improper profession for him, as from the cast in his eye it leads him differently to the object he intends."

71. His property was Vermont, which in the middle of the twentieth century remains in the Wentworth family, in direct descent, the one estate of the Macquarie age that has been kept in the direct male line of family ownership from the moment it was granted, apart from some other Wentworth lands.

72. NSWHR, VII, pp. 444-5: Meehan to Lloyd, 28 October 1810; Wentworth Papers, A752, p. 9 *et seq.*

73. Memoranda, A772, p. 27, 22 October 1810.

74. *Ibid.*, p. 28, 26 October 1810.

75. *Sydney Gazette*, 3 November 1810.

76. Journals, A778, p. 26.

77. *Ibid.*, p. 27.

78. *Ibid.*, p. 53.

79. Bigge Appendix, Box 13, p. 529.

80. See Chapter X.

81. Letterbooks, A797, p. 77: Baird to Macquarie, 30 March 1813.

82. Onslow, S. M., *Early Records of the Macarthurs of Camden*, p. 233: John M'Arthur to Mrs M'Arthur, 9 December 1812. He borrowed £400—his "last guinea"—from M'Arthur, £1200 from his own agent, Harrison, and secured merchandise and his passage on credit. A notable performance for one who had just been cashiered.

83. Wentworth Papers, A752: Kemp to D'Arcy Wentworth, 13 March 1811.

84. *Ibid.*, 18 August 1811.

85. See Chapter XIV, p. 218.

86. Letterbooks, A797, pp. 24-87, 25-93: Princes Edward and Frederick to Macquarie, 11 August and 19 August 1813; HRA, I. 7, pp. 502, 508 *et seq.*: Wilson's Remarks on Trade.

87. It was Camden to whom he had gone for support of his sheep-raising schemes in 1802-4, after he had been sent to England under arrest by King. Camden had secured for him at that time a grant of 5000 acres of land on which to develop the wool industry, but his ambition had soared far since then.

88. NSWHR, VII, p. 401: John M'Arthur to Eliz. M'Arthur, 3 August 1810.

89. Onslow, S. M., *Early Records of the Macarthurs of Camden*, p. 215: John M'Arthur to Elizabeth M'Arthur, 21 April 1811.

90. *Ibid.*, p. 219.

91. *Ibid.*, p. 214, 6 April 1811.

92. The system was first introduced in the days of Queen Elizabeth. It was, as Henry Grey Bennet pointed out, unknown to the Common Law and was born of various Statutes. Its more modern basis was 4 Geo. I, c. 2, which provided "that where any persons shall be convicted of grand or petit larceny, or felonious stealing of money or goods, and who by law shall be entitled to the benefit of clergy, it shall be lawful for the Court before whom they are convicted, to order them to be sent to his Majesty's plantations in America for seven years" This was extended to other crimes and other parts of the globe by 19 Geo. III, c. 74. An excellent account of the matter appears in Eris O'Brien's *The Foundation of Australia*, 2nd ed., pp. 47-63. See also Windeyer, *Lectures on Legal History*, p. 325 *et seq.*

93. H. of C. Papers, *Parliamentary Documents*, vol. I (1812), Report of the Select Committee on Transportation (ordered to be printed, 10 July 1812).

94. *Ibid.*, p. 3.

95. *Ibid.*, p. 13.

96. *Ibid.*, p. 14.

97. *Ibid.*, p. 8.

98. *Ibid.*, pp. 6-7.

99. HRA, I. 7, p. 772: to Bathurst, 28 June 1813.

100. *Ibid.*, pp. 780-1.

101. *Ibid.*, p. 781.

102. *Ibid.*, p. 780.

103. *Ibid.*, p. 675: Bathurst to Macquarie, 23 November 1812.

104. *Ibid.*, p. 780, Par. 6: to Bathurst, 28 June 1813.

105. *Ibid.*, pp. 774-7.

106. CSIL (1811) and other volumes contain numerous reports of inquisitions by coroners' juries, worth study, especially since the names of jurymen appear on the documents.

107. HRA, I. 7, p. 674: Bathurst to Macquarie, 23 November 1812.

108. *Ibid.*, p. 617: to Liverpool, 17 November 1812.

109. *Ibid.*, pp. 775-6: to Bathurst, 28 June 1813.

110. Missionary Papers, Box 49 (B.T.), 337: Rev. Pasco Crook to Rev. Tracey, 18 June 1813, describes the scene.

CHAPTER XVIII: "VERY LIVELY"

1. HRA, I. 8, pp. 30-6: Macquarie to Croker, 3 August 1813, with enclosures; pp. 36-55.

2. Bennet, *Letter to Viscount Sidmouth* (1st ed.), pp. 8, 9. In 1810-11 the influx had been 400 males and 99 females; in the next five years it was 3978 males and 681 females.

3. *Sydney Gazette*, 2 January 1813.

4. *Ibid.*

5. *Sydney Gazette*, Public Notice, 12 June 1813.

6. *Sydney Gazette*, 2 January 1813.

7. *Ibid.*

8. *Ibid.*

9. HRA, I. 7, p. 671: Bathurst to Macquarie, 23 November 1812.

10. *Sydney Gazette*, 2 January 1813.

11. *Sydney Gazette*, 2 January 1813, Simeon Lord (Chairman), John Blaxland, John Townson, Robt. Campbell, Robt. Jenkins and others.

12. *Sydney Gazette*, 30 January 1813.

13. Bigge Appendix, Box 11, vol. 142, 4358-74, 4 February 1821, Query 6.

14. *Ibid.*

15. British Museum (King's Library) MSS. 8958, 16 November 1816.

16. HRA, I. 8, p. 30, Macquarie to Croker, 3 August 1813; CSIL (1813), No. 43, p. 68: to Secretary, Board of Admiralty (original copy in Macquarie's writing).

17. *Ibid.*, p. 37: to Case, 5 December 1812.

18. *Ibid.*, p. 43: to Case, 7 December 1812.

19. *Ibid.*, p. 45: to Case, 16 February 1813.

20. *Ibid.*, p. 46: to Case, 22 March 1813; Case to Macquarie, 22 March 1813.

21. *Ibid.*

22. *Ibid.*, pp. 45-8: Case to Macquarie, 22-24 March 1813.

23. *Ibid.*, p. 54: to Lieutenant Butcher, 5 May 1813.

24. *Ibid.*, p. 53: Butcher to Macquarie, 5 May 1813.

25. *Ibid.*, p. 48.

26. HRA, I. 7, p. 364: Liverpool to Macquarie, 26 July 1811.

27. HRA, I. 7, pp. 364, 459, 608; NSWHR, VII, p. 463: to Liverpool, 28 November 1810, p. 572; 15 August 1811. He arrived in the *Minstrel*, 25 October 1812 (HRA, I. 7, p. 608).

28. HRA, III. 2, xii. The Colonial and War Secretary (Liverpool) made it clear that Foveaux's conduct in the Colony had not called for censure. He wrote that he would have no difficulty in assuring the Commander-in-Chief that there could be no objection to Colonel F.'s advance in rank as an officer, and that he should not suffer by the loss of opportunity which would have come his way had circumstances been otherwise.

29. HRA, III. 2, xii.

30. *Dictionary of National Biography*, L, pp. 43-4. Pitt at one stage considered him as his most likely successor.

31. Memoranda, A772, 31 January 1813.

32. HRA, I. 8, p. 458: to Bathurst, 22 March 1815.

33. HRA, I. 7, pp. 789-90: to Goulburn, 30 June 1813.

34. *Ibid.*, p. 790.

35. *Ibid.*, p. 708. Davey reached Sydney on 25 October 1812, and sailed for Hobart Town on 10 February 1813. For his instructions, see Mitchell Library, Safe, 15, Macquarie Papers.

36. HRA, III. 2, xiv; Calder Papers, A594, p. 595: "I have been told that he was one of those jolly fellows whom everybody likes and no-one esteems . . . He might be found quite as often at the Union Hotel, Campbell Street, as at Government House. When he arrived, the day was, as the good old fellow expressed it, 'as hot as hell,' and . . . he answered the huzzas of the crowd, not by taking off his hat, but his coat."

37. HRA, III. 2, pp. 23-5: Private Memorandums to Davey, 6 February 1813.

38. HRA, I. 8, p. 460: Macquarie to Bathurst, 22 March 1815.

39. HRA, III. 2, pp. 553-8, *Courtmartial of Fosbrook*; also HRA, I. 8, pp. 237 *et seq.*

40. HRA, III. 2, pp. 593, 611, 612, 614, 617, 618, 628, 633.

41. Wentworth Papers, A761, pp. 60-4: Contractor to Macquarie, 18 December 1812 (Contractors' office copy).

42. *Ibid.* The papers are in Wentworth Papers, A761, p. 20 *et seq.*, especially.

43. Bigge Appendix. Box 13, p. 510; Wentworth Papers, A761, p. 66, (orig.): J. T. Campbell to Contractors, 21 December 1812.

44. Bigge Appendix, Box 13, p. 622-3; Wentworth Papers, A761, p. 98 (orig.): to Contractors, 8 May 1813.

45. Wentworth Papers, A761, p. 84: to Contractors, 10 February 1813.

46. *Ibid.*: Contractors' copy, 15 October 1812. Bigge Appendix, Box 13, pp. 844, 847, 849, A761, p. 103: Campbell to Contractors, 29 September 1814; p. 112: Contractors to Macquarie, 5 October 1814, and 15 October 1814.

47. Wentworth Papers, A761, p. 103: Campbell to Contractors, 29 September 1814.

48. HRA, I. 8, pp. 259, 260: G. & G.O., 24 March and 30 April 1814, p. 157.

49. *Ibid.*

50. Memoranda, A772, 11 March 1813.

51. Bigge Appendix, Box 12: List of Works; Memoranda, A772, p. 59, 17 May, and p. 57, 15 April 1813.

52. *Ibid.*, A772, p. 58, 17 April 1813.

53. *Ibid.*, A772, p. 60, 18 May 1813.

54. *Ibid.*

55. *Ibid.*, p. 60, 25 May 1813.

56. *Ibid.*, A772, 2 February 1813.

57. *Ibid.*, A772, p. 59, 1 and 5 May 1813.

58. See Chapter XV, p. 324.

59. HRA, I. 7, pp. 558 *et seq.*: to Liverpool, 17 November 1812; all the originals correspondence of the dispute is in CSIL (1812), pp. 54-90.

60. HRA, I. 7, 559.

61. *Ibid.*, I. 8, p. 569: G. & G.O., 10 June 1815. There is another account—substantially a duplicate of that of 1823—among the Bigge Appendix papers, Box 20, pp. 3629, 3271 *et seq.*, entitled "A Narrative relating to the First Expedition over the Blue Mountains in New South Wales, containing the motives which first induced Mr. G. Blaxland to undertake it in the year 1813".

No historian apparently has noticed, hitherto, the remarks in the Settlers' Address to the Governor in January 1812, which refers to Macquarie's "proffers of patronage to every effort to surmount those obstacles so long considered to retard further discovery". Mainland exploration seems to have begun in earnest directly after the presentation of this address by the sending of George Evans to make a traverse from Jervis Bay to Broughton's farm near Appin through the Illawarra. The fact that those associated with the address included Blaxland and Wentworth seems to have important implications. There can be no doubt of Macquarie's interest in exploration from the beginning — his own expeditions, pushing out to the very limits of settlement and beyond, advertise it.

62. British Museum (King's Library) MSS. 8958, 16 November 1816.

63. Blaxland, G., A Journal of a Tour of Discovery Across the Blue Mountains in New South Wales (1823), C129, p. 5.

64. Ibid., p. 8.

65. Australian, 13 March 1827.

66. Mann, D. D., The Present Picture of New South Wales, p. 31.

67. Sydney Gazette, 22 May 1813. Lawson's Journal (C123) opens: "Mr Blaxland, Wentworth and myself with four men and four Horses Laden with Provisions etc. took our Departure on Tuesday the 11th May, 1813, Crossed the Nepean River at Mr. Chapman's Farm, Emu Island, at four o'clock and proceeded S.W. Two miles. Encamped at 5 o'clock at the foot of the first Ridge of Hills." The Gazette, of course, was a week out in the date in its report.

68. Henry Kendall.

69. Wentworth Journal, Mitchell Library, C122, Photostat, p. 7.

70. Ibid., p. 6.

71. Wentworth, W. C., Australasia.

72. Blaxland, A Journal of a Tour of Discovery Across the Blue Mountains in New South Wales (1823), C129, p. 36.

73. Lawson, Journal, C123, 31 May 1813. This passage contains almost no punctuation in the original.

74. Wentworth, Journal, C122, p. 13.

75. British Museum (King's Library) MSS. 8958, 16 November 1816.

76. Sydney Gazette, 18 June 1814.

77. Ibid.

78. Later this is exactly what happened. The bushrangers for some years had a royal time west of the ranges, even prior to the gold era. Bigge Appendix, Box 13, pp. 786-7; CSIL (1813), No. 63½, p. 113; No. 5, p. 8: Order, 13 February 1813.

79. The silence was peculiar. Even after the passage of the Mountains by Evans in December 1813 there is no evidence of their having given tongue. The original of Macquarie's order to pay Byrne is in the Wentworth Papers, A763, pp. 51, 73; Wentworth Accounts, D1, p. 88.

80. Sydney Gazette, 12 June 1813, p. 3.

81. Ibid.

82. HRA, I. 7, pp. 707-88: to Bathurst, 28 June 1813.

83. HRA, I. 8, p. 2: to Bathurst, 31 July 1813.

84. Sydney Gazette, February-March 1812.

85. Ibid., Governor's Proclamation to the Men of the 73rd Regiment.

86. HRA, I. 8, p. 2-26: to Bathurst, 31 July, 1813.

87. Ibid., pp. 9 et seq.

88. Ibid.

89. Ibid., pp. 3, 9, 10.

90. Ibid., p. 16.

91. Ibid., pp. 17-18: Evidence of Martin, Ross, and Luttrell.

92. Ibid., p. 26.

93. Ibid., p. 2.

94. Ibid., p. 3.

95. Ibid., p. 4. He particularly asked that officers of the 73rd should not be allowed to exchange into the succeeding regiment.

96. Piper Papers, A254: Birch to Piper, 13 August 1815.

97. HRA, I. 8, p. 36: Macquarie to Croker; p. 54: Blaxcell to Macquarie, 29 July 1813.

98. Ibid., p. 70: Macquarie to Case, 11 August 1813.

99. Sydney Gazette, Lord's advertisements, 1813.

100. Letterbooks, A797, p. 79: Baird to Macquarie, 30 March 1813; Memoranda, A772, p. 65, 9 October 1813. The brevet had been issued on 4 June 1813.

101. Memoranda, A772, p. 65, 9 October 1813.

102. Sydney Gazette, 1 January 1814. The news came in the Argo, and Mr M. M. Robinson wrote an ode about it.

103. Journals, A772, p. 66, 3 November 1813.

104. Ibid., p. 68, 13 December 1813.

105. Ibid.

CHAPTER XIX: NOONTIDE IN BOTANY BAY

1. Memoranda, A772, pp. 68-70, 28 March 1814.
2. Ibid., p. 71, 29 March 1814.
3. Ibid., p. 77, 24 May 1814.
4. Ibid., p. 78, 4 June 1814.
5. Ibid., p. 53, 18 December 1812.
6. HRA, I. 8, p. 58: to Bathurst, 14 August 1813; Bigge Appendix, Box 5, p. 2091: G. Blaxland; p. 1977: W. Cox; Sydney Gazette, 14 August 1813, p. 1: G. & G.O., 14 August.
7. HRA, I. 7, pp. 57-8, 593, 671, 772, 773.
8. HRA, I. 8, p. 58; Sydney Gazette: G. & G.O., 14 August 1813.
9. Ibid.
10. HRA, I. 8, p. 121: to Bathurst, 19 January 1814.
11. Ibid., p. 121, 19 January 1814.
12. Ibid., p. 121.
13. Sydney Gazette, 5 February 1814, and succeeding issues.
14. HRA, I. 8, p. 207: Oxley to Macquarie, 27 April 1814.
15. Ibid., p. 144: Macquarie to Bathurst, 28 April 1814.
16. Ibid., p. 122: Macquarie to Bathurst, 19 January 1814; p. 149, 28 April.
17. Ibid.
18. Ibid., p. 165: Assistant-Surveyor Evans's Journal, 1813-14.
19. Ibid., pp. 122, 149.
20. On 10 March; HRA, I. 8, p. 261: Macquarie to Bathurst, 28 May 1814.
21. HRA, I. 8, p. 152.
22. Ibid., p. 159.
23. Ibid., pp. 86, 160, 184, 250.
24. Ibid., pp. 160, 318, 644.
25. The 73rd Regiment sailed in four ships, beginning with the detachment in the Earl Spencer, embarked 17 January 1814. The first detachment of the 46th Regiment to arrive was on the General Hewitt, midday, 7 February 1814.
26. HRA, I. 8, p. 143.
27. Ibid., p. 207: Oxley to Macquarie, 27 April 1814.
28. Ibid., pp. 210-35.
29. Ibid., p. 211: Macquarie to Bathurst, 30 April 1814.
30. Ibid., p. 140, 244 et seq.; p. 276 et seq.; Surry, pp. 274, 279 et seq., 291, 295; Three Bees, pp. 253, 254, 278, 279.
31. Memoranda, A772, p. 77, 18 May 1814.
32. See Chapter XXIV.
33. Sydney Gazette, 10 September 1814, p. 1: G. & G.O.
34. Ibid., 23 July 1814, p. 1: G. & G.O., par. 4.
35. Ibid., par. 5.
36. Ibid., 8 January 1814.
37. Ibid.
38. Ibid., 23 July: G. & G.O.
39. Ibid., pars. 2 and 3.
40. HRA, I. 8, p. 72 et seq.; pp. 148, 241.
41. Ibid., pp. 148-9: to Bathurst, 28 April 1814.
42. Ibid., pp. 295-6.
43. Ibid., pp. 386, 591. The Betsey came on 22 October with 250 tons of grain; the General Browne on 20 October with about the same quantity.
44. Ibid., p. 314: Macquarie to Bathurst, 7 October 1814.
45. Ibid.
46. Ibid., p. 150: Macquarie to Bathurst, 28 April 1814.
47. Ibid.
48. Cox, Wm., Narrative of the Building of the Road Across the Blue Mountains, 1814-5 (1888 ed.), p. 1.
49. Sydney Gazette, 14 May 1814.
50. Ibid., 4 and 18 June 1814; CSIL (1814), No. 13, p. 21, Cox to Macquarie, 3 March 1814.
51. Cox, Narrative (1888 ed.), p. 1; Bigge Appendix, Box 13, p. 784: Return of Men Constructing the Blue Mts. Road, 8 July 1814; pp. 786, 788: Macquarie to Allan, 8 and 9 July 1814; p. 791: Macquarie to Cox, 14 July 1814.
52. Bigge Report, Convicts, p. 125; Bigge Appendix, Box 5, p. 1966, Cox's Evidence.
53. HRA, I. 8, p. 314: Macquarie to Bathurst, 7 October 1814.
54. Cox, Narrative, p. 5, 2 August 1814.

55. Cox, *Narrative*, p. 2; Bigge Appendix, Box 13, pp. 791-5: Macquarie to Cox, 14 July 1814. Cox left Clarendon on 17 July 1814 at 9 a. m. and arrived at the assembling point at noon.

56. Cox, *Narrative*; Bigge Appendix, Box 13, pp. 798-801, "List of Stores and Implements, etc.", (Signed) L. Macquarie, 14 July 1814.

57. Cox, *Narrative*, p. 13, Friday-to-Saturday, 1 October 1814; G. & G.O., 10 June 1815; HRA, I. 8, p. 315: Macquarie to Bathurst, 7 October 1814.

58. HRA, I. 8, p. 568: G. & G.O., 10 June 1815; Cox, *Narrative*, p. 31.

59. HRA, I. 8, p. 558: Macquarie to Bathurst, 24 June 1815.

60. *Ibid.* Macquarie, in his dispatch No. 7, 24 June 1815, asked Bathurst to sanction the payment of £300 to Cox as "pecuniary remuneration". Bathurst ignored the request and Macquarie repeated it in a private letter to Goulburn 17 May 1817, in which he says that he has not yet paid the money and is reluctant to do so without authority. However, he appears to have acted on his own initiative. A return in the Bigge Appendix, Box 14, p. 1234, shows "sums paid to Mr Cox from the Police Fund on account of the Bathurst Road and expenses incurred at Bathurst: July, 1815, Sundry Disbursements made by Mr Cox in constructing the Bathurst Road, £300; expense of depot at Emu Ford, £200. Jan., 1816, Expenses in connection with the depot at Springwood, £225. Dec., 1816, Expenses incurred in remuneration and payment of services in making the Bathurst Road, £179 8s. 1d." Mr Michael Robinson, poet laureate, wrote out the pardons of convicts who worked on the road and received £11 8s. 2d. in fees. And on 31 March 1817 the Police Fund is debited with the value of sixty head of cattle issued from the Government herds in payment of Mr Cox and others for services at Bathurst and on the road, £1200. See also Bigge Appendix, Box 11, Q. and A. 35 and 36.

61. HRA, I. 9, p. 114: Bathurst to Macquarie, 18 April 1816. In this dispatch, acknowledging Macquarie's dispatch of 24 June 1815, Bathurst does not mention either Cox or the road. It is ironic that the only reference to the road in this set of dispatches from home was in an anonymous letter of complaint which moved the Governor to tender his resignation. (See Chapter XXVI).

62. HRA, I. 8, p. 386: Macquarie to Bathurst, 12 December 1814.

63. HRA, I. 8, p. 601: Stock Returns, 17 October-16 November 1814; I. 9, p. 92: Stock Returns, 6 November 1814, 6 December 1815.

64. Journals, A779-A780: Journal of a Tour to the Western Districts of New South Wales, 1815 (2 vols); Antill, H.C., Journal of a Tour to the Interior.

65. HRA, I. 8, p. 574: G. & G.O., 10 June 1815.

66. *Ibid.*

67. *Ibid.*, p. 611 *et seq.*: The Journal of Assistant-Surveyor Evans, 13 May-12 June 1815.

68. HRA, I. 8, p. 150: Macquarie to Bathurst, 28 April 1814.

69. HRA, I. 8, p. 575: Macquarie to Bathurst, 24 June 1815.

70. *Ibid.*

71. *Ibid.*, p. 559: Macquarie to Bathurst, 24 June 1815. Here the proposed settlement conditions are set out in full.

72. Cox, Road Book, 21 July 1815: "Mr. Lawson crossed the River with 100 Head of Horn cattle for the West Country." CSIL (Bathurst Papers, 1815-23): R. Hassall to Macquarie, 18 August 1815.

73. HRA, I. 9, pp. 60, 850; CSIL (Bathurst Papers, 1815-23), No. 41: Hassall to Macquarie, 27 October 1815: "Two principal overseers to bring from thence 110 head of oxen . . . the men set off the latter end of last week."

74. HRA, I. 9, p. 60: Macquarie to Bathurst, 18 March 1816.

75. *Ibid.*

76. *Ibid.*; also Bigge Appendix, Box 10, pp. 4045-50: Evidence of Rodriguez; pp. 3989-96: Evidence of Wathen; CSIL (Bathurst Papers, 1815-23): Macquarie to R. Hassall, 3 February 1816, 1 March 1816.

77. HRA, I. 8, p. 569: "To G. Blaxland and W. Wentworth, Esqs., and Lieutenant Lawson, of the Royal Veteran Company, the merit is due of having, with extraordinary patience and much fatigue, effected the first passage over the most rugged and difficult part of the Blue Mountains"—G. & G.O., 24 June 1815.

78. Wentworth Papers, A752, p. 145: Memorandum to D'Arcy Wentworth, 27 February 1815. An earlier medicine chest had been destroyed by fire.

79. HRA, I. 8, p. 638: Bathurst to Macquarie, 4 December 1815.

80. HRA, I. 8, p. 310: Macquarie to Bathurst, 7 October 1814; p. 463: to Bathurst, 24 March 1815; p. 470: Government Public Notice, 31 December 1814; p. 471: G. & G.O., 31 December 1814.

81. HRA, I. 8, p. 310: Macquarie to Bathurst, 7 October 1814.

82. *Ibid.*, p. 641: Bathurst to Macquarie, 4 December 1815.

83. *Ibid.*, p. 464: Macquarie to Bathurst, 24 March 1815, p. 471.

84. *Ibid.*, p. 470: Government Public Notice, 31 December 1814.
85. *Sydney Gazette*, 3 and 17 June 1815.
86. HRA, I. 8, pp. 159, 663 (Note 45).
87. *Ibid.*
88. *Sydney Gazette*, 3 and 17 June 1815, p. 2.

BOOK FOUR

CHAPTER XX: THE DANGEROUS CONTAGION

1. Bent and others holding the same office were referred to in their commissions as "Deputy-Judge-Advocate" but the Statute 27 Geo. III c. 2 provided for them as "Judges Advocate", as did the Letters Patent (1787), and from the inception all holders of the office signed official documents as "Judge-Advocate". HRA, IV. 1, p. 181: J. H. Bent to Bathurst, gives his brother's age, at the time of his death on 10 Nov 1815, as 32 years.
2. HRA, IV. 1, 67: E. Bent to Liverpool, 30 November 1811.
3. HRA, I. 7, p. 81: Castlereagh to Macquarie, 14 May 1809.
4. National Library, A141: Bent, Ellis, Letters 1809-12, p. 157-8: E. to J. H. Bent, 2 May 1810.
5. HRA, I. 7, p. 395: to Liverpool, 18 October 1811.
6. *Ibid.*, IV. 1, p. 55: E. Bent to Cooke, 7 May 1810.
7. *Ibid.*, I. 7, p. 672 *et seq.*; p. 814: E. Bent to Liverpool, 19 October 1811; Acts of British Parliament, 27 George III, c. 2. [HRA, IV. 1, p. 3.] NSWHR, VII, p. 234: John Blaxland to Liverpool, 27 November 1809; HRA, IV. 1, pp. 799-802: Bigge Commission, Wylde's Examination.
8. HRA, IV. 1 p. 11, Charter of Justice.
9. HRA, IV. 1, p. 55: E. Bent to Cooke, 7 May 1810; CSIL (1810), p. 264.
10. *Ibid.*: CSIL (1812), No. 11: E. Bent to Macquarie.
11. *Ibid.*, I. 8, p. 390 *et seq.*: to Bathurst, 24 February 1815.
12. *Ibid.*; also CSIL (1812), No. 29, p. 95, Bent to Campbell; (1811), p. 96, 28 October 1811; p. 99, 23 June 1812.
13. HRA, I. 8, p. 390 *et seq.*: to Bathurst, 24 February 1815; CSIL (1812), p. 99, 23 June 1812.
14. HRA, I. 8, pp. 389-90: to Bathurst, 24 February 1815; p. 671, Note 91.
15. *Ibid.*, p. 393.
16. HRA, I. 7, p. 450: General Public Notice and Order, 12 October 1811.
17. *Ibid.*
18. NSWHR, VII, p. 402: G. & G.O., 11 August 1810.
19. HRA, I. 7, p. 818: E. Bent to Liverpool, 19 October 1811.
20. Mitchell Library, Am. 17: to Coutts, 10 November 1812.
21. HRA, I. 7, p. 777: to Bathurst, 28 June 1813.
22. *Ibid.*   23. *Ibid.*   24. *Ibid.*
25. HRA, IV. 1, p. 393: Wylde to Bathurst, 15 August 1821; pp. 394-5: J. Foster's Answers.
26. *Ibid.*, p. 53: E. Bent to Cooke, 7 May 1810.
27. HRA, I. 8, p. 391: to Bathurst, 24 February 1815; CSIL (1814), No. 24, p. 81: D. D. Mathew to Macquarie, 14 April 1814; also in HRA, I. 8, pp. 153, 178.
28. CSIL (1813), p. 179; HRA, I. 8, pp. 391-2.
29. HRA, I. 8, pp. 391-2.
30. *Ibid.*, p. 393.
31. *Ibid.*, p. 393.
32. CSIL (1813), No. 58, p. 96, 9 November 1813. The actual signature on the order is: "By Command of His Excellency, H. C. Antill, Major of Brigade". G. & G.O., 9 November 1813.
33. HRA, IV. 1, p. 127: Bent to Bathurst, 1 July 1815.
34. HRA, I. 8, p. 393: to Bathurst, 24 February 1815; E. Bent to Bathurst, p. 127.
35. HRA, IV. 1, p. 46: Commission for Deputy Judge-Advocate Bent, 1 January 1809.
36. HRA, IV. 1, p. 127; p. 171: Bathurst to E. Bent, 11 December 1815.
37. HRA, I. 8, p. 400: Extract from the Book of Proceedings of the Bench of Magistrates, dated Saturday, 31st of December, 1814.
38. HRA, I. 8, p. 401; HRA, I. 9, p. 110: Bathurst to E. Bent, 12 April 1816; CSIL (1815), No. 1, p. 3, 31 December 1814, Bent's original; No. 2, p. 14.
39. CSIL (1815), No. 1, p. 3: Bent's original letter of refusal in own handwriting, 31 December 1814; No. 2, p. 4: Answers to Mr Bent's Observations on the Proposed New Port Regulations, (Macquarie's handwriting); No. 3, p. 5: Macquarie to Bent, 9 January 1815, No. 4, p. 6; HRA, I. 8 pp. 401, 408, 409, 410, 422.

40. HRA, IV. 1, p. 124, par. 6: Bent to Bathurst, 1 July 1815.

41. HRA, I. 8, pp. 422–4: E. Bent to Macquarie, 11 January 1815. This letter, like some of the others written by Ellis Bent at this period, reeks of the diction of his brother, J. H. Bent—for instance, the language in HRA, IV. 1, p. 153: J. H. Bent to Bathurst.

42. *Ibid.*   43. *Ibid.*

44. HRA, IV. 1, p. 63: E. Bent to Liverpool, 19 October 1811, p. 908.

45. HRA, IV. 1, p. 108: E. Bent to Bathurst, 14 October 1814.

46. HRA, I. 9, pp. 216–17: to Bathurst, 29 March 1817.

47. CSIL (1810), p. 166; HRA, I. 9, p. 216: Proclamation of 30 June 1810; CSIL (1813), No. 31, p. 44: Proclamation, 1 July 1813; No. 51, p. 86: G. & G.O., 9 October 1813; HRA, I. 7, p. 722 *et seq.*; p. 750 *et seq.*: Proclamation, 1 July 1813.

48. *Ibid.*; CSIL (1813), No. 1 *et seq.*: correspondence and enclosures: Macquarie to Bathurst, 24 February 1815; HRA, I. 8, p. 389 *et seq.*

49. HRA, I. 9, p. 217.

50. *Ibid.*

51. HRA, I. 7, p. 393: Macquarie to Liverpool, 18 October 1811; p. 672 *et seq.*; HRA, IV. 1, p. 48 *et seq.*: E. Bent to Cooke, 7 May 1810; NSWHR, VII, p. 641 *et seq.*: E. Bent to Liverpool, 30 November 1811.

52. HRA, I. 7, p. 395: Macquarie to Liverpool, 18 October 1811.

53. HRA, IV. 1, p. 171: Bathurst to E. Bent, 11 December 1815.

54. *Ibid.*

55. HRA, IV. 1, p. 121: E. Bent to Macquarie, 17 February 1815.

56. NSWHR, V, VI, and VII.

57. HRA, IV. 1, pp. 77–94: Letters Patent Under the Great Seal of Great Britain (4 February 1814) to Establish Civil Courts of Judicature in New South Wales; pp. 3, 904: 27 Geo. III, c. 2, and 24 Geo. III, c. 56; p. 6: Warrant for Charter of Justice, 2 April 1787; p. 94: J. H. Bent's Commission, 7 February 1814.

58. HRA, I. 8, p. 597: List of Persons Holding Civil Employment; p. 139: Bathurst to Macquarie, 13 February 1814; IV. 1, p. 107: E. Bent to Macquarie, 13 February 1814.

59. HRA, IV. 1, p. 107.

60. *Ibid.*

61. Letterbooks, A797, p. 133: E. Macquarie to Drummond, 12 December 1817.

62. HRA, I. 8, p. 397 *et seq.*: to Bathurst, 24 February 1815.

63. *Ibid.*, p. 398.   64. *Ibid.*, p. 399.   65. *Ibid.*, pp. 396–7.

66. HRA, I. 7, p. 669 *et seq.*: Bathurst to Macquarie, 23 November 1812; p. 771 *et seq.*: to Bathurst, 28 June 1813; I. 8, pp. 134–5: Bathurst to Macquarie, 3 February 1814.

67. *Ibid.*   68. *Ibid.*, p. 135.

69. HRA, I. 8, p. 315: to Bathurst, 7 October 1814.

70. HRA, I. 8, p. 517: J. H. Bent to Broughton and Riley, 15 May 1815.

71. Bigge Appendix, Box 8, p. 3373: Marsden's evidence; HRA, I. 7, p. 277. The circumstances suggest that although the transcript of the evidence refers to "J. Bent", it more probably was Ellis Bent.

72. HRA, IV. 1, p. 95: J. H. Bent to Bathurst, 21 February 1814.

73. HRA, I. 8, p. 307: to Bathurst, 7 October 1814.

74. *Piper Papers*, A256, p. 94: Abbott to Piper, 11 April 1814.

75. HRA, IV. 1, p. 96.

76. Piper Papers, A256, vol. 1, p. 94.

77. *Ibid.*; Onslow, S.M., *Early Records of the Macarthurs*, p. 236.

78. HRA, IV. 1, pp. 94–5: J. H. Bent to Goulburn, 7 February 1814.

79. HRA, IV. 1, p. 241: Bent to Bathurst, 5 April 1817.

80. HRA, I. 8, p. 301: Macquarie to Bathurst, 7 October 1814. The offer of lodgings was upon the condition that Bent should pay the rent if the Colonial Office disapproved of what had been done. (Macquarie Papers, Safe, 15, No. 6: Macquarie to Bent, 1 December 1814).

81. *Sydney Gazette*, 4 February 1815; HRA, IV. 1, p. 309: J. H. Bent to Goulburn, 25 July 1818.

82. HRA, IV. 1, p. 241: J. H. Bent to Bathurst, 5 April 1817; p. 146: Bent to Bathurst, 1 July 1815.

83. HRA, IV. 1, pp. 91–2. The Charter generally defined the status of the Court and of the Judge.

84. HRA, I. 7, p. 395: to Liverpool, 18 October 1811.

85. HRA, I. 8, pp. 480–4: Macquarie to Bathurst, 22 June 1815; pp. 491, 493: Petitions of Crossley and Eagar; CSIL (1815), No. 15, p. 82: Macquarie to J. H. Bent, 18 April 1815, Office Copy in Michael Robinson's handwriting, "compared and certified correct. (Sgd.) J. T. Campbell". (HRA, I. 8, p. 489.)

86. HRA, IV. 1, pp. 394, 485: J. H. Bent to Wilmot, 3 July 1823; p. 838. Foster gave evidence before Bigge that he had "the entire management" of Ellis Bent's office and Court, as Principal Clerk or Registrar, from March 1813 till Ellis Bent's death in November 1815.

87. His story will be found in the vols. of NSWHR dealing with the periods of Governors King and Bligh; also HRA, IV. 1, pp. 268-71, his own version.

88. HRA, I. 4, pp. 352, 582 et seq.

89. NSWHR, VII, p. 225: J. Blaxland's Memorial; pp. 212-14: J. G. Harris's Report, 12 September 1809. Blaxland wrote (NSWHR, VII, p. 234), "The Judge-Advocate . . . gave his opinion and vote according to the advice he might receive of Gov'r Bligh, through George Crossley, and who was on particular occasions consulted, bullied, and brow-beat, by the Governor and his junto."

90. Bigge Appendix, Box 12, p. 435: Rev. Boyle Davies to Marsden, 23 November 1810; Missionary Papers, Box 49, p. 308: Eagar to Geo. Howe.

91. Bigge Appendix, Box 12, p. 439: Marsden's Memorandum re Eagar; Box 8, pp. 3320-1. Rev. Robt. Cartwright said that Eagar had for five years lived in his house, taught his children and dined at his own table when company were not present. "I sometimes go to his house," he said. "I have a very good opinion of him."

92. HRA, IV. 1, p. 788: Bigge Commission, Wylde's Evidence.

93. HRA, I. 8, p. 493: Eagar's Memorial, 11 April 1815.

94. Ibid.

95. Ibid.

96. HRA, I. 8, p. 466: to Bathurst, 24 March 1815.

97. Ibid., p. 554: Garling's alleged capture in the Francis and Eliza.

98. Ibid., pp. 466, 489, 495: Correspondence, Macquarie and Bent, 18-20 April 1815; HRA, IV. 1, p. 154: Statement of Mr Justice Bent.

99. CSIL (1815), No. 15, p. 82: Macquarie to J. H. Bent, 18 April 1815; HRA, I. 8, p. 489.

100. HRA, IV. 1, p. 50: Ellis Bent to Cooke, 7 May 1810.

101. HRA, IV. 1, p. 212: T. S. Amos to Bathurst, 14 October 1816; Goulburn to Amos, 17 October 1816.

102. HRA, I. 7, p. 186: Governor Macquarie's Commission.

103. HRA, I. 8, p. 482 et seq.: Macquarie to Bathurst, 22 June 1815.

104. Ibid., p. 495 et seq.: J. H. Bent to Macquarie, 20 April 1815.

105. Ibid. For his authorities, see pp. 497-9.

106. HRA, I. 7, pp. 394-5: to Liverpool, 18 October 1811.

CHAPTER XXI: SIR JEFFERY IN THE LISTS

1. HRA, I. 8, p. 480: to Bathurst, 22 June 1815.

2. Ibid., p. 510 et seq.: General Minutes of the Proceedings of the Supreme Court of New South Wales, 1, 5, 9, and 11 May 1815.

3. Ibid., p. 511, 9 May 1815.

4. Ibid., p. 513: Minutes of the Supreme Court, 9 May 1815. Macquarie's estimate was seven-eighths of the population (HRA, I. 8, p. 489). On 6 November 1819 Macquarie's estimate was above nine-tenths (HRA, I. 10, p. 223: to J. T. Bigge, 6 November 1819.)

5. Ibid., p. 515.

6. Ibid., p. 515 et seq.: Minutes of the Supreme Court, 11 May 1815.

7. Ibid., pp. 515-16: Minutes, 11 May 1815; Broughton and Riley to Bent, 12 May 1815.

8. Ibid., p. 519-20: J. H. Bent to Broughton and Riley, 15 May 1815.

9. Ibid., p. 521: Broughton and Riley to Bent, 22 May 1815.

10. Ibid., p. 526: Statement of Mr Broughton's Opinions; pp. 528-9, Minutes of the Supreme Court, 25 May 1815.

11. Ibid., p. 532: Memorandum enclosed in Bent to Riley and Broughton, 26 May 1815; pp. 532-4: Broughton and Riley to Bent, 30 May 1815.

12. Ibid., p. 536 et seq.: J. H. Bent to Macquarie, 31 May 1815. See also originals of this correspondence in the Bent Papers, Mitchell Library, Safe, 15.

13. Ibid., p. 537.

14. Ibid., pp. 539-40.

15. Ibid., p. 540: Macquarie to J. H. Bent, 2 June 1815.

16. Ibid., p. 541: to Ellis Bent, 17 June 1815: E. Bent to Macquarie, 19 June 1815.

17. HRA, IV. 1, p. 141: E. Bent to Bathurst, 1 July 1815.

18. HRA, I. 8, p. 488: to Bathurst, 22 June 1815.

19. Ibid., p. 489.

20. Ibid., p. 621: Macquarie to Bathurst, 1 July 1815.

21. HRA, IV. 1, p. 153: J. H. Bent to Bathurst, 1 July 1815.

22. CSIL (1815), p. 133: Proclamation, 30 March 1811; HRA, I. 9, pp. 5-6, 11-12; CSIL (1815), No. 29, p. 119: J. H. Bent to Macquarie 18 August, 1815. HRA, IV.1, pp. 162-4: J. H. Bent to Bathurst.

23. All the original correspondence is in CSIL (1815), No. 29-39, pp. 119-58, or in Mitchell Library, Safe, 15, Bent Papers; also in HRA, I. 9, pp. 11-30.

24. HRA, I. 9, p. 14: J. H. Bent to Macquarie, 25 August 1815.

25. HRA, I. 9, p. 14: to J. H. Bent, 26 August 1815.

26. *Ibid.*, p. 14: J. H. Bent to Macquarie, 28 August 1815.

27. *Ibid.*, p. 15.

28. CSIL (1815): Examinations of Michael Wyer, Patrick Cullen and Samuel Hockley, 6 September 1815. All the proceedings of the Court are in the documents comprised in CSIL (1815), No. 29 (a) *et seq.*, mainly in the handwriting of D'Arcy Wentworth, including the Judgment, CSIL (1815), p. 129. The papers are reprinted, HRA, I. 9, pp. 15-20.

29. HRA, I. 9, pp. 20-2, 9 September 1809. There is a copy of the original proclamation of the tolls (30 March 1811) in CSIL (1815), p. 133.

30. CSIL (1815), p. 127, and HRA, I. 9, p. 19. There is a slight difference in verbiage between Wentworth's holograph and the HRA text. The charge, however, of threatening the toll-keepers does not seem to have been proceeded with. It is not mentioned in the warrant for fine. (HRA, I. 9, p. 20.)

31. CSIL (1815), No. 39; HRA, I. 9, p. 25: J. H. Bent to Macquarie, 24 October 1815; CSIL 1815), No. 40, p. 159 (copy in Macquarie's hand); HRA, I. 9, p. 26: to Bent, 26 October 1815.

32. HRA, I. 9, p. 29: J. H. Bent to Macquarie, 9 January 1816. Garling had some diffidence about accepting the office because of "motives of delicacy on his part towards Mr. Justice Bent, and diffidence in his own qualifications arising out of his not having been bred up a Barrister". Macquarie had his own nominee for the permanent position — a "Mr James Moody, Dominick Street, Dublin" (HRA, I. 9, pp. 31, 32, 34: Macquarie to Bathurst, 24 February 1816; Garling to Macquarie, 11 December 1815. *Ibid.*, IV, 1, pp. 163 *et seq.*, 188-92.)

33. HRA, IV. 1, p. 184: J. Bent to Bathurst, 25 February 1816.

34. HRA, I. 9, pp. 3-4: Macquarie to Bathurst, 20 February 1816; I. 10, p. 223: Macquarie to Bathurst, 22 February 1820.

35. HRA, IV. 1, pp. 170-3: Bathurst to Ellis Bent, 11 December 1815.

36. *Ibid.*, p. 172.

37. *Ibid.*, pp. 173-4: Goulburn to J. H. Bent, 11 December 1815.

38. HRA, I. 9, pp. 110-11: Bathurst to Ellis Bent, 12 April 1816.

39. *Ibid.*, p. 112: Bathurst to J. H. Bent, 12 April 1816.

40. Journals, A773, p. 51, 5 October 1816; HRA, I. 9, p. 107: Bathurst to Macquarie, 18 April 1816.

41. HRA, I. 9, p. 108.

42. HRA, I. 8, p. 389 *et seq.*: Macquarie to Bathurst, 24 February 1815. The enclosure, p. 410: "Answers to Mr. Bent's Observations", 9 January 1815, is directly relevant and the views expressed are exactly those later expressed by Bathurst, whose words paraphrase Macquarie's opening sentences, making use of some of the Governor's actual expressions. Note Macquarie's request (HRA, I. 8, p. 399) for a draft of the Regulations by the Crown's legal advisers.

43. HRA, I. 10, p. 223: to Bigge, 6 November 1819.

44. HRA, IV. 1, pp. 783-4: Bigge Commission, Wylde's Evidence; CSIL (1817), p. 47: Wylde to Macquarie.

45. HRA, I. 9, p. 830: Bathurst to Macquarie, 24 August 1818.

46. The Privy Council sided with him in the end, but he lost his salary.

47. HRA, IV. 1, p. 215: Wylde to Goulburn, 17 November 1816.

48. *Ibid.*, pp. 308-9: J. H. Bent to Goulburn, 25 July 1818; Macquarie, *Letter to Viscount Sidmouth*, p. 67.

49. HRA, IV. 1, pp. 242, 308, 311, 328.

50. RAHSJ, XVI, Part 1, pp. 28-9, quoted by C. H. Bertie, 26 November 1929: Macquarie to Charles Macquarie, 2 July 1815.

Chapter XXII: HOLY WAR IN PARRAMATTA

1. *Dictionary of National Biography*, XXXVI, p. 205; Nicholas, J. L., *Narrative of a Voyage to New Zealand* (2 vols); *A Short Account of the Character and Labours of S. Marsden* (1844); Marsden, J. B., *Life and Work of Samuel Marsden*; Rusden, *History of New Zealand*, I, p. 102; NSWHR, VI, p. 380: to Cooke, 21 November 1807; Hassall Correspondence, A1677, II, pp. 41-2: to Mrs Stokes, 22 February 1800. Mackaness, G., *Some Private Correspondence of the Rev. Samuel Marsden and Family 1794-1824*; *Mitchell Library*, Am. 2, Letter from S. A. Donaldson.

Marsden entered Magdalene College as a scholar 7 December 1791 (*Magdalene College Register*, No. 3, p. 341).

2. Marsden Papers, C244, A1992-1993; NSWHR III, p. 439 *et seq.*: to Hunter, 25 July 1798.

3. Marsden, S., *An Answer to Certain Calumnies in Governor Macquarie's Pamphlet*, p. 9.

4. *Ibid.*, p. 9; Hassall Correspondence, A1677, II, p. 30: to Stokes, 3 December 1796: "I am a gardener, a Farmer, a Magistrate and Minister . . ."

5. NSWHR, III, p. 485: Letter dated 14 September 1798, addressee unknown. M. Péron came in 1802 with Baudin's expedition.

6. NSWHR, VI, pp. 406-7: Bligh's muster, 31 December 1807. He had 43 acres in cultivation, 500 acres of fallow, 2312 acres of pastoral land, 10 horses, 77 cattle, 1184 sheep, 8 goats and 39 pigs. John M'Arthur had 33 acres under cultivation and 400 of fallow in a total land-holding of 8533 acres. His stock consisted of 36 horses, 205 cattle, 5400 sheep and 22 pigs. Marsden had 17 servants, M'Arthur 30. In 1818 Marsden had 4150 acres, 520 cattle and 3400 sheep.

7. Marsden Papers, C244: Marsden to Stokes, 26 November 1811. The Mitchell Library, Sydney, owns a second copy of this letter on which the date appears to be 1816; but this date obviously is wrongly transcribed. (Hassall Correspondence, A1677, II, pp. 111-12, 117-18.)

8. *Ibid.*   9. *Ibid.*

10. Bennet, H. G., *Letter to Viscount Sidmouth* (1st ed.), p. 71 *et seq.*; Hassall Correspondence, 1677, II, p. 41: to Mrs Stokes, 22 February 1800.

11. Mann, D. D., *Present Picture of New South Wales*, p 97.

12. Bigge Appendix, Box 8, p. 3373: Marsden's Evidence; HRA, I. 7, p. 277: to Castlereagh, 30 April 1810. The circumstances suggest that it would more likely have been Ellis Bent, who had just then been appointed Judge-Advocate of the Colony; but Marsden says, "Mr. J. Bent." Marsden became resident chaplain at Parramatta, 15 September 1810.

13. Missionary Papers, Box 49, No. 22, p. 85: Transcript from Wilberforce Papers, Guildhall Library, London: Marsden to Wilberforce, 27 July 1810; HRA, I. 9, p. 499: to Bathurst, 1 December 1817.

14. Marsden, S., *An Answer to Governor Macquarie's Pamphlet*, p. 5.

15. *Hassall Correspondence*, A1677, II, p. 117: Marsden to Stokes, 26 November 1811 (or 1816).

16. Macquarie, L., *Letter to Viscount Sidmouth*, p. 17 *et seq.*; HRA, I. 7, p. 715: to Bathurst, 28 June 1813. Marsden's commission as a Justice of the Peace, *Sydney Gazette*, 31 October 1812.

17. Marsden Papers, C244, pp. 10-11: Marsden to Mrs King, 27 October 1810.

18. RAHSJ, XXIII, p. 484: Ann Marsden to Mrs Stokes, 18 June 1813; Hassall Correspondence, A1677, II, p. 121: Marsden to Mrs Stokes, 12 November 1812; p. 129, 25 June 1813.

19. HRA, I. 8, p. 257: G. & G.O., 5 February 1814; pp. 255, 259.

20. *Ibid.*, p. 256: to Bathurst, 24 May 1814.

21. *Ibid.*, pp. 256, 258.

22. *Ibid.*, p. 256; Marsden Papers, A1992, pp. 172-80: Good to Marsden, 25 December 1814.

23. Bigge Appendix, Box 12, p. 142: Proposals for Instituting a Lending Library for the General Benefit of the Inhabitants of N.S. Wales; NSWHR, VII, p. 161: Extract from the *Evangelical Magazine*, 1809.

24. Bigge Appendix, Box 12, p. 142.

25. *Ibid.*, p. 151.   26. *Ibid.*, pp. 145-50.

27. Missionary Papers, Box 49, p. 342: Rev. Pasco Crook to Rev. Tracey, 18 June 1813; Bigge Appendix, Box 8, pp. 3317-20: Cartwright's Evidence; pp. 3334-7: Thos. Bowden's Evidence; pp. 3366-7: Cowper's Evidence.

28. Missionary Papers, Box 49, p. 342.

29. Bigge Appendix, Box 12, p. 151: Butterworth to Bowden, 4 July 1811, and Bowden to Butterworth, 1 September 1813.

30. *Sydney Gazette*, p. 2, 5 March 1814. The Public Library had been toasted at the fête held in Mr Robert Jenkins's marquee on 29 January 1813. (See Chapter XVIII, and *Gazette*, 30 January 1813.)

31. *Ibid.*, p. 2, 12 March 1814.

32. *Ibid.*, p. 2, 19 March 1814. "Free Settler" declared that he "had indeed been informed that the Reverend Chaplain has a good collection of books, and that he occasionally lends them among his friends in a most obliging manner, which circumstances may possibly have led your correspondent to the erroneous belief that the books freely lent to him and others were public property".

33. *Ibid.*, p. 2, 26 March 1814.

34. *Ibid.*, 2 April 1814; Bigge Appendix, Box 12, p. 151 *et seq.*; Bowden to Butterworth.

35. Bigge Appendix, Box 13, p. 762-8: Marsden to Macquarie, 9 April 1814.

36. *Ibid.*, p. 767. 37. *Ibid.*, pp. 769–70.
38. Missionary Papers, Box 50, p. 236: Bowden to Butterworth, 14 March 1814; *Sydney Gazette*, 26 August 1810.
39. *Sydney Gazette*, p. 1, 10 September 1814; G. & G.O., 10 September 1814.
40. *Ibid.*, par. 9; Macquarie, L., *Letter to Viscount Sidmouth, Appendix*, pp. 82–3, 85–6; Marsden, S., *Answer to Governor Macquarie's Pamphlet*, p. 40.
41. Macquarie, L., *Letter to Viscount Sidmouth*, pp. 82–3: Circular to Magistrates, 20 September 1814.
42. On 28 July 1814.
43. *Sydney Gazette*, 13 August 1814. The ceremony took place in the Market Square on 12 August 1814. [G. & G.O., 13 August 1814.]
44. Marsden, *Answer to Governor Macquarie's Pamphlet*, pp. 41–2; HRA, I. 9, p. 505; Macquarie to Bathurst, 4 December 1817.
45. HRA, I. 7, p. 715: to Bathurst, 28 June 1813.
46. Missionary Papers, Box 49, No. 82, p. 326: Rev. W. P. Crook to London Missionary Society, 18 June 1813.
47. *Ibid.*, p. 329; Bigge Appendix, Box 8, p. 3497. Eagar mentioned Marsden's intolerance of dissenters.
48. HRA, I. 8, p. 337: to Bathurst, 7 October 1814. This was the work of the divine, William Goode the elder (*Dictionary of National Biography*, XXII, p. 120), and not of John Mason Good, who also was Marsden's friend.
49. *Ibid.* 50. *Ibid.* 51. *Ibid.*
52. *Ibid.*, p. 637: Bathurst to Macquarie, 2 December 1815; Journals, A773, p. 55, 14 October 1816.
53. HRA, I. 8, pp. 98–100: Proclamation, 1 December 1813.
54. Hassall Papers, A860, p. 113: Davies to Hassall, 18 September 1815; Missionary Papers, Box 49, p. 339; HRA, I. 7, pp. 264, 359, 706.
55. Missionary Papers, No. 22, p. 95: Missionaries of Eimeo to London Missionary Society, 21 October 1812; also p. 305.
56. Missionary Papers, Box 50, No. 97, pp. 213–14: Rev. S. Leigh to the Missionary Committee, 2 March 1816.
57. *Ibid.*
58. Marsden Papers, C244, p. 17: Marsden's Sermon on the Death of Ellis Bent. (Original in his own handwriting.)
59. See, Chapter XXIV.
60. Marsden Papers, A1993, p. 3: to Hardcastle, 25 October 1810.
61. Bigge Appendix, Box 11, p. 4435 *et seq.*: Points of Administration Submitted to Governor Macquarie, Q. amd A. 43: Hassall Correspondence, A1677, II, p. 212: Marsden to Mrs Stokes, 15 June 1815.
62. Marsden Papers, A1993, p. 4; Hassall Correspondence, A1677, II, pp. 210–16: to Mrs Stokes, 15 June 1815.
63. Marsden Papers, A1993, pp. 3–4: Marsden to Hardcastle, 25 October 1810. It is a curious fact that about the time that Mr Marsden developed hopes that "I shall be able to call the vessel my own, by paying the remainder of the money I was forced to borrow", he had learned that the Missionary Societies had agreed to vote subsidies totalling £500 towards the upkeep of the *Active* venture, which they obviously regarded as a pious public enterprise.
64. Missionary Papers, Box 50, pp. 1–163A: Observations on the Introduction of the Gospel into the South Sea Islands; Being my first visit to New Zealand in December, 1814. (Rev. S. Marsden.)
65. HRA, I. 8, pp. 561, 583 *et seq*: to Bathurst.
66. *Ibid.*, p. 582: Marsden's Report, 30 May 1815.
67. Ann Marsden to Mrs Stokes, March 1816, quoted by Dr G. Mackaness, RAHSJ, XXIII p. 488.
68. *Ibid.*
69. Hassall Correspondence, A1677, II, pp. 210–15: to Mrs Stokes, 14 June 1819. For the details of the *Active's* trading, as told by her officers, see Bigge Appendix, Box 28, p. 7236: Evidence of Jos. Thompson, master; p. 7251: Evidence of John Hunter, mate.
70. Hassall Correspondence, A1677, II, p. 176: to Mrs Stokes, 14 June 1819.
71. Bigge Appendix, Box 12, p. 317 *et seq.*: List Showing the Cost of Public Works done by Contract: 1812, Repairs to Old Parsonage at Parramatta, £237 4s. 3d.; Erection of New Parsonage, 1816–18, £2390; *Sydney Gazette*, 3 April 1813: Macquarie's commendation of Marsden for bringing criminals to justice.
72. Memoranda, A772, 5 June 1812. The name of St Andrew's Cathedral probably had its origin in the badge of Macquarie's Regiment, the 73rd Foot, and that of his brother's Corps,

the 42nd Foot (Black Watch), from which it was inherited. The design on the common badge
of these corps depicted St Andrew, with his cross.

73. Marsden Papers, A1993, p. 69: Marsden to Bigge, 24 September 1821.
74. Letterbooks, A797, p. 35: Wilberforce to Macquarie, 3 December 1810.
75. *Ibid.*, p. 105, Wilberforce to Macquarie, 15 March 1814.
76. Marsden Papers, C244, p. 13: Wilberforce to Marsden, 21 March 1814.
77. HRA, I. 8, p. 489: Macquarie to Bathurst, 22 June 1815.
78. Hassall Correspondence, A1677, II, pp. 210-16: Marsden to Mrs Stokes, 15 June 1815.

CHAPTER XXIII: THE NEW BALBUS

1. *Sydney Gazette*, 4 January 1817: "Philo Free's" letter.
2. The grant, 1000 acres, was issued on 10 July 1815, at the height of the quarrel with the
Bents. (Bigge Appendix, Box 12, p. 129.)
3. Bennet, H. G., *Letter to Viscount Sidmouth* (1st ed.), p. 71.
4. This was not, of course, William Goode the elder, the divine, but that prolific physician,
John Mason Good, whose *The Book of Job Literally Translated* appeared in 1812. (*Dictionary of
National Biography*, XXII, p. 110.)
5. *Dictionary of National Biography*, XXIII, p. 103. The volume was issued in 1811, while
the pious mathematician was master in his subject at the Royal Military Academy at Woolwich.
Marsden Papers, A1992, pp. 144-9: Good to Marsden, 10 March 1813.
6. Ho. of C. Select Committee (1812), Report, pp. 12-13.
7. HRA, I. 9, p. 504: to Bathurst, 4 December 1817; Bigge Appendix, Box 1, pp. 130-1:
William Hutchinson; pp. 245-8: Hannibal M'Arthur; pp. 282-3: Oakes, p. 335: Rouse;
HRA, I. 7, p. 252: to Castlereagh, 30 April 1810.
8. Bigge Report, Convicts, p. 68 *et seq.*; Bigge Appendix, p. 286: Oakes's Evidence;
Bennet, H. G., *Letter to Viscount Sidmouth* (1st ed.), Appendix, p. 132, Marsden's description.
He says there were forty-six women employed. He gives the dimensions of the room as 80
feet long by 20 feet wide. He says that about thirty girls and women sleep in the factory. Bigge
gives the dimensions of the room as 60 feet by 20 feet. For Marsden's responsibility, see Macquarie's Letter to Lord Bathurst, 10 October 1823, pp. 3, 27: "It was he [Marsden] who planned
and built the old factory."
9. Bigge Report, Convicts, p. 68, *et seq.*
10. *Ibid.*
11. Bigge Appendix, Box 12, pp. 230-61: Return of Punishments by the Parramatta
Bench.
12. Bigge Appendix, Box 14, pp. 1098-1105: Campbell to Marsden, 24 July 1815.
13. Bennet, H. G., *Letter to Viscount Sidmouth* (1st ed.), Appendix, p. 126 *et seq.* It would
appear that a remark by Greenway germinated Marsden's plan (Bigge Appendix, Box 1, p. 391).
14. Bennet, H. G., *Letter to Viscount Sidmouth*, p. 126: Marsden to Macquarie, 19 July 1815.
15. Bigge Appendix, Box 12, pp. 230-261: Return of Punishments by the Parramatta
Bench.
16. *Ibid.*
17. Bennet, H. G., *Letter to Viscount Sidmouth* (1st ed.), Appendix, p. 129.
18. *Ibid.*, pp. 129-30; Bigge Appendix, Box 1, p. 335: Rouse's Evidence.
19. Hassall Correspondence, 1677, II, p. 136: Marsden to Stokes, 8 October 1814.
20. HRA, I. 10, p. 453: Marsden's Evidence; Hassall Correspondence, A1677, II, pp. 210-17:
Marsden to Mrs Stokes. As for the sending of his memorial abroad, he declared that he waited
a year or two; but there is evidence that the substance of his complaints went home much
earlier. See p. 457 *et seq.*
21. RAHSJ, p. 487: Marsden to Stokes, 15 June 1815.
22. H of C. Select Committee on Jails (1819), Report, p. 83.
23. HRA, I. 7, pp. 614-15: to Bathurst, 17 November 1812; I. 8, p. 339, 7 October 1814;
p. 645: Bathurst to Macquarie. 4 December 1815.
24. Bennet, H. G., *Letter to Viscount Sidmouth* (1st ed.), p. 92.
25. HRA, I. 9, p. 353: to Bathurst, 4 April 1817. It came in the *Atlas.*
26. Macquarie, *Letter to Viscount Sidmouth*, pp. 17-18.
27. Marsden Papers, C244, p. 17: "Sermon preached at St. John's Church, Parramatta, by
the Revd. Samuel Marsden on the death of Justice Bent, for which the Governor (Macquarie)
gave Mr. Marsden a severe lecture in the presence of the Revd. Mr. Cowper and Major Antill
about a week or ten days after its delivery—stating that it was blasphemous to speak so highly
of any man." The manuscript is in Marsden's handwriting.
28. *Ibid.*
29. Hassall Correspondence, A1677, II, p. 142: Marsden to Mrs Stokes, 14 March 1816.

30. Hassall Correspondence, A1677, II, p. 147: Marsden to Mrs Stokes (copy), 14 March 1816.

31. HRA, I. 9, p. 249-50: to Bathurst, 1 April 1817; Bigge Appendix, Box 9, p. 3620 *et seq.*: Broughton's Evidence.

32. Bigge Appendix, Box 9, pp. 3752-825.

33. HRA, I. 9, p. 42: to Bathurst, 8 March 1816.

34. *Ibid.*, p. 43.   35. *Ibid.*, p. 42.   36. *Ibid.*, p. 43.   37. *Ibid.*, p. 46.   38. *Ibid.*, p. 43.

39. HRA, IV. 1, p. 160: Moore to J. H. Bent, 12 June 1815.

40. *Ibid.*, p. 161.

41. HRA, I. 8, p. 296: to Bathurst, 7 October 1814.

42. *Ibid.*, p. 299.

43. *Ibid.*, p. 300.

44. HRA, IV. 1, p. 193: J. H. Bent to Bathurst, 16 March 1816.

45. HRA, I. 9, 45-6; p. 48: Charges Preferred Against the Rev. Benjamin Vale.

46. *Ibid.*, p. 45; Proceedings of a General Court-martial ordered by Governor Macquarie to try the Rev. Benjamin Vale (1817), C470; Bigge Appendix, Box 14, p. 1284 *et seq.*

47. HRA, I. 9, p. 330: to Bathurst, 3 April 1817.

48. Bigge Appendix, Box 26, pp. 5920-3: Tompson to Macquarie, 29 January 1821.

49. HRA, I. 9, p. 410: to Goulburn, 17 May 1817.

50. *Ibid.*

51. *Ibid.*, pp. 334-5: Affidavits of Samuel Terry and Gustavus Lowe; also pp. 410-11.

52. HRA, I. 10, p. 684 *et seq.*: Report of Macquarie to Bathurst, 27 July 1822.

53. *Ibid.*, p. 687.

54. HRA, I. 9, p. 735: to Goulburn, 15 December 1817; Bigge Appendix, Box 1, pp. 177-9, Hutchinson's Evidence. Mrs Macquarie's road was finished by 13 June 1816.

55. *Australian*, Jack Vainspun to his "Dear Dolly Freelove".

56. Bigge Appendix, Box 11: Questions submitted to Governor Macquarie, Answer No. 31. For Macquarie's version in detail: Macquarie's *Letter to Viscount Sidmouth*, pp. 60-5.

57. HRA, I. 9, p. 735: to Goulburn, 15 December 1817; Bigge Appendix, Box 2, pp. 650-1. Willbow mentions the two convicts in his evidence, p. 599.

58. HRA. IV. 1, p. 209: Henshall's Deposition before J. H. Bent, 22 April 1816.

59. Bigge Appendix: Box 2, p. 599: D. Wentworth's Evidence.

60. *Ibid.*, p. 602.

61. NSWHR, VI, p. 278.

62. Bigge Appendix, Box 11: Questions Submitted to Governor Macquarie, Answer No. 31; Box 2, pp. 650-3: Willbow's Evidence; CSIL (1816), No. 49, p. 225, 6 July 1816.

63. HRA, IV. 1, p. 209: Henshall's Deposition; Bigge Appendix, Box 2, p. 652: Willbow's Evidence; p. 599: Wentworth's Evidence.

64. Bigge Appendix, Box 2, p. 600: Wentworth's Evidence; p. 644: Blake's Evidence; HRA, IV. 1, p. 211: Blake's deposition.

65. HRA, IV. 1, p. 210: D. Read's Deposition.

66. HRA, I. 9, p. 735: to Goulburn, 15 December 1816.

67. Bigge Appendix, Box 2, p. 644: Blake's Evidence.

68. HRA, IV. 1, p. 205: J. H. Bent to Macquarie, 21 May 1816.

69. HRA, I. 9, p. 171: Broughton's Deposition.

70. *Ibid.*, pp. 163-86: Proceedings of the Magistrates in the Case of Broughton; pp. 160-3: Macquarie to Bathurst, 31 August 1816.

71. Journals, A773, p. 27, 28 June 1816.

72. HRA, I. 9, pp. 164-76.

73. *Ibid.*, p. 186: Marsden to Campbell, 10 July 1816.

74. *Ibid.*, p. 493 *et seq.*: to Bathurst, 24 November 1817.

75. Bigge Appendix, Box 11: Questions to Governor Macquarie, Answer No. 32.

76. Bigge Appendix, Box 2, pp. 582-4: D. Wentworth's Evidence.

77. *Ibid.*, pp. 583-4.

78. *Ibid.*, Box 5, pp. 2151-2: Best's Evidence; Box 2, p. 586: Wentworth's Evidence.

79. *Ibid.*

80. HRA, I. 9, pp. 334-5.

81. *Ibid.*, p. 330: to Bathurst, 3 April 1817; Journals, A773, p. 44, 1 September 1816.

82. HRA, I. 9, p. 343: to Bathurst, 4 April 1817; Journals, A773, p. 52, 6 October 1816. He took the oaths of office 11 October 1816 and his commission was read in the Market Place.

83. *Dictionary of National Biography*, LXI, p. 228, under Thomas Wilde, Lord Truro.

84. HRA, I. 9, pp. 378-80: to Bathurst, 5 April 1817; Journals, A773, p. 77, 30 December 1816.

85. HRA, IV. 1, p. 783: Bigge Commission, Wylde's Evidence, pp. 802-4.

86. *Ibid.*, p. 383 *et seq.*: Wylde to Bigge, 23 July 1821. Bigge Appendix, Box 16, p. 1836: Wylde and Field, the two new judges, very sensibly asked in writing for Macquarie's instructions *re* convict attorneys.

87. HRA, IV. 1, pp. 788-9.

88. *Ibid.*, p. 826; CSIL (1816), No. 89, pp. 306-8.

89. Journals, A773, p. 73, 11 December 1816; HRA, I. 9, p. 311; IV. 1, p. 216: Riley to Campbell, 7 December 1816.

90. HRA, I. IX, pp. 312-13, 315-16; CSIL (1816), No. 92, p. 311: G. and G.O., 11 December 1816; No. 90, p. 309, 7 December, in Wylde's handwriting signed by Macquarie.

91. HRA, IV. 1, pp. 279, 297-310, 317.

92. *Ibid.*, I. 9, p. 320: Campbell to Mrs Bent, 15 March 1817; Journals, A773, p. 102, 18 May 1817.

93. Piper Papers, A256, p. 125: Eliz. Bent to Capt. Piper, 11 March 1825.

94. Wentworth Papers, A756, p. 21 *et seq.*: W. C. Wentworth to D'Arcy Wentworth, 16 August 1816.

95. HRA, I. 9, p. 411: to Goulburn, 17 May 1817.

96. It will be noted that, at this stage, he was no richer than he had been in 1802. His fortune consisted of £7500 in East India funds in Bengal; £1700 in East India stock in England; £6000 in 3 per cents reckoned at £65, a farther £3400 in 3 per cents; his salary, due to 4 December 1815, yet unpaid, £2200; and his pay as a Major-General in the hands of the Army Bankers, Cox and Greenwood, £1400. Total, £22,200.

Chapter XXIV: THE RED-SPATTERED TARTANS

1. CSIL (1812), No. 45, p. 131: Order, 5 December 1812; (1813), No. 31, p. 44: Proclamation, 1 July 1813; No. 51, p. 86, 9 October 1813; HRA, I. 7, p. 750 *et seq.*

2. The student who wishes to study this transaction will find its detail in RAHSJ, XXXII, No. V, pp. 273-93: M. H. Ellis, "*Governor Macquarie and the 'Rum' Hospital.*"

3. Bigge Appendix, Box 14, pp. 1302-4; Box 15, pp. 1385-99, 1410-21; Box 24, pp. 5046-8.

4. HRA, I. 9, pp. 397-9; Macquarie to Bathurst, 15 May 1817; pp. 416-28, 821; Journals, A773, p. 96, 10 April 1817.

5. Wentworth Papers, A752, p. 188: D'Arcy Wentworth to W. C. Wentworth, 6 April 1816; A756, pp. 13-16: W. C. Wentworth to D'A. Wentworth, 9 April 1816; pp. 21-36, 16 August 1816, and other correspondence to 1819, especially p. 145, 3 August 1819, and p. 153, 24 November 1819.

6. Riley had been on intimate terms with the Governor and in the inner Government House circle in 1814 and up to 1817, but for at least part of the time he was in secret league with Marsden and other enemies of Macquarie, especially after the Philo Free incident (see Chapter XXV). When he left for England in 1817 he carried letters from Macquarie "conveying the Governor's entire approbation of your upright impartial and zealous conduct" as a magistrate, and wishing that "other persons would fo'llow your good example" as an estate improver. (Riley Papers, A106, pp. 63-5, 69-72, 26 July and 12 November 1817.)

7. Boswell, *Journey to the Hebrides.*

8. British Museum, King's Library MSS., 104: "The Highlands of Scotland in 1750." Dundee, about the time of Killiecrankie—at which battle Lochiel was about the only clansman who owned a pair of shoes in his regiment—called the Highlanders "a gang of thieves".

9. The Disarming Act of 1725 illuminates the contemporary English view of the Highlanders.

10. Boswell, *Journey to the Hebrides.*

11. Kirke, Thomas, *Account of Scotland by an English Gentleman* (1679) gives a good picture of conditions.

12. The didgeridoo is a rough, hollow piece of wood cut from a branch, probably the world's most primitive and mournful wind instrument. The Macintyres, of course, were celebrated for their piping.

13. Adam, *Clans, Septs and Regiments of the Scottish Highlands*, p. 388.

14. Act of Scottish Parliament to punish theft, reiff, oppression, etc., 1601 (*Acts of Scotland*, IV., 71).

15. HRA, I. 9, p. 141: Proclamation, 4 May 1816; p. 363: Proclamation, 20 July 1816.

16. *Ibid.*, pp. 141, 363.

17. *Ibid.*, p. 363; Bigge Appendix, Box 26, p. 580: Bigge to Marsden, 20 January 1821.

18. This method was exactly that of James. In 1608, Lord Stewart of Ochiltree lured the chieftains (including Macquarie of Ulva) into his galley for a feast, weighed anchor and carried them to Iona, where they met in a conference not unlike those held by Macquarie at Parramatta, and signed a bond to assure that each became a peaceful Presbyterian and sent his eldest son or daughter to a Lowland school to learn English. (*Reg. Seg. Concilii*, 27 July 1610.)

19. HRA, I. 8, p. 368: Macquarie to Bathurst, 8 October 1814.
20. *Ibid.* 21. *Ibid.* 22. *Ibid.* 23. *Ibid.*
24. *Sydney Gazette,* 14 May, 4 June 1814; G. & G.O., 18 June 1814.
25. *Ibid.*; *Sydney Gazette,* 5 June 1814, p. 2: "The natives of Jarvis's Bay are reported on good authority to have coalesced with the mountain tribes; they commit no depredations in the cornfields, but have declared a determination that *when the Moon shall be as large as the Sun, they will commence a work of desolation,* and kill all the *whites* before them."
26. *Ibid.* 27. *Ibid.* 28. *Ibid.*
29. HRA, I. 8, pp. 367-73: Macquarie to Bathurst, 8 October 1814, enclosing plan of the institution; HRA, I. 10, pp. 140-1; Bigge Appendix, Box 26, p. 580: Bigge to Marsden, 20 January 1821.
30. HRA, I. 8, p. 373.
31. *Ibid.,* p. 467: Macquarie to Bathurst, 24 March 1815.
32. *Ibid.*
33. *Ibid.,* p. 645: Bathurst to Macquarie, 4 December 1815.
34. HRA, I. 9, p. 54: Macquarie to Bathurst, 18 March 1816.
35. *Ibid.*
36. CSIL (1816), No. 29, p. 95 (Macquarie's writing): Instructions for Captain W. G. B. Schaw; No. 30, p. 200, ditto to Lieut. Dawe; No. 31, p. 202: to Captain Wallis; HRA, I. 9, pp. 139-40: Macquarie to Bathurst, 8 June 1816; also p. 141 and Note 36 on p. 854. The Expedition went out under orders on 10 April 1816. Journals, A773, p. 1, *et seq.,* 10 April 1816: "I therefore, tho' very unwillingly, felt myself compelled, from a paramount sense of public duty, to come to the painful resolution of chastening these hostile tribes, and to inflict terrible and exemplary punishments upon them without further loss of time, as they might construe any further forbearance or lenity on the part of this Government into fear and cowardice." The force used consisted of two flank companies of the 46th Regiment.
37. CSIL (1816), No. 29, p. 98.
38. HRA, I. 9, p. 54: Macquarie to Bathurst, 18 March 1816.
39. *Ibid.,* pp. 139-40; CSIL (1816), p. 219B, No. 41: Wallis's Report and Journal, 9 May 1816. Macquarie's statement that Wallis "met with some resistance" does not appear to be borne out by Wallis's own report. No. 39, p. 215: Schaw's Report and Journal; No. 38, p. 214: Dawe's Report and Journal; Journals, A773, pp. 10-12, 4-7 May 1816; HRA, I. 9, p. 139 *et seq.*: Macquarie to Bathurst, 8 June 1816.
40. HRA, I. 9, p. 141: Proclamation, 4 May 1816.
41. *Ibid.,* p. 141. Charles Tompson, the younger, described its ruins ten years afterwards:

> "Thy once fair dawning beauties all are gone.
> Thy gardens fallow lie, with weeds o'ergrown;
> Wildflowers and spindling grass alone are seen
> Where cornfields waved their undulating green.
> Dark vines along the untrodden footpaths creep
> And all the desert landscape seems to weep."

42. *Ibid.,* pp. 144-5. 43. *Ibid.,* p. 362.
44. *Ibid.,* p. 363: Proclamation, 20 July 1816, and p. 365.
45. *Ibid.,* p. 342. The Scots, including Macquarie of Ulva, by making their marks on the documents at Iona in 1608, renounced their "bypast savageries".
46. *Ibid.,* p. 342: Macquarie to Bathurst, 4 April 1817.
47. HRA, I. 10, p. 95, 24 March 1819; Journals, A773, p. 76, 28 December 1816.
48. CSIL (1816), No. 100, p. 323, for names of Native Institution Committee; for Regulations, Bigge Appendix, Box 13, pp. 916-22; Missionary Papers, Box 49, No. 90, p. 379: Rev. W. P. Crook to Tracey, 5 October 1814; No. 91, p. 380: Shelley to Burder, 6 October 1814.
49. HRA, I. 10, p. 95.
50. Tompson, Charles, *Wild Notes from the Lyre of a Native Minstrel* (R. Howe, 1826); HRA, I. 10, p. 676 *et seq.*: Macquarie to Bathurst, 27 July 1822.
51. HRA, I. 10, pp. 262-6: Macquarie to Bathurst, 24 February 1820; pp. 263-72: Robert Cartwright's Plan; CSIL (1820), No. 8, p. 63: Cartwright to Macquarie, 18 January 1820; Journals, A773, p. 130, 1 January 1818; *Sydney Gazette,* 4 January 1817, p. 20.
52. HRA, III. 2, pp. 55, 448 *et seq.*; *Sydney Gazette,* 14 May 1814; HRA, I. 8, p. 264.
53. HRA, III. 2, pp. 238, 257, 262, 263, 269, 276.
54. *Ibid.,* pp. 56, 450, 556.
55. *Ibid.,* 202, 206, 207, 212, 214, 215 *et seq.,* 630.
56. *Ibid.,* pp. 284, 786; also *Michael Howe, the last and worst of the Bushrangers of Van Diemen's Land*; Calder Papers, A594, pp. 7, 70, 554, 561, 567, 569, 572, 576, 600-610, 661, 675-676, 827, 827a, 835; *Scraps of Tasmanian History* (Mitchell Library, 990C): Sketch of Howe's life by Calder.

57. HRA, III. 2, p. 568 *et seq.*; p. 132: Davey's Proclamation, 11 March 1813, called on the villains to bring with them "dogs, arms, ammunition, iron pots, tools, and whatever else they have with them in the woods".

58. HRA, I. 8, p. 264: Proclamation, 14 May 1814.

59. HRA, III. 2, pp. 77-8: Depositions of William Merry and W. H. Craig.

60. *Ibid.*, p. 79: Minutes of Hobart Magistrates, 30 August 1814. This outrage took place in the last week of August 1814. Many tales of Howe and his associates are in *Scraps of Tasmanian History*, p. 149 *et seq.*; his career, p. 155.

61. *Ibid.* One of the magistrates who signed the opinion was the Rev. Robt. Knopwood.

62. *Ibid.*, pp. 80-4: Depositions of Holsgrove and Lucas; *Scraps of Tasmanian History* p. 164 *et seq.*; Journals, A777, p. 29, 27 November 1811. Mr M'Carty actually presented one of the addresses, and when the Governor visited him at New Norfolk he found "a comfortable farm and a hearty, rural, honest welcome".

63. HRA, III. 2, p. 84: Deposition of William Lucas.

64. *Ibid.*, pp. 84-5. Mr M'Carty valued his losses at £546 7s. 6d.

65. *Ibid.*, p. 167, *et seq.*

66. *Ibid.*, pp. 92-108; *Scraps of Tasmanian History*, p. 641 *et seq.*

67. HRA, I. 8, p. 567. Davey had no power to execute martial law, though he based his action on Art. 4, Sect. 24, Articles of War. Dr Watson, in his commentary in the HRA, says that Davey had a precedent for his action in the proclamation of martial law on Norfolk Island when the *Sirius* went aground there. But that case certainly was no precedent. On Norfolk Island in 1790 there were no courts. As Macquarie pointed out (HRA, III. 2, p. 110), the Articles of War were "not at all applicable to the present case, there *being Courts of Justice* in this Territory of which Van Diemen's Land forms a part".

68. HRA, III. 2, pp. 110, 113, 125, 126, for Macquarie's censures; p. 126, revocation of martial law, 18 September 1815.

69. *Ibid.*, p. 294: Macquarie to Sorell, 10 January 1818.

70. *Ibid.*, p. 594: Broughton to Macquarie, 30 October 1816.

71. *Ibid.*, pp. 594-5.

72. *Ibid.*, p. 590: Peachey's Deposition.

73. *Ibid.*, p. 163: Howe to Davey.

74. *Ibid.*, 590-1: Peachey's Deposition.

75. HRA, I. 8, pp. 458 *et seq.*, 555 *et seq.*; I. 9, p. 338: Macquarie told Bathurst that "it would have saved a great deal of money to the Crown, had the Government given a pension of £200 or £300 a year to Davey, instead of sending him to V.D.L.".

76. HRA, I. 9, p. 113: Bathurst to Macquarie, 18 April 1816. Macquarie had asked Bathurst to make provision for the wretched man's "amiable but unfortunate wife and daughter," whose situations "were at best to be pitied".

77. HRA, I. 9, p. 339; III. 2, pp. 634-5: Davey to Harrowby, 14 December 1817.

78. HRA, III. 2, p. 634.

79. The Deed was dated 9 January 1821. HRA, I. 9, pp. 339, 822, 853; I. 10, p. 561.

80. He ultimately sailed for England in the *Regalia*, 15 August 1821. HRA, I. 10, p. 540.

81. E. Macquarie, Journal, C126, 23 September 1809; Journals, A773, p. 92, 27 March 1817.

82. HRA., III. 2, p. 240: Macquarie to Sorell, 24 May 1817.

83. *Ibid.*, p. 686: Kemp to Bathurst, 15 November 1818; p. 338: Mrs Sorell to Bathurst, 21 June 1818; *The Times*, 7 July 1817.

84. HRA, III. 2, pp. 376-7: Sorell to Bathurst, 20 January 1819. Sorell had been appointed by commission dated 3 April 1816. He had been in the Colony four months when damages were given against him by default. See also HRA, III. 3, p. 221; Bigge Commission, Kemp's Evidence, 9 November 1819; also pp. 228, 229, 675, 904, 917, 918.

85. HRA, III. 2, pp. 633-4: Davey to Bathurst, 14 December 1817.

86. *Ibid.*, pp. 684, 686: Kemp to Bathurst, 11 and 15 November 1818.

87. *Ibid.*, pp. 330, 350, 687.

88. *Ibid.*, p. 194: Sorell to Macquarie, 3 May 1817; HRA, I. 9, p. 348: Macquarie to Bathurst, 4 April 1817.

89. HRA, III. 2, p. 195.

90. *Ibid.*, pp. 194-241: Macquarie to Sorell, 24 May 1817; p. 275, Sorell to Macquarie, 13 September 1817; HRA, I. 9, p. 404.

91. HRA, III. 2, p. 234.

92. *Ibid.*, p. 363. Sorell, Orders, A1351, pp. 91-2; A1352, p. 242. Calder Papers, A594, pp. 605-11.

93. HRA, III. 2, p. 373: Macquarie to Sorell, 21 December 1818.

94. Mary returned to Port Jackson. Musquito was a Broken Bay (New South Wales) native, transported to Norfolk Island and then to Van Diemen's Land for murder. After his

adventures as a tracker, he became the leader of a band of outlaw blacks known as the "Tame Mob", which frequented the environs of Hobart and for several years was a source of trial to the authorities and of danger to settlers. In 1825 he was wounded by a fellow tracker and brought in to be hanged. He it was who introduced the boomerang to Van Diemen's Land, in which, before his time, it was unknown.

95. HRA, III. 2, p. 292: Macquarie to Sorell, 10 January 1818; I. 10, p. 90: Macquarie to Bathurst, 24 March 1819.

96. HRA, I. 10, p. 507: Macquarie to Bathurst, 17 July 1821.

97. *Ibid.*, p. 508.   98. *Ibid.*, p. 509.

CHAPTER XXV: THE LADS IN BLACK

1. Missionary Papers, Box 49, No. 81, p. 317: Rev. W. P. Crook to Rev. Tracey, 19 June 1813. Crook wrote, "Governor Macquarie says the missionaries at Otaheite have done more harm by this than they will ever do the natives good."

2. Hassall Papers, A860, p. 117: Rev. P. Crook to Rowland Hassall, 13 August 1816.

3. *Ibid.*   4. *Ibid.*

5. *Ibid.*, p. 121: Rowland Hassall to Crook, 26 November 1816.

6. *Sydney Gazette*, 4 January 1817.

7. *Sydney Gazette*, 4 January 1817. The text of the letter is reprinted in HRA, IV. 1, pp. 936-7.

8. See Chapter XXII. It will be remembered that the letters to the *Gazette* in that case were signed "Free Settler". Marsden suspected Campbell, the Governor's secretary, of having written them. The diction and curious brand of humour of the two sets of documents are strikingly similar. (Marsden Papers, C244, pp. 43-6: Marsden to Macquarie, 11 August 1818.) Robt. Jenkins to *Gazette*, 11 January 1817 (dated 9 January 1817): ". . . the sum received by me as collector to the Society amounts to £138 4s., the whole of which is now in my hands, no part of it having ever been called for either by the Committee or Treasurer."

9. *Sydney Gazette*, 18 January 1817: Government Notice, same date; HRA, IV. 1, pp. 796-7: Bigge Commission, Wylde's Evidence.

10. HRA, IV. 1, pp. 770-3, 794-9, 852-4.

11. HRA, I. 8, p. 468: to Bathurst, 24 March 1815; I. 9, p. 410: to Goulburn, 17 May 1817. Campbell's salary recently had been increased with the consent of the Colonial Office. (HRA, I. 9, p. 109 and pp. 358-9). Macquarie recommended his exaltation to the title of Colonial Secretary in his dispatch of 4 April 1817, three months after publication of the Philo Free letter and while Marsden's criminal prosecution of him was in train.

12. HRA, IV. 1, p. 797: Bigge Commission, Wylde's Evidence; Bigge Appendix, Boxes 15 and 16: Correspondence between Marsden and Wylde.

13. HRA, IV. 1, pp. 797-8: Bigge Commission, Wylde's Evidence; p. 833: W. H. Moore's Evidence.

14. Journals, A773, p. 81, 18 January 1817.

15. Wylde, the Judge-Advocate, disposed of the charge about Amos. W. H. Moore (HRA, IV. 1, p. 834) stated that Amos "he was afraid of making himself obnoxious and interfering in any public question". Wylde (p. 799) said that Marsden had told him, in 1820, that Amos would not consent to Moore leading in the case; hence his defection. Wylde added, "I believe at least that no other cause or influence occasioned the refusal." Moore said that he did not know that the above circumstances influenced the matter, but he thought Amos objected to the mode of proceeding (HRA, IV. 1, p. 834).

16. HRA, I. 10, p. 447 *et seq.*: Report of the Judge-Advocate, enclosed with Macquarie to Bathurst, 20 March 1821. The charge as given in this book is summarized.

17. HRA, IV. 1, p. 848. Williams made one of the two affidavits which Wylde demanded as grounds for the indictment. The Judge-Advocate presently threatened to commit Williams for perjury and contempt. (See his letter to Bigge, Bigge Appendix, Box 24, pp. 5263-6; Box 25, p. 5681.)

18. Bigge Appendix, Box 15, p. 1689: to George Howe, 21 February 1817; HRA, I. 10, pp. 452-4, 463-8: Marsden's Evidence. Note the discrepancy between this account and the one which he gave Hardcastle. See p. 327 of this book.

19. HRA, I. 10, pp. 458-61: Howe's and Jones's Evidence.

20. HRA, IV. 1, p. 853: Bigge Commission, Garling's Evidence; p. 468: Eagar's Evidence.

21. Bigge Appendix, Box 16, pp. 1986-2018.

22. HRA, I. 10, p. 472: Wylde's Report on the Trial.

23. *Ibid.*, pp. 443, 472: Wylde's Report; IV. 1, pp. 837-9, 794-5: Wylde's Evidence.

24. HRA, I. 10, p. 442 *et seq.*, 447 *et seq.*, for details of the two trials; p. 142: to Goulburn, 31 March 1819; p. 442: to Bathurst, 20 March 1821; Bigge Appendix, Box 8, p. 3441 *et seq.*: Marsden's account.

25. Journals, A773, p. 87, 24 February 1817; A773, p. 88, records his swearing in on 28 February 1817.

26. Barron Field, *First Fruits of Australian Poetry*: "Kangaroo." *First Fruits* was printed in Sydney in 1819 and was the pioneer Australian volume of verse—if volume it could be called. *The Times* owed one debt to Field—he introduced the great Barnes to its managers.

27. Charles Lamb's essay on "Distant Correspondents" was addressed to him under his initials. He was not yet "plump and friendly" as Lamb found him on his return to England.

28. HRA, I. 9, p. 381: to Bathurst, 8 April 1817.

29. *Dictionary of National Biography*, XVIII, p. 400. Storks was a well-known and voluble figure in London legal society. He was a friend or associate of Jeffery Bent, who, after his return to England, sometimes used his chambers as an address.

30. Dr Halloran's review of this Mr Field's extraordinary "flowers" of poesy in *The Gleaner* was more terse and apposite. He merely wrote in italics, *Jam satis!*

31. HRA, IV. 1, pp. 755-6: Bigge Commission, Piper's Evidence; Bigge Appendix, Box 28, p. 6754: Bigge to Bathurst, 9 September 1822.

32. Marsden Papers, C244, 50B, Bigge to Marsden, 20 January 1821, conveying the Governor's denial that he ever had seen the "Philo Free" letter before he was shown it in the *Gazette*; A1993, pp. 36-45: Marsden to Bigge, 29 December 1819.

33. HRA, I. 10, p. 443 *et seq.*: Field's Report on the Civil Court Trial, 9 December 1819.

34. HRA, IV. 1, p. 939; I. 10, p. 447; p. 141: Campbell to Macquarie, 31 March 1819.

35. Bigge Appendix, Box 11: Questions on Administration Submitted to Governor Macquarie, Q. and A. 48.

36. HRA, IV. 1, p. 938: Quotation from *Gazette*, 1 November 1817.

37. *Ibid.*, p. 799: Wylde's Evidence, in which is contained the report of the first judicial concession to the freedom of the Australian press. Wylde said that the "more proper mode", if any notice were taken of the *Gazette's* statement, would have been to bring the printer before the Court for contempt. "This measure," he said, "I was induced to forego, as the statement formed what is termed the leader of the paper and did not purport to be a formal report of the trial."

38. Journals, A773, 31 January 1818; A774, I, p. 23, 28 January 1819.

39. Marsden Papers, A1992, p. 205: Wilberforce to Marsden. Letter begun on 16 September 1816, and finished on 18 August 1818. Another supporter who took the trouble to write his congratulations was the pious Admiral Gambier (Mitchell Library, Am. 2, 8 April 1818 and 27 March 1819).

40. Marsden Papers, A1992, pp. 228-31: Bent to Marsden, 3 August 1818.

41. HRA, I. 9, p. 836: Bathurst to Macquarie, 18 September 1818.

42. HRA, I. 10, p. 140: J. T. Campbell to Macquarie, 31 March 1819.

43. Marsden Papers, C244, pp. 65-74: Marsden to Kendall, January 1822.

44. *Ibid.*, C244, pp. 79-82: Rev. J. Butler to Marsden, 8 January 1822.

45. Journals, A769, 31 March 1801; HRA, I. 9, p. 442: to Duke of York, 25 July 1817.

46. *Ibid.*, p. 442.

47. HRA, I. 8, p. 146-7: to Bathurst, 28 April 1814; p. 636: Bathurst to Macquarie, and Lushington to Goulburn.

48. *Ibid.*, pp. 375-6: to Torrens; pp. 376-8: Memorial of the Officers of the 46th Regiment.

49. *Ibid.*, p. 377.   50. *Ibid.*, p. 376.

51. HRA, I. 9, pp. 444-5: to the Duke of York, 25 July 1817.

52. *Ibid.*, p. 453: Sanderson, Forster and Grant to Molle, 13 June 1817. Molle himself, later a relation of Sir Thomas Brisbane, in whose brigade M'Arthur's son served, paid close attention to the M'Arthur family in New South Wales.

53. HRA, I. 9, p. 443.

54. *Ibid.*, p. 445. Macquarie names Major Mackenzie as the leader of the faction, but Sanderson appears to have been the active force behind all agitation.

55. *Ibid.*, p. 446.

56. *Ibid.*, p. 472. His letter dated 23 July 1817, was addressed to Molle, and the copy sent to Macquarie was annotated: "Read by Ensign Bullivant before all the Officers of the mess assembled by me. (Sgd.) G. Molle." Also pp. 473-4: to Macquarie, 15 July 1817.

57. Cramp and Mackaness, *History of the Grand Lodge of New South Wales*, I, p. 19 *et seq.*

58. See p. 43.

59. Cramp and Mackaness, *History of the Grand Lodge of New South Wales*, p. 19 *et seq.* For the case of Drummond, see Memoranda, A772, p. 115, 1 October 1817; HRA, III. 2, pp. 271 293, 294, 631.

60. Cramp and Mackaness, p. 19 *et seq.*, and *Sydney Gazette* 9 November 1816.

61. HRA, IV. 1, p. 448 *et seq.*; Bigge Appendix, Box 16, pp. 1900-31.

62. *Ibid.*

63. Bigge Appendix, Box 16, pp. 1900-31.   64. *Ibid.*
65. Bigge Appendix, Box 7 pp. 2912-15.
66. HRA, I. 9, p. 445.
67. *Ibid.*, p. 393: to Bathurst, 13 May 1817.
68. *Ibid.*, p. 446.
69. NSWHR, V, pp. 10, 119, 123.
70. Wentworth Papers, A758, p. 1. This version is in the handwriting of W. C. Wentworth.
71. HRA, I. 9, p. 447.
72. *Ibid.*, pp. 450, 453; 465: Captain Gill to Molle, 15 July 1817, and pp. 468-9.
73. Byron, *English Bards and Scotch Reviewers*, line 638. The Duke of Argyll had been old Mrs Macquarie's landlord at Oskamull. Lest purists are inclined to correct the spelling "Argyle" used for the most part in this book, let it be said that it is Macquarie's version.
74. HRA, I. 9, p. 446.
75. *Ibid.*, p. 447.
76. Wentworth Papers, A758. It is dated "March 16, 1816".
77. *Ibid.*
78. HRA, I. 9, p. 447; Wentworth Papers, A758, pp. 5-6.
79. *Ibid*; CSIL (1817), pp. 57, 59, 60: Wylde to Macquarie, 7, 10, 12, June 1817; CSIL (1817), p. 60: Wylde to Macquarie, 11 June 1817. CSIL (1816), p. 332: Murray to Macquarie, 29 March 1816, tells the sad story of his blighted life.
80. Bigge Appendix, Box 16, p. 1947: Extracts from Proceedings, 11 June 1817, on a complaint of Lieutenant-Governor Molle and Alexander Riley charging Robert L. Murray with being the author of certain scurrilous verses called Pipes, Examination of D'Arcy Wentworth.
81. *Ibid.*
82. HRA, I. 9, p. 448.
83. Wentworth Papers, A753, p. 53: D'Arcy Wentworth to Macquarie, 6 September 1817.
84. HRA, I. 9, p. 449; p. 453: Captain Sanderson and others to Molle, 13 June 1817.
85. *Ibid.*, p. 454.   86. *Ibid.*, p. 455.
87. *Ibid.*, p. 451: to Molle, 23 June 1817. See Molle's account (p. 456).
88. *Ibid.*, pp. 460-1: "Charges Intended to be Preferred by Major-General Macquarie against the officers of the 46th Regiment Generally"; and correspondence Macquarie-Molle and others, pp. 455-75.
89. *Ibid.*, p. 458: Molle to Macquarie, 24 June 1817.
90. Wentworth Papers, A753, pp. 51-3: D'Arcy Wentworth to Macquarie, 6 September 1817.
91. *Ibid.*, p. 53.
92. *Ibid.*, p. 35: Murray's Affidavit, 4 July 1817.
93. *Ibid.*, p. 49. The paper was marked, "Copy No. 5 . . . On His Majesty's Service. A True Copy, L. Macquarie." The date on Grose's letter allegedly was 25 June 1799. A753, p. 347: Macquarie's replies to Wentworth's queries.
94. *Ibid.*, p. 54: Wentworth to Macquarie, 6 September 1817.
95. *Ibid.*, pp. 54-5.
96. CSIL (1817): Macquarie to Molle (copy to D. Wentworth), 9 September 1817.
97. Wentworth Papers, A753, p. 57: Molle to D. Wentworth, 9 September 1817. Wentworth replied next day that he had no intention to threaten or insult the Lieutenant-Governor (p. 59).
98. *Ibid.*, pp. 63-5: Charges Preferred Against George Molle, Esq.
99. HRA, I. 9, pp. 463-71: Macquarie-Molle correspondence, 15-22 July 1817; A753, pp. 71, 77: Wylde to Wentworth; to Macquarie, 14 September 1817; p. 81: Macquarie to Wylde, 14 September 1817.
100. HRA, I. 9, pp. 554-5: to Bathurst, 11 December 1817; pp. 555-7: Wylde's Opinion, 17 September 1817; Memoranda, A772, pp. 107-9, 16-20 September 1817.
101. Wentworth Papers, A753, p. 87: Macquarie to D'Arcy Wentworth, 21 September, 1817; Mitchell Library, Am. 2, p. 1: Marsden to Molle, 18 October 1818, in reply to the Regiment's Public Letter, 14 May 1818.
102. Wentworth Papers, A757: Geo. Johnston, Jr., to W. C. Wentworth, 1 March 1819. A copy of the pipe about the M'Arthurs still existed in the possession of Miss Dorothy Wentworth in 1950. The authors had good cause to fear its falling into the hands of the "Archfiend" or his family, since it did not limit its derision to the males of the family.
103. *Ibid.*, A756, p. 103: W. C. Wentworth to Alex. Riley, 25 August 1818.
104. *Sydney Gazette*, 18 September 1818; Governor's Despatches, A1192, p. 507 *et seq.* Bigge Appendix, Box 17, p. 2221: Macquarie to Wylde, 26 August 1818.
105. RAHSJ, XXIX, p. 416.
106. CSIL (1817), p. 46: Wylde to Macquarie, dated "Saturday Evening".

CHAPTER XXVI: FAREWELL TO TOORALI-ADDITY

1. H. of C. Debates, XXXIII: Bill to Extend the Duration of the Transportation Acts (June 22), 55 Geo. III, c. 46.
2. HRA, I. 9, p. 797.
3. Liverpool, the Prime Minister, had himself seen the storming of the Bastille.
4. Sydney Gazette, 9 August 1817, p. 2; 16 August, pp. 3, 4: Report of the House of Lords Committee.
5. Ibid., 16 August 1817, pp. 3-4: Report of the Lords' Committee. Spa Fields Assembly took place on 2 December 1816.
6. House of Lords Debates: Report of the Secret Committee, respecting certain dangerous meetings and combinations (Hansard, XXXV, 411, 472, 531: Attack on the Prince Regent, 4, 37).
7. Ibid.; Gazette, 16 August 1817.
8. Greville Memoirs (1874 edition), I, p. 2.
9. H. of C. Hansard, XXXV, pp. 795, 825.
10. Wentworth Papers, A756, p. 53: W. C. Wentworth to D. Wentworth, 22 March 1817.
11. HRA, I. 9, pp. 732-6: to Goulburn, 15 December 1817.
12. Ibid., p. 736.
13. HRA, I. 8, p. 338 et seq.
14. Ibid.
15. Ibid. (see also p. 255 et seq. this book); HRA, IV, 1, pp. 205-8: J. H. Bent to Macquarie, 21 May 1816.
16. HRA, I. 9, pp. 733-4.
17. Ibid., p. 736.
18. HRA, IV. 1, p. 282 et seq.: Vale to Bathurst, 16 April 1818.
19. Bennet, H. G., Letter to Viscount Sidmouth (1st ed.), p. 11.
20. NSWHR, I, Part 2, pp. 386-9: Rev. R. Johnson to Thornton, undated, and written about July 1790. Report of H. of C. Select Committee (1812), p. 10: Between 1795 and 1801, out of 3833 convicts embarked, 385 died on the transports, or one in ten. From 1801 to 1811 only 52 out of 2398 died en voyage, or one in 46.
The Committee reported: ". . . However bad the treatment of convicts on board the vessel may formerly have been, the present system appears unobjectionable. The witnesses speak of it in terms of high commendation." The record of the system suffered a sad blow, however, in the Surry, General Hewitt and Three Bees cases in 1814. HRA, I. 10, p. 5: Bathurst to Bigge, 30 January 1819.
21. HRA, I. 8, pp. 140, 244 et seq.
22. HRA, I. 8, pp. 274-5: to the Commissioners of the Transport Board, 1 October 1814; pp. 275-93: Redfern to Macquarie, 30 September 1814; p. 640: Bathurst to Macquarie, 4 December 1815; I. 9, pp. 56-7: to Bathurst, 18 March 1816.
23. Bennet, H. G., Letter to Viscount Sidmouth, pp. 59-61, quoting evidence before the H. of C. Police Committee (1818).
24. Ibid., p. 61.
25. H. of C. Hansard, XXXV, 920.
26. Wentworth Papers, A756, p. 49: W. C. Wentworth to Bennet, 10 March 1817—written from "No. 22, opposite the Riding School at Pimlico".
27. Ibid., p. 54: W. C. Wentworth to D'Arcy W., 22 March 1817.
28. Ibid.
29. Ibid., p. 54: Sydney Gazette, 9 August 1817, p. 2, quoting "The Courier", 11 March 1817; H. of C. Hansard, 10 March 1817.
30. Wentworth Papers, A756, p. 56; Journals, A774, 4 June 1819 (King's Birthday), gives one example of the Governor's methods which was calculated to shock Regency London. On that day, opening the new Hyde Park Barracks for Convicts, Macquarie made a "short, plain speech" to the convicts, gave them a dinner of roast beef and plum pudding washed down with punch and drank himself to their "health and prosperity".
31. "And shall not such statues to Addington rise
    For service most timely—for warning most wise—
    For a treaty which snatched us from ruin away,
    When signed with a quill from the Bird of To-day."
                                        —GEORGE CANNING.

32. H. of C. Papers: Return to an Address of the Honourable the House of Commons to His Majesty, dated 3 July 1823, p. 5: Bathurst to Sidmouth, 23 April 1817.
33. Ibid.   34. Ibid.

35. Those which came on the *Almorah* included No. 82 (HRA, I. 9, p. 197) and No. 85 (p. 201), on the *Dick*, No. 86 (p. 206).

36. HRA, I. 8, p. 641: Bathurst to Macquarie, 4 December 1815.

37. HRA, I. 9, p. 206: Bathurst to Macquarie, 6 February 1817.

38. *Ibid.*, p. 207.

39. HRA, I. 7, p. 675: Bathurst to Macquarie, 23 November 1812.

40. HRA, I. 9, p. 111: Bathurst to E. Bent, 12 April 1816; *Proceedings of a general Court-martial ordered by Governor Macquarie to try the Revd. Benjamin Vale for seizing an American Vessel trading in Sydney Cove* (1817), C470.

41. HRA, I. 9, p. 492: to Bathurst, 24 November 1817.

42. *Ibid.*, p. 492. See also Note 39, *ante*.

43. *Ibid.*, p. 493.

44. *Ibid.*, p. 385: Bathurst to Macquarie, 22 April 1817. Bigge Appendix, Box 14, pp. 1284 *et seq.*: Moore and Campbell Correspondence, 4-5 March 1816.

45. *Ibid.*, pp. 385-6: Goulburn to Moore, 22 April 1817.

46. Letterbook, A797, pp. 129-32: Draft Dispatch; p. 136: E. Macquarie to Drummond, 12 December 1817; CSIL (1817), No. 92, p. 126: Moore to Macquarie, 29 September 1817, and Macquarie's holograph note of refusal thereon, together with Moore's subsequent pleading request.

47. HRA, I. 9, p. 493: to Bathurst, 24 November 1817.

48. *Ibid.*, pp. 494-5.

49. *Ibid.*, p. 198: "Extract from a Letter from . . . dated New South Wales, 13th March, 1816."

50. *Ibid.*, pp. 198-200, p. 856, Note 44.

51. *Ibid.*, p. 200.

52. *Ibid.*, p. 858.

53. *Ibid.*, p. 197: Bathurst to Macquarie, 24 Jan. 1817.

54. *Ibid.*, p. 484 *et seq.*: to Bathurst, 12 September 1817, Enclosures; p. 560 *et seq.*: to Bathurst, 12 December 1817, and Enclosures; pp. 562-707; CSIL (1817), II, pp. 1-70.

55. HRA, I. 9, p. 486.

56. *Ibid.*, p. 560; Journals, A773, pp. 126, 128, 22 December 1817.

57. *Ibid.*, p. 510: Field to Macquarie, 1 December 1817.

58. *Ibid.*, p. 503 *et seq.*: to Bathurst, 4 December 1817.

59. *Ibid.*

60. HRA, I. 7, pp. 614-15: to Bathurst, 17 November 1812; I. 8, p. 339: to Bathurst, 7 October 1814; Bank of New South Wales Manuscript Records, A329, p. 34: Autograph letter, Macquarie to J T. Campbell, 26 January 1821.

61. Letterbooks, A797, p. 135: E. Macquarie to Drummond, 12 December 1817.

62. *Sydney Gazette*, 23 August 1817, p. 3: Extract from *The Times*, 6 March 1817.

63. HRA, I. 9, pp. 520-2: J. T. Campbell to Magistrates and Chaplains, 20 November 1817; pp. 522-41: their replies, p. 515: G. & G.O., 10 September 1814.

64. *Ibid.*, p. 536: Marsden to Campbell, 28 November 1817.

65. *Ibid.*, pp. 540-1: H. M'Arthur to Campbell, 30 November 1817.

66. *Ibid.*, p. 509: to Bathurst, 2 December 1817.

67. *Ibid.*, p. 29: J. H. Bent to Macquarie, 9 January 1816; p. 513: Garling to Macquarie, 2 December 1817; pp. 511-13: Depositions.

68. *Ibid.*, pp. 512, 537-9.

69. *Ibid.*, p. 512.

70. *Ibid.*, pp. 512-13. Hoare was released on 12 August 1817. (See Bigge Appendix, Box 16, p. 1973: Macquarie to Oakes and Cullen, 11 August 1817.)

71. *Ibid.*, p. 506; Bigge Appendix, Box 8, pp. 3318-9, for Marsden's own account.

72. HRA, I. 9, p. 502. Bigge, in his report, substantiated the fact that Bayly had derived many of his complaints, second-hand, from his friend, Marsden.

73. *Ibid.*, pp. 856-8: Bayly to Bunbury.

74. NSWHR, VI, pp. 453, 587.

75. *Ibid.*, VII, p. 229.

76. *Piper Papers*, A256, p. 91: Bayly to Piper, 19 January 1816.

77. Journals, A778, p. 74, 15 December 1810. The grants were in addition to 1000 acres confirmed to him the day the Governor landed in Sydney (Bigge Appendix, Box 12, p. 127; Box 16, p. 66); Letters to Governor Macquarie, A1932, pp. 8-10.

78. NSWHR, IV, p. 915: Morgan to King, 11 December 1802; V, pp. 22, 71; p. 121: King to Hobart, 9 May 1803.

79. Bigge Appendix, Box 1, p. 81; HRA, I. 9, p. 509: Macquarie to Bathurst, 4 December 1817.

80. NSWHR, IV, p. 236: A Memorandum, 30 September 1800, sent by Governor King to the Duke of Portland. The careful F. M. Bladen, in his note, says that the paper was "apparently submitted to Governor King by the Revd. Samuel Marsden". The reference in the second paragraph of the document to "my servant George Lee" places the authorship beyond doubt.

81. Holt, *Memoirs*, II, p. 121.

82. HRA, I. 9, pp. 495-500: Macquarie (private letter) to Bathurst, 1 December 1817; pp. 501-2: Official letter of resignation; pp. 502-10: Commentary on Bayly's charges, to Bathurst, 4 December 1817.

83. *Ibid.*, pp. 509-10. 84. *Ibid.*, pp. 501-2. 85. *Ibid.*, p. 497 *et seq.*

86. *Ibid.*, p. 499-501. 87. *Ibid.*, pp. 500-1. 88. *Ibid.*, p. 499.

89. *Ibid.*, pp. 499-500. 90. *Ibid.*, p. 501.

91. *Ibid.*, p. 727: to Bathurst, 13 December 1817.

92. *Ibid.* 93. *Ibid.*, pp. 727-8.

BOOK FIVE

CHAPTER XXVII: THE FAVOURITE MEASURE

1. HRA, IV. 1, p. 254: Wylde wrote to Goulburn that Field conducted himself with hauteur and a tone of dictatorial authority. CSIL (1817), No. 98: Field told the Governor (12 November 1817) that a letter which he had received from Wylde was "such as he would despise me for pocketing. He must *retract* the having sent it to me."

2. HRA, I. 9, p. 797.

3. *Ibid.*, p. 710, 799, 800, 803, 881.

4. H. of C. *Hansard*, vol. XXXIX, p. 490, Goulburn.

5. HRA, I. 9, pp. 340-1: to Bathurst, 4 April 1817; Journals, A773, p. 19, 2 June 1816; p. 20, 3 June 1816; p. 111, 10 June 1817: Cox's Report.

6. HRA, I. 9, pp. 248-52, 549 *et seq.*

7. This practice was sanctified by the length of time it had been in vogue. See *Gazette*, 5 March 1803.

8. HRA, I. 9, p. 348: to Bathurst, 4 April 1817; pp. 714-15, 12 December 1817.

9. Bigge Appendix, Box 11, Questions submitted to Governor Macquarie, Q. & A. 62. For his outlook on organized settlement, see p. 491.

10. HRA, I. 10, pp. 96, 281, 368 *et seq.*, 719, 720; I. 9, p. 352. For references to churches, see Journals, A772, p. 121, 11 October 1817; A773, p. 109, 6 June 1817; p. 153, 7 April 1818; A774, II, p. 113, 19 March 1820. Macquarie laid the foundation stone of St Matthew's Church, Windsor, on 11 October 1817.

11. Bigge Appendix, Box 11, pp. 4358-74: Questions submitted to Governor Macquarie by the Commissioner of Inquiry, Q. and A. 63.

12. HRA, I. 9, p. 352, 720. The foundations for the Hyde Park Barracks were begun, 28 March 1817; foundation stone laid, 6 April 1817. Journals, A774, p. 43, 20 May 1819, record that the convicts slept then for the first time in the barracks.

13. HRA, I. 9, pp. 70-1, 205, 718-19.

14. Journals, A773, p. 29, 11 July 1816 (foundation stone laid); pp. 97, 125, 160. The whole matter of Macquarie's building programme is dealt with at full length in the author's *Francis Greenway*.

15. HRA, I. 9, pp. 352-4. 504: to Bathurst, 4 April and 4 December 1817.

16. *Ibid.*,pp . 832-3: Bathurst to Macquarie, 24 August 1818.

17. Bennet, H. G., *Letter to Viscount Sidmouth* (1st ed.), p. 77.

18. Bigge Appendix, Box 11: Questions Submitted to Governor Macquarie by Commissioner Bigge, Q. and A. 64.

19. *Ibid.*, Box 27, p. 6499: Report of the Work Done by the different government working gangs by F. H. Greenway.

20. Bigge Appendix, Box 11: Questions submitted to Governor Macquarie, Q. and A. 64.

21. *Ibid.*

22. *Ibid.*, Box 27, p. 6445 *et seq.* This report on St Matthew's church by the surveyors declared that a considerable part of the wall was insufficient and composed of bad material, and that it ought to be condemned and totally removed and its place supplied with better brick and lime. Two other churches in particular suffered from the same type of deficiency—those at Newcastle and Port Macquarie.

23. HRA, I. 10, pp. 684-701: Report of Governor Macquarie to Earl Bathurst, 27 July 1822.

24. HRA, I. 7, p. 242; p. 265: to Castlereagh, 30 April 1810; p. 343: to Liverpool, 27 October 1810; p. 478: Liverpool to Macquarie, 9 November 1812; CSIL (1811), No. 32, p. 60: Fawkener to Sir Robert Peel, 17 May 1811.

25. HRA, I. 9, pp. 217-18: to Bathurst, 29 March 1817.

26. *Ibid.*, p. 217.

27. See Chapter XX, pp. 290-1, 294-6; HRA, I. 9, p. 218.

28. *Ibid.*, p. 218; pp. 222-3: Proclamation, 23 November 1816.

29. HRA, I. 10, p. 676: Report of Governor Macquarie to Earl Bathurst, par. 18.

30. Minute Book of the Bank of New South Wales; Wentworth Papers, A752, p. 235: J. T. Campbell's circular letter, 19 November 1816. A preliminary private meeting seems to have been held at noon on Wednesday, 19 November 1816. Those invited were Wylde (Judge-Advocate), D. Wentworth, A. Riley, S. Lord, Robt. Campbell, sen., Chas. Hook, J. R. O'Connor, Wm. Browne, Thos. McVitie, Richd. Brooks, Jas. Birnie, Richd. Jones, Robt. Jenkins, and J. T. Campbell—"all magistrates and principal merchants". HRA, I. 9, p. 219, p. 861, Note 56.

31. *Ibid.*, pp. 219-20.

32. HRA, IV. 1, p. 787: Bigge Commission, Wylde's Evidence.

33. *Ibid.*

34. HRA, I. 9, pp, 861-2: Bank of New South Wales Minute Book, p. 1.

35. Bank of New South Wales Minute Book, p. 3.

36. *Sydney Gazette*, 7 December 1816; HRA, I. 9, pp. 234-5, Memorial of Campbell and Others; Bank of N.S.W. Minute Book, p. 3: Minutes of Meeting, 5 December 1816; Bigge Appendix, Box 27, p. 6285: List of Stockholders; CSIL (1818), p. 286: Michael Robinson to Macquarie, 16 January 1818.

37. Bank of New South Wales Minute Book, pp. 7-9: Minutes of Meeting, 18 December.

38. *Ibid.*, Minutes, 7 February 1817.

39. Bank of New South Wales Minute Book: Riley to Campbell, 27 February 1817; Campbell to Riley, 28 February 1817; Minutes, 15 February 1817.

40. HRA, IV. 1, p. 788: Bigge Commission, Wylde's Evidence; I. 9, p. 861; pp. 223-7: Charter of the Bank of New South Wales, 12 February 1817.

41. Bank of New South Wales Minute Book, p. 10, 22 and 25 March 1817.

42. Bank of New South Wales Minute Book, p. 28: Message from Governor Macquarie to the directors of the Bank at their inaugural meeting, 8 April 1817.

43. *Ibid.*, p. 8: Minutes of Meeting of Committee, 6 March 1817.

44. *Ibid.*, p. 28: Minutes of Meeting of Committee, 22 March 1817.

45. *Ibid.*, Minutes, 8 April 1817. The date of the foundation day was fixed as 8 April, at the meeting which elected the first Board of Directors, 7 February 1817. And that day was celebrated, though it is clear that the first deposit actually was accepted on 5 April.

46. Bigge Appendix, Box 27. p. 6290.

47. *Ibid.*, p. 6273.

48. Bank of New South Wales Minute Book, p. 10 Minutes of Meeting held at Mr J. T. Campbell's House, 25 March 1817.

49. *The Beginnings of Government in Australia* (Library Committee of the Commonwealth Parliament, 1913), Finance: First Ledger Entry, Bank of New South Wales, 1817:

"Dr. to JEREMIAH MURPHY, Sergt.

1817	£	s.	d.	1817	£	s.	d.
June 30 Balance	50	0	0	April 5 Cash 3	50	0	0
Sept. 11 Cash	50	0	0	July 1 Balance	50	0	0"

50. HRA, I. 9, pp. 840-1: Bathurst to Macquarie, 29 October 1818.

51. *Ibid.*, p. 841.

52. Bank of New South Wales Minute Book: Meeting, 3 February 1818; Bigge Appendix, Box 27, p. 6288.

53. Bank of New South Wales Minute Book: J. T. Campbell's Presidential Report, 21 July 1819.

54. HRA, I. 10, p. 348: to Bathurst, 1 September 1820; Wylde's Report, p. 350.

55. Bigge Appendix, Box 1, p. 279: Harris's Evidence.

56. *Ibid.*, Box 27, p. 6279: Evidence of Francis Williams.

57. *Ibid.*

58. Bank of New South Wales Minute Book.

59. Bigge Appendix, Box 27, p. 6280: Williams's Evidence.

60. *Ibid.*, pp. 6274-81.

61. *Ibid.*, p. 6275.

62. *Ibid.*, p. 6274.   63. *Ibid.*, p. 6282.

64. *Ibid.*, pp. 6284-5. At 26 January 1821, the Bank held Treasury Bills, £4741 17s 6d.; Colonial Duties, £2525; Spanish Dollars in bags, £1625; Dumps in bags, £312 10s.; further Treasury Bills, £11,368 13s. 2d.; store receipts, £12,500; dollars, dumps, and coppers, £2068 17s. 7d. Total, £35,141 18s. 3d. To this was hopefully added: Bills falling due in January, £1259 5s. 3d.; Ditto, February and the following months, £19,257 19s. 5d.; Due on Mortgage Deeds, £4172; Mr Williams's (late cashier's) furniture and property, £485 3s. 10d. Total, £60,316 6s. 9d. Against this very mottled backing, the responsibilities of the Bank at date of balance (31 December 1820) were itemized as follows: Bank Notes in circulation, £5902; Personal Balances, £26,867 17s. 10d.; Bank Stock Shares, £12,600; Profit and Loss: Dividends, £1038 10s. 1d.; Unclaimed Dividends, £81 14s. 7d. Total, £46,490 2s. 6d. Add "Losses from Mr. Williams's fraudulent conduct, balance may be reckoned at £6000. Grand Total, £52,490 2s. 6d." So that "there was a balance in favour of the Bank of £7826 4s. 3d". There were at the time 59 stockholders with a capital holding of £12,600, of which only £6287 was paid up, and the Directors (stout fellows!) had no hesitation in paying 6 per cent dividend, notwithstanding the opulent distributions of 12 per cent, 9 per cent, and 6 per cent which had been made since August 1819. Still, the position was a great improvement over that of 13 June 1818, when total share money received was £3625, personal balances stood at £1859 4s. 8d., and the Bank's discount and premium business brought in £281 7s. 5d. The Bank then had £1381 lent on mortgage and its holding of Treasury Bills, Store Receipts, and Specie totalled £3613 2s. 10d. The accounts balanced at £11,401 0s. 1d.

65. Bigge Appendix, Box 27, p. 6294 *et seq.*

66. *Ibid.*, p. 6290.

67. The Charter eventually was issued on 31 October 1823.

68. HRA, I. 10, p. 676: Macquarie to Bathurst, 27 July 1822; to Bathurst, 29 March 1817; I. 11, p. 586; Mitchell Library, C819, Charter of the Bank of New South Wales, signed 31 October 1823 (Printed by Robert Howe, Government Printer. Sydney, 1824).

69. Report and Balance Sheet of the Bank of New South Wales, 1956.

70. New South Wales Almanac, 1820: List of Bank Holidays.

71. Journals, A774, I, p. 64, 31 August 1819.

72. *Sydney Gazette*, 5 September 1818. It was recorded that the work was being done according to "the Edinburgh and London plans".

73. Journals, A773, p. 131, 1 January 1818; p. 138, 29 January 1818; p. 143, 17 February 1818.

74. Journals, A786: Journal of Voyage to Lake Bathurst.

75. Journals, A785: Journal of Voyage to Port Macquarie, 11 November 1821.

76. Journals, A774, II, pp. 119-23, 28 March 1820.

77. Arnold, Journal, C720, p. 396; CSIL (1819), No. 5, p. 21 *et seq.*: D. Allan to Macquarie, 19 January 1819; p. 24 *et seq.*: correspondence regarding the court martial of Broughton.

CHAPTER XXVIII: AN HABITATION AND A NAME

1. Journals, A773, p. 141, 2 February 1818; p. 157: List in W. Cox's handwriting signed "W. Cox, J.P.", endorsed by Macquarie, "Recd. 23rd April, 1818." Ellis, M. H., *The Beef Shorthorn in Australia*, Chapter XIII, p. 94 *et seq.*

2. Journals, A773, p. 137, 26 January 1818. The Governor ordered it to be celebrated as a special gala day, with a military review and a viceregal dinner to all the civil and military officers. Elizabeth gave a ball to the ladies of the settlement. HRA, IV. 1, p. 126. Ellis Bent had noted the stirrings of the new age: "A free generation is rising into existence." *Sydney Gazette*, 1 December 1821: "His Excellency's Address".

3. Journals, A773, p. 49, 30 September 1816.

4. HRA, I. 9, p. 747: Macquarie to Goulburn, 21 December 1817. See also pp. 356, 488, on which also he emphasizes the name.

5. HRA, I. 9, p. 867 *et seq.*, Note 84; p. 207: Bathurst to Macquarie, 8 February 1817. Macquarie on 4 April 1817, had similarly placed emphasis on the name in acknowledging a copy of Flinders's chart and journal which Lord Bathurst had sent out. Bathurst notified the sending of charts of "New Holland". Macquarie acknowledged the receipt of charts of *Australia*, with the word underlined. (HRA, I. 9, p. 105: Goulburn to Macquarie, 1 April 1816. Also p. 356: Macquarie to Bathurst, 4 April 1817.) The Governor used the name on 13 December 1817, when referring to "an enumeration of such remarkable plants as were discovered in the interior of Australia". Also, Wylde uses it as a matter of course in his doggerel on the discomfiture of Jeffery Bent, which must have been written *circa* April 1817. See also p. 825: Macquarie to Goulburn, 16 August 1818.

6. HRA, I. 9, p. 859, Note 52.

7. See Chapter I, Note 5. W. C. Wentworth wrote of the country as New Holland in a *Statistical Account of New South Wales* (1819), but in the third edition he records that "the most eminent modern geographers have given to it [the continent]the appropriate name of

Australia. . . ." Wentworth and his partner called their newspaper, founded the year of Macquarie's death, the *Australian*. It carried at its masthead the motto, "Advance Australia".

8. HRA, I. 9, p. 709: to Bathurst, 12 December 1817, includes a sample.
9. *Ibid.*, p. 797: to Bathurst, 16 May 1818.
10. *Ibid.*, pp. 114-7: Bathurst to Macquarie, 18 April 1816; p. 203, 30 January 1817.
11. *Ibid.*   12. *Ibid.*, p. 114.   13. *Ibid.*, pp. 730-1.
14. *Ibid.*, p. 808.   15. *Ibid.*, p. 356: to Bathurst, 4 April 1817.
16. *Ibid.*, p. 357.   17. *Ibid.*
18. *Ibid.*; Journals, A773, p. 95, 4 April 1817.
19. HRA, I. 9, p. 479 *et seq.*: Oxley to Macquarie, 30 August 1817.
20. Bigge Appendix, Box 5, pp. 1864-1934: Oxley's evidence; HRA, I. 9, p. 481.
21. HRA, I. 9, pp. 726-27: to Bathurst, 13 December 1817. Evans received £100 and Allan Cunningham, £50.
22. *Ibid.*, p. 501.
23. Letterbooks, A797, p. 138 *et seq.*: Eliz. Macquarie to Drummond, 12 December 1817.
24. HRA, I. 10, p. 23.
25. HRA, I. 10, p. 26: G. & G.O., 5 December 1818.
26. *Ibid.*, pp. 26-8.   27. *Ibid.*, p. 28.
28. *Ibid.*, p. 28: Oxley to Macquarie, 1 November 1818.
29. *Ibid.*   30. *Ibid.*, p. 29.   31. *Ibid.*   32. *Ibid.*
33. *Ibid.*, p. 30.   34. *Ibid.*   35. *Ibid.*   36. *Ibid.*
37. *Ibid.*, p. 26: G & G.O., 5 December 1818.
38. *Ibid.*, p. 24: to Bathurst, 1 March 1819.   39. *Ibid.*
40. RAHSJ, XXVI, pp. 515-18; XXVII, pp. 433-44: Notes of James Jervis and W. J. Goold; HRA, I. 10, p. 178.
41. Journals, A781: Journal of Tour to and from Newcastle pp. 1-35, 27 July-9 August 1818; A773, p. 34, 7 August 1816.
42. Journals, A781, pp. 16-17, 1 August 1818. John Maclaine was killed in Ceylon fighting against insurgents, 13 January 1818 (Journals, A774, I, p. 3).
43. Journals, A781, p. 19, 2 August 1818. The foundation stone had been laid by Captain Wallis on 1 January 1817, and on the following Christmas Day the captain had "assembled the People for Public Worship . . . in commemoration of the nativity of our Blessed Redeemer, in the newly erected edifice, to be dedicated to the adorable *Name*, and which is now called *Christ Church*". (*Sydney Gazette*, Supplement, 5 December 1818.) The plan (according to himself) was drawn by a convict named James Clohesy (or Clohasy), altered by Captain Wallis and finished by one, Wheatley (Bigge Appendix, Box 1, p. 483); but John Allan, who had charge of the building for a time (Appendix, Box 1, p. 502), declared the drawing to be the work of "a prisoner named Lycett, sent up for the forging of Commissariat bills". This is likely to be the truth. Lycett copied many plans for Mrs Macquarie.
44. *Sydney Gazette*, 15 August 1818, p. 4: Letter signed "W . . . . R, Newcastle, New South Wales, 5th August, 1818." This letter obviously was the work of Cowper.
45. *Ibid.*; Journals, A781, pp. 19-21, 2-3 August 1818.
46. Journals, A781, p. 24, 4 August 1818.
47. *Ibid.*, pp. 25-35, 5-9 August 1818.
48. HRA, I. 10, p. 13: to Bathurst, 15 February 1819; pp. 43-5.
49. RAHSJ, XXVI, pp. 515-18: The Route to the North, by James Jervis; XXVII, p. 433: Some Routes to the North, by W. J. Goold; p. 437, The Route to the North by James Jervis; HRA, I. 10, p. 43: to Bathurst, 8 March 1819.
50. Journals, A774, I, p. 12, 20 October 1818. It was designed by Greenway and contracted for in 1816.
51. Wentworth, W. C., Statistical Account of New South Wales (1st Ed.).
52. Mann, D. D., *The Present Picture of New South Wales*, p. 61.
53. Journals, A773, p. 107, 4 June 1817; CSIL (1820), No. 25, p. 98.
54. HRA, I. 9, p. 780: to Marsden, 20 April 1818; Journals, A774. p. 116, 23 March 1820.; Wentworth, W. C., *Statistical Account of New South Wales* (3rd ed.), I, p. 357 *et seq.*
55. Tompson, Charles, *Wild Notes from the Lyre of a Native Minstrel*, p. 9. "Retrospect".
56. *Ibid.*, p. 15.   57. *Ibid.*, p. 34: "Ode to Spring".

CHAPTER XXIX: THE RETURN OF THE EXILE

1. Wentworth Papers, A756, p. 53: W. C. Wentworth to D. Wentworth, 22 March 1817.
2. NSWHR, VII, p. 155; Memoranda, A772, p. 113. He had sailed from Sydney in the *Admiral Gambier*, 28 March 1809; and he returned in the *Lord Eldon*, which sailed from England, 21 April 1817, arriving Port Jackson, 30 September 1817. Onslow, S. M., *Early Records of the Macarthurs of Camden*, pp. 301-2: H. M'Arthur to John M'Arthur, 16 and 28 May 1814.

3. Onslow, S. M., *Early Records of the Macarthurs of Camden*, p. 244: John M'Arthur to Eliz. M'Arthur, 8 December 1814.

4. *Ibid.*, p. 245; NSWHR, VII, p. 144: Castlereagh to Macquarie, 14 May 1809.

5. Onslow, S. M., *Early Records of the Macarthurs*, pp. 245-6.

6. *Ibid.*, p. 246.

7. *Ibid.*, p. 246.

8. *Ibid.*, p. 261: John M'Arthur to Eliz. M'Arthur, 23 July 1816.

9. *Ibid.*

10. *Ibid.*, pp. 252-8. He left England in March 1815 and returned at the end of April 1816.

11. *Ibid.*, pp. 267-8: to Eliz. M'Arthur, 19 August 1816.

12. *Ibid.*, p. 273.

13. *Ibid.*, p. 276.

14. *Ibid.*, p. 276, 282: Goulburn to G. Watson-Taylor, 14 August 1816. 14 October 1816.

15. *Ibid.*, p. 279: John M'Arthur to Eliz. M'Arthur, 16 December 1816; p. 284, 9 December 1816; p. 286: John M'Arthur to Lieut. J. R. Smith, 16 January 1817; to Eliz. M'Arthur, 18 February 1817.

16. *Ibid.*, p. 286.

17. *Ibid.*, pp. 288-90: John M'Arthur to Eliz. M'Arthur, 18 February 1817.

18. *Ibid.*, p. 289.

19. *Ibid.*, p. 290.

20. Memoranda, A772, pp. 113-14; p. 125, 16 October 1817.

21. *Ibid.*, p. 18, 4 January 1810.

22. Onslow, S. M., *Early Records of the Macarthurs of Camden*, pp. 299 *et seq.*, p. 314; p. 308: Eliz. M'Arthur to Miss Kingdon.

23. *Ibid.*, p. 317: John M'Arthur to Davidson, 3 September 1818.

24. *Ibid.*, p. 187: John M'Arthur to Eliz. M'Arthur, 11 December 1809; p. 203, 3 August 1810. The quarrel began as soon as Marsden arrived in the Colony: "Your Excellency [Hunter] cannot be ignorant since your arrival of Captain J. M'Arthur's attempts privately to assassinate my character . . . Had his malicious intention succeeded, my authority, influence and respect must have been totally lost." (Bigge Appendix, Box 12, p. 112.)

25. Bennet, H. G., *Letter to Earl Bathurst* (1820), p. 122, Appendix: Marsden to Riley, 19 May 1818.

26. It is strange that in his letter to Riley, Marsden does not mention the decisive part played by Robert Campbell and Charles Hooke in the proceedings. They rebutted Hughes's statement at the Bigge Inquiry.

27. Bigge Appendix, Box 27, p. 6321: Marsden's affidavit; p. 6349: Hooke, affidavit; p. 6347: Robt. Campbell to Marsden, 10 February 1821.

28. Bigge Appendix, Box 2, p. 654 *et seq.*: Hughes's Evidence.

29. *Ibid.*

30. Bennet, H. G., *Letter to Earl Bathurst*, Appendix 3, p. 122 *et seq.*; Journals, A773, p. 133, 8 January 1818.

31. The furniture is catalogued in the Bigge Appendix, Box 27.

32. Bennet, H. G., *Letter to Earl Bathurst*, Appendix 3, p. 122 *et seq.*: Marsden to Riley, 19 May 1818.

33. *Ibid.*, p. 123.

34. *Ibid.*, pp. 123-4.

35. Letterbooks, A797, p. 141 *et seq.*: Address to Mr. Marsden, 8 January 1818.

36. *Ibid.*   37. *Ibid.*

38. Bennet, H. G., *Letter to Earl Bathurst*, p. 124; Journals, A773, p. 133, 8 June 1818.

39. *Ibid.*

40. Bennet, H. G., *Letter to Earl Bathurst*, p. 117: Marsden to Wilberforce, 5 February 1818.

41. HRA, IV. 1, pp. 813-16: Examination of J. Wylde, pp. 344-9: Wylde to Bathurst, 20 July 1821; Bennet, H. G., *Letter to Earl Bathurst*, p. 125.

42. *Sydney Gazette*, 28 March 1818; Bigge Appendix, Box 16, pp. 2028, 2145, 2160; Bennet, H. G., *Letter to Earl Bathurst*, p. 125.

43. *Ibid.*

44. *Ibid.*

45. Bennet, H. G., *Letter to Earl Bathurst*, p. 126.

46. Marsden Papers, A1992, p. 232: J. T. Campbell to Marsden, 3 August 1818; Bigge Appendix, Box 17, pp. 2205-8, including Macquarie to Marsden, 11 August 1818; Marsden Papers, C244, pp. 43-6: Marsden to Macquarie, 11 August 1818.

47. HRA, I. 10, p. 194: to Bathurst, 20 July 1819; p. 284: to Bathurst, 28 February 1820; Marsden Papers, A1992, p. 239: Bent to Marsden, 19 June 1819.

48. Journals, A774, I, p. 1, 9 July 1818.

49. Marsden Papers, A1993, p. 240: J. H. Bent to Marsden, 19 June 1819; HRA, I. 10, p. 806; Bonwick Transcripts (Biography), I, p. 259 et seq.: M. Biggé to Bonwick, 6 September 1897.

50. HRA, I. 10, p. 2: Bathurst to Macquarie, 30 January 1819; p. 4 et seq.: Bathurst to Bigge, 6 January 1819; p. 806, Note 3; Wentworth, Statistical Account of New South Wales (3rd ed.), I, p. 387; National Library, A141, Ellis Bent Correspondence, p. 238.

51. HRA, I. 10, p. 4, pp. 8-11.

52. Ibid., pp. 4-8.

53. Ibid., p. 6-7.

54. HRA, I. 2, pp. 94, 166.

55. HRA, I. 5, pp. 513, 552, 578, 579.

56. NSWHR, VI, pp. 23, 26, 172, 248, 358, 740; HRA, I. 5, pp. 577, 632, 675, 681, et seq.; Onslow, S. M. Early Records of the Macarthurs of Camden, p. 135.

57. Bligh described M'Arthur as "a disturber of public society and a venemous serpent to His Majesty's Governors. He has hitherto overcome them with his artifice." (NSWHR, VI, p. 609.)

58. In November 1808, a few months before M'Arthur sailed for England, the sheep population of Australia was 32,251. Despite bad droughts in the interval, the number had risen to 250,000 less than three years after his return.

59. Onslow, S. M., Early Records of the Macarthurs of Camden, p. 327-8.

60. He had proposed the formation of a sheep-raising company as far back as the days of Governor King.

61. Onslow, S. M., Early Records of the Macarthurs of Camden, p. 329.

62. Ibid.

63. Ibid., p. 317: John M'Arthur to Davidson, 3 September 1818.

64. Ibid., p. 62.

65. Ibid., pp. 325, 338, 473.

66. Memoranda, A772, p. 113. It was an ironic fact that it was Macquarie himself who, by introducing Bowman to Bathurst and recommending him for his meritorious services, enabled him to supplant Redfern. (HRA, I. 9, p. 494.)

67. HRA, I. 10, pp. 39-40: to Bathurst, 8 March 1819; pp. 65-7: to Bathurst, 22 March 1819; I. 8, p. 131: Bathurst to Macquarie, 3 February 1814.

68. Ibid., p. 295: Bathurst to Macquarie, 24 March 1820.

69. Ibid; Bigge Appendix, Box 14, p. 1292. The figure is for 1820.

70. HRA, I. 10, pp. 823-4. Major Goulburn was soon the most unpopular official in the Colony and was treated somewhat roughly by the emancipists in their rousing ditty, called "The Old Viceroy":

> "Freeman and bondsman, man and boy,
> Are all agreed, I'll wager,
> They'd sell their last slop shirt to buy
> A ticket for the Major.
> Here's to Sir Thomas's release,
> The Old Viceroy's return,
> And fourteen years beyond the seas
> For thee, Frederick Goulburn."

71. Bigge Appendix: Various letters to Goulburn, 1821-2.

72. Piper Papers, A256, pp. 137-8: J. H. Bent to Piper, 3 August 1818.

73. Select Committee on Jails (1819).

74. Piper Papers, A256, pp. 141-3: Bent to Piper, 27 November 1819. There is a curious phrase bearing on the rumoured appointment of Bigge as Governor, in the dispatch (HRA, I. 10, p. 149) in which Bathurst tells Macquarie that "in the event of Mr Bigge signifying his intention of returning to this country", etc.

75. HRA, I. 10, p. 147, for dates.

76. Bigge had been Chief Justice of Trinidad (HRA, I. 10, p. 806, Note 3). His nephew, Matthew Bigge, told Bonwick that he had also served in Mauritius. (Bonwick Trans., Biography, I, p. 259 et seq.)

77. John M'Arthur, Junior, had retailed the story to his father. See Onslow, Macarthurs of Camden, p. 325.

78. Onslow, S. M., Early Records of the Macarthurs of Camden, pp. 279, 284.

79. H. of C. Hansard, XXXIX, pp. 464-509.

80. Ibid.   81. Ibid.

82. Ibid., pp. 478-84: Castlereagh, pp. 478-84; Wilberforce, pp. 485-7.

83. Ibid., pp. 480-1.

84. Ibid., p. 1124, 23 March 1819: Brougham; Wentworth Papers, A756, p. 135: W. C. Wentworth to D'Arcy Wentworth, 13 April 1819.

85. *Hansard*, XXXIX, p. 1125.
86. HRA, I. 9, p. 775: Field to Macquarie, 23 February 1818; IV. 1, p. 321: Field to Goulburn, 13 November 1818.
87. HRA, I. 9, p. 774.
88. *Ibid.*, pp. 774-5.
89. *Ibid.*, p. 775.
90. *Ibid.*, pp. 772-4: to Bathurst, 15 May 1818.
91. *Ibid.*, p. 773.
92. HRA, IV. 1, pp. 330-1: Opinions of Shepherd and Gifford, 15 February 1819.
93. H. of C. *Hansard*, XXXIX, p. 1125: Brougham.
94. *Ibid.*, p. 1124.
95. *Ibid.*, p. 1127.
96. HRA, I. 9, pp. 761-2: Bathurst to Macquarie, 12 May 1818.
97. H. of C. *Hansard*, 1128-38.
98. *Ibid.*, 1130-1, 1133-4.
99. *Ibid.*, 1134-5.
100. HRA, I. 10, p. 196: Bathurst to Macquarie, 4 August 1819; 59 Geo. III, c. 114. The right was reserved to the Crown of imposing a duty on spirits in the Colony. It brought policy to the point at which the Governor might establish his distillery—of course with Mr Bigge's consent.
101. Wentworth Papers, A756, p. 145: W. C. Wentworth to D'A. Wentworth, 8 August 1819; p. 153, 24 November 1819; *Hansard*, XXXV, pp. 491, 551, 825.
102. H. of C. Select Committee (1812): Report, p. 11. The other matters were ventilated in Parliament that year.
103. NSWHR, VI, p. 267: G. & G.O., 25 May 1807. The ration was usually 10 pound of wheat, 8 pounds of flour, 3 pounds of maize, or 3 pints of peas, 7 pounds of beef or 4 pounds of pork, 6 ounces of sugar, or 1 pound of rice.

CHAPTER XXX: JOHN M'ARTHUR HOLDS TRUMPS

1. Wentworth Papers, A756, p. 157: W. C. Wentworth to D'Arcy Wentworth, 24 November 1819; Letterbooks, A797, p. 173: Drummond to Macquarie, 6 June 1820. See Chapter XXXI, Note 32.
2. HRA, I. 9, pp. 838-40: Bathurst to Macquarie, 18 October 1818.
3. Journals, A774, I, p. 45, 29 May; p. 61, 5 August 1819; HRA, I. 10, p. 190; I. 9, p. 824: Bathurst to Macquarie, 26 July 1818; Mitchell Library: Macquarie to Charles Macquarie, 1 March 1820.
4. HRA, I. 10, p. 2: Bathurst to Macquarie, 30 January 1819.
5. *Ibid.*, p. 3.
6. *Ibid.*, pp. 3-4.
7. *Ibid.*, p. 149: Bigge to Goulburn, 18 April 1819.
8. *Ibid.*, pp. 52-4: to Bathurst, 22 March 1819; pp. 55-65: text of Petition.
9. *Ibid.*, pp. 53-6.
10. *Ibid.*, pp. 52-4. The collection of signatures was hampered by the flood rains.
11. *Ibid.*, pp. 295-6: Bathurst to Macquarie, 24 March 1820.
12. Piper Papers, A256, pp. 64-5: Allan to Piper, 29 November 1819. For Drennan's case, HRA, I. 10, p. 101: Macquarie to Bathurst, 24 March 1819; pp. 629-30: Brisbane to Bathurst, 6 April 1822.
13. H. of C. Papers: Report of Select Committee on Jails, etc. (1819) with Appendix of Evidence.
14. Marsden Papers, A1992: Sir T. F. Buxton to Marsden, 7 May 1819.
15. *Ibid.*
16. HRA, I. 10, pp. 210-14: to Bathurst, 22 February 1820.
17. Journals, A774, p. 65, 31 August 1819; Bigge Appendix, Box 24, p. 4956 *et seq.*: Bigge to Macquarie, 31 March 1820. Bigge spoke of the proposed church as a "very large edifice", and expressed preference for "a new gaol calculated to meet the demands of a rapidly augmenting population".
18. *Ibid.*; HRA, I. 10, p. 211: to Bathurst, 22 February 1820.
19. *Ibid.*
20. *Ibid.*; Bigge Appendix, Box 17, p. 2966 *et seq.*: Bigge to Bathurst, 18 October 1819.
21. HRA, I. 10, pp. 283-4: to Bathurst, 28 February 1820; Journals, A774, p. 81, 18 November 1819.
22. Journals, A774, p. 71, 7 October 1819; H. of C. Papers (1828), p. 24: Extract of a letter from Major-General Macquarie to Earl Bathurst, 10 October 1823.
23. *Ibid.*

24. Onslow, S. M.; Early Records of the Macarthurs of Camden, p. 321: J. M'Arthur to ¹. M'Arthur the younger, 20 February 1820.

25. *Ibid.* 26. *Ibid.*, p. 322. 27. *Ibid.* 28. *Ibid.*, p. 323.

29. HRA, I. 10, pp. 2-3: Bathurst to Macquarie, 30 January 1819.

30. H. of C. Papers (1828), p. 25: Macquarie to Bathurst, 10 October 1823.

31. *Ibid.*

32. Redfern was "heir apparent" by a precedent established in the days of Sir Robert Dundas's rule as Secretary for War. See HRA, I. 2, p. 458: Dundas to Grose, 15 November 1793: "It may be proper to add that it is intended that the assistant-surgeons shall succeed to the office of Chief Surgeon by rotation and according to their seniority from the dates of their commissions." HRA, I. 10, p. 146: Bathurst to Macquarie, 14 April 1819; p. 214 *et seq.*: to Bathurst, 22 February 1820; p. 273: Redfern to Macquarie, 18 October 1819; p. 274: Redfern's Memorial. On Redfern's appointment as assistant surgeon, Macquarie had written (HRA, I. 7, p. 787) that "Mr. Redfern . . . unquestionably looks forward to filling the highest situation in the Medical Department of New South Wales in the regular rotation of seniority."

The Governor later (in 1820) wrote (*Letter to Sidmouth*, pp. 38-40). "Mr. Redfern was, at his own particular request to Sir Jeremiah Fitzpatrick, the Inspector of the Transport Department, sent to this Colony in 1801. During the passage, he assisted the Surgeon and kept the Journal of the treatment of the sick. A few days after his arrival in this Colony, he was sent to Norfolk Island as Assistant to the Surgeon stationed there. General Foveaux, shortly after his arrival, appointed him to the sole charge of the hospital . . . General Foveaux personally introduced, and recommended Mr. Redfern to my notice in the strongest terms, as to his conduct, character and professional abilities, stating that, in order to secure to the Settlement the advantage of his professional skill, he had appointed him Assistant Surgeon in the Colony, and solicited Lord Castlereagh for his confirmation. His appointment was confirmed by . . . the Prince Regent in 1811. So far as my opinion goes, no man in this Colony is better qualified to execute the duties of magistrate with credit to himself and benefit to the Public Service."

33. HRA, IV. I, p. 152: Bent to Bathurst; Bigge Appendix, Box 26, p. 6190: Redfern to Bigge, 5 February 1821. He refers to Bowman as "your obsequious, intimate and humble protégé".

34. NSWHR, VII, pp. 306, 561: Liverpool to Macquarie, 26 July 1811. It was granted by Royal Commission under seal in the usual form and addressed to "our trusty and well beloved William Redfern, gent."

35. HRA, I. 10, pp. 221-2: Macquarie to Bigge, 6 November 1819; G. & G.O., 23 October 1819 and 12 November 1819; Bigge Appendix, Box 28: Redfern to Wilmot, 10 December 1822.

36. Onslow, S. M., *Early Records of the Macarthurs of Camden*, p. 192: to Eliz. M'Arthur, 3 May 1810.

37. HRA, I. 10, p. 218: Macquarie to Bigge, 30 October 1819; IV. I, p. 789: Wylde's Evidence.

38. HRA, I. 10, pp. 219-20: Bigge to Macquarie, 2 November 1819, and other correspondence.

39. *Ibid.*, p. 221: Macquarie to Bigge, 6 November 1819.

40. *Ibid.*, pp. 220-2, 224, 557-8.

41. *Ibid.*, p. 227.

42. *Ibid.*, See also Note 34.

43. HRA, I. 10, p. 223: Macquarie to Bigge 20 November 1819; Bigge Appendix, Box 20, p. 3206: Bigge to Bathurst, 19 December 1819.

44. Bigge Appendix, Box 26, p. 6199: Redfern to Bigge, 5 February 1821.

45. *Ibid.*

46. HRA, I. 10, p. 222. See also pp. 217-18.

47. *Ibid.*, pp. 217-18, 223-4.

48. *Ibid.*, p. 224.

49. Onslow, S. M., *Early Records of the Macarthurs of Camden*, p. 325, 331: John M'Arthur to John M'Arthur, the younger, 20 February 1820.

50. *Ibid.*, p. 331.

51. *Ibid.*

52. *Ibid.*, pp. 331-2.

53. *Ibid.*, p. 323.

54. HRA, I. 10, p. 288: to Bathurst, 28 February 1820; III. 2, p. 744: Sorell to Loane, 22 November 1819.

55. Onslow, S. M., *Early Records of the Macarthurs of Camden*, p. 325 *et seq.*

56. *Ibid.*

57. *Ibid.*, p. 327.

58. *Ibid.*, pp. 341-2: Sorell to M'Arthur, 26 November 1819, and 21 January 1820.

59. HRA, III. 3, p. 15: Sorell to Macquarie, 1 May 1820: ". . . of the whole the number of 300, 185 only remain." Contrary to M'Arthur's estimate of the value of the sheep, Sorell wrote that "having consulted with persons on whose opinion I could rely, I conclude it to be quite impossible to fix a higher price than seven guin's on each ram", which was about what the original 300 cost the Government in terms of land at 7s. 6d. per acre plus freight. HRA, I. 10, p. 823: Grant, 27 May 1823.

60. NSWHR, VI, pp. 23, 26, 248.

61. HRA, I. 10, pp. 91-2, 280, 682.

62. Onslow, S. M., *Early Records of the Macarthurs*, p. 340.

63. *Ibid.*, p. 330.   64. *Ibid.*

65. *Ibid.* Bigge Appendix, Box 28: Report on Marsden.

66. Onslow, S. M., *Early Records of the Macarthurs*, p. 324-5.

67. *Ibid.*, p. 338.

68. *Ibid.*, pp. 338-46.

69. Macquarie Papers, A800-¹: Macquarie to Bathurst, 10 October 1823, p. 2.

70. Bennet, H. G., *Letter to Viscount Sidmouth*.

71. *Ibid.*, p. 64.   72. *Ibid.*, p. 71.   73. *Ibid.*, pp. 71-2.   74. *Ibid.*, p. 77.

75. *Ibid.*, p. 75; *Sydney Gazette*: G & G.O., 24 July 1813.

76. NSWHR, VII, p. 340: Macquarie's outline of the method he has adopted for "keeping female convicts separate till they can be properly distributed amongst the inhabitants in such manner as they can best derive the advantages of industry and good character".

77. Bennet, H. G., *Letter to Viscount Sidmouth*, p. 79. On arriving in 1810, Macquarie had reduced the number of licensed houses in Sydney from 75 to 20. (HRA, I. 7, p. 250.)

78. *Ibid.*, p. 79. In actual fact, the average number of funerals per quarter in Sydney fell by nearly 50 per cent during the period of the contract. (HRA, I. 7, pp. 434, 654, *et seq.*, 771.)

79. *Ibid.*, pp. 91, 93, 94.

80. *Ibid.*, pp. 94-5.

81. HRA, I. 10, pp. 235-6: to Bathurst, 22 February 1820.

82. *Ibid.*, p. 236.

83. Wentworth, *Statistical Account of the Colony of New South Wales* (3rd ed.), I, p. 387.

84. Journal, A774, I, p. 90, 27 December 1819.

85. Lowe, R., Letter to J. T. Bigge, 15 July 1820; HRA, I. 10, p. 236: to Bathurst, 22 February 1820, with enclosures; pp. 239-40: Circular to the Magistrates and Clergymen of the Colony; Queries submitted for answers to the same; CSIL (1820), No. 7, p. 61: Queries, 15 January 1820. Bigge's questions were directed to obtain evidence that convicts were best reformed on large estates.

86. HRA, I. 10, p. 242: Bigge to Macquarie, 5 February 1820; Journals, A774, I, pp. 100-3, 1-6 February 1820; Bigge Appendix, Box 20, pp. 3215-23: Minutes of conversation with Governor Macquarie; Box 24, pp. 4960-80.

87. Journals, A774, p. 102, 5 February 1820.

88. He returned on 6 June 1820. HRA, I. 10, p. 346: to Bathurst, 31 August 1820.

89. HRA, I. 10, p. 506: F. Goulburn to Bathurst, 17 July 1821; H. of C. Papers (1828): Macquarie to Bathurst, 10 October 1823.

90. HRA, I. 10, p. 142, 31 March 1819.

91. *Ibid.*, p. 291: to Bathurst, 28 February 1820.

92. *Ibid.*, pp. 314-15: Bathurst to Macquarie, 15 July 1820.

93. *Ibid.*, p. 314: Bathurst to Macquarie, 14 July 1820.

94. *Ibid.*, p. 479: to Bathurst, 20 March 1821.

95. *Ibid.*, I. 9, p. 761; p. 822: Bathurst to Macquarie, 24 July 1818.

96. HRA, I. 10, pp. 292-3: to Goulburn, 29 February 1820: Moore's Apology.

97. *Ibid.*, p. 292. Dr John Dunmore Lang (*Historical Account of New South Wales*, 4th ed., I, p. 49) wrote, "The late John M'Arthur stated in my hearing [in 1824], and with evident feelings of self-satisfaction, that he had been the means of sending home every Governor of the Colony but the last." The facts contradict this statement.

CHAPTER XXXI: SIC SEMPER TYRANNIS

1. HRA, I. 10, p. 239-42: to Bathurst, 22 February 1820. H. of C. Papers Relating to New South Wales (1828), pp. 42-3.

2. *Ibid.*, pp. 41-2.   3. *Ibid.*, pp. 52-3.   4. *Ibid.*, p. 63.

5. Macquarie, L., *Letter to Viscount Sidmouth*.

6. *Ibid.*, pp. 7-8.   7. *Ibid.*, p. 14.   8. *Ibid.*, pp. 17-18.   9. *Ibid.*, p. 18.

10. *Ibid.*, pp. 19-20.   11. *Ibid.*, pp. 21-2.   12. *Ibid.*   13. *Ibid.*, pp. 22-3.

14. *Ibid.*, pp. 53-4, 72-3, 77-8.

15. *Ibid.*, pp. 73, 77.

16. *Ibid.*, pp. 79-80.

17. Bigge Appendix, Boxes 1-10, provides fair examples of the mean tittle-tattle which Mr Bigge encouraged.

18. Bigge Appendix, Box 11: Questions to Governor Macquarie on Administration, Qs. and As. 12, 13, 14, 15, 16, etc.

19. *Ibid.* 20. *Ibid.* 21. *Ibid.* 22. *Ibid.*

23. Onslow, S.M., *Early Records of the Macarthurs of Camden*, pp. 349-50: Enclosed with M'Arthur to Bigge, 7 February 1821, Suggestions.

24. *Ibid.*, p. 350.

25. *Ibid.*, pp. 350-1.

26. *Ibid.*, p. 347: M'Arthur to Bigge, 7 February 1821.

27. *Ibid.*, p. 325. For references to buildings, in next papagraph, see H. of C. Papers (1828): Macquarie to Bathurst, 10 October 1823: "Had I followed Mr Bigge's advice, I should have altered almost every erection to a purpose for which it was never intended, condemning every one already completed, and leaving unfinished every improvement."

28. Wentworth Papers, A756, p. 159: W. C. Wentworth to D'Arcy Wentworth, 24 November 1819.

29. *Ibid.*, pp. 153-4.

30. *Ibid.*, pp. 155-6.

31. *Ibid.*, p. 157.

32. *Ibid.*, p. 157. His viewpoint was supported by Drummond (Letterbooks, A797, p. 173), who wrote to Macquarie as late as 6 June 1820, "We begin to despair of your return, for tho' many in Parliament have thrown out most infamous and unjust aspersions, you have been well defended, and Government are perfectly satisfied that they possess a most valuable representative."

33. *Ibid.*, pp. 164: W.C. Wentworth to D'Arcy Wentworth, 6 December 1819.

34. *Ibid.*, p. 165. Writing on 28 December, young Mr Wentworth announced,"I have not yet sent a challenge to Jeffery Bent because I have hitherto been unable to procure a friend." Mr Wentworth's anger was particularly hot since Mr Jeffery Bent had secured the publication in the Appendix of the Report of the Committee of Jails (1819) his letters of 1815, in which he had referred to D'Arcy Wentworth as a highwayman. The voice of Henry Goulburn (a member of the Committee) was loud in Whitehall after Mr W. C. Wentworth found out about it.

35. In the second edition of his *Letter to Sidmouth*, p. 110, Bennet stated that "in the first copies of this letter I wrote upon an authority which I thought could not mislead, that the Surgeon-General, Mr. Wentworth, had, in the earlier part of his life, been transported to this Colony; having learned the incorrectness of this statement, I hasten to contradict it, and to make the reparation which it is my duty to do, for the unintentional injustice which I have committed .... I learn that Mr Wentworth has passed a long life in the Settlement with a character of probity and honour . . . the office he fills . . . administered faithfully and justly." Wentworth Papers. A756, p. 135: W. C. Wentworth to D'Arcy Wentworth, 13 April 1819. Mr Wentworth told his father, "If I had followed the first dictates of my feelings on perusing it, I should not have called on him myself, but have sent a third person and have attempted ere this to wash out the foul stain which he had put on your character in his blood . . . If he was mistaken I should have it in my power to stigmatise him as an infamous slanderer and that I should not fail to profit by my situation to the utmost unless I was satisfied with his subsequent conduct." Mr Bennet "repeatedly changed colour and was very much agitated". Young Mr Wentworth told his father that "no doubt he had to thank that dark villain, Samuel Marsden", for the aspersions upon his character, but added that it was impossible that anyone could make a more handsome apology than Mr Bennet, who was so much affected that the House cheered him. It seems likely that Bennet may have been Bigge's informant.

36. *Ibid.*, p. 172: W. C. Wentworth to D'Arcy Wentworth, 1 May 1820. There was some delay in confirming the pension while matters connected with stores belonging to the Victualling Board were investigated. (HRA, I. 10, p. 146). Colonel Molle was at the bottom of the trouble. (Wentworth Papers, A756, pp. 171-2.)

37. HRA, I. 10, p. 310: Bathurst to Macquarie, 10 July 1820.

38. *Ibid.*

39. *Ibid.*

40. HRA, I. 10, p. 11: Bathurst to Bigge, 30 January 1819, Instructions.

41. *Ibid.*, pp. 354-5: Complaint of Eagar v. Barron Field; p. 356: Affidavit of Mr Justice Field; p. 362: Wylde's Report on the Decision in Eagar v. Field.

42. *Ibid.*, p. 354.

43. *Ibid.*, pp. 354-5. 44. *Ibid.*, p. 363.

U

45. *Ibid.*, p. 352: Macquarie to Bathurst, 1 September 1820; p. 353: Form used in Granting Pardons; 8 Geo. III, c. 15; 30 Geo. III, c. 47.

46. *Ibid.*, pp. 351-64, pp. 553-5.

47. *Ibid.*, p. 361: Minutes of Argument in Eagar v. Field.

48. *Ibid.*, p. 357: Petition of Mr Justice Field's Solicitor; p. 358: Order of the Court, pp. 362-4, Judge-Advocate Wylde's Report, 1 September 1820.

49. *Ibid.*, pp. 352, 354; Journals, A774, p. 200, 23 January 1821. Bigge gives a detailed version of the whole affair (Report, Legal, p. 132 *et seq.*), and suggests that Eagar deliberately misled the emancipists as to effects of the decision to inflame their minds. Actually, he averred, the ruling only affected property held or transmitted by emancipated convicts guilty of treason or murder, and of persons attainted for felony prior to the passing of the Statute 54 Geo. III, c. 145 (27 July 1814). Property of attainted convicts acquired since the passing of the Statute remained subject to the claim of the Crown for profits during lifetime, but was inheritable.

50. *Ibid.*, p. 550: to Bathurst, 22 October 1821; pp. 549-56, The Humble Petition of the Emancipated Colonists of the Territory of New South Wales and its Dependencies.

51. *Ibid.*, p. 550; Bigge Appendix, Box 16, p. 78: The muster at the end of 1819 analysed the New South Wales population: Those who came free, 794 men, 245 women, and 463 children, with 13,133 acres in cultivation. Those who came prisoner, but had been freed totalled 4002 men, 2005 women, and 3854 children, with 38,840 acres in cultivation.

52. *Ibid.*, p. 554.

53. *Ibid.*, pp. 554-5.

54. *Ibid.*, p. 557: to Bathurst, 22 October 1821.

55. *Ibid.*, pp. 557-8: to Bathurst, 22 October 1821.

56. Journals, A774, pp. 142-3, 22-23 July 1820: "This morning previous to our meeting at Government House a reconciliation took place between the Honourable Commissioner Bigge and myself of the Differences subsisting between us for some time past"; pp. 144-7, 24 July 1820.

57. *Sydney Gazette*, 3 November 1821; O'Brien, Eris, *Life and Letters of Archpriest John Joseph Therry*, pp. 43, 47.

58. *Ibid.*, p. 47; Kenny, *Progress of Catholicity in Australia*, p. 41.

59. O'Brien, *Life of Therry*, p. 51.

60. HRA, I. 10, p. 304: Bathurst to Macquarie, 13 May 1820.

61. Journals, A782: A Tour of Inspection of the Western and Southern Countries Some Time Since Discovered by Charles Throsby, Esq., in Oct. and Nov., 1820.

62. Journals, A774, II, pp. 168-9.

63. *Ibid.*, pp. 173-7, 1 December 1820.

64. *Ibid.*, pp. 178-9, 1 December 1820.

65. *Ibid.*, p. 186, 23 December 1820.

66. Journals, A774, II, pp. 203-8, 5-14 February 1821.

67. *Ibid.*, III, p. 211, 17 March 1821, 21 March 1821. The expedition consisted of Captain Francis Allman, Commandant and Magistrate, Lieutenant William Wilson, Acting Engineer, A. Fenton, Assistant Surgeon, three sergeants, two corporals, one drummer, thirty-three privates, Stephen Partridge, Superintendent of Convicts and Public Labour, one convict doctor (Cooke), sixty convict artificers, women and children. (Journals, A774, III, p. 212, 17 March 1821.)

68. Journals, A784: Journal of a Visit to Van Diemen's Land in 1821; CSIL (1820), No. 78, p. 62: Throsby to Macquarie, 25 August 1820; (1821), No. 1: Throsby to Macquarie, 3 February 1821; No. 18, p. 115: to Throsby, 26 February 1821; No. 32, p. 139: Throsby, 10 May 1821. For Broughton's death, see Mitchell Library, AC87, Extracts from Register of St Luke's Church, Liverpool, 22, 25 July 1821.

69. Journals, A785: A Voyage and Tour of Inspection from Port Jackson to the Settlements of Port Macquarie and Newcastle in November, 1821.

70. Journals, A774, III, p. 239, 1 November 1821, and 21 November 1821; p. 243, 30 November 1821.

71. Journals, A774, p. 246; A783: Journal of a Journey to Bathurst in 1821; A786: Journal of Tour to the Cowpastures and Illawarra in January, 1822.

72. Journals, A774, pp. 259-60, 11 February 1822.

73. *Ibid.*, pp. 260-1, 12 February 1822.

74. *Sydney Gazette*, 15 February 1822.

75. Journals, A775, pp. 9, 20, 12-23, 12 February 1822. The quotation about his drive: *Nugae Australes*, No. 4, in the *Australian*, 28 July 1825.

76. Journals, A775, 12 February.

CHAPTER XXXII: THE OLD VICEROY

1. Journals, A775: Journal of a Voyage from New South Wales to England in 1822, pp. 1-104.
2. *Ibid.*, p. 105 *et seq.*, 5 July 1822.
3. *Ibid.*, p. 112.
4. H. of C. Papers (1828): Report of Governor Macquarie to Earl Bathurst, 27 July 1822, p. 2. Also HRA, I. 10, pp. 672-701.
5. HRA, I. 10, p. 675.
6. *Ibid.*, p. 793 *et seq.*: Bathurst to Macquarie, 10 September 1822.
7. Journals, A776, I: Journal Commencing at London on 30 November 1822. On their return journey they arrived at Boulogne on 26 July 1823.
8. Bigge Report, Convicts, pp. 81, 82, 83. H. of C. Papers (1828), p. 31: Macquarie to Bathurst, 10 October 1823, p. 31 and Appendix C thereto, p. 67; also Mitchell Library, A800-¹.
9. Farley, Felix, *Bristol Journal*, 21 and 28 March 1812.
10. Bigge Report, p. 147.
11. *Ibid.*, pp. 80-2. H. of C. Papers (1828), pp. 31-2: Macquarie to Bathurst, 10 October 1823. Macquarie denied Bigge's statement that he had actually offered Bell office a, a Justice. He said that Bell was ordered home for having taken part in the Bligh Rebellion, and therefore would have been unsuitable.
12. Bonwick Transcripts, A2000, I, Biography, p. 259 *et seq.*
13. H. of C. Papers (1828), p. 25: Macquarie to Bathurst, 10 October 1823.
14. Wentworth, W. C., *Statistical Account of New South Wales* (3rd ed.), I, pp. 388-9. Mr Wentworth added that Bigge's "sentiments had been formed previously to his departure from England", and that he was actuated by two motives—his desires to oblige his patron in England, and to support the pretensions of his party in Australia. See Bigge Appendix, Box 28, pp. 6694, 6698: Bigge to Bathurst, 29 July and 3 August 1822, for some other reasons for Mr Wentworth's heat.
15. It was Elizabeth who forced the issue. Mitchell Library, Am. 15, C.O., 201/188: E. H. Macquarie to Goderich, 11 May 1827, and subsequent correspondence. *Ho. of Commons Papers*, XXI, 1828. No. 1: Copy of a Report by the late Major-General Macquarie on the Colony of New South Wales to Earl Bathurst, in July, 1822; No. 2: Extract of a Letter from Major-General Macquarie to Earl Bathurst in October, 1823, in answer to certain parts of the Report of Mr. Commissioner Bigge, on the state of the said Colony (Manuscript certified copy of No. 2: Mitchell Library, A800-¹). The only known full transcript was one prepared and sworn to from the documents in Elizabeth Macquarie's possession, by Wm. Stafford and John Wood, who sent their sworn copy to Bathurst, 24 July 1826. The only things missing from the version printed by order of the House of Commons were: (1) Paragraphs in which Macquarie said that Bigge's demeanour to him became such that respect for his Royal Commission "alone prevented me from resenting it by breaking off all private intercourse with him. My forbearance under the influence of those feelings was indeed forced to the utmost limit." (2) The paragraph which exposed the treachery of John M'Arthur, who, while "particularly intimate" with Bigge, was warning Macquarie against his methods of inquiry. (See Chapter XXX, Note 69.)
16. M'Garvie, Rev. J., Memoranda, C254: Narrative of the Last Days of General Macquarie, by Mrs Macquarie. (Copy made by the Rev. J. M'Garvie from Mr Richard Fitzgerald's copy.) The manuscript is a copy of a letter from Elizabeth Macquarie, dated Barns, Surrey, 3 November 1825. It was written to friends in New South Wales on the anniversary of her wedding day and was finished apparently (or perhaps dispatched) on 23 March 1826. A copy of this letter printed in the *Sydney Morning Herald* in 1868 was quoted before the Royal Australian Historical Society in 1929 by Mr C. H. Bertie and is printed in RAHSJ, XVI. Mr Bertie's version (from the *Sydney Morning Herald*) misses out one or two names of persons and towns mentioned, but otherwise coincides with Mr M'Garvie's version, which is marked: "A true copy signed Rd. Fitzgerald." "Correct copy from Mr. Fitzgerald's copy. J. M'Garvie, Minister, 4 October 1832."
17. The song is quoted in the notes at the end of Dr J. D. Lang's "Poems, Sacred and Secular."
18. RAHSJ, XVI, p. 39.
19. *Ibid*
20. Journals: Journal Commencing Thursday, 15 April 1824, pp. 1-9.
21. *Ibid.*, pp. 8-9. The rent of the rooms included that of a bedroom for his servant, George.
22. *Ibid.*, pp. 11, 23 *et seq.*
23. *Ibid.*, p. 19.
24. *Ibid.*, p. 11; Macquarie Papers, Mitchell Library, Safe, 15, No. 7: Bathurst to Macquarie, 29 April 1824.
25. Mitchell Library, Am. 15, CO 201/188, 2790, N.S.W

26. *Ibid.*; Journals, A776, II, pp. 20-1.
27. *Ibid.*, 17-18 May 1824.
28. RAHSJ, XVI, p. 43.
29. Journals, A776, II, p. 16.
30. *Ibid.*, p. 24.
31. *Ibid.*, p. 27.
32. RAHSJ, XVI, pp. 45-6.
33. *Ibid.*, p. 46.
34. Memoranda, A772, p. 222.
35. *Sydney Gazette*, 28 October 1824, p. 2; 11 November 1824, pp. 2, 4; 18 November 1824, p. 2; *Australian*, 28 November 1824, for "letter to Wentworth". It had come in the *Mangles* and apparently had been written on 22 June, ten days before Macquarie died. Journals, A776, p. 19, 15 May 1824.
36. Charles Tompson, "Ode on the Death of Governor Macquarie".
37. *Sydney Gazette*.
38. *Oban Times*, 22 June 1940.
39. Missing Dispatches, Mitchell Library Transcripts, A1267, Pkt. 4, p. 126: CO 201/166: Forbes and Money to Bathurst, 6 and 25 July 1825.
40. Mitchell Library, Am. 15: E. Macquarie to Horton, 25 June 1825; W. T. Money, 12 July 1825.
41. Mitchell Library, *ibid.*: Forbes and Money to Bathurst, 6 July 1825.
42. Wentworth Papers, A757, pp. 31-3: Elizabeth Macquarie to W. C. Wentworth.
43. *Australian*, 17 July 1835. She died on Mull 11 March 1835. Brisbane had offered her a grant of 2000 acres of land in New South Wales after Macquarie's death, but when, a decade later, she attempted to secure the deed of grant, it was found that there was no record. However, through Governor Bourke's intervention, it was secured for her son after her death.
44. In 1957 Macquarie's tomb, which holds the bodies of his wife, son and daughter, had been repaired with the proceeds of a fund raised as a result of the efforts of the late Mr A. E. Heath and the author and now (1964) administered by the National Trust of Australia.

INDEX